ЗА ОТВАГУ
СССР
ЗА БОЕВЫЕ ЗАСЛУГИ
FOR MILITARY MERIT

Blue Seas, Red Stars

Soviet Military Medals to U.S. Sea Service Recipients in World War II

David A. Schwind

Schiffer Publishing Ltd
4880 Lower Valley Road • Atglen, PA 19310

Published by Schiffer Publishing, Ltd.
4880 Lower Valley Road
Atglen, PA 19310
Phone: (610) 593-1777; Fax: (610) 593-2002
E-mail: Info@schifferbooks.com

For our complete selection of fine books on this and related subjects, please visit our website at www.schifferbooks.com. You may also write for a free catalog.

This book may be purchased from the publisher. Please try your bookstore first.

We are always looking for people to write books on new and related subjects. If you have an idea for a book, please contact us at proposals@schifferbooks.com

Schiffer Publishing's titles are available at special discounts for bulk purchases for sales promotions or premiums. Special editions, including personalized covers, corporate imprints, and excerpts can be created in large quantities for special needs. For more information, contact the publisher.

Library of Congress Control Number: 2015939937

Designed by RoS
Type set in Trajan Pro/Garamond Premier Pro

ISBN: 978-0-7643-4829-7
Printed in China

Dedication

This book is dedicated to the memory of the recipients of Soviet medals who never lived to see their awards:

Robert Buckbee
Kendall Cram
Harold Handshuh
Elbert Heim
Paul Lessard
Don Moon
Howell Murray
John Ours
Percy Spann
William Tepuni

It is also dedicated to the following recipients who passed away during the writing of this book:

Romuald Holubowicz, January 1, 2013
Thomas Kinaszczuk, January 13, 2013
Charles Dole, June 21, 2013
Willard Brown, July 15, 2013
Dallas Jones, December 8, 2013
Robert Baughan, January 8, 2014
Milton Sherbring, April 5, 2014
Wilbur Collins, June 15, 2014
Cecil Graff, October 18, 2014.

Fair winds and following seas, shipmates.

Contents

Part III

Part IV

Appendices

Foreword

by the Honorable William L. Ball III

The naval historian faces challenges of an entirely different order than those who study and analyze the history of military events, people, and conflict ashore. Significant actions at sea can be veiled in obscurity for understandable reasons involving time, distance, the rigors of sea service and constraints on modes of communication.

Occasionally, a work of new scholarship reveals little known dimensions of war at sea that over the years have failed to receive the attention that their consequences deserve. In this vein, Dave Schwind's illuminating and consequential work in this new volume is a singular triumph of diligence and determination to document the largely untold story of a group of decorated naval officers and men who served on the Murmansk Run in 1942-43.

That their decoration was bestowed upon them by the Soviet government prior to the onset of the Cold War makes this account an all the more remarkable tale of bravery, naval leadership, and unheralded sacrifice.

The attack on Pearl Harbor and the subsequent entry of the United States into the Second World War led to an unusual alliance. In spite of the mutual distrust of the United States and Great Britain toward the Soviet Union, the three nations were united by a common enemy: Nazi Germany. With the Soviets reeling from the German attack of August 1941, the Lend-Lease convoys made it possible for them to defend their nation against the attackers and eventually take the offensive, finally marching into the heart of Berlin in May 1945. The Soviets of the time were profoundly grateful for the aid rendered by Great Britain and the United States and in an unusual and relatively unknown occurrence in the history of those nations, quietly bestowed well-deserved medals upon a handful of the men of their allies who made the convoys possible. The 217 recipients recorded in this book represent a small fraction of the thousands of brave men who risked their lives to deliver the much-needed war materiel to the Soviet Union, particularly in the dark days of 1942 and 1943, when a victory over Nazi Germany appeared all but impossible.

The events of June 1944 at Normandy were over a year away, while in the Pacific the U.S. Navy had just broken Japan's eastward advance at the pivotal Battle of Midway in June 1942. This gave Roosevelt the green light fora major shift of American resources to the war in Europe.

Following the end of the war, the majority of these recipients returned to their civilian occupations and worked hard to build the American dream. For many, like my uncle, Albert Maynard, the mementos and memories of the war were quietly put away while they raised families, started businesses, and provided the foundation for decades of economic progress in our nation. Sadly, for far too many, their heroism and sacrifice in the defense of our freedoms were never discussed or recorded and went with them to the grave.

Through the pages of this book, Dave Schwind vividly illustrates each of the men from the US Navy, Coast Guard, and Merchant Marine who received medals from the Soviet Union in 1944 and 1945. The thousands of hours he spent researching these men, tracking down the surviving recipients or the families of those who have passed on, and illuminating their deeds and lives are evident in this book. It was truly a remarkable undertaking, one unparalleled by contemporary authors.

This book serves as a memorial to the bravery, valor, and sacrifice made by the men who gave their all to their nation and Allied cause during the Second World War, many of whom returned home from the war and continued on with their lives, only to have been forgotten or overlooked in the last seven decades. As you read through the book, keep in mind these were just ordinary men who were called upon to do the extraordinary: lay down their lives to ensure the safe transport of war materiel to the Soviet Union and prevent Nazi Germany from securing an outright victory in Europe. The world truly owes an unpayable debt of gratitude to these men, and through this book, we trust they will never be forgotten.

William L. Ball III
Alexandria, Virginia

Foreword

by Dr. Anatoly L. Lifshits, PhD.,
Captain, First Rank, Soviet Navy, Retired.

The Second World War ended many years ago, and the day when its last participant leaves this world may be right around the corner. However, their experience, their actions, their memories of past battles must be carefully preserved in the memory of their descendants.

History has shown that an important factor in ensuring victory was the union of forces of progress: the joint actions of the USSR, the United States, and Great Britain.

Perhaps the most remarkable, most glorious page of this collaboration was the polar convoys.

The severe conditions through which the convoys had to navigate are well known. It seemed that everything was in favor of the enemy. In the last third of the journey, the convoy routes ran through a relatively narrow passageway, limited on one side by the coasts of Norway and Murmansk, and on the other side by the edge of polar ice that ran about four hundred miles from the coast in summer and two hundred miles in winter.

Enemy aerial reconnaissance, which could detect the convoys relatively easily, provided continuous information to the submarines and strike aircraft. It took enemy planes between thirty minutes to an hour to fly from their bases to the convoys. Moreover, the convoys' maneuvers were limited. The resulting battles were fierce and resulted in numerous casualties on both sides. Many participants of convoys paid for victory with their lives.

Despite all the difficulties, dangers, and losses, the goals set for the convoys were generally successfully achieved; the important military goods were delivered to the Russian ports.

The value of these goods for the victory was very significant.

Under the Lend-Lease agreement, the convoys delivered 3,632 bombers, 13,853 fighter aircraft (approximately twenty percent of the total amount produced in the USSR), high octane gasoline that covered more than half of the army's needs, 11,800 tanks, 400,000 cars, machine tools, a substantial amount of food, etc. Much of this cargo was delivered specifically by the Arctic convoys during the most difficult time for our country.

The Soviet government praised the heroism of the Allied seamen. Many participants of the convoys were awarded Russian orders and medals, to include those in this book. In honor of their service seventy years ago, awards continue to be awarded to convoy participants, as demonstrated by the recent awarding of the Ushakov Medal to surviving American convoy participants.

I hope this book will serve to further rapprochement of the people of our great countries.

Participant of twenty-three polar convoys,
Professor A. Lifshits
St. Petersburg, Russia

PREFACE

This book is the culmination of a journey that commenced with my winning bid on an eBay auction in 1999. I was the only bidder on an Order of Glory, Third Class, awarded to a U.S. Navy Chief Petty Officer being sold by an estate liquidator in Florida. At the time, no one (or at least anyone I talked to) knew anything about Soviet awards to the US Navy during the Second World War. By pure luck, two years later I was able to reunite the medal with its original documents, and in 2003 I began researching the topic in earnest. My research led to the eventual authoring and publishing of the article *Soviet Military Decorations to Americans during World War II* in the September/October 2007 issue of the "Journal of the Orders and Medals Society of America."

With the article published, I honestly believed I had gone as far as anyone could in the researching of this topic and I went about pursuing the other demands of my military career and family. In 2011, now in a new career, I came across my old research while organizing my garage. On a whim, I decided to see if any further information was available about the award recipients, now with so much information available from digital sources online. I was stunned at what I found. I initially thought another article was justified, but I soon had far too much information. A book was warranted, and the rest, as they say, is history.

When I started researching this topic, all I had was the list of the 190, 1945 U.S. Navy and Coast Guard recipients from the February 1946 *All Hands* magazine. The list had no units assigned, no biographical information, and in about twenty percent of the names on the list, a plethora of spelling mistakes. It was only after starting my research that I found the list of 1944 recipients, and later, from the National Archives, the list of Merchant Marine awardees. I had to not only properly identify all of the recipients, but the units they served with, what they did to earn their awards, and find enough information for their biography. A lucky break came about when the list of citations for each of the 1945 recipients was discovered in the State Department files at the National Archives (these are included in Appendix 2). However, this list was unclassified as it was intended to be provided directly to the Soviets, and thus all of the unit names were removed and their content was extremely general in nature. While I could now identify pilot from Armed Guard gunner, the linking of the unclassified citation to the correct unit, and subsequently correct action, was venturing into uncharted territory.

At first, the task of creating the correlation between unit and individual, then, between individual and their biography, and finally between the individual and their family or (if they were still alive) themselves, appeared to be far less of a daunting task than it actually turned out to be. Although period lists existed of most of the recipients, nearly all of them had lost touch with their fellow shipmates over the course of seventy years (save for three who were related by marriage). There were no veterans associations to contact, nor were there contemporary contact rosters of former officers or men of various units. For many of these recipients, they served together for a matter of weeks or months, barely knowing each other at the time, let alone remaining in contact after their discharge from the Navy. This required me to track down the surviving recipients and the families of those who had passed on both during, and since, the Second World War; each one a separate and distinct research project. Countless thousands of hours were spent poring through public records, genealogical websites, through archival newspapers and records, and even creating family trees, often going back two and three generations for some awardees, in order to find someone related to the recipient.

Contact with each of these recipients or their families represented an entire pursuit in its own right. I sent out nearly eight hundred letters as my initial form of contact. Of those, over two hundred were returned to sender. I made hundreds of phone calls, many times hearing the all-too-familiar tone preceding the statement: "... this phone number is no longer in service." When the families did contact me, in some cases up to a year after they received my initial letter, I then had to convince them of the merits of my book and the benefit of their participation. At first, many were (appropriately) skeptical and some required a considerable amount of effort to convince them to help me with this book. The families represented all walks of life: young and old, rich and poor, cordial and rigid. I visited homes and locations that ranged from tiny and worn to breathtakingly palatial, and my visits ranged in length from thirty minutes to well over half a day. Some of the families had retained mountains of material from the veterans, and some only had the single Soviet medal and nothing else. Some of the families could never be moved beyond their suspicions or unwillingness to help and unfortunately their relative was not as well represented as others.

For nearly every family willing to participate in the book, I paid a personal visit, accumulating in excess of twenty-two thousand miles on rental cars and visiting forty out of the fifty states. Many of the families knew little to nothing about their relative's service in the war, and less than a handful knew anything about the Soviet medal and why it was awarded. Quite often, these medals sat in storage or out of sight for decades, only to have my inquiry bring new attention to the medal and the veteran's service. Most of the recipients simply "moved on" after the war, to include those who remained on active duty, and it was thus incumbent on me to assemble the stories of these men from contemporary, archival, and other sources.

With that in mind, the records I referenced to create this narrative may or may not have been error free. I have done the best I can to reduce the number of egregious errors by using multiple sources and eyewitness statements. If unable to come to a firm conclusion on the validity of the factual statements, I have done my best to either avoid using them, or when they have been highly pertinent to the relaying of an episode or story, erring on the conservative side. Most of these conflicts were found in the Armed Guard reports, though the books referenced throughout my work were not without conflict between their own details and that of the ship or Armed Guard reports. Even statements taken from the same recipient at different times provided conflicting information. Events were often recorded as having taken place at different times and this was compounded by some of the Armed Guard reports written with reference to local time and others written based on GMT (Greenwich Mean Time). For the purposes of this narrative, I recounted the details as they took place in local time in order to convey, as much as possible, the feel of the event.

One common error with the Armed Guard reports dealt with the number of attacking aircraft. In several instances, I had access to the ship's master's report as well as the Armed Guard report and the numbers were incongruent (with the Armed Guard commander's report often being more conservative than that of the civilian master). The same can be said for the reports of the Armed Guard commanders on ships in the same convoy: attacks were recorded differently based on their perspective of the attacking aircraft, as well as whether or not their ship sank. In the cases of the latter, the reports were often compiled over a week (up to a month) later with information gleaned from the memories of the participants. This created an often skewed assessment of the battle as the exact times and details of engagements were remembered differently by participants. For example, the death of Ensign Cram on the SS *Wade Hampton* was retold differently by each member of the civilian and Navy crew interviewed. I did my best at combining the information recorded and presenting it accurately within the context of this narrative.

In several cases, I had access to the uncensored, personal journals of the participants, and relied on their recorded entries, so long as I was confident that they were recorded within a reasonable amount of time following the event. However, as with the above reports, these too had to be verified by other sources as the perspectives of one participant varied greatly depending on their status and position.

The information received from the National Personnel Records Center (NPRC) was likewise not without error (and sometimes extensive errors). For those recipients who remained on active duty or reserve (including inactive reserve) status past 1953, I had to request their records through a Freedom of Information Act (FOIA) request. This meant the quality of the information I received was directly dependent on the generosity of the particular archivist handling my request. In some cases, the information received was minimal, at best, and multiple FOIA requests were made. Even with those, I still received records of assignments in incorrect order, or responses laden with spelling errors or random omissions. I did everything possible to ensure a proper retelling of the veteran's service history based on the information I received. For the families I located and established communication, I sent a draft of the recipient's biography to ensure my accuracy prior to publication. However, quite a number of the families were not aware of what the veteran did during the war, or in the case of some, still remained unresponsive, so I had to rely on what I was able to piece together from my sources. With this said, the information I used to construct the history of some of these recipients may or may not have been perfect and thus, errors may exist, despite my extensive efforts to avoid them.

In some cases, families had retained clippings from articles that appeared in local newspapers published during the war or from men's magazines published in the 1950s and 1960s. Some of these stories were far more exciting to read than the official after action report. However, not having any other sources available to verify their accuracy, and not knowing if they were the actual "uncensored" version of the event or if they may have been written with sensationalism as their intent, I avoided including them as part of the narrative to the greatest extent possible.

Several exceptional books have been published about anti-submarine duty as well as the Murmansk convoys and I was able to use them to develop my narrative. Those books have been have been listed in the Bibliography and any direct quotations have been annotated in the endnotes. If there are any statements that were not properly cited, it was a completely unintentional failure on my part and no ill intent should be assumed by the lack of a reference. I must also give a caveat with regard to these references as on several occasions, the comparison of one book to another, or a book to the original eyewitness report, led to the discovery of errors even within the most foundational of references on the topic.

Countless websites were used to ascertain the information in this book. Google.com was consulted thousands of times, and websites such as uboats.net, warsailors.com, uboatarchive.net, and convoyweb.org.uk, provided detailed information that assisted in pointing me in the right direction to determine the units, personnel, published materials, and archival records eventually used as sources throughout this book. For example, in almost every after action report referenced, none of the enemy forces are named. This was because they were not known at the time: knowing that the ship was "attacked by a U-boat" was the best that could be determined from the eyewitness statements. Countless scholars and researchers over the last seven decades have dedicated their time to determining just who was where and when. Today, the antagonists in most of the actions discussed in this narrative have been identified. This is particularly helpful in the case of situations like the SS *Henry Wynkoop* that remained a mystery for decades after the event actually happened, and was even listed as a "mystery of the sea" in John Bunker's *Heroes in Dungarees*. Had they struck a U-boat? Were they torpedoed with a dud torpedo? It wasn't until recently that the ship was actually determined to have been damaged by the underwater explosions of the SS *William C. Gorgas* that also damaged *U-757*. My contribution has been to add the bit of information that the steadfast Armed Guard commander on the *Henry Wynkoop* later became a chief advisor to the Secretary of Defense during the Vietnam War and the designee to become the fifty-ninth Secretary of the Navy.

One additional note must be made with reference to nautical and military terminology. I have tried my best to limit the use of nautical and military-specific jargon as much as possible throughout the text. Unfortunately, having personally served as a naval officer, this is often a very difficult mission to accomplish, as terms in my everyday vernacular come from many years at sea. Attempting to ensure every reader can understand all of the narrative has been a challenge, but I have done what I can to limit as many extraneous uses of jargon as possible. With that said, many of the scenarios could not be told coherently without the use of at least a minimal amount of naval or military vernacular and I apologize in advance for any confusion these may cause.

Finally, two statements must be made to clarify some of the terminology used for awards and medals in the book. First, the Letter of Commendation from the Secretary of the Navy was, during the course of the war, just that: a piece of paper, signed by the Secretary. Any commanding officer could award a Letter of Commendation; however, only the ones from the Secretary of the Navy entitled the recipient to wear a green and white striped Commendation Ribbon when the ribbon was created in 1943. It wasn't until the 1950s that the planchet was developed for the ribbon and the Letter of Commendation became the Navy Commendation Ribbon with Metal Planchet (it was later renamed the Navy and Marine Corps Commendation Medal). Recipients of a Letter of Commendation could request a Navy Commendation Medal from the government, and several of the recipients took advantage of the ability to do so in the 1950s, 1960s, and even later.

Second, intrinsically important to the medals issued is the presence of the recipient's name engraved on the reverse of the medal. With the exception of William Tepuni's Air Medal, I included images of all of the named medals I encountered while writing the book. It can be assumed that if the reverse of a medal is not shown, it was not engraved with the recipient's name or other information.

For those medals that were named on the reverse, two kinds of engraving exist: official, as done by an engraver specifically for the Navy Department, and unofficial, done by a jeweler or engraver retained by the recipient. During the Second World War, the Navy's engravers were terrifically skilled and each medal was a work of art. Official engraving was always done on posthumous awards that were given to the recipient's next of kin, and in this book, can be seen on the Purple Hearts to Kendall Cram and William Tepuni. Officially engraved awards were not always for posthumous recipients, as the beautifully engraved Air Medal to David Puckett can testify. (The Air Medal to Tepuni was similarly engraved, but no amount of photographs could capture the engraving through the patina on the medal, and thus the image was sadly not included.)

Other awards were engraved unofficially, to include the Silver Stars to Ralph Boucher, George Lennig, and Jeremiah Mahoney, the Distinguished Flying Crosses to Joseph Horn and Leonard Harmon, and most peculiarly, the Order of Glory awarded to Norman Hyams. These were often done by the individual awarding command by a jeweler they selected (as in the case of the Silver Stars to Boucher and Mahoney, believed to have been engraved by the Armed Guard Center) or may have been commissioned by the recipients themselves at their own expense (as in the case of Horn's Distinguished Flying Cross and Hyams' Order of Glory). Either way, they represent an aesthetically pleasing tribute to the valor exhibited by the men who received them.

I originally planned on retaining a collector-centric focus in this book, with only including discussion of the actual events that took place as a matter of editorial clarification for each of the biographies in a "biographical dictionary" format. What I did not realize at the time was that what these recipients did during the Second World War was far more important than could be captured in a side note retelling of the circumstances around their deeds. Thus, this book took on the format of a narrative, with the stories of each of the recipients woven throughout, much like actors on a worldwide stage. In many of these events, the lives and actions of the recipients are intertwined, sometimes on more than one occasion, and I have attempted to highlight those interactions whenever possible. I have done my best to present these events in a visually stimulating format that I believe best suits the retelling of the stories of these brave men. As I wrote this book, my respect and admiration for what all of these men did dramatically increased. My hope is that, as the reader, your appreciation will likewise grow. It was truly an honor for me to record their deeds in order to preserve and share them with future generations.

I sincerely hope you will enjoy the content of this book and the memorial it serves to these 217 men. I would appreciate hearing of any omissions, errors, or additional information I may have overlooked during my research or writing.

Dave Schwind
daveschwind@aol.com

Acknowledgments

This book is the first of its kind. To my knowledge, no one has ever attempted to create a book and illuminate it with images and biographical details taken directly from the families of so many unassociated and diverse participants. It would have been easy to write if all of these medals resided with collectors or in my personal collection and if all of the personnel and archival files were open and available locally. But that was far from reality. In fact, only one of the Soviet medals in this book is owned by a collector and two are in museums; the other medals photographed are still in the possession of the veterans or their immediate relatives. Through the course of my research, in addition to contacting seven still-living recipients, I was able to locate and communicate with the families of 176 of the 217 recipients. Unfortunately, not all of them knew the location of the medal or could assist with my research due to a plethora of reasons or events that had taken place in the last seven decades. In the end, I was able to visit 121 families and five still-living recipients in order to gain the majority of images included in this book.

It is with the greatest appreciation and deepest gratitude that I acknowledge the help of the veterans and their families, whose names are included in the captions for each image as well as elsewhere in the book. I absolutely could not have done this book without their dedicated support, encouragement, and assistance. Several families had life-changing events take place directly because of my research (such as reuniting several families, separated for many decades) and it was because of those positive events that I was able to maintain the momentum to finish this book.

Visiting families was only the tip of the iceberg with regard to the information in this narrative. Thousands of images and hours were accumulated conducting research in the National Archives and the National Personnel Records Center (NPRC). For the former, I had never conducted research physically at the Archives. However, Kevin Mahoney not only taught me how to conduct my research there, but also spent countless hours pulling and discovering new material for me due to my lack of proximity to the Archives. For the latter, when I first told Geoff Gentilini (owner of Golden Arrow Research) that I planned on pulling the service records of over two hundred individuals from the NPRC, it didn't seem like too much of a daunting task. That is, until it took almost two years to accomplish! I believe we both learned a considerable amount about the intricacies and the bureaucracy of the NPRC, and I appreciate his patience and willingness to "request that record again," when we didn't get the results we were hoping for the first, second, third, fourth, and sometimes, fifth time. Without Kevin and Geoff, this book would have been impossible to complete.

I am likewise indebted to a number of collectors and researchers for their help with various aspects of the book including Mark Adamic, Andreas Blischke, Robert Bottie, Tim Frank, Allan Henderson, Ian Henry, Tom Nier, Gary Putnam, Adam Rohloff, George Wilhelmsen, Dave Zeller, and several additional members of the US Militaria Forum, an exceptional online resource for the study and preservation of military memorabilia from the United States.

I also wish to thank Captain First Rank Igor Kozyr, Russian Navy (Retired) for his assistance and generous help with research in the Russian archives. Captain Kozyr also paved the way for my relationship with Nikolai Efimov, who not only allowed me to use his published data on Ushakov and Nakhimov medals, but generously supplied me with considerable amounts of further research from the State Archives of the Russian Federation.

I would also like to note the help of Tom Poullin, who maintains a blog dedicated to John McNaughton, for his assistance in obtaining quotes about McNaughton's receipt of his Soviet medal from his FBI background investigation.

Special thanks goes to Paul McDaniel and Paul Schmitt, my mentors in the world of Soviet medals and the authors of *The Comprehensive Guide to Soviet Orders and Medals* (Historical Research, 1997), for allowing me to use their translations of the Statutes for the Soviet medals as the foundation for writing Appendix 3. Additionally, thanks go to Helen Arends, who assisted with the final translation of the award documents in Appendix 4.

I appreciate the assistance of Evan Smith, whose grandfather, Paul Gill, kept an excellent diary of his experiences during convoy PQ-18 and the excerpts have been invaluable in illuminating some of the stories in Chapter 11.

Because my naval experience has been confined to ships, Marc Frattasio, of the VP Association, and Commander Doug Siegfried, USN (Retired) of the Tailhook Association took time out of their very busy schedules to review and provide their opinions on Part I of the book to ensure my aviation jargon and nomenclatures were correct. Thank you!

I must also mention the office of my Congressman, John Garamendi, specifically his constituent liaison Brandon Thomson, who was instrumental in obtaining biographical records of thirteen of the previously unresearchable officers from the Navy Operational Archives.

My wife once said: "Now you know why people write books when they are retired" due to the excessive stresses and time consumption of writing a book like this while holding a full time career (to include a job relocation just as the book was coming due!) I am extremely appreciative of my superiors, my employees, and my company, Iberdrola Renewables, for allowing me the opportunity to make this book a reality.

I would also like to thank my father, Rodger Schwind, and my father in law, Captain George McMichael, United States Navy (Retired), for their patience, assistance, and advice during the writing of the book, as well as their encouragement along the way. I am certain they eventually grew weary of the daily updates as I wrote the book, but I truly appreciate their help.

Finally, I am most indebted to my wife and children, who not only put up with but encouraged me during my absence on countless evenings when I "got on a roll" with research or writing and during my extended road trips visiting families and veterans all across the United States. Thank you!

Introduction

The Second World War was the first and only time the weapons of modern warfare were put in use globally. The Japanese invasion of Asia, and the German invasion of Western Europe, followed by the Soviet Union, brought the first-hand experience of the horrors of war to the majority of the world's population. Tens of millions of men and women were mobilized to fight for their nations, and combat occurred in all climes and places. Very few locations were untouched by the war, and men of dozens of counties fought, transited through, passed nearby, or died within the air and sea boundaries of nearly every nation. The movements of armies and navies affected nations on a global scale, with the fates and futures of entire countries and continents hanging precariously in the balance.

The first years of the war saw the Axis powers of Japan and Germany with a nearly unbroken string of decisive, major victories over the nations who would later form the Allied powers. Core to the Allies were the nations of Great Britain, the United States, and the Soviet Union. Two of the three already had a close bond, with alliances and partnerships between Great Britain and the United States in place for decades prior to the war. In contrast, the Soviet Union had little in common with its soon-to-be partners. The Tsarist government was overthrown in 1917 and shortly thereafter, Communism was violently planted and aggressively cultivated in its place. Their leader in the years up to the Second World War, Joseph Stalin, was an absolute dictator who would murder (technically "purge") anyone he believed may have cause or ability to overthrow the regime. Economic development had taken place by force, with the people of Russia and the other Soviet republics paying for it in blood.

On June 22, 1941, Adolf Hitler, leader of Nazi Germany and until then, an ally of the USSR, crossed the Soviet border intent on overthrowing the Communist regime and taking the land and resource-rich country by force. Despite global warnings, the Soviets were ill-prepared to fight against the overwhelmingly superior German forces. Chaos reigned on the frontlines while hundreds of thousands of Soviet soldiers and citizens were mowed down before the Nazi juggernaut. While the losses of manpower were nearly catastrophic for the Soviets, even more immediately irreplaceable was the USSR's ability to produce the basic needs for a nation at war: food, fuel, and war materiel. The fate of the Soviet Union, and with it, a large portion of the world's population, daily hung in the balance with continuing losses of men and materiel.

As the people of the Soviet Union made up for the human losses through their own bodily sacrifices numbering on the tens of millions, Great Britain and the United States came to the material aid of the USSR through the advent of Lend-Lease. These goods were brought to the Soviet Union in heavily laden ships through hundreds of convoys across the Atlantic and through the Arctic and Arabian Gulf. It was the men of these convoys; both the civilian mariners who manned the merchant vessels, the Navy Armed Guard who defended them, the pilots, and the destroyermen, who made these convoys a reality, and in their very definite and tactile way helped the Soviet Union turn the tide of the war and eventually conquer Nazi Germany. These are the men this book is about: 217 who were selected by the Soviets to represent the thousands who heroically ensured the delivery of war materiel in their time of darkest and most desperate need.

PART I

CHAPTER 1

ANTI-SUBMARINE OPERATIONS: PATROL AND PATROL BOMBING SQUADRON RECIPIENTS

Donald Mason receives his Order of Glory, Third Class, in a ceremony on April 6, 1946. *Official US Navy photo via the National Archives.*

January 28, 1942: The First Claimed U-boat Sinking

The United States had been in a state of war against Nazi Germany for less than two months when Aviation Machinist's Mate (Naval Aviation Pilot) first class Donald Mason was flying a routine anti-submarine patrol over the North Atlantic in a twin-engine Lockheed PBO-1 Hudson patrol bomber. The war hadn't started off well for the United States; by this point, Pearl Harbor had been bombed and it seemed as though the Japanese were invincible in their invasion of the Philippines and the Far East. In Europe, the Germans occupied land from the French coastline to the outskirts of Moscow. They too appeared unstoppable in their conquest of the European and African continents. At sea, the Germans controlled the North Atlantic sealanes; any merchant vessel underway from the coast of the United States to the coastline of Great Britain was subject to being on the receiving end of a torpedo or projectile from a U-boat or surface raider. Times were tough, and the American people needed at least a glimmer of hope that they could, indeed, reverse the losses experienced thus far in the war. Their first taste of hope came on January 28, 1942.

Mason was following the wake of convoy HX-172 heading eastbound from Newfoundland, searching for any signs of U-boat activity. The air was frigid, the seas were rough, and the winds were reading over thirty-five miles per hour. Visibility was low, roughly five nautical miles with a ceiling around one thousand feet. The plane was buffeted by turbulence, causing the crew to concentrate on staying in position as much as searching for the enemy. Airborne for almost two hours at this point, they adjusted uncomfortably in their seats for the remainder of the mission. Suddenly a flash was seen on the surface. Coming in for a closer look, Mason and his crew discovered the periscope of a German U-boat. Preparing for an immediate attack, Mason brought the plane down as far as he could, and the crew let go two depth bombs from an altitude of twenty-five feet, surprising the submarine. Massive spouts of water caused by the explosions bracketed the U-boat and it seemed as though it were brought bodily out of the water. It stopped, dead in the water, and as Mason and his crew circled the wounded vessel, they observed it sink vertically. Oil bubbled to the surface where the submarine had gone under: a sure sign of the end of a U-boat. With darkness descending, Mason radioed back to base in plain language: "Sighted sub, sank same."[1] On that day, he earned worldwide fame for the first United States Navy sinking of a U-boat in the Second World War.

Reverse of Donald Mason's Navy Good Conduct Medal. *Courtesy of the Mason family.*

Donald F. Mason, *Order of Glory, Third Class*

Donald Francis Mason was born on May 26, 1913, in Rochester, Minnesota, far from the sea and very far from his future career as a Naval Aviator. However, learning about aircraft as a young man, he made up his mind to pursue his dream: serving as a Navy pilot. He enlisted in the Navy on August 9, 1935, and following recruit training, was assigned to the USS *San Francisco* (CA-38) under the command of then-Captain Royal E. Ingersoll, who later served as the approving authority for many of Mason's future decorations in his role as Commander in Chief, Atlantic Fleet during the war. By March 1936, Mason had transferred to the *San Francisco's* aviation unit, and shortly thereafter, earned his way to flight school in Pensacola, Florida. In February 1938, he earned his wings as a Naval Aviation Pilot and a rank advancement to Aviation Machinist's Mate, third class. On Christmas Day 1941, now-Aviation Machinist's Mate, first class, Donald Mason shipped out for Naval Air Station Argentia, Newfoundland, flying the Lockheed Hudson PBO-1, delivered to Patrol Squadron (VP) 82 in October of the same year. Immediately following his encounter with the U-boat on January 28, 1942, he was awarded the Distinguished Flying Cross and promoted to Chief Aviation Machinist's Mate.

On March 15, 1942, flying another anti-submarine patrol, this time with convoy ON-72, Mason spotted *U-503* on the surface. Using tactics similar to those employed on January 28, he bombed the U-boat and watched it sink below the waves, taking all fifty-one of her crew with her. For the sinking of *U-503*, Mason was awarded his second Distinguished Flying Cross and was promoted to Ensign on the direct recommendation of Commander, Task Force Twenty-Four.[2]

Following his successful wartime duty with VP-82, later redesignated as VP-125 on March 1, 1943, Donald Mason joined VPB-200, the latter requiring a change of scenery from the Atlantic to the Pacific theater. Flying out of Naval Air Station Kaneohe Bay, Territory of Hawaii, he saw the end of the war and transitioned to staff billets, serving with Commander, Fleet Air Hawaii and Commander, Fleet Air Wing Two. His final job before retirement was as the commanding officer, Naval Air Missile Test Center, Point Mugu. Retiring from the Navy as a Commander on September 30, 1955, he spent the rest of his days as a golf instructor in Oxnard, California, proud of his trademark knickers and knee socks on the course. He passed away just short of Christmas, on December 23, 1990, and is buried in Los Angeles National Cemetery.

Although some question was later raised as to the validity of Mason's first claimed submarine kill as no U-boat was reported lost that day in the post-war evaluation of *Kriegsmarine* records, Mason became a virtual celebrity upon his homecoming, taking part in a thirty-day war bond tour. The nation, still reeling from the losses early in the war, needed a glimmer of hope, and Mason delivered. To his death, Mason claimed the sinking of the submarine, with his crew as witnesses.

Donald Mason's Soviet order book. *Courtesy of the Mason family.*

Donald Mason is congratulated by President Roosevelt for sinking two U-boats. Seated to Roosevelt's right is Lord Halifax, Ambassador of Great Britain to the United States. *Courtesy of the Mason family.*

Order of Glory, Third Class, number 387902, awarded to Donald Mason. *Courtesy of the Mason family.*

Donald Mason's Distinguished Flying Cross, Air Medal, and Navy Good Conduct Medal. *Courtesy of the Mason family.*

March 1, 1942: The Sinking of *U-656*

With debate surrounding Donald Mason's U-boat sinking on January 28, 1942, the first undeniably confirmed U-boat kill of the Second World War by United States forces was claimed by Ensign William Tepuni, flying the same model aircraft in the same squadron as Mason. As with Mason, Tepuni was conducting a routine anti-submarine patrol when he spotted *U-656* south of Cape Race, Newfoundland, on March 1. Racing in for the kill, Tepuni dropped two Mk.17 depth bombs just short of the submarine's starboard bow from an altitude of fifty feet. The subsequent explosions badly damaged *U-656,* and she sank with all hands. He was awarded his first Distinguished Flying Cross for this accomplishment.

William Tepuni, *Order of Glory, Third Class*

William Tepuni as an Aviation Cadet. *US Navy photo.*

William Tepuni (born William De Puni) had a very different background from Donald Mason. Born on October 30, 1915 as the second son to parents who had recently emigrated from Australia to San Francisco, his childhood was shattered by the untimely death of his father when he was two years old. William's mother was able to provide a meager living by working as a theater usher while attempting to raise two young boys into men. William and his brother, Thomas, joined the Navy in 1939. Attending flight school, and then re-assigned to the West Coast together, his brother Thomas was killed in a tragic crash of a torpedo plane in June 1941. Six months later, Tepuni transferred to Argentia, Newfoundland, where he served with Mason and the rest of VP-82.

Following his attack on *U-656,* Tepuni continued his anti-submarine patrols in the inhospitable weather and freezing conditions of the North Atlantic through 1943 until his rotation to the United States. In January 1944, now-Lieutenant Tepuni reported to squadron VPB-128, flying the twin engine Lockheed PV-1 Ventura in the Pacific theater. Flying out of Samar, VPB-128 conducted anti-submarine and convoy escort duties throughout submarine-infested Pacific waters.

On March 22, 1945, Lieutenant Commander Tepuni, now the executive officer of VPB-128, led a five-plane mission to destroy a Japanese midget submarine moored at Cebu City. He had led a mission two days before with only limited success; striking the submarine with two of his rockets, but not causing irreparable damage. Locating the submarine again, he made a direct hit on his first bombing run. However, having lost the element of surprise by their previous attack, the Japanese anti-aircraft emplacements in the city had been heavily reinforced and his plane was mortally hit. Tepuni's aircraft was last seen, in flames, tumbling to the ground. There were no survivors from his six-man crew. He was posthumously recommended for the Navy Cross, but this was reduced to a second award of the Distinguished Flying Cross.[3] William Tepuni is buried in Manila American Cemetery and Memorial in the Philippines.

Close-up of the reverse of William Tepuni's posthumous Purple Heart.

The Distinguished Flying Cross, Air Medal, and posthumous Purple Heart awarded to William Tepuni.

August 20, 1942: The Sinking of *U-464*

Much like Donald Mason's iconic radio transmission of "Sighted sub, sank same," Robert Hopgood was responsible for the statement: "Sank sub, open club." VP-73 had a miserable operational record since their transfer to Iceland several months earlier: they failed to achieve a single victory against a U-boat. Captain (later Rear Admiral) Daniel Gallery, Jr., the Fleet Air Base commander, believed this was due to the late nights the squadron pilots were spending at the base officer's club: their flying skills were dulled by a combination of alcohol and lack of sleep. Thus, he closed the club until the squadron could perform to his level of expectation.

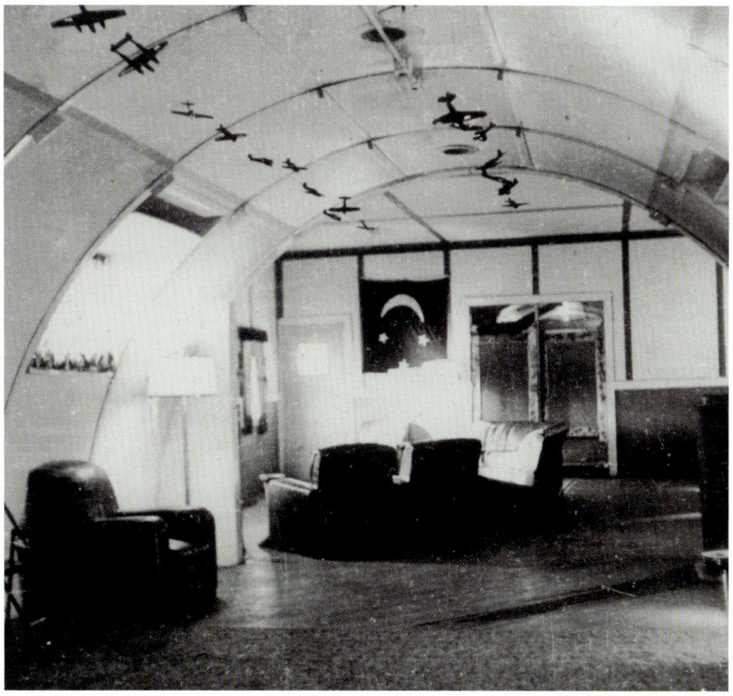

Inside of the officer's club at the Fleet Air Base in Iceland, closed on the orders of Captain (later Rear Admiral) Daniel Gallery due to VP-73's failure to sink U-boats. *Courtesy of the Dyer family.*

On August 20, 1942, Hopgood was flying PBY-5A Bureau number 2459 (later gaining notoriety as the PBY-5A with the highest number of U-boat kills during the Second World War[4]) with Bradford Dyer as his second pilot. Flying down the path of an eastbound convoy on their early morning mission, Dyer spotted a shape about a mile and a half away. In the overcast, dawn sky, Hopgood first thought it was a friendly destroyer, so he fired a flare and received a flare from the submarine in return. However, the response was incorrect, prompting Hopgood to investigate the contact. Dropping in altitude to visually identify the vessel, they were stunned to see the shape of a U-boat, and even more surprised when they noted men waving at them from the conning tower!

Hopgood and his crew had located *U-464*, one of ten "milk cow" U-boats built to resupply other submarines while out at sea. These were extremely valuable targets: sinking one meant the disruption of the entire logistical chain for dozens of other U-boats. *U-464*, commanded by *Korvettenkapitän* Otto Harms, was on her first deployment approximately 175 nautical miles south of Hofn, Iceland. She was completely surprised by the attack. Harms had been warned previously about transiting on the surface due to the presence of enemy aircraft, but ignored the warnings and did so anyway. This was to prove his undoing: immediately going into the attack, Hopgood let go five Mk.17 325-pound depth bombs. Three landed on the sub's deck and were rolled off by the crew, later exploding when their pre-set depth was achieved. One landed to port and immediately exploded. The final landed to starboard, the explosion blowing in the diving tanks and causing the submarine to take a considerable list. *U-464* was mortally wounded, but Hopgood still received heavy anti-aircraft fire from the struggling beast until he lost track of her in a rainsquall. Harms made the determination she could not be rescued, and ordered the crew to abandon the submarine. Fifty-one of her fifty-four-man crew were rescued by an Icelandic fishing vessel and then transferred to the HMS *Castleton* as prisoners of war. In his excitement over the U-boat kill, and in direct response to the now-famous saying by Donald Mason, Hopgood radioed back to base in plain language: "Sank sub, open club!" And they did.[5] Hopgood was awarded the Navy Cross for his heroism, and earned the sound appreciation of his fellow officers.

Captain Gallery congratulates Bradford Dyer and the rest of his aircrew on the sinking of *U-464*. Robert Hopgood is in the back row, center. *Official US Navy photo, courtesy of the Hopgood family.*

Robert Hopgood, on leave in the United States shortly after the sinking of *U-464*. *Courtesy of the Hopgood family.*

Robert B. Hopgood, *Order of the Red Star*

Robert Brown Hopgood was born to Roy Caldwell Hopgood, an attorney for the International Western Electric Company, Inc., on June 30, 1919. Growing up in Africa and England, being educated at Yale, Hopgood fit the mold as a classic Ivy-league representative upon his arrival to flight school on December 29, 1940. Following his designation as a Naval Aviator in July 1941, and after operational training, he reported to VP-73 flying the Consolidated PBY-5A Catalina amphibious aircraft. Several months following the sinking of *U-464*, VP-73 was transferred to North Africa, flying anti-submarine patrols out of French Morocco and Algeria. Rotating stateside in July 1943, Hopgood received orders to serve as the assistant to the aviation ordnance officer, testing smoke tanks and bomb clusters in Dahlgren, Virginia. After a period of retraining in the FM-2 Wildcat fighter in 1945, the war came to an end and he was discharged from active duty. Remaining in the Naval Reserves, he became the commanding officer of VF-832 and VF-836, both Reserve jet squadrons. He retired on June 30, 1979 as a captain.

As a civilian, Hopgood worked as an independent management consultant. His primary focus was on the reorganization and turnarounds of small to mid-sized manufacturing corporations. A brilliant tinkerer, he also patented several inventions, including several new types and styles of lipstick containers, some still commonly found today. While not working or inventing, he played amateur competitive tennis and greatly enjoyed singing, being involved with the "Master Singers" of Worcester, Massachusetts, for many years before his retirement in 1985. Following his retirement, he moved to Florida and passed away on April 15, 2000. He is memorialized at the United Church of Christ Memorial Gardens in Naples, Florida.

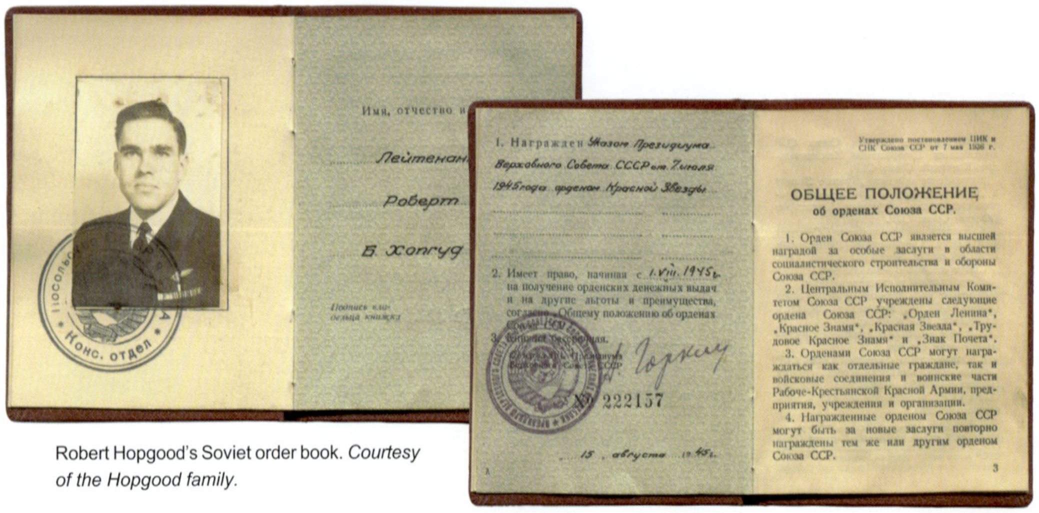

Robert Hopgood's Soviet order book. *Courtesy of the Hopgood family.*

Robert Hopgood's Navy Cross in the original box of issue. *Courtesy of the Hopgood family.*

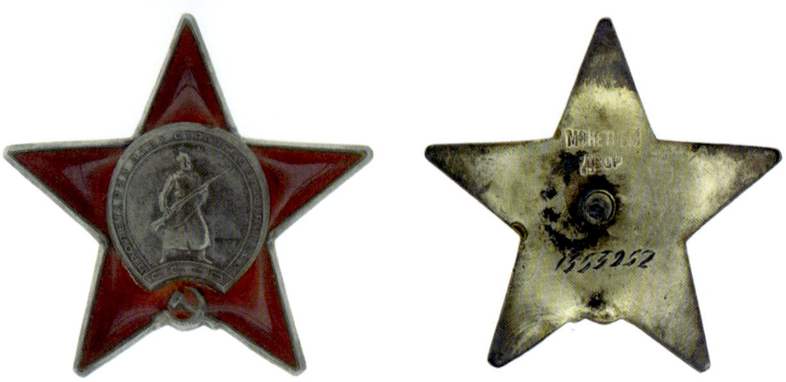

Order of the Red Star number 1553952 awarded to Robert Hopgood. *Courtesy of the Hopgood family.*

Robert Hopgood's Navy Cross. *Courtesy of the Hopgood family.*

June 20, 1942: Friendly Fire Incident

For the sinking of *U-464*, Hopgood's second pilot, Bradford Dyer, was awarded a Letter of Commendation from the Secretary of the Navy. This was his second Commendation earned while serving with VP-73. His first, along with his Purple Heart, was earned two months before, while flying another PBY-5A, Bureau number 2458, out of Iceland when tragedy struck.[6]

On June 20, 1942, future Soviet medal recipients Lieutenant William Cole, Dyer, Chief Aviation Machinist Mate Cecil Haycraft, and Aviation Machinist Mate, second class William B.C. Smith, along with five other crewmembers, took off on a routine anti-submarine patrol in preparation for the Iceland-bound British convoy UR-29. Three hours into the flight, Cole was flying at three thousand feet, above the layer of broken clouds, when a group of ships was detected about seven miles away. They presumed this to be the convoy and descended in order to gain visual contact. Conducting their prescribed homing procedures, they maneuvered to within two miles of the ships, coming down below five hundred feet in altitude. However, no contact was received from the ships, so Cole decided to turn outbound and climb back into his position above the cloud layer. At approximately seven hundred feet, while still in their turn and ascending in the clouds, they were hit by a sudden burst of gunfire from the ships below. Shrapnel flew throughout the aircraft, wounding all but four of the crew, destroying their airspeed meter and disabling their auto pilot system. Outside, the plane had sustained serious damage to the tail, one engine, the hull, and one wing, not to mention several of the cables leading to the control surfaces. Fortuitously, Cole was not wounded, but looking next to him, he saw blood covering Dyer's clothing, flowing from a large gash in his left hand.

The plane's navigator, Ensign Clay, received a severe chest wound from shrapnel and was bleeding profusely from multiple wounds caused by the disintegration of the navigation table and floorboards when they were hit. The plane's first radioman, Aviation Chief Radioman Rollins, was next to Clay and had sustained severe wounds on his hands and back. The second radioman and second mechanic were both likewise severely wounded. The mechanic had large pieces of shrapnel protruding from his back and required serious medical attention immediately. The second radioman, though wounded, remained at his post, his arm unusable and bleeding, continuing in vain to raise the convoy on the radio for help. Haycraft and Smith were lucky: they escaped without being wounded. Haycraft immediately went about rendering first aid to the wounded crewmen, while Smith went to the cockpit to assist Cole and Dyer with the plane's controls.

PBY-5A Bureau number 2458 rests on Kossandr Beach, Iceland, after the friendly fire incident on June 20, 1942. *Courtesy of the Dyer family.*

Breaking out of the clouds and narrowly avoiding a fatal stall, Cole assessed their condition. With the help of Dyer and Smith forcing the unwieldy controls, he made the decision to fly the aircraft as far as possible toward Iceland before ditching in the sea. With the third radioman taking bearings, they flew in this damaged condition for thirty minutes before being forced into a bank of clouds with no visibility. Relying on what instrumentation he had left, Cole flew the plane blindly for another hour and a half, an absolutely remarkable feat of flying skill. Finally, the damaged engine cut out. Feathering the prop, they were forced to descend with a single engine to look for a suitable area to ditch the plane. Breaking out of the clouds, they discovered they were thirty miles from the coast of Iceland. Squeezing every last moment of airspeed and altitude from the wounded plane, Cole ditched the plane in the sea less than a mile from Kossandr Beach on the south coast of the island.

Despite the picture-perfect landing, it was obvious the plane would not stay afloat due to the many holes caused by shrapnel in its keel and fuselage. With the plane rapidly filling with water, Cole, Haycraft, and Smith deployed the two available life rafts and placed the wounded men in them. However, once away from the plane, one of the rafts collapsed and began to take on water due to the weight of the occupants and leaks caused by shrapnel damage. With land so close, Dyer, although wounded, and Smith, jumped out of the good raft and began to propel it to shore by pushing it while swimming in the frigid waters. They were still not safe: by this time, another PBY-5A from VP-73, which had been dispatched to render assistance, saw the situation and dropped a new life raft to the men on the collapsing raft. The rescue aircraft's crew assumed this would be appreciated; however, Smith observed the new raft tumbling through the air directly toward the survivors. Thinking quickly, he leapt aboard the old raft and shielded the wounded men with his own body. This undoubtedly prevented considerable further injury to the wounded men, but resulted in a sprained arm and concussion for Smith. Moving with utmost speed, Dyer and Smith managed to place the wounded men in the new raft just as the other sunk below the waves. With a push of superhuman strength, they finally propelled the two lifeboats ashore.

Meanwhile, Cole and Haycraft remained in the plane, even though it was filling with water and the rafts had already left. This action put them at the risk of almost certain death, as they would have had to traverse a mile of icy water in order to make it to land while still dressed in their unwieldy flight clothing and without the benefit of a life raft. They valiantly attempted to restart the one good engine on the plane and finally, it started. Even though the hull of the plane was now rapidly taking on seawater, they maneuvered the plane the remaining mile and onto the beach. By this point, the plane was low enough in the sea where water was coming up over the windshield and had almost reached the auxiliary power unit (APU) inside the plane. However, by sheer luck and considerable skill, they beached the aircraft on the sandy coastline.

Once ashore, Cole and Haycraft removed the top two bunks from the plane and turned them into makeshift stretchers for the wounded. Despite their injuries, Dyer and Smith assisted them in carrying each of the wounded men across four miles of uneven coastline to a small, and very poor, Icelandic fishing village. There, the locals sacrificed their own meager rations and medical supplies to tend to the wounded men.

William Cole, *Order of Glory, Third Class*

William Cole, pilot of PBY-5A Bureau number 2458. *Courtesy of Weston and Brooke Robinson.*

Following the friendly fire incident, Cole was recommended for the Distinguished Flying Cross for his heroism and unparalleled flying skill. It was downgraded to an Air Medal.[7] William Cole was a New Englander by birth. Born on July 9, 1915, in Danbury, Connecticut, he enlisted in the Navy in July 1938 following his graduation from Dartmouth, where he played football and majored in sociology. He was designated a Naval Aviator on September 30, 1939. He was an "old hand" with VP-73, having spent his entire career with them to that point. Likewise, he was the most experienced pilot in the squadron, receiving a Commendation in both 1940 and 1941 for logging the most accident-free flight hours of any pilot in the Navy, an extremely impressive record. In late summer 1942, he was transferred back to the United States where he became an instrument flight instructor in Jacksonville, Florida, and at Whidbey Island, Washington. A year and a half later, he was retrained to the four-engine PB4Y-1, the Navy's version of the Army Air Force B-24, and was assigned to VPB-104. In June 1945, he became the commanding officer of the squadron and led it to an absolutely remarkable record of over 1,000 operational flights above the South China Sea, accounting for 262 vessels sunk, forty-nine aircraft destroyed, and twelve thousand hours of flight time. By the end of the war, he had added an additional four Air Medals and one Distinguished Flying Cross to his credit. He left active duty in December 1947 and remained in the Naval Reserves through his retirement on March 1, 1961, with the rank of Commander. Following the war, he established a scholarship fund to send one of the young men from the Icelandic fishing village to college, paying his way out of his own pocket.

As a civilian, he lived in Sandy Hook and Newtown, Connecticut, and became the third generation to run the Fabric Fire Hose Company, a family business specializing in the manufacture of fire hoses. He patented two new designs for fire hoses, based on the original woven rubber fire hose patented by his father. Their innovations with freeze-resistant and high-pressure fire hoses are still in wide use today. Retiring from the company in the 1970s, he passed away on September 20, 2009, and is buried in Newtown, Connecticut.

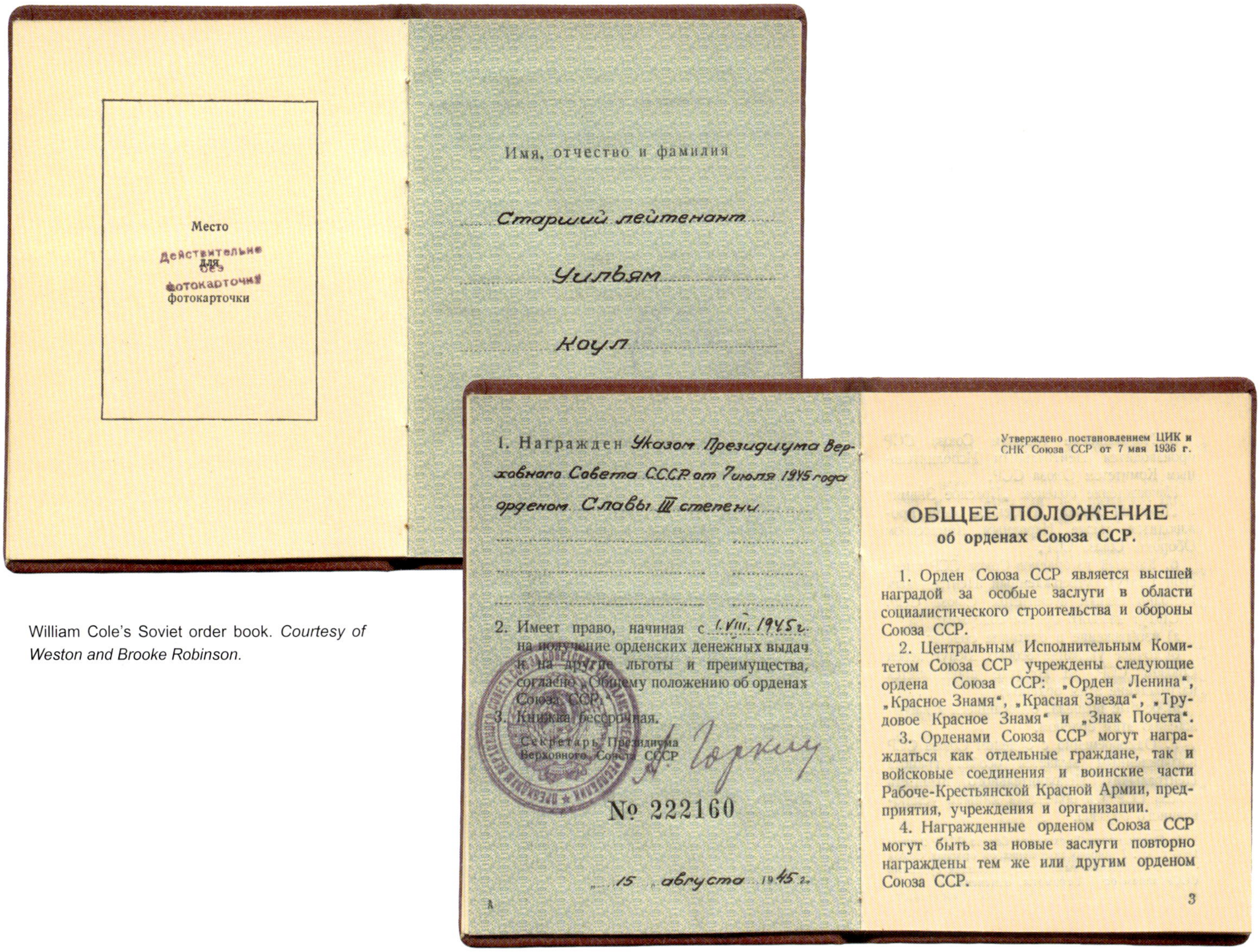
Место
Действительно без фотокарточки
Действительно для фотокарточки

Имя, отчество и фамилия
Старший лейтенант
Уильям
Коул

1. Награжден Указом Президиума Верховного Совета СССР от 7 июля 1945 года орденом Славы III степени

2. Имеет право, начиная с 1.VIII.1945 г. на получение орденских денежных выдач и на другие льготы и преимущества, согласно Общему положению об орденах Союза ССР.

3. Книжка бессрочная.

Секретарь Президиума Верховного Совета СССР

№ 222160

15 августа 1945 г.

Утверждено постановлением ЦИК и СНК Союза ССР от 7 мая 1936 г.

ОБЩЕЕ ПОЛОЖЕНИЕ
об орденах Союза ССР.

1. Орден Союза ССР является высшей наградой за особые заслуги в области социалистического строительства и обороны Союза ССР.

2. Центральным Исполнительным Комитетом Союза ССР учреждены следующие ордена Союза ССР: „Орден Ленина", „Красное Знамя", „Красная Звезда", „Трудовое Красное Знамя" и „Знак Почета".

3. Орденами Союза ССР могут награждаться как отдельные граждане, так и войсковые соединения и воинские части Рабоче-Крестьянской Красной Армии, предприятия, учреждения и организации.

4. Награжденные орденом Союза ССР могут быть за новые заслуги повторно награждены тем же или другим орденом Союза ССР.

3

William Cole's Soviet order book. *Courtesy of Weston and Brooke Robinson.*

William Cole's Distinguished Flying Cross, Air Medal, and Order of Glory, Third Class, number 387901.
Courtesy of Weston and Brooke Robinson.

William B.C. Smith, *Order of Glory, Third Class*

One of these mechanics trained by Haycraft was William Smith, an Aviation Machinist's Mate, second class. He was serving as the first mechanic on the aircraft when it was hit by friendly fire. William Benton Conway Smith considered himself a Texan, having lived there most of his life. Born February 24, 1916, he joined the Navy on May 18, 1936, and served with VP-6F at Pearl Harbor and later on the USS *Broome* (DD-210) in the Atlantic. He reported to VP-73 in October 1941. Smith transferred from VP-73 to VP-53 a month after the incident in June 1942. He remained with VP-53 until his transfer to Carrier Aircraft Service Unit (CASU) 22 in June 1943. He then served in Night Fighter (VFN) 78 and Fighter Squadron (VF) 20, flying from the USS *Enterprise* (CV-6) and taking part in the invasion of Okinawa and the Philippines. He served the remainder of his career in the Navy with Transportation Squadron (VR) 2, flying out of Naval Air Station Alameda. Smith retired as a Chief Aviation Machinist's Mate on March 15, 1956. Shortly thereafter, he was hired by the Los Alamos Scientific Laboratory to work as a maintenance man in the Weapons Neutron Research Operations Group (P-9), where he worked for the next twenty-two years. On June 9, 1978, while conducting routine maintenance in the tank holding the Van de Graaf particle accelerator, he collapsed due to a lack of oxygen in the atmosphere. Rushed to the hospital, he died eight days later from brain damage resulting from oxygen deficiency.[8] He is buried in the Santa Fe National Cemetery, Santa Fe, New Mexico.

Cecil Haycraft's Order of Glory, Third Class, number 387911, in the original case of issue.

Front page of Cecil Haycraft's Soviet order book.

Cecil R. Haycraft, *Order of Glory, Third Class*

Rivalling Cole with his level of expertise, Chief Haycraft was the most experienced mechanic in the squadron and he served as the plane captain on the doomed flight. Cecil Ray Haycraft was born in Glen Dean, Kentucky, on May 30, 1909, and joined the Navy on January 20, 1930. He had served in Panama with VP-3, and in 1934 was selected to become the Aviation Machinist's Mate assigned to the personal aircraft for the Secretary of the Navy. Heading back to sea in 1937, he served as a plane captain on the USS *Enterprise* (CV-6) prior to reporting to VP-73 in May 1939 as their engineering chief. No one could argue with his level of experience around aircraft, and he was the mentor to the junior technicians in the squadron. Transferring from VP-73 in April 1943, Cecil Haycraft later served with Leonard Harmon and James Delhom in VB-105 flying over the Bay of Biscay. Now a commissioned officer, he served as the engineering and maintenance officer for Headquarters Squadron (HEDRON) 5 before his transfer in July 1945 to serve as an engineering officer on the USS *Corregidor* (CVE-58) and later, USS *Franklin* (CV-13). His subsequent tours took him to Washington, DC, Seattle, and finally, on the staff of the Chief of Naval Education and Training in Pensacola, Florida. He retired on January 31, 1957 as a Lieutenant Commander. He spent his retirement years active in the Antique Car Club of America, and passed away in Pensacola on June 5, 1981. He is buried in Barrancas National Cemetery, Pensacola, Florida.

Cecil Haycraft's Navy Good Conduct Medal. *Courtesy of Adam Rohloff.*

Bradford M. Dyer, *Order of Glory, Third Class*

Bradford Mayo "Tex" Dyer was born on October 15, 1914, and was raised in Boston (despite his nickname). He became an Aviation Cadet in May 1941, and in December, earned his designation as a Naval Aviator. Following initial training, he reported to VP-73 in March 1942.

Following the incident, Dyer continued to serve in VP-73 until July 1944. He then transferred to Naval Air Station Deland, Florida, where he became a flight instructor. In May 1945, he received orders to Night Torpedo Squadron (VTN) 55, flying the TBM-1D. By the time they made it into the Pacific theater, the war was over. Dyer became the executive officer of the squadron as they rotated back to the United States. Unlike many of his peers, he remained on active duty, spending the remainder of his career in various billets ashore, as well as serving as the air operations officer on the USS *Midway* (CV-41), and as executive officer of Fleet Air Service Squadron (FASRON) 2, meteorological squadron VW-15, and global transport squadron VR-22. He retired in March 1964 with the rank of Commander. Following retirement from the Navy, he worked as an engineer for Newport News Shipbuilding and drydock for fifteen years. He passed away on November 13, 1994, and is buried in Arlington National Cemetery.

Order of Glory, Third Class, number 387941, awarded to Bradford Dyer. *Courtesy of the Dyer family.*

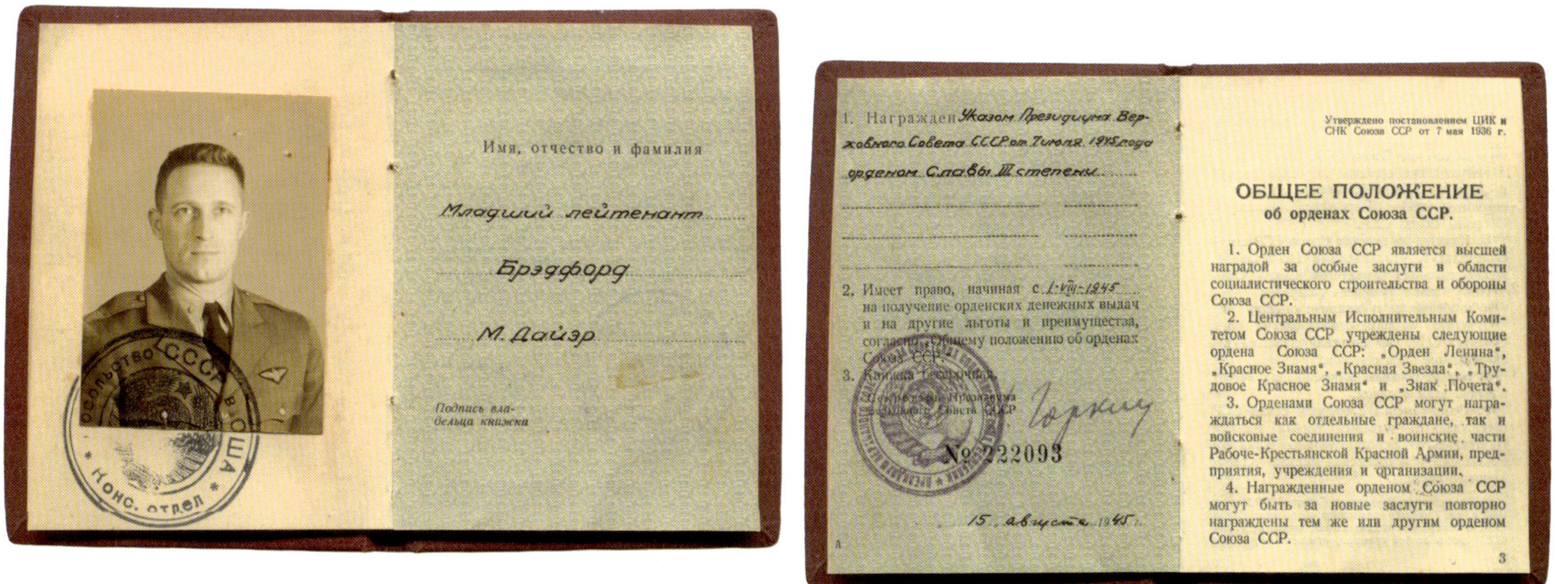

Bradford Dyer's Soviet order book. *Courtesy of the Dyer family.*

December 10, 1942: The Sinking of an Unknown U-boat

As the temperature dropped lower and the weather worsened, Navy patrol aircraft remained in the skies to defend the convoys bound for the Soviet Union. Flying out of Iceland, Lowell Davis was serving with VP-84, along with fellow Soviet medal recipient Robert Millard, conducting anti-submarine and convoy coverage patrols. On December 10, operating approximately 350 nautical miles south of Reykjavik, Davis' co-pilot spotted a surfaced U-boat at a distance of six miles. Closing in for the kill, they dropped one 650-pound depth bomb in close proximity of the U-boat while avoiding deadly anti-aircraft fire. The aircraft's navigator watched as the submarine lifted from the water and collapsed beneath the waves, her last position being marked by an oil slick and what appeared to be a handful of survivors, though none were ever recovered. Considered a positive kill, Davis was awarded the Distinguished Flying Cross for the destruction of what was believed to be *U-611*. Postwar analysis called his kill into question, however, as *U-611* was claimed to have been sunk by the Royal Air Force (RAF) two days prior.[9] On April 5, 1943, Davis again had his opportunity to register a U-boat kill, this time with *U-592*. His bombing pattern was well done, but not enough to sink the submarine. However, he did achieve an effective "mission kill," as *U-592* was forced to abort her mission several days later due to the extensive damage caused by his attack.

Lowell L. Davis prior to joining the Navy. *Courtesy of the Davis family.*

Lowell L. Davis, *Order of Glory, Third Class*

Lowell Levon Davis was born on October 11, 1918, in Vina, Alabama. He left college before graduation and joined the Navy. In January 1941, he reported to Pensacola, Florida for flight school as an Aviation Cadet. On June 3, he was designated a Naval Aviator, and shortly thereafter reported to VP- 81, flying PBY-5 aircraft out of Naval Air Station, Key West. He served with them until March 1942, when he transferred to VP-84. Following the U-boat sinking on December 10, he returned to the United States and was assigned to Air Anti-Submarine Development, Atlantic Fleet, conducting testing of experimental rockets and bombs. While here, he developed the Navy's first airborne anti-submarine searchlight (an anti-submarine weapon first developed by the British and known as a "Leigh Light"), an invaluable tool used in future submarine engagements.[10] The remainder of the war was spent training and ferrying PB4Y-1 aircraft from England back to the United States following the end of the war in Europe. The subsequent sixteen years of his career were spent in training positions and dealing with Naval Reserve policy matters in Alabama, Florida, New York, and Washington, DC Davis retired from the Navy as a Captain on April 30, 1961. Shortly thereafter, he joined the Federal Aviation Administration, eventually becoming the chief of the Civil Aviation Security Division before his second retirement. Lowell Davis passed away on September 24, 1980, and was buried at sea.

Место для фотокарточки

Имя, отчество и фамилия

1. Награжден

2. Имеет право, начиная с

на получение орденских денежных выдач и на другие льготы и преимущества, согласно „Общему положению об орденах Союза ССР".

№ 222076

Утверждено постановлением ЦИК и СНК Союза ССР от 7 мая 1936 г.

ОБЩЕЕ ПОЛОЖЕНИЕ
об орденах Союза ССР.

1. Орден Союза ССР является высшей наградой за особые заслуги в области социалистического строительства и обороны Союза ССР.

2. Центральным Исполнительным Комитетом Союза ССР учреждены следующие ордена Союза ССР: „Орден Ленина", „Красное Знамя", „Красная Звезда", „Трудовое Красное Знамя" и „Знак Почета".

3. Орденами Союза ССР могут награждаться как отдельные граждане, так и войсковые соединения и воинские части Рабоче-Крестьянской Красной Армии, предприятия, учреждения и организации.

4. Награжденные орденом Союза ССР могут быть за новые заслуги повторно награждены тем же или другим орденом

Lowell Davis' Soviet order book. *Courtesy of the Davis family.*

The Distinguished Flying Cross, American Defense, Asiatic-Pacific Campaign, World War II Victory, Korean Service, and National Defense medals awarded to Lowell Davis. *Courtesy of the Davis family.*

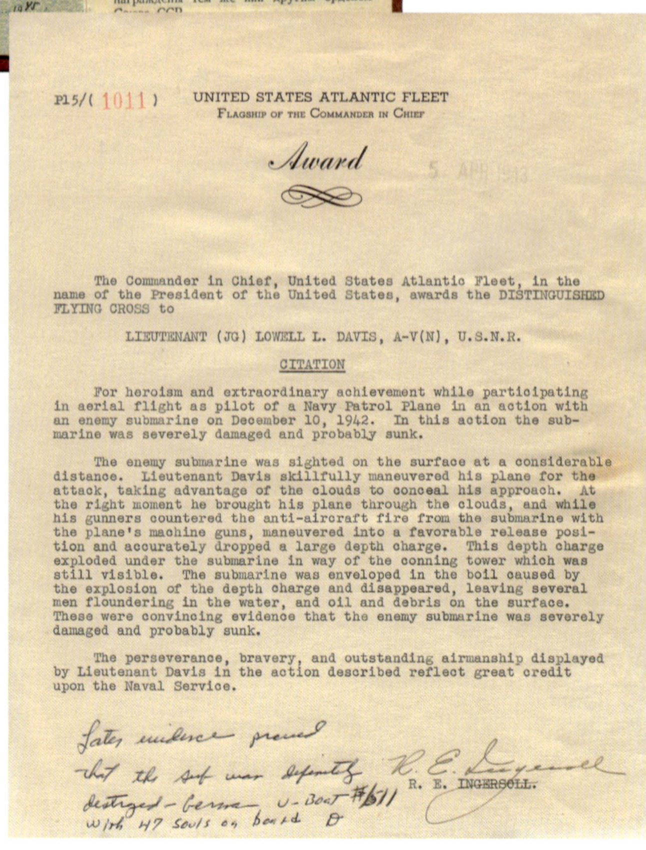

P15/(1011) UNITED STATES ATLANTIC FLEET
FLAGSHIP OF THE COMMANDER IN CHIEF

Award

5 APR 1943

The Commander in Chief, United States Atlantic Fleet, in the name of the President of the United States, awards the DISTINGUISHED FLYING CROSS to

LIEUTENANT (JG) LOWELL L. DAVIS, A-V(N), U.S.N.R.

CITATION

For heroism and extraordinary achievement while participating in aerial flight as pilot of a Navy Patrol Plane in an action with an enemy submarine on December 10, 1942. In this action the submarine was severely damaged and probably sunk.

The enemy submarine was sighted on the surface at a considerable distance. Lieutenant Davis skillfully maneuvered his plane for the attack, taking advantage of the clouds to conceal his approach. At the right moment he brought his plane through the clouds, and while his gunners countered the anti-aircraft fire from the submarine with the plane's machine guns, maneuvered into a favorable release position and accurately dropped a large depth charge. This depth charge exploded under the submarine in way of the conning tower which was still visible. The submarine was enveloped in the boil caused by the explosion of the depth charge and disappeared, leaving several men floundering in the water, and oil and debris on the surface. These were convincing evidence that the enemy submarine was severely damaged and probably sunk.

The perseverance, bravery, and outstanding airmanship displayed by Lieutenant Davis in the action described reflect great credit upon the Naval Service.

R. E. INGERSOLL.

The citation for Lowell Davis' Distinguished Flying Cross. It is interesting to note the hand-annotated update on the bottom of the page. *Courtesy of the Davis family.*

November 5, 1942: The Sinking of *U-408*

Davis' fellow pilot and only other Soviet medal recipient in VP-84, Robert Millard, flew his first action against U-boats on November 1, 1942. Flying in a two-plane section, he discovered *U-613* and *U-644* surfaced at a rendezvous location. Millard went in for the attack. Unfortunately, *U-613*, his target, was quick to respond and disappeared below the waves before she could be destroyed. *U-644* likewise escaped total destruction, but was sufficiently damaged by Millard's fellow pilot to force its return to France for repair (*U-644* was later sunk on August 9, 1943, by Soviet medal awardees Gerald Hogan, Junior Forney, and Norman Hodson of VC-1).[11] Millard's first confirmed kill took place four days later on November 5, 1942. Conducting an anti-submarine patrol one hundred miles north of Iceland, Millard's PBY-5A spotted *U-408* (who had sunk the SS *Oliver Ellsworth* of convoy PQ-18 two months earlier) on the surface and took her completely by surprise. His four depth bombs straddled the hapless vessel and within minutes she went to the bottom of the sea. There were no survivors. He was later awarded the Distinguished Flying Cross for the sinking of *U-408*.

Robert C. Millard, *Order of Glory, Third Class*

Robert Millard as a Navy Captain. *Courtesy of the Millard family.*

Robert Carpenter Millard was born on September 22, 1915, and entered the Naval Academy with the class of 1938. Upon graduation and commissioning, he first reported to the USS *Tennessee* (BB-43) followed by a tour as the engineering officer on the USS *Gilmore* (DE-18). He then reported to flight school and after completing his operational training was sent to his first squadron, VP-84. Earning the Distinguished Flying Cross and British Distinguished Flying Cross for his actions against enemy U-boats, he finished out the war with the Anti-Submarine Development Force, Atlantic Fleet, and then commanded Headquarters Squadron (HEDRON) 3 and Fleet Aircraft Service Squadron (FASRON) 108. His next tour took him to Experimental Squadron (VX) 4, followed by service as the assistant director of tests at the Naval Air Missile Test Center, Point Mugu, California. He returned to sea as executive officer of the USS *Windham Bay* (CVE-92), serving off the coast of Korea during the war. Next, he served as executive officer of Naval Auxiliary Air Station Monterey, later becoming the commanding officer until his transfer in October 1954. He was then ordered to command Utility Squadron 3, followed by Guided Missile Group One. His final duty stations included serving with the guided missile project at North Island and at the Bureau of Aeronautics as the assistant bureau chief for programs and management plans. He retired in June 1961 as a Captain.

Following his retirement, Millard went to work first for the Radio Corporation of America (RCA), and then became manager of the Charles S. Draper Laboratory in the NASA Apollo shuttle program at the Massachusetts Institute of Technology. Robert Millard passed away on March 10, 1981, in Pensacola, Florida, and is buried in Arlington National Cemetery.

Robert Millard's Distinguished Flying Cross, Order of Glory, Third Class, number 387903, and his British Distinguished Flying Cross. *Courtesy of the Millard family.*

April 27, 1943: The Sinking of *U-174*

Commencing his overseas tour of duty in May 1942 with Mason and Tepuni in VP-82, Thomas Kinaszczuk remained with the squadron when it redesignated to VB-125 on March 1, 1943, and switched to the Lockheed PV-1 Ventura aircraft. The squadron had not had a kill since transitioning to the Venturas, but on April 27, 1943, they had their first. Kinaszczuk spotted a surfaced U-boat at eight miles and went in for the kill. Rather than dive, the submarine, *U-174*, decided to fight it out on the surface. Her captain, *Oberleutnant zur See* Wolfgang Grandefeld, had been in command for just forty-one days and was in need of proving himself to the crew. The submarine's previous commander, the swaggering Ulrich Thilo, had survived a five-hour depth charge and two aerial attacks previously, and had sent over thirty thousand tons of shipping to the bottom of the sea, leaving Grandefeld with some very large shoes to fill. Valiantly manning the submarine's guns, the crew opened fire on the inbound Ventura, confident in their ability to add an aircraft credit to their impressive list of kills.

Despite the hail of incoming fire, Kinaszczuk pressed home his attack: he descended to twenty-five feet and released his depth bombs in a perfect pattern. Three of the four bombs exploded below the submarine, sending up an incredible mountain of spray and causing immeasurable internal damage to the vessel and crew. For the next fourteen minutes, Grandefeld fought valiantly to keep the submarine afloat. However, the damage proved too much and *U-174* slipped below the waves, bow first, taking her entire crew with her. For this action, the first U-boat sunk by a PV-1 Ventura, Kinaszczuk was awarded the Navy Cross.

Images of the attack on *U-174*. *Official US Navy photos via the Kinaszczuk family.*

Thomas Kinaszczuk, *Order of Glory, Third Class*

Born to Ukrainian immigrant parents in New Jersey on October 21, 1920, Kinaszczuk graduated from high school in 1938 and with the minimum requirement of two years of college completed, enlisted in the Navy in 1941 as an Aviation Cadet. Earning his Naval Aviator designation on December 30, he was sent to the fleet as soon as his operational training was complete. Two months after earning his Navy Cross, VPB-125 was rotated back to the United States and commenced operations out of Boca Chica, Florida. Conducting many anti-submarine missions out of the Azores, Kinaszczuk survived what could have been a potential disaster when both engines on his Ventura gave out four hundred miles off the coast of Brazil while on a non-routine mission ferrying sensitive communication equipment to Europe. Surviving for five days in a small raft, they were finally rescued at sea after being located by a Pan American World Airways C-54 and US Army B-24, who directed a crash boat to their location. They were incredibly lucky: their odds of survival four hundred miles off the coast, alone in a small boat in the middle of the South Atlantic, were practically none.

In February 1945, he transferred to VPB-114, flying anti-submarine patrol missions out of the Azores. He remained there for the rest of the war. Kinaszczuk left active duty on October 11, 1945, and entered the Naval Reserve, eventually retiring as a Commander. As a civilian, he joined Pan American World Airways in March 1946, eventually flying 747 jets until his retirement in October 1980. Thomas Kinaszczuk passed away on January 15, 2013, and is buried with full military honors at Arlington National Cemetery.

Thomas Kinaszczuk at the award ceremony for his Navy Cross. *Courtesy of the Kinaszczuk family.*

Order of Glory, Third Class, number 387929, awarded to Thomas Kinaszczuk along with his Soviet order book. *Courtesy of the Kinaszczuk family.*

The Navy Cross awarded to Thomas Kinaszczuk. *Courtesy of the Kinaszczuk family.*

Thomas Kinaszczuk with his aircrew in front of their Lockheed PV-1 Ventura. *Courtesy of the Kinaszczuk family.*

August 12, 1943: The Attack on *U-760*

Shortly before Kinaszczuk sank *U-174*, Theodore Thueson was transferred from the Pacific theater to the Atlantic for service with VB-103, flying the converted Consolidated B-24, known to the Navy as the PB4Y-1, out of Argentia, Newfoundland. On August 12, 1943, Thueson spotted a surfaced U-boat, believed to be *U-760*, and went in for the attack. Although he strafed the U-boat and dropped three depth bombs, the submarine managed to submerge and escape. One member of the U-boat crew was killed in the attack; no injuries were reported amongst Thueson's crew, despite receiving heavy anti-aircraft fire from the submarine. For this action, the only U-boat attack for VB-103 up to that time, Thueson was awarded the Air Medal.

Theodore S. Thueson, *Order of Glory, Third Class*

Theodore Thueson receives the Distinguished Flying Cross from Admiral Halsey for his actions during the Battle of Midway. *Official US Navy photo via the National Archives.*

Theodore Stanley "Swede" Thueson was born on October 31, 1915, in Newburgh, New York. At the age of eighteen, he volunteered for the Navy and reported for active duty on April 23, 1934. His first duty was as a gun pointer on the USS *Raleigh* (CL-7), an *Omaha*-class light cruiser. Finding a fascination with aircraft, he became an Aviation Machinist's Mate and served as the plane captain for one of the ship's scouting aircraft. Leaving the *Raleigh* in 1938, he was offered the opportunity to attend flight school while conducting maintenance on aircraft ashore. He was designated as an enlisted Naval Aviation Pilot on May 17, 1940. His first squadron was VP-23, flying out of Pearl Harbor, Territory of Hawaii. Here, he qualified as first pilot of a PBY-type aircraft, conducting routine missions around the islands. Peace was shattered on the morning of December 7, 1941, and Thueson received his first taste of war as a hastily-assembled crewmember on Lieutenant Commander James Ogden's PBY-5; one of only four PBY-5s from VP-23 to survive that fateful day. Promoted to Ensign in April 1942, he began flying as plane commander in the PBY-5 aircraft. He earned his first Distinguished Flying Cross for his actions during the Battle of Midway on June 4, 1942, when he discovered the Japanese fleet and alerted Admiral Nimitz to their location and disposition for a period of over two hours until his aircraft ran out of fuel. He was able to successfully land his plane and was eventually rescued by the USS *Monaghan* (DD-354) approximately eighty miles from Midway Island.

Reporting to VB-103 in April 1943, he spent the next year flying anti-submarine patrols out of Dunkeswell, England, along with fellow future Soviet medal recipients Kenneth Wright, Roy Johnson, Phillip Anderson, George Enloe, Paul Kinney, and Dallas Jones. Thueson served as the squadron's material and navigation officer. Returning to the United States in July 1944, he served with Transportation Squadron (VR) 2 out of Naval Air Station Alameda as a plane commander. He was stationed here when the war ended. Requesting to remain on active duty, he held many operational billets throughout the remainder of his career, to include serving with VP-42 during the Korean War, earning his second Distinguished Flying Cross and three additional Air Medals while flying from August to December 1950. Thueson retired on May 1, 1956, tombstoned to the rank of Captain due to his extensive combat experience and decorations.[12] He passed away on January 3, 1989, and is buried in Arlington National Cemetery.

Theodore Thueson and his aircrew receive a post-flight intelligence debrief after conducting an anti-submarine mission over the Bay of Biscay in February 1944. *Official US Navy photo via the National Archives.*

November 10, 1943: Attacks on *U-966*

Kenneth Wright and Roy Johnson marked VB-103's next encounter with a U-boat in the attack on *U-966* on November 10, 1943. This action later became known as one of the longest-running surface battles of aircraft against a U-boat in the Second World War.

However, before Wright and Johnson got into the fray, two other future Soviet medal recipients spotted the same submarine. November 10 was a beautiful day, with no cloud cover and choppy seas. At 8:00 AM, a PB4Y-1 from VP-105, piloted by Leonard Harmon and James Delhom, sighted *U-966* on the surface with a steady wake. Closing in for an attack, they were met by heavy anti-aircraft fire from the submarine. Still determined to let go their depth bombs, Harmon pressed in. However, the explosions of subsequent shells from the submarine's anti-aircraft guns wreaked havoc on the thin aluminum structure of the bomber and damaged the plane's bomb release system. Undaunted, Harmon and Delhom positioned the plane to make the best possible strafing runs at close range, making not one, but two strafing passes at the U-boat. Feeling their luck about to expire, they turned away from the submarine and broke off the attack. Circling out of range of the U-boat's weapons, they watched an RAF fighter make a strafing run at the submarine, only to be repulsed by the heavy anti-aircraft fire. At this point, having already attacked once and dangerously low on fuel, Harmon and Delhom would have been justified in returning to base. However, they closed in again, making one final strafing run before breaking off the attack and returning to base due to their fuel level.

At 10:40 AM, Kenneth Wright and Roy Johnson, flying another PB4Y-1, also spotted *U-966* on the surface. As with Harmon and Delhom, they closed in to attack. Experiencing waves of heavy anti-aircraft fire, they pursued their target and laid a pattern of five depth bombs in the vicinity of the submarine, causing heavy damage. With the bombing run complete, they circled around. Taking advantage of the confusion on the deck of the submarine, they commenced yet another strafing run before heading outside the range of the U-boat's guns. Also running low on fuel, Wright and Johnson had to return to base but observed *U-966* trailing oil and moving significantly slower through the water as they departed the scene. Finally, another PB4Y-1 from VB-110 and an RAF Liberator arrived on scene at 12:30 PM. The Navy PB4Y-1 dropped a pattern of six depth bombs and the RAF Liberator launched a rocket attack on the almost-stopped and battered U-boat. Even with this dramatic escalation of force, *U-966* refused to sink. With extensive damage resulting from the multitude of attacks, her captain made for the Spanish coastline and scuttled her that evening. The brave crew of *U-966*, save for six who were killed during the running battle that day, were interred in Spain.[13]

Leonard E. Harmon, *Order of Glory, Third Class*

Leonard Edward Harmon was born in Danvers, Massachusetts, on February 2, 1915. He joined the Naval Reserve in February 1933 and was accepted into the Naval Academy as a midshipman in June 1934. Graduating with the class of 1938 along with Robert Millard, Harmon's first assignment was to the USS *Saratoga* (CV-3), where he served in multiple departments before receiving orders to flight school in August 1940. Receiving his Naval Aviator designation in March 1941, he reported immediately afterward to VP-31, operating out of Puerto Rico, flying the PBY-2 Catalina. He remained with this squadron throughout the entire Second World War; a relatively unusual career path for a wartime pilot. With the commencement of the war in December, VP-31 began anti-submarine patrols in the Caribbean, continuing these through 1943; first out of Puerto Rico, and later with the squadron headquarters in Elizabeth City, North Carolina. A single detachment of the squadron, now designated VB-105, was sent to Argentia, Newfoundland, and subsequently, Greenland, but the squadron did not permanently change station until October 1943. At this time, they transferred to RAF Station Dunkeswell, England, to patrol the Bay of Biscay and Western Approaches in the PB4Y-1. It was while flying out of Dunkeswell that Harmon and his co-pilot, James Delhom, made their encounter with *U-966*. Harmon assumed command of VB-105 in October 1944 and remained in that position until May 1945, supervising the continued anti-submarine patrols of his squadron throughout the Bay of

Close-up of the engraving on the reverse of Leonard Harmon's Distinguished Flying Cross.

Biscay and the English Channel. Reporting to the Naval Academy in June 1945, he served as an ordnance and gunnery instructor until entering the aeronautical engineering curriculum at the Naval Postgraduate School. That was followed by another stint at postgraduate education, this time at the California Institute of Technology, where he graduated in June 1949. He went on to hold multiple command positions to include squadron VR-24, USS *Rankin* (AKA-103), and Airborne Early Warning Wing, Atlantic. He retired from the Navy as a Captain on April 30, 1968. Leonard Harmon passed away on July 9, 1998, and is buried in Calverton National Cemetery, Calverton, New York.

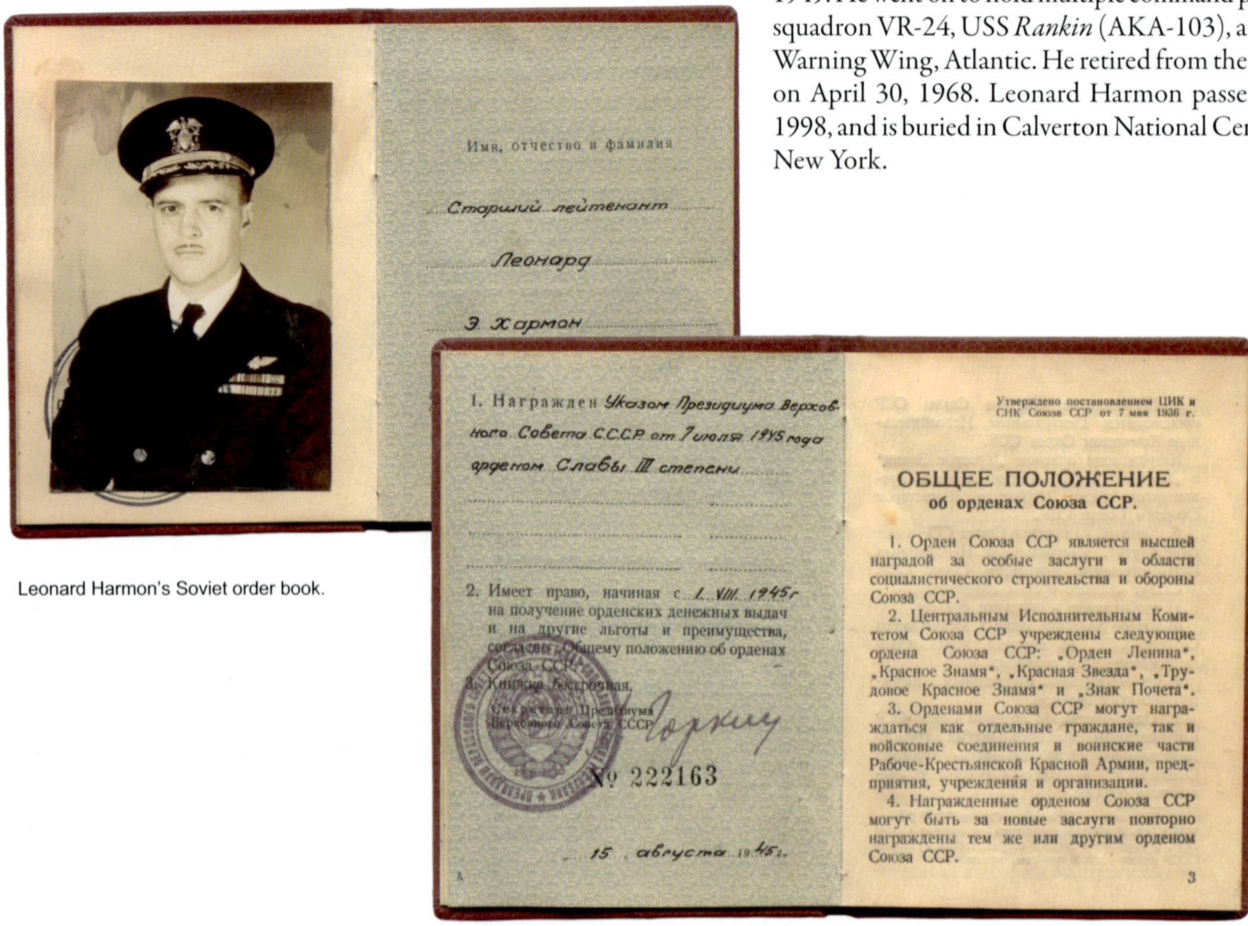

Имя, отчество и фамилия

Старший лейтенант

Леонард

Э. Харман

1. Награжден Указом Президиума Верховного Совета С.С.С.Р от 7 июля 1945 года орденом Славы III степени

2. Имеет право, начиная с 1. VIII. 1945 г на получение орденских денежных выдач и на другие льготы и преимущества, согласно Общему положению об орденах Союза ССР.

3. Книжка бессрочная.

Секретарь Президиума Верховного Совета СССР

№ 222163

15 августа 1945 г.

Утверждено постановлением ЦИК и СНК Союза ССР от 7 мая 1936 г.

ОБЩЕЕ ПОЛОЖЕНИЕ
об орденах Союза ССР.

1. Орден Союза ССР является высшей наградой за особые заслуги в области социалистического строительства и обороны Союза ССР.

2. Центральным Исполнительным Комитетом Союза ССР учреждены следующие ордена Союза ССР: „Орден Ленина", „Красное Знамя", „Красная Звезда", „Трудовое Красное Знамя" и „Знак Почета".

3. Орденами Союза ССР могут награждаться как отдельные граждане, так и войсковые соединения и воинские части Рабоче-Крестьянской Красной Армии, предприятия, учреждения и организации.

4. Награжденные орденом Союза ССР могут быть за новые заслуги повторно награждены тем же или другим орденом Союза ССР.

3

Leonard Harmon's Soviet order book.

Leonard Harmon and his aircrew pose in front of his PB4Y-1 aircraft named *White Witch*.

Leonard Harmon's medal bar, including the Distinguished Flying Cross, Bronze Star Medal, Air Medal, American Defense Medal, and British Distinguished Flying Cross.

James J. Delhom, *Order of Glory, Third Class*

Unlike his New England-native pilot, James Joseph Delhom was born in New Orleans on May 13, 1918. Raised in Louisiana, he attended Loyola University and made a name for himself as a distance runner on their track team. He was a member of the 1939-40 and 1940-41 Dixie Conference championship track teams, serving as the captain of the latter. Prior to joining the Navy after his graduation in 1941, he held the Conference records in the mile and two-mile runs. Designated a Naval Aviator as the war began, he was sent to VP-31, and served with Harmon throughout the squadron's varied duty stations and locations. Following the action with *U-966*, Harmon and Delhom did not lack for adventure. On December 28, 1943, while on routine patrol, they encountered a surface force of eleven German destroyers. Relaying the position of the ships to the RAF, three Royal Navy ships were vectored to the location and in the ensuing battle three of the German vessels were sunk. At the same time, while shadowing the surface ships, Harmon and Delhom were attacked by a force of six German Ju 88 bombers. Outmatched for agility, they fought as bravely as they could, resulting in one probable kill of a Ju 88 before they could escape.

James Delhom returned to New Orleans and remained in the Navy Reserve, where he retired as a Captain on September 1, 1972. He worked as the sales manager for several local companies and was very involved in the New Orleans community, eventually rising to become the president of the Exchange Club and vice commander of the New Orleans chapter of the Military Order of the World Wars. He passed away on February 17, 1973, at Chalmette, Louisiana, and is buried in Greenwood Cemetery, New Orleans.

James Delhom as a Captain later in his career. *National Personnel Records Center.*

Kenneth L. Wright, *Order of Glory, Third Class*

Kenneth L. Wright, approximately 1942. *Courtesy of the Wright family.*

As the pilot of the PB4Y-1 from VB-103 who attacked *U-966*, Kenneth Leon Wright was born in Burlington, Kansas, on September 20, 1917. Graduating from Burlington High School in 1935 and attending Kansas University, he enlisted in the Navy on October 2, 1941. Accepted for flight training, he reported to Kansas City, Kansas, for initial training on February 5, 1942, and received his Naval Aviator designation at Corpus Christi, Texas, on August 20. Reporting shortly thereafter to VP-11 in the Western Pacific, he transferred again on March 27, 1943, this time to the newly-commissioned VB-103, serving as the squadron's assistant operations officer. He had been with the squadron for seven months by the time he earned the Distinguished Flying Cross for bravery demonstrated in the attack on *U-966*.

On February 14, 1944, Wright was again in combat, this time against a well-coordinated surprise attack by two German Ju 88s. Although his crew was credited with one possible kill during the action, he was forced to ditch his plane in the water due to fatal hits from enemy gunfire that knocked out one engine and subsequently caused a second to be lost. He was personally responsible for saving eight of his crewmembers upon evacuating the plane, though three died from wounds received during the exchange of fire and injuries sustained during the landing. In May 1944, he was rotated back to the United States and served as a flight instructor on the PBY4-1 aircraft for the remainder of the war, flying out of the US Naval Auxiliary Air Station, Chincoteague, Virginia.

Discharged on September 13, 1945, he moved to Salina, Kansas and founded the Wright-Lorenz Grain Company, where he worked until he retired as the company's president. He was very involved in the community, being a director of the First National Bank & Trust, a board member of the St. Francis Boy's Home, a trustee of St. Johns Military School and commander of his American Legion post. He suffered a heart attack while working in his yard and died the same day, November 10, 1983. He is buried in Roselawn Memorial Park in his hometown of Salina.

Kenneth Wright's medals, including the Distinguished Flying Cross, Air Medal, Purple Heart, and Order of Glory, Third Class, number 387933. *Courtesy of the Wright family.*

Roy W. Johnson, *Order of Glory, Third Class*

Roy W. Johnson, taken in 1954.
Courtesy of the Johnson family.

Roy Walter Johnson, Wright's co-pilot, was born on December 2, 1921, and became an Aviation Cadet on February 21, 1942. Reporting to VB-103 for his first operational tour, he was only slightly junior to Kenneth Wright with regard to time and flight experience. Following the attack on *U-966*, he continued to serve with VB-103 until transferring to VB-107. He joined his new squadron at the same time as Soviet medal recipient Paul Kinney, becoming an instructor pilot when they received the PB4Y-1 aircraft. He served with VB-107 for the remainder of the war. Discharged from active duty in September 1945, he remained in the Navy Reserves, holding various billets in transportation squadrons, to include command of Naval Reserve Transport Squadron (VR) 704. He retired in March 1973 as a Captain.

Following his discharge, he was quickly hired by the Federal Aviation Administration, first serving as an air traffic controller, and then as an airway flight inspector. In the latter capacity, he earned his commercial pilot license in command qualifications in the DC-3, C-18, T-33, C-135 and B-57 aircraft. He further served as chief of the High Altitude Flight Office, Flight Inspection and Logistics Branch in Honolulu, the Aircraft Management Branch for twelve midwestern states, and finally on the regional director's staff for the FAA Central Region. Retiring from the FAA after twenty-nine years of service on January 1, 1975, he moved to Ozark, Missouri, to raise registered Angus cattle, and occasionally flew as a corporate pilot for the Caterpillar Company. He finally retired completely in June 1983 and passed away on June 8, 2007.

Roy Johnson's bar-mounted medals, including the Distinguished Flying Cross, Air Medal, European African Middle Eastern Campaign Medal, American Campaign Medal, and Order of Glory, Third Class, number 387942.
Courtesy of the Johnson family.

December 28 and 29, 1943: Attacks on German Warships.

The group of ships sighted by Harmon and Delhom on December 28 were on their way to escort a blockade runner, the name for a merchant ship attempting to reach the German-occupied coastline in order to discharge its cargo for the Nazis. Harmon radioed the ships' position to the RAF, and the Royal Navy vectored ships to intercept the German units. Additionally, a flight of fifteen aircraft from the combined squadrons of VB-103 and VB-105 took off to seek out and destroy the German ships. Following the combined air and surface attack, three of the German ships had been sunk by the Royal Navy; and the remainder were scattered by heavy bombing from VB-103 and VB-105 aircraft.

Philip R. Anderson, *Order of Glory, Third Class*

On December 29, two PB4Y-1 aircraft from VB-103 returned to search the attack area for survivors. One of these aircraft was piloted by Philip Anderson, a relative newcomer to the squadron. Philip Randolph Anderson was born in Washington, DC, on March 23, 1916, to Peter Melvin Anderson, a US Army Quartermaster Corps officer. Living in Maryland, he applied for, and was accepted into, the class of 1940 at the Naval Academy. However, he decided to leave the Academy without graduating and continued his education at the University of Maryland, where he studied electrical engineering for two years. However, again he left without graduating and became a manufacturer's representative for the Wood Conversion Company out of St. Paul, Minnesota. He learned to fly on his own, and with the start of the war, joined the Navy as an Aviation Cadet. Following a year of flight school and secondary training, he arrived at VB-103 in mid-1943.

On that late December day, he sighted a single German destroyer that had escaped the previous day's attack. Determined to at least damage, if not sink the destroyer, he flew in at a low altitude to ensure a successful bombing run. Unfortunately, the German destroyer fired back, severely damaging his plane and disabling his bomb release mechanism. Not to be deterred, he pressed home a second attack, strafing the destroyer. Once away from the ship, they discovered a punctured and leaking fuel tank from anti-aircraft fire. With his fuel level decreasing rapidly, he made the decision to fly the aircraft over neutral Spain in an attempt to land and repair the leaking tank. However, a severe weather front blocked his landing area, so he decided to allow his crew to bail out over a small stretch of mountainous Spanish land. Being the last to leave the plane, he steered the aircraft out to sea and armed its load of depth bombs to ensure destruction of the aircraft upon landing. Only then did he bail out of the disabled plane and rejoin his crew. They were repatriated after two weeks in Spain via Gibraltar, and he was awarded the Air Medal for his heroism and devotion shown under the most extreme circumstances. He continued to fly anti-submarine missions through June 1944, earning a second Air Medal and the Distinguished Flying Cross before returning to the United States. He was discharged on September 8, 1945, and continued to live in the Washington, DC area until his death on February 7, 1967, at the age of fifty. He is buried in Arlington National Cemetery.

January 28, 1944: The Sinking of *U-271*

VB-103 would have one more notable success while stationed out of England. On the morning of January 28, 1944, crew number ten, consisting of Soviet medal recipients George Enloe, Paul Kinney, and Dallas Jones, along with eight other crewmembers, were given the mission of patrolling the path of an eastbound US convoy approximately five hundred miles due west of the southern tip of Ireland. This was to be an "easy" day. As Francis "Red" Dean, the tail gunner remembered:

> *An operational flight going out west into the Atlantic Ocean seemed to the crew like having the day off. We had originally been scheduled to fly down the coast of France to Spain and back. Going out over the Atlantic where we didn't have to worry too much about looking out for enemy planes was good news.*[14]

Midway through the flight, at 11:47 AM and approximately two hundred miles from the west coast of Ireland, the crew moved about as they started to eat lunch. Ensign Pohling, the navigator, stood up and as he did, yelled out over the intercom that he spotted a submarine. George Enloe, the pilot, took the plane into a steep dive from eight hundred down to fifty feet, directly out of the sun and downwind, and Aviation Chief Ordnanceman Dallas Jones, the bombardier, quickly dropped six depth bombs precisely on target: four on the port side, and two on the starboard, resulting in a near simultaneous explosion of impressive proportions. By the time the spray and smoke cleared, *U-271* was settling by the stern and within minutes slid stern-first into the sea. All fifty-one of her crew perished that day. The plane remained on station for forty-five minutes, but the seas were too choppy to detect any wreckage or debris. For this action, Enloe was awarded the Distinguished Flying Cross and the remainder of the crew, to include Kinney and Jones, the Air Medal.

The attack on *U-271*. *US Navy photo, courtesy of the Jones family.*

Paul B. Kinney, *Order of the Red Star*

Roy Johnson (left) and Paul Kinney (right) receive the Air Medal and Distinguished Flying Cross (respectively) in an award ceremony in Natal, Brazil, on December 19, 1944. *Official US Navy photo via the National Archives.*

Paul Bruce Kinney, born September 26, 1916, in New England, was working as the assistant Canton District traffic superintendent in Canton, Ohio, when the war started. He joined the Navy on January 1, 1942, and reported immediately to flight school. Upon completion of operational training, he reported to VB-103, and had only been there a short time before his mettle was tested in combat. On September 4, 1943, they were five hours into a ten-hour anti-submarine patrol when his PB4Y-1 was attacked by six Ju 88 aircraft. During the course of the fight, the PB4Y-1 crew shot down one Ju 88 and damaged two others. However, the toll was great: three of four engines on the PB4Y-1 were on fire, as was the port fuel tank; the port rudder and aileron were shredded and unusable, and due to an explosion of a shell inside the cockpit that wounded both Kinney and his pilot, all of the instruments were destroyed. Remarkably, the pilot was able to keep the plane flying for the next twenty minutes but maintaining airspeed proved impossible. The decision was made to ditch the plane in the open water off the coast of Spain. Upon landing, the nose was crushed, the tail disintegrated, and the plane split in two, but the crew were able to escape into a life raft. They spent the next thirty-six hours at sea before being rescued by a Spanish fishing vessel. They were returned to their base in England on September 17.[15] For this event, the pilot, Lieutenant James Alexander, received the Navy Cross, and Kinney received the Distinguished Flying Cross.

No. 170

Certificate in Lieu of a

PASSPORT

This is to certify that Paul Bruce Kinney is a Lieutenant (j.g.) in the Navy Air Force of the United States of America and was born at Hopkinsville, Kentucky on April 12, 1918.

Paul Bruce Kinney
Signature

He is being repatriated from Spain and this document is valid in lieu of a passport for travel to Gibraltar, via Madrid.

Issued at the Embassy of the United States of America, Madrid, Spain on September 9, 1943.

Niles W. Bond
Third Secretary of Embassy

Document issued by the US Embassy in Spain to assist Paul Kinney in returning to US forces after being shot down off the coast of Spain on September 4, 1943. *Courtesy of the Kinney family.*

Following the sinking of *U-271* on January 28, 1944, Kinney was rotated back to the United States and joined VB-107 together with Roy Johnson, and flew missions out of Natal and Ascension Island in the South Atlantic. Discharged from active duty on November 1, 1945, he settled in Connecticut. Working first for General Electric, he eventually worked his way into the publishing industry, selling commercial advertisement space in magazines such as *Missiles and Rockets* and *Aviation Week*. Well known for his skill in tennis and racquetball, Kinney passed away on October 13, 1985.

George A. Enloe, *Order of Glory, Third Class*

George Albert Enloe attended the University of Minnesota and enlisted in the Navy on January 3, 1938. In January 1940, he received orders to flight training at Pensacola, Florida, and completed his aviation training in November 1941. He was stationed at Naval Air Station Kaneohe with VP-11 when the Japanese attacked on December 7, 1941. Until his transfer in December 1943, he flew combat patrol missions throughout the Southwest Pacific. Flying with Dallas Jones, Enloe flew during the Battle of Midway and in July 1942, began patrolling around Guadalcanal and the adjacent islands. Becoming a "Black Cat" squadron specializing in night operations, Enloe earned his first Distinguished Flying Cross during a nighttime attack on a Japanese heavy cruiser on October 23, 1942. Although the cruiser was not mortally damaged, it was sufficient to prove the worth of Black Cat squadrons and earn Enloe and Jones the admiration of their fellow flight crews.[16] Following his tour in the Western Approaches, Enloe returned to the United States and spent the remainder of the war as a flight instructor in Florida and Texas. He was discharged in September 1945, but remained in the Naval Reserves, eventually rising to the rank of Captain.

As a civilian, he began working for Bradlo Construction in Los Angeles in 1953, and in May 1961, became a maintenance service salesman for Alaska Airlines, operating out of Paine Field in Washington. He was in Florida on business and was scheduled to return home on Northwest Orient Flight 705 from Miami to Chicago on February 7, 1963. The day was stormy; rainsqualls frequently passed through the area and wind gusts were measured at forty miles per hour. In spite of these factors, the plane was cleared for departure.[17] At 12:42 PM, seven minutes after takeoff, the flight crashed into the Florida everglades, killing everyone on board: a tragic ending for a man who fought so bravely for his country.

Dallas H. Jones, *Order of Glory, Third Class*

Enloe's bombardier was Dallas Harding Jones, a tall young man born in Halifax, North Carolina, on March 14, 1922. Entering active duty in the Navy on April 15, 1940, he lied about his age to enlist, but was soon on his way to becoming an Aviation Ordnanceman. Upon completion of Ordnanceman School in January 1941, the majority of his class received orders to Pearl Harbor. He was fortunate in receiving orders to a land-based patrol squadron; the remainder of his classmates received orders to the USS *Arizona* (BB-39), and are still entombed in the ship. Promoted quickly, he began to be regularly assigned to Enloe's aircraft. Jones went on to serve with Enloe throughout much of the remainder of the war. Following the sinking of *U-271*, Jones was rotated back to the United States after completing thirty missions with VB-103. For the remainder of the war in Europe, he was a flight crew instructor for future PB4Y-1 crews flying out of England. In mid-1945, he was transferred to Bermuda and flew patrol aircraft during the final days of the war. He followed this with a tour as an instructor at the Aviation Ordnance School in Jacksonville, Florida. In June 1951, Jones was promoted to Warrant Officer and served as Air Ordnance Officer on the USS *Midway* (CV-41). This was followed by additional tours, ashore, at sea, and overseas. He remained in the Navy, on active duty, until his retirement on July 1, 1960, as a Chief Warrant Officer (CWO) 3. Following his retirement from the Navy, he worked as the Logistics Support Manager for Aero-Jet General Corporation in Azusa, California, working on projects including the Mk.46 torpedo system and aircraft-mounted infrared systems. He retired from Aero-Jet in 1972 and returned to North Carolina, where he founded the Roanoke Valley Veterans Center in Roanoke Rapids. Dallas Jones joined his shipmates who perished at Pearl Harbor almost exactly seventy-two years before, passing unexpectedly on December 8, 2013. He is buried in Tarboro, North Carolina.

Order of Glory, Third Class, number 387910 awarded to Dallas Jones. *Courtesy of the Jones family.*

Soviet order book to Dallas Jones. Note his wearing of the Order of Glory. *Courtesy of the Jones family.*

CHAPTER 2

ANTI-SUBMARINE OPERATIONS: COMPOSITE SQUADRON RECIPIENTS

The concept of the hunter-killer squadron was born from experience during the previous year and a half of being at war. Composite Squadrons, better known as VC squadrons, consisted of multiple types of aircraft. In most cases, the aircraft were the F4F Wildcat fighter plane and the TBF-1 Avenger torpedo bomber, stationed on one of the small "Jeep" CVE escort carriers. The mission of these squadrons was singular: to find and destroy submarines. In concept, the single-seat F4F would be the "hunter" and, once finding a submarine running on the surface or snorkeling, would report it. He would then be reinforced by the TBF-1, the "killer," armed with a torpedo or depth bombs. The TBF would then make the attack run on the submarine, escorted by the F4F for protection. Traditionally armed, the single-seat F4F could not support the heavy ordnance required to sink a submarine, and the three-man crew of the TBF was less than suitable at self-defense while making their attack run. Thus, the two aircraft worked in coordination to drive home their successful attack.

August 7, 1943: The Sinking of *U-117*

VC-1 left Bermuda on August 1, 1943, and began conducting their trans-Atlantic passage with convoy UGS-13. The squadron was embarked on the escort carrier USS *Card* (CVE-11) for hunter-killer anti-submarine duty during the crossing. On the morning of August 7, two submarines were detected on the surface: *U-66*, homeward bound after a long deployment, and refueling her, *U-117*, a "milk cow" logistical resupply submarine. *U-66* had survived an attack by VC-1's aircraft the previous day. This time too, she reacted quickly and escaped. However, *U-117* was doggedly attacked by Lieutenant (jg) Asbury Sallenger, one of the pilots of VC-1, preventing her from doing the same. Minutes later, shortly after 7:30 AM, two Avengers and two Wildcats appeared on the scene. One of the Avengers was flown by Lieutenant (jg) Junior Forney; one F4F by Lieutenant Norman Hodson. In conjunction with their fellow squadron pilots, they vigorously attacked *U-117* by strafing and torpedo attacks. Finally, she began to wallow on the surface. Her bow came up, and then she slid stern first below the waves, taking her entire crew with her. Hodson and Forney were both awarded the Distinguished Flying Cross for their demonstrated heroism in the sinking of *U-117*.

The attack on *U-66* and *U-117* on the morning of August 7, 1943. *Official US Navy photo via the National Archives.*

The pilots of VC-1. Soviet medal recipients include: J.C. Forney (second row, far right), Norman Hodson (front row, fourth from left), Gerald Hogan (second row, far left), and Jack Stewart (second row, fourth from right). *Courtesy of the Forney family.*

J.C. Forney, approximately 1944. *Courtesy of the Forney family.*

Junior C. Forney, *Order of Glory, Third Class*

Junior Clyde "J.C." Forney was born on June 13, 1920, in Hoisington, Kansas. Spending three years at the Kansas State Teachers College of Emporia, where he excelled in physical education courses (and not particularly in academics), he joined the Navy as soon as he could be admitted into the Aviation Cadet program. On August 6, 1941, he reported to primary training in Kansas City, Kansas, and later received his flight school training in Corpus Christi. Following his initial operational training in San Diego, he reported to VC-1 as a torpedo bomber pilot, flying the TBF-1 aircraft. Through much of the war, he served with VC-1, alongside fellow Soviet medal recipients Norman Hodson, Gerald Hogan, and Jack Stewart. This included actions against German U-boats in the North Atlantic and his subsequent transfer to VF-74 with Gerald Hogan, where they conducted ground attack missions against targets during the invasion of Southern France as part of Operation Dragoon. By the end of the war, he was a flight instructor at Patuxent River, Maryland. Discharged on March 26, 1946, he sold life insurance for a brief time before pursuing a career as a petroleum landman. He went on to found Forney Oil, Inc., and spent the next forty years of his life in the oil industry in both Oklahoma and Colorado. He passed away on October 11, 1987, in Rogers, Arkansas.

Order of Glory, Third Class, number 387922 awarded to J.C. Forney. *Courtesy of the Forney family.*

Order of the Red Star number 1553951 awarded to Norman Hodson. *Courtesy of the Hodson family.*

Norman D. Hodson, *Order of the Red Star*

Forney's fellow pilot, Norman Douglas "Doug" Hodson, entered the Navy from San Bernardino, California, on October 14, 1940. He commenced flight school in Pensacola, Florida, in January 1941, and by July 1941, received orders to report to the USS *Enterprise* (CV-6) for service with Fighter Squadron (VF) 6. It was while serving with the *Enterprise* that he earned a Letter of Commendation from Admiral Chester Nimitz for his part in the Battle of Midway from June 4 to 6, 1942. With the start of the war and the bloom of new squadrons, he was transferred to the newly commissioned Escort Scouting Squadron (VGS) 1 in August 1942, redesignated VC-1 on March 1, 1943. With VC-1, he served on the USS *Long Island* (CVE-1), the USS *Card* (CVE-11), USS *Block Island* (CVE-21) and the USS *Croatan* (CVE-25). While on the latter ship, he was promoted to executive officer of VC-1 before his transfer in March 1944. That same month, he reported to VC-8 as the commanding officer. He spent the rest of the war in this capacity in both the Atlantic and Pacific theaters. In June 1944, he earned a Bronze Star Medal for his role in the now-famous capture of *U-505*, while on USS *Guadalcanal* (CVE-60), directing his aircraft to its location and strafing the submarine to prevent her crew from manning their weapons. In the Pacific, he earned an Air Medal for taking part in the invasion of Okinawa and patrols in the Sakishima islands.

Following the end of the war, he served in a number of important positions afloat and ashore, to include serving as an aviation officer detailer at the Bureau of Personnel, an instructor in the aviation department at the Naval Academy, as chief of staff to Commander, Naval Forces Marianas, and inspector general of the Thirteenth Naval District. At sea, he was commanding officer of Attack Squadron (VA) 55 during the Korean War, earning his third Distinguished Flying Cross and four additional Air Medals. He later served at sea as the operations officer and the executive officer of the USS *Wasp* (CVS-18). He then served as commanding officer, Azores Antisubmarine Warfare Group. Hodson's final tour was as commanding officer, US Naval Reserve Center, Wichita Falls, Texas. He retired as a Captain on June 30, 1972. Retiring to Iowa Park, Texas, he purchased a thirty-acre farm where he raised cattle, goats, and birds. Additionally, he volunteered in the pharmacy at Sheppard Air Force Base, helping other veterans. Norman Hodson passed away on September 10, 1988, in Iowa Park.

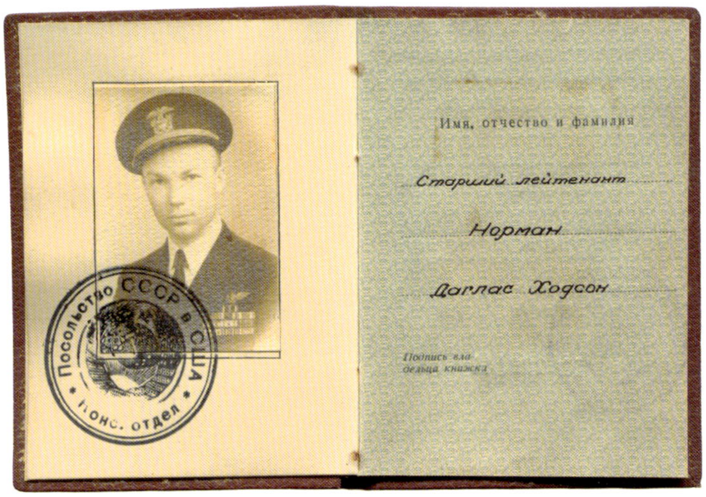

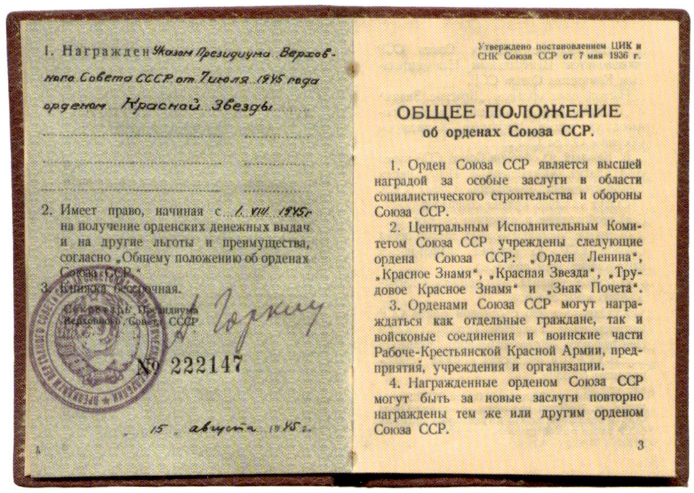

Soviet order book to Norman Hodson. *Courtesy of the Hodson family.*

Norman Hodson's medal bar, including the Distinguished Flying Cross, Bronze Star Medal, Air Medal, Navy Commendation Medal, and American Defense Medal. *Courtesy of the Hodson family.*

August 27, 1943: The Sinking of *U-847*

On August 27, Lieutenant (jg) Gerald Hogan, flying an Avenger, spotted *U-508* on the surface. This was not Hogan's first encounter with a U-boat. On August 9, he had assisted Forney and Hodson with the sinking of *U-664*, and earned his first Distinguished Flying Cross. But this time, he was alone. As he sped toward *U-508*, she opened fire at him. Fortunately for him, their flak remained far enough away from his aircraft to not deter his inbound approach. What did save the U-boat, however, was its sudden maneuvering, causing Hogan's air launched torpedo to miss its target when the submarine submerged. Previous to making his attacking run, he had requested reinforcements from the carrier, and as *U-508* slipped below the surface, they arrived. One of these reinforcements was Ensign Jack Stewart, flying a Wildcat. Stewart already had one U-boat to his credit, assisting with the sinking of *U-525* on August 11.

Resuming the patrol for additional submarines, Hogan and Stewart soon detected another surfaced submarine, *U-847*. Going in for the attack, Stewart received heavy anti-aircraft fire initially, but then the submarine attempted to submerge and escape. It was too late: *U-847* was struck by a torpedo and exploded beneath the surface, taking her entire crew to a watery grave. Hogan earned the Distinguished Flying Cross for this action and Stewart the Silver Star.

U-847 explodes beneath the surface of the water after being struck by a torpedo. *Official US Navy photo via the National Archives.*

Gerald G. Hogan, *Order of the Red Star*

Hailing from Brooklyn, Gerald Griffin "Jerry" Hogan was born on March 7, 1918. Upon completion of high school, he attended Notre Dame University, where he enlisted in the Marine Corps. Serving as a Private and then Private First Class, he applied for a commission in the Navy and entered active service on October 16, 1941. Following completion of flight training in June 1942, he reported to VC-1. He served with VC-1 through March 1944, when he was transferred, along with J.C. Forney and Jack Stewart, to VF-74, participating in the invasion of Southern France. In October 1944, he was transferred to Scout Observation Service Unit (SOSU) 2 in Norfolk, Virginia, testing and developing new tactics and techniques for catapult-launched floatplanes. This is where he was stationed when the war ended, and he was discharged in October 1945. After the war, he partnered with his brother-in-law and formed a Catholic religious goods and publishing business. Retiring from publishing, he went back to school, earned a master's degree in English, and taught for ten years before retiring altogether. Gerald Hogan passed away on January 11, 1989.

Gerald Hogan and Jack Stewart shake hands, approximately 1945. *Courtesy of the Hogan family.*

Order of the Red Star number 1553958 awarded to Gerald Hogan. *Courtesy of the Hogan family.*

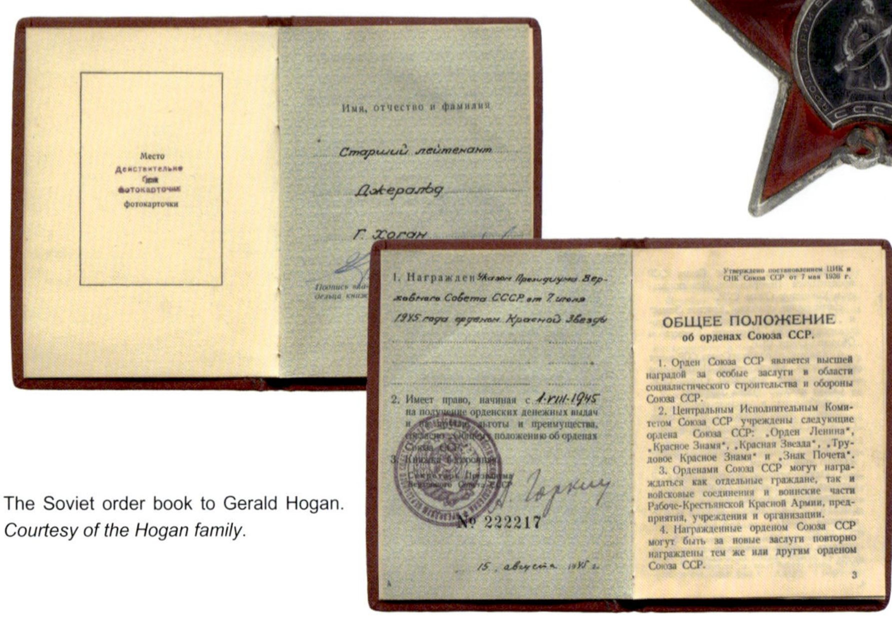

The Soviet order book to Gerald Hogan. *Courtesy of the Hogan family.*

Jack H. Stewart, *Order of the Red Star*

Hogan's fellow attacking pilot, Jack Howard Stewart, was born in Washington, DC in 1920. He joined the Navy on February 11, 1942, following two years at the University of Maryland and reported immediately thereafter for flight training in Pensacola, Florida. Completing operational training in March 1943, he reported to VC-1, where he served for the following year on hunter-killer anti-submarine cruises in the Atlantic. Transferring to VF-74 in March 1944 along with Gerald Hogan and J.C. Forney, he flew from the USS *Kasaan Bay* (CVE-69), taking part in the invasion of Southern France. Here, he earned a Distinguished Flying Cross for leading a division of five fighter aircraft against a land-based enemy column in the vicinity of Lussan. Strafing the column until he was forced to withdraw, he found a railway locomotive and destroyed it. Returning to the column, he led his division on multiple strafing runs until all five of the aircraft were damaged and forced to return to base.

In October 1944, he transferred with Gerald Hogan to SOSU-2, and remained there as a flight instructor until August 1945. He then reported to Fleet Aircraft Service Squadron (FASRON) 201, as the officer in charge of a detachment. Following the end of the war, he served on the USS *Kearsarge* (CVA-33) followed by command of photographic squadron VFP-61 on the *Kearsarge* in 1957 and VF-151, flying from the USS *Hancock* (CVA-19) in 1958 and 1959. Subsequent tours included serving as the operations officer for the commissioning of Naval Air Station Lemoore, California, where he served as a direct subordinate for fellow Soviet medal recipient Howard Avery. He continued to serve on active duty until his retirement on March 1, 1972 with the rank of Commander. Following retirement, he spent thirteen years as a civilian on the staff of Commander, Naval Air Forces Pacific before retiring again. In his later years, he was an active volunteer at the San Diego Aerospace Museum, and spent his free time traveling in his motor home, taking his final trip at age ninety-one. Jack passed away on August 15, 2012 in Bonita, California.

Jack H. Stewart as a Commander in the 1960s. *Courtesy of the Stewart family.*

The Soviet order book to Jack Stewart. *Courtesy of the Stewart family.*

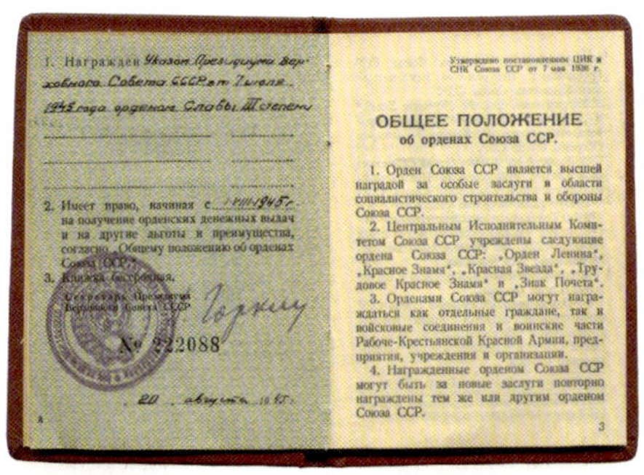

Jack Stewart's medal bar, including the Silver Star, Distinguished Flying Cross, American Campaign Medal, European, African, and Middle Eastern Campaign Medal, and the World War II Victory Medal. *Courtesy of the Stewart family.*

Order of Glory, Third Class, number 387935 awarded to Jack Stewart. *Courtesy of the Stewart family.*

October 28, 1943: The Sinking of *U-220*

The subsequent notable cruise of VC-1 was on the USS *Block Island* (CVE-21), which later became victim of a U-boat. Departing Norfolk on October 15, 1943, the *Block Island* was vectored to a known concentration of U-boats close to the center of the Atlantic. Their first action came on the night of October 25, but the submarine escaped. Three days later, on the morning of October 28, Ensign Harold Handshuh was flying a Wildcat on patrol north of the carrier when his fellow pilot spotted a pair of U-boats some twenty miles distant. Descending for an attack run, they discovered the two submarines, *U-220* and *U-256*, approximately two hundred yards apart, transiting on the surface at approximately eight knots. Making a simultaneous attack, Handshuh strafed the conning tower of *U-220*, the closest submarine, and his fellow pilot Lieutenant Franklin Murray, flying a TBF, dropped two Mk.47 depth bombs, bracketing the same. Both aircraft ascended to survey damage and contact the carrier. Meanwhile, *U-256* increased her anti-aircraft fire, aiming for the TBF, and *U-220* commenced a slow turn to starboard. Watching *U-220* make her turn, both pilots saw the submarine's stern rise abruptly and then disappear into a mass of violent bubbles. She was never heard from again. The pilots' attempt to keep *U-256* on the surface until reinforcements could arrive, despite heavy anti-aircraft fire, proved fruitless as she submerged and escaped unharmed. For sinking *U-220*, Handshuh was awarded the Distinguished Flying Cross.

Harold Handshuh, *Order of Glory, Third Class*

Born in San Francisco on December 4, 1921, Harold Leo Handshuh enlisted in the Navy on July 6, 1942, after attending the University of Oregon from 1940 to 1942. Shortly thereafter, he became an Aviation Cadet and commenced flight training in Corpus Christi, Texas. Following the completion of his flight training, he was commissioned on June 12, 1943, and reported to VC-1 on September 27. He had been with the squadron one month when he had his first submarine kill, an enviable record even amongst veteran pilots. In March 1944, he was transferred to VC-9, under the command of Soviet medal recipient Howard Avery, one of the most successful anti-submarine squadrons of the war. Embarked on the USS *Solomons* (CVE-67) and operating approximately five hundred miles south of St. Helena in the South Atlantic, they were notified of a located U-boat on June 15. This was *U-860*, and it was discovered by one of VC-9's pilots. She was ultimately to prove a costly target to the squadron.

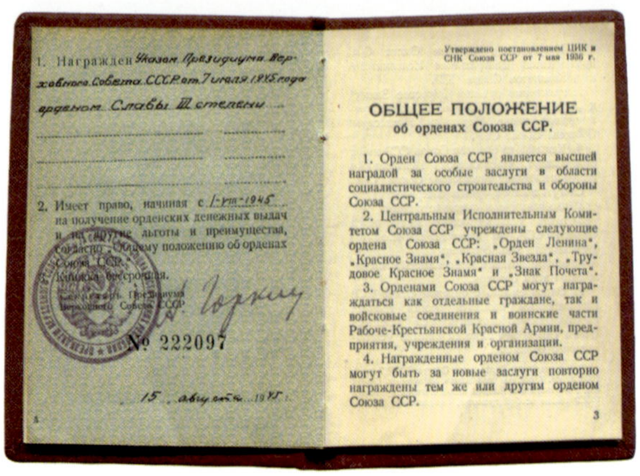

The Soviet order book to Harold Handshuh. *Courtesy of Christina Christensen.*

After reporting the position of *U-860*, Ensign George Edwards closed in to make a total of four strafing runs with his TBF. Unfortunately, it proved to be one too many and he was shot down by the submarine on his final run; the German crew watching the aircraft catch fire and spin into the sea, killing the crew instantly. Launching on Edwards' initial report, two aircraft were sent as reinforcements from the carrier, with Handshuh flying one of them. After being aloft for several hours and unable to locate the submarine, Handshuh radioed back to the carrier that both aircraft were running low on fuel. That was his last report. Hearing nothing for two more hours, it was assumed that both planes ran out of fuel and were forced to ditch, somewhere in the Atlantic. Despite a concerted two-day search, they were never seen again. Harold was later declared dead on June 16, 1945, a year and a day from his date of loss.

That same day, the attacks on *U-860* continued. Unbeknownst to *Fregattenkapitän* Paul Büchel, *U-860's* commanding officer, additional aircraft had been launched from the *Solomons* to locate him as well as the survivors from the three missing aircraft. Unhappy with the performance of his gunnery crew during the previous attack, Büchel decided to surface and afford them the benefit of additional practice. *U-860* was spotted by VC-9's commanding officer, Howard Avery, upon surfacing and he commenced one of two strafing runs on the submarine, keeping her from maneuvering until additional reinforcements could arrive.

Within minutes, *U-860* was viciously mauled by multiple aircraft, taking twelve rockets forward of the conning tower, the damage causing massive flooding inside the boat, resulting in a pronounced starboard list as well as a chlorine gas leak that killed many of the crew inside. As *U-860* began to wallow in the seas, Navy Cross recipient William Chamberlain, a veteran pilot of VC-9, flew in on what would be his last attack: descending to just fifty feet over the conning tower when he dropped his depth bombs, his plane caught fire from the resulting thunderous explosions. He was witnessed flying through the fire with flames licking through his cockpit glass and was seen ditching his aircraft into the sea, but neither he nor his crew were ever located. However, Chamberlain's depth bombs had their desired effect on *U-860*: when the few lucky crewmembers taken prisoner were interrogated, they stated the bombs had exploded on contact and force of the explosion was so violent they were all temporarily dazed. When they came to, they were in the water and the submarine was nowhere to be found; it had sunk instantly from damage sustained from the bombs.[1] With the sinking of *U-860*, Howard Avery earned the Navy Cross and Harold Handshuh's loss was avenged.

October 20, 1943: The Sinking of *U-378*

VC-1 was not the only squadron having multiple successes against U-boats in the North Atlantic. Three Soviet medal recipients, Robert Hayman, Bert Hudson, and William McLane sank several U-boats while flying with VC-13. Taking the place of the USS *Card* (CVE-11) while she pulled in to Casablanca for supplies, the USS *Core* (CVE-13) had been at sea for just about two weeks and had not yet seen action. On the afternoon of October 20, 1943, that changed. Lieutenant (jg) Robert Hayman was flying a TBF-1C in tandem with an F4F aircraft when they spotted *U-378* on the surface. The fighter made a strafing run that ignited the submarine's topside ready ammunition locker, causing a blinding explosion on the conning tower of the submarine. Hayman followed, straddling the U-boat with his depth bombs, as well as strafing the length of the submarine. *U-378* quickly dived, but it was too late. Hayman made a second attack, dropping his Mk.24 aerial torpedo. Scoring a direct hit and exploding under the surface of the water, the submarine sank. For his valor and aggressive attack, Hayman was awarded the Distinguished Flying Cross.

Robert Hayman, *Order of Glory, Third Class*

Robert William Hayman was born in Minnesota on May 25, 1918. Learning the value of hard work, he spent his time outside of school working on his father's farm near Red Wing. Enrolled in the Naval ROTC program at the University of Minnesota, Hayman was selected for flight training and entered active duty in July 1941. Earning his wings on June 14, 1942, he reported to VC-13 in November, and remained there for the entirety of his wartime career. Following several successful cruises in the Atlantic, VC-13 was transferred to the Pacific in late 1944, arriving at Pearl Harbor in January 1945. While in the Pacific, he flew off the USS *Anzio* (CVE-57), taking part in the invasion of Okinawa and conducting anti-submarine operations off the coast of the Philippines. Here, he earned two Air Medals. Remaining in proximity to Okinawa, they conducted numerous night anti-submarine patrols in preparation for the possible Japanese submarine attacks. This never happened, but Hayman did earn his third, and final, Air Medal for his superb vigilance and flying skill.

With the end of the war and the decommissioning of VC-13, Hayman was transferred to Naval Air Station Ft. Lauderdale in November 1945 as a flight instructor, and along with Howard Roberts, the executive officer of the base, participated in the search for the missing fliers of Flight 19, lost in the infamous Bermuda Triangle. Finally discharged from active duty in September 1946, he began employment with Pan American World Airways as a navigator, flying out of Miami, Florida. He went on to spend his civilian flying career with Pan American, eventually retiring as a 707 aircraft captain flying international flights from New York. He passed away on December 11, 2003, and is buried in Oakwood Cemetery, Red Wing, Minnesota.

Robert Hayman shortly after the war. Note his top right ribbon is for the Order of Glory. *Courtesy of the Hayman family.*

Robert Hayman's Distinguished Flying Cross and Air Medal. *Courtesy of the Hayman family.*

Order of Glory, Third Class, number 387938, awarded to Robert Hayman. *Courtesy of the Hayman family.*

January 16, 1944: The Sinking of *U-544*

Departing on January 3, 1944, for another anti-submarine cruise on the carrier USS *Guadalcanal* (CVE-60) under the command of Captain Daniel Gallery, things went wrong from the start for VC-13. They lost two pilots, three enlisted aircrew, six aircraft, and damaged nine more during their six-week embarkation. It was not without success, however. On January 16, Ensigns Bert Hudson and William McLane, later reinforced by Hayman and several other pilots, came across *U-544* refueling *U-129* and *U-516*. *U-129* submerged immediately, but *U-544* and *U-516* had refueling hoses attached and could not submerge. With their crews scrambling to release the hoses, Hudson raced in, firing rockets, and depth bombs. His rockets holed *U-544*, one passing through the hull, exiting aft of the conning tower, and his depth bombs straddled *U-516*. At an altitude of seventy-five feet, he let go his final rockets which both penetrated the hull of *U-544*. Finally free of the hoses, *U-516* disappeared from sight; her disposition unknown. The crew of *U-544* began to abandon ship and both Hudson and McLane reported seeing twenty to thirty-five men jumping over the side before the submarine slipped, stern first, beneath the waves. A search for survivors later that day by US destroyer escorts regretfully yielded none.

Returning to the *Guadalcanal* after the attack, however, was not easy. The sun was going down and darkness was descending. The first four aircraft, including McLane's, landed safely. However, the fifth aircraft was not so fortunate and crashed into a catwalk, fouling the deck. By the time the deck was clear, both Hudson and Hayman were critically low on fuel. Hayman was too low on fuel to attempt a landing, so he ditched his plane at sea alongside a destroyer escort that expeditiously plucked the crew from the ocean. Hudson attempted to land, but was not successful. Breaking through all of the barriers on the flight deck, his plane flipped over and went straight into the sea. Their luck held out: all three of the crewmen survived and were rescued by another destroyer escort within minutes.

Bert Hudson (gesturing) and William McLane (to Hudson's right) describe the sinking of *U-544* to Captain (later Rear Admiral) Daniel Gallery. *Courtesy of the Hudson family.*

William M. McLane, *Order of Glory, Third Class*

William McNair McLane, a native Floridian, was born on January 26, 1919, and entered active duty on February 19, 1942, following graduation from the University of Florida with a major in zoology and a brief stint in their master's program. Reporting to VC-13 in April 1943, he remained with them, alongside Robert Hayman, for the entire duration of the war. Prior to sinking *U-544*, he seriously damaged a U-boat (possibly *U-406*) while flying patrol on August 23, 1943. His first Distinguished Flying Cross was awarded for the sinking of *U-544*. Subsequent awards were from action in the Pacific theater. During the invasion of Okinawa, and preparation for the invasion of the Japanese homeland, he earned his second and third Air Medals. He earned his second Distinguished Flying Cross for damaging a Japanese submarine on July 16, 1945. Diving through a cloud, he strafed the submarine and launched six rockets. The submarine escaped, but left an oily trail and was subsequently located and sunk by a US Navy destroyer.

Returning to the United States, he was discharged from active duty on November 5, 1945, and returned to Florida. Remaining in the Naval Reserves, he retired in September 1958, promoted to Lieutenant Commander based on his wartime awards. As a civilian, he returned to school, finishing his master's degree in 1947, and earning his PhD in biology in 1955. He went on to found Florida Aquatic Nursery in 1959. They are still in business today, as the United States' largest aquatic nursery. He also founded V & W Enterprises, conducting biological consulting work for federal, state, and local agencies, in addition to those who are engaged in research and development both in the United States and abroad. Dr. William McLane passed away on March 24, 1973, in Plantation, Florida.

William McLane discusses a flight plan with his aircrew onboard the USS *Core* (CVE-13) August 11, 1944. *Official US Navy photo via the National Archives.*

Bert J. Hudson, *Order of Glory, Third Class*

The pilot responsible for the final blow to *U-544* was Bert J. Hudson. Born in Coeur d'Alene, Idaho on December 29, 1917, he attended Coeur d'Alene High School, North Idaho, Junior College, and Gonzaga University before joining the Navy as an Aviation Cadet on March 16, 1942. He reported to VC-13 in July 1943, and served with them throughout their time in the Atlantic. He received a Distinguished Flying Cross for the sinking of *U-544*, and in December 1944, transferred to the Night Attack and Combat Training Unit (Atlantic), reporting on January 1, 1945. He served here as an instructor pilot until his discharge from active duty on November 23, 1945. He remained in the Reserves, but eventually took his leave of the Navy in October 1954. Returning to Coeur d'Alene after the war, he became a Shell Oil Company distributor and owned Coeur d'Alene Tire Service until his retirement. Bert Hudson passed away on November 29, 2001, and is buried in Forest Cemetery, Coeur d'Alene, Idaho.

The Distinguished Flying Cross awarded to Bert Hudson. Also in the original blue presentation case is Hudson's Presidential Unit Citation ribbon. *Courtesy of the Hudson family.*

Order of Glory, Third Class, number 387944, awarded to Bert Hudson. *Courtesy of the Hudson family.*

August 20, 1944: The Sinking of *U-1229*

VC-42 was commissioned on April 15, 1943, at Naval Air Station Alameda, California, with the standard Pacific theater complement of anti-submarine operations aircraft. By early June, however, their aircraft numbers had changed to the standard for Atlantic operations. Six months later, in December 1943, they were officially reassigned to the East Coast and Atlantic Fleet anti-submarine operations. Their patrols were relatively uneventful through most of 1944. In fact, sailing on the USS *Croatan* (CVE-25) in April, VC-42 had missed multiple opportunities to attack surfaced submarines, to include *U-856*, whose fate was later sealed by surface ships commanded by Soviet medal recipients Robert Wanless and Robert Baughan. Embarking the USS *Bogue* (CVE-9) in July, they commenced their next anti-submarine cruise, getting underway at 11:00 AM on July 24. Among the pilots in the squadron, there were six who received Soviet awards for their participation in the sinking of *U-1229*.

Lieutenant (jg) John Sulton's cruise did not start off well. VC-42 had been allotted four brand new General Motors built TBM-1D aircraft, built for use during night anti-submarine activity with the addition of a searchlight and improved radars. Unfortunately, none of the pilots had flown these before, and were expected to train and qualify in them at sea. On the morning of July 26, Sulton was taking his first flight in one of the new aircraft, and upon landing, his arresting hook pulled out after being weakened by striking the ramp. He scooted through multiple barriers, clipping the wing and tail of John Watson's recently landed Avenger and smashing two of the new TBMs before coming to a stop.

The *Bogue* had been at sea for nearly a month with nothing to show for it, in contrast to her previous cruises. This was not entirely the fault of the luckless VC-42; weather was a major contributing factor, preventing air operations for most of the period. However, this changed on August 20. Entering an area of better weather, flight operations renewed. At the same time, *U-1229*, on a special mission to land a German agent on the coast of Maine, was travelling on the surface. This was in spite of the fact that she was outfitted with a snorkel, allowing her to remain submerged while charging her batteries during transits. Her captain, Armin Zinke, was extremely stubborn and preferred traveling on the surface, in spite of the new technology. His crew later blamed him for destroying their morale with his heavy drinking and lack of ability to communicate effectively, refusing to heed the advice of both his superiors and his crew. As a result, Zinke had spent the last few days traveling exclusively on the surface during daylight hours.[2] By his ineptitude and arrogance, *U-1229* became the first U-boat with snorkel sunk by the US Navy.

U-1229 as she appeared on the surface before the first attack by Alex Brokas. *Official US Navy photo, courtesy of the Sherbring family.*

At 12:27 PM Alex Brokas was flying a routine patrol when his radioman detected a radar blip at a distance of five miles. Closing in to look, Brokas spotted *U-1229*, fully surfaced, and went in for the attack, despite continuous anti-aircraft fire from the submarine. Dropping two Mk.54 depth bombs at an altitude of one hundred feet, he completely bracketed the U-boat, blowing the anti-aircraft gun and several crewmen over the side. However, *U-1229* escaped, fully submerging as quickly as possible. Dropping a sonobuoy pattern at the location where the U-boat was last seen, Brokas was relieved at 1:55 PM at the scene by Bernard Sissler, Milton Sherbring, Wallace Porter, Watson, and Sulton. Damaged and flooding, *U-1229* had descended to nearly two hundred feet to escape the attacking aircraft. At this point, the survivors of *U-1229* later testified that their primary concern was the possibility of a fatal explosion of their batteries due to the damage they had sustained, coupled with rising seawater in the compartments. Unable to start their diesel engines to provide power, they decided to blow tanks and surface.[3]

At 2:21 PM, Watson sighted the submarine below the surface, and at 2:30 PM, two periscopes and the snorkel appeared. Sherbring and Sissler made a simultaneous depth

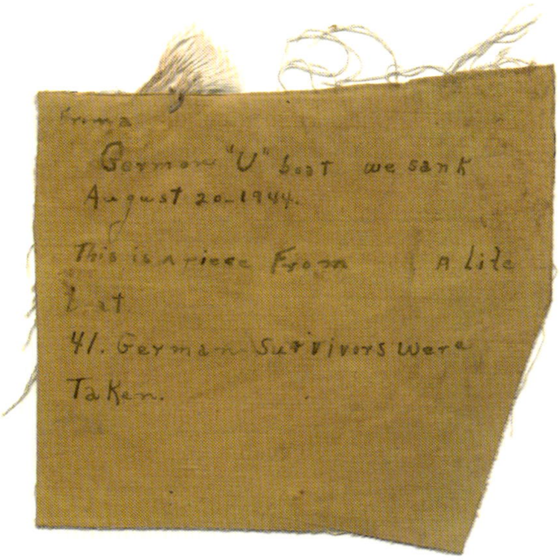

A piece of the *U-1229* survivor's life raft, taken as a souvenir by Milton Sherbring. *Courtesy of the Sherbring family.*

bomb attack, but were unsuccessful. As the submarine surfaced, Sissler fired seven rockets. All of them found their target, causing considerable damage. By 2:34 PM, *U-1229* was fully surfaced and the crew began appearing on deck to jump overboard. All of the planes took turns making continuous strafing runs on the submarine, killing Zinke and many others as they scrambled on deck. Six minutes after surfacing, a large explosion rocked the boat. Later, it was determined that this was caused by the batteries, just as her crew had feared. Within minutes, the stern lifted and *U-1229* slid below the surface in its final dive. Not content to go quietly, the submarine exploded once again under the surface, spectacularly shooting water and debris one hundred feet into the air.

On August 24, the six pilots were personally commended by Admiral Royall Ingersoll for finding and destroying *U-1229*. Brokas received the Distinguished Flying Cross, and the others, the Air Medal. After a short training period, the squadron headed for the Pacific theater, arriving in Pearl Harbor on December 9, and transferred to the USS *Corregidor* (CVE-58). However, multiple anti-submarine patrols in the vicinity of Eniwetok yielded no success, and in May 1945, the squadron was decommissioned upon their return to the United States.

John R. Sulton, *Order of Glory, Third Class*

John Rueben Sulton was born on September 22, 1921, in Okemah, Oklahoma. He graduated from Preston High School in 1938. Entering the Navy on April 20, 1942, following the minimum of two years of college, he was assigned to VC-42 upon their commissioning. Serving with VC-42 through the end of the war, Sulton was discharged from active duty in 1946 and returned to his native Oklahoma. In 1949, he graduated with his bachelor's degree from the University of Tulsa. He went on to have a successful career in the business world, rising to become the vice president of sales for the Frank Wheatley Company. Later, he worked for, and then purchased, the J.W. Johnston Company. He eventually retired as the owner of the Sulton Group, an oil and gas industry supplier and manufacturer. He passed away in Tulsa, Oklahoma, on August 24, 2009.

John Sulton. *Courtesy of the Sulton family.*

John B. Watson, *Order of Glory, Third Class*

John Belton Watson, who Sulton missed by inches on his landing, was born on June 26, 1920, in Anderson, South Carolina. He graduated with the class of 1938 at Boys High School, and spent three years at Clemson before leaving college to join the Navy as an Aviation Cadet on April 1, 1941. Following flight school in Pensacola, Florida, he reported to the fleet and soon after, to VC-42 as one of its original six pilots. Shortly after returning to Virginia after their successful cruise, John Watson was promoted to executive officer of VC-42. He oversaw all preparation for transition into the Pacific, embarking on the USS *Shamrock Bay* (CVE-84), simultaneous with VC-9 embarking on the USS *Wake Island* (CVE-65), to replace the two escort carriers just recently sunk during the battle of Leyte Gulf in late October. On the night of embarkation, November 10, all pilots in the squadron were required to qualify for night operations on the USS *Charger* (CVE-30). At 7:46 PM, a new pilot, suffering from vertigo, crashed in the water while attempting to land his Wildcat and was killed. Despite this mishap, operations continued. At 8:03 PM, John Watson, also apparently suffering vertigo, crashed his Wildcat into the sea, killing him instantly. His body was recovered and is buried in Silver Brook Cemetery in Anderson, South Carolina.

John B. Watson. *US Navy photo.*

Alex X. Brokas. *Courtesy of the Brokas family.*

Alex X. Brokas, *Order of Glory, Third Class*

Alex Xavier Brokas, VC-42's specialist in night flying tactics, was born on September 21, 1919, in the rural village of Shtike, Albania. At age six, he came to the United States and settled in New York. Immediately following graduation from Allegheny College, he joined the Navy on February 5, 1942, as an Aviation Cadet. After flight training in Pensacola, Florida, and operational training at NAS Fort Lauderdale, he reported to VC-42 in April 1943. Remaining with VC-42 through the end of the war, Brokas was discharged in September 1945. Though he never flew again, he remained in the Naval Reserves until October 1956, retiring as a Lieutenant Commander. Returning to the civilian world, he became an accountant for the Meadville Telephone Company in Pennsylvania. He then moved to Merritt Island, Florida, in 1953 and later to Keystone Heights in 1956, where he worked as a liquor salesman for Darnall and Company. Alex Brokas passed away on February 17, 2005, in Keystone Heights.

The Soviet order book to Alex Brokas. *Courtesy of the Brokas family.*

The Distinguished Flying Cross and Order of Glory, Third Class, number 387926, awarded to Alex Brokas. *Courtesy of the Brokas family.*

Reverse of the Order of Glory, Third Class, awarded to Alex Brokas. *Courtesy of the Brokas family.*

Bernard C. Sissler, *Order of Glory, Third Class*

Bernard Charles "Bernie" Sissler was born on November 12, 1921, in New York City. He joined the Navy on March 16, 1942, and with his counterparts, reported to VC-42 following the completion of training. Discharged in late 1945 after remaining with VC-42, Sissler returned to New York and enrolled in Manhattan College, where he received a bachelor's degree in electrical engineering. Before retirement, he served as the assistant vice president of construction engineering for New York Telephone in New York. He passed away on July 14, 2005, and is buried in St. Johns Cemetery in Goshen, New York.

At the award ceremony on board the USS *Bogue* (CVE-9) on August 2, 1944, Admiral T.L. Sprague pins the Air Medal on Milton Sherbring while Bernard Sissler is handed the box for his medal from the admiral's aide. *Official US Navy photo via the National Archives.*

Milton J. Sherbring, *Order of Glory, Third Class*

Sissler's good friend and fellow chess player was Milton John Sherbring. He was born on August 21, 1920, in Jefferson, Iowa, but grew up in Ogden. He graduated from Ogden High School and attended Boone Junior College for two years; enough time to qualify to become an Aviation Cadet. He joined the Navy on May 5, 1942, only after he was turned down for the Army Air Corps due to a lack of available openings. He completed his operational training on March 1, 1943, before reporting to VC-42. Following the squadron's decommissioning, Sherbring transferred to Naval Air Station Jacksonville and was trained as a Landing Signals Officer (LSO). He served in this capacity at Naval Air Station Miami and Naval Air Station Quonset Point until his discharge in July 1946. Remaining in the Naval Reserves, he went on to command one of the early Reserve jet squadrons, VA-761, and retired as a Commander on August 21, 1980, with nearly forty years of service, active and reserve. As a civilian, he returned to college, graduating in June 1949 with a degree in forestry from the University of Iowa. Working for Northern Natural Gas Company as a district clerk, he settled in Omaha in 1967, where he eventually retired from Northern Natural Gas. Milton Sherbring passed away on April 5, 2014.

Milton Sherbring as a Commander, later in his career. *Courtesy of the Sherbring family.*

1. Награжден Указом Президиума Верховного Совета СССР от 7 июля 1945 года орденом Славы III степени

2. Имеет право, начиная с 1-VIII-1945 г. на получение орденских денежных выдач и на другие льготы и преимущества, согласно „Общему положению об орденах Союза ССР."

3. Книжка бессрочная.

№ 222091

15 августа 1945

Утверждено постановлением ЦИК и СНК Союза ССР от 7 мая 1936 г.

ОБЩЕЕ ПОЛОЖЕНИЕ

об орденах Союза ССР.

1. Орден Союза ССР является высшей наградой за особые заслуги в области социалистического строительства и обороны Союза ССР.

2. Центральным Исполнительным Комитетом Союза ССР учреждены следующие ордена Союза ССР: „Орден Ленина", „Красное Знамя", „Красная Звезда", „Трудовое Красное Знамя" и „Знак Почета".

3. Орденами Союза ССР могут награждаться как отдельные граждане, так и войсковые соединения и войские части Рабоче-Крестьянской Красной Армии, предприятия, учреждения и организации.

4. Награжденные орденом Союза ССР могут быть за новые заслуги повторно награждены тем же или другим орденом Союза ССР.

Имя, отчество и фамилия

Лейтенант

Милтон

Джон Шёрбринг

Подпись владельца книжки

The Soviet order book to Milton Sherbring. *Courtesy of the Sherbring family.*

The Air Medal presented to Milton Sherbring in its original green presentation box. *Courtesy of the Sherbring family.*

Order of Glory, Third Class, number 387939, awarded to Milton Sherbring. *Courtesy of the Sherbring family.*

Lieutenant (Junior Grade) Wallace S. Porter on his wedding day, June 10, 1945. Courtesy of the Porter family.

Wallace S. Porter, *Order of Glory, Third Class*

Finally, Wallace Stevens "Wally" Porter hailed from Pittsburgh, Pennsylvania. He was born on Christmas Eve, 1919, and after graduation from the University of Pittsburgh in June 1941, had worked as a chemical engineer at Corundite Refractories, Inc. in Massillon, Ohio. He left his job in December 1941 and reported for active duty service in the Navy as an Aviation Cadet on January 6, 1942. As with his peers, he commissioned VC-42 at Alameda and traveled with them to their stations on the East Coast and Pacific. Porter was released from active duty on September 29, 1945, and enrolled in Cornell University. Following his graduation, he moved to Hondo, Texas, where he worked as the plant manager of the Universal-Rundle bath fixture factory. Wallace Porter passed away in Hondo on August 30, 1984, and is buried in Hondo Cemetery.

May 21, 1943: The Sinking of *U-569*

In the fight against U-boats in the Atlantic, one squadron achieved the most remarkable record. This was VC-9, commanded by Lieutenant Commander Howard Avery for much of their time in anti-submarine duty. VC-9 was commissioned on August 6, 1942, and following training on the West Coast, arrived in the Atlantic just after Christmas. They began their official role of anti-submarine warfare and convoy escort in the Atlantic in January 1943, spending most of their first year stationed between the USS *Bogue* (CVE-9) and Argentia, Newfoundland.

Following a visit to Belfast, Ireland, in May 1943, VC-9's fight against U-boats started in earnest as the convoy headed directly toward a then-coalescing multi-wolfpack group of forty-two U-boats. The squadron's first kill came by way of Lieutenant Howard Roberts, one of the most senior and experienced pilots in the squadron.

May 21 and 22 were trying days for fighting U-boats. Pilots from VC-9 found *U-231*, *U-468*, and *U-305* within one hundred miles of each other and proceeded to attack them all. None of them, however, were definitively sunk though they were damaged by the accurate attacks of VC-9's pilots. It wasn't until just after 5:00 PM on the second day that they scored their first confirmed kill. *U-569*, a relatively luckless U-boat who had spent her entire war without a single kill, had been cruising on the surface for about one hour.[4] She was discovered by another VC-9 pilot, Lieutenant (jg) William Chamberlain (who would later perish while attacking *U-860* in 1944, as recounted earlier) and attacked at 5:04 PM, but submerged to escape. Reporting on station at 5:25 PM, Roberts relieved Chamberlain and searched for the submarine. He was not disappointed. Fifteen minutes later, *U-569* surfaced again, almost directly under Robert's aircraft. Immediately attacking, he dropped his two Mk.44 and two Mk.17 depth bombs from six hundred feet and observed them exploding near the stern of the submarine. *U-569* was now wounded and taking in water. She floundered, rolling on her side, and then righted herself. Regaining control long enough to escape the flooding vessel, her crew, already suffering extremely low morale due the overall lack of wartime success, readily commenced abandoning the ship and a tied white flag on the periscope in surrender. This was the first time in history an enemy submarine surrendered to an aircraft.[5]

The pilots of VC-9 before the arrival of Howard Avery. Soviet medal recipients include: Roberts (front row, fourth from right), Balliett (front, second from right), Fowler (front, far right), Puckett (back, fifth from right), Heim (back, seventh from right), and Horn (middle, far left). *Courtesy of the Fowler family.*

Despite Roberts' best efforts to prevent them from scuttling the submarine and take her as a prize, her crew succeeded in doing so and she slid beneath the waves. Approximately ninety minutes after the attack, the HMCS *St. Laurent* arrived on scene to pick up the twenty-five survivors in the water and Roberts returned to the carrier. He was awarded the Distinguished Flying Cross from the US and the Distinguished Service Cross from Great Britain for his skill and tenacity in the sinking of *U-569*.

Howard S. Roberts, *Order of the Red Star*

Howard Stowe Roberts was born in Oklahoma City on February 28, 1914. He attended high school in Webster Grove, Missouri, and graduated with a bachelor's degree in mechanical engineering from Purdue. He was employed at Beech Aircraft before enlisting in the Navy on December 17, 1935. Following his designation as a Naval Aviator, Roberts served with Torpedo Squadron (VT) 2 on the USS *Lexington* (CV-2) and on the USS *Salt Lake City* (CA-25). Leaving active duty in 1939, Roberts joined Pan American Airlines, flying commercial aircraft. With war on the horizon, he was called back to active duty in 1940 and shortly thereafter, returned to the fleet. Assigned to VC-9 as a newly commissioned squadron, he had already participated in several anti-submarine cruises on the *Bogue* prior to May 1943. Roberts remained with VC-9 until transferred that summer to assume command of VT-14, commissioning her on September 1, 1943. While in command of VT-14 and flying from the USS *Wasp* (CV-18), Roberts participated in forty strikes against Japanese forces. He earned the Air Medal for a strike on Guam on June 19, 1944, the Silver Star on September 21, 1944, for torpedoing a large oiler in Manila Bay, and finally, the Navy Cross on October 25, 1944, during the Battle of Leyte Gulf, for damaging a Japanese battleship despite terrific resistance.

With the end of the war, he received orders to serve as the executive officer of Naval Air Station Fort Lauderdale, Florida. During a period in December 1945 when he was serving as the acting commanding officer, he spearheaded the search for the five missing aircraft of the infamous Flight 19 over the Bermuda Triangle. He was subsequently assigned to the USS *Suisun* (AVP-53) in the Pacific, followed by service on the staff of the Chief of Naval Air Training in Pensacola, Florida. Roberts then assumed the duties as executive officer of Naval Air Station Bermuda before heading to Italy, serving with the Commander, Fleet Air Eastern Atlantic and Mediterranean.

Returning to the United States, Roberts then served on the staff of the Chief of Naval Personnel in Washington, DC Here, he attended law school in the evenings at the George Washington University, graduating with his Juris Doctorate in 1958. Heading to Hawaii for his final tour, he served as the fleet personnel officer on the staff of Commander in Chief, US Pacific Fleet. Roberts retired from the Navy as a Captain in June 1961. Returning to Pensacola, he practiced law until his passing on October 3, 1984. In 1996, the Howard Stowe Roberts Cultural Life Center at Roberts Wesleyan College was dedicated in his honor.

Howard Roberts receives his British Distinguished Service Cross from Lord Halifax, ambassador of Great Britain. *National Archives.*

Howard Roberts' medals on display in the Howard Stowe Roberts Cultural Life Center at Roberts Wesleyan University, Rochester, New York. *Courtesy of the Howard Stowe Roberts Cultural Life Center, Roberts Wesleyan University.*

October 4, 1943: The Sinking of *U-460*

U-422, as she is attacked by Stewart Holt and Donald Horn. *Courtesy of the J.D. Horn family.*

On September 23, 1943, VC-9, now embarked on the USS *Card*, began the most dramatic anti-submarine cruise of the war. With Howard Avery newly in command, the squadron went on to make attacks on ten U-boats, sinking four and seriously damaging the other six. The cruise was quiet until October 4, when one of VC-9's pilots spotted not one, but four U-boats refueling on the surface. These were *U-460*, the "milk cow," *U-264*, who had just finished fueling, *U-422* getting ready to fuel, and *U-455*, awaiting her turn. Surprised by the inbound aircraft, the captains of *U-460* and *U-264* got into an argument about who should dive first, and as a result, neither did. *U-422* submerged in haste, leaving the other three submarines to fight it out on the surface. Shortly thereafter, *U-455* also dove, just as Lieutenant (jg)s Elbert Heim and David Puckett arrived in their Wildcats. Fighting through heavy anti-aircraft fire from the remaining surfaced U-boats, they pushed through their attacks, despite significant damage to Puckett's plane. *U-264* dove and avoided destruction that day, but Puckett, along with an Avenger flown by Lieutenant (jg) Robert Stearns, pressed home the attack on *U-460*. An aerial torpedo dropped by the Avenger ran a direct path toward *U-460* as she tried to escape, but it was too late. The torpedo found its mark and *U-460* sunk with all hands. Both Heim and Puckett received the Navy Cross for their part in the action.

The day wasn't over. Three hours later, *U-422*, thinking the aircraft had departed the location, surfaced. Unfortunately for her, an Avenger, flown by Lieutenant (jg) Stewart Holt, and a Wildcat, flown by Ensign Joseph Horn, were circling above her in scattered cloud cover. Horn, flying the fighter, began strafing and continued all the way into the target, zooming off above *U-422* at an altitude of fifty feet. The submarine dove, but Holt was right on Horn's heels and let go his torpedo. Within seconds, *U-422* exploded, throwing a dramatic column of water and debris in the air, signaling her demise. Holt and Horn both received the Distinguished Flying Cross for sinking *U-422*.

Elbert S. Heim and David Puckett reading their Navy Cross award citations. *Official US Navy photo via the National Archives.*

Elbert S. Heim, *Order of the Red Star*

Elbert Stewart "Stew" Heim was born on April 8, 1920, in Alba, Texas, the only child of Elbert Stewart Heim, Sr., and Minnie Ruth Heim. Raised in Bossier, Louisiana, and having attended Louisiana State University, he enlisted in the Navy on July 18, 1941. Becoming an Aviation Cadet in December 1941, he was designated a Naval Aviator on June 5, 1942. He received orders in November 1942 to VC-9, and flew with them until transferred in March 1944 to form the cadre of VF-82, preparing to embark to the Pacific theater. Departing December 29 on the USS *Bennington* (CV-20), they headed to Pearl Harbor. By mid-February, the squadron was attacking targets on mainland Japan, to include attacks on future US installations, Yokosuka and Atsugi. By February 19, 1945, they were to the south, making attack runs on Iwo Jima, and by March, were over Okinawa. On March 19, Heim shot down two Japanese fighters over Kyushu, earning his second Distinguished Flying Cross. On March 27, on a mission against Japanese shipping at Sase Ko, Kakeroma Shima, Heim dove on a target and released his bombs. He then pulled up from the bombing run and disappeared into a cloud. That was the last time he was ever seen alive.[6] His body was later found on Kakeroma; the exact cause of death was never determined.[7] He was reburied in Centuries Memorial Park in Shreveport, Louisiana, on March 31, 1949.

David O. Puckett, Jr., *Order of the Red Star*

David Oliver "Son" Puckett Jr. was a lifelong resident of Tupelo, Mississippi. Born there on May 5, 1920, he graduated from Tupelo High School in 1937, followed by the University of Mississippi. Entering active duty on June 14, 1941, he was commissioned on May 31, 1942. Reporting to VC-9 as his first squadron, he held an extraordinary record, earning his Navy Cross for the sinking of *U-422*. With Stew Heim, Puckett transferred out of VC-9 and became one of the veteran pilots in VF-82. Like Heim, luck was on his side in the Atlantic theater, but ran out in the Pacific. On their first mission to bomb Atsugi airfield on February 16, 1945, two divisions of VF-82 fighters were jumped by sixteen Japanese *Oscar*, *Zeke* and *Tojo* aircraft. In the ensuing dogfight, eleven Japanese aircraft were shot down. However, this was at a cost of the loss of three VF-82 Grumman F6F-5 Hellcats with a fourth so badly damaged that it had to be jettisoned upon return to base. Flying one of the aircraft that failed to return was Puckett. He was captured on the ground and became a prisoner of war at the Shinjuku POW Camp near Tokyo for the next six months. Following his release from the camp, he returned home and was discharged on April 27, 1946. A consummate businessman, he owned the Tupelo Lumber Company until his retirement. He was likewise active in his community, earning the Boy Scouts' Silver Beaver award for his work on the Board of Directors for Yocona Area Boy Scouts, and was the former chairman of the Lee County Chapter of the American Red Cross. He passed away on October 29, 2005, and is buried in Tupelo Memorial Park, Tupelo, Mississippi.

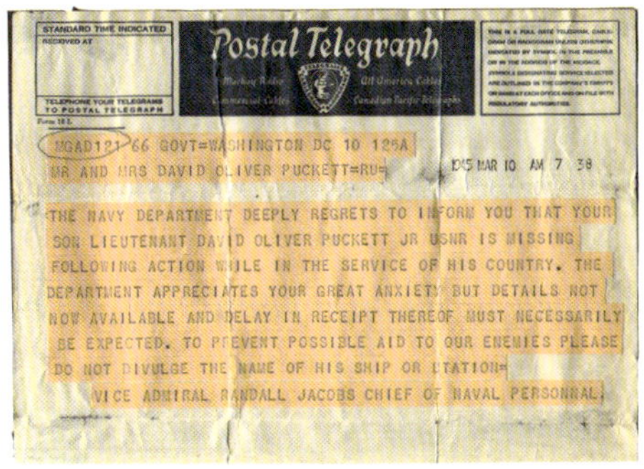

Postal Telegraph

MGAD121 66 GOVT=WASHINGTON DC 10 125A
MR AND MRS DAVID OLIVER PUCKETT=RU= 1945 MAR 10 AM 7 38

THE NAVY DEPARTMENT DEEPLY REGRETS TO INFORM YOU THAT YOUR SON LIEUTENANT DAVID OLIVER PUCKETT JR USNR IS MISSING FOLLOWING ACTION WHILE IN THE SERVICE OF HIS COUNTRY. THE DEPARTMENT APPRECIATES YOUR GREAT ANXIETY BUT DETAILS NOT NOW AVAILABLE AND DELAY IN RECEIPT THEREOF MUST NECESSARILY BE EXPECTED. TO PREVENT POSSIBLE AID TO OUR ENEMIES PLEASE DO NOT DIVULGE THE NAME OF HIS SHIP OR STATION=
VICE ADMIRAL RANDALL JACOBS CHIEF OF NAVAL PERSONNAL.

The telegram notifying David Puckett's family of his Missing in Action status. *Courtesy of David O. Puckett III.*

Close up of the engraving on the reverse of David Puckett's Air Medal. *Courtesy of David O. Puckett III.*

Order of the Red Star number 1553963 awarded to David Puckett. *Courtesy of David O. Puckett III.*

David Puckett's medals, to include the Navy Cross, Air Medal, Purple Heart, and Prisoner of War Medal. *Courtesy of David O. Puckett III.*

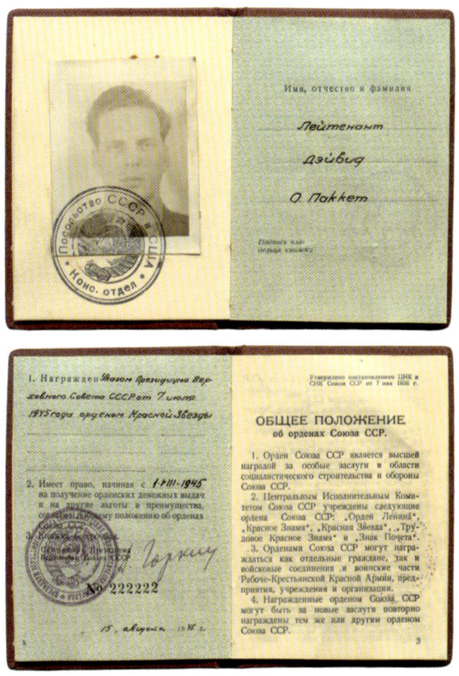

Имя, отчество и фамилия.
Лейтенант
Дэйвид
О. Паккет

1. Награжден Указом Президиума Верховного Совета СССР от 7 июля 1945 года орденом Красной Звезды

2. Имеет право, начиная с 1-VIII-1945 на получение орденских денежных выдач и на другие льготы и преимущества, согласно Общему положению об орденах Союза ССР.

№ 222222

Утверждено постановлением ЦИК и СНК Союза ССР от 7 мая 1936 г.

ОБЩЕЕ ПОЛОЖЕНИЕ
об орденах Союза ССР.

1. Орден Союза ССР является высшей наградой за особые заслуги в области социалистического строительства и обороны Союза ССР.

2. Центральным Исполнительным Комитетом Союза ССР учреждены следующие ордена Союза ССР: „Орден Ленина", „Красное Знамя", „Красная Звезда", „Трудовое Красное Знамя" и „Знак Почета".

3. Орденами Союза ССР могут награждаться как отдельные граждане, так и войсковые соединения и воинские части Рабоче-Крестьянской Красной Армии, предприятия, учреждения и организации.

4. Награжденные орденом Союза ССР могут быть за новые заслуги повторно награждены тем же или другим орденом Союза ССР.

The Soviet order book to David Puckett. *Courtesy of David O. Puckett III.*

The Distinguished Flying Cross in the blue presentation case awarded to Stewart Holt. *Courtesy of the Holt family.*

Stewart B. Holt, *Order of Glory, Third Class*

Stewart Baldwin Holt was born on May 19, 1919, in Oglethorpe, Georgia, but grew up in Savannah and Norfolk, Virginia, graduating from Maury High School. He attended the Norfolk Division of the College of William and Mary (now Old Dominion University) for two years prior to joining the Navy in February 1941. Entering flight training, he earned his Naval Aviator designation on August 19, 1941. After a year as a flight instructor in Hutchison, Kansas, he reported to VC-9 upon completion of operational training in Jacksonville, Florida. He served with VC-9 through 1944 before transferring to Carrier Aircraft Service Unit (CASU) 21 and CASU-25. He left active service in September 1945 and enrolled at Virginia Tech, graduating with his bachelor's degree in civil engineering in 1946. He worked at the University of Georgia in 1947 followed by the Seaboard Railroad (later CSX) eventually becoming the chief of buildings for the railroad, and retired from their new headquarters in Jacksonville in 1983. Stewart Holt passed away on July 13, 1988, and is buried in Athens, Georgia.

Order of Glory, Third Class, number 387923 awarded to Stewart Holt. *Courtesy of the Holt family.*

The Soviet order book to Stewart Holt. *Courtesy of the Holt family.*

Joseph D. Horn, *Order of the Red Star*

Born in Palm City, California, on April 26, 1922, Joseph Donald Horn enlisted in the Navy on February 3, 1942. Qualifying as a Naval Aviator, he reported to his first and only squadron for the war, VC-9. Following his service in the Atlantic, VC-9 was transferred to the Pacific theater, where they used Guam as their base of operations, participating in the invasion of Okinawa and anti-submarine operations. During the assault on Miayko Jima, VC-9 was serving on the USS *Natoma Bay* (CVE-62). She was hit on June 7, 1945, by a kamikaze, but the resourceful crew repaired her flight deck sufficiently to commence flight operations the same day. The squadron returned to the United States that summer, and Horn was released from active duty on October 26, 1945. Returning to school, he graduated from the University of Southern California Dental School and worked as a dentist in Long Beach, California, for thirty years. He passed away on March 15, 2000, and is buried in Westminster Memorial Cemetery, Westminster, California.

Joseph Donald Horn receives his Distinguished Flying Cross from Rear Admiral Albert C. Reed, Commander, Naval Air Forces, US Atlantic Fleet. *Official US Navy photo, via the J.D. Horn family.*

Место для фотокарточки

Имя, отчество и фамилия

Младший лейтенант

Джозеф

Д. Хорн

1. Награжден Указом Президиума Верховного Совета СССР от 7 июля 1945 года орденом Красной Звезды

2. Имеет право, начиная с 1-VIII-1945 г. на получение орденских денежных выдач и на другие льготы и преимущества, согласно Общему положению об орденах Союза ССР.

№ 222133

15 августа 1945 г.

Утверждено постановлением ЦИК и СНК Союза ССР от 7 мая 1936 г.

ОБЩЕЕ ПОЛОЖЕНИЕ
об орденах Союза ССР.

1. Орден Союза ССР является высшей наградой за особые заслуги в области социалистического строительства и обороны Союза ССР.

2. Центральным Исполнительным Комитетом Союза ССР учреждены следующие ордена Союза ССР: „Орден Ленина", „Красное Знамя", „Красная Звезда", „Трудовое Красное Знамя" и „Знак Почета".

3. Орденами Союза ССР могут награждаться как отдельные граждане, так и войсковые соединения и воинские части Рабоче-Крестьянской Красной Армии, предприятия, учреждения и организации.

4. Награжденные орденом Союза ССР могут быть за новые заслуги повторно награждены тем же или другим орденом Союза ССР.

3

The Soviet order book to Donald Horn. *Courtesy of the J.D. Horn family.*

Close up of the engraving on Donald Horn's Distinguished Flying Cross. He had the date of the sinking of *U-422* and the date he received his medal engraved on the reverse. *Courtesy of the J.D. Horn Family.*

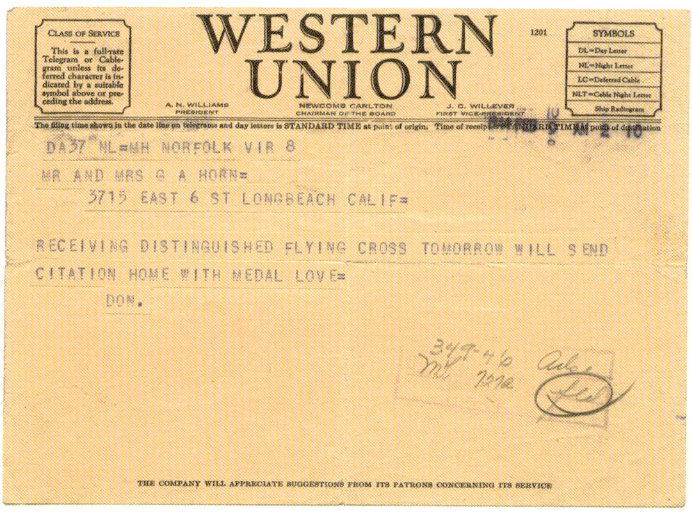

CLASS OF SERVICE
This is a full-rate Telegram or Cablegram unless its deferred character is indicated by a suitable symbol above or preceding the address.

WESTERN UNION

1201

SYMBOLS
DL=Day Letter
NL=Night Letter
LC=Deferred Cable
NLT=Cable Night Letter
Ship Radiogram

A. N. WILLIAMS, PRESIDENT — NEWCOMB CARLTON, CHAIRMAN OF THE BOARD — J. C. WILLEVER, FIRST VICE-PRESIDENT

The filing time shown in the date line on telegrams and day letters is STANDARD TIME at point of origin. Time of receipt is STANDARD TIME at point of destination

DA37 NL=MH NORFOLK VIR 8

MR AND MRS G A HORN=

3715 EAST 6 ST LONGBEACH CALIF=

RECEIVING DISTINGUISHED FLYING CROSS TOMORROW WILL SEND

CITATION HOME WITH MEDAL LOVE=

DON.

THE COMPANY WILL APPRECIATE SUGGESTIONS FROM ITS PATRONS CONCERNING ITS SERVICE

Donald Horn sent this telegram to his parents the day before the ceremony, informing them of receiving the Distinguished Flying Cross. *Courtesy of the J.D. Horn family.*

The Distinguished Flying Cross and Air Medal awarded to Donald Horn. *Courtesy of the J.D. Horn family.*

Order of the Red Star number 1553976 awarded to Donald Horn. *Courtesy of the J.D. Horn family.*

October 31, 1943: The Sinking of *U-584*

Just over a week later, October 12 brought another round of attacks on U-boats. That morning, Lieutenant (jg) Letson Balliett attempted an attack on *U-488*, but she evaded him and got away. The same day, her luck again played a factor: spotted by Lieutenant (jg) Wilma Fowler, he pressed home an attack, but just as before, she escaped. The next day, October 13, was different. At 8:00 AM, Fowler was again on patrol when he found *U-378* and attacked it. However, he again missed his target. The squadron commander, Howard Avery, had taken off to assist and upon reaching Fowler's vicinity, he spotted a surfaced U-boat: *U-402*, commanded by Knights Cross holder *Korvettenkapitän* Freiherr Siegfried von Forstner, one of the most successful U-boat commanders of 1943. Sighting the submarine with her decks awash in heavy seas, Avery planned to conduct an attack with his torpedo. However, von Forstner did not continue his dive, preventing Avery from having a good target. Unable to launch, Avery strafed the submarine's deck. What von Forstner did not see was another VC-9 plane on his stern that dropped a five hundred pound bomb close enough to distract him and to force him to dive. This was Avery's chance. Coming around for the attack the second time within fifteen seconds of the submarine diving, he let go his homing torpedo and it ran true. *U-402* exploded and disappeared below the surface forever. Avery was awarded his first Distinguished Flying Cross.

This was not the last U-boat sunk this cruise. On October 31, shortly after 4:00 PM, Fowler discovered two U-boats riding together on the surface about one thousand yards apart. These were *U-91* and *U-584*. Fowler called for reinforcements, and they arrived in the form of Balliett and Lieutenant (jg) Alexander McAuslan. At this juncture, *U-91* submerged, surviving this attack to come back and wreak havoc on the force that same night. However, *U-584*, commanded by Joachim Deecke, nicknamed "Battleship Deecke" for attempting to attack a destroyer with his deck gun (and being able to escape to tell the tale) paused on the surface, possibly deciding whether or not they should fight it out, despite orders to submerge and escape. Opting to dive, he was too late: Fowler and Balliett both raced in, launching torpedoes on both the starboard and port sides of the submarine. She had nowhere to go. A large explosion was her last statement before heading to the depths of the sea.

Wilma S. Fowler, *Order of the Red Star*

Wilma S. "Monk" Fowler in his summer white uniform at the end of the war. *Courtesy of the Fowler family.*

Wilma Sim "Monk" Fowler was born on January 10, 1920 in Gustine, Texas. Prior to joining the Navy, he graduated from John Tarleton A&M Junior College in Stephensville, Texas, and reported for active duty service on April 17, 1941. Originally assigned to VGS-12 embarked on the USS *Copahee* (CVE-12) following his graduation from flight school, he was transferred to VC-9 prior to the *Copahee's* departure for action in the Pacific theater. With VC-9, he earned a Silver Star for damaging *U-641* in June 1943, and two Distinguished Flying Crosses, one for the attack on *U-758*, the same week as *U-641*, and then for sinking *U-584*. Following this remarkable career, where he earned the nickname "King of the Sub Killers," he transferred to the staff of Fleet Air Wing (FAW) 2, stationed at Naval Air Station Kaneohe, Territory of Hawaii. Subsequently, he reported as a staff officer for the Hawaiian Aircraft Rocket Training Unit (HARTU), stationed at NAS Kahului in December 1944, where he adopted a young dog named "Little Dipper," who routinely flew with him during missions. He remained here until December 1945 before reporting to Naval Proving Ground, Dahlgren, Virginia, to continue working on aerial rocket and missile testing. He was discharged from active duty service on April 18, 1946. Fowler remained in the Reserves and retired as a Lieutenant Commander in December 1958.

Having played football on the NAS Kaneohe team during the war, he caught the eye of Babe Wood, star of the 1939 Tennessee Orange Bowl victory. Babe recruited Fowler to the University of Tennessee at Knoxville, where he played as a wingback on the university's team. Little Dipper, his dog, who had accumulated 117 Navy flight hours during the war, served as the team's first mascot. Graduating from college, he tried his hand at coaching football, but soon discovered that coaching was not for him. Ever an entrepreneur, Fowler opened the Dr. Pepper Bottling Company in Kosciusko, Mississippi, in December 1954. Moving forward from there, he started a successful life insurance company, which he later sold. He retired at age fifty-seven, and spent the rest of his life tending Liberty Hall, the family's antebellum ancestral plantation, until he passed away on July 27, 1990. He is buried on the family estate, along with his beloved Little Dipper.

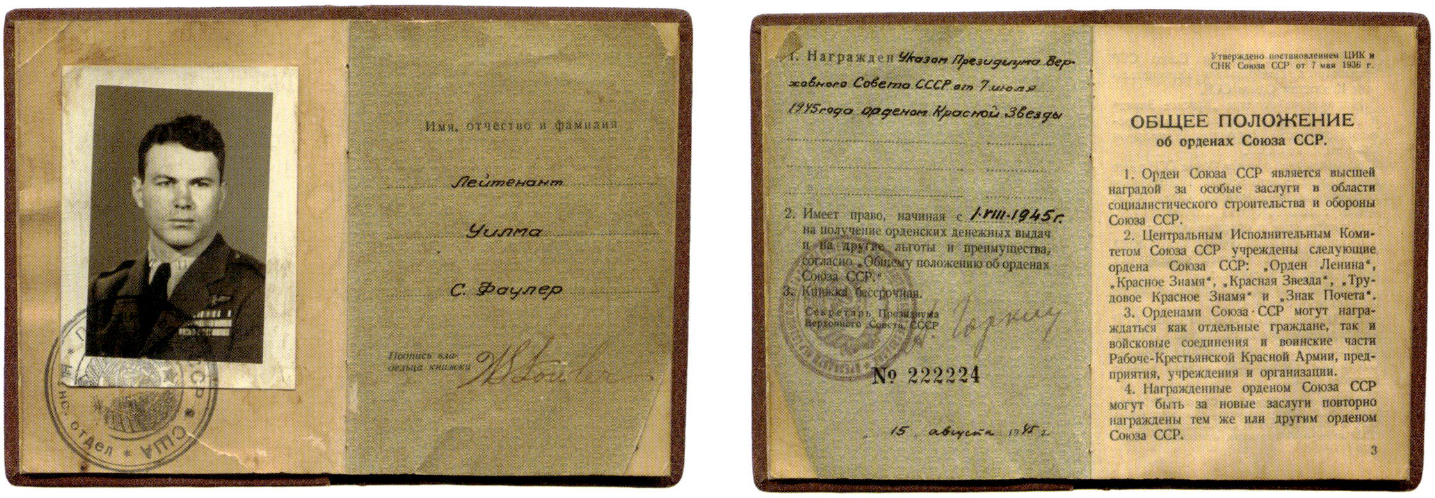

Имя, отчество и фамилия

Лейтенант

Уилма

С. Фаулер

Подпись владельца книжки

1. Награжден Указом Президиума Верховного Совета СССР от 7 июля 1945 года орденом Красной Звезды

2. Имеет право, начиная с 1.VIII.1945 г. на получение орденских денежных выдач и на другие льготы и преимущества, согласно „Общему положению об орденах Союза ССР."

3. Книжка бессрочная.

Секретарь Президиума Верховного Совета СССР

№ 222224

15 августа 1945 г.

Утверждено постановлением ЦИК и СНК Союза ССР от 7 мая 1936 г.

ОБЩЕЕ ПОЛОЖЕНИЕ

об орденах Союза ССР.

1. Орден Союза ССР является высшей наградой за особые заслуги в области социалистического строительства и обороны Союза ССР.

2. Центральным Исполнительным Комитетом Союза ССР учреждены следующие ордена Союза ССР: „Орден Ленина", „Красное Знамя", „Красная Звезда", „Трудовое Красное Знамя" и „Знак Почета".

3. Орденами Союза ССР могут награждаться как отдельные граждане, так и войсковые соединения и воинские части Рабоче-Крестьянской Красной Армии, предприятия, учреждения и организации.

4. Награжденные орденом Союза ССР могут быть за новые заслуги повторно награждены тем же или другим орденом Союза ССР.

3

The Soviet order book to Monk Fowler. *Courtesy of the Fowler family.*

Monk Fowler sometime in 1943. Note the early, wide, Presidential Unit Citation ribbon bar. *Courtesy of the Fowler family.*

The Silver Star and Distinguished Flying Cross awarded to Monk Fowler. *Courtesy of the Fowler family.*

Order of the Red Star number 1553965 awarded to Monk Fowler. *Courtesy of the Fowler family.*

The Silver Star and Distinguished Flying Cross awarded to Letson Balliett. *Courtesy of the Balliett family.*

Letson Balliett, *Order of the Red Star*

A native of Reno, Nevada, Letson Balliett was born into the family of a noted mining entrepreneur on February 4, 1917. Graduating from the University of California at Berkeley prior to joining the Navy, he entered active duty on June 2, 1941, as an Aviation Cadet. Ordered to VC-9 following completion of flight training, he went on to make a name for himself in Atlantic anti-submarine operations. Along with Fowler, he was awarded the Silver Star for the attack on *U-641*, and the Distinguished Flying Cross for *U-584*. Transferring for future duty in the Pacific as a member of VT-80, they arrived at Pearl Harbor on August 27, 1944, following seven months of East Coast operational training. Flying off the USS *Ticonderoga* (CV-14), Balliett earned his second Distinguished Flying Cross on a mission to sink a *Mogami*-class Japanese cruiser on November 25. Finding the IJN *Kumano* at Santa Cruz, already missing her bow from a torpedo hit taken during the Battle of Samar, she took a direct torpedo hit from Balliett, along with four others from fellow VT-80 aircraft. The *Kumano*, mortally wounded, proceeded to roll over and sink.[8] Balliett's next two Distinguished Flying Crosses were awarded for sinking two large freighters on January 12 and 16, 1945, in the China Sea.

Returning to the United States in April 1945, Balliett was discharged from active duty. Remaining in the reserves, he retired as a Lieutenant Commander on June 30, 1961. As a civilian, he first found employment with the Flying Tigers Line, but soon went to work for Standard Oil Company, where he worked at locations in the United States and Thailand until his retirement in the early 1960s. Subsequently, he moved to Hawaii, where he spent the remainder of his life. Letson Balliett passed away on May 14, 1978, and is buried in the Punchbowl Cemetery in Honolulu.

Order of the Red Star number 1553959 awarded to Letson Balliett. *Courtesy of the Balliett family.*

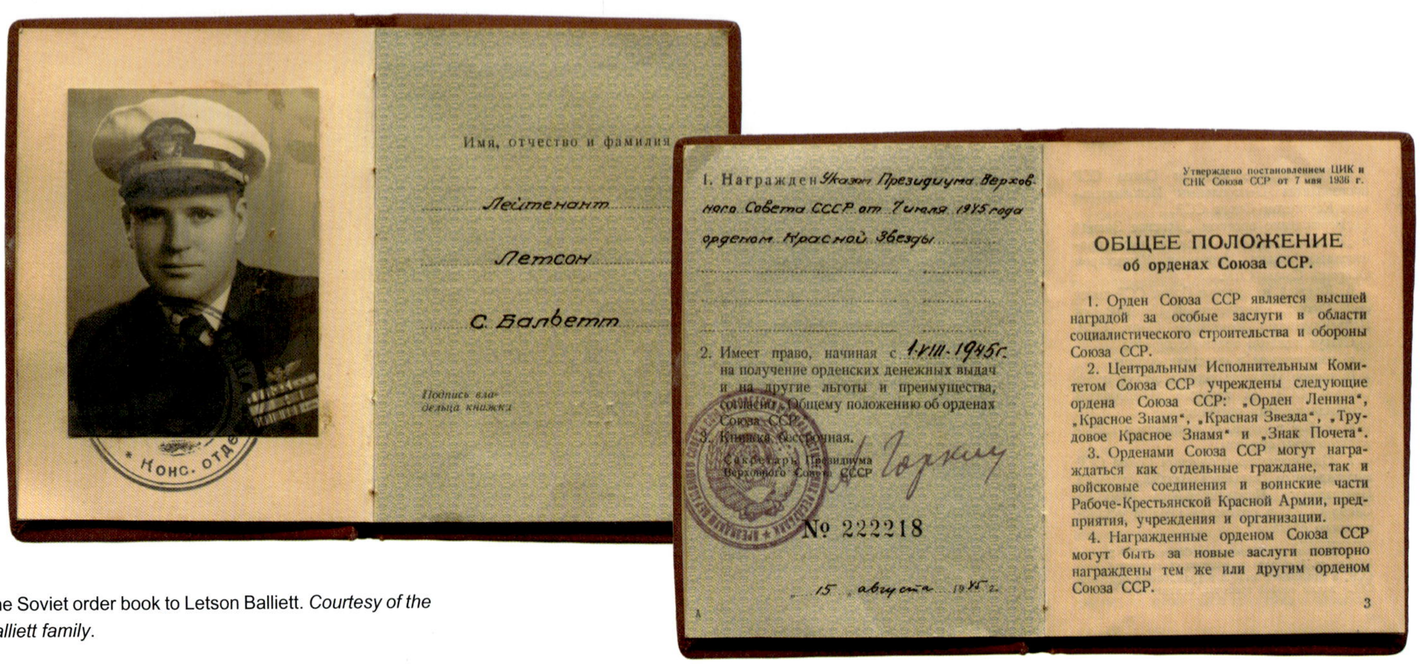

Имя, отчество и фамилия

Лейтенант

Летсон

С. Балветт

Подпись владельца книжки

1. Награжден Указом Президиума Верховного Совета СССР от 7 июля 1945 года орденом Красной Звезды

2. Имеет право, начиная с 1-VIII-1945 г. на получение орденских денежных выдач и на другие льготы и преимущества, согласно „Общему положению об орденах Союза ССР".

3. Книжка бессрочная.

Секретарь Президиума Верховного Совета СССР

№ 222218

15 августа 1945 г.

Утверждено постановлением ЦИК и СНК Союза ССР от 7 мая 1936 г.

ОБЩЕЕ ПОЛОЖЕНИЕ
об орденах Союза ССР.

1. Орден Союза ССР является высшей наградой за особые заслуги в области социалистического строительства и обороны Союза ССР.
2. Центральным Исполнительным Комитетом Союза ССР учреждены следующие ордена Союза ССР: „Орден Ленина", „Красное Знамя", „Красная Звезда", „Трудовое Красное Знамя" и „Знак Почета".
3. Орденами Союза ССР могут награждаться как отдельные граждане, так и войсковые соединения и воинские части Рабоче-Крестьянской Красной Армии, предприятия, учреждения и организации.
4. Награжденные орденом Союза ССР могут быть за новые заслуги повторно награждены тем же или другим орденом Союза ССР.

3

The Soviet order book to Letson Balliett. *Courtesy of the Balliett family.*

Howard Avery, *Order of the Patriotic War, First Class*

Howard Malcolm Avery was born in King Ferry, New York, on September 15, 1908, and joined the Navy as an Aviation Cadet in November 1935 following his graduation from Stanford University. His first sea duty assignment following commissioning was on the USS *Salt Lake City* (CA-25), alongside Howard Roberts, serving three years until transferring in March 1940 to instructor duty at Naval Air Station, Pensacola. With the war raging, he returned to fleet duty in October 1942 as the executive officer of VC-6 on the USS *Bogue* (CVE-9) and in August 1943, became the commanding officer of VC-9. For the remarkable success of VC-9 on this cruise, Avery was awarded the Legion of Merit for enabling the task group to "achieve an unparalleled record of sinkings and damage to the enemy."[9] Transferring to the USS *Solomons* (CVE-67) VC-9 continued their fight against Nazi Germany, and Avery claimed his second U-boat on June 15, 1944 with the sinking of *U-860*. For his valor and leadership exhibited during the vicious fighting with the submarine that cost the squadron the lives of four pilots, he was awarded the Navy Cross. Transferring to the Pacific, Avery assumed command of CVG-91, flying from the USS *Bon Homme Richard* (CV-31). Flying night strikes against the Japanese homeland, Avery went on to earn the Bronze Star Medal and his second Distinguished Flying Cross.

Following the end of the Second World War, Avery held staff positions in Pearl Harbor and the Pentagon before returning to sea as the executive officer of the USS *Bennington* (CV-20) in 1953. Here he earned his Navy and Marine Corps Medal for lifesaving during the May 26, 1954, fire on board that took the lives of 102 men. His later career included service in London and in Paris, as well as serving as the commissioning commanding officer of Naval Air Station Lemoore, serving with fellow Soviet medal recipient Jack Stewart. Howard Avery retired from the Navy on July 1, 1967, and passed away almost exactly twenty years later, on July 4, 1987. He is buried in San Francisco National Cemetery in San Francisco, California.

Howard Avery as a Captain while in command of Naval Air Station Lemoore. *Courtesy of the Avery family.*

The Soviet order book to Howard Avery. *Courtesy of the Avery family.*

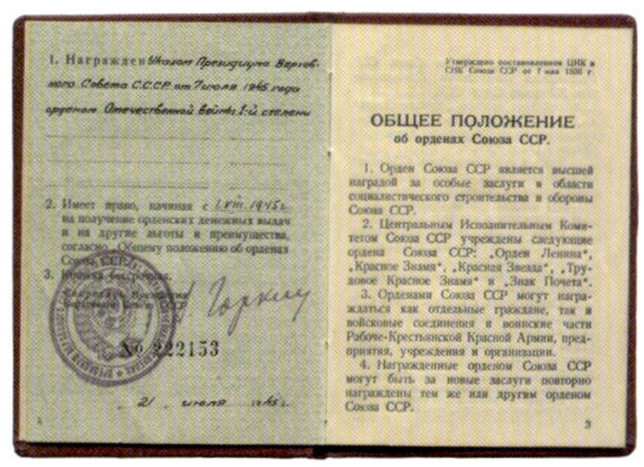

Order of the Patriotic War, First Class, number 247527 awarded to Howard Avery. *Courtesy of the Avery family.*

Howard Avery's Navy Cross. *Courtesy of the Avery family.*

Howard Avery conducts a meeting with his department heads at NAS Lemoore. Jack Stewart, his operations officer and fellow Soviet medal recipient, is at his immediate left. *Courtesy of the Stewart family.*

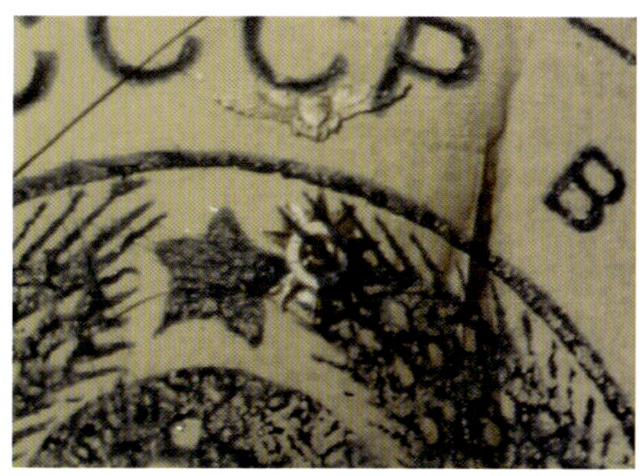

Close-up of the photo in Avery's order book. Note he is wearing his Order of the Patriotic War through the pocket flap of his uniform. *Courtesy of the Avery family.*

Chapter 3

Anti-Submarine Operations: Destroyer and Destroyer Escort Recipients

October 31, 1943: The Sinking of *U-405*

U-boat victories weren't only confined to pilots and aircraft. The mission of the Navy's destroyers and destroyer escorts assigned to convoys was to provide an anti-submarine screen and conduct attacks against discovered U-boats. Often, these battles became fierce as the ship's commanding officers fought the submarine with every means available, to include ramming with their own ship. One of the most ferocious fights between a surface vessel and a U-boat took place on the evening of October 31, 1943, between *U-256*, *U-405*, and the aging First World War-vintage destroyer, USS *Borie* (DD-215). *U-256* had escaped destruction on October 28 by attacks from VC-1 aircraft, to include Harold Handshuh.[1] *U-405*, commanded by *Fregattenkapitän* Rolf-Heinrich Hopmann, was on her eighth war patrol and had five previous sinkings to her credit, to include the SS *Wade Hampton*, sunk in February 1943.[2]

The *Borie*, commanded by Charles Hutchins, at the time a thirty-year-old Lieutenant and the youngest destroyer captain in the Navy, and Lieutenant Philip Brown, his executive officer, was commissioned shortly after the end of hostilities in the First World War. Her earliest service had taken place during the Russian Civil War as a refugee transport in the Black Sea, followed by years of duty in the Far East and the Panama Canal Zone. On the night of October 31, she was sent to track down *U-91*, which had escaped from the attack of Letson Balliett and Monk Fowler earlier in the day. At 8:10 PM, *Borie* picked up a radar contact in the area believed to be *U-91*. However, this turned out to be *U-256*. The *Borie* conducted three depth charge attacks, and hearing a large underwater explosion, believed they had sunk the submarine. Later, it was determined this was not the case as *U-256*, though badly damaged and unable to carry on her mission, was able to limp back to Germany for repair and refit.

For the successful anti-submarine cruise of Task Group 21.14 in October and November 1943, the ships and squadron were presented the Presidential Unit Citation. Admiring the award pennant are Howard Avery (second from left) and Charles Hutchins (third from left). *Official US Navy photo via the National Archives.*

Continuing her patrol, *Borie* found another contact at 2:00 AM. Dropping depth charges, *Borie* forced *U-405* to the surface, just off her port quarter. As *U-405's* crew manned her deck guns to fight on the surface, *Borie* fired her aft four-inch gun, obliterating the submarine's deck gun. Coming to full speed, Hutchins ordered the ship turned to bring all of *Borie's* guns to bear on the surfaced U-boat. Firing everything they could, the crew of *U-405* conducted themselves fearlessly in an attempt to man her remaining topside weapons and maneuver to escape the onslaught of *Borie's* firepower. At the same time, Hutchins noted a man at the top of the conning tower of the battered submarine waving as if to surrender. Calling a ceasefire on *Borie*, they watched as *U-405* again began evasive maneuvers. Frustrated by their apparent deception, Hutchins could stand no more. He gave the order to immediately ram the submarine. *U-405* attempted to submerge but was too late; the *Borie* cut directly over her bow at a thirty-degree angle.

For ten minutes, the two ships were locked together in a deadly embrace. In a scene almost reminiscent of a battle between sailing ships of old, the two crews fought in hand-to-hand combat illuminated only by the beams of searchlights, flares, and flashlights. They were in such close quarters that a five-inch sheath knife, thrown by a member of *Borie's* crew, found its mark in the belly of a German submariner. At the same time, an empty four-inch shell, thrown off *Borie's* bow, claimed yet another victim. On the bridge wing, *Borie's* executive officer, Philip Brown, calmly grabbed a Thompson forty-five-caliber machine gun and began methodically firing magazine after magazine of bullets into the chaos on the deck of the submarine below.

Finally freed from their deadly embrace, *U-405's* captain decided that he would turn the tables and ram the *Borie*. Turning to dodge a torpedo fired by *Borie*, he aimed directly for her starboard quarter. The quick maneuvering of the ship and the launch of three depth charges jarred the sub and stopped the U-boat in her tracks. The Germans who had survived the onslaught quickly poured out of the sinking submarine and clambered for lifeboats thrown down by the crew of the *Borie*. *U-405*, settling fast in the water, at once slid below the waves and exploded, leaving a wake of debris and survivors on the surface. Unfortunately for their fellow countrymen, an unknown U-boat was in the area and attempted to extract revenge. Firing a torpedo at *Borie*, the ship took evasive action and the torpedo missed. However, during her maneuvering, she cut through the cluster of *U-405's* survivors, killing many of them as they attempted to swim out of the path of the ship. Racing away from the area as fast as she could to avoid yet another torpedo, *Borie* left the remaining survivors at sea. Later, not a single survivor was found.

The victory over *U-405* was not without cost. During the ramming, almost the entire port side of the ship had been crushed. *U-405's* diving fin had sliced into the hull, tearing a gash in the forward engine room, manned by six of *Borie's* crew, including Soviet medal recipients Chief Machinist's Mate William Green and Fireman, first class Mario Pagnotta. Water began pouring into the space faster than the bilge pumps could remove it. A damage control party arrived on scene that included future Soviet medal recipient, Machinist's Mate, second class Irving Saum. They stuffed mattresses in the gash in an attempt to stop the flooding. They were successful to a point, but the water crept higher and during the bloody fight topside, *Borie's* engineers were operating her propulsion plant in waist-deep water. Due to the high-speed maneuvering following the engagement with *U-405*, the mattresses could no longer stem the flooding and the forward engine room began to flood uncontrollably. Chief Green and Fireman Pagnotta were still manning their stations in water up to their necks, working underwater and then only returning to the surface for air. Finally, they could fight it no longer and were ordered to leave the space by the chief engineer.

Because of the pump cross-connects, the flooded engine room presented a massive problem to the other spaces: water began rising in them as well. Saum, who had already broken his hand during previous damage control efforts, volunteered to dive into the murky water and swim forward, under the ship's water tank, and close the connection to the forward engine room: a near-suicidal mission. Despite being in considerable pain, he survived, closed the cross-connects, and brought the aft flooding under control.

However, this only bought the crew time as the *Borie* was ultimately doomed. By 4:30 PM on November 1, already having not slept for the better part of two days and worried about capsizing in the twenty-foot seas, Hutchins made the call to abandon ship. Although not a single member of the crew had been killed in the battle with *U-405*, twenty-seven were lost at sea during the subsequent rescue attempt, leaving a bitter reminder of the cost of war.

The USS *Borie* (DD-215) receives the *coup de grace* from aircraft of VC-9 after being abandoned at sea following the severe damage sustained in the battle with *U-405. National Archives.*

Charles H. Hutchins, *Order of the Patriotic War, First Class*

Charles Hutchins receives the Navy Cross for his heroism in the battle between the USS *Borie* (DD-215) and *U-405*. *Official US Navy photo via the National Archives.*

Charles Harris Hutchins was born in Indiana on January 28, 1913, and entered the Naval Academy with the class of 1936. Commissioned on June 4, 1936, he served on the USS *Nevada* (BB-36), USS *Arizona* (BB-39), and USS *Dorsey* (DD-117) prior to the start of the Second World War. He conducted minesweeping operations in the Pacific on USS *Boggs* (DMS-3) and was subsequently transferred to command the USS *Borie* (DD-215) in the Atlantic. In command of *Borie* through her sinking on November 1, 1943, he earned the Navy Cross for his aggressive attacks and exceptional command ability. Following two months of recovery, he was promoted to Lieutenant Commander and took command of the USS *J. Fred Talbott* (DD-156), where he also served as Commander, Destroyer Division (COMDESDIV) 53 following his change of command on October 12, 1944. From March 1945 he commanded the USS *Doran* (DMS-41) a high-speed mineseweeper and took her into the Pacific in preparation for conducting minesweeping operations for the eventual invasion of the Japanese mainland. On November 20, he was relieved of command and returned to the United States for discharge from active duty.

As a civilian, he worked for his father-in-law's company, Wabash Fibre Box, eventually retiring from there as the vice president of sales in 1964. He moved to Naples, Florida, to escape the winters in Indiana, and later relocated to Hilton Head, South Carolina. He passed away there on August 30, 1992.

Philip B. Brown, *Order of the Patriotic War, Second Class*

Lieutenant Philip B. Brown following the battle between the USS *Borie* (DD-215) and *U-405*. *Courtesy of the Brown family.*

Hutchins' executive officer on *Borie* was Philip Bosche Brown. Brown was born in North Carolina on August 25, 1915, and graduated from the Naval Academy with the class of 1939. His first ship was the *Borie*, where he earned the Legion of Merit for his bravery and leadership exhibited on October 31 and November 1, 1943. Subsequently, in an unusual twist, he received orders to the USS *J. Fred Talbott* (DD-156), under the command of his former captain, Charles Hutchins. When Hutchins was promoted to command COMDESDIV 53 in October 1944, Brown took command of *Talbott*. He commanded the ship, then redesignated AG-81, as a target ship for torpedo bombers, all the way through the end of the war. He was relieved of command on November 1, 1945, and was discharged to civilian life shortly thereafter. He remained in the Reserves, retiring in 1954 as a Lieutenant Commander.

As a civilian, he established the Brown-Lucius Wood Preserving Company in 1946. He later owned the radio station WDSC and opened the first cucumber market in Dillon, South Carolina. As a politician, he served in the South Carolina state legislature from 1949 to 1951, and was appointed a South Carolina highway commissioner, representing the Fourth Judicial District, by Governor Richard Riley in 1981. Deeply involved in his community, he served as the chairman of the Dillon District Two school board and chairman of the Dillon County Board of Education for fourteen years. He passed away in South Carolina on May 29, 2002.

Order of the Patriotic War, Second Class, number 557263 awarded to Philip Brown. *Courtesy of the Brown family.*

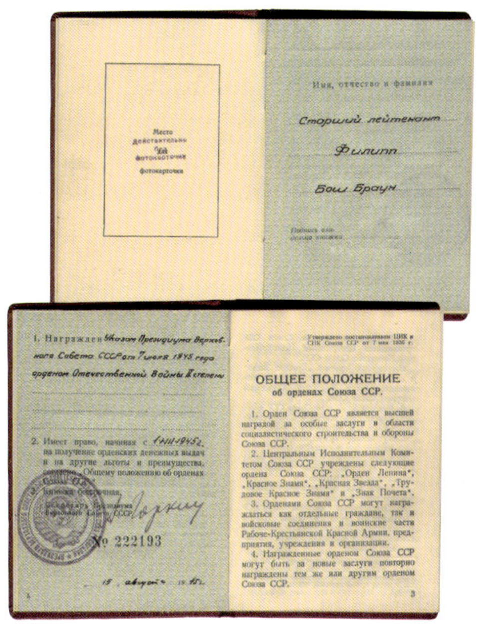

The Soviet order book to Philip Brown. *Courtesy of the Brown family.*

William J. Green, *Order of Glory, Third Class*

Born in New Jersey on April 22, 1897, Chief Machinist's Mate William Joseph Green was one of the oldest members of *Borie's* crew. He had enlisted in the Navy on May 24, 1918, and served on USS *S.C. 63*, followed by the USS *Kaiserin Auguste Victoria*, a converted cruise ship to troop transport bringing troops back from France after the end of the First World War. He was discharged on September 30, 1921, but enlisted again on July 27, 1922, and served on USS *Eagle 48* and *55*, two early anti-submarine patrol craft. He was promoted to Chief Machinist's Mate on July 27, 1926. Chief Green reported to the *Borie* on November 25, 1940, while she was still serving in the Panama Canal Zone, before her Atlantic Ocean service. Earning a Silver Star for his efforts to save the *Borie* in November 1943, he spent the remainder of the war stationed at the US Navy Frontier Base in Tompkinsville, New York. Being placed on "Retired on Active Duty" as of September 3, 1945, he served in the Headquarters, Third Naval District in New York. He remained in the inactive reserves and retired on September 1, 1957, with almost thirty-nine years of active and reserve service. He lived in Jersey City, New Jersey, where he passed away on March 15, 1967.

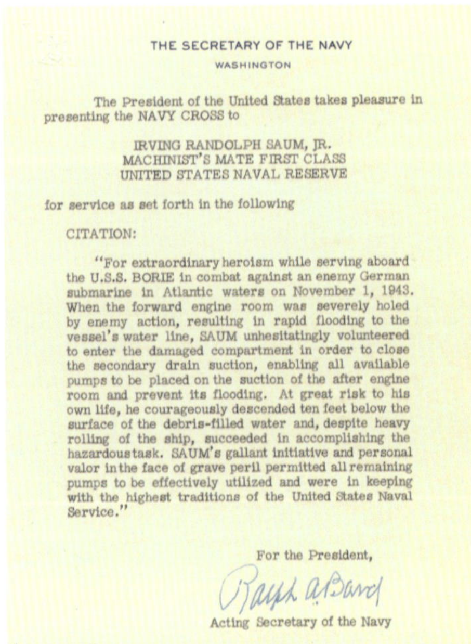

THE SECRETARY OF THE NAVY
WASHINGTON

The President of the United States takes pleasure in presenting the NAVY CROSS to

IRVING RANDOLPH SAUM, JR.
MACHINIST'S MATE FIRST CLASS
UNITED STATES NAVAL RESERVE

for service as set forth in the following

CITATION:

"For extraordinary heroism while serving aboard the U.S.S. BORIE in combat against an enemy German submarine in Atlantic waters on November 1, 1943. When the forward engine room was severely holed by enemy action, resulting in rapid flooding to the vessel's water line, SAUM unhesitatingly volunteered to enter the damaged compartment in order to close the secondary drain suction, enabling all available pumps to be placed on the suction of the after engine room and prevent its flooding. At great risk to his own life, he courageously descended ten feet below the surface of the debris-filled water and, despite heavy rolling of the ship, succeeded in accomplishing the hazardous task. SAUM's gallant initiative and personal valor in the face of grave peril permitted all remaining pumps to be effectively utilized and were in keeping with the highest traditions of the United States Naval Service."

For the President,
Ralph A. Bard
Acting Secretary of the Navy

Original citation for Irving Saum's Navy Cross. *Courtesy of the Saum family.*

Irving R. Saum, *Order of Glory, Third Class*

Working as an apprentice surveyor for the District of Columbia Transit Authority in Washington, DC prior to the war, Irving Randolph Saum was born on July 15, 1918, in the same city and graduated from Western High School. He had already served a previous enlistment in the Navy from March 31, 1936 to March 30, 1940. He was working on his engineering degree from the University of Maryland when he decided to reenlist on October 22, 1940. His first assignment was on the *J. Fred Talbott*, the same ship both Hutchins and Brown would command later in the war. He transferred to the *Borie* in October 1941, and served on her throughout her time in the Atlantic. Receiving the Navy Cross for his exceptional bravery at the risk of his own life while attempting to save the ship, he spent the next four months in the hospital, recovering from complications resulting from his broken hand (he later applied, and was disapproved, for a Purple Heart because of his broken hand). In March 1944, he was assigned to Amphibious Base Little Creek, Virginia, assisting with the development, maintenance, and repair of new equipment for amphibious landings. He was discharged on September 7, 1945, and settled in Bethesda, Maryland. Saum became a self-employed cabinet and custom furniture maker, skilled enough to be offered a coveted position on the cabinet crew tasked with rebuilding the cabinets of the White House during the Kennedy Administration. Irving Saum died of a heart attack on August 23, 1984, and is buried in Arlington National Cemetery.

Место для фотокарточки

Имя, отчество и фамилия
Помощник машиниста II статьи
Орвинг
Рэндолф Соом
Подпись владельца книжки

1. Награжден Указом Президиума Верховного Совета СССР от 7 июля 1945 года орденом Славы III степени

2. Имеет право, начиная с 1.VIII.1945 г. на получение орденских денежных выдач и на другие льготы и преимущества, согласно „Общему положению об орденах Союза ССР".

3. Книжка бессрочная.

Секретарь Президиума Верховного Совета СССР
№ 222168
15 августа 1945 г.

Утверждено постановлением ЦИК и СНК Союза ССР от 7 мая 1936 г.

ОБЩЕЕ ПОЛОЖЕНИЕ
об орденах Союза ССР.

1. Орден Союза ССР является высшей наградой за особые заслуги в области социалистического строительства и обороны Союза ССР.
2. Центральным Исполнительным Комитетом Союза ССР учреждены следующие ордена Союза ССР: „Орден Ленина", „Красное Знамя", „Красная Звезда", „Трудовое Красное Знамя" и „Знак Почета".
3. Орденами Союза ССР могут награждаться как отдельные граждане, так и войсковые соединения и воинские части Рабоче-Крестьянской Красной Армии, предприятия, учреждения и организации.
4. Награжденные орденом Союза ССР могут быть за новые заслуги повторно награждены тем же или другим орденом Союза ССР.

3

The Soviet order book to Irving Saum. *Courtesy of the Saum family.*

Irving Saum (center) stands with Rear Admiral F.W. Rockwell and his flag aide during an award ceremony at Little Creek Amphibious Base on July 22, 1944. *Official US Navy photo via the National Archives.*

Irving Saum's Navy Cross. *Courtesy of the Saum family.*

Order of Glory, Third Class, number 387913 awarded to Irving Saum. *Courtesy of the Saum family.*

Mario Pagnotta (lower left) poses with three shipmates while on leave in 1945. *Courtesy of the Pagnotta family.*

Mario J. Pagnotta, *Order of Glory, Third Class*

Born on October 23, 1916, to recently-immigrated Italian parents in Hoboken, New Jersey, Mario James Pagnotta enlisted in the Navy in August 1940 following three years of working for the Lever Brothers Company. Remaining a Reservist until August 1941, he joined the *Borie* on September 30, 1941. He served on her for the following twenty-six months, and earned the Silver Star for his heroism in the flooded forward engine compartment with Chief Green. He was subsequently transferred to the *J. Fred Talbott* in December 1943, serving there with both his former commanding officer and executive officer. He was subsequently assigned to the newly commissioned USS *Rooks* (DD-804) in September 1944, and took part in shore bombardments during the invasions of both Iwo Jima and Okinawa. During the invasion of Okinawa, they conducted shore bombardment for eighty-seven consecutive days, and shot down six Japanese aircraft, four of whom were kamikazes deliberately targeting her.[13] Pagnotta returned to the United States in November 1945 and was assigned to the USS *General A.E. Anderson* (AP-111), conducting trans-Atlantic troop transport duties. Finally, he was assigned to the USS *Wallace L. Lind* (DD-703), conducting naval reserve training cruises out of New Orleans. He was discharged as a Machinist's Mate, first class from active duty on May 25, 1947. He settled in Weehawken, New Jersey, but moved to Maywood and resumed his duties as a machinist for Lever Brothers in Edgewater. Mario Pagnotta passed away on April 3, 1972, and buried in Holy Cross Cemetery, North Arlington, New Jersey.

Mario Pagnotta's Silver Star in the original case of issue. *Courtesy of the Pagnotta family.*

Mario Pagnotta's Navy Good Conduct Medal, dated 1946. *Courtesy of the Pagnotta family.*

Order of Glory, Third Class, number 387950 awarded to Mario Pagnotta. *Courtesy of the Pagnotta family.*

March 1, 1944: The Sinking of *U-709* and *U-603*

Sailing on February 16, 1944, from Norfolk, the USS *Block Island* (CVE-21), along with one destroyer and four destroyer escorts, including the USS *Bronstein* (DE-189), USS *Thomas* (DE-102), and USS *Bostwick* (DE-103), headed into the U-boat infested waters of the Atlantic on a mission to destroy German submarines. The first two weeks of the cruise were quiet, as the weather up to that point had made sub hunting nearly impossible. With heavy seas and near gale-force winds, several of the ships had to repair damage caused by the tumultuous ocean. The evening of February 29, with weather more supportive of the deadly hunt, would test the mettle of the task group. At 5:57 PM, an aircraft from *Block Island* reported a visual sighting of a U-boat ahead of the group. Vectoring in that direction for the attack, *Thomas*, with Lieutenant Commander David Kellogg as her commanding officer, picked up a sonar contact at 10:16 PM. The *Bostwick*, commanded by Lieutenant Commander John Church, maintained about 4,500 yards separation from *Thomas* to conduct a second search and protect *Thomas* if needed. *Thomas* dropped a depth charge pattern as she closed, but lost the contact and maneuvered away.

Meanwhile, Lieutenant Commander Sheldon Kinney in the *Bronstein*, having already badly damaged *U-441* by gunfire earlier that night, rushed in, firing star shells at the last known location of the contact. Much to everyone's surprise, the illumination revealed *U-709* on the surface, preparing to attack *Bostwick* and *Thomas*. She submerged, and the contact was lost. *Bostwick* and *Thomas* began a search and at 11:50 PM, gained contact again. What followed were eight depth charge attacks, continually pounding the submarine until just before 4:00 AM, when a secondary explosion was heard and *U-709* made her final dive. At the same time, *Bronstein* had found another submarine, *U-603*, preparing to make a torpedo attack on the *Block Island*. Following a successful depth charge attack, *U-603* sank to the depths at approximately 1:22 AM on March 1. Kinney became the first destroyer escort captain to participate in three successful U-boat engagements in one night and was awarded the Navy Cross for his actions in damaging *U-441* and sinking both *U-709* and *U-603*. David Kellogg and John Church were both awarded the Bronze Star for their part in the sinking of *U-709*.

This was not the last time Kinney and Kellogg would have encounters with U-boats. On March 16, the *Bronstein* went on to sink *U-801*, and shortly thereafter, participate in one of the more unusual events of the Second World War, the transportation of $68 million worth of gold, the Reserves of the Bank of Poland, from Dakar to New York. These were but a handful of notable events in the career of Sheldon Hoard Kinney.

The USS *Bostwick* (DE-103) at sea in 1943. *Official US Navy photo via the National Archives.*

Rear Admiral Sheldon Kinney. Note he wears the ribbon for the Order of the Patriotic War, First Class, on his ribbon bars (third row from the bottom, far right). *Official US Navy photo via the National Archives.*

Sheldon H. Kinney, *Order of the Patriotic War, First Class*

Born on August 27, 1918, in Pasadena, California, Kinney left high school before his senior year in order to enlist in the Navy. Serving as a Signalman on the USS *New York* (BB-34), he was selected from the fleet to attend the Naval Academy, where he graduated with the class of 1941. His first ship was the USS *Sturtevant* (DD-240), where he earned the Navy and Marine Corps Medal for saving the lives of two aviators in submarine-infested waters. Following the sinking of the *Sturtevant*, he took command of the training ship USS *Edsall* (DE-129), followed shortly thereafter by command of the *Bronstein*, where he earned his Navy Cross. Leaving the *Bronstein*, he finished the war as the Anti-Submarine Warfare Officer on the staff of Commander Destroyers Atlantic.

Later, he commanded the USS *Ludlow* (DD-438), the USS *Taylor* (DD-468), USS *Mitscher* (DL-2), USS *Mississinewa* (AO-144), Amphibious Squadron Twelve, and Cruiser Destroyer Flotilla Eleven during Vietnam. Ashore, one of his most notable tours was as the Commandant of Midshipmen at the Naval Academy, followed by service as the Deputy Chief of Naval Personnel and as Chief of Naval Education and Training. Rear Admiral Kinney finally served as Commander, Cruiser Destroyer Pacific prior to his retirement in 1972.

Following retirement, he served as the president of the State University of New York Maritime College for ten years followed by president of the World Maritime University (WMU) of the International Maritime Organization (IMO) of the United Nations. He also served as special advisor to the Secretary General of the IMO in London. Because of his tremendous work and dedication, a doctoral fellowship and a memorial prize lecture were established at WMU in his honor. He also served as editor of the United States Naval Institute *Proceedings*. Sheldon Kinney passed away on December 11, 2004, and is buried in the Naval Academy Cemetery, Annapolis, Maryland.

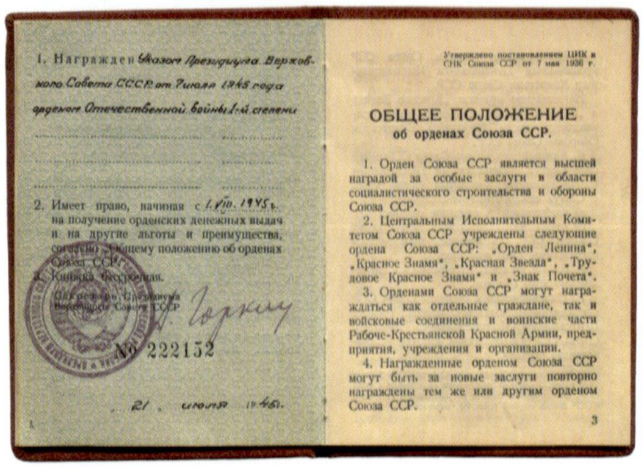

1. Награжден Указом Президиума Верховного Совета СССР от 7 июля 1945 года орденом Отечественной войны 1-й степени

2. Имеет право, начиная с 1.VIII.1945 г. на получение орденских денежных выдач и на другие льготы и преимущества, согласно „Общему положению об орденах Союза ССР".

3. Книжка бессрочная.

Секретарь Президиума Верховного Совета СССР

№ 222152

21 июля 1945 г.

Утверждено постановлением ЦИК и СНК Союза ССР от 7 мая 1936 г.

ОБЩЕЕ ПОЛОЖЕНИЕ
об орденах Союза ССР.

1. Орден Союза ССР является высшей наградой за особые заслуги в области социалистического строительства и обороны Союза ССР.
2. Центральным Исполнительным Комитетом Союза ССР учреждены следующие ордена Союза ССР: „Орден Ленина", „Красное Знамя", „Красная Звезда", „Трудовое Красное Знамя" и „Знак Почета".
3. Орденами Союза ССР могут награждаться как отдельные граждане, так и войсковые соединения и воинские части Рабоче-Крестьянской Красной Армии, предприятия, учреждения и организации.
4. Награжденные орденом Союза ССР могут быть за новые заслуги повторно награждены тем же или другим орденом Союза ССР.

3

The Soviet order book to Sheldon Kinney. *Courtesy of the Kinney family.*

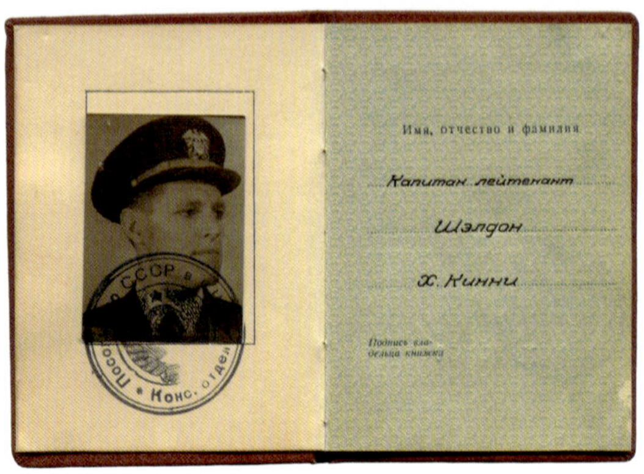

Имя, отчество и фамилия

Капитан лейтенант

Шэлдон

Х. Кинни

Подпись владельца книжки

Order of the Patriotic War, First Class, number 247526 awarded to Sheldon Kinney. Notable are the modifications Admiral Kinney had a jeweler make to the medal in order to wear it as a hanging award. These include the addition of the hanging ring and hand-made ribbon. *Courtesy of the Kinney family.*

John H. Church, Jr., *Order of the Patriotic War, Second Class*

John Howard Church Jr., the commander of *Bostwick*, was born in Germantown, Pennsylvania, on April 9, 1904, a bona-fide *Mayflower* descendent. He joined the Naval Reserve as a Lieutenant on August 10, 1939, a senior rank due to his experience working as a pilot on the Delaware River, following in the footsteps of his father. He reported for active duty on August 25, 1941, serving as the executive officer of the USS *Coral* (PY-15), a former steam yacht owned by Henry Ford, but pressed into military service. He was promoted to commanding officer on May 21, 1943, and remained on board through her decommissioning. Church then reported to the *Bostwick* on December 1, 1943, and stayed with her until relieved on May 28, 1944 when he went to take command of the USS *Enright* (DE-217), taking her to the Pacific theater and later participating in the invasion of Okinawa. Finally, he returned to the United States to commission the USS *Cybele* (AKS-10), serving as her commanding officer through February 18, 1946, transporting supplies for occupation forces around the Japanese islands. Leaving active duty, he later retired from the Naval Reserves as a Captain on June 30, 1961. Following the war, Church returned to Bowling Green, Pennsylvania, and spent the remainder of his career as a river pilot on the Delaware River. John Church passed away in Swarthmore, Pennsylvania, on July 28, 1977.

John H. Church as a Commander. *National Personnel Records Center.*

April 7, 1944: The Sinking of *U-856*

About 350 miles off the coast of Massachusetts, the USS *Huse* (DE-154) commanded by Lieutenant Commander Robert Wanless and the USS *Champlin* (DD-601), under the command of Commander John Schaffer, with Lieutenant Robert Baughan as the executive officer, began searching for a reported U-boat at dawn on April 7, 1944. *Champlin* made first contact at 3:42 PM, but lost it soon thereafter. At 4:10 PM, contact was regained and *Huse* dropped a pattern of depth charges at 4:14 followed by a series from *Champlin*. These depth charge attacks caused considerable damage in the *U-856's* control room, with the hand wheel from the main blowing valve being "torn from its socket...and hurled across the control room."[3] Flooding was out of control in the stern, and the decision was made to surface and abandon ship, as the crew knew the boat was doomed.[4] At 4:52, the excitement on the surface began, as a periscope, rising from the water, was sighted just forward of the port beam by a sharp-eyed lookout on *Champlin*. Commander Schaffer made the decision to ram the surfacing U-boat and began to batter the now-visible conning tower with rounds from her forward five-inch gun. At 5:06, *U-856* was rammed in the stern by *Champlin's* port bow, causing considerable damage to both ships. Backing away from the now-injured U-boat, Wanless, on *Huse,* closed in and maintained gunfire on the submarine. Preparing to make a second ram, Shaffer brought the *Champlin* around, but in the process was mortally wounded by the accidental detonation of a twenty-millimeter projectile from their bridge gun on the top of an open ammunition locker. The resulting detonation sent burning shrapnel in the direction of the captain and three enlisted crew, causing carnage on the bridge. Baughan, the executive officer, took charge of the attack and by 5:14 PM, it was over: the German crew was already abandoning their U-boat and many were in the water, anxious to surrender. At 5:23, *U-856*, a new submarine who had not yet fired her first torpedo, sank, taking twenty-seven of her fifty-five man crew to the bottom with her.

Robert H. Wanless, *Order of the Patriotic War, First Class*

Robert Wanless as a Captain later in his career. *Courtesy of the Wanless family.*

Commanding the *Huse*, Robert Hume Wanless was born in Pennsylvania on July 6, 1911. He was part of the Naval ROTC at Northwestern University from 1929 through his graduation in June 1933, when he was commissioned as an Ensign, United States Naval Reserve. Remaining in Chicago, he was called to active duty in November 1940, with his first duty being commanding officer of USS *YP-68*, a small patrol craft stationed in Chicago. June 1941 brought orders to become executive officer of Section Base in Cristobal, Canal Zone, where he remained until April 1943. He reported to the newly commissioned *Huse* in August as the executive officer, serving under the command of fellow Soviet medal recipient William Sessions. In December, Wanless took command as Sessions headed to take command of the USS *Gandy* (DE-764). Following his command tour on *Huse*, Wanless then commanded USS *Flaherty* (DE-135), and later, finished the war as commanding officer of the USS *Pratt* (DE-363). After the war, he commanded Escort Divisions (CORT DIV) Thirty-six and Six, Surface Antisubmarine Development Detachment at the Key West Naval Base Annex, followed by the USS *Harry E. Hubbard* (DD-748), and USS *Samuel N. Moore* (DD-747), where he earned the Bronze Star Medal twice for meritorious service during the Korean War. From September 1951, he commanded the Administrative Command at Naval Training Center Great Lakes, and reported in December 1954 as the readiness officer on the staff of Commander, First Fleet. In February 1957, Wanless assumed command of the USS *Caliente* (AO-53). A year later, he reported to the OPNAV staff, where he served as the Deputy Chief of Naval Operations (Fleet Operations and Readiness). Robert Wanless retired as a Captain on June 30, 1961, and died on January 17, 1962. He is buried in Arlington National Cemetery.

Robert Wanless' US medal bar. It includes the Legion of Merit with "V" device, Bronze Star Medal with "V" device and star for second award, Navy Commendation with "V" device, Naval Reserve Medal and the American Defense Medal with "Fleet" bar. *Courtesy of the Wanless family.*

Reverse of Robert Wanless' medal bar. *Courtesy of the Wanless family.*

Order of the Patriotic War, First Class, number 247504 awarded to Robert Wanless. *Courtesy of the Wanless family.*

Robert L. Baughan, *Order of the Patriotic War, Second Class*

Robert Louis Baughan was born in Huntington, West Virginia, on September 6, 1919. Graduating from Huntington High School in January 1937, he was appointed to the United States Naval Academy and graduated in February 1941. In March 1942, Baughan reported to the USS *Lexington* (CV-2) and took part in the Battle of Coral Sea, where the *Lexington* was later sunk. Rescued from the sea, he returned to the United States and was reassigned to the USS *Champlin* (DD-601) as the Gunnery Officer on September 12, 1942. The *Champlin* took part in convoy duty in the Atlantic, sinking their first U-boat, *U-130*, with all hands on March 14, 1943. For this action, Baughan was awarded the Bronze Star Medal. Next, they took part in the invasion of Sicily in July 1943, and in November 1943, Baughan became the executive officer. On April 7, 1944, during the action with *U-856* and the fatal wounding of the commanding officer, Baughan took command. He was awarded his second Bronze Star Medal for his valor during the sinking of *U-856*. Returning overseas, the ship served as the marker ship for the amphibious invasion of Southern France in August 1944, and for this, Baughan received his third Bronze Star Medal. Returning to the United States, he then transferred to the USS *Wyoming* (AG-17), a converted battleship tasked with experimental anti-aircraft firing to defend against kamikaze attacks in the Pacific. Following the end of the Second World War, Baughan held several other positions afloat and ashore, to include service as the executive officer of the USS *Shelton* (DD-790) and USS *Salem* (CA-139), and command of USS *Porterfield* (DD-682), USS *Leahy* (DLG-16), Destroyer Squadron Six, and Cruiser Destroyer Flotilla Nine. Ashore, Baughan's duties concentrated on gunnery and ordnance. Following the earning of a master's degree at the Massachusetts Institute of Technology, he served in the Bureau of Ordnance, Office of the Chief of Naval Operations under Admiral Arleigh Burke, the Joint Chiefs of Staff, and the Naval Ordnance Systems Command. His final billet before retirement in September 1975 was the Vice Chief of Naval Material. Representing over thirty-eight years of service, his decorations included the Navy Distinguished Service Medal, three awards of the Legion of Merit, and four awards of the Bronze Star Medal. Following retirement, Baughan attended seminary and in June 1981 was ordained as a Lutheran minister. He served in active ministry at parishes in Pennsylvania until he fully retired in 1994. Robert Baughan passed away on January 8, 2014, and is buried in the Augustus Lutheran Cemetery in Trappe, Pennsylvania.

Rear Admiral Robert Baughan. *Official US Navy photo.*

The Soviet order book to Robert Baughan. *Courtesy of the Baughan family.*

Order of the Patriotic War, Second Class, number 557260, awarded to Robert Baughan. *Courtesy of the Baughan family.*

April 16, 1944: The Sinking of *U-550*

Just over a week after *U-856* was sunk, five destroyer escorts got underway on the foggy afternoon of April 15 to escort convoy CU-21 across the Atlantic from New York to Barry, Wales. This group of destroyer escorts included the USS *Gandy* (DE-764), under the command of Lieutenant Commander William Sessions, the USS *Peterson* (DE-152), commanded by Lieutenant Sidney Hay, United States Coast Guard, and the USS *Joyce* (DE-317), with Lieutenant Robert Wilcox, United States Coast Guard, in command. April 16 was a normal morning, with *Gandy* holding a General Quarters drill before settling down for breakfast. After one day at sea, approximately seventy-five miles from Nantucket, this was appearing to be yet another uneventful convoy bringing more war material in preparation for the upcoming invasion of Europe. That changed at 8:05 AM. Out of nowhere, the eleven-thousand-ton steamer *Pan Pennsylvania*, laden with 140,000 barrels of eighty-octane gasoline, was struck by a torpedo on her port side. The ship could be seen sinking by the stern and her engine room was on fire from burning fuel. Despite the chaos taking place on the merchant, *Gandy*, *Peterson*, and *Joyce* leapt into action, attempting in vain to find the now-submerged U-boat. Having no success, they were ordered to return to the *Pan Pennsylvania* to pick up survivors. By 9:50, they had finished retrieving the civilian mariner crew and Navy Armed Guards, noting that twenty-five of the eighty-one members of the crew perished during the torpedoing.

The USS *Gandy* (DE-764) at sea. *Official US Navy photo via the National Archives.*

With the survivors retrieved, it was now time to extract revenge. The *Peterson* gained contact first, and then the *Joyce*, dropping a thirteen depth charge pattern that disabled *U-550* and brought her to the surface. Suddenly, at 10:00, the submarine's bow broke through the surface, six hundred yards from *Gandy*. Sessions immediately ordered gunfire on the submarine and told the crew: "Stand by to ram."[5] At 10:02, the *Gandy* rammed *U-550* about thirty feet from her stern, cutting off part of her after section and causing massive, uncontrollable flooding on the boat. At 10:34, *U-550* slipped under the sea, and by 10:45, *Joyce* completed picking up survivors, a total of thirteen from the submarine's crew of forty-four (one perished after being retrieved from the water).

Captain (later Rear Admiral) William Sessions. *Courtesy of the Sessions family.*

William A. Sessions, *Order of the Patriotic War, First Class*

William Alton Sessions was born on August 3, 1897, and with an eighth-grade education, enlisted in the Navy on November 27, 1916, from New York. Discharged in July 1918, he returned to the Reserves, earning a commission as an Ensign in July 1927. Working as a bail bondsman in New York City during the day, he educated himself at night, eventually earning a degree in engineering. Going to work for an insurance company in Buffalo, he was in charge of a unit in the New York Naval Militia when he was called up for active duty on October 25, 1940. His first duty was to collect civilian yachts and craft for Navy use, pressing them into patrol roles off the coast of the United States. He then served on the USS *Republic* (AP-33), and had his first command in USS *PC-473*. This was next followed by the *Huse* where Robert Wanless served as his executive officer, then *Gandy*, where he had his encounter with *U-550*. His final command was the USS *Eisner* (DE-192), taking it into the Pacific theater in May 1945 in preparation for the invasion of Japan. Discharged from active duty service on October 23, 1945, he returned to the Naval Reserve, retiring in September 1957 as a Rear Admiral. As a civilian, he became an officer in a major insurance company and held that position until retirement. William Sessions passed away on December 15, 1973, and is buried in Woodlawn Cemetery in the Bronx.

Robert Wilcox, *Order of the Patriotic War, First Class*

Robert Wilcox was born on March 17, 1914 in Portland, Maine. Commissioned in the Coast Guard on June 8, 1936 following his graduation from the Coast Guard Academy, he served at the Coast Guard Base San Juan, Puerto Rico before the start of the war. For the remainder of his career, aside from a tour at the Naval Postgraduate School in Annapolis in 1948 and 1949, he held multiple commands, to include the USCGC *Campbell* (WPG-32), USCGC *Barataria* (WAVP-381), USCGC *Yamacraw* (WARC-333) in addition to the USS *Joyce* during the sinking of *U-550.* He went on to spend a thirty-year career in the Coast Guard, retiring as a Captain on June 30, 1966. After his retirement, he worked for twelve years with the Maryland Port Authority in Baltimore before retiring permanently and moving to Delray Beach, Florida. He passed away in Delray Beach on May 26, 1995, and is buried in Arlington National Cemetery.

Lieutenant Commander Robert Wilcox conducts the funeral ceremony for a German crewman of *U-550* who died from wounds sustained during the battle on April 16, 1944. *Photo from Captain Robert Wilcox, USCG (Ret.) via the US Coast Guard.*

Sidney M. Hay, *Order of the Patriotic War, Second Class*

The commanding officer of the USS *Peterson* was Sidney Miller Hay, who was born on October 17, 1905. Growing up in Salem, Massachusetts, he graduated from Staunton Military Academy in 1924. Following graduation, he worked as a quartermaster on millionaire William Vanderbilt's yacht, the *Ara*, during her round-the-world cruise in 1928. Subsequently, he worked for the boat division of the American Car and Foundry Company, and came on active duty in August 1941. His first assignment was as the navigator on the USCGC *Duane* (WPG-33) on convoy escort duty between Iceland and Greenland. Leaving *Duane*, he was assigned to the USS *Peterson* as executive officer, and a year later, became her commanding officer. He remained in this job until *Peterson* was decommissioned in May 1946 and he returned to inactive duty. He was recalled in 1950, and later served as executive officer of the *Duane*, as well as commanding officer of the USCGC *Dexter* (WHEC-385) and USCGC *Sebago* (WHEC-42). He later served as Reserve Director for the Thirteenth Coast Guard District. Retiring as a Captain, he lived in Mystic, Connecticut, and passed away on September 28, 1972. He is buried in Arlington National Cemetery.

The medals awarded to Sidney Hay, including the Navy Commendation Medal for the battle with *U-550*.

July 5, 1944: The Sinking of *U-233*

With the invasion of France in full swing, convoys continued their resupply of the air, ground, and naval forces in theater. At sea, the U-boat war continued, with the Allies slowly taking the upper hand. Patrolling off the coast of Nova Scotia, Task Group 22.10, including the *Bronstein*, commanded by Sheldon Kinney, the *Thomas*, commanded by David Kellogg, and the *Baker* (DE-190), with Lieutenant Commander Norman Hoffman in command, had experienced little excitement since departing Norfolk on June 25, 1944. That would change on the evening of July 5. *Baker* and *Bronstein* were patrolling ten miles ahead of the carrier when, at 7:07 PM, *Baker* acquired a sonar contact. Going to General Quarters, Hoffman prepared and launched a shallow depth pattern at 7:13. Adjusting course to maintain sonar contact, *Baker* then dropped a second depth charge pattern at 7:20. This resulted in a huge explosion of seawater mixed with oil. *U-233* had been wounded. She descended, out of control, to almost four hundred feet. Water was quickly filling her stern and the situation appeared hopeless to her poorly trained and led crew, classified later as "the dregs of the reserve pools in Germany."[6] They blew her tanks and surfaced at 7:27, ready to abandon ship. Hoffman ordered his guns to open fire, and they did, scoring several direct hits on and near the submarine's conning tower.

Racing in to assist, Kellogg in *Thomas* opened fire on *U-233* at 7:35, and the submarine became obscured from smoke and spray. Both Kellogg and Hoffman believed *U-233* was sinking at this point and stopped firing. To their surprise, however, as the smoke cleared it was clear she was still very much alive and making about twelve knots on the surface. Many of her crew were already on the stern and were seen to be jumping into the water in order to escape the ship. Hoffman closed in and fired side-mounted depth charges at the escaping prey, straddling the U-boat and causing massive explosions around her. At 7:44, Kellogg opened fire with everything *Thomas* could bring to bear and charged in at *U-233*. Slowing from flank speed and then backing down the ship, he rammed the submarine two minutes later, twenty feet behind the conning tower. The submarine rolled at least seventy degrees to port, her bow high out of the water as *Thomas* came to a rest on top of her, spelling certain doom. The U-boat crewmen who had the chance to escape scrambled out from wherever they could as the submarine disappeared beneath the waves one minute after she was rammed. Of her crew of sixty, thirty-one found watery graves in the depths of the Atlantic.

Still images taken from film footage created as the USS *Thomas* (DE-102) rammed *U-233*. *National Archives.*

The Soviet order book to David Kellogg. *Courtesy of Tom and Kathie Kellogg, Seattle, Washington.*

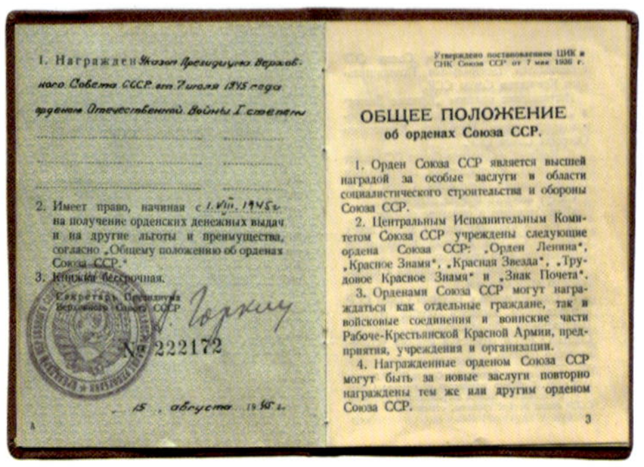

1. Награжден Указом Президиума Верховного Совета СССР от 7 июля 1945 года орденом Отечественной Войны I степени

2. Имеет право, начиная с 1.VIII.1945 г. на получение орденских денежных выдач и на другие льготы и преимущества, согласно „Общему положению об орденах Союза ССР."

3. Книжка бессрочная.

Секретарь Президиума Верховного Совета СССР

№ 222172

15 августа 1945 г.

Утверждено постановлением ЦИК и СНК Союза ССР от 7 мая 1936 г.

ОБЩЕЕ ПОЛОЖЕНИЕ
об орденах Союза ССР.

1. Орден Союза ССР является высшей наградой за особые заслуги в области социалистического строительства и обороны Союза ССР.

2. Центральным Исполнительным Комитетом Союза ССР учреждены следующие ордена Союза ССР: „Орден Ленина", „Красное Знамя", „Красная Звезда", „Трудовое Красное Знамя" и „Знак Почета".

3. Орденами Союза ССР могут награждаться как отдельные граждане, так и войсковые соединения и воинские части Рабоче-Крестьянской Красной Армии, предприятия, учреждения и организации.

4. Награжденные орденом Союза ССР могут быть за новые заслуги повторно награждены тем же или другим орденом Союза ССР.

3

David M. Kellogg, *Order of the Patriotic War, First Class*

The commanding officer of the *Thomas*, David McDougall "Dave" Kellogg, was born on September 16, 1913. A native of Seattle, Washington, he joined the Navy as a Reserve officer following his graduation from the University of Washington in 1938 and entered active duty on July 1, 1940. Serving first on the USS *Fairfax* (DD-93), he remained on board until she was decommissioned and given to the Royal Navy as part of Lend-Lease in November 1940. Kellogg was then transferred to the USS *DuPont* (DD-152), a First World War-vintage destroyer conducting convoy escort duty in the North Atlantic. He remained on *DuPont* until his transfer on May 31, 1943. Finally, in October 1943, he received orders to the USS *Thomas* (DE-102) as the commanding officer. Remaining on *Thomas* through the end of the war and participating in the sinkings of *U-709*, *U-233*, and *U-879*, he left active duty on November 20, 1945. Returning to Seattle, he remained in the Reserves, retiring on September 1, 1958, with the rank of Commander.

As a civilian, he worked as the sales manager for the United States Steamship Company from 1953 to 1969, living in Seattle, Los Angeles, and San Francisco, followed by working as the marine traffic manager for the Alaska State Ferry System in Juneau, Alaska, until 1973. Finally, he was a real estate agent with Sam Hess Realtors in Bellevue, Washington, until his final retirement in 1976. He was an avid fan of University of Washington football, holding season tickets for over fifty years. He was also the president of the Seattle chapter of the SKÅL Club of the International Association of Travel and Tourism Professionals, where a scholarship fund named in his honor is awarded each year to a student focusing on hospitality and travel as a career. For many years, he attended annual reunions held by the surviving crewmembers of the *Thomas* and *U-233*, with his final attendance in 1995. Dave Kellogg passed away on December 10, 1996. He is buried in Lake View Cemetery, Seattle, Washington.

Norman C. Hoffman, *Order of the Patriotic War, First Class*

Norman C. Hoffman as a Commander. *National Personnel Records Center.*

Norman Cutten Hoffman was born on June 7, 1913, and raised in Milton and Dennisport, Massachusetts. Following his graduation from Harvard with a degree in business administration, he was commissioned on May 19, 1934, but remained in the Reserves, working as a stockbroker for the First Boston Corporation until called to active duty in December 1939. As an Ensign, he was a turret officer on the USS *Oklahoma* (BB-37) at Pearl Harbor on December 7, 1941 and miraculously survived that fateful day. Transferred to the commissioning crew of the USS *South Dakota* (BB-57), Hoffman saw combat during the Battle of Santa Cruz and the Battle of Savo Island. Returning to the United States on December 18, 1942, he conducted North Atlantic patrols on the *South Dakota* until mid-April 1943. Subsequently, the *South Dakota* served with the British Home Fleet based in Scapa Flow until returning to the United States in August 1943. Prior to the *South Dakota* leaving for her next tour in the Pacific, Hoffman detached with orders to the pre-commissioning unit for the *Baker* as her first lieutenant, but shortly became her executive officer with the departure of Lieutenant Commander R.J. Reynolds (of tobacco fame) as he went to hold command in the Pacific theater. Hoffman later commanded *Baker* through her actions in the North Atlantic before receiving orders to serve as an NROTC instructor at the University of Mississippi. He left active service on July 7, 1946, but remained in the Reserves, retiring on July 1, 1961, as a Captain. As a civilian, he returned to the banking industry, retiring from New England Merchants National Bank in 1978. After spending thirty-two years living in Wellesley, Massachusetts, he moved to Florida in 1983. Norman Hoffman passed away in Florida on September 6, 1995.

David Kellogg's Legion of Merit and Bronze Star awarded during the Second World War. *Courtesy of Tom and Kathie Kellogg, Seattle, Washington.*

Order of the Patriotic War, First Class, Number 247502, awarded to David Kellogg. *Courtesy of Tom and Kathy Kellogg, Seattle, Washington.*

Chapter 4

Anti-Submarine Operations: Arctic Cutter and Submarine Recipients

Francis Pollard, *Order of the Patriotic War, First Class*

Far to the north, patrolling off the coast of Greenland was the USCGC *Northland* (WPG-49), commanded by Commander Francis Costello Pollard, United States Coast Guard. Born in Seattle on September 14, 1899, he joined the Coast Guard on July 12, 1920, following an enlistment in the Navy during the First World War. On July 4, 1941, he reported to the *Northland* as the commanding officer, operating out of Greenland. Before he left command in February 1943, he may have had one of the most eventful tours of any commanding officer during that time. Rescuing a Danish settlement in September 1942, they went on to further conduct a daring rescue of three members of the Royal Canadian Air Force who crashed on the Greenland Ice Cap in November 1942. In the same theme, they rescued twenty-six US Army Air Force aviators also stranded on the Greenland Ice Cap.[1] For his actions in Greenland, Pollard was awarded the Legion of Merit, the Navy and Marine Corps Medal, and the Order of the British Empire, in addition to the Order of the Patriotic War from the Soviets.

It was on June 18, 1942, that the *Northland* discovered a submarine contact. Using all resources at his disposal, Pollard positively identified the contact as a U-boat and dropped a limited depth charge pattern. The contact was lost and in the concerted search that followed, it was determined that *Northland* had destroyed the contact due to the presence of a large oil slick and rising air bubbles over the location of the attack.[2]

Unfortunately, according to *Kriegsmarine* records, no U-boats were lost on this date. However, at the time it was considered yet another success for the brave crew of the *Northland*, and Pollard was awarded the Legion of Merit for sinking a submarine. Pollard left the ship and was ordered to the USCGC *Tampa* (WPG-48), commanding her from June 1943 until she entered the shipyard for repairs in February 1944. His arduous wartime service took its toll on his health and he was retired on September 1, 1944, promoted to Commander based on his wartime awards. Settling in Seal Beach, California, he passed away on January 19, 1986. Francis Pollard is buried in Holy Cross Cemetery, Culver City, California.

John Corbus, *Order of the Patriotic War, First Class*

The sinking of U-boats wasn't confined to aircraft and surface ships. Off the coast of Spain, Lieutenant Commander John Corbus and the crew of the USS *Herring* (SS-233) claimed the first U-boat sinking by another submarine during an attack on March 21, 1943. Just after midnight, they spotted a greenish-white flare off the port bow. Going to investigate, they discovered what they believed to be a German 530-ton U-boat at a range of 2,500 yards.[3] Turning on the surface to make a straight stern shot, Corbus fired the number nine and ten tubes and quickly dove. Two minutes later, they recorded a heavy explosion, followed by a second explosion fifteen seconds later, coincidental with the torpedo run times to the target. The screw noises from the target stopped suddenly and cracking noises were heard as the target fractured from the two direct hits.[4] At the time, the kill was listed as a "B-probably sunk" due to lack of submarine evidence in the area of the attack.[5] Initially, this submarine contact was believed to be *U-163*. However, postwar assessment determined that she was sunk by the HMCS *Prescott* on March 13, 1943. The *Herring's* contact was later classified to have been a "nonsub" contact – perhaps an unfortunate Spanish fishing vessel.

John Corbus receiving the Navy Cross after his record-breaking patrol on the USS *Bowfin* (SS-287). *Official US Navy photo via the National Archives.*

John Corbus, *Herring's* acting commanding officer, was born on October 25, 1907, in Vallejo, California, and entered the Naval Academy on July 6, 1926. Graduating with the class of 1930, he served the battleship USS *California* (BB-44) before being selected for submarine duty in 1938. He was serving as the executive officer of *Herring* at the time of the attack on *U-163*, and was awarded the Legion of Merit with "V" device for his valor. He later became commanding officer of the *Haddo* (SS-255) on December 14, 1943, taking the sub on her third and fourth war patrols with his change of command on February 18, 1944. In his next command, Corbus became a household name. On April 15, 1944, he took command of the USS *Bowfin* (SS-287), leading her on an exceptionally successful war patrol until he was relieved on September 23, 1944. While in command of *Bowfin*, he earned the record for the most enemy shipping sunk during any war patrol from 1943 to 1944, sinking 26,700 tons of shipping on the sub's sixth war patrol. For this amazing feat, he was awarded the Navy Cross and the submarine received the Presidential Unit Citation. From October 1944 through the remainder of the war, he served on the staff of Commander Submarines, Pacific, earning his second Legion of Merit.

Corbus went on to command Submarine Division Eighty-one, followed by the Submarine School in New London, Connecticut, from 1949 to 1951. He was then ordered to Hawaii, where he commanded Submarine Squadron Seven and subsequently the ammunition ship USS *Wrangell* (AE-12) until 1955. His final assignment was as Director of Military Personnel Security at the Bureau of Naval Personnel in Washington, DC Retiring in 1958 with the rank of Rear Admiral, he moved to Santa Rosa, California, in 1962. John Corbus passed away on March 22, 1966, and is buried in Golden Gate National Cemetery.

PART II

CHAPTER 5

CONVOY OPERATIONS

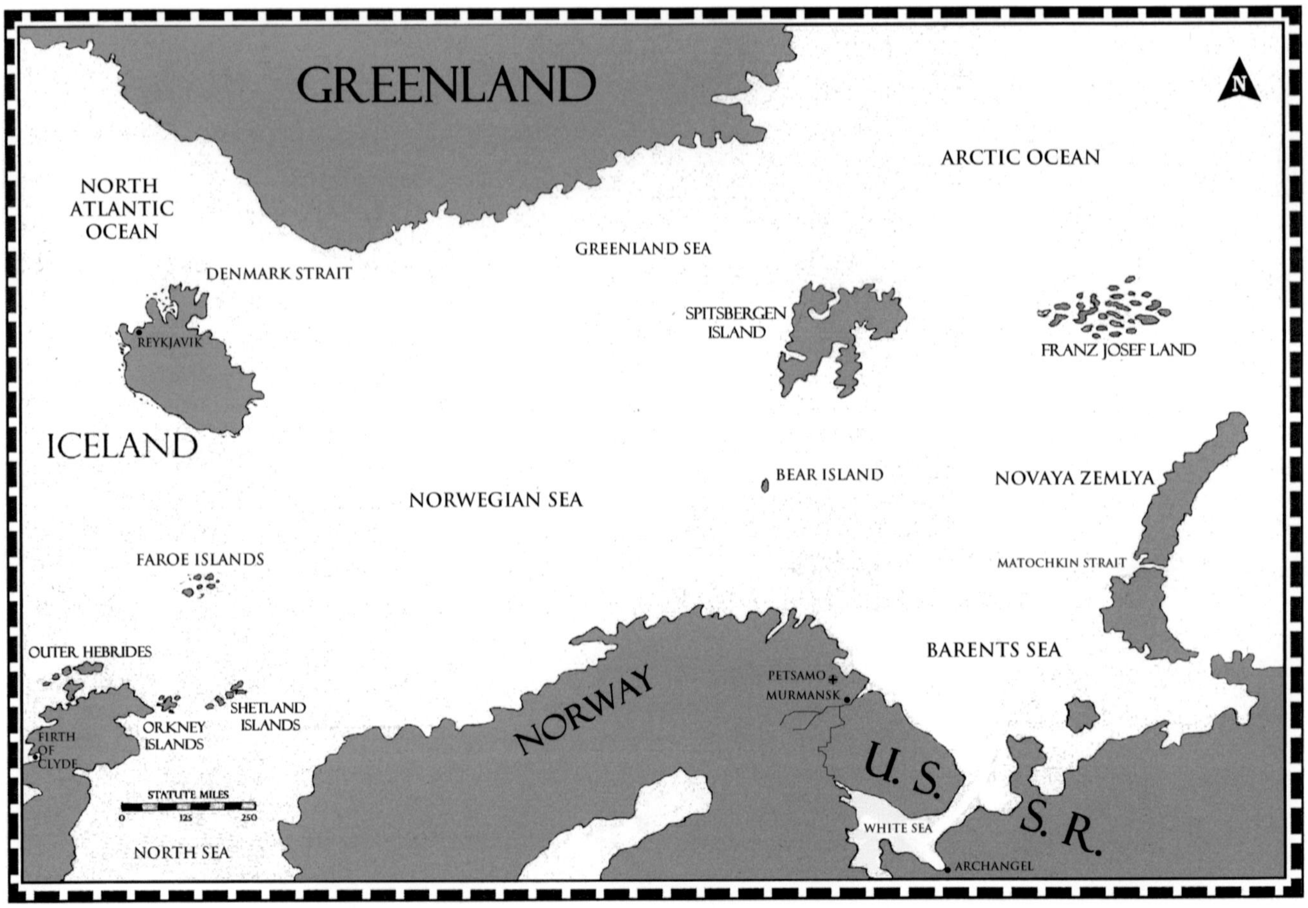

The area transited by the convoys and patrolled by the *Luftwaffe* and *Kriegsmarine*. It was across these near-frozen waters that the brave men of the convoys transited in constant danger of the enemy and elements. *Original map courtesy of Richard Carter.*

The attire worn by merchant seamen and Armed Guard alike, often for days at a time without changing, causing irritation, rashes, and foul odor. Here, John Grotenrath sports the survival gear he was wearing at the time the SS *City of Joliet* sank. *Courtesy of the Grotenrath family.*

The office of the Assistant Naval Attaché in Archangel, taken in 1945. *Courtesy of the Roullard family.*

The German invasion launched against the USSR on June 22, 1941, forced the urgent necessity of material aid from the United States and Great Britain to the Soviet Union. Within weeks, the Soviets lost much of their ability to produce the raw and manufactured goods required to stop the onslaught of the German war machine. By November 1941, the land occupied by the Germans contained forty percent of the total population of the Soviet Union and produced sixty-three and fifty-eight percent of her coal and steel, respectively.[1] The losses in Soviet military manpower had reached nearly two million killed, wounded, and taken prisoner.[2] By the time the Japanese bombed Pearl Harbor, the Germans were at the door of Moscow and were advancing rapidly. The imminent danger to the balance of world power was ascertained immediately by the governments of the United States and Great Britain and a vital lifeline of material from the west into the Soviet ports of Murmansk and Archangel was quickly established. On August 31, the first convoy, made up of six British and one Dutch merchant vessel, arrived in Archangel.[3] They were the first vessels to transit on what would eventually become known over the next four years as the treacherous "Murmansk Run."

As unglamorous the role of the logistician may seem in the history of warfare, a nation cannot fight or win wars without the ability to supply the front lines. This was the case in the Soviet Union, and Hitler was well aware of how the losses were affecting the Soviet's crumbling infrastructure. By removing the ability to sustain combat operations, he could force Stalin to surrender, paving the way to a German-Japanese alliance and control of the entirety of the European and Asian continents.[4] From there, Hitler could overcome the weary resistance in Great Britain, control Africa, and make plans for an invasion of the eastern United States, or at a minimum, determine a diplomatic solution to gain the United States as an ally. Japan, simultaneously, could consume the remaining western outposts in the Pacific and concentrate on the western United States, creating a multi-axis attack on the last remaining great power.[5] In order to make this strategy a reality, Stalin had to surrender. The key factor in forcing him to abdicate was to remove, or sufficiently derail and delay, the tenuous lifeline of supplies arriving via the Lend-Lease convoys.[6]

History shows the modern reader that Stalin and the USSR did survive the German onslaught, but it was due in no small part to the contributions of the United States and Great Britain. During the course of the Lend-Lease agreement, the following were delivered to the ports of the USSR: over 14,000 aircraft, 43,000 ¼-ton Jeeps, 13,000 tanks and armored cars, 1,900 steam locomotives, 10,000 railway flat cars, 112,000 submachine guns, 638,000 tons of wheat flour, 532,000 tons of sugar, 365,600 tons of steel plate, and fourteen-million pair of boots. These are but a handful of the thousands of items carried by the Lend-Lease convoys during the war.[7]

There were three primary routes for delivering Lend-Lease goods to the USSR. The first route was via Vladivostok in the Pacific. However, this required a lengthy trip via rail across Siberia before the goods could arrive at the front. Similarly, the hazardous and long seaborne trip across the Atlantic, around the Cape of Good Hope and through the Persian Gulf, then via the tenuous rail line through the Persian Corridor in Iran into Azerbaijan had its fair share of challenges. In contrast, the sea route from Great Britain and Iceland around Norway and into Murmansk or Archangel appeared to be the most feasible in theory, as the amount of goods sent were only limited by the ability to unload them at the destination ports. Once unloaded, they were within close proximity to the frontlines and could be put into action almost immediately.

With this Arctic route, Hitler was clearly at an operational and tactical advantage having taken Norway and moved his well-trained air and naval forces to the far north, where they held uncontestable control of the air and sea for most of the passage to the Soviet Union. Coupled with the weather and environmental extremes present throughout the route, the perpetual daylight during the summertime and the constant darkness of the winter, the Arctic convoy route was by far the most dangerous and deadly of any of the other routes to deliver Lend-Lease goods to the USSR. One historian bluntly explained the rationale for the choice of using the northern sea route for Lend-Lease convoys: "... the decision to use the Arctic route to send supplies to the Soviet Union was a triumph of political expediency over military reality."[8]

The Royal Navy, already stretched thin by concurrent operations in the Pacific, Atlantic, and Mediterranean, was tasked with providing protection for the large, slow, aging merchant vessels of the Lend-Lease convoys against the technologically superior, locally based, and well-maintained German battle forces. The often aged civilian ships were manned by civilian mariners and seamen, men from dozens of countries (many occupied by the Axis powers) some of whom had served decades at sea. Those ships under United States flag were commanded by officers from the United States Merchant Marine, professional merchant mariners who were often also commissioned officers in the United States Naval Reserve.

To give these merchant ships a fighting chance, the US Navy placed a small (initially, six to ten man, and later, up to thirty-man) contingent of Sailors as their Naval Armed Guard detachment, under the charge of a young Ensign or Lieutenant (jg) (and later, full Lieutenants). The first Armed Guard commanders were pulled directly from gunnery duty on a cruiser or battleship. Thomas Delate, who served as the Armed Guard commander on the SS *Deer Lodge*, recalled a message sent out in December 1941 to all cruisers and battleships requesting they detach and send two USNR (Naval Reserve) officers with "at least six months of gunnery experience" to serve as Armed Guard commanders.[9] They were placed in charge of enlisted Sailors who often had less than two months service in the Navy and tasked with the defense of the ship against determined and experienced enemy surface, subsurface, and aerial attacks.

A German bomber at mast head height makes an attack on a ship in convoy PQ-17. *National Archives.*

Around the globe during the Second World War, 144,970 Navy personnel served tours in the Naval Armed Guard, in a strange and often thankless limbo, completely separate from the merchant seaman crews of the vessels yet not on the grey-hulled Navy fighting ships of their peers. Over eight thousand men of the Armed Guard earned Navy medals and decorations, including five Navy Crosses, two Legions of Merit, seventy-five Silver Stars, twenty-four Navy and Marine Corps Medals, fifty-four Bronze Stars, and 563 Letters of Commendation from the Secretary of the Navy. Eighteen hundred would pay the ultimate price, forever resting beneath the waves and never returning to their loved ones or partaking in the freedom for which they gave their lives.[10]

Nowhere did the brave men of the Merchant Marine and the Armed Guard distinguish themselves more, or pay so dearly, than in the transport of Lend-Lease material to the Soviet Union. In these convoys, initially prefixed "PQ" followed by the convoy number, the men braved not only the unimaginable torment of Arctic elements, but they withstood the round-the-clock onslaught of German aerial, surface, and subsurface attacks.

Many who left Iceland or Scotland in an eastbound convoy did not survive. They died terrible deaths torn apart by shrapnel, burned alive by the ignition of fuel and explosives, or frozen into solid, unspeakable forms in the icy waters of the Arctic Circle. Those who survived the sinking of their ships, crammed into overloaded lifeboats or on rafts, suffered from intense hunger and thirst, contracting frostbite on their extremities, even during the summer months, causing the eventual amputation of hands, arms, feet, and legs. Others died from exhaustion and the onset of despair after weeks of floating aimlessly in the frigid waters. And they were

The British merchant *Navarino*, sailing in convoy PQ-17, receives a direct torpedo hit, the explosion blowing water and debris high into the air. *National Archives.*

the lucky ones; the stories of their demise were known. For some, they escaped their sinking vessel and were never heard from again; dying an unknown death in an unknown place, alone above the Arctic Circle. And those who did survive, their lives were forever changed, shattered by constant nightmares or plagued by poor health to their last days, having witnessed the utmost brutality and inhumanity of war and the elements.

Deliveries of the vital war cargo were made to the ports of Murmansk and Archangel, the latter also having the small port of Molotovsk nearby. Archangel was the preferred port, being somewhat protected from the nearby German invaders and better able to support the level of war material being delivered by the convoys. However, it was only navigable five months out of the year, with thick ice present for the remainder. The smaller port of Murmansk, accessed via the Kola Inlet, remained open throughout the year, but was sufficiently close to the frontlines to receive daily bombing raids from the Germans in Norway.

After the ships arrived at either Murmansk or Archangel, the mettle of their crews was continually tested through the intense bombing raids, impoverished living conditions in the wartime USSR, and the occasional inhospitality of their Soviet hosts. The Naval Armed Guard reports and historical accounts are replete with stories of the heroism of the Armed Guard and merchant crews, as well as the tales of conflict between the Navy and civilian crews, disagreements with the ships' masters, unlawful activity at sea and in port, starvation both of Soviets and US forces alike, and the continual spectre of death in the ice-bound Arctic. The westward return voyage to Iceland or Scotland (known as a "QP" convoy) was often as dangerous as the initial trip to Murmansk or Archangel. Those ships lucky enough to survive the German onslaught still had to run the same gauntlet in order to return home, facing the same threats throughout their voyage. Many of the ships that departed ports on the East Coast of the United States bound for the USSR never returned. The handful that did carried the survivors of many other vessels whose remains rested in watery graves.

Naval Armed Guard survivors rarely made a second trip to the USSR, as a single voyage was considered enough of a sacrifice. Armed Guard commanders were often transferred

Pack ice near the Arctic Circle, present even during the twenty-four hour sunlit days of summer. *Courtesy of Weston and Brooke Robinson.*

shortly following their return to the Armed Guard Center in Brooklyn, receiving orders to flight or submarine training, or to warships in the fleet. Some of the enlisted Armed Guard personnel opted to remain with the Armed Guard, and several finished the war still serving with the Armed Guard, having made dozens of voyages in both the Atlantic and Pacific. Others transferred to a multitude of commands at sea and ashore. Unlike their Navy counterparts, the Merchant Marine survivors, as professional merchant mariners, would be assigned to new ships and many returned to the USSR as part of subsequent convoys.[11]

The SS *Laranaga*, the first American-flagged merchant vessel in a Lend-Lease convoy, left Iceland on January 8, 1942, bound for Murmansk as part of convoy PQ-8. She survived and returned from her voyage on April 20. Her tiny Armed Guard detachment saw comparatively little action, but others would not be so lucky. Subsequent American vessels departed in convoys PQ-11 and PQ-12, but the first convoy that truly experienced the fury of German attacks was PQ-13.

If the men were lucky enough to survive the sinking of their ship, they would be forced to survive for days on end in crowded lifeboats while seeking rescue. These survivors from the SS *Washington* spent almost a week in lifeboats before reaching land. *Courtesy of the McDonald family.*

Once in the ports of the USSR, Soviet crews were continually at work to maintain an ice-free passage. This photograph shows the results of icebreaking in the port of Archangel. *Courtesy of the Roullard family.*

CHAPTER 6

CONVOY PQ-13 RECIPIENTS

The SS *Dunboyne*, originally slated to become the first American merchant to the USSR, started the war in a most conspicuous way: taking extensive damage during a storm between Boston, Massachusetts, and Sydney, Nova Scotia, her master and crew were investigated by the Bureau of Marine Inspection and Navigation.[1] By 1941, she was already an old ship, built in 1919 for the purpose of hauling cargo to and from the Allied Expeditionary Forces in France during the First World War. During her overhaul period back in the United States, where most of her crew was changed out and a new master brought on board, she was fitted out with six thirty-caliber machine guns, two fifty-caliber machine guns, and one four-inch deck gun. Her Armed Guard consisted of one officer, Ensign Rufus Brinn, and ten enlisted men, including Boatswain's Mate, second class Eaton DeCottes as the most senior enlisted Sailor, and Seamen Edward Hoban, Gustav Schill, Thomas Dixon, and Edwin Newman. Of the ten members of the Armed Guard, these five enlisted men had all served together as Naval Reservists in Jacksonville, Florida, prior to the start of the war. Having arrived at the Armed Guard Center in November 1941, they had embarked *Dunboyne* on December 5, but due to the storm damage sustained off the coast of Nova Scotia, their actual sailing was delayed until January 30, 1942.

Departing Halifax on February 10, the *Dunboyne* arrived in the Firth of Clyde on the coast of Scotland on March 4, and remained there until March 10, when she got underway for Iceland in order to rendezvous with the other ships of convoy PQ-13, to include the SS *Eldena* and SS *Mormacmar*.

The voyage of the *Mormacmar* had already been considerably eventful. Shortly after arrival in South Boston, her Armed Guard commander, Harrison Smith, had to enlist the aid of the Army, Navy, and Coast Guard in order to put down a disturbance, to include death threats towards the ship's officers, by four drunken members of the ship's crew. Leaving a week after *Dunboyne* with a five-million-dollar cargo consisting mostly of phosphorous, they received a distress call from a nearby merchant vessel that had been torpedoed. Considering the *Mormacmar* could not effectively "darken ship"; extinguishing all topside lights to make submarine targeting difficult because of her aged and ill-fitting hatches, as well as the fact that both of her lifeboats had been condemned two years previously and never repaired, her master decided to leave their convoy and achor indefinitely in Portland, Maine, to avoid any further exposure to possible U-boat attacks. This decision cost him his command, and his replacement took the ship to sea on February 25.

On March 3, just after midnight in heavy seas, some of her deck cargo, consisting of barrels of phosphorous, broke loose and caught on fire. The Armed Guard detachment was able to extinguish the fire, just before it reached the number five hatch, holding additional cargo of TNT and high explosives. Over the next five days, they rejoined the convoy and things were quiet. That did not last long, as on March 8, some of the merchant crew broke into the ship's liquor stores and stole and subsequently consumed a case of rum. This caused them to be unable to stand their watches, and several were temporarily relieved by members of the Armed Guard.

Ensign Frederick Fink and Coxswain Francis Shipley boarded the *Eldena* with their twelve-man Armed Guard detachment on January 24, 1942, and departed for Halifax on February 11. Similarly, Coxswain Charles Dole took his five gunners and left the United States on the SS *Effingham*. Much unlike their fellow ship *Mormacmar*, their voyage was relatively uneventful and they arrived in Reykjavik, Iceland, on March 15. Here, along with *Dunboyne* and *Mormacmar*, they joined the twenty-ship convoy PQ-13. The night before their planned underway on March 18, the crew of the *Mormacmar* decided to test Harrison Smith yet again, by refusing the master's orders to load cargo in preparation for their trek to Murmansk. Calling in the Coast Guard and Marines to arrest the dissenters, they were replaced with local Icelanders. However, they still missed the sailing of the convoy. It was all for naught however, as the convoy returned to Reykjavik on March 20, supposedly due to the presence of the German battleship *Tirpitz* in vicinity of the convoy's route. Finally back underway several days later, the convoy ran into a North Atlantic gale on March 25, scattering the ships for the next two days and causing considerable damage, including the removal of the port and starboard catwalks on the *Dunboyne*. As March 28 dawned, only five of the original twenty ships were present. The convoy was scattered along a 150-mile stretch near Bear Island. This day marked the start of the German attacks on PQ-13, when the British and Panamanian merchants, *Empire Ranger* and *Raceland*, respectively, were sunk by aircraft that afternoon.

To the men of the other ships in convoy, both ships appeared to have disappeared with their crews. However, it was later discovered that sixty-one of the crew of the *Empire Ranger* had been taken prisoner by the Germans.[2] They were the fortunate ones: the majority of the crew of *Raceland* (who had already sustained considerable damage during the gale and had fallen behind the rest of the convoy prior to the German attack) were never heard from again. Only a pitiful, frozen handful survived an eleven-day journey at sea before landing on the Norwegian coast.

Harrison Smith noted that the morning of March 29 was "as beautiful a day as I ever hope to witness"[3] with four destroyers and one cruiser, the HMS *Trinidad*, joining the increasing ranks of the convoy. Within two hours, however, it began to snow and they found themselves in the middle of a surface battle between the British ships and multiple German destroyers. Though no merchants were hit, one of the German destroyers was sunk and the HMS *Trinidad* was disabled by one of her own torpedoes, causing her to limp into Murmansk for repairs. Before the day was done, the British merchant *Induna*, the flagship of the convoy's vice commodore, became stuck in the ice. Finally freeing herself, she was torpedoed and sunk the following day.

The SS *Mormacmar* at sea, taken on August 1, 1944. *National Archives.*

March 30 was also a bad day for the *Effingham* and Charles Dole. She was following the *Dunboyne*, maintaining station 150 feet behind her. Suddenly, at 10:28 AM, she was struck by a torpedo on her port side by the number four hatch. Having a significant cargo of TNT, the crew made haste to abandon ship in two lifeboats. Attempting to get as far from the ship as possible, they watched her explode, fold in two, and disappear from the surface of the sea in less than a minute at 12:20 PM. Dole and his five gunners were part of the twenty-three occupants in the master's lifeboat, rocking in the heavy seas, blanketed by snow and ice. After the first nineteen hours, twenty-two occupants remained as one of the merchant seamen died from exposure and was buried in sea. Seven hours later, between 4:00 and 4:45 PM, four additional crewmembers perished from exposure and were lowered over the side. That evening, the remaining eighteen members of the crew were rescued by the HMS *Harrier*, with one additional crewmember passing away that evening due to the effects of exposure. The following day, the survivors of the *Effingham* were delivered to Murmansk for treatment and eventual passage back to the United States.

Charles E. Dole, *Medal "For Valor"*

Charles Everett "Chuck" Dole, the Coxswain on the *Effingham*, was born in Corry, Pennsylvania, in January 1920 and enlisted in the Navy soon after his eighteenth birthday on May 4, 1938. He spent his first three years in the Navy on the USS *Texas* (BB-35) and USS *Trippe* (DD-403) prior to reporting for Armed Guard duty in December 1941. Surviving the sinking of the *Effingham*, and earning a Silver Star for the valor he exhibited, he returned to the United States on the *Mormacmar* in May 1942 and continued duty as an Armed Guard through November 1944, shipping out of San Francisco on the SS *Robin Doncaster* from March 28, 1944, to October 25, 1944. He spent the remainder of the war attached to Carrier Air Service Unit (CASU) 6 on the West Coast of the United States. Following the war, he remained on active duty in the Navy, and as a Chief Boatswain's Mate, served on multiple ships to include the USS *Wyandot* (AKA-92), the *Amphion* (AR-13), the *Allagash* (AO-97), the *Kimberly* (DD-521) and the *Conechu* (AOR-110). His last tours included serving with Landing Craft Squadron (LCURON) 2 where he was officer in charge (OIC) of an LCU, and on the staff of Amphibious Training Unit, Atlantic, in Little Creek, Virginia. He retired on January 7, 1958, and went to work for Renault Inc., USA as a parts manager where he again retired in the late-1970s to become a real estate agent in Port St. Lucie, Florida. He passed away in Melbourne, Florida, on June 21, 2013 and was buried at sea.

As the survivors of the *Effingham* fought to survive in their lifeboats, the *Dunboyne*, *Mormacmar*, and *Eldena* continued their passage to Murmansk. Despite aerial attacks, they arrived at Kola Inlet on the evening of March 30, and were pierside by the morning of April 1. Their safe arrival was only the beginning. Over the next twenty-eight days, the three ships were subject to one hundred ten air raid alerts and fifty-four actual bombing attacks on the city, piers, and harbor. The *Dunboyne* alone manned her guns fifty-eight times during the four-week period, and were credited with destroying two German aircraft. The *Eldena* scored the record with three aircraft to her credit, and her entire crew was rewarded with one month's pay by the Soviets.[4] Surviving this onslaught, the three ships left Murmansk on April 28 and arrived in Iceland on May 7, dodging multiple aerial torpedo and U-boat attacks, including one that sank a Soviet merchant vessel traveling with them. The ships all arrived in New York harbor at the end of May.

Charles Dole, taken shortly after his return from convoy duty. *Courtesy of the Dole family.*

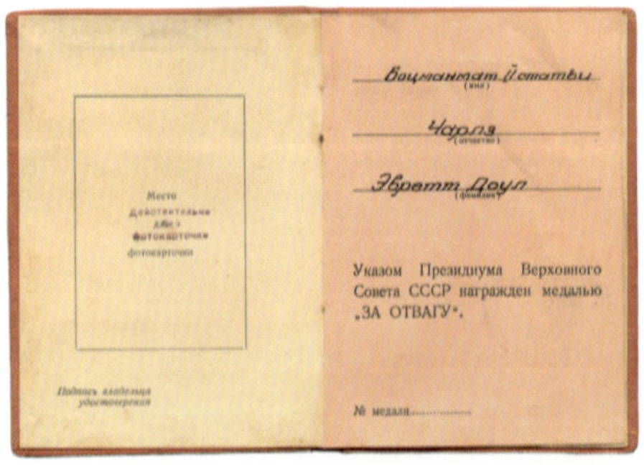

The Soviet medal book to Charles Dole. *Courtesy of the Dole family.*

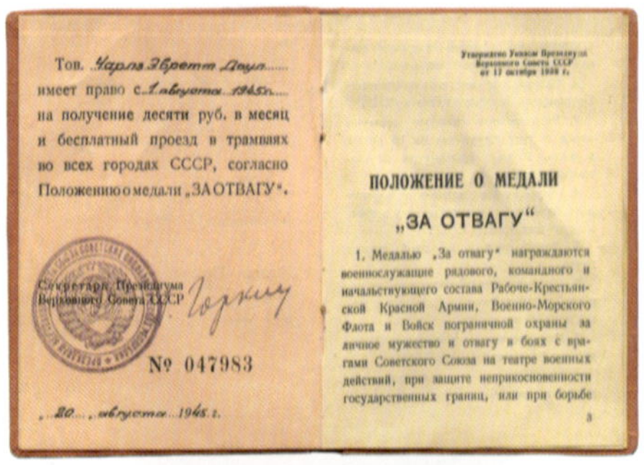

The Silver Star awarded to Charles Dole for his actions on the Murmansk Run. *Courtesy of the Dole family.*

The Navy Good Conduct Medal awarded to Charles Dole. *Courtesy of the Dole family.*

Medal "For Valor" number 2075701 awarded to Charles Dole. *Courtesy of the Dole family.*

Frederick S. Fink, Jr., *Order of the Patriotic War, First Class*

Ensign Frederick Fink, Armed Guard commander on the SS *Eldena*. *US Navy photo*

Returning to the United States on the *Eldena* were Frederick Fink, the Armed Guard commander, and Francis Shipley, the senior enlisted person in the detachment. Frederic Strong "Fred" Fink Jr. was born on April 16, 1917, in Kenton, Ohio, to Frederic Sr., who later retired as president of the Kenton Telephone Company. He attended Ohio Wesleyan University before joining the Navy on August 30, 1940. Commissioned on May 15, 1942, Fink served at the Twelfth and Eleventh Naval Districts before being assigned to the Armed Guard in December 1941. He was immediately sent to the *Eldena* as the Armed Guard commander, earning the Silver Star for his bravery on convoy PQ-13. Like many of his peers, he transferred out of Armed Guard duty following his return from Murmansk and reported as the gunnery officer on the USS *Bell* (DD-587), conducting anti-submarine and convoy escort patrols in the North Atlantic. In November 1943, the *Bell* was transferred to the Pacific theater, and shortly thereafter, Fink became the executive officer. Here, he earned nine battle stars for campaigns in the Pacific, including participation in the Wake Island raid, Truk and Marianas attacks, Morotai landings, capture of Saipan, battle of the Philippine Sea, the battle of Surigao Strait, Okinawa attacks, and the sinking of the Japanese submarine *RO-115* in January 1945. He left active service on September 28, 1945, but remained in the active Reserves, commanding several reserve units and being recalled from September 1951 to January 1953 for the Korean War. He retired from the Navy on July 1, 1967, as a Commander. Leaving Ohio, he spent his remaining years in Cooper City, Florida, and passed away on March 18, 1995.

Francis M. Shipley, Jr., *Medal "For Valor"*

Fink's second in command was Coxswain Francis Marion Shipley, Jr., who was born on April 1, 1919, in Baltimore, Maryland. He attended Mount Saint Joseph's College and enlisted in the Navy on November 2, 1938. Spending the first years of his enlistment in the Far East on the USS *Pecos* (AO-6) and the USS *Chaumont* (AP-5), he later reported to the Armed Guard Center and served on the *Eldena,* where he earned a Silver Star Medal for his bravery during the Murmansk Run, and later on the SS *Musa*. He finished the war in Tsingtao, China, as a member of the Chinese Amphibious Training Group, responsible for training Chinese crews for the amphibious vessels given to them by the United States at the end of the Second World War. Remaining in the Pacific, he also served on the USS *Estes* (AGC-12), the flagship of Seventh Fleet, and the USS *Agawam* (AOG-6) out of Pearl Harbor. Finally, he served in the Philippines with Service Craft, US Naval Forces Philippines. He retired from the Navy as a Chief Boatswain's Mate on December 15, 1958. Shipley returned to Maryland and passed away in Indian Head on November 6, 1998. He is buried in Arlington National Cemetery.

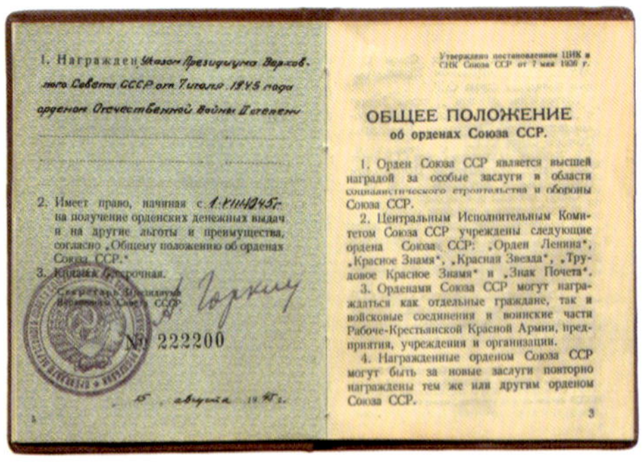

1. Награжден Указом Президиума Верховного Совета СССР от 7 июля 1945 года орденом Отечественной Войны II степени

2. Имеет право, начиная с 1.VIII.1945 г. на получение орденских денежных выдач и на другие льготы и преимущества, согласно „Общему положению об орденах Союза ССР."

3. Книжка бессрочная.

Секретарь Президиума Верховного Совета СССР

№ 222200

15 августа 1945 г.

Утверждено постановлением ЦИК и СНК Союза ССР от 7 мая 1936 г.

ОБЩЕЕ ПОЛОЖЕНИЕ
об орденах Союза ССР.

1. Орден Союза ССР является высшей наградой за особые заслуги в области социалистического строительства и обороны Союза ССР.

2. Центральным Исполнительным Комитетом Союза ССР учреждены следующие ордена Союза ССР: „Орден Ленина", „Красное Знамя", „Красная Звезда", „Трудовое Красное Знамя" и „Знак Почета".

3. Орденами Союза ССР могут награждаться как отдельные граждане, так и войсковые соединения и воинские части Рабоче-Крестьянской Красной Армии, предприятия, учреждения и организации.

4. Награжденные орденом Союза ССР могут быть за новые заслуги повторно награждены тем же или другим орденом Союза ССР.

3

Имя, отчество и фамилия

Лейтенант

Харрисон

Смис

Подпись владельца книжки

The Soviet order book to Harrison Smith, Armed Guard commander on the SS *Mormacmar. Courtesy of his son, Todd Smith.*

Harrison Smith, *Order of the Patriotic War, Second Class*

Returning with *Effingham* survivor Charles Dole on the *Mormacmar* was her Armed Guard commander, Harrison Smith, hailing from Atchison, Kansas. He was born on January 16, 1914, and was a practicing lawyer prior to joining the Navy on August 6, 1940. Following his initial training, he served at the Destroyer Base in San Diego, as well as on the USS *Pensacola* (CA-24). On January 22, 1942, he reported to the Armed Guard Center in Brooklyn, was assigned to the *Mormacmar* for her trip on the Murmansk Run. For his heroism during the transit to and from the USSR, he received a Commendation from the Secretary of the Navy. Remaining with the Armed Guard, he later became the Armed Guard commander on the SS *William Johnson*, taking her on a successful convoy crossing from New York to Liverpool, then to Algeria, and back to New York. For his service, he earned his second Commendation. Leaving the Armed Guard, Smith transferred to the Pacific, where he became a specialist in amphibious operations and later served on the USS *Marvin H. McIntyre* (APA-129) during the invasion of Okinawa. Discharged from active duty on August 22, 1945, he returned to Kansas where he resumed his practice of law, residing in Garden City from 1947 onward. He became an associate district judge of the Twenty-Fifth Judicial District in 1977 and he remained in that position until his retirement in 1984. Following retirement, he remained an active lawyer, hearing cases for the Kansas Supreme Court and on assignment with the Twenty Fifth Judicial District. He is perhaps best known for his role as the court-appointed attorney for Richard Eugene Hickock, one of the main subjects in the Truman Capote book *In Cold Blood*. Harrison Smith died on Christmas Day 1987.

The heroic crew of the *Dunboyne* returned to New York on June 2. Promised ten days of leave following their voyage, it was cancelled and they were immediately sent to the SS *Robin Tuxford*, en route to the Middle East. They finally returned to New York on October 7, 1942. Six days later, Brinn, DeCottes, Dixon, Hoban, and Schill all received Silver Star Medals for their heroism shown on the Murmansk Run. Her Armed Guard commander, Rufus Brinn, whose Silver Star had been downgraded from an original recommendation for the Navy Cross,[5] forwarded a list of twenty-four recommendations for improvements for the Armed Guard of future convoy vessels. Many of these improvements found their way into subsequent convoys, undoubtedly saving numerous lives and cargoes. Quite possibly, they contributed to the continued existence of the *Dunboyne*, who went on to survive subsequent trips to Murmansk, meeting her end not by enemy force but by the cutting torch of the scrap yard in 1948.

Lieutenant (jg) Rufus Brinn is presented the Silver Star in October 1942 for his heroism on the SS *Dunboyne*. *Courtesy of the Brinn family.*

Rufus T. Brinn, *Order of the Red Star*

Rufus Timothy Brinn was born on January 30, 1919, in Hertford, North Carolina. He attended the Marion Military Institute and graduated from Duke University. Joining the Navy on November 21, 1940, he was commissioned on May 15, 1941. That June, he became the commanding officer of the USS *Nawat*, a harbor tug, where he remained until he reported to the Armed Guard Center in Brooklyn. Following his service as an Armed Guard commander, he reported to the USS *Hopping* (DE-155) as the executive officer, serving under future Rear Admiral Frank Giambattista, her commanding officer at the time. After one year of service on *Hopping*, he transferred to flight school in March 1944 and was awarded his wings in May 1945. He spent the remainder of the war flying with VF-97 out of Atlantic City, New Jersey, and later with VF-98. In February 1946, he became the assistant operations officer for Operation Crossroads, the testing of the atomic bomb at Bikini Atoll in the Pacific. Subsequently he served as the officer in charge and executive officer of Naval Air Station, Edenton, North Carolina; Naval Air Station Weeksville, Elizabeth City, North Carolina; and VF-12, followed by operations officer on the staff of Air Group Six. Following a tour as an intelligence officer assigned to the Office of the Chief of Naval Operations in Washington, DC, he was sent to Lighter-than-Air flight training, and became executive officer of Airship Squadron Two in September 1954. In 1955, he became the commanding officer of the same squadron and remained there until reporting to the Bureau of Aeronautics in July 1957. Two years later, he reported to the USS *Tarawa* (CVS-40) as her executive officer and in January 1960, became her final commanding officer before decommissioning.

His subsequent tours were on the staff of NATO in Europe, and finally, on the staff of the Industrial College of the Armed Forces in Washington, DC He retired from the Navy as a Captain on March 1, 1965. Returning to North Carolina, he became active in the anti-poverty efforts led by the North Carolina Fund, working with government and private organizations to raise the quality of life in the state. While on a trip to celebrate his thirty-fifth wedding anniversary, Rufus Brinn unexpectedly passed away in Bremerhaven, Germany, on September 30, 1984. He is buried in his hometown of Hertford, North Carolina.

Order of the Red Star number 366451 awarded to Rufus Brinn. *Courtesy of the Brinn family.*

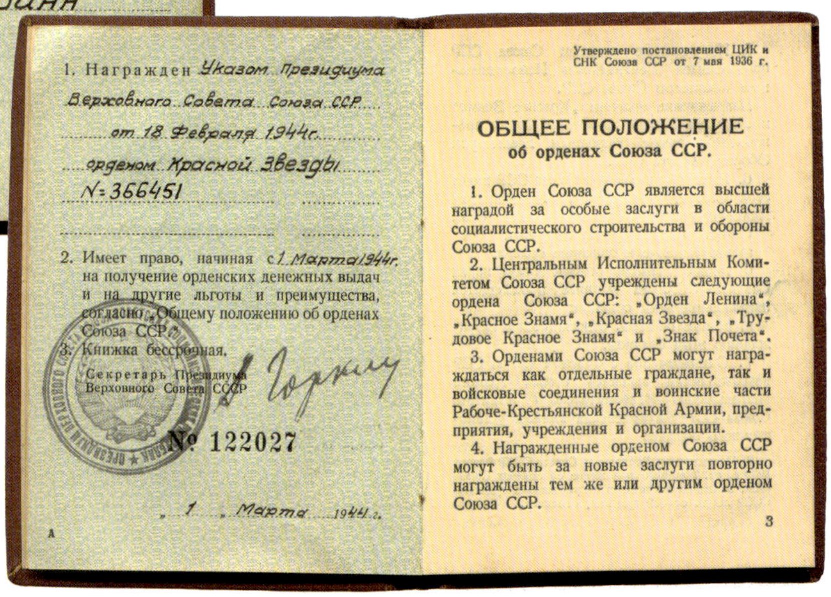

The Soviet order book to Rufus Brinn. Note his wearing of the ribbon for the Order of the Red Star above his other ribbons. *Courtesy of the Brinn family.*

Eaton P. DeCottes, *Medal "For Military Merit"*

A veteran of multiple services, Eaton Pleasants DeCottes was born in Vancouver, Washington, in 1909. Moving to Florida when his mother married into a prominent Jacksonville family, he served in the Florida National Guard from July 27, 1924 to November 26, 1927, followed by an enlistment in the Marine Corps on December 2, 1927. Trained as an artilleryman, he joined General Smedley Butler's Third Brigade in China, serving there until they were withdrawn to the United States in 1929. He then served as part of the Marine guard detachment at Naval Station Mare Island Prison, followed by almost two years on the Marine detachment of the USS *Nevada* (BB-36). Subsequently, he served in Quantico, Virginia, and in Washington, DC prior to his discharge on December 1, 1933. Returning to Florida, he worked as an elevator repairman for a short time, and enlisted in the Naval Reserves on April 8, 1936, serving on the USS *Dallas* (DD-199) as part of his Reserve duty from Jacksonville. Following the outbreak of war, he was transferred to Armed Guard duty, where he served on the *Dunboyne*, and later, the *Robin Tuxford*, in the Mediterranean and the Middle East. Reporting to the USS *Stewart* (DE-238) as part of the commissioning crew in May 1943, he served on her in the Atlantic before commissioning the USS *Day* (DE-225) in June 1944. Transferring to the Pacific, the *Day* conducted escort duties around the islands in the Philippines. On April 19, 1945, he was sent to USS *LST-464* for medical treatment, where he remained until June 1945. DeCottes later claimed that while he was recuperating ashore from surgery, the field hospital was attacked by the Japanese. He escaped and joined the Philippine guerillas, with whom he fought in the mountains against the Japanese for several months before returning to the ship. Because of this action, he was eventually made an honorary member of the Philippine Guerrillas.[6] Returning to the *Day*, he transferred to the USS *Rudderow* (DE-224) in May 1946, followed by a subsequent transfer to the *Herbert C. Jones* (DE-137) in February 1947. He continued active duty service in the Navy until his retirement on April 9, 1957, as a Chief Boatswain's Mate. Residing in the San Diego area, he became a property inspector for the Land Title Insurance Company. Eaton DeCottes died of a sudden heart attack on December 8, 1963, and is buried in Fort Rosecrans National Cemetery.

Edwin B. Newman, *Medal "For Military Merit"*

Edwin Newman with his wife Muriel during the war. *Courtesy of the Newman family.*

Edwin Booth Newman was born on June 6, 1921, in South Orange, New Jersey. He joined the Naval Reserve in Jacksonville on May 3, 1939, and reported for Armed Guard duty on November 18, 1941. While attached to the Armed Guard, he served on several ships, to include the *Dunboyne*, *Robin Tuxford*, and *Hawaiian Shipper*, until his transfer to Naval Auxiliary Air Station, Mayport, Florida, on April 1, 1944. Moved to another air station in Green Cove Springs, Florida, he transferred to Naval Air Station Port Lyautney, French Morocco, on April 12, 1945, and finished the war here as a Boatswain's Mate, first class, in September 1945. Released from active duty, he returned to Jacksonville, Florida. Enlisting in the Coast Guard in 1948, he worked on buoy tenders on Florida's west coast. Then he was transferred to Cape May, New Jersey, as a gunnery instructor, and after several years was transferred to Portsmouth, Virginia, to resume his buoy tender work. Subsequently, he served on the USCGC *Mendota* (WHEC-69). Finally, he served as the commanding officer of the lifeboat stations at Cape Lookout and Oak Island near Wilmington, North Carolina. He retired as a Master Chief Boatswain's Mate in 1964. Ever a stickler for discipline and details, he went to work for Carolina Nitrogen as a safety supervisor, ensuring their compliance with government safety regulations. Edwin Newman passed away on January 10, 1988, and is buried in Wilmington, North Carolina.

The three other Soviet medal recipients on the *Dunboyne* became joined by more than just their service on the Murmansk Run. In an unusual twist that could only happen during a time of war, Thomas Dixon, Edward Hoban, and Gustav Schill, three friends from Jacksonville, married three sisters they met while stationed at the Armed Guard Center in Brooklyn.

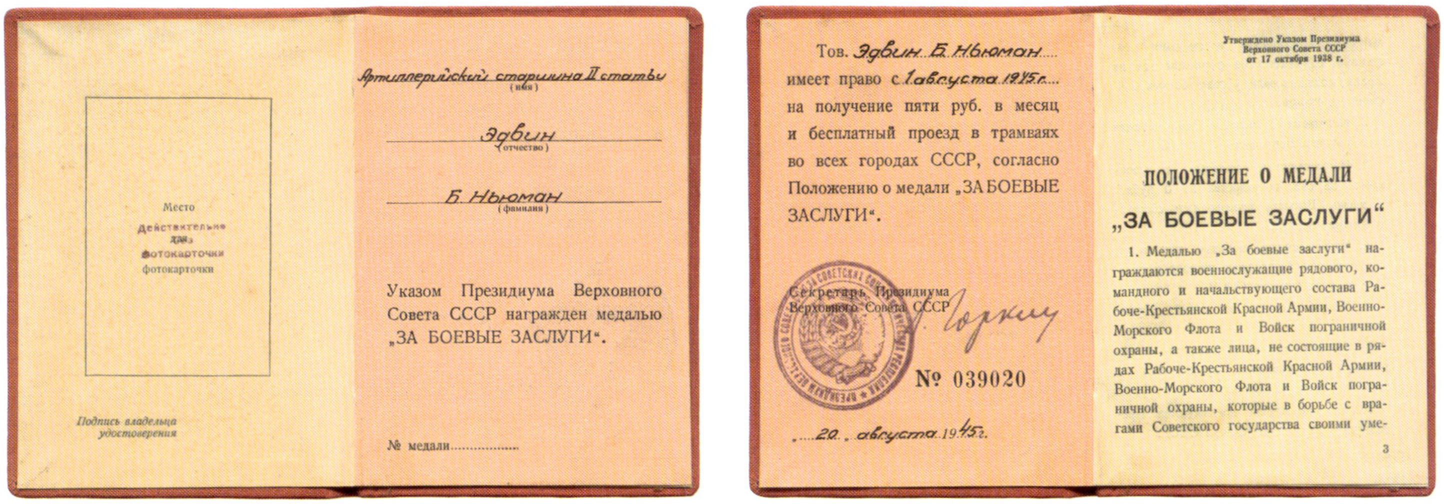

Место для фотокарточки

Действительно без фотокарточки

Подпись владельца удостоверения

Артиллерийский старшина II статьи
(имя)

Эдвин
(отчество)

Б. Ньюман
(фамилия)

Указом Президиума Верховного Совета СССР награжден медалью „ЗА БОЕВЫЕ ЗАСЛУГИ“.

№ медали...............

Тов. Эдвин Б. Ньюман имеет право с 1 августа 1945 г. на получение пяти руб. в месяц и бесплатный проезд в трамваях во всех городах СССР, согласно Положению о медали „ЗА БОЕВЫЕ ЗАСЛУГИ“.

Секретарь Президиума Верховного Совета СССР Горкин

№ 039020

20 августа 1945 г.

Утверждено Указом Президиума Верховного Совета СССР от 17 октября 1938 г.

ПОЛОЖЕНИЕ О МЕДАЛИ „ЗА БОЕВЫЕ ЗАСЛУГИ“

1. Медалью „За боевые заслуги“ награждаются военнослужащие рядового, командного и начальствующего состава Рабоче-Крестьянской Красной Армии, Военно-Морского Флота и Войск пограничной охраны, а также лица, не состоящие в рядах Рабоче-Крестьянской Красной Армии, Военно-Морского Флота и Войск пограничной охраны, которые в борьбе с врагами Советского государства своими уме-

3

The Soviet medal book to Edwin Newman. *Courtesy of the Newman family.*

Medal “For Military Merit” number 2551010 awarded to Edwin Newman. *Courtesy of the Newman family.*

The Silver Star Medal in the original case of issue awarded to Edwin Newman. *Courtesy of the Newman family.*

(l. to r.) Edward Hoban, G.W. Schill, and Thomas Dixon with their wives in 1945. *Courtesy of the Schill family.*

The Silver Star awarded to Thomas Dixon. *Courtesy of the Dixon family.*

Thomas J. Dixon, *Medal "For Military Merit"*

Thomas Jackson Dixon was born on September 5, 1920 in Merdian, Mississippi, and joined the Navy on October 16, 1940. Reporting with the others to the Armed Guard Center in Brooklyn, he spent the majority of his war as a member of Armed Guard detachments, rising to the rank of Gunner's Mate, second class. Detached from the Armed Guard Center on June 25, 1945, he spent two months in Bremerton, Washington, before being released from duty out of Miami, Florida, on September 12, 1945. Returning to Jacksonville, but remaining in the Naval Reserves, he was recalled for active duty and served from September 1950 to September 1951 on the USS *Rochester* (CA-124), conducting naval gunfire support off the coast of Korea. Returning to civilian life, he worked as a machinist for King Edward Cigars for over thirty years. Following his retirement, he spent his time hunting and fishing on his property along the Santa Fe River. He passed away on May 27, 1988 and is buried in Riverside Memorial Park, Jacksonville, Florida.

The Soviet medal book to Thomas Dixon. *Courtesy of the Dixon family.*

Medal "For Military Merit" number 2551009 awarded to Thomas Dixon. *Courtesy of the Dixon family.*

Edward C. Hoban, *Medal "For Military Merit"*

Edward Connor Hoban was born in Orangeburg, South Carolina, on February 14, 1916. A plasterer by trade, he enlisted out of Jacksonville on October 9, 1940. Following his service on the *Dunboyne* and *Robin Tuxford*, he too served on the *Hawaiian Shipper*, where he was promoted to Gunner's Mate, first class, in 1943. Commissioned in October 1944, he spent the first five months of 1945 at the Amphibious Training Base, Coronado, California, preparing for the future invasion of the Japanese homeland. In May, he was assigned to Amphibious Training Base Oceanside as a boat officer, and finally, was assigned to CUB Eighteen, a special unit designated to build and repair airfields in Sasebo, Japan. Returning to the United States, he was discharged from active duty on March 24, 1947.

Remaining in the Naval Reserves, he was recalled during the Korean War, serving on the USS *Greenwich Bay* (AVP-41), and later, serving as commanding officer of the USS *Hunt* (DD-674) in the months leading up to the Cuban Missile Crisis. He eventually retired as a Commander in the Naval Reserves, but remained active in the Military Sea Transportation Service (MSTS), periodically going to sea as a chief yeoman or chief steward from 1966 through 1979. As a civilian, he started and operated the Jacksonville Plastering Company until the mid-1950s, followed by becoming a salesman for the Friden Calculating Machine Company. Retiring to Jacksonville, he became very active in charitable work, serving as president of the Jacksonville Interdenominational Ministerial Alliance (even though he was not a minister). He also volunteered in a soup kitchen in downtown Jacksonville, routinely feeding close to five hundred people. Known as the "Candy Man," he would purchase all the candy on clearance at supermarkets and drugstores after holidays to give it out freely to children who came to eat at the soup kitchen. Edward Hoban passed away on Good Friday, April 17, 2006. He is buried in Riverside Memorial Park in Jacksonville.

Edward Hoban as a Commander. *Courtesy of the Hoban family.*

Edward Hoban's medals mounted on a bar, including his Silver Star and the Soviet Medal "For Military Merit" number 2551013. Why he did not mount the other medals he was entitled to wear is unknown. *Courtesy of the Hoban family.*

Gustav W. Schill, Jr., *Medal "For Military Merit"*

Gustav William "G.W." Schill, Jr. was born on March 24, 1917, in St. Augustine, Florida, where he worked as an insurance policy examiner for the Florida Inspection and Rating Bureau prior to enlisting in the Navy on August 26, 1939. Like Thomas Dixon, he spent his entire wartime career with Armed Guard detachments, eventually being discharged from Bremerton, Washington, on August 25, 1945, as a Gunner's Mate, second class. Returning to his native Florida, he also returned to the insurance industry, where he worked until his retirement. Subsequently, he moved onto a canal on the St. Johns River where he spent his time fishing and reading until he passed away on July 15, 2000. G.W. Schill is buried in Sampson Cemetery, St. Augustine, Florida.

Medal "For Military Merit" number 2551014 awarded to G.W. Schill. *Courtesy of the Schill family.*

The Silver Star Medal awarded to G.W. Schill. *Courtesy of the Schill family.*

Место
Действительно без фотокарточки
фотокарточки

Подпись владельца удостоверения

Артиллерийский старшина III статьи
(имя)
Густав
(отчество)
У. Шилл, мл.
(фамилия)

Указом Президиума Верховного Совета СССР награжден медалью „ЗА БОЕВЫЕ ЗАСЛУГИ".

№ медали..................

Тов. Густав У. Шилл, мл. ......
имеет право с 1 августа 1945 г. ....
на получение пяти руб. в месяц и бесплатный проезд в трамваях во всех городах СССР, согласно Положению о медали „ЗА БОЕВЫЕ ЗАСЛУГИ".

Секретарь Президиума Верховного Совета СССР

№ 039377

„20" августа 1945 г.

Утверждено Указом Президиума Верховного Совета СССР от 17 октября 1938 г.

ПОЛОЖЕНИЕ О МЕДАЛИ „ЗА БОЕВЫЕ ЗАСЛУГИ"

1. Медалью „За боевые заслуги" награждаются военнослужащие рядового, командного и начальствующего состава Рабоче-Крестьянской Красной Армии, Военно-Морского Флота и Войск пограничной охраны, а также лица, не состоящие в рядах Рабоче-Крестьянской Красной Армии, Военно-Морского Флота и Войск пограничной охраны, которые в борьбе с врагами Советского государства своими уме-

3

The Soviet medal book to G.W. Schill. *Courtesy of the Schill family.*

Chapter 7

Convoy PQ-14 Recipients

By mid-February 1942, the next ships were preparing to make the transit from the United States to Murmansk. Following their convoy assembly, twenty-four ships left Iceland on April 8 in convoy PQ-14. However, within the first day, this convoy ran into difficulties. Underway in a storm the first evening, a signal was passed to change the course of the convoy. However, twelve of the ships did not receive the signal and were separated from the rest of the convoy. With the location of the remaining portion of the convoy in doubt, these ships returned to Iceland. The next two days brought about heavy fog, dense pack ice, and to make matters worse, a blizzard. While making a turn during the blizzard, four additional ships were lost on April 10. By the time the remaining ships were headed to Murmansk, only two ships with Armed Guard detachments remained: the SS *Yaka*, who had suffered a damaged bow and hold from the heavy ice, and SS *West Cheswald*. Other than the convoy commodore's ship being torpedoed and sinking in less than forty seconds on April 16, the voyage saw a very limited amount of enemy activity, partially due to the extreme weather the ships faced. By nightfall on April 19, both *Yaka* and *West Cheswald* arrived in Murmansk and by midnight began discharging cargo.

Although their voyage to Murmansk was less costly than others, the men of the *Yaka* and *West Cheswald* endured an onslaught of German bombing while in Murmansk. Walter Gudat, the Armed Guard commander, and Coxswain Harry Wilson, the senior enlisted member of the Armed Guard detachment on the *West Cheswald*, experienced their first bombing raid within an hour of being tied to the pier. On April 22, the bombs fell close enough to destroy a floating crane in the process of offloading tanks from the deck of the *West Cheswald*. Unloading as quickly as possible, she was away from the pier by April 26 and two days later joined a return convoy to Iceland. Blessed by blizzards and fog on the return voyage, they made it through without the loss of a single ship. The *West Cheswald* arrived in port New York on May 31. She went on to survive other hazardous trips across the Atlantic, finally meeting her fate as part of the artificial breakwater off the Normandy beaches on June 7, 1944.[1]

Order of the Patriotic War, Second Class, number 557278 awarded to Walter Gudat. *Courtesy of the Gudat family.*

Walter J. Gudat, *Order of the Patriotic War, Second Class*

Walter John Gudat was born on January 24, 1919, in Somerville, Massachusetts, the son of a career Navy Chief Petty Officer. Graduating from Northwestern University, he joined the Navy on September 16, 1940, and was commissioned on January 3, 1941. At the time the younger Gudat joined the Navy, his father was serving as the bandmaster on the USS *Arizona* (BB-39) in Pearl Harbor (he later transferred from the *Arizona* to his next duty station in San Diego six months before the fateful attack). Reporting the same month of his commissioning, Gudat served on the USS *Antares* (AG-10), followed by the USS *Idaho* (BB-42), and the USS *Lea* (DD-118) before reporting for Armed Guard duty in February 1942. Assigned to the *West Cheswald* on February 11, he served on her until transferred to the SS *Benjamin Hawkins* on November 13. Returning to the United States, he served as an instructor at the Armed Guard School before reporting to the newly commissioned USS *Biloxi* (CL-80). Sent to the Pacific theater, he participated in the bombardment of Wotje and Roi Island in the Marshall Island chain. Back in the United States, Gudat received orders to serve on the commissioning crew of the USS *Atlanta* (CL-104). Again in the Pacific theater, he participated in the fighting for Okinawa and conducted shore bombardment on the Japanese home islands in preparation for the eventual invasion. Japan surrendered, and Gudat transferred off the *Atlanta* to return to the United States on the USS *Antietam* (CV-36).

Gudat was discharged from active duty on November 22, 1946. Remaining in the Naval Reserves, he retired as a Commander on July 1, 1965. While on leave before his discharge in November 1946, he began his civilian career in the Bank of America's San Francisco headquarters as part of the Bond Investment Department. He later transferred to their Municipal Bond Department and on July 1, 1984, retired from nearly thirty-eight years with Bank of America. For the last fourteen years of his life, he was a much-loved tutor at his granddaughter's grade school. Walter Gudat passed away on July 26, 2009, in Santa Clara, California.

Walter John Gudat in approximately 1947. Note his wearing of the Order of the Patriotic War, Second Class, below the pocket on the left side of his uniform. *Courtesy of the Gudat family.*

Harry P. Wilson, *Medal "For Valor"*

Harry Wilson as a Chief Boatswain, approximately 1945. *Courtesy of the Wilson family.*

Harry Parks Wilson was born on November 21, 1918, in Gibson County, Tennessee. Completing all twelve years of school, a relative rarity at the time for many of his enlisted peers, he joined the Civilian Conservation Corps, serving with Company 490 in Brownsville, Tennessee. With the CCC, he planted trees, terraced local farm fields, improved roads, and after the flood of 1937, helped homeless families and rebuilt the Obion Levee. Planning on making the Navy a career, he enlisted on November 13, 1939. Reporting to the Armed Guard Center, Brooklyn, New York, on January 22, 1942, as a Boatswain's Mate, second class, he served on multiple ships in both the Atlantic and the Pacific. In addition to the Letter of Commendation from the Secretary of the Navy he received for the Murmansk Run, he earned another Commendation following intense anti-aircraft action off the coast of Sicily in July 1943. Promoted to Chief Boatswain on June 15, 1945, he was discharged from active duty on January 7, 1946. As a civilian, he worked for Standard Oil in Whiting, Indiana, until 1962. He then worked for Carolina Nitrogen in Wilmington, North Carolina, and eventually worked for Hawkeye Chemical in Clinton, Iowa, as the chief operator in the ammonia plant. Harry Wilson passed away from lung cancer on May 26, 1978, still working for Hawkeye Chemical as their chief shift operator.

Although the *West Cheswald* returned from her nine-day stay in Murmansk relatively unscathed, the *Yaka* was not as fortunate. Because of the damage caused by pack ice sustained during the transit, she missed the outgoing convoy on April 28 because of ongoing repair work. By mid-May, due to her immobile state, *Yaka* became a favorite target of German bombers. May 12 brought the first in a series of raids specifically targeted at the ship, and a near miss by a bomb dented the bulkhead on the port side and ruptured her deep tank water lines. Two days later, the concussion caused by close bombing broke her compass binnacle. The following day, ten German bombers unloaded their bombs directly above and in the vicinity of *Yaka*. One bomb, exploding three feet above the waterline, ripped open the port side of the ship, and shrapnel destroyed much of the ship's number two boiler. The engine room and fire room were open to the sea and flooded to a depth of eighteen feet. Finally, with repairs complete, *Yaka* headed out to anchor on May 27, waiting for the next convoy, but her luck ran out again. On June 13, another series of bombers hit the ship, tearing fourteen holes in her port side and rupturing the deep tank. This time, however, *Yaka's* Armed Guard repaid the damage in kind: they were officially credited with shooting down one German bomber and damaging a second. After enduring 156 air raid alarms, forty-eight full-scale bombing raids, and five direct attacks on the ship, *Yaka* got underway on June 27 for Iceland. Those who breathed a sigh of relief were premature: the day before the convoy entered port in Iceland, a navigation error in dense fog sent the convoy through an Allied minefield, sinking six ships and costing the lives of dozens of Royal Navy and merchant sailors.[2] *Yaka* arrived safely in New York on July 26, 1942. She would not serve her country much longer, however. *Yaka* was sunk on November 18, 1942, by two torpedoes from *U-522* (*Kapitänleutnant* Herbert Schneider) while returning from her next convoy assignment.

Medal "For Valor" number 2075718 awarded to Harry Wilson. *Courtesy of the Wilson family.*

The Soviet medal book to Harry Wilson. *Courtesy of the Wilson family.*

Lieutenant (jg) George T. Smith, Armed Guard commander of the SS *Yaka*. *Courtesy of the Smith family.*

The Soviet order book to George Smith. *Courtesy of the Smith family.*

George T. Smith, *Order of the Patriotic War, Second Class*

Yaka's Armed Guard commander was George Thornewell Smith, a Southern gentleman born and raised in the Greenwood community in Mitchell County, Georgia. Born on October 15, 1916, he was valedictorian of his class at Hopeful High School, and attended Middle Georgia College and Abraham Baldwin Agricultural College. Joining the Navy on August 26, 1940, he reported for active duty on March 15, 1941, and was commissioned on June 12. His first duty assignment was on the USS *Antaeus* (AS-21), a submarine tender operating off the east coast of Panama. Transferring on February 2, 1942, Smith reported for Armed Guard duty at Brooklyn, New York, on March 6, and found himself assigned to duty on the *Yaka*, where he reported the next day. Detaching from the *Yaka* after her voyage to Murmansk on July 31, he next reported for Armed Guard duty on the USAT *Arrow*, a former commercial passenger steam liner built in 1909 and pressed into wartime Army transport service. On *Arrow*, he transited the Panama Canal and spent the remainder of 1942 stationed in Pearl Harbor, conducting island-hopping runs between the Hawaiian Islands. Transferring from Armed Guard duty, Smith spent the remainder of the war assigned to the Twelfth Naval District, first at Mare Island, California, and then at the Naval Landing Force Equipment Depot (NLFED) in Albany, California, in charge of the hundreds of landing craft preparing for use during the invasion of the Japanese home islands. Discharged from active duty as a lieutenant commander on October 26, 1945, he returned to Georgia and in 1948 received his LLB from the University of Georgia School of Law.

Entering private practice in Cairo, Georgia, he additionally served as the county attorney, solicitor of the State Court of Grady County, the Cairo city attorney and the attorney for the Grady County Board of Education. In 1958, he was elected into the Georgia House of Representatives, where he served for eight years, becoming the speaker of the House of Representatives in 1963. In 1966, he was elected lieutenant governor of the state of Georgia, where he served until 1971. After returning to private practice in Marietta, Georgia, he was elected in 1976 as a judge on the Georgia Court of Appeals. With this election, he became the first person in Georgia history to win contested elections in all three branches of state government. In recognition for his outstanding service to the state of Georgia, his portrait was unveiled in the rotunda of the state Capitol on May 12, 1980.

His career did not stop here, however. On January 1, 1981, he joined the Supreme Court of the State of Georgia and became the presiding justice on January 1, 1990. On December 20, 1991, he resigned his position after thirty years of service to the state. Returning to private practice in 1992, he joined the law firm of Barnes, Browning, Tanksley, and Casurella as counsel. George Smith passed away in Marietta, Georgia, on August 23, 2010, and was buried with full military honors, commemorating a life of service to his nation and state.

George Smith's Cross of Military Service for World War II from the United Daughters of the Confederacy. *Courtesy of the Smith family.*

Order of the Patriotic War, Second Class, number 557283 awarded to George Smith. *Courtesy of the Smith family.*

Gifford H. Starnes, *Medal "For Military Merit"*

Assisting George Smith in his duties on *Yaka* was Gifford Harmon Starnes, born December 22, 1913, in Spigner, Alabama. Working as a delivery truck driver and salesman for the A.G. Henry 7-Up Bottling Company in Guntersville, Starnes had already served in the Army from 1932 to 1933 as a Private in Company E, Second Battalion, 66th Infantry (Light Tanks) at Fort Benning, Georgia, and to 1936 in the Alabama National Guard. He enlisted in the Navy on August 3, 1941, and in September, was assigned to the USS *Ruby* (PY-21), a converted motor yacht assigned to escort duties in Charleston, South Carolina. In January 1942, he was assigned to the Armed Guard duty.

His first ship as a member of the Armed Guard was the SS *West Jaffrey*, under the command of Ensign Thomas Delate. She ran aground on Peases Island off the coast of Nova Scotia and subsequently sank on February 8, 1942. Returning to Brooklyn, he was assigned to the *Yaka*, taking her to and from Murmansk. Following his safe return, he became a gunnery instructor at the Armed Guard School at Dam Neck, Virginia, until he transferred to the USS *Willard Keith* (DD-775) on November 22, 1944. Transiting to the Pacific theater in convoy with the *Atlanta* (with Walter Gudat in her crew), they were assigned radar picket duties for the invasion of Okinawa. Here, they experienced their baptism by fire, shooting down two Japanese aircraft, including one who launched a torpedo directly at the ship. Luckily, the torpedo was a dud, merely denting the hull. With the post-war drawdown, Starnes was discharged as a Chief Gunner's Mate on December 17, 1947.

Returning to Guntersville, Starnes started as a meter reader for the city Electric Department, and eventually became the department manager. Retiring after twenty-two years of service, he spent much of his time traveling, covering almost all of the United States. Active in the community, he served on the city planning board and was actively involved in the Boy Scouts and his church. Gifford Starnes passed away on August 22, 1986.

Gifford H. Starnes. *Courtesy of the Starnes family.*

Medal "For Military Merit" number 2551011 awarded to Gifford Starnes. *Courtesy of the Starnes family.*

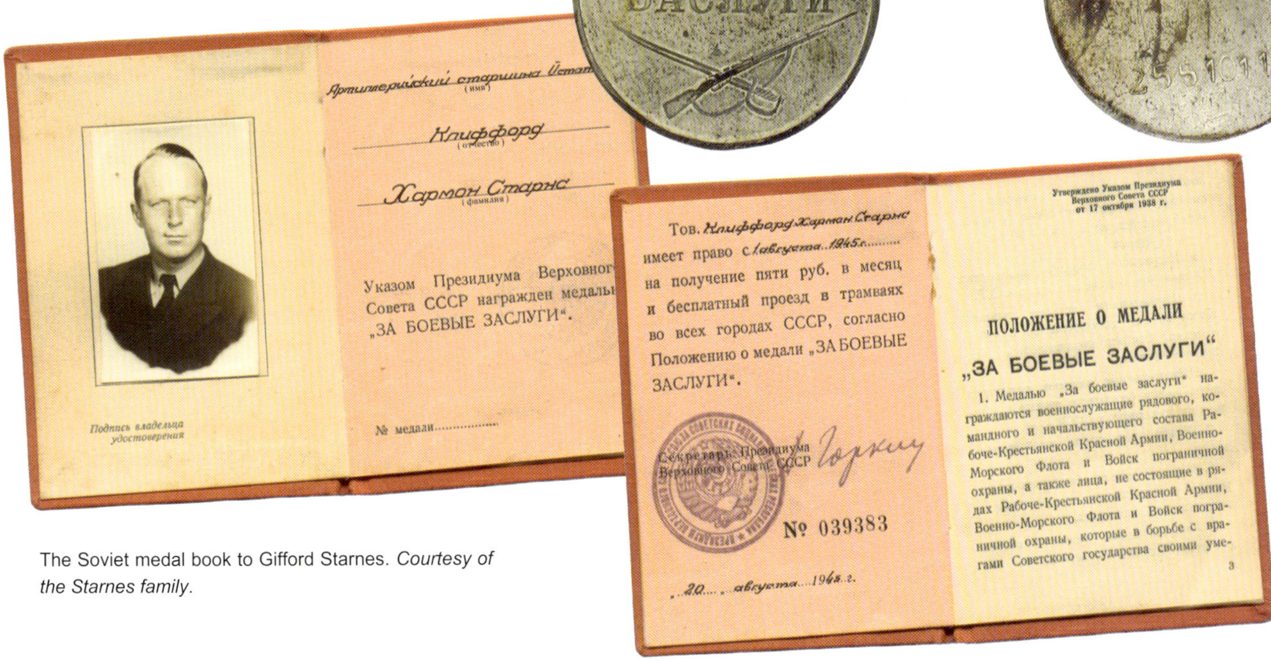

The Soviet medal book to Gifford Starnes. *Courtesy of the Starnes family.*

Chapter 8

Convoy PQ-15 and Task Group 39 Recipients

With loses ever increasing due to the growing ferociousness of German attacks on the convoys, PQ-15, consisting of twenty-three ships with fifteen being American merchant vessels, left Reykjavik on April 26, 1942. Among these ships were the SS *Deer Lodge*, *Expositor*, *Francis Scott Key*, *Mormacrio*, and the *Zebulon B. Vance*, all with Navy Armed Guard detachments on board. Additionally, PQ-15 was the first convoy to have American warships assigned, including the battleship USS *Washington* (BB-56), the heavy cruisers USS *Wichita* (CA-45) and *Tuscaloosa* (CA-37), the aircraft carrier USS *Wasp* (CV-7), and Destroyer Squadron Eight, embarked in the USS *Wainwright* (DD-419). Together, they made up Task Group (TG) 39. Aside from *Wasp*, who was later pulled to assist with supply convoys to Malta, these ships remained on USSR-bound convoy duty for multiple voyages between Iceland and Murmansk in 1942.[1]

Robert C. Giffen, *Order of Suvorov, Second Class*

Commanding TG 39 was Rear Admiral Robert Carlisle "Ike" Giffen, who had taken command following the untimely and accidental death of Rear Admiral John Wilcox on March 27, 1942, the second day underway from the United States. Born at West Chester, Pennsylvania, on June 29, 1886, Giffen graduated from the United States Naval Academy in 1907 and was commissioned on February 12, 1909, following his obligatory two years of sea time as a Passed Midshipman on the USS *Virginia* (BB-13) and the three-masted bark, USS *Severn*. An accomplished rifle marksman, the first four years of his commissioned duties revolved around participation and competition with the Navy Rifle Team, to include participation in the 1912 Olympic Games in Stockholm, until he was detached in August 1913. His first command was the USS *Wainwright* (DD-62), seeing her commissioned in May 1916. Next, he commanded the USS *Trippe* (DD-33), where he earned the Navy Cross for conducting anti-submarine patrols during the First World War, followed by the USS *Schley* (DD-103). Transferred to duty on the Asiatic Station for the next three years, he served as the executive officer of the USS *Huron* (CA-9) patrolling the waters around China and the Philippines. After a stint on the staff of the Naval Academy from 1924 to 1927 (he later served there from 1934 to 1937), Giffen returned to the Asiatic Station to command the USS *Sacramento* (PG-19), followed by command of Destroyer Squadron Forty-Five, the USS *Neches* (AO-5), USS *Boise* (CL-47), USS *Savannah* (CL-42) and Cruiser Division Seven. He was subsequently promoted to Rear Admiral, effective March 29, 1941.

Admiral Robert C. Giffen. Note his ribbon for the Order of Suvorov, Second Class, in the far right of his bottom row of ribbons. *Official US Navy photo via the National Archives.*

Following his command of TG 39 on the Murmansk Run, well-chronicled by his flag aide, Hollywood star Douglas Fairbanks Jr., he commanded the Covering Group of the Western Naval Task Force during the landings and occupation of French Morocco in November 1942, successfully defending the invading Task Force and destroying all enemy surface ships in the port of Casablanca. Transferred to the Pacific theater, he commanded the US naval forces during the Battle of Rennell Island in January 1943 and participated in the Guadalcanal campaign as Commander, Task Force Eighteen. Subsequently, he was the officer in tactical command of Covering Forces, North Pacific Force for the Aleutian Islands Campaign, to include the capture of Attu and bombardment and capture of Kiska, followed by the assault on the Palau Islands as Commander, Supporting Cruisers. At the end of 1943 and the beginning of 1944, he served as Commander, Fire Support Groups, Fifth Amphibious Force for the capture of the Gilbert and Marshall Islands, and as Commander, Supporting Cruisers, US Pacific Fleet, participated in the attacks on Kwajalein, Truk, Saipan, and Tinian. Promoted to Vice Admiral, he became Commandant of the Tenth Naval District and Commander, Caribbean Sea Frontier, in May 1944, and remained there until the end of the war. His final command was Commander, Service Force, US Atlantic Fleet from August 1945, and he retired from active duty, after a remarkable career, in September 1946.

Admiral Giffen retired to his eighty-nine-acre Masque Farm in Annapolis that he had purchased while serving at the Academy as athletic director in 1937. Here, he devoted his full attention to agriculture, specializing in the cultivation of tobacco, until his passing on December 10, 1962. Robert Giffen is buried in the Naval Academy Cemetery in Annapolis.

Harry W. Hill, *Order of Kutuzov, Second Class*

Admiral Harry W. Hill. He is wearing his ribbon for the Order of Kutuzov, Second Class, as the topmost ribbon on his bars. *Official US Navy photo via the National Archives.*

Commanding the cruiser USS *Wichita* (CA-45) was Captain Harry Wilbur Hill. Born in Oakland, California, on April 7, 1890, he graduated from the Naval Academy in 1911, after playing forward on the Academy's first varsity basketball team. Commissioned in March 1912, he served tours in the Pacific on the USS *Maryland* (ACR-8), the torpedo boat tender USS *Iris*, USS *Perry* (DD-11), and the USS *Albany* (CL-23). During the First World War, he served on the USS *Texas* (BB-35) and the USS *Wyoming* (BB-32), where he was eyewitness to the surrender of the German High Seas Fleet on November 11, 1918. Leaving sea duty, he became aide to the Chief of Naval Operations, and served in Washington, DC for the subsequent four years. Back to sea, he served as the gunnery officer on the USS *Maryland* (BB-46), earning a Commendation from the Secretary of the Navy for winning the Gunnery Trophy. His following tours included service on the staff of the Naval Academy, as force gunnery officer for Commander, Battle Force, Pacific Fleet, in the Office of the Chief of Naval Operations, and as a student at the Naval War College in Newport, Rhode Island. Upon his graduation in May 1938, he assumed command of the *Wichita*, where he served on escort duty for the Murmansk-bound convoys. In September 1942, he became commander, Battleship Division Four, with the *Maryland* as his flagship, serving a year in the South Pacific. Subsequently, he was promoted to the position of Commander, Amphibious Group Two, in charge of the assault on Tarawa. Changing from the traditional tactics of naval gunnery, he spearheaded the concept of up-close naval gunfire support, bringing his ships within a mile of the coastline to destroy the enemy.[2] He later participated in operations against the Gilberts, Marshalls, Marianas, Iwo Jima, and Okinawa. He relieved the Commander, Fifth Amphibious Force at Okinawa in April 1945, and commanded amphibious operations there until the island was secured at the end of June.

In August, his amphibious force landed the Sixth Army in Southwestern Japan for occupation duty. Leaving the Pacific, he assumed duty as commandant, Army-Navy Staff College in November and in June 1946 established National War College, serving as its first commandant. In September 1949, he reported as chairman of the General Board, Navy Department, where he remained for the next six months. He subsequently became superintendent of the Naval Academy and commandant, Severn River Naval Command in April 1950. He continued to serve after his retirement and from May 1952 to May 1954 was governor of the Naval Home in Philadelphia, Pennsylvania. Harry Hill passed away in Annapolis, Maryland, on July 19, 1971, and is buried in the Naval Academy Cemetery.

Norman C. Gillette, *Order of Suvorov, Third Class*

Captain Norman Campbell Gillette was in command of *Tuscaloosa* during the Arctic voyages. Born in Chicago, Illinois, on December 13, 1889, he graduated from the Naval Academy with the class of 1913. He served on the USS *Texas* (BB-35) with Harry Hill, and reported to the USS *Wyoming* (BB-32), as she returned to the United States in 1919. Following this assignment, he spent the next three years training as a specialist in ordnance with the Bureau of Ordnance in Washington, DC, the Midvale Steel Company in Nicetown, Pennsylvania, and at Edgewood Arsenal in Maryland. Reporting for sea duty, he served on the USS *California* (BB-44), the USS *Shirk* (DD-318), and USS *Bainbridge* (DD-217) before returning to the Naval Gun Factory in Washington, DC After two years ashore, he was assigned to the USS *Lexington* (CV-2) as gunnery officer before accepting a posting at the Bureau of Ordnance. His first command was of the USS *Manley* (DD-74) a *Caldwell*-class four-stack destroyer from June 1932 to May 1934. As an ordnance expert, he again returned to the Bureau of Ordnance for a three-year tour before reporting to the USS *Omaha* (CL-4) as executive officer in June 1937. His next two years were spent as a professor of naval science at Northwestern University, instructing future officers, including Walter Gudat. He then served in the Office of the Chief of Naval Operations during the dark days following the attack on Pearl Harbor and took command of *Tuscaloosa* on February 9, 1942, a month before departing for convoy escort duty.

On April 20, 1943, he was relieved of command and spent the next seventeen months commanding the Naval Ordnance Plant in Center Line, Michigan, and serving as the naval inspector of ordnance at the Pontiac Division of General Motors and at the Chrysler Corporation. Next, he headed to the Pacific to become the chief of staff to the commander,

Philippine Sea Frontier, on October 15, 1944. Promoted to Commodore, he served in New Guinea, Leyte, and Luzon, directing the flow of materials and men in the defense of the Philippines and forward movement toward the Japanese home islands. With the end of the war, he detached from the Philippine Sea Frontier in December 1945 and assumed command of the Naval Ammunition Depot, Hawthorne, Nevada, in April 1946. Following his retirement, he moved to Long Beach, California, and passed away on November 2, 1956. He is buried in Arlington National Cemetery.

Howard E. Orem, *Order of Kutuzov, Third Class*

The executive officer of the *Wichita* was already experienced at dealing with the North Atlantic. Captain Howard Emery Orem was serving as the senior liaison officer between the United States and the Royal Navy in Icelandic, British, and North Sea waters from August 1941 onward. Born in Klamath Falls, Oregon, on November 1, 1900, he graduated from the Naval Academy with the class of 1922. His first four years were spent at sea on the USS *Idaho* (BB-24), the USS *Tracy* (DD-214), USS *William B. Preston* (DD-344), USS *Tennessee* (BB-43), and the USS *Lawrence* (DD-250). With a two-year break before returning to sea, he attended the Postgraduate School at the Naval Academy and received a master's degree in electrical engineering from Columbia University. Subsequently, he was assigned to the USS *Maryland* (BB-46) in 1929 and served on her until he transferred to the USS *Waters* (DD-115) as chief engineer. This was followed by a tour at the Navy Yard in Philadelphia, then returning to sea on the USS *New York* (BB-34), where he served as the gunnery officer until July 1937. Ordered next to the Naval Academy, he served as an instructor before starting his tour on the staff of Commander, Cruiser Division Seven. Prior to embarking on their trans-Atlantic crossing, Orem assumed the duties as executive officer of the *Wichita* under the command of Harry Hill, and served in this position until May 1943 when he was transferred to the Pacific to become chief of staff for Cruiser Division Six. In August, he was selected by Admiral Ernest King, the Chief of Naval Operations and Commander in Chief, US Fleet, to serve as his aide and flag secretary, and he remained in that job through July 1945. Taking command of the USS *Houston* (CL-81) during her stateside repairs and subsequent post-war goodwill deployment to the Mediterranean, he was selected for the National War College and graduated in August 1947. His subsequent tours included assistant chief of staff for logistics for Commander, Pacific Fleet, in the Office of the Chief of Naval Operations, where he started the Office of Foreign Affairs, and in command of Amphibious Group Four and US Naval Forces, Germany. In April 1954, he became the Assistant Chief of Naval Operations for Plans and Policy before serving in the Office of the Joint Chiefs of Staff. Here he served in multiple billets until his retirement on December 1, 1961, with the rank of Vice Admiral. After his Navy service, he was the vice president of research at the Stevens Institute in Hoboken, New Jersey, and retired from there in 1966. Howard Orem passed away in Williamsburg, Virginia, on June 21, 1995. He is buried in the Naval Academy Cemetery.

Admiral Howard E. Orem, photo taken in approximately 1950. He is wearing his ribbon for the Order of Kutuzov, Third Class, on the far right of his bottom row of ribbons. *Courtesy of the Orem family.*

Order of Kutuzov, Third Class, number 6654 awarded to Howard E. Orem. *Courtesy of the Orem family.*

Admiral Don P. Moon, taken at the Amphibious Training Base, Algiers, Algeria in early-1944. *Official US Navy photo via the National Archives.*

Don P. Moon, *Order of Alexander Nevsky*

Embarked on the *Wainwright*, Captain Don Pardee Moon was in command of Destroyer Squadron Eight. Moon was born on April 18, 1894, in Kokomo, Indiana, and entered the Naval Academy in August 1912. Commissioned in June 1916, he served on the USS *Arizona* (BB-39) from her commissioning through all of her operations in the Atlantic and Mediterranean, eventually detaching at the end of 1920. Returning to the Naval Academy for postgraduate school, he transferred in August 1921 to the University of Chicago for a course in ballistics, followed by continued instruction at Naval Proving Ground, Indian Head, Maryland, and Army Proving Ground, Aberdeen, Maryland, through the end of 1922. After seven months at the Naval Gun Factory, Navy Yard, Washington, DC, he reported to the USS *Colorado* (BB-45) for two years, followed by a tour on the USS *Nevada* (BB-36). Returning to the Naval Gun Factory in July 1927, he remained there until ordered to Destroyer Squadron Eleven in February 1929, followed by a tour on the staff of Destroyer Squadrons Six and Four. The years 1932 and 1933 were spent at the Naval War College before taking command of the USS *John D. Ford* (DD-228) with the Asiatic Station in China. He remained on *Ford* for almost three years before returning for instruction at the Naval War College. In 1940, he took command of Destroyer Division Fifteen, followed by Destroyer Squadron Twenty-Seven in August 1941 and Destroyer Squadron Eight in November. A year later, following his time on the Murmansk Run, he participated in the assault on and occupation of French Morocco from November 8 to 11, 1942, and immediately reported to the staff of Admiral Ernest J. King, Commander in Chief, US Fleet. He was detached from Admiral King's staff on January 25, 1944, four days after his promotion to Rear Admiral, retroactive to November 21, 1942.

Returning overseas, he began preparation in earnest for the upcoming invasion of the European mainland. As commander of Assault Force "U," he directed the assault on Utah Beach on June 6, 1944, landing the US Army VII Corps and earning the Army Distinguished Service Medal. Ever vigilant, the crew of his flagship, the USS *Bayfield* (APA-33) stood watch for three weeks off the coast of Utah Beach, providing anti-aircraft cover and direction for the assault force. On July 5, *Bayfield* began her transit to Italy. At Naples, Moon assumed command of Task Force Eight in preparation for the invasion of Southern France, codenamed Operation *Dragoon*. During rehearsals on August 5, 1944, for the full-scale invasion near Salerno, suffering from severe combat fatigue, Rear Admiral Moon took his own life. He received a posthumous Legion of Merit, and his body was returned to the United States for burial in Arlington National Cemetery.

Escorted by Admiral Giffen's TG 39, the ships of PQ-15 departed Iceland in relative calm save for the occasional sighting of floating mines along the convoy's initial path. This had not originally been the case for the SS *Francis Scott Key* with Jules Bloch as her Armed Guard commander and Renald Blake as her senior gunner, nor for the SS *Mormacrio*, with Wilbur Collins on board as the Armed Guard commander. They had initially left Iceland with convoy PQ-14, but due to heavy ice and even heavier weather, were forced to return to Iceland and wait for the next convoy.

Four days into the transit, on April 30, the first German scout plane was spotted by the convoy. From that time forward, until they returned to Iceland, they were under continual surveillance or attack by the Germans. May 1 brought the first attempted attack on the convoy, but it was unsuccessful. Two German aircraft attempted to bomb the convoy, but one was shot down and the other disappeared into the clouds. Subsequent attacks would not be defeated as easily. With the nearly twenty-four hours of daylight, foul weather was desperately prayed for to ground the enemy. An attack at 1:27 AM on May 3 during the course of a snowstorm resulted in two British merchant ships, the *Bothaven* and *Jutland*, being torpedoed and sunk by an attack from six He 111 torpedo planes attacking at wavetop height. They were not the only ships to be sunk during the attack. Almost simultaneously, according to Robert Ricks, the Armed Guard commander on the SS *Expositor*, who was loaded with five thousand cases of TNT and ten thousand rounds of tank ammunition, the "midship section of the SS *Cape Corso*, British merchantman, blew skyward in a hundred and fifty foot flame."[3] Just like Ricks' *Expositor*, the *Cape Corso* carried an all-explosive cargo of high-octane fuel and ammunition. Ricks was awestruck as he watched *Cape Corso* disappear in seconds, taking her entire crew of fifty with her.[5]

Just then, the aft lookout on the *Expositor* sighted the conning tower of a U-boat just off their starboard quarter. Swinging into action, Ricks' crew of five Armed Guards, with Coxswain Joseph O'Savage as the senior enlisted member, attempted to fire their four-inch deck gun at the submarine but could not depress the barrel sufficiently to hit the target. Opening range, Ricks ordered his crew to keep firing and at twenty-five yards, they placed a four-inch round directly into the conning tower of the U-boat, blowing off the topmost portion. The submarine submerged, leaving bubbles and an oil slick where she once was on the surface. Celebration was premature, as another lookout spotted a torpedo heading directly toward their bow. Only the quick response of the engine room and a full backing bell allowed the torpedo to miss the ship's bow by a matter of feet. At the same time, on the other side of the convoy, one of the British corvettes escorting the merchant ships was attacked, torpedoed, and sunk by another aircraft. The attack was over, but it was costly: four ships had been sunk, and the casualties were high.

Heavy seas and weather embraced the convoy from then onward and save for one additional attack at 11:25 PM on May 3, the convoy was allowed to transit quietly, finally arriving at Kola Inlet at 9:00 PM on May 5, and anchored in Murmansk on May 6. However, the ships of the convoy could not find peace there. Marcel Desgalier, the Armed Guard commander on the SS *Zebulon B. Vance*, recorded forty-five air raid alarms during the period from May 9 to May 21. At midnight on May 10, a formation of German aircraft dropped bombs all around his ship, recording hits between thirty and one hundred feet away jarring the ship and crew to the core.[4] On May 12, ten German He 111 aircraft attacked the *Mormacrio*, with Wilbur Collins as her Armed Guard commander, while she was at anchor in Murmansk harbor. They were the only ship able to fire on the aircraft, in spite of the barrage of enemy bombs. Four bombs landed within fifty yards of the ship, covering the ship with spray and knocking crewmen off their feet. As a result of the hail of fire from the *Mormacrio*, one of the attacking planes was shot down, crashing into the water in flames.

Continually conducting air attacks throughout the city and harbor, the German pilots were almost successful against one of the merchant ships on May 18. Five Ju 88 bombers attacked in formation, and bombs encircled the ships anchored in the harbor, including the SS *Deer Lodge*. The *Deer Lodge* had Thomas Delate on board as the Armed Guard commander, Frank Townsend as the chief engineer, and Alexander Henry as her master. Several of the bombs landed near the stern of the ship and as they exploded, the force of the blast lifted the aft end of the ship out of the water, buckling and twisting the twenty-three year old vessel. Feeling the ship settling by the stern, Townsend rushed to shaft alley and closed the watertight door, stemming the flow of seawater through her ruptured stern plates and saving the engine and boiler rooms from flooding entirely. With her stern now touching bottom of the harbor, Henry ordered the forward-most number one hold flooded, counterbalancing the effect of the flooded stern compartments. Doing their utmost to repair the damage to the slowly sinking vessel caused by a gash in the hull twelve feet long by ten feet wide, Townsend and Henry knew they had to get the ship into shallow water as soon as possible. Ingeniously using wire ropes attached to boulders and stumps to inch the ship stern-first onto a mud flat, they were able to haul her into position to repair the damage without fear of sinking.[5]

Even in her damaged condition, she was still a considerable target for the German bombers and on May 27, she was attacked again. This time the bombs blew in close to seven hundred square feet of shell plating on the port side, with a ten-foot hole in the middle of this damage. Ever resourceful, the crew maintained their heroic effort, working continuously between the tides and eventually repairing and refloating the ship.[6] The *Deer Lodge* returned to New York on November 11, 1942. Unfortunately, her luck would only hold out for three more months: on February 16, 1943, the *Deer Lodge*, with a new crew on board, was sunk by two torpedoes fired from *U-516*, sinking approximately sixty miles off the coast of South Africa.

Alexander S. Henry, *Order of the Red Star*

Alexander S. Henry reviews his citation for the Merchant Marine Distinguished Service Medal. *War Shipping Administration Photo.*

Following their return from the USSR, Alexander Henry and Frank Townsend became two of the 148 recipients of the Merchant Marine Distinguished Service Medal during the Second World War. Alexander Smith Henry was born in Paisley, Scotland, on August 15, 1902. He was educated as a draftsman but could not find work and thus immigrated to the United States, arriving on September 2, 1923. For two years, he labored as a coppersmith for a sugar refinery in Yonkers, New York. Joining the US Coast Guard in 1925, he served for three years, achieving the rank of Boatswain's Mate, second class, and becoming a naturalized citizen in November 1928. Finding his calling, he headed to sea as a civilian. Working his way through the ranks, he became a licensed mariner, achieving his license as a master for all types and sizes of vessels in February 1942. With his new license, he became master of the *Deer Lodge* in on April 6, 1942. Following his most eventful mission to Murmansk, he went on to serve as master of SS *Lancaster*, *African Star*, *Cape Blanco*, *Cape Blas*, and *Pomona Victory* – all before the end of the Second World War. (It is interesting that he never made another voyage on the Murmansk Run.) It was while on *Pomona Victory* that he became a Commander in the United States Merchant Marine on July 14, 1945. Spending his entire career at sea, he eventually retired to West Palm Beach, Florida. Alexander Henry passed away in January 1969.

Frank F. Townsend, *Medal "For Valor"*

The quick-thinking chief engineer on *Deer Lodge* was Frank Floyd Townsend. Born on April 17, 1895, in Lumberton, North Carolina, his life was spent at sea. An imposing man at six-foot, two-inches and weighing in at 250 pounds, he was not one to be trifled with: he was known for winning fights using only the palm of his hand as a weapon. He also had a brilliant mind, able to adeptly solve complex engineering problems despite a lack of formal training. Going to sea for the first time on July 8, 1915, he served as a civilian mariner on the USS *Arethusa* (AO-7), the Navy's first official oiler. Serving on *Arethusa* through the entire First World War, he was discharged from her in June 1919. Townsend became a chief engineer for the first time in 1923 and served in that capacity for the next thirty-five years. In 1929, he served on the SS *Chickasaw*, owned by the Moore-McCormack Company and from that time onward, he served on Moore-McCormack ships. Townsend was assigned to the *Deer Lodge* in March 1942 and stayed with her until she sank on February 17, 1943. Retiring from the Merchant Marine, he lived in multiple locations, finally settling in Latta, South Carolina. He passed away on March 4, 1973, and is buried in Greenlawn Cemetery, Dillon, South Carolina.

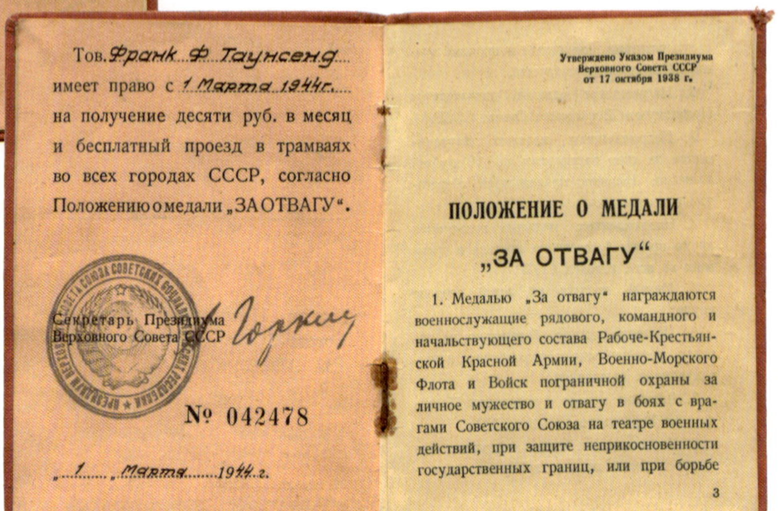

The Soviet medal book to Frank Townsend. Note, as a 1944 award, the number of the medal is recorded on the second page of the book. *Courtesy of the Townsend family.*

The Merchant Marine Distinguished Service Medal awarded to Frank Townsend. Along with his Soviet Medal "For Valor," it was later turned into a neck bolo for everyday wear. *Courtesy of the Townsend family.*

U. S. MARITIME COMMISSION

This is to certify that

Mr. Frank F. Townsend

HAS BEEN AWARDED THE

MERCHANT MARINE

DISTINGUISHED SERVICE MEDAL

16—40219-1

E S Land

CHAIRMAN

The identification card certifying Frank Townsend as one of the 148 recipients of the Merchant Marine Distinguished Service Medal in the Second World War. *Courtesy of the Townsend family.*

Medal "For Valor" number 525483 awarded to Frank Townsend. Like his Merchant Marine Distinguished Service Medal, it also has been converted to a neck bolo for daily wear. *Courtesy of the Townsend family.*

Thomas E. Delate, *Order of the Red Star*

Ensign Thomas Delate, Armed Guard commander on the SS *Deer Lodge*. *National Personnel Records Center.*

The *Deer Lodge's* eleven-man Armed Guard detachment was under the command of Thomas Edward Delate. Born in New Jersey on December 12, 1917, he graduated from Villanova University in 1939 prior to joining the Navy on July 15, 1940. Following his commissioning, he was assigned to the USS *Memphis* (CL-13), making her voyage from Alaska to the East Coast. Reporting for Armed Guard duty in December 1941, he was first assigned to the SS *West Jaffrey* along with Gifford Starnes. The *Jaffrey* ran aground on February 8, 1942, along the Canadian coastline. Sending off the crew and the Armed Guard gunners, he remained behind with the master and ship's officers. Rocking in the heavy weather, the ship began to crack and break apart on the rocks. The decision was made to abandon ship and she subsequently sank. This allowed the Navy to offer him the opportunity to head back to sea on the *Deer Lodge*, where he earned a Commendation from the Secretary of the Navy for his valor on the Murmansk Run. After four months of training at the Submarine Chaser Training School in Miami, Florida, he reported as part of the pre-commissioning crew for the USS *Jacob Jones* (DE-130). Commissioning her at the end of April 1943, he served on board as the gunnery officer, and later, the executive officer, for multiple escort voyages across the Atlantic before detaching in March 1944. He next reported to the USS *General J.H. McRae* (AP-149) in August as navigator and served in the Pacific theater until February 1945.

Released from active duty in September, he returned to school, earning his Juris Doctorate degree from Fordham University and his master's degree in taxation from New York University. He was admitted to the New York Bar in 1949. In 1955, following a two-year active duty recall where he commanded a Naval Reserve facility in Bridgeport, Connecticut, he began working for the Exxon Corporation. Here, he traveled with the exploration group to Egypt, the Middle East, and India, exploring tax requirements for the licenses relating to oil exportation. He retired in 1982 and opened his general practice law firm, practicing law in New York and Pennsylvania.

Robert B. Ricks, *Order of the Patriotic War, First Class*

Secretary of the Navy Frank Knox awards the Silver Star Medal to Robert Ricks on November 16, 1942. *Official US Navy photo via the National Archives.*

On the SS *Expositor*, a twenty-three year-old Hog Island freighter, Robert Ricks commanded the Armed Guard detachment with Joseph O'Savage as his senior enlisted Sailor on board. Robert Byron Ricks was born on August 14, 1918, and joined the Navy on September 14, 1940. Activated for officer training on March 17, 1941, he was commissioned on June 12. Following a brief tour at sea on the USS *Heywood* (APA-6) transporting troops to Iceland, he was assigned to Armed Guard duty and served on the *Expositor*, where he earned the Silver Star for valor on the Murmansk Run. Serving on surface ships, by the end of the war he was a Lieutenant Commander serving on the USS *Scania* (AKA-40), decommissioning her in 1947. He then served on the USS *Chipola* (AO-63) in the Pacific, followed by a year at the General Line School at Monterey, California. Next, he was assigned to the USS *Tingey* (DD-539) as she was recommissioned and headed to the east coast of Korea. Here, she supplied gunfire support for United Nations ground troops, and conducted anti-mining and shore bombardment patrols off Hungnam. Subsequently, he was stationed on the USS *Sierra* (AD-18), a destroyer tender out of Norfolk, Virginia, until being transferred to become part of the Navy Unit on the Dugway Proving Ground in Utah until 1956.

In 1957, he reported to the USS *Cowell* (DD-547) as executive officer, detaching two years later to report to Fleet Training Group, Western Pacific. He remained in the Far East until July 1962, when he took command of the USS *Mathews* (AKA-96), delivering eighteen hundred Marines in Thailand during the Communist insurgency in Laos, and then transiting to the Caribbean to take part in the Cuban Missile Crisis before returning to the Pacific. His final tours were at the Headquarters of the Eighth Naval District in New Orleans, and finally at the San Francisco Naval Shipyard. He retired on June 30, 1965, and went to work for the state of California as a hospital administrator for the next ten years. Retired again, he spent his time boating at Oceanside Harbor, California, to include purchasing and operating Ricks Yacht Sales for six years. Robert Ricks passed away on November 9, 2009.

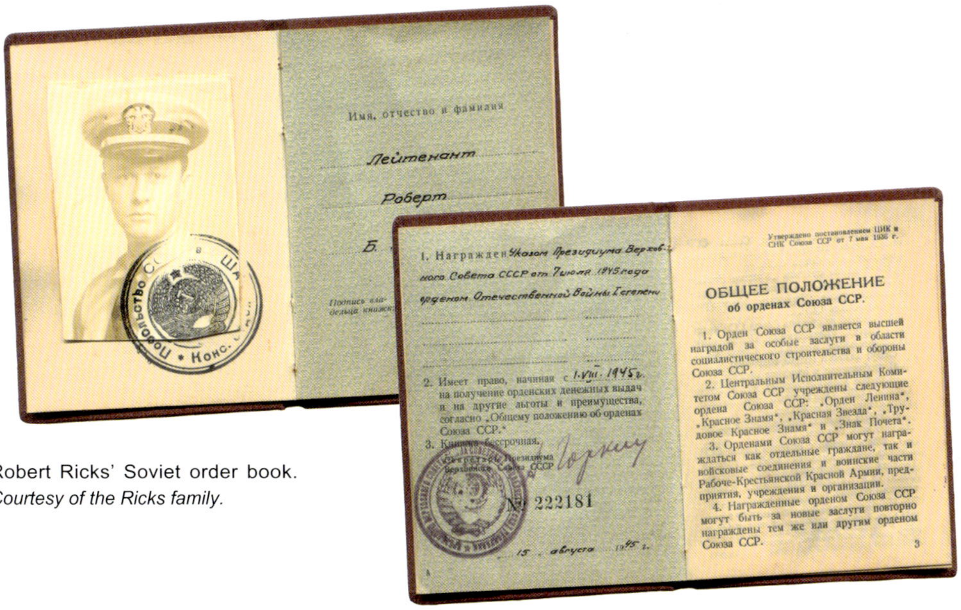

Robert Ricks' Soviet order book.
Courtesy of the Ricks family.

Order of the Patriotic War, First Class, number 247511.
Courtesy of the Ricks family.

The reverse of Robert Ricks' U.S. medal bar.
Courtesy of the Ricks family.

The bar-mounted U.S. medals of Robert Ricks including the Silver Star, Navy Commendation Medal, American Defense with "A" device and the American Campaign Medal. *Courtesy of the Ricks family.*

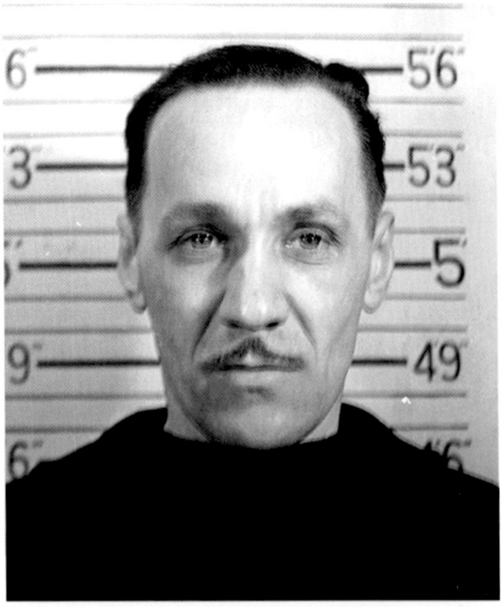

Joseph O'Savage. *National Personnel Records Center.*

Joseph O'Savage, *Medal "For Valor"*

Coxswain Joseph O'Savage, who earned his Silver Star in the same action as Robert Ricks, was born on February 1, 1904, in Coal Center, Pennsylvania. With an eighth-grade education, he lied about his age and first enlisted in the Navy in January 1920, just before his sixteenth birthday, and served on the submarine USS *S-5*, where he advanced to Gunner's Mate, second class. Leaving the Navy after two years, he reenlisted in February 1923 and served in Panama, first spending two years as a coxswain on a captain's gig and later, two years on the USS *Camden* (AS-6), a submarine tender in Norfolk, Virginia. He was discharged in December 1927 and worked as a building maintenance man for the Arcadia Ballroom on Broadway in New York City, making $22 a week. With the war starting, he enlisted in the Navy on January 13, 1942, and reported directly to the Armed Guard Center in Brooklyn. His first four months were spent on four different ships, finally arriving on the *Expositor* for her trip to Murmansk. He continued service with the Armed Guard throughout the war, and was discharged as a Boatswain's Mate, first class, on September 21, 1945. He returned to Rockaway, New Jersey, and passed away on August 22, 1983.

Jules H. Bloch, Armed Guard commander on the SS *Francis Scott Key. National Personnel Records Center.*

Jules H. Bloch, Jr., *Order of the Patriotic War, Second Class*

Ensign Jules Bloch and Gunner's Mate, second class, Renald Blake led the Armed Guard detachment on the SS *Francis Scott Key*. Jules Hirsch Bloch Jr. was born on July 15, 1915, in Oklahoma. He attended the New Mexico Military Institute in Roswell, New Mexico, before returning to Oklahoma City to graduate from Classen High School. Following his graduation from the University of Oklahoma and Oklahoma City University with a bachelor's degree in Business Administration in 1936, he was employed by the First National Bank in Oklahoma City. With war on the horizon, he enlisted in the Navy on July 19, 1940, and was discharged to accept his commission on December 15. Serving on the USS *Chicago* (CA-29) out of Pearl Harbor, he was one of many junior officers reassigned following the United States entry into World War II. He received orders to the Armed Guard Center in Brooklyn, and was quickly assigned as the Armed Guard commander on the SS *Francis Scott Key*. Underway from Baltimore on January 29, 1942, they arrived in Gourock, Scotland, on March 16. The following day, a letter from the officers and crew of the *Key* was submitted to the British Naval Control at Gourock and the US Consul at Glasgow, attesting to the incompetence of the master of the *Key*. However, it is not known if he was removed from command. Ten days later, they departed for Iceland, and on March 31, the *Key* collided with a Royal Navy destroyer. After repairs in Reykjavik, the *Key* departed on April 8 with convoy PQ-14. However, due to heavy fog, she lost the convoy and was forced to return to Iceland and join convoy PQ-15. Finally, on April 26, the *Key* commenced her voyage to Murmansk. For his actions during the month of May 1942, like the rest of his crew, he was awarded a Letter of Commendation from the Secretary of the Navy.

Shortly thereafter, Bloch was sent to the Submarine Chaser Training Center in Miami, Florida, and was assigned to the newly-commissioned USS *Port Clinton* (PC-1242). Throughout the fall and into December she provided convoy escort, patrol and training services between Galveston, Key West, and Guantanamo Bay, Cuba. In December 1943, she transited the Panama Canal, arriving at Bora Bora on February 26, 1944. Her Pacific patrol and escort operations took her between Bora Bora, Tutuila, Samoa, Funafuti, Ellice Islands, and Milne Bay, New Guinea. Bloch was then transferred to the USS *Hennepin* (AK-187) where he served from July through November 1945. He was discharged on June 6, 1946, and returned to Oklahoma City. Remaining in the Reserves, he was finally discharged as a Lieutenant Commander on July 16, 1954. Following a short time in the investment securities business, he became a petroleum geologist, serving in that capacity until his retirement. Remaining active in community and civil affairs, Jules Bloch passed away on July 26, 1999, and is buried in the Memorial Park Cemetery in Oklahoma City.

Renald H. Blake, Jr., *Medal "For Valor"*

Renald H. Blake. *Courtesy of the Blake family.*

Born on March 7, 1921 in Jamaica, New York, Renald Henry "Hank" Blake enlisted in the Navy on May 17, 1939, and following his initial training in Newport, Rhode Island, he joined the crew of the USS *Lexington* (CV-2). In July 1940, he transferred to the USS *Neches* (AO-5), where he served until it departed for Pearl Harbor and later sunk in January 1942. First assigned to the Armed Guard Center, San Francisco, he was later transferred to Brooklyn, and assigned as the lead Gunner's Mate for the Armed Guard detachment on the SS *Francis Scott Key*. Returning from Murmansk, Blake, now a Gunner's Mate, second class, served on two subsequent merchant vessels as part of the Armed Guard detachment: SS *Tidepenn* and SS *Hannis Taylor*. In October 1943, he was next ordered to the minesweeper USS *Hawk* (YMS-362), where he served until his transfer to the USS *General Leroy Eltinge* (AP-154) in October 1944. His final assignment of the war was on the attack transport USS *Hansford* (APA-106), where he took part in the invasion of Iwo Jima in February 1945. Discharged as a Gunner's Mate, first class, on August 23, 1946, he returned to civilian life. With the pending war in Korea, he reenlisted in 1951, but was only allowed to return as a Gunner's Mate, third class. He served on the USS *Ashland* (LSD-1), the USS *Red River* (LSMR-522), and USS *Sierra* (AD-18). Ashore, he served in Washington, DC, the Naval Training Center, Bainbridge, Maryland, and at Great Lakes Naval Training Center. He retired as a Chief Fire Control Technician (FTC) on December 21, 1962. He retired again after a career as a Navy civilian with the Naval Sea Systems Command. Hank Blake passed away on September 4, 2006.

The Soviet medal book to Renald Blake. *Courtesy of the Blake family.*

Renald Blake's Medal "For Valor" number 2075708. *Courtesy of the Blake family.*

Renald Blake's US-awarded medal bar, including his Navy Commendation Medal, Navy Good Conduct, American Defense, American Campaign and Asiatic-Pacific Campaign. *Courtesy of the Blake family.*

Wilbur Collins, Armed Guard commander on the SS *Mormacrio. National Personnel Records Center.*

Wilbur P. Collins, *Order of the Patriotic War, First Class*

Serving as the Armed Guard commander on the *Mormacrio*, Wilbur Plummer Collins was born on April 1, 1919, in Ellisville, Mississippi. He graduated from Mississippi State University and reported to Northwestern University for midshipman training on October 24, 1940. Commissioned on March 14, 1941, he served on the USS *Colorado* (BB-45) in the Gunnery Division until transferring to Armed Guard duty. While on the *Mormacrio*, he earned his Silver Star for the destruction of one German aircraft on May 12, 1942. Returning to the United States, he remained with the Armed Guard, serving on the SS *Alcoa Pioneer*, until his transfer to Fire Control School in March 1943. Following schooling at the Submarine Chaser Training Center in Miami, he reported to the Naval Training Station, Norfolk, Virginia, in August 1943. Here, he served as the assistant officer in charge of the Pre-Commissioning Destroyer and Destroyer Escort Gunnery School. With the concentration of the war into the Pacific theater, he received orders to become a beachmaster on the staff of Commander, Amphibious Forces, Pacific in February 1945. He remained in the Pacific, taking part in the liberation of the Philippines, until returning to the United States in November 1945. Becoming a staff officer at the Officer Separation Center in Great Lakes, Illinois, he served there until attending the General Line School in July 1946. Following his graduation in May 1947, he served on the USS *Wyoming* (BB-32) until her decommissioning in August. He then transferred to the USS *Dayton* (CL-105), serving as the first lieutenant and later as the damage control officer. This was followed by an assignment on the Staff of Commander, Middle Eastern Forces on the island of Bahrain. Reporting in April 1949, he served there until his transfer in July 1950 to the Naval War College in Newport, Rhode Island. After his graduation, he served as the assistant operations officer on the staff of Commander in Chief, Atlantic Fleet, and later, as the training officer on the staff of Strategic Allied Commander, Atlantic. In July 1953, he reported to the office of the Chief of Naval Operations in Washington, DC, where he served as the current logistics plans officer for the Atlantic Fleet. Returning to the fleet in February 1956, he served as the gunnery officer on the USS *Valley Forge* (CVS-45) before transferring to the USS *Olmsted* (APA-188) as the executive officer in November 1957. Leaving the Olmstead after a year, he received orders to command the USS *Betelgeuse* (AK-260), where he remained until the summer of 1960. His final tour was on the staff of Commander, Fifth Naval District in Norfolk, Virginia. He retired from the navy as a commander on June 30, 1962 and settled in Miami, Florida. Attending the University of Miami, he earned a masters degree in education and taught school in Dade County for the following nine years. Changing careers, he then sold real estate before joining the county in the office of the real estate appraiser, where he worked for five years before retiring. Wilbur Collins passed away on June 15, 2014, and is buried in Arlington National Cemetery.

Marcel Desgalier, Jr., *Order of the Patriotic War, Second Class*

On board the *Zebulon B. Vance* was Ensign Marcel "Des" Desgalier, on his first, and only, voyage as an Armed Guard commander. He was born in Washington, DC on March 18, 1917, and following his graduation from George Washington University in March 1941, he reported to his first ship, the USS *Mississippi* (BB-41), where he received officer training before commissioning. In January 1942, Ensign Desgalier reported to the Armed Guard Center in Brooklyn and received orders to serve as the Armed Guard commander on the SS *Zebulon B. Vance*. For his voyage to Murmansk, he was awarded a Commendation from the Secretary of the Navy and the opportunity to attend flight school, where he reported in January 1943. He returned to the fleet as a patrol plane commander with VPB-54, flying reconnaissance and rescue patrols from Midway Island, Guadalcanal, Peleliu, and Leyte, among others, from February 1944 to February 1945, earning two Air Medals. In his later years, he recounted the horror of having to leave the survivors of the sinking ships on the Murmansk Run behind in order to avoid the possible torpedoing of his own ship. Conducting rescue missions in the Pacific was his way of being able to finally help others who may have considered themselves doomed to a similar fate.[7] Continuing his service after the war, he served as the executive officer of VP-MS-5 out of Bermuda, as navigator on the USS *Kula Gulf* (CVE-108), on the OPNAV staff at the Pentagon, as executive officer and commanding officer of Naval Technical Training Unit, Olathe, Kansas, Naval Aviation Technical Training Command in Memphis, Naval Air Station Barber's Point in Hawaii, and Fleet Air Service Squadron (FASRON) 103. He retired in 1968 as a Commander. Following retirement, he served as the president of the Paola, Kansas, Chamber of Commerce and worked in the housing administration at the University of Colorado from 1971 through his final retirement in 1981. Marcel Desgalier passed away on June 1, 2004, and is buried in Mountain View Memorial Park, Boulder, Colorado.

Marcel Desgalier as a Commander later in his career. *Courtesy of the Desgalier family.*

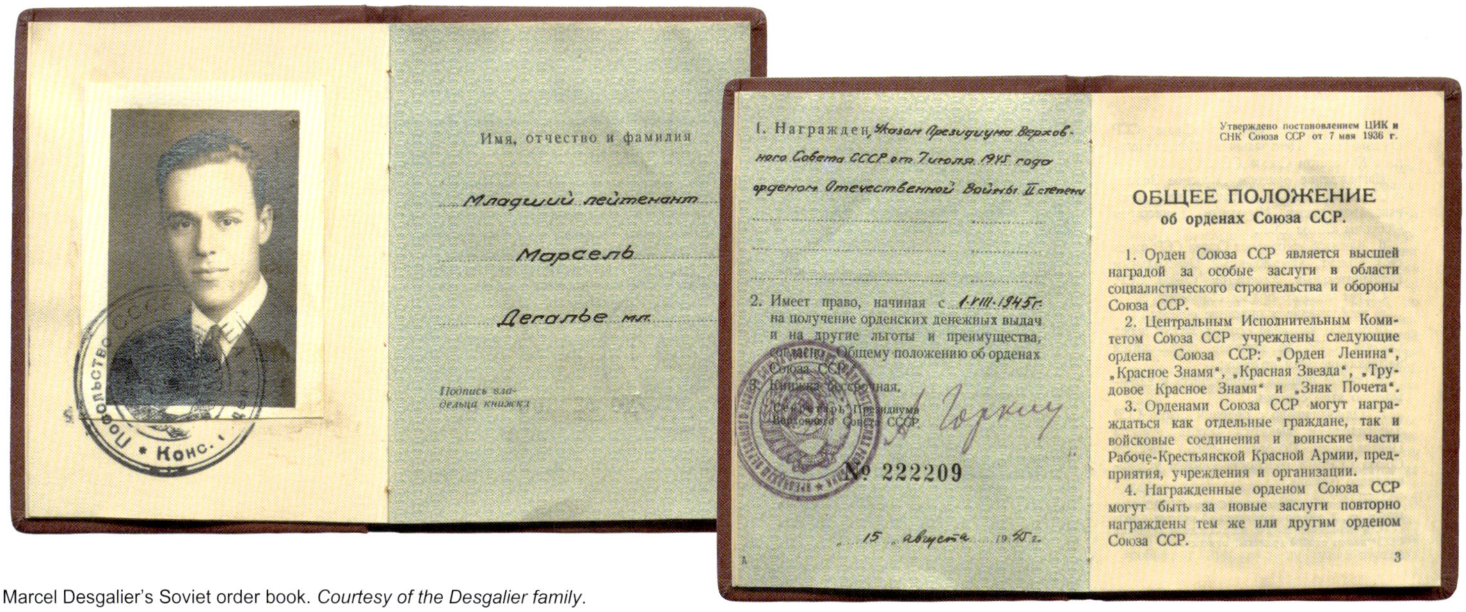

Имя, отчество и фамилия

Младший лейтенант

Марсель

Дегальe мл.

Подпись владельца книжки

1. Награжден Указом Президиума Верховного Совета СССР от 7 июля 1945 года орденом Отечественной Войны II степени

2. Имеет право, начиная с 1·VIII·1945 г. на получение орденских денежных выдач и на другие льготы и преимущества, согласно „Общему положению об орденах Союза ССР".

3. Книжка бессрочная.

Секретарь Президиума Верховного Совета СССР

№ 222209

15 августа 1945 г.

Утверждено постановлением ЦИК и СНК Союза ССР от 7 мая 1936 г.

ОБЩЕЕ ПОЛОЖЕНИЕ
об орденах Союза ССР.

1. Орден Союза ССР является высшей наградой за особые заслуги в области социалистического строительства и обороны Союза ССР.
2. Центральным Исполнительным Комитетом Союза ССР учреждены следующие ордена Союза ССР: „Орден Ленина", „Красное Знамя", „Красная Звезда", „Трудовое Красное Знамя" и „Знак Почета".
3. Орденами Союза ССР могут награждаться как отдельные граждане, так и войсковые соединения и воинские части Рабоче-Крестьянской Красной Армии, предприятия, учреждения и организации.
4. Награжденные орденом Союза ССР могут быть за новые заслуги повторно награждены тем же или другим орденом Союза ССР.

3

Marcel Desgalier's Soviet order book. *Courtesy of the Desgalier family.*

Order of the Patriotic War, Second Class, number 557275 awarded to Marcel Desgalier. *Courtesy of the Desgalier family.*

Chapter 9

Convoy PQ-16 Recipients

Convoy PQ-16 consisted of thirty-five ships, departing from Iceland on May 20, about the same time the PQ-15 ships were being battered in Murmansk. For the first few days, things were quiet, save for the spotting of numerous floating mines, increasing as time went by. It wasn't until May 25 that the German attacks began in earnest. The first indication of German presence was the spotting of a German Fw 200 *Condor* arriving over the convoy at 6:00 AM. This meant only one thing: the Germans knew where the convoy was. The attacks from the air, surface, and subsurface would commence at any time. Ships called away general quarters; gunners across the convoy manned their weapons. For the men of PQ-16, the stories they had heard about the Murmansk Run were about to become their reality.

The SS *Syros* in better days. She later sank in a massive explosion during convoy PQ-16.
Courtesy of the Holubowicz family.

The SS *City of Joliet* was not a new ship, having been in service since 1920, but this was her maiden voyage on the Murmansk Run. No one on board, merchant or Navy, had ever been under attack before. Her Armed Guard commander, John Grotenrath, had been in the Naval Reserves since 1932, but had been commissioned as an officer and on active duty for less than a year. For everyone on board, May 25 would be a day they would remember for the rest of their lives. With the Fw 200 circling overhead and relaying their position to the German bases in Norway, a Bv 138 flying boat appeared at 2:00 PM and began to shadow the convoy. An hour later, a U-boat was spotted, but submerged before it could be attacked. The weather was partially cloudy, and the sea was smooth. The *City of Joliet* was making eight knots and had all of her weapons manned: four gunners on her four-inch surface gun, one on the number one machine gun, and two stationed as lookouts.

At 6:30 PM, the convoy commodore hoisted the "Repel Aircraft" signal. All was quiet, but across the convoy, pulse rates were soaring and adrenaline was pumping. Ten minutes later, as predicted, eight He 111 torpedo planes, flying close to the water, and eighteen Ju 88 dive-bombers, estimated by Arthur Maddalena, *Michigan's* Armed Guard commander, to be flying at fifteen thousand feet, approached on the starboard side of the convoy in a line abreast, approximately seventy-five feet apart. Maddalena's senior enlisted Sailor, Gunner's Mate, third class George Norton, had trained his fellow Armed Guard gunners to hold their fire and wait until the aircraft were in range before shooting in order to conserve the small amount of ammunition allotted to the ship. They waited impatiently for the planes to come their direction. They did not have to wait long. Suddenly, the Ju 88s broke formation and the raced in at a fifty degree angle, releasing their bombs from approximately one thousand feet in the air. Excited shots were fired from the ships but they were of no use on the departing and ascending bombers. Next, the torpedo planes screamed over the surface of the water at an altitude of thirty feet, releasing their torpedoes simultaneously three thousand yards away from the convoy. Maneuvering to avoid the torpedoes, the convoy was spared. More damage was done during this attack to the nerves of the men on the ships than to the ships themselves. But this was only a harbinger of attacks to come.

At 8:00 PM, the Germans attacked again. The *City of Joliet* narrowly avoided a torpedo using a hard right rudder; as the ship swung to starboard, the torpedo missed her stern by a matter of feet. Her gunners fired at the passing bombers, putting as many bullets into them as they possibly could while they raced overhead. In the midst of the attack, the gun manned by Coxswain William Sharp jammed. Despite the bombs falling near the ship and the evasive maneuvers to avoid torpedoes, he calmly repaired his gun and with the utmost coolness, completed his repairs and began shooting at the enemy again, never missing a beat. At 8:40 PM, another flight of twelve bombers attacked, with bombs landing close to many ships in the convoy. Despite the estimated one hundred bombs and twenty torpedoes that were dropped during the attacks on May 25, no ships were seriously damaged or sunk. But the convoy had been christened in combat.

By 10:30 PM, most of the ships had secured from General Quarters, but it would not last long. Eighteen-year-old Deck Cadet Romuald Holubowicz of the Merchant Marine was on watch on the bridge of the SS *Syros*, who was starting to lag behind the convoy. At 1:15 AM on May 26, Holubowicz spotted the dirty white wake of a torpedo coming directly at the ship, fired by *U-703*. Without time to sound the ship's general alarm, the torpedo hit the engine room, killing everyone on watch instantly. A subsequent torpedo, fired only seconds after the first, found its way to the number two hatch, detonating the ship's cargo of ammunition. Norman Adams, the Armed Guard commander on the SS *American Robin*, *Syros'* partner in the last column of ships, saw something hit the *Syros*, and recalled that after, "... the slightest interval, there was a violent explosion in her number two hold containing TNT. There followed a burst of flame and in less than a minute, the entire ship had disappeared."[1] Witnesses from the *City of Joliet* saw:

> *... a column of blinding flame rise to nine thousand feet, followed by a deafening roar, a suffocating displacement of air, and a searing wind to the face. The pillar of fire grew larger, became a gigantic egg, and changed color. From a blinding white it turned carmine, scarlet, and yellow. Then nothing. Not even a wisp of smoke against a pale blue sky.*[2]

Miraculously, Holubowicz, carried down with the wreckage of the ship, was able to break free and swim to the surface. Along with twenty-seven of his fellow crewmembers out of the original crew of thirty-seven, he was eventually plucked from the frigid waters.

Save for one aerial attack that was quickly driven off, the rest of May 26 was relatively quiet. Since the arrival of the Fw 200 at 6:00 AM on May 25, most of the men had not slept. Many were still in the same clothes they had worn for several days. Merchant sailors and Navy Armed Guard crews lightly dozed near hatches and scuttles, ready to defend their ships at a moment's notice. Or, more importantly for some, abandon ship if they had been unlucky enough to cross the path of a lurking U-boat. The peace was broken just after midnight on May 27. At 12:55 AM, six torpedo planes rode the wavetops and launched an attack at the convoy. Two hours later, another attack came, this time from dive-bombers and lasting for thirty minutes. Remaining on station, the vigilant crews detected another attack at 10:30 AM, from high altitude bombers, well out of range of the ships' weapons. John Grotenrath calculated at this point that one hundred eight planes had attacked the convoy in over two hundred separate attacks.[3] But the day wasn't over.

At 11:24 AM, another enemy attack took place. Norman Adams, on *American Robin*, noted that this one was "a much more daring and systemized raid."[4] In order to avoid another burning merchant, the *Robin* fell behind the convoy and became a prime target. One plane dropped three bombs just off her starboard quarter. Three other planes dived at the ship, straddling her with seven bombs, shaking the ship and jarring pieces of pipe lagging and engine fittings loose. At 12:20 PM, the SS *Alamar*, a US-flagged merchant vessel with an Armed Guard detachment on board, suffered a direct bomb hit from a Ju 88, just aft of the ship's mainmast. Piercing the deck, it ruptured the main steam line and the steering engine. The master made the call to abandon ship as she began to burn uncontrollably. Twenty minutes later, a group of three Ju 88s took aim at the US-flagged SS *Mormacsul*, and one bomb found its mark, exploding underneath the hull, amidships on the port side. Her Armed Guard crew was covered in oil and water from the explosion, and the ship lost all steam and power. Afraid the cargo of TNT would detonate due to sparks and flame on board caused by the blast, the crew left the ship. She sank twenty-five minutes later. Shortly thereafter, the SS *Empire Lawrence*, a British merchant armed with a catapult for launching a Royal Air Force fighter as a means to defend the convoy, was likewise sunk by the attack of six Ju 88s.[5]

Across the convoy, the *Heffron*, a US-flagged merchant vessel who had gotten underway from the United States with only two Navy Radiomen, two light thirty-caliber machine guns, and no Armed Guard detachment, was surrounded by spouts of water from exploding German bombs. Twisting and torqueing, joints loosened and pipes burst throughout the ship. On one side of her deckhouse, Second Mate Clyde Andrews of the Merchant Marine manned one of the machine guns in an unprotected mount. On the other side, Third Mate Edward Fetherston likewise manned his gun, completely unprotected against the German onslaught. Although not their official duty on the ship, Fetherston and Andrews manned the guns around the clock, braving the horrible effects of weather, fatigue, and aerial strafing. Their helmets were creased and dented by shrapnel and debris, their life jackets torn and the filling exposed. They fired at the attackers with every ounce of energy they could muster as their lives, and the survival of the *Heffron*, depended on them. The attack was over by 1:00 PM, and three merchant ships, with their precious cargo, were on their way to the bottom of the sea. The day still wasn't over.

At 1:45 PM, the Germans returned with a high altitude raid. Another raid commenced at 3:20 PM. This time, one of the bombers got lucky, dropping a bomb so close to the *City of Joliet* that the concussion knocked the crew off their feet, the machine gun emplacement on the bridge was filled with water, and the ammunition storage locker on the other side of the bridge was broken off its mounts and lost overboard. The hull yielded to the blast, and within an hour, the ship had taken sixteen feet of Arctic water in number one hold. Fighting to keep the ship afloat, the crew was able to keep ahead of the flooding, even during the subsequent attacks at 6:30 PM and 8:00 PM. Two more British merchants, the *Empire Purcell* and the *Lowther Castle*, had sunk or were sinking due to hits received from these attacks. By this point, Grotenrath noted in his report: "All hands dead tired from almost continuous attacks."[6]

No one slept on any ship. All hands waited for the next attack, or, worse yet, the sight of a torpedo's wake. They did not wait long. At 3:57 AM on May 28, the Germans returned for a brief bombing raid. This was the last raid the *City of Joliet* would endure: by 5:40 AM, the ship was taking on more water than the pumps could discharge. She was going down by the head, had a starboard list, and steering was nearly impossible. A dense fog had rolled in and the convoy was temporarily safe from the threat of German aircraft. Captain Miller, her master, made the decision to abandon ship at 5:42 AM, and organized an expeditious, but careful, exodus from the groaning hull. Within ten minutes, the survivors were rescued by the HMS *St. Elsten* and the Free French corvette *Roselys*, where they spent the next two days before arriving in Murmansk.

The fog gave other ships the chance to take care of the solemn duties of tending to the wounded and repairing their vessels, without the immediate threat of aerial attack. At 9:50 AM, Howell Murray, the Armed Guard commander on the SS *Richard Henry Lee*, attended the burial at sea service for John Tomson, Ship's Carpenter. He had died the morning before from heart failure, undoubtedly brought on by the constant bombardment. Until 8:30 PM that night, the day was quiet. A one-plane aerial raid was conducted by an Fw 200, but it was met by a wave of anti-aircraft fire. Murray noted in his report that pieces of the plane's wing were later found on deck.[7] Friday, May 29 began with an attack by seven torpedo bombers at 4:30 AM, and by three more at 3:35 PM. No damage was done to the ships. At 8:00 PM, the surviving members of the convoy were split, one column to Murmansk, the other to Archangel. By mistake, the *Richard Henry Lee* was sent with the Archangel convoy and travelled with them for an hour. Realizing the mistake, they headed back across open water to rejoin the Murmansk convoy, only to be met by three He 111 bombers, dropping bombs within ten yards of the ship, deluging all onboard with geysers of water and knocking the crew off their feet.

The following day, the survivors of PQ-16 arrived in Murmansk, tired, cold, and battle hardened. The ships and their crews went on to discharge their cargo, braving enemy bombing raids while in port. The majority left for their return voyage to Iceland with convoy QP-13 on June 28. It was during this return convoy that one of the greatest tragedies of the Murmansk Run took place. On the night of July 5, nineteen of the returning ships which had been transiting through heavy weather and unable to obtain accurate navigational fixes for the previous forty-eight hours, neared the coast of Iceland. The next morning, they were scheduled to enter the relative peace of the harbor and enjoy a well-deserved rest. Leading the single column of convoy ships, the HMS *Niger* believed they sighted Iceland's North Cape and gave a course correction to the convoy. Unfortunately, instead of land, this turned out to be an iceberg. Not only had they committed a grave navigational error, they found themselves in the middle of an Allied minefield! Just as she discovered the mistake, the *Niger* struck a mine and within minutes, had "turned turtle" and was sinking. Her commanding officer and 148 of his crew went to the bottom of the sea that night.[8] Norman Adams' *American Robin* was the flagship of the convoy commodore, transiting astern of the *Niger*. Seeing the *Niger* explode and initially believing the convoy was under attack from submarines, Adams yelled for the ship to change course, but in doing so, she too struck a mine.[9] The *Heffron*, previously defended only by the sheer bravery of Fetherston and Andrews, likewise hit a mine and began rapidly sinking. In the ensuing attempt to escape the minefield, both the *Hybert*, carrying Deck Cadet Holubowicz and the other survivors of the *Syros*, and *Massmar*, struck mines and sunk. The SS *John Randolph*, with *City of Joliet* survivors John Grotenrath and William Sharp on board, was rocked by a mine detonation just forward of the bridge. While attempting to conduct damage control, she was hit by another mine four minutes later. Water began pouring in uncontrollably and the groaning hulk began to sink rapidly. The order was given to abandon ship. With her survivors away in lifeboats, they watched in horror as the ship broke apart; the stern and midships sinking rapidly, and the bow staying afloat, as if by some unearthly hand. What should have been a calm evening before a warm homecoming became one of the greatest preventable disasters of the Second World War, at the cost of hundreds of lives together with the loss of five ships and serious damage to three others.

John Grotenrath as a Lieutenant Commander at the end of the war. *Courtesy of the Grotenrath family.*

John G. Grotenrath, Jr., *Order of the Red Star*

The Armed Guard commander on the *City of Joliet* was John Gellert Grotenrath, Jr. Born in Ohio but raised in Grand Rapids, Michigan, he enlisted in the Naval Reserve on July 13, 1932. Along with his brother, they served under their father, the commanding officer of their Naval Reserve unit. An engineer by training, he worked as an assistant operating engineer at the water and light plant for the city of Grand Rapids. Commissioned in the Reserves on August 10, 1937, Grotenrath entered active duty on March 12, 1941, and served on the USS *Salamonie* (AO-26) before transferring to Armed Guard duty. As an Armed Guard commander, he took the *City of Joliet* on the Murmansk Run, but she never arrived in the USSR. In Murmansk and without a ship to defend, he was first assigned as officer in charge of a camp of merchant marine and US Navy survivors from other ships, ensuring discipline as well as arranging transport back to the west in departing convoys. After the final survivors found ships to return with, he was assigned to the staff of the Assistant Naval Attaché. While here, he assisted the Attaché wherever he could, to include evacuating the offices during bombing raids and ensuring the welfare of the ships and Armed Guard detachments on the waterfront. He received a commendation for assisting Soviet citizens during multiple bombing raids, rendering first aid and, in one case, personally saving the life of a senior Soviet officer whose arm was amputated by shrapnel during a violent bombing attack.

Following his return to the United States after the sinking of the *John Randolph* off the coast of Iceland, he was assigned to the Naval Reserve Midshipman School at Fort Schuyler, New York, where he remained for the duration of the war. Both his father and brother served in the Pacific theater. His brother, a Chief Pharmacist Mate, survived the torpedoing and devastating fires on the USS *Alchiba* (AKA-6), while his father, who spent most of the war as commanding officer of Naval Diesel Training Station at the University of Missouri, finished the war by spending eighteen months in New Guinea. Unfortunately, he succumbed to liver disease in theater before returning to the United States. With the death of his father, John Grotenrath requested a transfer to New Guinea as the war in the Pacific was winding down and his request was granted. He was discharged from active duty on March 29, 1946, but remained active in the Naval Reserves, retiring as a Commander on September 1, 1967. As a civilian, he returned to the city of Grand Rapids, continuing to work for them as an engineer at the city's water filtration plant until his retirement. John Grotenrath passed away in Grand Rapids, Michigan, on December 10, 1991. He is buried in Resurrection Cemetery, Wyoming, Michigan.

Order of the Red Star number 1553960 awarded to John Grotenrath. *Courtesy of the Grotenrath family.*

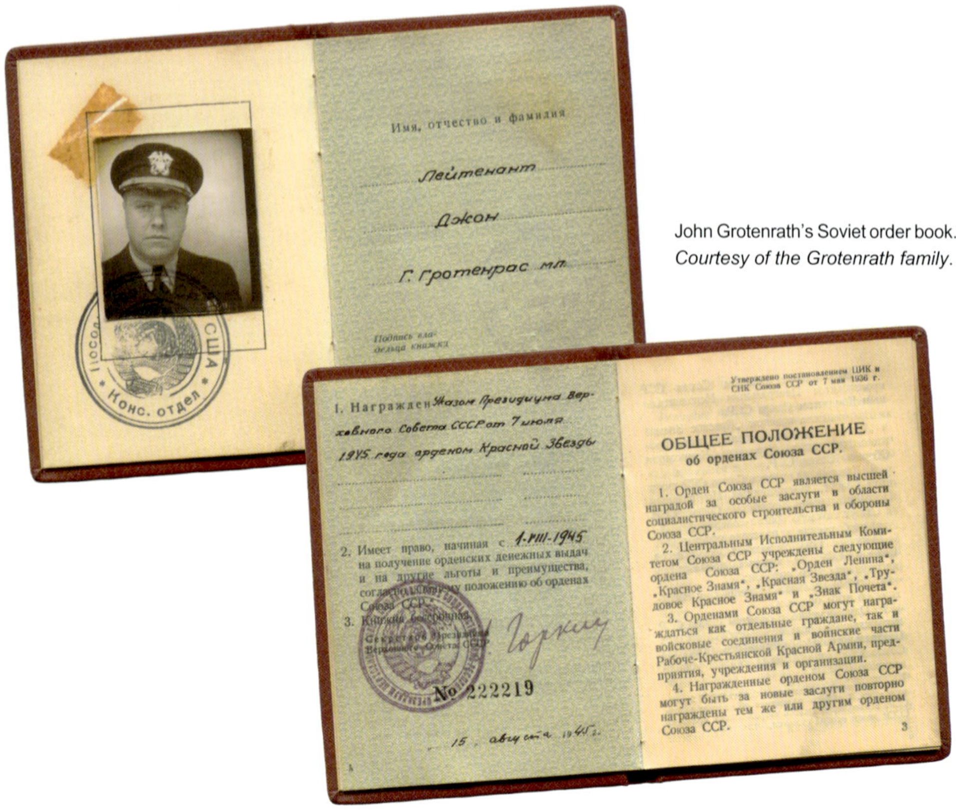

John Grotenrath's Soviet order book. *Courtesy of the Grotenrath family.*

William S. Sharp, *Medal "For Military Merit"*

William Sharp from his merchant mariner's license. *Courtesy of the Sharp family.*

William Stewart Sharp was also on the *City of Joliet*. Born on February 27, 1917, in Baltimore, Maryland, he left high school after finishing ninth grade to work as a blacksmith helper. After five years, he went to work for E.I. DuPont in Wilmington, Delaware, and Martinsville, Virginia, serving in their machine shop as a rigger for three years before entering the Navy on January 5, 1942. By Valentine's Day, he started Armed Guard training in Little Creek, Virginia, and on March 1, reported for duty on the *City of Joliet*. Following his return to the United States, he continued to serve with the Armed Guard through the duration of the war. He earned his second Commendation for service on the SS *Asa Gray*, where he fought a fire caused by ruptured gasoline containers on the deck during the night of August 8, 1944. He was discharged from active duty on November 4, 1945, and joined the Merchant Marine shortly thereafter. He went on to serve on civilian ships at sea, both in the Atlantic and the Pacific, for the next thirty-six years. Retiring in 1981, he moved to Florida and passed away on March 17, 1989.

Medal "For Military Merit" number 2551020 awarded to William Sharp. *Courtesy of the Sharp family.*

Norman O.W. Adams, Jr. *Order of the Patriotic War, Second Class*

Norman O.W. Adams, Jr., later in life as a college professor. *Courtesy of Mankato State University.*

On the *American Robin*, Norman Owens Whitehurst Adams Jr. served as the Armed Guard commander. Adams was born in Virginia on September 19, 1919, and on January 16, 1942, was selected to attend Naval Reserve Midshipman Training School in Chicago, Illinois, following his graduation from Randolph-Macon College. Four months later, he received orders to report to the Armed Guard School, and shortly thereafter, found himself as the Armed Guard commander on the *American Robin*, with a cargo hold full of TNT and bound for Murmansk. For gallantry exhibited on the voyage, Adams received a Commendation from the Secretary of the Navy. Returning to the United States, Adams made one more trip as an Armed Guard commander, this time commanding the Armed Guard detachment on the transport USAT *Borinquen* between New York and Oran, Algeria. Following his discharge from the Navy on February 26, 1946, Adams attended Northwestern University and later the University of Wisconsin, earning his PhD in English in 1955. Joining the faculty of Mankato State University in 1958, he retired in 1981 after spending twenty-three years teaching his specialty: nineteenth-century English literature. He passed away after a short illness in Hendersonville, North Carolina, on May 22, 1992.

Clyde N. Andrews, *Order of the Red Star*

Clyde Andrews and Ed Fetherston of the *Heffron* became two of the 148 recipients of the Merchant Marine Distinguished Service Medal for their valor exhibited during the attacks and later sinking of their ship. Clyde Neil Andrews was born on August 13, 1910, and went to sea at the age of nineteen. Learning to be a quartermaster, he sailed throughout the Orient on the SS *President Taft* and *President McKinley*. With the start of the Second World War, he shifted to the Atlantic. Making his run to the USSR on the *Heffron* in 1942, he returned to the United States along with Holubowicz and Fetherston on the USAT *Siboney*. His next voyage was on the SS *Wendell Phillips* as the chief officer, followed by serving as the master of the SS *John Fitch*. With Fetherston as his chief officer, he took the *Fitch* to Archangel as part of convoy JW-54B. Returning to New York in March 1944, he subsequently served as the master of the *Robert McBurney* and as the war ended, the *George G. Meade*. His postwar career took him onto the SS *F.S. Bell*, serving as the second mate on voyages from 1948 to 1954. Retiring from the merchant navy, he settled in North Bend, Oregon, and passed away on February 10, 1987.

Edward Fetherston during the presentation of his Merchant Marine Distinguished Service Medal. *War Shipping Administration Photo.*

Edward M. Fetherston, *Order of the Red Star*

Edward Michael Fetherston was born in New York City on April 2, 1916, and went to sea following his graduation from Columbia High School in Maplewood, New Jersey, in 1935. Serving as the third mate on *Heffron*, he returned to the United States and made his subsequent trip to the USSR with Clyde Andrews on the *John Fitch*. Upon his return, he was appointed a Lieutenant in the United States Merchant Marine, and was later promoted to Lieutenant Commander in 1946. Following a career at sea, he retired to New York City and passed away on November 29, 2000.

Arthur D. Maddalena, *Order of the Patriotic War, First Class*

On board the *Michigan*, Arthur Maddalena served as the Armed Guard commander and Gunner's Mate, third class George Norton, served as the senior enlisted Sailor for the gun crews. Arthur Daniel Maddalena, Jr. was born on May 9, 1918, in Cambridge, Massachusetts. He graduated from St. Ann's High School in Gloucester, Massachusetts, and attended Notre Dame, where he graduated magna cum laude from their pre-med program. Joining the Navy on July 8, 1940, he began his reserve midshipman training at the Naval Academy in January 1941. Commissioned on May 15, 1941, he was assigned to the repair ship USS *Vulcan* (AR-5) as a communication watch officer. Transferring from the *Vulcan* in December 1941, he arrived on board the SS *Michigan* as the Armed Guard commander in March 1942. He survived the Murmansk Run and brought the *Michigan* back to the United States, earning the Silver Star in the process. From October 1942 to February 1943, he served as the Armed Guard commander on the USAT *Mexico*, making two Atlantic crossings to North Africa, prior to taking command of the USS *PC-820*, a submarine chaser in the Pacific theater, conducting patrols and convoy escort duties up the West Coast of the United States. On April 12, 1945, he took command of his second ship, *PCE-900*, the USS *Groton II*. He took her to Hawaii and spent the remainder of the war conducting plane guard duties out of Pearl Harbor, Territory of Hawaii. Maddalena's final tour was on the USS *Kishawaukee* (AOG-9), a fleet oiler also based out of Pearl. He was placed on the medically retired list as of June 1, 1947, with the rank of Lieutenant Commander.

Arthur D. Maddalena, Armed Guard commander on the SS *Michigan*. *US Navy photo.*

Returning to Massachusetts and entering the real estate business, he founded Arthur D. Maddalena Real Estate of Centerville, Massachusetts, in 1947. Active in community and professional organizations, he served as the president of the New England Chapter of the American Institute of Real Estate Appraisers, president and director of the Cape Cod Board of Realtors, director of the Sandwich Cooperative Bank, a trustee of Our Lady of Victory Church, and long-serving board member for the Kennedy Memorial Youth Hockey League. He passed away on October 6, 1981, in Hyannis, Massachusetts.

Romuald P. Holubowicz, *Medal "For Military Merit"*

The lucky survivor of two sinkings during PQ-16, Romuald Paul "Ray" Holubowicz was born on January 24, 1924, in Cudahy, Wisconsin. He graduated from St. Bonaventure High School in 1941 and attended one semester at Marquette University before transferring to the Merchant Marine Academy at Kings Point. He graduated in 1942 as a member of their first class and served as a Cadet Midshipman (Deck) at sea, taking part on the Murmansk Run. Commissioned as an Ensign in the United States Maritime Service on August 2, 1943, he was quickly promoted to Lieutenant Commander, USMS, on June 20, 1946. During the war, he earned his Chief Mate license, and following service on the *Syros* and *Hybert*, he made yet another trip to Murmansk on the *J.L.M. Curry* as part of convoy JW-51A. The *Curry* also proved to be an unlucky ship: she foundered during heavy seas, splitting her hull, and on March 8, 1943, sunk 187 miles northeast of Scotland.[10]

Following his return to the United States, he served on the SS *Tyson Lykes* and SS *Marine Wolf* through the end of the war. Because his service in the Merchant Marine did not classify as wartime military service, he joined the Navy after the war as a commissioned officer, serving with naval intelligence. Returning to school upon discharge, he graduated from Georgetown University, was selected as one of the first Fulbright Scholars, and attended the London School of Economics. Returning to the United States, he served as the director for port development in the New York Port Authority, followed by a stint as the assistant to the president of Grace Lines. Subsequently, he became a vice president of Ingalls Shipbuilding and helped found the International Cargo Handling Coordination Association (ICHCA), where he became known as the "Father of Shipping Containerization" for his determined advocacy of the worldwide use of uniform steel containers to transport goods.[11] In 1971, he became the president of the McGregor Hatch Cover Corporation in London, and two years later, founded his own company, Marine Ventures Limited, which is still in business today. Ray Holubowicz passed away in London on January 1, 2013.

Medal "For Military Merit" 598609 awarded to Romuald Holubowicz. *Courtesy of Romuald Paul Holubowicz II.*

Romuald Holubowicz's Soviet medal book. As a 1944 award, note the addition of the medal's serial number on the right side page. *Courtesy of Romuald Paul Holubowicz II.*

Merchant Marine ribbons worn by Romuald Holubowicz. From left to right, they are the Combat Bar with three silver stars (indicating subsequent awards), the Atlantic War Zone Medal, and the Mediterranean and Middle East War Zone Medal. *Courtesy of Romuald Paul Holubowicz II.*

George J. Norton receives his Silver Star in a ceremony at the Armed Guard Center. *Official US Navy photo via the National Archives.*

George J. Norton, *Order of the Red Star*

Arthur Maddalena's gun captain was George James Norton. Born on March 15, 1923, in Carbondale, Illinois, he joined the Navy on September 24, 1940. Following his entry training at Great Lakes, Illinois, he was assigned to the USS *Maryland* (BB-46), reporting on November 15, 1940. He served on *Maryland* until transferred on August 26, 1941, to the USS *Fox* (DD-234) a World War I-vintage four-stack destroyer in the Pacific Fleet. With the commencement of hostilities, he was ordered to Armed Guard duty, and in early 1942 reported to the Armed Guard Center in Brooklyn. After serving on the *Michigan*, where he earned the Silver Star, he continued service with the Armed Guard in both the Atlantic and Pacific theaters through the duration of the war. During the postwar years, he served on the USS *Blue Ridge* (AGC-2), the USS *Romulus* (ARL-12), USS *Jason* (ARH-1), USS *Maurice J. Manuel* (DE-351), USS *Small* (DDR-838), and USS *PCE-874*. He additionally served at Naval Air Station, Pensacola, Florida, and at Submarine Group Three in San Diego. He retired on April 1, 1960, as a Chief Gunner's Mate. Settling in Long Beach, California, he passed away of a sudden heart attack on April 28, 1971. George Norton is buried in Sailors Cemetery, Long Beach, California.

Howell S. Murray, *Order of the Patriotic War, Second Class*

Howell Murray, taken while serving on the USS *Turner* (DD-648). *Courtesy of the Murray and Herman Families.*

Because of the spirited anti-aircraft defense from the Armed Guard crew serving under Howell Murray on the *Richard Henry Lee*, they were able to survive the five-mile gauntlet of determined German attackers between the split convoys on the last day before entering Murmansk. Howell Sherer Murray was born in Chicago, Illinois, on April 29, 1918. He attended Amherst University, and belonged to the Chi Psi fraternity. With war imminent, he enlisted in the Navy on July 8, 1941, and on September 18 reported for duty at the Naval Reserve Midshipman School, Abbott Hall, Northwestern University. He was commissioned on January 16, 1942, and reported to the Armed Guard School on March 9. After less than a month at the command, he was detailed as the Armed Guard commander on the SS *Richard Henry Lee*, reporting on March 26. For his valor on the Murmansk Run, he was awarded a Commendation from the Secretary of the Navy. Returning to the United States on July 31, Murray remained attached to the Armed Guard Center until ordered to the USS *Turner* (DD-648), still in construction, on February 17, 1943. *Turner* was commissioned on April 15, and following a shakedown period, embarked on convoy escort duty on June 22. She was on her second trans-Atlantic patrol when they detected a surfaced German U-boat on the night of October 23. After a brief exchange of fire, the U-boat submerged, depriving the *Turner* credit for an official sinking. Following completion of convoy duty, *Turner* anchored off Ambrose Light in New York at 3:30 AM on Monday, January 3, 1944, to await follow-on orders. While the engineers were making preparations for a 7:00 AM underway time, the officers, including Murray, gathered in the wardroom for breakfast. At 6:18 AM, a series of what could be best described as volcanic explosions, caused by an unknown ignition source, ripped apart the *Turner*, killing everyone in the wardroom instantly. Fire swept through the ship and despite the best efforts of the crew to save the ship from sinking, a subsequent massive explosion at 7:50 AM caused her to roll to starboard and sink.[12] She was last seen slipping beneath the waves at 8:27 AM, taking fifteen officers and 102 crewmen, including Howell Murray, with her.[13]

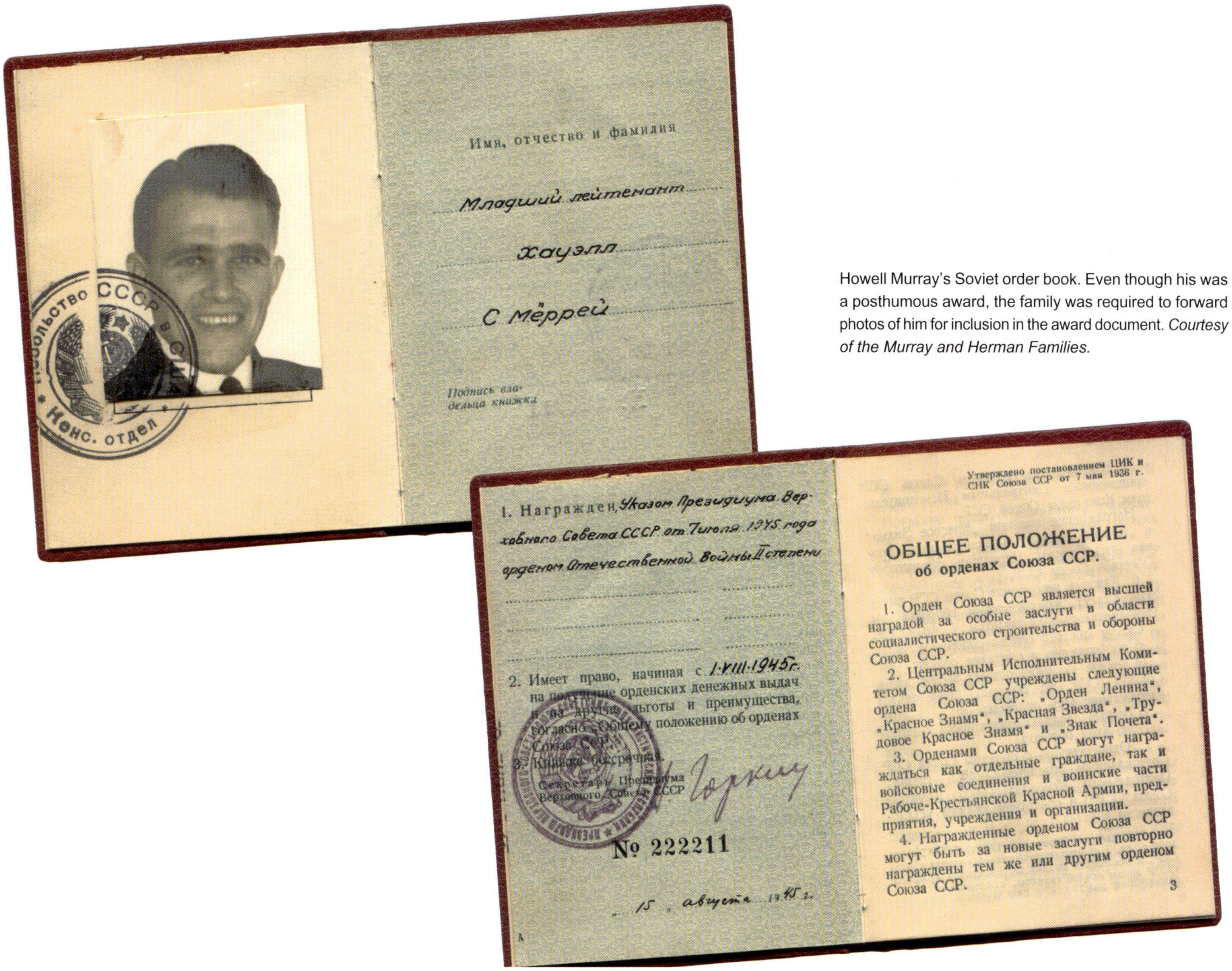

Howell Murray's Soviet order book. Even though his was a posthumous award, the family was required to forward photos of him for inclusion in the award document. *Courtesy of the Murray and Herman Families.*

Order of the Patriotic War, Second Class, number 557282 awarded posthumously to Howell Murray. *Courtesy of the Murray and Herman Families.*

CHAPTER 10

CONVOY PQ-17 RECIPIENTS

This photo was taken of Admiral Giffen the day the battle force headed out to sea from Hvalfjord to cover PQ-17, June 29, 1942.

The day before the ships of PQ-16 began their return transit to Iceland, the next convoy, PQ-17, departed Iceland. Many of the ships, like the SS *El Capitan*, had been anchored in Iceland for a period of a month or more, waiting for their opportunity to make the eastbound convoy to Murmansk. The crews of the merchant vessels and their Armed Guard detachments weren't the only ones anticipating the departure of convoy PQ-17: the Germans had prepared, and were about to launch, Operation *Rösselsprung*. In German, this was translated as the "Knight's Move," in the fashion of chess. This operation had been in the works for some time, but the operational orders were issued verbally by Admiral Carls, commanding *Gruppe Nord*, on June 4.[1] The goal of the plan was to destroy an entire convoy and prevent any ships from entering port in the USSR.The Germans wanted to make the cost of Murmansk-bound convoys so heavy the Allies would be forced to stop them and allow the USSR to accept defeat by force and starvation. In theory, the plan was tactically brilliant: the convoys and their escorts would be destroyed by round-the-clock attacks from aircraft, surface ships, and submarines, all operating within close proximity to their bases to readily refuel and re-arm in order to attack multiple times. The extreme amount of weaponry available to the Germans in Norway, coupled with the slow movement of the large, nearly defenseless, merchant vessels made this plan almost foolproof.[2]

In a paraphrase of the words of the great tactician, Helmuth von Moltke: "No plan stays intact after the first contact with the enemy."[3] In short, despite the devastation that eventually took place amongst the participants in the convoy, they were spared total destruction due to over-cautiousness on the part of both Hitler and several of his subordinate commanders, as well as damage to some of the participating German units during the course of the operation. Conversely, on the side of the Allies, mistakes were made that almost ensured a complete German victory had Hitler allowed his commanders freedom to execute the plan as they saw fit. While a complete historical discourse on the operation of the convoy is beyond the scope of this book and has filled multiple books since the end of the Second World War, the central decision to scatter the convoy on July 5 because of an unfounded fear by the British Admiralty of the location of the *Kriegsmarine* surface fleet has gone down in history as one of the most unsound decisions made during the course of the war.[4]

The convoy initially left Iceland on June 27, traveling in standard formation, just as convoy PQ-16 had done before them. Thirty-five merchant vessels, along with nearly fifty Royal Navy, United States Navy, Free French, and Polish warships in the escort and covering force, to include the battleships HMS *Duke of York*, USS *Washington* (with Rear Admiral Giffen on board), the cruisers HMS *London*, HMS *Norfolk*, HMS *Cumberland*, HMS *Nigeria*, HMS *Manchester*, USS *Wichita* (Harry Hill and Howard Orem), USS *Tuscaloosa* (Norman Gillette), the aircraft carrier HMS *Victorious*, and finally, Destroyer Squadron Eight, under the command of Don Moon on the USS *Wainwright*. The first few days of the convoy were relatively uneventful, save for the grounding of the SS *Richard Bland*, which had to return to Iceland for repair. (The *Bland* eventually went to the USSR with convoy JW-51A and is discussed in further detail later.)[5] It wasn't until noon on July 1 that the convoy was first spotted by a long-range German Bv 138 reconnaissance plane about two hundred miles west of Bear Island. The following day, an aerial attack was made, but was driven off before damage could be done to the convoy. July 3 was likewise comparatively quiet, as the convoy continued its way eastward to the USSR.

For the Americans in the convoy, July 4 was Independence Day, but the fireworks they saw that day weren't what any of them expected. It was a typical day in the Arctic summer: overcast, foggy, and three degrees below zero. The men of the convoy had been on alert due to the inevitable arrival of the German attack, and it came at 3:15 AM on July 4. Twenty-six He 111 torpedo bombers flew through the fog and, hugging the wavetops at an altitude of no more than thirty feet, let loose their weapons on the convoy. One of the aircraft was directly on the starboard beam of the SS *Christopher Newport* in the first row of convoy ships, and she dropped her two torpedoes directly at the *Newport*. The HMS *Palomares*, an anti-aircraft ship, was in the line of fire from the *Newport's* Armed Guard, so they could only watch as the bomber banked steeply and flew back into the fog. The maneuverable warship *Palomares* turned to remain clear of the torpedoes. Unfortunately, the ungainly *Newport* could not. Dodging one torpedo, the crew could only watch as the second torpedo raced toward them. With the torpedo clearly visible, skimming on the surface of the water, the order was given for the Armed Guard to fire at it in a desperate attempt to stop it from reaching the ship. Seamen Hugh Wright and Paul Webb, the latter being the youngest member of *Newport's* Armed Guard at age seventeen, opened fire with their thirty and fifty caliber machine guns in an attempt to destroy the torpedo before it struck the ship. On Wright's mount, the merchant seamen loaders ran for their lives, stricken with panic, while Wright, seeing his bullets ineffectively bounce off the water, cursed loudly at his "BB gun."[6] Nearby, Webb's machine gun jammed, and he desperately attempted to reload it as the torpedo came ever closer. Despite the confusion, Wright and Webb stayed at their mounts, firing as fast as they possibly could, even though it was readily apparent that they could not destroy the torpedo with their weapons.[7]

Despite the heroics of the two sailors, the torpedo impacted the *Newport*, tearing a hole in the engine room and flooding the adjoining spaces. Wright was blown off his gun mount and landed two decks below; miraculously only spraining his ankle and being knocked unconscious. Webb was blown into the air and was slammed "like a rag doll"[8] into the ship's stack, twenty feet away. Seeing the wounded ship, German aircraft approached within one thousand yards, bombing and strafing while the crew of the *Newport* attempted to abandon ship. The Armed Guard remained at their posts, firing at the aircraft until the Germans turned and headed back in the direction of Spitsbergen. With the exception of three men killed in the engine room, the crew of the *Newport* were rescued by the rescue vessel SS *Zamalek*. The slowly flooding but not sinking *Newport* was finished off by a British submarine and escort vessel to prevent her from falling into German hands.

The Soviet merchant *Azerbaijan* is torpedoed on July 4, 1942. *National Archives*.

Paul Neil Webb, brave gunner of the SS *Christopher Newport*. *National Personnel Records Center*.

Paul N. Webb, *Order of the Red Star*

Paul Neil Webb was born on December 3, 1924, in the town of Millville, West Virginia. With the start of the war, he rushed to enlist. With the written permission from his father, his age was waived, and he entered active duty on January 14, 1942, a month after his seventeenth birthday. Reporting directly to Armed Guard duty on April 3, he was assigned to the Armed Guard detachment under the command of Ensign Peter M. Coy on the *Christopher Newport*. After the sinking of the *Newport* on July 4, he was commended for his effective manning of the gun mounts on the *Zamalek* until they were put ashore in the USSR. Returning to the United States, he went on to serve as a member of the Armed Guard on the SS *Zoella Lykes* in the Pacific theater. Following his Armed Guard duty, Webb reported to the USS *ATA-215*, a fleet tug out of Norfolk, and subsequently, to CUB 8, an airfield construction unit based at Camp Allen, Virginia. His final tour during the war was as a newly minted Gunner's Mate, first class attached to USS *PC-1212*, an anti-submarine patrol craft operating in the Atlantic. Discharged on January 2, 1946, he returned to West Virginia. He subsequently moved to Southern California and passed away in Monrovia, on May 30, 1997.

Hugh P. Wright, *Order of the Patriotic War, Second Class*

Hugh Patrick Wright enlisted in the Navy on January 5, 1942, from Little Rock, Arkansas. Like most of his contemporaries, he reported directly for Armed Guard duty following his initial training. His ship, like Paul Webb, was the *Christopher Newport*, and he would also spend his time with PQ-17 on board the *Zamalek,* taking charge of a quad fifty-caliber mount when its Royal Navy gunner was wounded during an aerial raid. For his valor exhibited during PQ-17, both on the *Newport* and the *Zamalek*, he was awarded the Silver Star and the Purple Heart. Returning to the United States, he served on the SS *Colorado* as a member of her Armed Guard detachment. Leaving Armed Guard duty in 1943, he served on the USS *Varuna* (AGP-5) a motor torpedo boat tender in the South Pacific. He was discharged from active duty on January 21, 1946, but was recalled for the Korean War and served from April 1951 to August 1952 on the USS *Bairoko* (CVE-115), conducting raids off the Korean peninsula. He was finally discharged from the Navy at the rank of Gunner's Mate, first class in September 1954.

The *Christopher Newport* was not the only ship sunk on Independence Day: a similar fate later befell the SS *Navarino* and the SS *William Hooper*. Following the early morning attack, the convoy was offered a brief respite by the sudden appearance of a heavy fog for part of the morning. By 2:00 PM, the convoy entered a field of heavy ice. Robert Henderson, one of the communications personnel on the SS *Washington*, commented: "... they were one of the most beautiful sights I've ever seen. They were in all sorts of fantastic shapes, and were composed of bright blue and milky white stripes."[9] At 6:30 PM, the convoy was again attacked. On the *Washington*, according to Henderson, "everybody cut loose."[10] Ensign Charles Ulrich and Seaman Emmett Anderson fired the fifty caliber machine guns, with Albert Friday and Arthur McDonald as the loaders. George Cooper fired the twin Marlin machine gun with William Harkins as his loader. Finally, the last two members of her Armed Guard, Paul Lessard and James Guyton manned the Lewis guns. They watched as a German aircraft flew across the entire convoy, no more than seventy-five feet in altitude, and made a direct hit on the *Navarino*, a British merchant near the center of the convoy. Continuing directly at the *Washington,* Cooper and Anderson let go with a continued stream of tracers and bullets, causing the aircraft to burst into flames and spin into the ocean.

German aircraft, flying at masthead height, attack the convoy on July 4, 1942. *National Archives.*

With the *Navarino* in flames, a group of three He 115 bombers directed their attention on the farthest aft ship in the convoy, the *Hooper*, carrying 268 tons of TNT, her decks covered with brand-new tanks and trucks. The first aircraft veered away without launching his weapon while he was four thousand yards away. The second dropped his torpedo and flew over the bow of the *Hooper*. His port engine was hit by anti-aircraft fire and he was seen traveling away from the convoy with his engine on fire. The third aircraft made a run directly at the ship and dropped his torpedo five hundred yards away. Concentrating their fire on the airplane, the Armed Guard almost failed to notice the wake of the torpedo coming directly at the ship. Brian Welch, *Hooper's* Armed Guard commander, yelled "Torpedo, starboard!" and braced himself against the stack.[11] He could feel the concussion of the torpedo slamming into the hull and then ... nothing. Several seconds went by that seemed like hours before the delayed-timing fuse on the torpedo detonated with such force that it blew one of the ship's boilers out through the stack. The *Hooper* began to settle immediately at the stern as she filled with water. There was no power in the ship and the passageways were filled with smoke from internal fires. Welch attempted to reach the three bags of Office of Naval Intelligence mail, bound for the Naval Attaché in Archangel, in his stateroom, but by the time he arrived, the paint on the bulkheads was bubbling and burning from the intense heat of the fire, and he could not enter the room. Abandoning ship at 7:00 PM, they were picked up by the HMS *Rathlin* at 7:30 PM and continued the voyage with the convoy. The HMS *Leda* shelled the burning remains of the *Newport* and sunk her shortly thereafter.

Brian Welch, Armed Guard commander on the *Hooper*. *US Navy photo.*

Brian G. Welch, *Order of the Patriotic War, First Class*

Brian Grant Welch, the Armed Guard commander on the *Hooper*, was born in New York, on March 29, 1920. Commissioned via the Naval Reserve Midshipman School at the Naval Academy in July 1941, he was assigned to the USS *Dunlap* (DD-384) in Pearl Harbor, Hawaii, as the assistant gunnery and torpedo officer. Following the start of the war, he was reassigned to Armed Guard duty and was trained at the Destroyer Base in San Diego. Upon completion, he was then assigned to the Armed Guard Center in New Orleans in March 1942, and then to the *Hooper*. Having survived the sinking of the ship and after spending several months in the USSR awaiting transport, he found his way back to the United States. Volunteering for submarine duty, he was assigned to the USS *O-4* as the assistant communications officer before attending the Submarine School in New London, Connecticut. His first assignment was to the USS *Bang* (SS-385) as the communication officer on the pre-commissioning crew in October 1943. He participated in the *Bang's* first and second war patrols in the Pacific. In August 1944, he was reassigned to the USS *Skate* (SS-305) for her sixth war patrol as the gunnery and torpedo officer. Prior to *Skate's* seventh war patrol, Welch was again transferred, this time to the USS *Halibut* (SS-232), taking the damaged submarine from Pearl Harbor to New London, where she became a school ship at the Submarine School. On *Halibut*, he served as the torpedo officer, assistant executive officer, and navigator. Finally, after attending Prospective Commanding Officer School in New London in May 1945, he was assigned to the USS *Dolphin* (SS-169), then serving as a school ship, as the executive officer. Released from active duty on December 11, 1945, he returned to New York. However, he was recalled by the Navy and on October 9, 1946, returned to active duty, working at the Submarine School as head of the Reserve Training Department until October 1947 when he was once again released from active duty. Finally returning to the civilian world, he remained in New York until his passing on December 3, 1989.

With the conclusion of the last attack, the Independence Day fireworks were over. However, the most historically significant event of that day had yet to occur. At 9:11 PM, the British Admiralty gave the order to have the cruiser and battleship covering force withdraw to the west at high speed. This was followed by another message ordering the convoy to scatter at 9:23 PM. To Rear Admiral Hamilton, the Royal Navy commander, the receipt of these messages could only mean one thing: the *Kriegsmarine* heavy surface fleet had set sail from Norway, enroute to challenge the convoy and their escorts in the open sea.[12] Although well-endowed with considerable firepower, the Allied Navy component was nearing the limits of their safe fuel range and further, lacked control of the skies. Conversely, the German naval units, comparable in firepower, and not burdened by thirty-two slow merchant vessels, would be close to their bases, and most importantly, their fuel and logistical supplies. To compound matters, the *Luftwaffe* held clear control of the skies. The chances of significant Allied naval losses were far too much for the British Admiralty to accept, and the call was made to withdraw the heavy naval support from the convoy. In an attempt to confound the potential success of the German surface force, the scatter order intended to spread the convoy as widely as possible to avoid total annihilation by the *Kriegsmarine* surface ships.

What was not known at the time, and has since been subject to a considerable amount of scrutiny under the cold light of history and hindsight was this: the Germans did not have their entire battle fleet underway.[14] More importantly, during the course of operations against PQ-17, the entire German surface fleet never arrived in the open sea. Consequently, instead of making difficult targets for German surface ships to find as the scatter order was intended to do, the order resulted in a multitude of large, slow targets perfectly vulnerable to aerial and subsurface attacks. Thus, on the evening of Independence Day 1942, one of the greatest Allied maritime blunders of the Second World War took place.

As the order was given, Charles Ulrich, the Armed Guard commander on the SS *Washington*, watched as the remaining escort vessels (several trawlers and two anti-aircraft ships) "ran away from us at superior speed."[15] The *Washington*, along with the British merchant SS *Bolton Castle* and the Dutch SS *Paulus Potter*, decided to head as far north as possible before angling back eastward, and then dropping down from Novaya Zemlya, a rocky and nearly uninhabited archipelago forming the eastern border of the Barents Sea. Unfortunately, in the early morning fog on July 5, they discovered that they were blocked in to the north by heavy ice flows. Adjusting course to the south, Ulrich reminded the ship's master of the three hundred fifty tons of TNT on the port side of the ship, and the decision was made to shield that side as much as possible from torpedo attack by remaining close to the ice. Things were relatively quiet for the little convoy, and they bunched together to provide covering fire for the eventual aerial attacks. At 3:00 PM, the first attack came; a Ju 88 swooped down, straight out of the sun, and strafed the deck of the *Washington*. Bullets landed "within inches" of where Ulrich was manning his gun.[16] Forty-five minutes later, nine Ju 88s attacked out of the clouds. The *Bolton Castle* was hit and began to immediately sink. Within another minute, the *Paulus Potter* received a fatal blow. Counting twenty-one bombs dropped around them, the *Washington* miraculously avoided any direct hits. However, the massive concussion from the explosions close to the ship knocked out their steering gear and opened up their hull plating. The ship began taking on water rapidly and the master gave the order to abandon ship. The merchant crew, shoving their way past the Armed Guard Sailors, launched the lifeboats so quickly that Ulrich was almost left on the ship when he went to retrieve his first aid kit.[17] They watched the German aircraft riddle the ship with incendiary bullets and then depart above the clouds. Remembering the TNT onboard, they "rowed like hell"[18] to get as far away from the ship as possible before it exploded.

At 10:30 PM, the SS *Olopana*, a US-flagged merchant, came across the forty-six survivors of the *Washington* and offered to take them on board. Deciding they had a better chance in the lifeboats than on another large ship, the crew of the *Washington* declined the invitation, opting instead to take their chances in the open sea. This was a wise choice: two days later, on July 7, the *Olopana* was torpedoed and sunk by *U-255*, taking all but twelve of her crew with her.[19] Watching the doomed *Olopana* transit over the horizon, the crew of the *Washington* decided to make their way to Novaya Zemlya, three hundred eighty miles away. In his journal, Robert Henderson wrote:

> *This was a nightmare period that seems more like a dream than a reality when one looks back on it. But there was plenty of grim reality out there in that vast ocean in a little open boat. We rowed and rowed, and sailed and sailed. There were twenty-three men in each boat and we were so crowded that you couldn't stretch out at any time. Fellows started getting frozen feet a couple of days out. The deck engineer was the first to discover that his were black, and others examined theirs, and several found them to be badly swollen. Harkins' are the worst of the naval crew. We had less than a blanket apiece, and at times we nearly froze. We had snow, rain, sunshine at midnight, and almost every kind of weather conditions imaginable. At the same time fellows were suffering with frost bitten feet, their faces were peeling from sunburn.*[20]

Finally, after six excruciating days in the cramped lifeboats, they spotted the coast of Novaya Zemlya at 2:12 AM on July 11. Landing on the rocky coast, the steward quickly built a fire and made a soup from four cans of tomatoes, four cans of corn, and one can of sardines: all the food remaining for forty-six survivors. It wasn't until two days later, after they were joined by the survivors of the *Paulus Potter* and on the verge of starvation, that they discovered a large population of Common Eider, or as they called them: "Arctic ducks."[21] Assisted by Ulrich's service sidearm, they were able to capture nearly three hundred for the burgeoning colony of approximately 110 survivors from the two ships. Ultimately, the group survived, and by plane and ship, made their way to Archangel, arriving on July 24. They remained in Archangel, along with hundreds of other survivors, until they could make it back to the United States with a return convoy.

While the *Washington* was sinking, Arthur McDonald remembered his camera and collected these incredible images. The first two photos show the survivors crammed on lifeboats where they lived for six days. The next photos show the survivors cooking Eider on Novaya Zemlya. *Courtesy of the McDonald family*.

Additional photos from Arthur McDonald and the crew of the SS *Washington*. These poignant scenes are those of survival against the elements and against the enemy. The lower right image is believed to be of Captain Julius Richter, the master of the *Washington*. *Courtesy of the McDonald family*.

Charles M. Ulrich, *Order of the Patriotic War, First Class*

Leading the men of the Armed Guard on the *Washington* was Charles Monroe Ulrich. Born in Pittman, New Jersey, on September 30, 1919, he entered active duty on June 23, 1941, and was commissioned on January 15, 1942. Reporting immediately for Armed Guard duty following his initial training, he took the *Washington* overseas, and then led his men to survival following the sinking of the ship and stranding on Novaya Zemlya. For his bravery and leadership, Ulrich was awarded the Silver Star. Upon his return to the United States, he became an Armed Guard gunnery instructor in Little Creek, Virginia, until reassigned to the Submarine Chaser Training Command (SCTC) in Miami, Florida, in preparation for anti-submarine warfare duty. In February 1944, he reported to the pre-commissioning crew of the USS *Samuel B. Roberts* (DE-413). Ulrich served as the gunnery officer on the *Roberts* until his transfer on October 11, 1944, just two weeks short of their epic stand during the Battle of Samar, where the crew of the *Roberts* heroically charged multiple Japanese cruisers at point-blank range, eventually sinking with massive casualties. Ulrich spent the remainder of the war attached to the staff of Commander Destroyers, Pacific Fleet, and separated from active duty on December 17, 1945.

Returning to the civilian world, Ulrich remained in the Naval Reserves, eventually retiring as a Commander in April 1959. As a civilian, he graduated from Temple University and went on to gain progressive prominence within the milk industry, eventually becoming the public relations director for the Milk Industry Foundation in Washington, DC Charles Ulrich passed away in Sewell, New Jersey, on July 31, 1985.

Emmett D. Anderson. *Courtesy of the Anderson family.*

Emmett D. Anderson, Jr., *Medal of Nakhimov*

Emmett Dotson Anderson Jr. was born in Rock Hill, South Carolina, on July 14, 1920, and enlisted in the Navy on December 16, 1941. Reporting to Armed Guard duty, he remained with the Armed Guard following his service on the *Washington* and later served on the oiler SS *Five Forks* from December 1943 to July 1944. Detached from the Armed Guard, he reported to the USS *Swan* (YMS-470) a motor minesweeper commissioned in October. On *Swan*, Anderson conducted minesweeping duties on the East Coast of the United States until the ship was transferred to the Pacific in March 1945. Operating in the vicinity of New Caledonia and the New Hebrides until the end of the war, they participated in occupation duty in Japan, sweeping the ports and harbors in Okinawa and on the Japanese mainland. He was discharged from active duty on November 27, 1946, as a Gunner's Mate, third class, and returned to Rock Hill. With the outbreak of the Korean War, he was recalled to active duty on August 2, 1950. In August 1951, he was assigned to the USS *Boxer* (CV-21), where he was again discharged on November 27, 1954, as a Boatswain's Mate (Guns), second class. Returning back to his home in Rock Hill, he worked as a security guard in the textile mills until his retirement. Emmett Anderson passed away on April 20, 1988, and is buried in Neely's Creek Associate Reformed Church Cemetery in Rock Hill.

George C. Cooper. *National Archives.*

George C. Cooper, *Medal of Nakhimov*

Seaman second class George Clifford Cooper, the gunner on *Washington's* twin Marlin machine gun, was born on March 7, 1924, in Staley, North Carolina. Leaving school after ninth grade to work in the upholstery business, he enlisted in the Navy on November 4, 1941, not yet eighteen years old. Reporting directly to Armed Guard duty, he was attached to the Armed Guard detachment on the SS *Santa Elisa*. However, he missed the sailing of the *Elisa* (she was later torpedoed in the Mediterranean) and was reassigned to the SS *Washington*. Returning from the USSR, he went on to serve on the SS *Sonney Point*, *Brooksfield*, *Gilbert M. Hitchcock*, *Benjamin Bonneville*, and the *Fort Casper*. His voyages took him though both the Atlantic and Pacific theaters. Finally he served on the USS *Floyds Bay* (AVP-40) prior to his discharge on June 29, 1947. He returned to civilian life, living in Ramseur, North Carolina. On the night of January 14, 1950, he lost control of his car and hit a bridge piling next to a rural highway, killing him instantly. George Cooper is buried in Staley Cemetery, Staley, North Carolina.

Albert D. Friday, *Medal of Nakhimov*

Albert Friday's Soviet medal book. *Courtesy of the* Friday *family*.

Born in Holdridge, Nebraska, on June 23, 1923, Albert DeLloyd Friday was raised in West Point, Mississippi. Upon graduation from high school, he enlisted in the Navy on January 6, 1942, in New Orleans, Louisiana. Sent directly to Armed Guard training, he reported to the Armed Guard Center in Brooklyn on February 27. Spending ten months on the *Washington* and later recovering from exposure in a hospital in Archangel, he finally returned to the United States, becoming an instructor in gunnery at the Armed Guard School. He then applied for and was accepted into the Navy's V-12 commissioning program at Duke University in July 1943. However, this did not last long. Leaving school after four months, he returned to the fleet and served in temporary duty billets in Miami while awaiting the approval of his request to change his rate from Gunner's Mate to Musician. This was finally approved and he reported to the US Navy School of Music in Washington, DC, where he perfected his already-present skill in playing the clarinet and saxophone. He reported to the USS *Tennessee* (BB-43) as a member of the ship's band in November 1944 and served on *Tennessee* through all of her engagements in the Pacific theater. He then transferred to the band on the USS *Vixen* (PG-53) and USS *Pocono* (AGC-16) the flagships of Commander in Chief, Atlantic Fleet. Friday was released from active duty on June 22, 1946.

Friday entered the civilian world as a musician and attended a music college for three of four years but did not complete the course. During this time, Friday toured with a singing quartet as well as played his clarinet with another small group of performers. Unfortunately, his big break in the music industry never materialized, and he went to work for Battelle Memorial Institute in Columbus, Ohio, where he became an expert electron microscopist. Recruited by the Lockheed-Georgia Company (known today as Lockheed-Martin), he began their electron microscopy laboratory in Marietta, Georgia, in 1964. After working for Lockheed for nearly twenty-five years, he retired and moved back to his hometown of West Point, Mississippi, to care for his ancestral home (now the Friday House Museum). Following his attempted murder during a robbery in the late 1980s, he moved to Texas to be with his family, spending his last days there. Albert Friday passed away in Magnolia, Texas, on May 26, 2003.

Edge numbering of Albert Friday's Medal of Nakhimov. *Courtesy of the Friday family.*

Albert Friday with his band following the end of the war. He is second from left holding the clarinet. *Courtesy of the Friday family.*

Medal of Nakhimov number 5600 awarded to Albert Friday. *Courtesy of the Friday family.*

William Harkins. *Courtesy of the Harkins family.*

William T. Harkins, *Medal of Nakhimov*

Albert Friday's best friend on the *Washington* was William Thomas Harkins. Born in Gloucester, New Jersey, on May 15, 1924, he was one of the youngest in the Armed Guard detachment on the ship. Enlisting in the Navy after completing St. Mary's High School on January 28, 1942, he reported to the Armed Guard Center on March 12. His experience surviving the *Washington* was the most dramatic. Henderson recorded in his diary that Harkins' legs were the worst off of any of the Navy crew on the ship.[22] When on land, he could barely walk, and had to be carried by his fellow Sailors while they were in search of other survivors. It did not help that he was one of the biggest members of the Armed Guard detachment at six-foot one-inch and weighing 165 pounds. Once they were able to locate help, Harkins was flown to Archangel, where he was immediately sent to a Soviet hospital. The decision was made upon admittance to amputate both of his legs due to the extent of his frostbite. However, the quick intervention of a British doctor saved his legs: they placed him in rubber gaiters, like those used for wading in a river, and poured in hot wax. This allowed the heat to penetrate his frozen flesh and, over time, restore circulation in his legs. He survived his stay in the Soviet hospital and was able to walk when he returned to the United States. Joining the MS *Idaho* as a member of her Armed Guard, he spent the next two years conducting convoy transits across the Atlantic, in the Indian Ocean, and the Pacific. In November 1944, he left Armed Guard duty, and now as a Boatswain's Mate, second class, he served as a Master at Arms at Naval Station Norfolk, Virginia. He was discharged from active duty on October 5, 1945, and moved to Chicago, where he had a career with TRI-R Vending, eventually retiring as a sales manager. He moved to Florida in 2004 and passed away on April 19, 2010. William Harkins is buried in Florida National Cemetery in Bushnell, Florida.

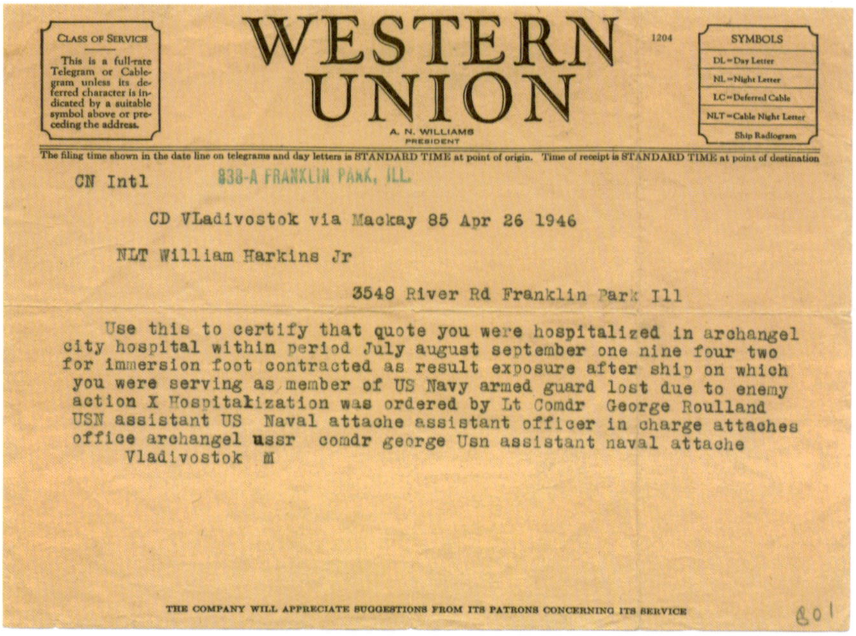

CLASS OF SERVICE
This is a full-rate Telegram or Cablegram unless its deferred character is indicated by a suitable symbol above or preceding the address.

WESTERN UNION

A. N. WILLIAMS
PRESIDENT

1204

SYMBOLS
DL=Day Letter
NL=Night Letter
LC=Deferred Cable
NLT=Cable Night Letter
Ship Radiogram

The filing time shown in the date line on telegrams and day letters is STANDARD TIME at point of origin. Time of receipt is STANDARD TIME at point of destination

CN Intl 838-A FRANKLIN PARK, ILL.

CD VLadivostok via Mackay 85 Apr 26 1946

NLT William Harkins Jr

3548 River Rd Franklin Park Ill

Use this to certify that quote you were hospitalized in archangel city hospital within period July august september one nine four two for immersion foot contracted as result exposure after ship on which you were serving as member of US Navy armed guard lost due to enemy action X Hospitalization was ordered by Lt Comdr George Roulland USN assistant US Naval attache assistant officer in charge attaches office archangel ussr comdr george Usn assistant naval attache Vladivostok M

THE COMPANY WILL APPRECIATE SUGGESTIONS FROM ITS PATRONS CONCERNING ITS SERVICE

801

A telegram from George Roullard, former Assistant Naval Attaché in Archangel (now in Vladivostok) certifying the frostbite and hospitalization received by Harkins while in Archangel. *Courtesy of the Harkins family.*

Paul O. Lessard, *Medal of Nakhimov*

The youngest in the Armed Guard detachment, Paul Oscar Lessard did not live to see the end of the war. Born August 24, 1924, in Woonsocket, Rhode Island, he entered active duty on January 29, 1942, from Fall River, Massachusetts. Following basic training in Newport, Rhode Island, he reported to the Armed Guard Center on March 12. Assigned to the *Washington* as his first ship, he returned to the United States after his hospitalization in the USSR and remained with the Armed Guard until March 1943. He was subsequently assigned as part of the crew on the USS *Haste* (PG-92), taking it over from the Royal Canadian Navy on April 6, and taking part in anti-submarine cruises on the East Coast. After two months, he attended a series of schools to prepare him for duty on the USS *AFD-25*, a floating drydock. Transferring in September 1944, he reported to USS *YMS-341*, a motor minesweeper in the South Pacific. In March 1945, he reported to the USS *Terror* (CM-5), a fleet minelayer and the flagship of Rear Admiral Alexander Sharp in the battles off Iwo Jima and Okinawa. Just before 4:00 AM on May 1, 1945, as the *Terror* lay at anchor in Kerama Retto, she was hit by a kamikaze. The resulting explosion extracted a terrible toll on the ship: forty-one dead, seven missing, and 123 wounded. Paul Lessard was one of the dead. He is buried in the National Memorial Cemetery of the Pacific, Honolulu, Hawaii.

Arthur McDonald, Jr., *Medal of Nakhimov*

Arthur McDonald. *Courtesy of the McDonald family.*

Like Lessard, Arthur McDonald Jr. entered service from Fall River, Massachusetts. He was born on June 27, 1923, and spent most of his early years living in Newport, Rhode Island. Enlisting in the Navy on January 13, 1942, after briefly working as a survey rodman for the United States Coast and Geodetic Survey, he reported to the Armed Guard Center in March 1942. Following his service on the *Washington*, he performed duties maintaining the weapons and drilling guns at the Armed Guard Center in Brooklyn and at the Armed Guard School in Little Creek, Virginia, until April 1944. He then reported to the advanced Gunner's Mate school in Dearborn, Michigan, in preparation for duty to the USS *Springfield* (CL-66). Reporting just after the launching of the *Springfield* in March 1944, McDonald remained on board through her commissioning and campaigns in the Pacific theater, to include bombardments on Okinawa and on the Japanese home islands. Transferred to the USS *South Dakota* (BB-57) on October 1, 1945, he returned to the United States and was discharged on January 19, 1946.

Returning to civilian life, McDonald became a firefighter on the Newport Naval Base and remained in that job until his retirement in 1977. Active in town government, he served as chairman of the Tiverton Housing Authority, a member of the Zoning Board, Water Commission, and served as the town moderator for Tiverton for ten years. Arthur McDonald passed away on December 21, 1990, and is buried in Our Lady of Fatima Cemetery, Little Compton, Rhode Island.

Edge numbering on Arthur McDonald's Medal of Nakhimov. *Courtesy of Arthur McDonald Jr.*

Reverse of Arthur McDonald's Navy Good Conduct Medal. *Courtesy of Arthur McDonald Jr.*

Medal of Nakhimov 5590 awarded to Arthur McDonald. *Courtesy of Arthur McDonald Jr.*

Arthur McDonald's US-awarded medals, including the Navy Commendation, Purple Heart, and Navy Good Conduct Medal. *Courtesy of Arthur McDonald Jr.*

James N. Guyton, *Medal of Nakhimov*

The *Washington's* Armed Guard detachment included two communications personnel: James Guyton and Robert Henderson. James Nathan Guyton Jr., was born in Council, North Carolina, on June 11, 1924. He enlisted in the Navy on August 5, 1941, and attended recruit and signalman training at Naval Training Station Norfolk, Virginia, until December 5. Reporting for communication school in Norton Heights, Connecticut, in February 1942, he remained there for a month before reporting to the Armed Guard Center in Brooklyn. Following his transit on the *Washington*, he returned to the United States and remained with the Armed Guard through the rest of the war. Guyton was discharged as a Signalman, first class on October 4, 1945. As a civilian, he worked for the Victor Welding Equipment Company as a salesman and retired after twenty-two years of service. James Guyton passed away on November 3, 2000, and is buried in Memory Hill Gardens, Tuscaloosa, Alabama.

Robert G. Henderson, *Medal of Nakhimov*

Robert Glenn Henderson was born in Frankfort, Indiana, on October 28, 1922. He joined the Navy on August 6, 1941 and following his recruit training at Great Lakes, attended radio communication school in Indianapolis. Reporting to the Armed Guard Center, he served on the *Washington* and returned to the United States in September 1942. In November, he was transferred to the Armed Guard Center at Treasure Island, California, and served on ships in the Pacific theater until June 1944. Returning to the Armed Guard Center in Brooklyn, now as a Radioman, first class, he remained there until his transfer to the newly commissioned USS *Renate* (AKA-36), an *Artemis*-class attack cargo ship. Taking *Renate* to the Pacific theater, he remained on board until his discharge from the Navy on October 1, 1945.

Following his return to civilian life, he enrolled at Indiana University under the GI Bill and graduated in May 1949 with a bachelor's degree in psychology. Moving to Southern California, he worked in the human resources and personnel field until 1970. He then switched careers and became the sales manager of the Rose Hills Memorial Park in Whittier, California, until his retirement in 1988. Residing in Pasadena, California, until 1991, he moved to Atascadero, and later, Nevada City, California, where he passed away on August 22, 2005. Robert Henderson is buried in Rose Hills Memorial Park, Whittier, California.

The *Washington* wasn't the only ship to take the final plunge to the bottom of the sea that fateful day. Two of the other thirteen ships that sank on July 5 were the SS *Daniel Morgan* and the SS *Peter Kerr*. Following the order to scatter the convoy, the *Peter Kerr*, loaded with 6,600 tons of trucks, steel, food, and four bomber aircraft on deck, ventured out along with one other vessel, the British merchant SS *Earlston*. The *Earlston* turned to the north and was sunk shortly thereafter by a U-boat. The *Peter Kerr*, travelling independently, observed perfect weather for the Arctic: smooth seas, no wind, and almost unrestricted visibility.[23] She was maintaining constant lookouts, zigzagging, and altering speed to do everything possible to avoid becoming the next U-boat victim. Her Armed Guard detachment, under the command of Coxswain Norbert Schwartz, slept and ate at their stations. However, at 6:00 PM, seven torpedo planes and four dive-bombers came out of the southeast, aimed directly at her. The torpedo planes came first: flying no higher than fifty feet above the water, they simultaneously dropped thirteen torpedoes at the freighter. Fighting valiantly, the *Kerr* miraculously maneuvered to avoid all of them. Next came the dive-bombers, dropping a total of thirty-six bombs on or near the ship. Evasively maneuvering just as they had for the torpedoes, the ship avoided all but three. These three bombs were incendiaries: alone, they would not have sunk the ship, as the fires, engulfing the on-deck cargo, the radio shack, and the number three hatch, could have been fought by members of the crew and the Armed Guard. However, it was the concussion from the thirty-three other bombs that fell within ten to fifty feet from the ship that destroyed the ship's steering gear, caused steam lines to rupture, destroyed all of the instruments on the bridge, and ruptured seams in the hull near the bow of the ship, causing massive flooding. *Kerr's* master made the decision to abandon ship; despite the fact that they had "fought like hell"[24] there was nothing else they could do. All thirty-eight of her crew and ten members of the Armed Guard climbed into two lifeboats and rowed away from the burning ship. At 2:00 AM, they watched her explode and sink on the horizon, as the fire had finally reached the explosives stored in the number two hold. For the next seven days, the crew remained in their lifeboats, finally landing at Kola Inlet, where they were rescued by a Soviet patrol boat and brought into Murmansk on July 13.

Имя, отчество и фамилия

Радист Iстатьи

Роберт

Глэнн Хендерсон

Подпись владельца удостоверения

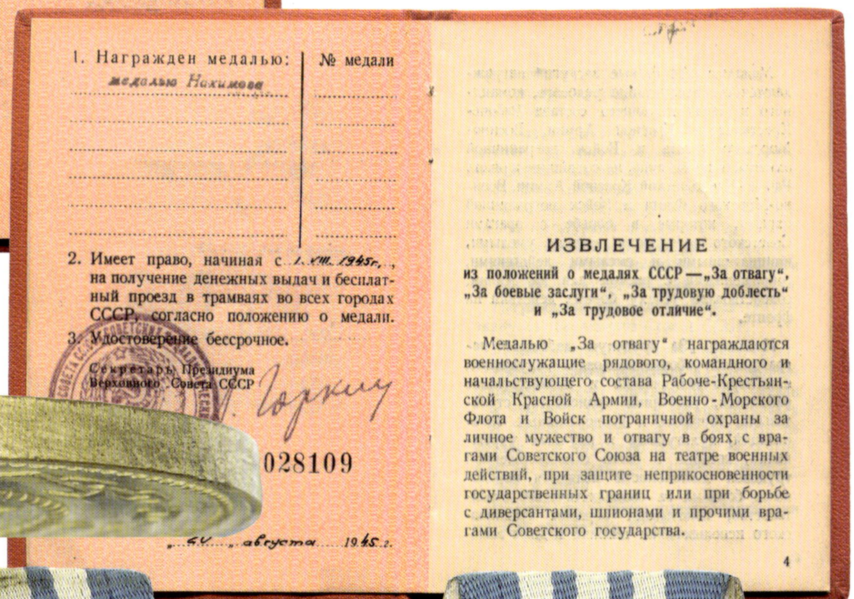

1. Награжден медалью: медалью Нахимова | № медали

2. Имеет право, начиная с 1.XII.1945г., на получение денежных выдач и бесплатный проезд в трамваях во всех городах СССР, согласно положению о медали.

3. Удостоверение бессрочное.

Секретарь Президиума Верховного Совета СССР

028109

„20" августа 1945 г.

ИЗВЛЕЧЕНИЕ

из положений о медалях СССР — „За отвагу", „За боевые заслуги", „За трудовую доблесть" и „За трудовое отличие".

Медалью „За отвагу" награждаются военнослужащие рядового, командного и начальствующего состава Рабоче-Крестьянской Красной Армии, Военно-Морского Флота и Войск пограничной охраны за личное мужество и отвагу в боях с врагами Советского Союза на театре военных действий, при защите неприкосновенности государственных границ или при борьбе с диверсантами, шпионами и прочими врагами Советского государства.

4

The medal book to Robert Henderson. *Courtesy of the Henderson family*.

Edge numbering for Robert Henderson's Medal of Nakhimov. *Courtesy of the Henderson family*.

Medal of Nakhimov number 5591 awarded to Robert Henderson. *Courtesy of the Henderson family*.

Order of Glory, Third Class, number 387956 awarded to Norbert Schwartz. *Courtesy of the Schwartz family.*

Norbert L. Schwartz, *Order of Glory, Third Class*

Norbert Lewis Schwartz was born to German immigrants in Chicago, Illinois, on March 18, 1923. Growing up in a bi-lingual household, he was fluent in both German and English. His parents passed away when he was young, leaving him in charge of raising his younger brother. At age twelve, he went to work for Sprout and Davis in Whiting, Indiana, finally becoming a truck driver before joining the Navy on January 27, 1942. Quickly promoted, he was a nineteen-year-old Coxswain when he took command of the Armed Guard detachment on the *Peter Kerr* on April 21, 1942. Due to the shortage of commissioned officers in the early days of the Armed Guard service, a small handful of mature enlisted personnel were put in charge of the detachments. Schwartz, with his seven previous years of labor experience, was one of these leaders. Following the sinking of the *Kerr*, Schwartz took charge of the welfare of the civilian and Navy survivors of the crew, and remarkably, every crewmember survived the voyage, a testament to his enduring leadership abilities even in the most stressful of times. Returning to the United States in September 1942, he was promoted to Boatswain's Mate, second class, and received a Commendation from the Secretary of the Navy for his heroism and leadership shown during PQ-17. Remaining with the Armed Guard, he served on the USAT *State of Maryland*, the USAT *General George S. Simonds*, and the SS *Orpheus*. He left the *Orpheus* on October 31, 1945, and was discharged from active duty on December 7, 1945. Returning to Chicago, he maintained his relationship with the water, eventually becoming harbormaster for Jackson Park Harbor in 1962. Norbert Schwartz passed away on September 8, 1989.

The *Daniel Morgan* had weathered through vicious attacks on July 4, avoiding a massed torpedo attack by the "skillful maneuvering of the ship and by the Grace of God."[25] Her three-inch deck gun, commanded by Gunner's Mate, third class, William Schilbe, fortuitously hit on a torpedo bound for the *Carlton*, and shortly thereafter, took down a He 111 by a direct hit to the plane's belly. When the command came to scatter, Ensign Morton Wolfson and the *Morgan's* master, George Sullivan, made the determination to head directly to Novaya Zemlya and pick their way along the coast, using the fjords and fog to shield themselves from the Germans. However, they did not adhere to this plan as they spotted a small convoy of three warships and three merchant vessels early on the morning of July 5. Deciding to stay with this mini-convoy for group protection, they proceeded on a route direct to Archangel. Unfortunately, shortly after the *Morgan* joined, the warships left the convoy, and the four merchants were left to defend themselves. Seeking any protection, the ships spotted a fog bank and changed their course to intercept it. However, they were spotted by a *Luftwaffe* Bv 138 patrol plane prior to entering the fog, and despite the anti-aircraft fire provided by the *Morgan*, the plane escaped to report their position. Realizing the untenable nature of their position, the *Morgan* again headed in the direction of Novaya Zemlya, leaving the other three merchant vessels to fend for their own defense.

Racing through the fog at her top speed of thirteen knots, they could hear gunfire erupting around them, and on several occasions, spotted U-boats through the fog. The men on the *Morgan* were nearing exhaustion, having been at battle stations for nearly twenty-eight continual hours by this point. Suddenly, at 3:00 PM, the fog lifted, and another ship, the *Fairfield City*, was spotted on a parallel course. Not five minutes later, Wolfson, Schilbe and their crew watched as three Ju 88 bombers dropped their bombs on the ship, despite her heavy anti-aircraft fire. The bombs of the second and third aircraft made direct hits on the *Fairfield City* and she began to quickly sink. But the men of the *Morgan* could only watch in horror as they had no time to stop or render aid to the survivors in the water. Three additional *Luftwaffe* bombers joined the first trio and all six now made bombing runs on the *Morgan*. Captain Sullivan excelled at evasive maneuvering, and Schilbe's gun crew, with John Gannon as the pointer, Merlin Houdeshell as the trainer, and Elden Kirby as the relief man for them both, were firing at a next-to-impossible rate of thirty rounds a minute. The six planes dropped their bombs, splashing on either side of the ship, and departed. For the first time in nearly an hour, there was silence. But this would not last long.

Fifteen minutes after the initial aircraft left, they spotted five more Ju 88 bombers, flying directly out of the sun. Individually, each bomber came screaming at the *Morgan*, dropping their bombs. The first and third bombers were blown from the sky by Schilbe's three-inch gun. The bombs from all four of the first aircraft fell well outside the danger area for the *Morgan*. However, the fifth bomber was lucky: the *Morgan's* three-inch gun jammed while he made his dive from four thousand feet, directly at the ship. A round did not seat correctly in the gun's breech due to the overheating of the barrel and when the crew attempted to clear the round, the case came loose from the projectile, leaving it in the barrel. With no time to loose, Schilbe swung the gun around and commanding his crew to leave the mount, attempted to clear the bore himself.[26] Pushing past the crew hurriedly leaving the mount, Wolfson ran to assist as Schilbe attempted to clear the round with the cleaning rod. But their efforts were for naught: the fifth bomber dropped his two bombs directly along the starboard quarter of the ship, rupturing the plates between the number four and five holds. The *Morgan* began to settle aft, and developed a list to starboard as she began to fill with water. They lost rudder control, and their supply of ammunition was nearly exhausted. The master determined it was best to abandon ship. The crew, with a loss of only three men, departed the ship in lifeboats.

When they were a half-mile from the ship, they saw a torpedo hit the port side of the ship, followed almost simultaneously by a torpedo on the starboard side. The *Daniel Morgan* sank stern first at 5:30 PM. An hour later, a U-boat surfaced and asked the men in the lifeboats about their cargo and gave them the direction to land. After remaining on the surface for quite some time, the U-boat finally submerged and the survivors of the *Morgan* were left alone in the Arctic.

At 2:00 AM the following day, the Soviet tanker *Donbass* rescued the *Morgan* survivors. Two of the Armed Guard, Eli Bourg and Senua Trahan, were hospitalized from exposure as a result of their time in the lifeboats. The other members of the Armed Guard volunteered to man the *Donbass* weapons, including the ship's three-inch deck gun, a twin to the one they had used with such incredible effect on the *Morgan*. At 3:30 PM that afternoon, they were attacked by a Ju 88, and at 4:00 AM on the morning of July 7, they were again attacked by two Ju 88s. At 1:30 AM on July 8, the *Donbass* anchored in Iokanka, near the entrance to the White Sea. After being at their battle stations since July 2, the *Morgan's* Armed Guard was finally stood down. The men were beyond exhausted when they were admitted to the Soviet hospital in Archangel to be treated for exposure. Given civilian clothes to wear, they remained in Archangel for the next seven weeks before making their transit to the United States.

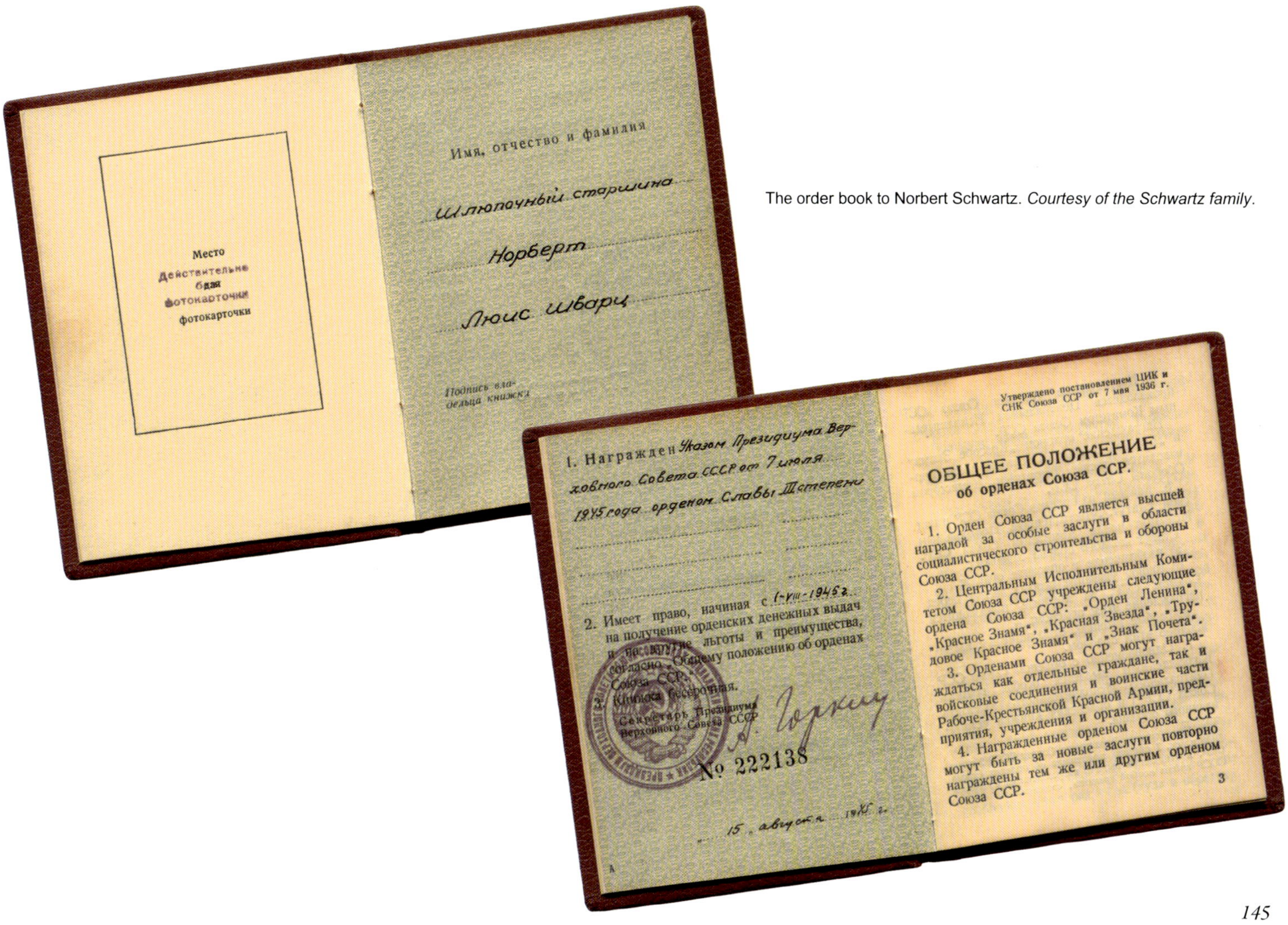

The order book to Norbert Schwartz. *Courtesy of the Schwartz family.*

ОБЩЕЕ ПОЛОЖЕНИЕ
об орденах Союза ССР
№ 222178

The Soviet order book to Morton Wolfson. *Courtesy of the family of Morton E. Wolfson.*

Morton E. Wolfson, *Order of the Patriotic War, First Class*

A native of Chicago, Morton Eugene Wolfson was born on March 27, 1916. He attended Hyde Park High School, Michigan State University, the University of Utah, and George Williams College. After a short stint in the National Guard from April 1939, he joined the Navy on September 26, 1940, and attended Naval Reserve Midshipman School at Annapolis, Maryland. Commissioned in January 1941, he was initially assigned to the USS *U.S. Grant* (AP-29) a converted Army Transportation Service ship in the Pacific. Following the outbreak of the war, he was quickly assigned to Armed Guard duty, and spent the majority of his tour with the Armed Guard on the *Daniel Morgan* and in Archangel as a survivor. Because of his valor and leadership, he was awarded the Silver Star Medal and the Distinguished Service Cross from Great Britain. Returning to the United States via the USS *Emmons* (DD-457) and USS *New York* (BB-34) he was then assigned to the commissioning crew of the USS *James O'Hara* (APA-90), where he took part in the invasion of Sicily and Italy. Off the coast of Italy, he was badly injured in a non-combat accident. As a result, he returned to the United States and spent the following eleven months at Bethesda Naval Hospital. Discharged from active duty on November 18, 1946, he remained in the Naval Reserves, retiring with the rank of Commander on July 1, 1954.

As a civilian, he worked as the general manager for Charm Tread Mills in Monticello, Arkansas, from 1951 to 1954. Subsequently, he worked for Powell Muffler, and finally, for Illinois Baking. While working for Illinois Baking, they became part of the Keebler Corporation, and he eventually became the director of military and international sales for the company. He also served as the president of the American Logistics Association. Retiring in 1982, he became involved with Aunt Martha's Youth Services, working closely with disadvantaged youth in the Chicago suburbs. Morton Wolfson passed away in Tucson, Arizona, on November 21, 1997, and was buried with full military honors at Arlington National Cemetery.

Order of the Patriotic War, First Class, number 247508 awarded to Morton Wolfson. *Courtesy of the family of Morton E. Wolfson.*

Morton Wolfson's Silver Star and British Distinguished Service Cross. Note the engraving of his name on the reverse of the DSC. It was initially incorrectly engraved with the last name of "Wilson," so it was replaced with another with the correct spelling. *Courtesy of the family of Morton E. Wolfson.*

William A. Schilbe, *Order of the Red Star*

The petty officer in charge of the *Morgan's* extraordinary three-inch gun was William Alfred Schilbe. He was born on April 1, 1916, in Detroit, Michigan. Following the completion of eleventh grade, he joined the Michigan National Guard on January 24, 1933, and served as a machine gunner in the 106th Cavalry until his discharge on June 10, 1940. In 1938, for his civilian occupation, he began working as a salesman for the Dearborn Furniture Company, but left to enlist in the Navy on February 3, 1942, as a Gunner's Mate, third class. His first assignment with the Armed Guard was on the SS *Bethare*, followed by reporting to the *Daniel Morgan* for the Murmansk Run. He earned the Silver Star for his heroism from July 2 to July 9. Returning to the United States, he was next assigned to the merchant tanker SS *Bennington*, followed by duty on the SS *Paul Hamilton Hayne*, taking him to North Africa in 1943 and to Wales in 1944. On February 17, 1944, he was transferred to the Port Director of New York, supervising the loading and unloading of shipboard ammunition as a Gunner's Mate, first class. Leaving active duty on September 17, 1945, he first worked as a salesman for the War Assets Administration, responsible for the sale of surplus furniture in the Detroit area. In 1949, he went to work as the district manager for Ajax Distributing Company, overseeing the distribution and maintenance of vending machines for the company in the eastern US. Two years later, Schilbe went into business for himself as a general contractor, specializing in commercial and residential kitchens and bathrooms. Tired of the instability of the home improvement market, he then became a car salesman for McGuire Rambler, followed by Rancho Rambler and Kelly Chevrolet in Warren and Detroit, Michigan. He passed away on September 1, 1968, and is buried in Grand Lawn Cemetery in Detroit.

Gunner's Mate, second class, William Schilbe, who put the *Morgan's* deck gun to use with deadly accuracy. *Courtesy of the Schilbe family.*

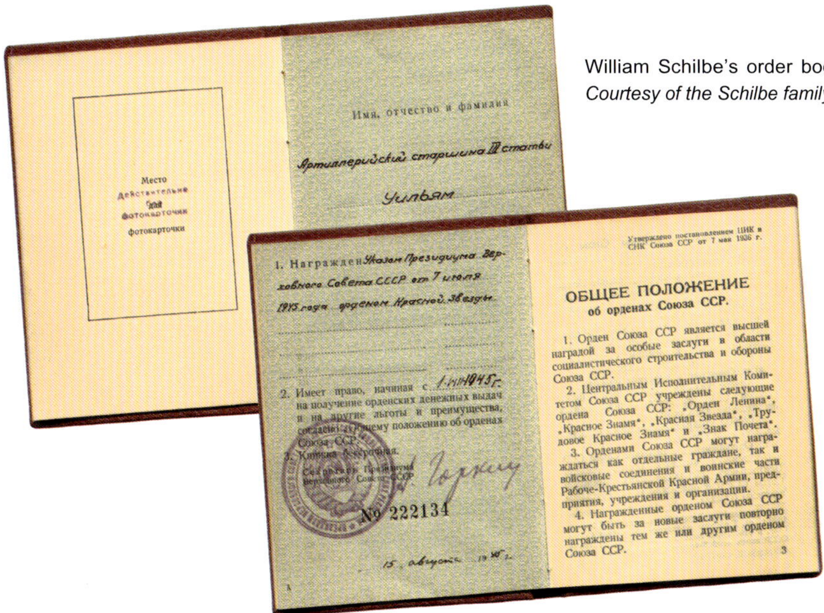

William Schilbe's order book. *Courtesy of the Schilbe family.*

William Schilbe's Silver Star Medal in the original case of issue. *Courtesy of the Schilbe family.*

Order of the Red Star number 1553978 awarded to William Schilbe. *Courtesy of the Schilbe family.*

Senua Trahan as he appeared in the 1941 *L'Acadien* yearbook. *Courtesy of the University of Louisiana at Lafayette.*

Senua Trahan, *Medal "For Military Merit"*

Senua Trahan joined the Navy from Kaplan, Louisiana. He was born on October 17, 1914, and graduated from the Southwestern Louisiana Institute of Liberal and Technical Learning (now University of Louisiana at Lafayette) in 1941 with a bachelor's degree in agriculture. Enlisting on October 7, 1941, he was tapped for Armed Guard training and reported to the Armed Guard Center in Brooklyn on December 30, 1941. His first assignment was the *Daniel Morgan*. Upon his return from the USSR, he was assigned to the SS *Del Rio*. Subsequently, he was promoted to Storekeeper (Disbursing), third class, and remained at the Armed Guard Center as a disbursing clerk until assigned to the USS *Cotten* (DD-669) in May 1945. He took part in the raid on Wake Island in August 1945, and ended the war in Tokyo Bay in September. Discharged from active duty on January 25, 1946, he returned to Louisiana. Senua Trahan passed away in New Iberia, Louisiana, on February 4, 1999.

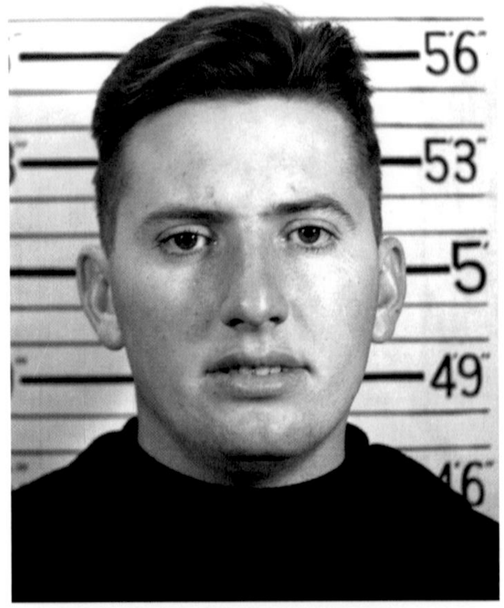

Eli P. Bourg. *National Personnel Records Center.*

Eli P. Bourg, *Medal "For Military Merit"*

A fellow Louisianan, Eli Philip Bourg was born on June 15, 1919, in Lafayette, Louisiana. He was an electrician by trade and joined the Navy to carry on his training in the field on September 17, 1941. Promoted to Seaman, second class, he reported to the Armed Guard Center in Brooklyn on January 25, 1942. He reported to the *Daniel Morgan* on April 15, 1942. He remained in the USSR until picked up with his fellow *Morgan* survivors by the USS *Emmons* (DD-457) and then transferred to the USS *Tuscaloosa* (CA-37) for his return trip to the United States. He remained as an Armed Guard crewmember through the rest of the war, serving on the SS *Del Rio*, SS *Beacon Oil*, and the SS *Alcoa Leader*. He was discharged as a Gunner's Mate, second class, on October 15, 1945. Returning to Louisiana, he found work as a pipefitter with the Texas and Pacific Railroad, where he worked until he passed away suddenly on February 12, 1966, at the age of forty-six. He is buried in McDonough Cemetery in Gretna, Louisiana.

Milton C. Casey. *National Personnel Records Center.*

Milton C. Casey, *Medal "For Military Merit"*

Assigned to the same Armed Guard detachment as Eli Bourg, Milton Clayton Casey hailed from Huntsville, Alabama. Born on November 26, 1919, in Fayetteville, Tennessee, he had been unemployed before joining the Navy on October 7, 1941. Like Bourg, after his tour on the *Daniel Morgan*, he sailed on the *Del Rio*, *Beacon Oil*, *Alcoa Leader*, as well as the MV *Saturnia*, before being discharged from the Navy as a Gunner's Mate, second class, on October 15, 1945. Residing in New Jersey for the majority of his life, he passed away in Clarksburg, West Virginia, on March 6, 1996.

Edward T. Anderson, *Medal "For Military Merit"*

Edward Thomas Anderson was born in Virginia on August 13, 1921. With war imminent, he enlisted in the Navy on April 10, 1941, and was ordered to the Armed Guard School on September 12, 1941. His first duty as a member of an Armed Guard crew was on the SS *Del Rio*, where he served as a fifty-caliber machine gunner. He was then transferred to the SS *Daniel Morgan*, and reported on April 15, 1942. Returning from the USSR, he was ordered to the SS *West Cheswald*, a fellow Murmansk Run veteran on October 20, 1942, before subsequently serving on the SS *Mary Lyon*. Leaving the Armed Guard service, he received orders to the USS *Mertz* (DD-691) on November 19, 1943, and served in the Pacific theater. There, he earned six campaign stars for his service in the landings and attacks on Yap, Palau, Tinian, Saipan, Angaur Island, Leyte, Iwo Jima, and Okinawa, among others. He ended the war in the Pacific with ten campaign stars on his Asiatic Pacific Campaign Medal and as a Signalman, third class. He was discharged on December 14, 1946, and lived in New York City. Shortly thereafter, he moved to Coleman Falls, Virginia, and was killed in a tragic car accident on March 26, 1966.

Hubert Williams, *Medal "For Military Merit"*

Hubert Williams joined the Navy from Gainesville, Florida, on October 7, 1941. Attending recruit training in Norfolk, Virginia, he reported to the Armed Guard Center in Brooklyn on New Year's Eve, 1941. Attached first to the *Daniel Morgan*, he then served on the SS *Del Rio*, along with his peers. In January 1943, he was assigned to the SS *West Maximus*. Williams survived her sinking on May 4, 1943, when she received three torpedoes between 11:00 PM and 1:00 AM while in convoy westbound ONS-5 traveling from Wales to Boston, Massachusetts.[27] He was picked out of the water at 7:00 AM by the HMS *Northern Spray*, and was safely delivered to St Johns, Newfoundland. Remaining there for two weeks, he received transport back to the United States on the SS *Yarmouth*, arriving in New York on May 29. Williams was detached from Armed Guard duty in August and spent the next two months working at the Naval Reserve Armory in Detroit, Michigan. He ended the war serving on shore patrol in Pearl Harbor, Territory of Hawaii. Continuing to serve, he transferred to shore patrol in Norfolk, Virginia, before reporting to the minesweeper USS *Grosbeak* (AMS 14) as a Gunner's Mate, second class. Williams remained in the Navy until June 30, 1961, when he retired as a Gunner's Mate, second class.

Thomas E. Brown, *Medal "For Military Merit"*

Thomas Edward Brown was born on May 7, 1923, in Buckatunna, Mississippi. Joining the Navy on September 25, 1941, he received recruit training in Norfolk, Virginia, and was sent directly to Armed Guard service with the *Daniel Morgan* as his first ship. Following service on the Murmansk Run, he served on the *Del Rio*, the *Bering*, *William R. Day*, and the *John B. Gordon*. In addition to a Commendation from the Secretary of the Navy for his service on the *Daniel Morgan*, he received a subsequent Commendation for actions against German aircraft off the coast of Norway on February 25, 1943. He was discharged from active duty on October 27, 1946, and his stated intentions were to become a mechanic in Brooklyn, New York. He followed his passion, finally retiring as a machinist and becoming very active in the Antique Automobile Club of America and the Antique Truck Society. Thomas Brown passed away on June 13, 1995, in Citronelle, Alabama, and is buried in the local Methodist Cemetery.

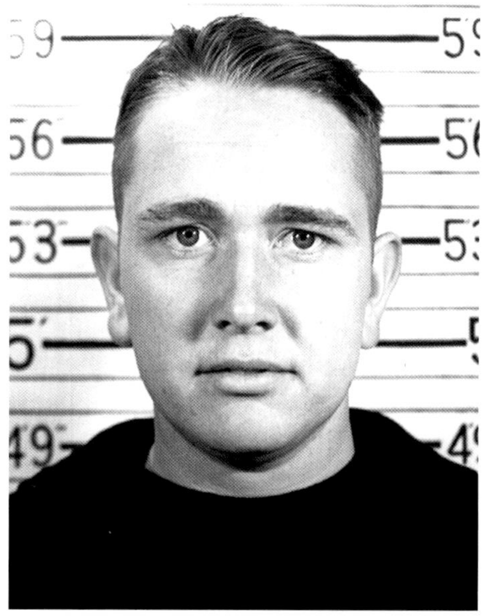

Thomas E. Brown. *National Personnel Records Center.*

Merlin Houdeshell, taken while on the USAT *James Parker* in 1944. *Courtesy of the Nelson family.*

Merlin G. Houdeshell, *Medal "For Military Merit"*

One of the *Morgan*'s three-inch gun experts was Merlin Gaylord Houdeshell. Born in Council Grove, Kansas, on April 20, 1921, he entered the Navy from Kansas City, Missouri, on December 18, 1941. Following his recruit training in San Diego, he was assigned to the Armed Guard Center and subsequently to the *Daniel Morgan*. Surviving the Murmansk Run, Houdeshell was assigned to the USAT *James Parker*, an Army troop transport, along with Oman Nelson. While on board, they made twenty-seven trans-Atlantic crossings, docking in seventy-five ports in the Mediterranean, Europe, and South America. Following the end of the war, he was discharged on September 18, 1945. Taking up residence in Brighton, Colorado, he used the GI Bill to train for electric motor repair. With these skills, he worked as a journeyman electrician for forty years, retiring in November 1985 to Aurora, Colorado. Merlin Houdeshell passed away on June 5, 1993.

Elden S. Kirby, *Medal "For Military Merit"*

Elden Samuel "Bud" Kirby was born on February 9, 1914, in Bemidgi, Minnesota and enlisted from Minneapolis on January 16, 1942. Like the others, he was immediately sent to Armed Guard training. Following his service on the *Daniel Morgan*, he was assigned to the USAT *James Parker* along with Merlin Houdeshell and Oman Nelson. However, unlike the other two, who remained on the *Parker* through the end of the war, he served on the MV *Cape Nun*, SS *Henry Austin*, and the SS *Portland*. While aboard the *Portland*, she ran aground on February 11, 1943, off the coast of South Carolina. Breaking apart in the heavy seas, the crew were rescued by the US Coast Guard and taken ashore. Discharged on October 28, 1945, he remained in Brooklyn where he was employed in the construction of federal housing projects, later becoming the maintenance manager of a group of houses. Moving to Hannibal, NY in 1952, he built his own house and worked as a self-employed heating and air-conditioning contractor, as well as owned and managed a trailer park he purchased. Retiring from the heating and air-conditioning business after twenty-five years, he relocated to Florida in 1975. Following the passing of his wife, he moved to Texas. Elden Kirby passed away on November 12, 1992, and is buried in Algoma Cemetery, Marshall, Texas.

Medal "For Military Merit" number 2551022, awarded to Elden Kirby. Courtesy of the Kirby family.

Матрос 1статьи
(имя)
Элден
(отчество)
Сэмьюэл Кёрби
(фамилия)

Указом Президиума Верховного Совета СССР награжден медалью „ЗА БОЕВЫЕ ЗАСЛУГИ".

Подпись владельца удостоверения

Тов. Элден Сэмьюэл Кёрби имеет право с 1 августа 1945 г. на получение пяти руб. в месяц и бесплатный проезд в трамваях во всех городах СССР, согласно Положению о медали „ЗА БОЕВЫЕ ЗАСЛУГИ".

Секретарь Президиума Верховного Совета СССР

№ 039360

„20" августа 1945 г.

Утверждено Указом Президиума Верховного Совета СССР от 17 октября 1938 г.

ПОЛОЖЕНИЕ О МЕДАЛИ „ЗА БОЕВЫЕ ЗАСЛУГИ"

1. Медалью „За боевые заслуги" награждаются военнослужащие рядового, командного и начальствующего состава Рабоче-Крестьянской Красной Армии, Военно-Морского Флота и Войск пограничной охраны, а также лица, не состоящие в рядах Рабоче-Крестьянской Красной Армии, Военно-Морского Флота и Войск пограничной охраны, которые в борьбе с врагами Советского государства своими уме-

3

Elden Kirby's Soviet medal book. Courtesy of the Kirby family.

Maurice E. Larson, *Medal "For Military Merit"*

Born in Harlow, North Dakota, on October 3, 1916, Maurice Elvin Larson left school after eighth grade to become a truck driver. In 1937, he joined the Civilian Conservation Corps, serving with Company 4756 in Upland, California, as a truck driver. Upon his discharge that same year, he began to work as a truck driver for the Midland Produce Company in Devils Lake, North Dakota. With the war starting, he joined the Navy on January 20, 1942, and was processed through Minneapolis, Minnesota. After recruit training at Great Lakes, he was stationed at the Armed Guard Center in New Orleans, and from there was assigned to the *Daniel Morgan*. Upon his return to the United States, he remained with the Armed Guard, eventually transferring to the Armed Guard Center in Brooklyn. He was discharged from the Navy as a Gunner's Mate, second class, on September 8, 1945. Returning to Devils Lake, he worked for Jerome Wholesale until his retirement in 1980. In 1990, he moved to Rocklin, California, and passed away on June 6, 2001.

Oman A. Nelson, *Medal "For Military Merit"*

Hailing from North Dakota like Maurice Larson, Oman Ambrose Nelson was born on October 15, 1916, in Maddock, North Dakota. Fluent in Norwegian, he moved to California following his graduation from high school and worked for Douglas Aircraft. In 1937, he returned to North Dakota and worked as a parts man at the General Supply Company in Maddock from 1937 until he joined the Navy, out of patriotism, on January 23, 1942. Receiving his recruit training at Naval Training Station Farragut, Idaho, he was sent to the Armed Guard Center in New Orleans, where he was subsequently assigned to the *Daniel Morgan* for his first experience at sea. Returning from the USSR, he remained with the Armed Guard until the end of the war, assigned to the USAT *James Parker*, an Army troop transport along with Merlin Houdeshell. Discharged in November 1945, he returned to North Dakota and purchased the Walhalla Hardware Store in 1946. He operated the business until he sold it in 1979. In 1982, he moved to Jamestown, North Dakota, and in 1993, moved to Fargo. Oman Nelson passed away on April 22, 1998, and is buried in Riverside Cemetery, Fargo.

Oman A. Nelson. *Courtesy of the Nelson family.*

John W. Gannon, *Medal "For Military Merit"*

Responsible for finding the targets for the *Morgan's* three-inch gun, John Walter Gannon was born on January 29, 1921, in Washington, DC He grew up in Mount Rainier, Maryland, but attended Central High School in Washington, DC While still in high school, he joined the National Guard, rising to the rank of Corporal in the Coast Artillery, Anti-Aircraft section, prior to his discharge in May 1940. Working as a settlement clerk at the National Metropolitan Bank in Washington, DC, he spent his free time watching aircraft at the local airports. He enlisted in the Navy on January 9, 1942, and attended recruit training in Norfolk, Virginia. Assigned to the Armed Guard Center in Brooklyn, the *Daniel Morgan* was his first ship. It would also be his only ship: following his return to the United States, he received orders to attend Aviation Machinist Mate School in Chicago. Promoted to Aviation Machinist Mate, third class, upon graduation in April 1943, he was selected for flight training and redesignated as an Aviation Cadet. He was transferred to the University of Washington flight school to begin flight training. He completed flight preparatory school and primary training, but sadly washed out of intermediate training in November 1943. Redesignated to Aviation Machinist Mate, third class, he served in the aviation engine cylinder shops in Norfolk and in San Diego before being transferred to Barbers Point, Hawaii, where he assembled Stromberg carburetors for aircraft. He ended the war with Carrier Aviation Support Unit (CASU) 6, specializing in hydraulic repair. Discharged from active duty on September 22, 1945, he attended Benjamin Franklin University in Washington, DC and spent his career as a salesman for Montgomery Ward. Moving to Normal, Illinois, following his retirement, he passed away on February 2, 1999. John Gannon is buried in Holy Cross Cemetery, Normal, Illinois.

John W. Gannon. *Courtesy of the Gannon family.*

Francis L. Duncan, *Medal "For Military Merit"*

Francis Lee Duncan was born in Huntington County, Indiana on November 25, 1922. He entered the Navy directly from high school in Peru, Indiana, on September 11, 1941. Receiving his recruit training in Great Lakes, he was assigned to the Armed Guard Center in Brooklyn as a signalman. His first ship was the *Daniel Morgan*. Upon his return to the United States, he was assigned to the SS *Esso Augusta*. Due to his specialty as a signalman, he rotated quickly through numerous ships, including the SS *Polonaise*, *Jalapa*, *Golden Eagle*, *Amos Kendall*, and the *David F. Honston* prior to the end of the war. He was discharged from active duty on June 1, 1946, with the rank of Signalman, third class. Returning to Peru, he became a conductor with the Norfolk and Western Railroad. Francis Duncan passed away due to a short illness on August 15, 1981. He is buried in Ever-Rest Memorial Park Cemetery in Peru.

Medal "For Military Merit" number 2551004 awarded to Francis Duncan. *Courtesy of the Duncan family.*

Матрос 1 статьи
(имя)
Фрэнсис
(отчество)
Ли Данкан
(фамилия)

Указом Президиума Верховного Совета СССР награжден медалью „ЗА БОЕВЫЕ ЗАСЛУГИ".

№ медали.........

Тов. Фрэнсис Ли Данкан имеет право с 1 августа 1945г. на получение пяти руб. в месяц и бесплатный проезд в трамваях во всех городах СССР, согласно Положению о медали „ЗА БОЕВЫЕ ЗАСЛУГИ".

Секретарь Президиума Верховного Совета СССР

№ 039003

„20" августа 1945г.

Утверждено Указом Президиума Верховного Совета СССР от 17 октября 1938 г.

ПОЛОЖЕНИЕ О МЕДАЛИ „ЗА БОЕВЫЕ ЗАСЛУГИ"

1. Медалью „За боевые заслуги" награждаются военнослужащие рядового, командного и начальствующего состава Рабоче-Крестьянской Красной Армии, Военно-Морского Флота и Войск пограничной охраны, а также лица, не состоящие в рядах Рабоче-Крестьянской Красной Армии, Военно-Морского Флота и Войск пограничной охраны, которые в борьбе с врагами Советского государства своими уме-

3

The Soviet medal book to Francis Duncan. *Courtesy of the Duncan family.*

Allan A. Thompson, *Medal "For Military Merit"*

Allan Anthony Thompson was born on September 14, 1924, and was raised in San Francisco. Entering the Navy on September 15, 1941, the day after his seventeenth birthday, he was sent to Radioman training prior to entering the Armed Guard. Following his service on the *Daniel Morgan*, he returned to the United States and served on the USS *Augusta* (CA-31), taking part in her actions in the Mediterranean and off North Africa. He was subsequently transferred to the USS *Ancon* (AGC-4), where he became part of the admiral's communication detachment for Commander, Amphibious Forces, Atlantic Fleet. Returning to the United States, he was assigned to the USS *Dade* (APA-99) and took part in the Okinawa landings in the Pacific theater. With the end of the war, he was discharged on December 13, 1945. Returning to San Francisco, he decided to rejoin the Navy and on October 11, 1948, re-entered active duty service. Initially assigned to the USS *Tatnuck* (ATA-195), he was reassigned to the USS *Hampden County* (LST-803) in time for her recommissioning and service transporting troops, cargo, and prisoners of war along the Korean coastline. He subsequently served at NAS Alameda before returning to sea on the USS *Polaris* (AF-11) in 1955. Redesignated a Metalsmith, he was reassigned to the USS *Sirius* (AF-60) in 1957, followed by assignments on the USS *Pine Island* (AV-12) and the USS *Midway* (CVA-41). Redesignated again to Shipfitter, first class (Aviation), he was assigned to the USS *Piedmont* (AD-17), where he was promoted to Chief Petty Officer in 1963. He retired from the Navy on July 16, 1964, and returned to San Francisco, where he became a cab driver for the next eight years in his native city. Allan Thompson passed away on March 1, 2005, and is buried in the San Joaquin National Cemetery.

July 5, 1942, was a bloody day in the history of the Murmansk Run. But the carnage continued as the Germans actively sought out the remaining scattered merchant vessels. About 7:00 AM on July 5, the SS *John Witherspoon*, an American merchant that had been traveling independently since the call to scatter the convoy, joined a small group of ships, consisting of the SS *Fairfield City*, *Benjamin Harrison*, and several Royal Navy escorts. At 11:00 AM, the escorts instructed the merchant vessels to maintain their course, while they ventured in a different direction at high speed (eight hours later, they would pass by the SS *Bellingham*, sailing independently in an attempt to avoid attacks). The merchants, now alone, proceeded into a fog bank for protection. The fog was sufficiently dense that when it lifted at 2:00 PM, the *John Witherspoon* was alone. John McDole and Percy Spann, the Armed Guard communication group, listened intently to the radio as distress signals from other vessels came in as they were being slaughtered. However, other than the spotting of a U-boat on the horizon at 3:00 PM, they were untouched. At 5:00 PM, they discovered another fog bank, and were able to transit through it until 3:30 AM on the morning of July 6. Their plan, like that of the *Washington* and others, was to travel due east to Novaya Zemlya hoping for safety among its fjords and cliffs. As they were heading east, Armed Guard lookouts spotted what appeared to be the wake of a U-boat, and fired their four-inch deck gun at the leading edge of the wake on several occasions. The wake would disappear, and the process would start over again.

They were approximately twenty miles off the coast of Novaya Zemlya, and the master made the determination to change course due south in order to intercept the Soviet coastline. The weather was beautiful: cloudless and bright, with only a slight swell. The transit was almost peaceful. That is, until 2:50 PM when a torpedo slammed into the *Witherspoon's* starboard side between holds number four and five. While responding to the splitting hull, a second torpedo exploded directly below the bridge, throwing up a column of water over two hundred feet high, causing the main deck to be awash, destroying two lifeboats, and temporarily flooding the Armed Guard weapons. The crew frantically launched the two serviceable lifeboats while the members of the Armed Guard attempted to spot their attacker. But they could not. They were alone, and the ship was sinking fast. Ensign Rudolph Kroetz, the Armed Guard commander, and Latney Farmer, his Coxswain, left the ship in the number four lifeboat, following the other lifeboat away from the sinking hulk. As soon as they were clear of the ship, a third torpedo exploded amidships and the *Witherspoon* broke in two, slipping beneath the waves.

Minutes later, *U-255*, commanded by *Kapitänleutnant* Reinhart Reche, came to the surface within a hundred feet of the lifeboats. Having followed the *Witherspoon* for over thirty hours, he had fired a four-torpedo spread at the hapless ship, followed by a fifth to ensure her destruction. The spokesman on the U-boat spoke perfect English, and mentioned that he had gone to university in New York. He asked the men with Kroetz if they needed food or water and supplied them with packs of American cigarettes, cognac, and water. The German then offered directions to the nearest land. With that, the U-boat crew hurried below and the submarine dropped out of sight, as quickly as it had appeared. Reinhart Reche, captain of the *U-255*, was on a mission: the *Witherspoon* was his first kill. Before the debacle of convoy PQ-17 was over, he would claim the destruction of the *Alcoa Ranger*, *Olopana*, and the *Paulus Potter*. To thoroughly compound his victory, he would later sink the SS *Richard Bland*, which had originally started with convoy PQ-17 and eventually arrived in the USSR with convoy JW-51A, as she carried the last survivors from PQ-17 westward in March 1943.[28]

Following the sinking of the ship, a heavy fog rolled in and the two lifeboats were separated. Kroetz and Farmer, who were both later awarded the Silver Star for valor, and Seaman Milton Parker, were picked up by the *El Capitan* at 7:00 PM on July 8; fifty-three hours after the *Witherspoon* had sunk. At the request of Louis Marks, the *El Capitan's* Armed Guard commander, they manned the starboard forward fifty-caliber machine gun on the *El Capitan* before she too was sunk. The remaining crew and Armed Guard gunners were picked up by the HMS *Lamuline* at 3:30 AM on July 9, after sixty-one hours in their lifeboat, and taken to Archangel.

Rudolph H. Kroetz, Armed Guard commander on the SS *John Witherspoon*.

Rudolph Kroetz, *Order of the Patriotic War, First Class*

Rudolph Kroetz, the *Witherspoon's* Armed Guard commander, was born in Milwaukee, Wisconsin, on July 2, 1913. His grandfather owned the Hercules Knitting Company and the family made regular trips to Germany in his younger years to gain expertise in the industry, giving him the chance to become fluent in German. Attending Lake Forest University in Chicago, he was immensely popular and graduated with the class of 1935. Following graduation from the University of Wisconsin Law School and after practicing law in Milwaukee, he volunteered for naval service. In September 1941, Kroetz attended the Naval Reserve Midshipman School in Chicago, receiving his commission in January 1942. Reporting for Armed Guard duty in March, he was assigned as the Armed Guard commander attached to the steamship *John Witherspoon*, reporting on April 28, 1942. Following his time on the Murmansk Run, Kroetz returned to the United States and made another Atlantic transit, this time on the *Robin Tuxford* to North Africa, before his eventual transfer to the USS *Stewart* (DE-238) in October 1943. In September 1945, following service as the executive officer of the *Stewart*, he became a Navy Judge Advocate General (JAG) officer, serving in various capacities in Subic Bay, Philippines, Newport, Rhode Island, and Washington, DC, until leaving active service in September 1951. Returning to Chicago, he remained active in the Navy Reserves, retiring as a Commander on July 1, 1961. As a civilian, he practiced corporate law in the Chicago area for several firms until he retired. Rudolph Kroetz passed away on January 7, 1988.

The Silver Star awarded to Rudolph Kroetz.

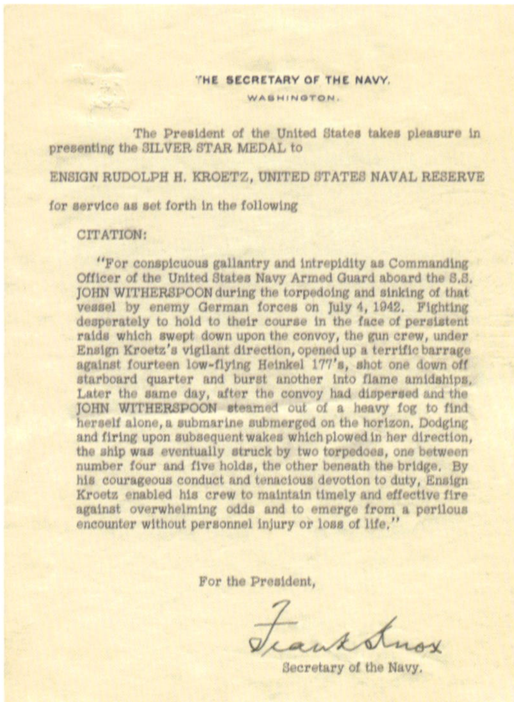

THE SECRETARY OF THE NAVY.
WASHINGTON.

The President of the United States takes pleasure in presenting the SILVER STAR MEDAL to

ENSIGN RUDOLPH H. KROETZ, UNITED STATES NAVAL RESERVE

for service as set forth in the following

CITATION:

"For conspicuous gallantry and intrepidity as Commanding Officer of the United States Navy Armed Guard aboard the S.S. JOHN WITHERSPOON during the torpedoing and sinking of that vessel by enemy German forces on July 4, 1942. Fighting desperately to hold to their course in the face of persistent raids which swept down upon the convoy, the gun crew, under Ensign Kroetz's vigilant direction, opened up a terrific barrage against fourteen low-flying Heinkel 177's, shot one down off starboard quarter and burst another into flame amidships. Later the same day, after the convoy had dispersed and the JOHN WITHERSPOON steamed out of a heavy fog to find herself alone, a submarine submerged on the horizon. Dodging and firing upon subsequent wakes which plowed in her direction, the ship was eventually struck by two torpedoes, one between number four and five holds, the other beneath the bridge. By his courageous conduct and tenacious devotion to duty, Ensign Kroetz enabled his crew to maintain timely and effective fire against overwhelming odds and to emerge from a perilous encounter without personnel injury or loss of life."

For the President,

Frank Knox

Secretary of the Navy.

The original Silver Star citation awarded to Rudolph H. Kroetz.

Order of the Patriotic War, First Class, number 247517, awarded to Rudolph Kroetz.

Arthur L. Farmer, *Order of Glory, Third Class*

Arthur Latney Farmer. *Courtesy of the Farmer family.*

Rudolph Kroetz' Coxswain was Arthur Latney Farmer. Born in Richmond, Virginia, on May 27, 1914, he joined the Navy on July 23, 1931. Following recruit training, he served on the USS *Omaha* (CL-4) until the end of his enlistment on April 22, 1935. He moved to Tacoma, Washington, and was working as a musician when the war started. Enlisting on January 9, 1942, as a Coxswain, he was immediately sent to Armed Guard duty. However, he had developed a habit of not showing up at his designated place of duty and lost his place on the modern oiler MS *Pacific Sun* when he failed to muster in time for her departure. Subsequently assigned to the *John Witherspoon* heading to the USSR, he demonstrated his aptitude for valor on the Murmansk Run. Returning to the United States after seven weeks in the USSR, he was awarded the Silver Star after being released from the hospital, still suffering from exposure as a result of the extended period of time in the lifeboat. He was transferred to the Armed Guard Center, New Orleans, and finally, Naval Air Station, Corpus Christi, Texas, before his separation from the Navy on January 24, 1944. Returning to the music industry as a traveling country western singer, Latney Farmer was performing in Tacoma when he received an accidental blow to the head, resulting in his death, on April 15, 1949. He was returned to his family farm in North Carolina and is buried in the Old Smithville Cemetery in Southport, North Carolina.

Latney Farmer poses with his band at a honky-tonk, shortly after the end of the war. *Courtesy of the Farmer family.*

The Silver Star awarded to Latney Farmer. *Courtesy of the Farmer family.*

Harry Jones, Jr., *Medal "For Valor"*

Born in Jonesboro, Indiana, on June 13, 1917, Harry Jones Jr. joined the Navy on January 15, 1942. Following recruit training in Newport, Rhode Island, on February 11, he was assigned to Armed Guard duty and subsequently to the *Witherspoon* for service on the Murmansk Run. Surviving his transit to the USSR and return, he remained with the Armed Guard until his transfer to LION Four, based at Moffett Field, California, and later at Pearl Harbor, on August 13, 1943. Transferring from LION Four prior to the unit's departure for the Eastern Pacific, he was assigned to the personal staff of Commander, Air Force Pacific Fleet, where he served until October 1944. His following assignments were on the staff of the Headquarters Squadron, Fleet Air Wing Two, and with the admiral's personal staff for Commander, Fourteenth Naval District, both stationed at Pearl Harbor. His final two assignments during the war were serving on the staff of the Commander, Naval Air Station Honolulu and Naval Air Station Johnston Island. Following the end of the war, Jones then served on the USS *Johnston* (DD-821) and later, the USS *Tidewater* (AD-31). In February 1957, he graduated from Navy salvage diver training and in November 1960, received orders to the USS *Preserver* (ARS-8). Following this tour, he was stationed as a dive instructor in Washington, DC, where he was promoted to Chief Boatswain's Mate in 1963. In August 1965, he retired from the Navy with twenty-three years of service. Moving to Oceanside, California, he passed away on October 20, 1987.

Thomas Nightingale, *Medal "For Valor"*

Born in Garrett, Pennsylvania, on November 11, 1920, Thomas Nightingale joined the Navy on January 28, 1942, after working for five years as a coal miner. Attending recruit training in Norfolk, he was assigned to the Armed Guard Center in Brooklyn, and subsequently, to the *John Witherspoon*. Upon his return from the USSR, he continued service with the Armed Guard through the end of the war in both the Atlantic and Pacific theaters. He was discharged on December 19, 1945. Taking up residence in Clinton, Indiana, he became a truck driver and pipeline construction worker. Thomas Nightingale passed away on November 19, 1989 and is buried in Hall Cemetery, Universal, Indiana.

John W. McDole. *Courtesy of the McDole family.*

John W. McDole, *Medal "For Valor"*

John Wallace McDole was born in Springfield, Illinois, on January 21, 1920. Attending Flint Junior College, he was called up for the Army, but instead volunteered for the Navy in October 1941. Following five months of Radioman School, he reported to the Armed Guard Center on April 18, 1942. Ten days later, he reported to the steamship *John Witherspoon* as one of the two communications group (along with Percy Spann) in the Armed Guard detachment. Returning to the United States, now a Radioman, third class, he reported to the Q-ship (anti-submarine decoy) USS *Asterion* (AK-100) in October. He served on her until she was decommissioned and transferred to the US Coast Guard in January 1944. Leaving *Asterion* as a Radioman, second class, he next was ordered to the Sub Chaser Training School and upon graduation, reported to the rescue tug USS *ATR-82* for the next six months. Finally promoted to Radioman, first class, he spent the last year of his time in the Navy at the Amphibious Training Base, Little Creek, Virginia, and attached to the medium rocket landing ship, USS *LSM(R)-516* upon her launching in May 1945. With the end of the war, he was discharged that September, and returned to Illinois. The rest of his life was dedicated to helping people. In 1952, he attended George Williams College in Chicago, and following graduation, became the youth director for the West Suburban YMCA in LaGrange, Illinois. This was followed by becoming the executive director of Isham Memorial YMCA. Finally, he served as the executive director of the Division Street YMCA where he retired in 1980. John McDole passed away on December 28, 1982.

The Soviet medal book to John McDole. *Courtesy of the McDole family*.

Medal "For Valor" number 2075710 awarded to John McDole. *Courtesy of the McDole family*.

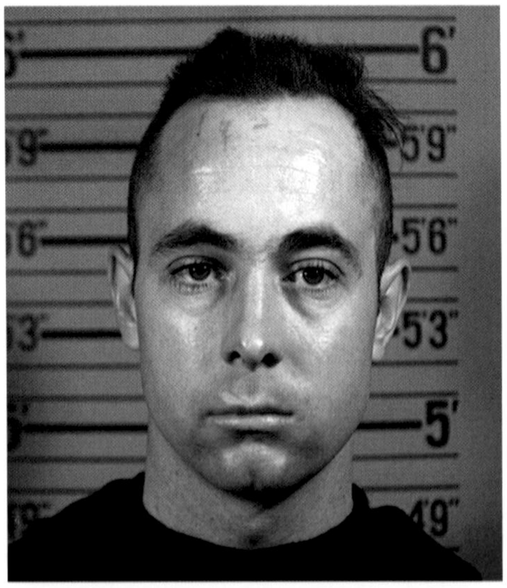

John J. Ours. *National Personnel Records Center.*

John J. Ours, *Medal "For Valor"*

John Jacob Ours was born on January 28, 1917, in Cabins, West Virginia, the eighth child of Marcellus Columbus Ours. He completed the eighth grade and went to work for his father. Joining the Civilian Conservation Corps, he served with Company 519 in Petersburg, West Virginia, but received his discharge to join the Navy on January 19, 1942. Reporting for duty at the Armed Guard Center in Brooklyn on April 24, he had less than a week before he was underway on the *John Witherspoon*. Surviving the transit of the Murmansk Run, he returned to the United States and was subsequently assigned to the SS *Meriwether Lewis*, a 7,176-ton Liberty ship built in January 1942. En route to Great Britain in convoy HX-227 with a cargo of ammunition and tires, they fell behind the convoy escorts. At 4:43 AM on March 2, 1943, she was torpedoed by *U-634*. She sunk instantly, taking her entire crew of forty-four civilians and twenty-eight Navy Armed Guard with her to the bottom of the sea.[29] Coxswain John Ours' body was never recovered, and he was officially listed as killed in action as of March 3, 1944.

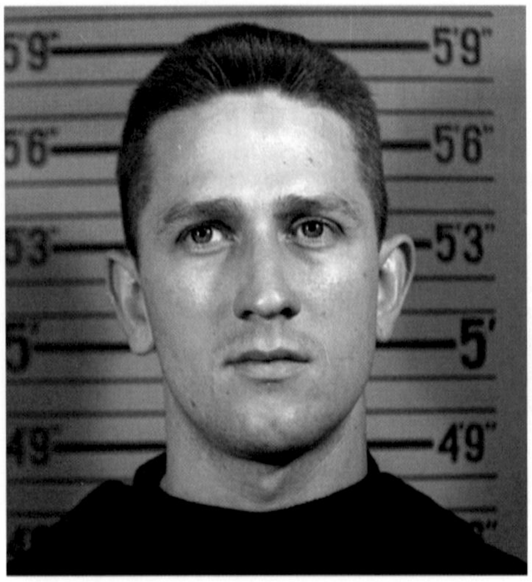

Milton Parker. *National Personnel Records Center.*

Milton Parker, *Medal "For Valor"*

Enlisting from Baltimore, Maryland, Milton Parker had worked as a handyman, painter, and sheet metal worker for the Maryland Drydock Company since age sixteen. Born in Baltimore on January 22, 1918, to a Polish father and German mother, he left school after the sixth grade to provide money to support his family. He enlisted in the Navy on January 16, 1942 in order to "keep out of the Army."[30] Following his recruit training in Norfolk, he was sent to the Armed Guard Center in Brooklyn and assigned to the *John Witherspoon*. Following his time in the USSR and his return, he was promoted to Gunner's Mate, third class, and continued to serve with the Armed Guard. Sent to the USAT *Mexico*, he made multiple trips across the Atlantic, ferrying troops for the invasions of Italy and France. He was discharged from the Navy on November 1, 1945, and returned to Baltimore. Milton Parker passed away on August 2, 1996 in Baltimore, Maryland and is buried in Holy Cross Cemetery.

Luther W. Perdue, *Medal "For Valor"*

Luther William Perdue was born on March 12, 1915, in Blue Knob, Ohio, and raised in the Vincent, Ohio, area. Enlisting in the Navy on February 11, 1942, he entered active duty on February 17. Following recruit training, he reported to the Armed Guard Center in Brooklyn, and subsequently to the *John Witherspoon* as his first ship. Following his time on the Murmansk Run, he remained in the Armed Guard for a short time before reporting to the destroyer tender USS *Hamul* (AD-20) in early 1943. With a shortage of crewmembers following her commissioning, Perdue, now Gunner's Mate, third class, was transferred to the USS *Cogswell* (DD-651) on September 24, 1943. Serving under the command of future Vice Admiral (then Commander) H.T. Deutermann as the commanding officer, and under future astronaut (and Rear Admiral) Alan Shepard as the gunnery officer, Perdue participated in the assaults on the Marshall Islands, Paulaus, Yap, Hollandia, the Marianas, Iwo Jima, Peleliu, Okinawa, Leyte, and others. And the end of the war, the *Cogswell* was given the honor of being the first US Navy ship to enter Tokyo Bay before the surrender. Perdue earned nine battle stars for his service in the Pacific theater during the war. He transferred off *Cogswell* on September 8, 1945, as a Gunner's Mate, second class and returned to civilian life on November 2, 1945. Lured by the sea, he rejoined the Navy and returned to active duty, now a Gunner's Mate, third class, and served on the USS *Tarawa* (CVS-40) and on the USS *McCaffery* (DD-860) until he was again discharged on February 25, 1959.

Returning to Ohio, he went to work for Union Carbide, retiring from there in 1977. On October 17, 1992, he was brutally murdered by two teenagers during the robbery of his house. Both suspects were caught and brought to justice: one is currently serving a life sentence; the other was murdered in prison. Luther Perdue is buried in Veto Cemetery, Washington County, Ohio.

James W. Pernell, *Medal "For Valor"*

James William Pernell joined the Navy on January 28, 1942, from Charleston, West Virginia. Born on August 6, 1924, in Big Chimney, West Virginia, he had an eighth grade education and worked as a laborer and farmhand on the 270-acre farm owned by H.R. Young in Dickinson until his enlistment in the Navy. Entering recruit training at Norfolk on February 16, 1942, he was assigned Armed Guard duty and reported to the *John Witherspoon* on April 10. Following his return to the United States, he was assigned to the Liberty ship SS *Nathan Hale* in October, where he served until mid-1943. Pernell was subsequently reassigned to the SS *Bloody Marsh*, a 10,195-ton fuel tanker on June 9, 1943. Around midnight on July 2, 1943, the *Bloody Marsh* was approximately seventy-five miles east of Savannah, Georgia, carrying a cargo of 102,500 gallons of fuel en route New York. *U-66* found her to be an irresistible target and launched a single torpedo, impacting at the engine room on the port side. The explosion ruptured the hull from amidships to the engine room, destroying the latter and killing all the men on watch. The Armed Guard attempted to fire on a contact they believed to be the submarine, but found their deck gun inoperable due to the explosion. The master made the determination to abandon ship, and they were subsequently rescued by the subchaser USS *SC-1048* at 9:00 AM the same day.

Now a survivor of two merchant vessel sinkings, he was assigned to the SS *Pan Pennsylvania*, another fuel tanker, on August 9, 1943. Pernell served on her through multiple transits in the Atlantic and transferred on April 5, 1944. He was lucky: the *Pan Pennsylvania* was torpedoed by *U-550* on April 15, becoming the catalyst for the notable action with the destroyers *Gandy*, *Peterson*, and *Joyce*.[31] Finally avoiding the sinking of yet another merchant vessel, he was reassigned to the Amphibious Training Base at Solomons, Maryland, where he trained to become part of the crew of USS *LCT-870*, and was later assigned to USS *LST-751* in the Pacific for the end of the war. Released from active duty on November 26, 1945, he returned to West Virginia but later moved to Georgia, where he worked first as a farmer, then as a school bus driver for the Gordon County School System until he retired. James Pernell passed away on October 13, 1997, and is buried in Gordon Memorial Gardens, Calhoun, Georgia.

Medal "For Valor" number 2075717 awarded to James Pernell. *Courtesy of the McWilliams family.*

Шлюпочный старшина
(имя)
Джэймс
(отчество)
Уильям Пёрнелл
(фамилия)
Указом Президиума Верховного Совета СССР награжден медалью „ЗА ОТВАГУ".
Подпись владельца удостоверения

Тов. Джэймс Уильям Пёрнелл имеет право с 1 августа 1945 г. на получение десяти руб. в месяц и бесплатный проезд в трамваях во всех городах СССР, согласно Положению о медали „ЗА ОТВАГУ".
Секретарь Президиума Верховного Совета СССР
№ 048280
20 августа 1945 г.

Утверждено Указом Президиума Верховного Совета СССР от 17 октября 1938 г.

ПОЛОЖЕНИЕ О МЕДАЛИ „ЗА ОТВАГУ"

1. Медалью „За отвагу" награждаются военнослужащие рядового, командного и начальствующего состава Рабоче-Крестьянской Красной Армии, Военно-Морского Флота и Войск пограничной охраны за личное мужество и отвагу в боях с врагами Советского Союза на театре военных действий, при защите неприкосновенности государственных границ, или при борьбе

3

The Soviet medal book to James Pernell. *Courtesy of the McWilliams family.*

Willie H. Phillips. *Courtesy of the Phillips family.*

Willie H. Phillips, *Medal "For Valor"*

Willie H. Phillips was born on March 26, 1918, in Gaffney, South Carolina. Leaving school at age fifteen, he worked as a diesel-dragline operator and truck driver for the W.C. Shepherd Construction Company in Charleston, South Carolina, and served in the Civilian Conservation Corps before enlisting in the Navy in January 1942. Attending recruit training in Norfolk, he was assigned to the Armed Guard and his first ship was the *John Witherspoon*, where he was the pointer on the four-inch deck gun. Returning from the USSR, he was subsequently assigned to the SS *Colorado*, followed by the SS *Nemaha* in April 1943, the *Howard E. Coffin* in January 1944, and the *Mary A. Townsend* that March. He continued to serve with the Armed Guard through the end of the war, and was discharged as a Coxswain on September 13, 1945. Moving to High Point, North Carolina, he went to auto body school on the GI Bill. He first opened a paint shop in High Point, but after several years moved back to Gaffney, where he worked in the cotton mills. In the late 1950s, he went to work for Pilot Freight Carriers in Charlotte, North Carolina, doing body and paint work on their semi-trucks. He worked for Pilot for twenty-six years before he retired. Returning to Gaffney, he opened Philips Truck Service and Phillips Paint and Body Shop. Willie Phillips, a lifelong Christian and family man, passed away on August 31, 1992, and is buried in Crestview Baptist Church in Gaffney.

Medal "For Valor" number 2075722 awarded to Willie Phillips. *Courtesy of the Phillips family.*

Percy L. Spann, *Medal "For Valor"*

The *Witherspoon's* Signalman was Seaman Percy Leon Spann. Born in Georgiana, Alabama, on January 22, 1919, he served in the Civilian Conservation Corps before enlisting in the Navy on October 14, 1941. The Spann family was like many during the Second World War: the young men of military age joined the war and as a family, shared in the sacrifices of the nation. Percy's cousins both joined the Army Air Force; one served as a navigator on a B-17, the other an engineer on a B-24. Both were shot down and became prisoners of the Germans during the war. Percy's older brother, Army Private First Class Jamie Spann, was killed in action fighting on Luzon in 1945. Percy, following his recruit training, was assigned to Armed Guard duty, and subsequently to the *John Witherspoon* as part of her communications group. Treated for exposure following his sixty-one-hour ordeal in the lifeboat, he developed a deep cough upon his return to the United States. Believed at first to be a result of smoking, the cough became more pronounced, and he was finally admitted to the US Naval Hospital, Portsmouth, New Hampshire, where he was diagnosed with tuberculosis. On May 25, 1943, Signalman, third class Percy Spann passed away. He is buried with full military honors in his hometown of Georgiana, Alabama.

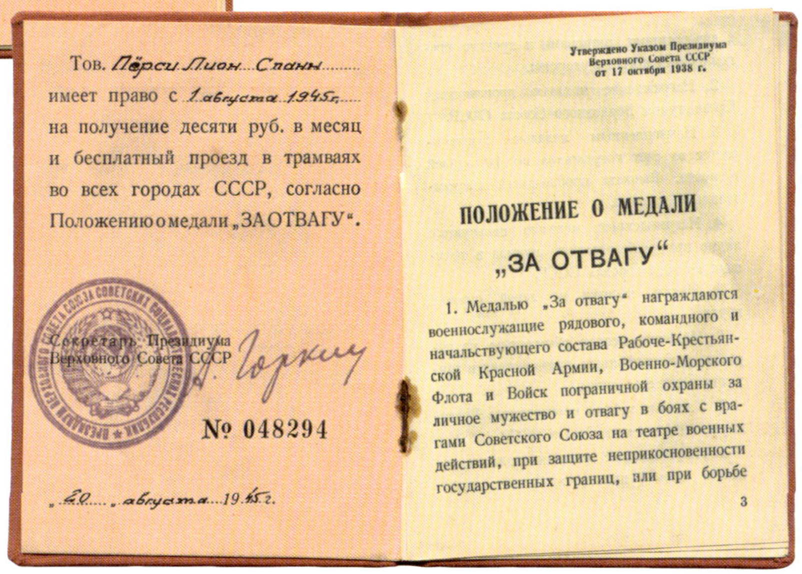

Percy Spann's medal book. As with the other posthumous recipients, the family was still required to supply a photo of him for the document. *Courtesy of the Spann family.*

Medal "For Valor" 2075719 awarded posthumously to Percy Spann. *Courtesy of the Spann family.*

The posthumous Purple Heart awarded Percy Spann's brother, Jamie Spann, killed in action while serving with the 251st Field Artillery Battalion in the Philippines on April 20, 1945. *Courtesy of the Spann family.*

The SS *El Capitan*, a Panamanian-flagged merchant with a US Navy Armed Guard detachment on board, survived the carnage of July 5 by following the summertime fog banks. Throughout July 6, they listened to the distress calls of the ships around them. They knew of ships sinking off their bow, stern, and off each quarter, and in the process, they rescued nineteen survivors from the *John Witherspoon*. Her master decided to head for Novaya Zemlya and take cover in Matochkin Strait, where they could wait a week and hopefully outlast the German attackers. They arrived in the Strait on July 7, and discovered nearly all of the escorts there, along with an anti-aircraft ship and six other merchants, including the *Ironclad*, *Benjamin Harrison*, and *Troubadour*. Underway from the strait at 6:00 PM the same day as a newly formed convoy, they proceeded south with relatively little fanfare. However, a dense fog closed in on the evening of July 8, preventing the convoy from the detecting the heavy pack ice in their path. With the lead ship impacting the ice and becoming stuck fast, the other ships turned and made their way out of the ice field in an attempt to avoid a similar fate. By the time the fog lifted, however, only the *El Capitan*, along with the SS *Hoosier*, a US-flagged merchant, and the military escort vessels were present. The other merchant vessels had gone missing in the fog.

In a race against time and the enemy, the slightly smaller remnant of PQ-17 headed south to the USSR. At 6:45 PM on July 9, a U-boat surfaced astern of the convoy. However, no one fired on it, hoping to outrun it on the surface. Shortly thereafter, two reconnaissance planes arrived above the convoy. For the ships not yet at battle stations, all preparations were made to fend off an expected determined enemy attack. At 10:00 PM, just eighty miles from the Soviet coastline, the attack arrived in the form of five Ju 88 dive-bombers. With the first wave, the *Hoosier* was mortally wounded, falling behind as her crew abandoned the sinking vessel. But that attack was just the beginning. From 10:00 PM on July 9 to 5:30 AM on July 10, the remaining ships were unceasingly attacked by German aircraft. Lieutenant (jg) Louis Marks, the Armed Guard commander on the *El Captain*, estimated thirty-five to forty planes took part in these attacks, with his Armed Guard gunners and the *Witherspoon* survivors firing their two fifty caliber, thirty caliber, and twin Marlin machine guns throughout the entire ordeal. However, despite watching their bullets impact the aircraft, they appeared to have little effect, as the same aircraft were watched returning to base in the direction of Petsamo.[32]

As the attacks continued, at 1:50 AM three five hundred pound bombs fell less than forty feet away from the stern of the ship, causing her to take water in the after peak and in the gun crew quarters and rupturing the number four hold. The starboard side of the engine room was destroyed. However, this was not necessarily fatal and her master determined to keep the ship afloat. At 5:30 AM, three more bombs landed within twenty feet of the ship, just abreast of the bridge. The concussion rocked the ship, causing the sea valves to blow in and the fuel and water pipes to the engines to burst. This was the end of the *El Capitan*. The order to abandon ship was given, and in a very orderly fashion, the crew and the Armed Guard detachment, as well the nineteen survivors from the *John Witherspoon*, boarded the HMT *Lord Austin* for eventual recovery in Archangel.

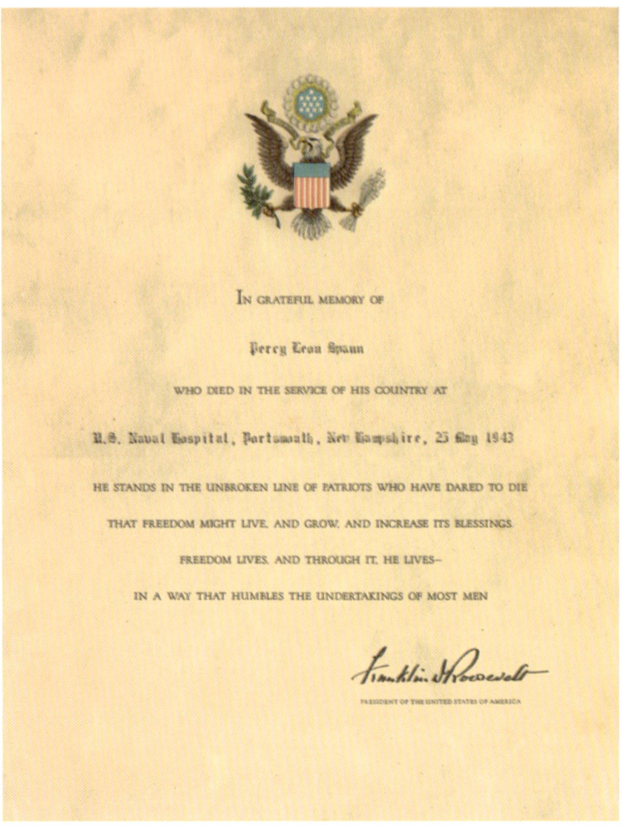

IN GRATEFUL MEMORY OF

Percy Leon Spann

WHO DIED IN THE SERVICE OF HIS COUNTRY AT

U.S. Naval Hospital, Portsmouth, New Hampshire, 25 May 1943

HE STANDS IN THE UNBROKEN LINE OF PATRIOTS WHO HAVE DARED TO DIE

THAT FREEDOM MIGHT LIVE, AND GROW, AND INCREASE ITS BLESSINGS.

FREEDOM LIVES, AND THROUGH IT, HE LIVES–

IN A WAY THAT HUMBLES THE UNDERTAKINGS OF MOST MEN

Franklin D Roosevelt

PRESIDENT OF THE UNITED STATES OF AMERICA

The memorial accolade given to Percy Spann's mother upon his death. *Courtesy of the Spann family.*

Louis D. Marks, *Order of the Red Star*

Louis Marks, later in life, the former Armed Guard commander on the SS *El Capitan*. *Courtesy of the Marks family.*

Louis Davidson Marks, *El Capitan's* Armed Guard commander, was born in Memphis, Tennessee, on June 10, 1920. Graduating from the University of Tennessee in 1940 with a degree in business administration, he volunteered for the Navy on August 26, 1940, and was commissioned on March 14, 1941. Serving first on the USS *Nashville* (CL-43), he was sent to Armed Guard duty in January 1942. His first ship was the SS *City of Dallas*, where he made a convoy to Iceland and back. He survived the sinking of the *El Capitan*, and upon his return from the USSR, was decorated with the Silver Star Medal for his valor during the Murmansk Run. His final ship was the SS *Irene DuPont*, taking part in convoys to England and French Morocco. Leaving Armed Guard duty in March 1943, he reported to the USS *Mobile* (CL-63) in the Pacific theater, conducting strikes on Marcus Island and Tarawa Atoll. Transferred to the USS *Astoria* (CL-90) in October as part of her pre-commissioning crew, he took her from the Atlantic to the Pacific, serving with Task Force 38 (later 58) under the commands of Admirals Halsey and Spruance for much of the remainder of the war. Here, he took part in the raids in the South China Sea, bombarding Chi Chi Jima, Iwo Jima, and later Okinawa. Returning to the United States, he was discharged on February 2, 1946, at the rank of Lieutenant Commander.

Returning to civilian life, he worked for Bell Helicopter-Textron for nineteen years as an aircraft spares administrator before retiring in 1985. Active in the community, he was a volunteer amateur boxing judge and arbitrator for the Better Business Bureau. In 1992, Marks and his wife earned the title of "Volunteer Couple of the Year" in Richland Hills, Texas. Louis Marks passed away on January 12, 1996, and is buried in Mount Olivet Cemetery, Fort Worth, Texas.

Ward L. Gemmer, *Order of the Patriotic War, Second Class*

Ward Gemmer, as a Chief Petty Officer toward the end of his career. Note the faintly visible small ribbon for his Order of the Patriotic War on the right breast of his uniform jacket. *Courtesy of the Gemmer family.*

Ward Leverne Gemmer served as the Coxswain on the Armed Guard crew of the *El Capitan*. Born on August 29, 1914, Gemmer enlisted in the Navy on October 24, 1934, and served in the Asiatic Fleet on the USS *Henderson* (AP-1), USS *Elliot* (DD-146), USS *Asheville* (PG-21), USS *West Virginia* (BB-48), and the USS *Pennsylvania* (BB-38). Discharged from the Navy after almost six years of service, he decided to reenlist in March 1941 and was subsequently assigned to the USS *Ericsson* (DD-440) before his assignment to the Armed Guard in March 1942. On April 9, 1942, he reported to the *El Capitan* for their voyage to Archangel. Following three months in a Soviet hospital, he returned to the United States and was awarded the Silver Star for his heroism during the final days of the *El Capitan*. He was next assigned to the SS *Nortun*, a Panamanian-flagged merchant vessel that was sadly torpedoed at 4:58 AM on the morning of March 20, 1943, off the coast of Namibia with a great loss of life. Injured during the attack, Gemmer earned the Purple Heart. Recovered from his second sinking, he was selected for a war bond tour, where he was partnered with Medal of Honor recipient Marine Sergeant John Basilone.

Completing the tour, Gemmer went on to serve on three merchant ships in the Pacific theater without incident: SS *Samuel T. Tilden*, *Pierre Laclede*, and *Berwindglen*. Leaving the latter on July 2, 1945, now a Chief Boatswain's Mate, he reported for duty at the Receiving Station, Boston, for an almost three-year tour before transferring to the USS *Mississippi* (EAG-128). Subsequently, he was assigned to Naval Air Station Norfolk before returning to sea on the USS *Latimer* (APA-152), followed by the USS *Chief* (AM-315), where he operated off the coast of Korea conducting peacekeeping and patrol operations. Gemmer retired on August 17, 1954, but remained in the Fleet Reserve until February 1, 1965. Following his retirement, he moved to Dayton, Ohio, and passed away on December 1, 1973.

The *El Capitan* had an unusually senior communications detachment, made up of Signalman, first class, Floyd Eugene Richards and Radioman, second class, Joseph Donald Leahy. Both earned the Silver Star for their valor exhibited on the *El Capitan* during the countless raids of July 10.

Имя, отчество и фамилия

Помощник боцмана II класса

Уорд

Л. Джеммер

Подпись владельца книжки

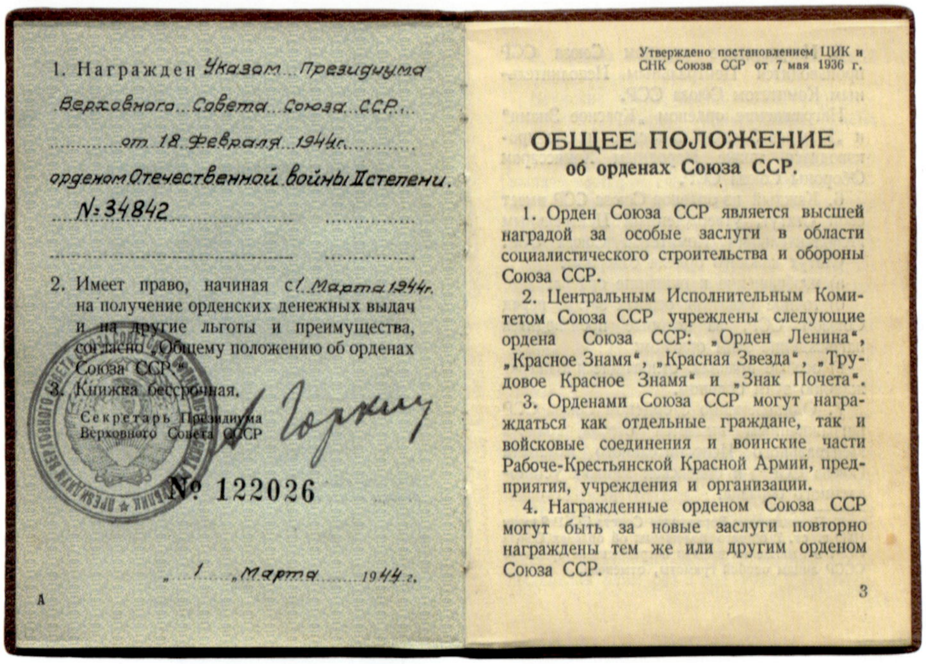

1. Награжден Указом Президиума Верховного Совета Союза ССР от 18 февраля 1944г. орденом Отечественной войны II степени. №34842

2. Имеет право, начиная с 1 марта 1944г. на получение орденских денежных выдач и на другие льготы и преимущества, согласно „Общему положению об орденах Союза ССР."

3. Книжка бессрочная.

Секретарь Президиума Верховного Совета СССР

№ 122026

„1" марта 1944 г.

A

Утверждено постановлением ЦИК и СНК Союза ССР от 7 мая 1936 г.

ОБЩЕЕ ПОЛОЖЕНИЕ
об орденах Союза ССР.

1. Орден Союза ССР является высшей наградой за особые заслуги в области социалистического строительства и обороны Союза ССР.

2. Центральным Исполнительным Комитетом Союза ССР учреждены следующие ордена Союза ССР: „Орден Ленина", „Красное Знамя", „Красная Звезда", „Трудовое Красное Знамя" и „Знак Почета".

3. Орденами Союза ССР могут награждаться как отдельные граждане, так и войсковые соединения и воинские части Рабоче-Крестьянской Красной Армии, предприятия, учреждения и организации.

4. Награжденные орденом Союза ССР могут быть за новые заслуги повторно награждены тем же или другим орденом Союза ССР.

3

Ward Gemmer's order book. Note, as a 1944 award, the medal number is included in the document. *Courtesy of the Gemmer family.*

Order of the Patriotic War, Second Class, number 34842 awarded to Ward Gemmer. *Courtesy of the Gemmer family.*

The Silver Star and Purple Heart awarded to Ward Gemmer. *Courtesy of the Gemmer family.*

Floyd E. Richards, *Medal of Ushakov*

Floyd Richards was born on July 26, 1918, but for the purposes of joining the Navy, he lied about his age and for the remainder of his naval career, his birthday was listed as July 26, 1917. Joining the Navy on December 3, 1935, he served as a Signalman on several ships, to include the USS *Wasmuth* (DD-338) through 1939, followed by the USS *Williams* (DD-108), USS *Sciota* (AT-30) and in October 1941, to the USS *Wyoming* (BB-32) as a Signalman, first class. He wasn't on *Wyoming* long. On January 9, 1942, he was transferred to New York to take part in operation *Magnet-Indigo*, the transportation of US Army troops to Iceland and Ireland to support an early 1942 invasion of North Africa. With the operation cancelled, he was transferred to Armed Guard duty and assigned to the SS *El Capitan*. Earning a Silver Star on the way to Russia during PQ-17, he returned to the United States and was commissioned on August 24, 1943. His first assignment following amphibious operations training was command of USS *LST-133*, commissioning her on November 29 of the same year. Sent to England in preparation for the upcoming Normandy invasion, *LST-133* became the first tank landing ship on Omaha Beach on D-Day plus 1, June 7, 1944. A week later, in the early morning of June 15, 1944, they were transporting three batteries of the 113th Field Artillery Battalion, 30th Infantry Division from England to France. Halfway across the English Channel, *LST-133* was struck by a *Gnat* torpedo fired by *U-621*. Initially believing they hit a floating mine, the entire stern of the ship was demolished. The force of the explosion blew off both forty-millimeter Bofors guns mounts, demolished the steering room, tore off most of the fantail, and destroyed the screws and rudder. Most remarkable was the aft anchor of the ship: it had been blown into the air and embedded itself in the deckhouse. Fifteen Navy crew and twenty-eight Army and Navy Seabee passengers were killed. Because of his calmness and leadership exhibited during the course of the damage control efforts, Floyd Richards received his second Silver Star.

With repairs made to the ship in England, they were transferred to the Pacific, where they later took part in the invasion of Okinawa. With the end of the war, he became commanding officer of USS *LST-579* in December 1945 followed by USS *LST-461* in February 1946. On May 2, 1947, Richards took command of USS *Jekyl* (AG-135), a cargo ship responsible for resupply missions for the small US outposts and bases throughout the Western Pacific. A year later, she was decommissioned and following a brief time ashore at Twelfth Naval District Headquarters, Richards took command of USS *LST-840* in July 1952, making shuttle runs between Korea and Japan at the end of the Korean War. His final award was for his leadership during Operation Passage to Freedom, evacuating thousands of refugees from northern Vietnam in October and November 1955 with USS *LST-803*. For this, he received a Letter of Commendation from Commander, Task Force Ninety. After twenty years of service, with nearly all of it at sea, Richards retired from the Navy as a Lieutenant Commander on February 29, 1956, but was promoted to Commander based on his wartime awards. Floyd Richards passed away on September 12, 1991.

Joseph D. Leahy, *Medal of Nakhimov*

Joseph Leahy was born in Canandaigua, New York, on January 17, 1918, attended West High School in Rochester, and enlisted in the Navy as an inactive reservist on May 17, 1938. He was employed by Ritter Dental Manufacturing Company as a production clerk until called up for active duty on April 28, 1941. He first served at the Naval Radio Station for the Third Naval District, but was subsequently assigned to the communication school in Noroton Heights, Connecticut, for twelve weeks of training in shipboard communication. His first and only ship with the Armed Guard was the *El Capitan*. Following his return from the USSR, he was subsequently assigned to the USS *Bond* (AM-152) in the Pacific, conducting patrols off the coast of Alaska. Reassigned to the USS *Arenac* (APA-128) in 1944, he took part in the invasion of Okinawa, followed by a transfer to the USS *Mifflin* (APA-207) transporting troops to the Philippines and later, back to the United States at the conclusion of the war. Released from active duty on September 12, 1945, as a Radioman, first class, he returned to Rochester and to the Ritter Company. He worked as an automatic screw machine operator and set-up man at the company for nearly twenty-four total years.

Joseph Leahy. *Courtesy of the Leahy family.*

Edge numbering of the Medal of Nakhimov awarded to Joseph Leahy. *Courtesy of the Leahy family.*

Medal of Nakhimov number 5594 awarded to Joseph Leahy. *Courtesy of the Leahy family.*

On June 21, 1963, after an illness, he suffered a major heart attack while driving to the doctor for a return-to-work physical. Exiting his car, he collapsed, and was pronounced dead at the scene. Joseph Leahy is buried in White Haven Memorial Park, Rochester, New York.

A handful of ships survived convoy PQ-17 and arrived safely in Archangel. The SS *Bellingham*, which was initially passed by the Royal Navy escorts, finally came across the convoy rescue ship RFA *Rathlin* on July 7 and proceeded in tandem with her. At 6:05 AM that morning, the *Bellingham* was struck starboard side amidships by a German torpedo. They were exceptionally lucky: the torpedo failed to explode and merely left a "tin hat" indentation into the side of the ship, twelve feet below the waterline. Had it exploded, the ship would have undoubtedly sunk. At 10:30 PM the same day, they were attacked by a single German bomber. Despite thoroughly ravaging her with the Armed Guard's weapons on the ship, the aircraft still managed to drop three bombs twenty yards astern of the ship and fired at them with its twenty-millimeter cannon, causing an ammonia tank to explode before crashing in flames into the sea. Seaman Raymond Peer, manning the aft gun mount, was thrown to the deck and sustained multiple shrapnel wounds from the explosions. Further, the ammonia caused the engine room to require evacuation, but armed with respirators, the engineers had the ship back underway in fifteen minutes, and Peer's wounds were treated onboard. On July 8, the *Bellingham* spotted several Soviet warships that escorted her into port safely. The *Bellingham* had survived, and as the other ships were still attempting to remain hidden from the Germans, she began off-loading cargo on the morning of July 10.

The SS *Benjamin Harrison*, which had steamed alongside the ill-fated *Daniel Morgan* and *Fairfield City* on July 5, was a ship that survived mostly due to luck and heavy fog. When the *Daniel Morgan* was able to see the destruction of the *Fairfield City* as they exited the fog bank, the *Benjamin Harrison* was able to stay in the fog. Lieutenant (jg) Paul Thompson, *Harrison's* Armed Guard commander, noted that the fog was sufficiently thick that they were so well hidden from the attacking German aircraft that they were never discovered, despite being sufficiently close to the attack on the other two ships to feel the concussions from the bomb blasts that eventually claimed them both.[33] But the *Harrison* survived. She made it to Matochkin Strait on the coastline of Novaya Zemlya at 2:00 PM on July 6, and found multiple convoy survivors anchored in the Strait. At 8:10 PM on July 7, an attempt was made to leave the strait, but a dense fog rolled in, and the *Harrison* was instantly alone. Remaining in place until the fog lifted the following day, they returned to the strait to await further orders.

On July 11, the Royal Navy trawler HMS *Ayreshire*, escorting the surviving SS *Ironclad*, *Silver Sword*, and *Troubador* arrived in the strait. These four ships had decided to head to the north on July 4, where they had waited for a time in the ice. To prevent discovery by the lurking U-boats, their crews painted the ships white, undoubtedly saving them from a fate similar to many others in the convoy. The *Ironclad* and *Troubador* had both provided sufficient excitement before convoy PQ-17 even left Iceland. On *Troubador*, Ensign Howard Carraway, the Armed Guard commander, recorded an initial, and continued, friction between the Armed Guard and the ship's civilian crew. Two days into their voyage to the USSR, an unknown member of the crew opened the ship's flood valves, filling the Armed Guard ammunition magazine with four feet of water and submerging almost their entire onboard ammunition allowance. Ensign Carraway requested, and was given, four additional pistols for the members of the Armed Guard, in order to arm each of them. He considered this "necessary in view of the conduct of the ship's crew, which was from the first antagonistic, unruly and irresponsible."[34] The crew likewise had considerable friction with their civilian officers, and at one point while anchored in Iceland, twenty members of the crew refused to work and the master was forced to confine them below, with members of the Armed Guard filling their jobs, until the civilian crew acquiesced. These events were not helped by Carraway's contraction of pneumonia during the voyage across the Atlantic, leaving him in a considerably weakened state throughout the remainder of the transit to the USSR, nor the fact that much of the water logged ammunition was never fully replaced. In order to remedy their ammunition shortfall, Carraway ordered the on-deck M3 Lee medium tanks on deck unsealed and their thirty-seven millimeter guns put into use in the defense of the ship.

The SS *Troubador*. *National Archives.*

Due to their shortage of ammunition on the *Troubador*, Howard Carraway put the M3 tanks on deck to use. This image shows one of the crew giving target coordinates to the gunners inside the tank. *National Archives.*

On the *Ironclad*, Ensign William Carter and his Armed Guard detachment had reported on January 19, 1942, prior to the enlistments of many of the Armed Guard Sailors on other ships in the convoy. They had departed New York on January 31, and arrived in Scotland on March 16. They initially departed Iceland on April 8 with the *Yaka* and *West Cheswald* of convoy PQ-14, but missed a communication during a heavy snowstorm and failed to turn with the remainder of the convoy. Ordered to return to Iceland, they arrived on April 21. For the next month, they sat at anchor, with no liberty allowed ashore. The civilian crew and Navy gunners grew restless, and on May 19, some of both groups were caught with stolen whiskey that had been part of the cargo intended for the American Embassy in Moscow. An altercation required the intervention of a squad of Marines from the USS *Washington* (BB-56). Two of the most unruly crew were shackled by the master to the ship's rail, and the rest of the crew was placed under armed guard, with fourteen of the crew placed under arrest in the forecastle. Because of this, they missed the opportunity to sail with convoy PQ-16 and were rescheduled to become part of PQ-17.

Since receiving the scatter order on July 4, their time with the *Ayreshire* had been relatively uneventful save for a collision between the *Silver Sword* and the *Ironclad* on July 8, when the former attempted to avoid an iceberg and steered into the bow of the latter. They followed the edge of the icefields and waited patiently to arrive unscathed at Matochkin Strait on July 10 at 2:00 PM. Undamaged, that is, until the *Ironclad* ran aground on a hidden reef and had to wait until high tide to refloat herself. The small convoy of surviving ships moved further inland on July 13 to avoid discovery by German aircraft or surface vessels. And here they waited. Three days later, they attempted to head back out to sea, but both the *Troubador* and the *Ironclad* ran aground. Despite refloating themselves, the convoy was ordered to return far into Matochkin Strait and continue to wait. At 5:14 AM on July 20, sixteen days after the order to scatter had been given, the convoy, consisting of the *Benjamin Harrison*, *Ironclad*, *Troubador*, *Silver Sword*, three Soviet merchant ships, and four British escorts, got underway for Archangel. The following day, they were joined by the British merchant *Empire Tide* that had been hiding in a more southern bay. On July 22, seven escorts including one British anti-aircraft ship, five Soviet destroyers and one corvette joined the growing group. By July 25, they were all anchored in Archangel.

Convoy PQ-17 had begun with thirty-six merchant vessels, of which twenty-four were American. One ran aground and one turned back. Of the remaining ships, only six American merchant vessels reached Archangel. Even fewer would make it back to the United States. Returning with convoy QP-14 along with *Benjamin Harrison*, *Deer Lodge*, and *Troubador*, the *Bellingham* was sunk by *U-435* four days away from her arrival in Loch Ewe, Scotland. She was approximately forty-five miles west of Jan Mayen Islands with a Lend-Lease repayment cargo of mineral ore and animal skins. At 6:15 AM, a torpedo struck number four hold on the starboard side without warning and without a wake, causing serious damage below the waterline. Her master made the decision to abandon ship and the survivors were picked up immediately by the convoy escort vessels. The brave ship that had been through so much slipped stern first below the waves.

The *Ironclad*, on the other hand, had a far less glorious departure. Returning with convoy QP-15 on November 17, she ran aground at the entrance to the White Sea on November 24, 1942, due to a combination of navigational errors caused by poor weather, communication failure, and pilot incompetence. Unable to return to port, the crew was removed from the ship and negotiations began with the Soviets with regard to repairing the ship. George Roullard, the Assistant Naval Attaché in Archangel, recommended repatriating the civilian crew immediately in a message to the Navy staff in Washington, DC, on December 6:

> *Judging from past experience, repair equipment available ice conditions and usual prompt Russian way of handling American ships after they have discharged war cargo,* Ironclad *will be in North Russian another 6 months. Because of past events, officers' and crews' morale at breaking point. Suggest ship and equipment be chartered to or entirely turned over to Soviet government and crew repatriated at first opportunity before general mutiny or loss of life occurs.*[35]

Badly damaged, the decision was made to sign the ship over to the Soviets effective January 25, 1943, for them to repair and place in service as they deemed appropriate. Her voyage to, and stay in, the USSR had been nothing short of tumultuous, due mainly to the attitude of her master, Captain Philip Moore. As Roullard wrote of him to the War Shipping Administration:

> *The Office of the Assistant US Naval Attaché at Archangel, USSR, made every effort to assist the master of the SS* Ironclad, *but he repeatedly failed in his duty as master to straighten out problems concerning his, as well as his ship's, welfare. During his stay in the Soviet Union he was particularly antagonistic toward the Soviets and therefore received a minimum of cooperation from them. He broke many Soviet laws ... After almost daily contact with Captain Philip Moore, his ship, and his most troublesome problems for over six months while in the Soviet Union, the Assistant Naval Attaché believes him mentally incompetent, thoroughly unfit to command and that the best interest of the United States would be jeopardized if he is permitted to retain his master's license.*[36]

The luck of those who survived the voyage of the *Ironclad* didn't improve. Her Armed Guard commander, William Carter, along with three Navy gunners and the *Ironclad's* second officer, left Archangel for their return voyage on the SS *Richard Bland*. The *Bland* had initially started with convoy PQ-17, but had been holed by an iceberg on June 29 and was forced to return to Iceland for repairs. She later arrived in Archangel on December 27 as part of convoy JW-51A. Returning with the survivors of the *Ironclad*, the last remaining veterans of PQ-17 in the USSR, she was hit by a torpedo at 4:30 AM on March 10, 1943. The torpedo had been fired by *U-255*, the same submarine responsible for the sinkings of the *John Witherspoon*, *Alcoa Ranger*, *Olopana*, and the *Paulus Potter* during convoy PQ-17. The *Richard Bland* took thirty-three of her sixty-eight-man crew, including fifteen members of the Navy Armed Guard, to the bottom of the sea: the final losses of the ill-fated convoy.

William A. Carter, *Order of the Patriotic War, First Class*

William A. Carter, the Armed Guard commander on the SS *Ironclad*. *Courtesy of the Carter family.*

William Allen "Bill" Carter, the Armed Guard commander on the ill-fated *Ironclad* and passenger on the *Richard Bland*, was born on January 23, 1919, and raised on Maryland's Eastern Shore and in Southern Delaware. He attended St. Johns College in Annapolis, graduating with the class of 1940. He enlisted in the Navy's V-7 officer candidate program on September 10, 1940, and started his active duty service in the Navy on February 14, 1941. Commissioned from the Naval Reserve Midshipman School at the Naval Academy in May 1941, he was assigned to the submarine tender USS *Antaeus* (AS-21) as her gunnery officer before being transferred to the Armed Guard Center in Brooklyn on January 14, 1942. Assigned to the SS *Ironclad*, he took her to the USSR, earning the Silver Star for his heroism and devoted leadership. Returning to the United States, he became the pre-commissioning gunnery officer on the USS *Roche* (DE-197). Serving on *Roche* and taking part in Atlantic convoy-escort duties, Carter transferred on February 16, 1945, to the tender USS *Black Hawk* (AD-9), where he became the gunnery officer and served with her in the Pacific theater. Detached on August 30, 1945, he returned to Delaware and was discharged from active duty on November 11, 1945. Remaining in the Naval Reserves, he commanded Naval Reserve Ordnance Company 4-6 in Seaford, Delaware, and retired on June 1, 1960, as a Commander.

As a civilian, Carter became plant superintendent and later sales manager for the Houston-White Company, manufacturer of wood veneer fruit and produce baskets. Later, he served as president of the Millsboro Town Commission, where he led efforts to construct the town's first sewage treatment system. He additionally served as chairman of the state Water and Air Resources Commission and of the Delaware Industrial Building Commission, and the state's Higher Education Scholarship Commission. Following the integration of Delaware's schools, he chaired a committee to find a new use for the former William C. Jason High School for Sussex County's black students, recommending that it be turned into a community college campus for Sussex County. This school became known as the Owens Campus of the Delaware Technical and Community College. He was named by Governor Sherman W. Tribbitt as chairman of the statewide College Board, a position he held for nearly ten years under two governors. In 1998, the Owens Campus named its new higher education building the "William A. Carter Partnership Center" in his honor.

William Carter in his later years was a staunch advocate for positive relations between the people of the United States and Russia. He is photographed here in the Russian Embassy in Washington, DC. *Courtesy of the Carter family.*

In addition to his interest in education, he served for over fifty years as an agent and district agent for the Northwestern Mutual Life Insurance Co., and co-developed a Millsboro shopping center. At age seventy-nine, he returned to college, earning a PhD in higher education and public policy. In 2008, he published a memoir of his experiences on the Murmansk Run, (to include a comprehensive and impassioned defense to the character of the previously derided master of the *Ironclad*) entitled: *Why Me, Lord? The Experiences of a US Navy Armed Guard Officer in World War II's Convoy PQ-17 on the Murmansk Run*. In his later years, he devoted much of his time to efforts to improve relations between citizens of Russia and the US. He was an honored guest at the Russian Embassy in Washington several times and had been invited to participate in festivities in Moscow's Red Square in May 2010, but his declining health forced the cancellation of his trip. Bill Carter passed away on September 11, 2010.

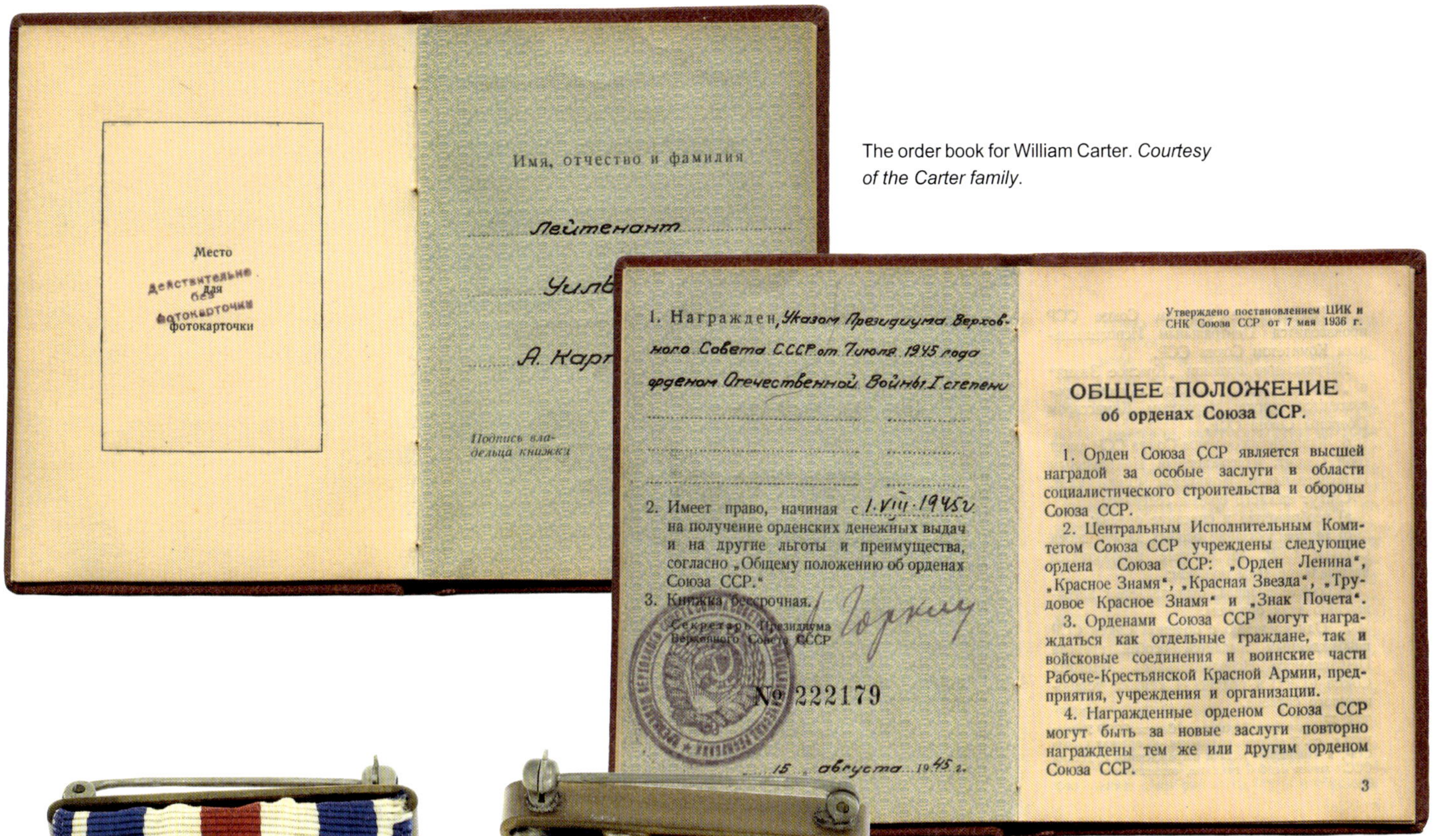

The order book for William Carter. *Courtesy of the Carter family*.

The Silver Star Medal awarded to William Carter. *Courtesy of the Carter family*.

Order of the Patriotic War, First Class, 247509 awarded to William Carter. *Courtesy of the Carter family*.

Paul W. Thompson, *Order of the Patriotic War, Second Class*

Paul Waite Thompson, the Armed Guard commander on the SS *Benjamin Harrison. National Personnel Records Center.*

A native of Syracuse, New York, Paul Waite Thompson was born on August 20, 1918. He attended the Western Reserve Academy in Hudson, Ohio, and graduated from the College of Wooster in Wooster, Ohio, in 1940, with a degree in political science. Thompson joined the Navy on December 18 of the same year. Selected to serve as an Armed Guard detachment commander, he was assigned to the SS *Benjamin Harrison* during PQ-17. Returning to the United States on October 20, 1942, he was reassigned to the USAT *Uruguay*, transporting US Army troops across the Atlantic. Following his release from the Armed Guard in January 1943, he was assigned to the USS *Paducah* (PG-18), a pre-First World War vintage gunboat used for training Armed Guard crews in the Chesapeake Bay. Detaching from *Paducah* after four months, he attended the Submarine Chaser Training School in Miami and reported to the USS *Breeman* (DE-104) as the gunnery officer. On *Breeman*, Thompson took part in hunter-killer operations against U-boats in the Atlantic in task groups including the USS *Bogue* (CVE-9) and the USS *Card* (CVE-11). At the end of 1944, he reported to the USS *Madera County* (LST-905), assuming the duty as commanding officer upon her commissioning in January 1945. In February, Thompson took the *Madera County* into the Pacific, and by June, was operating off the coast of Okinawa. He remained on board the ship until his change of command in October. Returning to the United States, he was discharged from the Navy and settled in Morristown, New Jersey. He first worked in the personnel department of Random House publishers, but in 1957, moved to RCA. He worked for RCA for the next twenty-five years, retiring as a personnel director in 1982. About fifteen years later, he moved to Convent Station, New Jersey and passed away there on October 31, 2002. He is buried in the First Presbyterian Churchyard in Morristown.

Howard E. Carraway, *Order of the Red Star*

Howard Carraway, Armed Guard commander on the SS *Troubadour. Courtesy of the Carraway family.*

On board *Troubador*, Howard Ernest Carraway was serving as the Armed Guard commander. Born on October 22, 1917, in Olanta, South Carolina, and working as a newspaperman when the war started, he volunteered for the Navy. He was commissioned on January 16, 1942, after attending the Naval Reserve Midshipman School at Abbott Hall, Northwestern University. Reporting to the Armed Guard Center in Brooklyn following his initial gunnery training in Little Creek, Virginia, he was immediately assigned to the Armed Guard detachment for the SS *Troubador*. Taking her to Archangel, he earned a Commendation from the Secretary of the Navy for his valor during the inbound and outbound voyages. Returning to the United States, he transferred from the Armed Guard and spent the remainder of the war developing training programs at the Naval Mine Warfare School in Yorktown, Virginia, as well as at the Naval Training and Distribution Center at Camp Peary, Virginia.

Returning to Pageland, South Carolina on March 27, 1946, he remained in the Naval Reserves, being recalled in 1950 to serve as the officer in charge of the US Naval Magazine, Theodore, Alabama, for two years. He eventually retired as a Commander on December 15, 1976. As a civilian, he returned to the newspaper business, working as a staff writer for the Florence, South Carolina, *Morning News*, and later becoming the co-owner of the Pageland Press and Pageland Journal until 1959. Selling the Journal, he moved to Fort Pierce, Florida, where he purchased the Fort Pierce Press. He also worked for the Fort Pierce News-Tribune, writing a column called "The Cracker Barrell" as well as conducting investigative reporting. In 1962, he published a series of acclaimed articles on the inequities of the Florida trucking industry, entitled *Florida's Freight Rate Fiasco*, earning him the "National Headliner Award"[35] and the Associated Press award for public service.[36] This brought him to the attention of the Florida Public Service Commission, which hired him for their staff. Starting as the administrative secretary and assistant to the commissioners, he was selected to be the executive director of the Florida Telephone Association in 1972. He retired from this position in 1985. In his retirement, he wrote *Telephony in Florida Since 1877 and a History of the Florida Telephone Association*, which was published in 1991. Active in the community, he served as the governor of the Florida Kiwanis Clubs and as president of the Kiwanis International Foundation. Howard Carraway passed away on March 19, 2003, and is buried in Florida National Cemetery in Bushnell, Florida.

Имя, отчество и фамилия
Младший лейтенант
Хауард
Э. Карауэй
Подпись владельца книжки

I. Награжден Указом Президиума Верховного Совета СССР от 7 июля 1945 года орденом Красной Звезды
2. Имеет право, начиная с 1-VIII-1945 г. на получение орденских денежных выдач и на другие льготы и преимущества, согласно Общему положению об орденах Союза ССР.
3. Книжка бессрочная.
Секретарь Президиума Верховного Совета СССР
№ 222228
15 августа 1945 г.

Утверждено постановлением ЦИК и СНК Союза ССР от 7 мая 1936 г.

ОБЩЕЕ ПОЛОЖЕНИЕ
об орденах Союза ССР.

1. Орден Союза ССР является высшей наградой за особые заслуги в области социалистического строительства и обороны Союза ССР.
2. Центральным Исполнительным Комитетом Союза ССР учреждены следующие ордена Союза ССР: „Орден Ленина", „Красное Знамя", „Красная Звезда", „Трудовое Красное Знамя" и „Знак Почета".
3. Орденами Союза ССР могут награждаться как отдельные граждане, так и войсковые соединения и воинские части Рабоче-Крестьянской Красной Армии, предприятия, учреждения и организации.
4. Награжденные орденом Союза ССР могут быть за новые заслуги повторно награждены тем же или другим орденом Союза ССР.
3

Howard Carraway's Soviet order book. *Courtesy of the Carraway family*.

Order of the Red Star number 1553971 awarded to Howard Carraway. *Courtesy of the Carraway family*.

Willard Brown receives his Silver Star for gallantry exhibited on the SS *Bellingham*. *Courtesy of the Willard W. Brown family.*

Willard W. Brown, *Order of the Patriotic War, First Class*

The crew of the *Bellingham* fought bravely throughout their transit, but their luck ran out before their safe arrival on Allied territory. *Bellingham's* Armed Guard commander was Willard Wilkins "Bill" Brown. Born on May 6, 1918, in Newark, New Jersey, he attended Columbia High School in Maplewood and Williams College in Williamstown, Massachusetts, lettering in football, hockey, and lacrosse. In the summer before his senior year at Williams, he took a group of students to Europe and what he saw there gave him the chills: he knew war was on the horizon. Upon graduation, he volunteered for officer training and was enlisted in the Navy on September 30, 1940. Commissioned on February 28, 1941, he served on the USS *Colorado* (BB-45) before being sent to Armed Guard duty in New Orleans. Taking the *Bellingham* to Archangel, he earned the Silver Star for his bravery and ensuring the survival of the ship. Returning to the United States, he reported to the USS *New Jersey* (BB-62), and became the starboard five-inch gunnery officer, supervising the installation and use of the guns on the newly commissioned ship. Taking the ship to the Pacific, he served through her first actions around the Marshall and Caroline Islands before volunteering for flight school. Following his fifty-four weeks of flight training, he reported to squadron VPB-91 for operational training before his ultimate assignment to VPB-1. Discharged from active duty on November 12, 1945, he remained in the Naval Reserves until his retirement on October 1, 1959, as a Commander.

As a civilian, Brown completed an internship at Chase Bank following his Navy service and went on to spend the majority of his career in the investment and brokerage field. In 1956, he built Pheasant Ridge farm in Gladstone, New Jersey, where he spent much of his free time with his beloved wife of fifty-nine years and his many horses and dogs. Bill Brown passed away on July 15, 2013.

Willard Brown (right) with his brother during a chance meeting in Pearl Harbor, February 1944. *Courtesy of the Willard W. Brown family.*

Francis P. Perret. *National Personnel Records Center.*

Francis P. Perret, *Medal "For Valor"*

The gun captain on the *Bellingham* was Francis Peter Perret, who was born in Los Angeles, California, on April 21, 1923. Enlisting in the Navy, he went through recruit training in San Diego, graduating on January 14, 1942. He reported to the Armed Guard Center in New Orleans, Louisiana, on March 2 and was sent directly to the *Bellingham*. Surviving the Murmansk Run, he was promoted to Gunner's Mate, third class and further served on the SS *Miguel Hidalgo*, *James B. Hickock*, *Hans Heg*, and *Richard Yates* in both the Atlantic and Pacific theaters until the end of the war. As a Gunner's Mate, second class, he was retained on active duty and served at the Armed Guard Center on Treasure Island, California. On September 4, 1946, he boarded the destroyer tender USS *Prairie* (AD-15) and remained there until he was discharged on December 16.

Residing in the Los Angeles area after his discharge, he became a truck driver and shortly thereafter moved to Tacoma, Washington. In Tacoma, he became a driver for Mayflower Cab and worked with them for seventeen years before he retired. Moving back to California, he spent the rest of his life in Oceanside, an active member of the US Power Squadrons and the Elks Lodge. Francis Perret passed away on November 25, 2001.

Raymond P. Peer, *Medal "For Valor"*

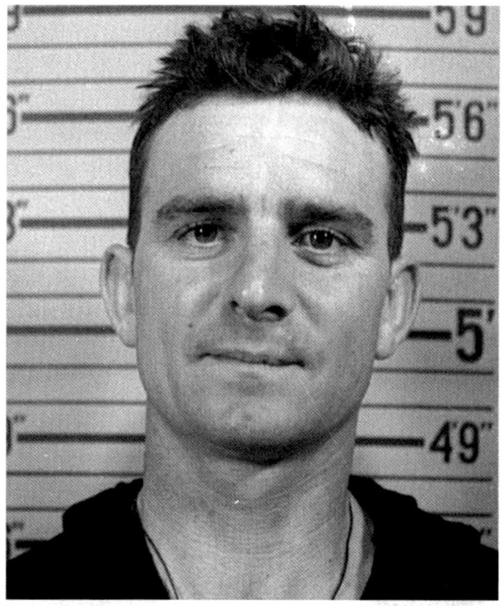

Raymond P. Peer. *National Personnel Records Center.*

The *Bellingham* had six Navy gunners attached to the Armed Guard detachment, all of whom later received Soviet medals. Raymond Peter Peer was born on November 6, 1916, in Green Bay, Wisconsin. He was raised by his uncle and dropped out of school after seventh grade to work on a farm. His background wasn't perfect: he had been arrested twice for disorderly conduct while drunk. With the start of the war, he felt it was his patriotic duty to enlist, and he arrived at recruit training in Great Lakes on January 27, 1942. Sent to the Armed Guard Center in New Orleans on February 22, he was immediately placed on the list for duty on the *Bellingham*. Surviving the Murmansk Run, he reported to the Armed Guard Center in Brooklyn in December, and was assigned to the SS *Cornelius Harnett*, serving under fellow Soviet award recipient Lieutenant (jg) Richard Stone, the *Harnett's* Armed Guard commander in convoy JW-52.[37] Surviving the concentrated attacks of the Germans a second time, he was subsequently assigned to the SS *John Davenport* and promoted to Coxswain on May 3, 1943. If two trips to the USSR weren't sufficient excitement, he was on the *Davenport* on the morning of July 6, 1943, moored in the harbor of Wellington, New Zealand, full of explosives and with aircraft secured to the top of the hatches holding the explosives. She was undergoing welding repairs to her deck when a fire broke out in number three hold. Only the quick thinking of the ship's master and the harbormaster saved the day and took the ship out to sea and extinguished the fire before the ammunition could explode and quite possibly flatten much of the city of Wellington.[38]

In October ,while the ship was in Ceylon, he was transferred off the *Davenport* due to reoccurring issues from his shrapnel wounds received during PQ-17, he was transferred back to the United States and assigned to the Naval Training School at the University of Chicago in February 1944. Shortly thereafter, he was promoted to Boatswain's Mate, second class. His wounds again resulted in hospitalization, and he was unable to perform additional service. Peer received his honorable discharge on February 8, 1945, and he returned to Green Bay. Moving to Chicago, he worked as a laborer until he was admitted to the Veterans Affairs Westside Medical Center due to lung cancer. He died of a heart attack on July 16, 1985, and is buried in Queen of Heaven Cemetery in Hillside, Illinois.

Albert Yingling, approximately 1943. Courtesy of the Yingling family.

Albert O. Yingling, *Medal "For Valor"*

Albert Oney Yingling was born in Muncie, Indiana, on January 22, 1922. Enlisting from Indianapolis, he attended recruit training at Great Lakes before being sent to the Armed Guard Center in New Orleans and assigned to the *Bellingham*. Surviving the voyage to the USSR, he remained with the Armed Guard throughout the war, ending up as Boatswain's Mate, second class, by August 1945. Remaining in the Navy, he transferred to the USS *Philadelphia* (CL-41) in January 1946, and in July, received orders to the USS *Prince William* (CVE-31). His final command was the USS *Pentheus* (ARL-20). He was discharged from Jacksonville, Florida, in 1947 and settled in West Palm Beach. He became a firefighter and spent the next twenty-five years serving with the West Palm Beach Fire Department before his retirement. Albert Yingling passed away on March 7, 2001, and is buried in Hillcrest Memorial Park in West Palm Beach.

Oswald I. Cassidy, *Medal "For Valor"*

Oswald I. Cassidy. *National Personnel Records Center.*

Oswald Irvin Cassidy was born on March 19, 1924, in Dickinson, North Dakota. He finished eighth grade and served in Company 2772 of the Civilian Conservation Corps. He was working as a bellhop at a hotel in Mandan, North Dakota, prior to enlisting in the Navy on January 17, 1942. Following recruit training, he was assigned to the Armed Guard and spent the entirety of the war sailing from the Armed Guard Centers in both Brooklyn and New Orleans. Discharged as a Seaman, first class, on October 7, 1945, he moved to Van Port City, Oregon, to live with his brother. Following his job location, he lived most of his life in Philadelphia, Pennsylvania, but after his retirement and the sudden death of his wife, he returned to live with his brother in Oregon, where he spent the remainder of his life. Oswald Cassidy passed away on May 19, 1998.

Lewis W. Kroeger, *Medal "For Valor"*

Lewis William "Lewey" Kroeger was born on April 11, 1918, in Sumatra, Montana, but moved to Minnesota at a young age. He dropped out of school after the eighth grade to help his family and from the age of sixteen, worked for the Hanson Silo Company in Lake Lillian, Minnesota as a truck driver. He worked for Hanson until he enlisted in the Navy on January 6, 1942. Reporting to Great Lakes for recruit training, he received orders to the Armed Guard Center in New Orleans, and subsequently, to the *Bellingham*. Surviving the Murmansk Run, he was transferred to the Armed Guard Center in Brooklyn where he served on the SS *Caquetta*, *Altair*, *Hawaiian*, *James Gordon Bennett*, and the MS *Sun*. He was discharged on October 6, 1945, and returned to Lake Lillian, Minnesota. As a civilian, he worked as a carpenter and crane operator for Nelson Construction in Willmar, Minnesota, for his entire career. Lewis Kroeger died on January 10, 2011, and is buried in Fort Snelling National Cemetery in Minneapolis.

The Soviet medal book awarded to Leland Hall, along with his dog tag. *Courtesy of the Hall family.*

Leland Hall, *Medal "For Valor"*

Leland Hall was born at Elbowoods, North Dakota, on October 28, 1920, and was raised in the Independence District of the Fort Berthold Indian Reservation on the Hall family ranch. He attended Elbowoods Elementary School and Pipestone Indian Boarding School, in Pipestone, Minnesota, but left after the eighth grade. Hall enlisted on January 20, 1942, and was assigned to the Armed Guard Center in New Orleans following recruit training at Great Lakes. His first, and only, ship was the SS *Bellingham*. Upon his return to the United States, his health was severely affected by the transit, and he was discharged on October 26, 1943. He returned to Elbowoods and worked at Elbowoods Hospital as a fireman before buying cattle for his own ranch. Proud of his ranch, he worked all day, seven days a week, to care for his livestock until his health could no longer support it. He passed away on June 1, 2001, in Dickinson, North Dakota.

Leonard Horton. *Courtesy of Leonard Horton.*

Leonard D. Horton, *Medal "For Valor"*

Leonard Durwood Horton was born on May 27, 1919, in Whitewright, Texas. He began working for the Santa Fe railroad, working as a fireman on freight locomotives in New Mexico. He joined the Navy on December 21, 1941, following in the footsteps of his stepfather, who he greatly respected. After recruit training in San Diego, California, he was assigned to the Armed Guard service at the Armed Guard Center in New Orleans. His first ship was the SS *Bellingham*, and he took it to the USSR, with his responsibility being the pointer on the four-inch deck gun. After the sinking of the *Bellingham*, he returned to the United States and continued with the Armed Guard service until January 18, 1944, when he received orders to advanced gunnery school in Washington, DC He reported to the USS *Otus* (ARG-20), an internal combustion engine repair ship stationed in the South Pacific, in July 1944. Returning to Washington, DC in December, he became an instructor at the gunnery school and remained there through his discharge in September 1945. Returning to New Mexico, he assumed his former position with the Santa Fe Railroad and worked as a fireman and engineer for the next thirty years. Following his retirement from the railroad, he settled in Clovis, New Mexico, and worked on home construction and remodeling projects for others as a hobby, eventually building his own home where he spent his remaining years.

Ernest E. Grandey, Jr., *Medal "For Valor"*

Bellingham's communications group consisted of Ernest Grandey as the Radioman and Charles Harris as the Signalman, both of whom later were awarded Soviet medals. Ernest Edwin Grandey, Jr., was born on February 9, 1919, in McMinnville, Tennessee. He worked for his father's dairy business from 1936 until he joined the Navy on September 3, 1941. Following recruit training in Norfolk, and then radio communication training in Indianapolis, Indiana, and Noroton Heights, Connecticut, he reported to the Armed Guard Center in Brooklyn. Assigned to the *Bellingham* as his first ship, he survived the Murmansk Run to continue his service in the Armed Guard as a Radioman throughout the entire duration of the war. He was discharged on November 9, 1945, as a Radioman, third class, and returned to McMinnville to work as a dairy farmer.

In 1950, he enrolled in David Lipscomb College in Nashville, Tennessee, and graduated in 1953. He taught in the Warren County, Tennessee, schools until 1964, when he decided to move to Florida, where he taught at the Apopka High School for eight years. He decided to return to Warren County and worked as a math teacher until he became a high school principal prior to his retirement in 1985. Becoming interested in body building while in the Navy, he continued his weight training and three-mile daily run until age seventy, two years before his death. Following his retirement, he became interested in small engine repair and gardening, and became extremely adept at both. Ernest Grandey passed away on February 18, 1991.

Матрос II статьи
(имя)
Орнст
(отчество)
Э. Грэнди, мл.
(фамилия)

Указом Президиума Верховного Совета СССР награжден медалью „ЗА ОТВАГУ".

Тов. Орнст Э. Грэнди
имеет право с 1 августа 1945 г.
на получение десяти руб. в месяц и бесплатный проезд в трамваях во всех городах СССР, согласно Положению о медали „ЗА ОТВАГУ".

Секретарь Президиума Верховного Совета СССР

№ 048268

„20" августа 1945 г.

Утверждено Указом Президиума Верховного Совета СССР от 17 октября 1938 г.

ПОЛОЖЕНИЕ О МЕДАЛИ „ЗА ОТВАГУ"

1. Медалью „За отвагу" награждаются военнослужащие рядового, командного и начальствующего состава Рабоче-Крестьянской Красной Армии, Военно-Морского Флота и Войск пограничной охраны за личное мужество и отвагу в боях с врагами Советского Союза на театре военных действий, при защите неприкосновенности государственных границ, или при борьбе

3

The Soviet medal book to Ernest Grandey. *Courtesy of the Grandey family.*

Medal "For Valor" number 2075724 awarded to Ernest Grandey. *Courtesy of the Grandey family.*

Andrew O. Mathson, *Medal "For Valor"*

The final gunner on the *Bellingham* was Andrew Oliver "Andy" Mathson. Born on September 9, 1921, in Halliday, North Dakota, he graduated from high school in 1939 and attended the Minot State Teachers College prior to joining the Navy. An amateur boxer, he won the Golden Gloves Championship for the state of North Dakota in 1939. He joined the Navy on January 20, 1942 and completed recruit training at Great Lakes before reporting to the Armed Guard Center in New Orleans on February 22. Serving first on the *Bellingham*, he was later attached to the SS *Cortago* in December 1942 and served on her until May 1943. His next assignment was the USS *Cotten* (DD-669), where he briefly crossed paths with fellow Soviet medal recipient Senua Trahan in May 1945. Mathson then transferred to the Small Craft Training Center in San Pedro, California, on June 19. This was followed by a course at the Submarine Chaser Training Center at Treasure Island before he reported to the USS *Arcadia* (AD-23) on September 13. He was discharged from the Navy on November 16, 1945, as a Boatswain's Mate, second class.

Returning to North Dakota, he worked at the St. Charles Hotel in Dickinson, and then managed the Farmer's Union Oil Company in Rhame. Leaving there after three and a half years, he worked for Gates Rubber Company in Denver for seventeen years (alongside fellow Soviet medal recipient Frank Gay) eventually becoming the territorial manager for the company. This was followed by another seventeen years working for the Amarillo Hardware Company in Amarillo, Texas, as a salesman prior to his retirement. Andrew Mathson passed away on February 14, 2007, and is buried in Llano Cemetery, Amarillo.

The Soviet medal book to Andrew Mathson. *Courtesy of the Mathson family.*

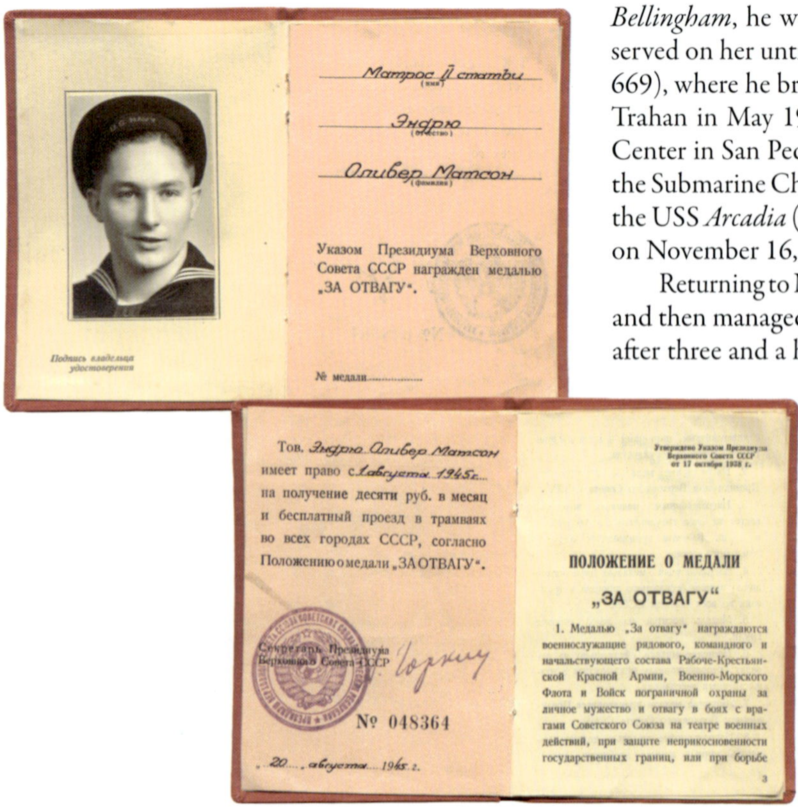

Medal "For Valor" number 2075731, and Navy Good Conduct Medal awarded to Andrew Mathson. *Courtesy of the Mathson family.*

Charles C. Harris, *Medal "For Valor"*

Bellingham's signalman was Charles Clayton Harris, who was born in Moberly, Missouri, on June 17, 1924. Dropping out of high school, he enlisted in the Navy on December 15, 1941. As he told the local newspaper: "Gotta [sic] protect the country, that's more important than going to school right now. The quicker I get to the fight, the better."[39] He was sent through recruit training at San Diego, where he subsequently attended Signalman school before being assigned to the Armed Guard Center in Brooklyn. His chance to get in the fight came on the *Bellingham*; and there was plenty of "fight" to go around. Surviving the sinking of the *Bellingham* and returning to the United States, he continued his service in the Armed Guard through the rest of the war, serving on the SS *Reverdy Johnson*, *John T. Holt*, *China Mail*, and *Thomas Eakins*. He was discharged on October 30, 1945, and returned to Moberly. However, he subsequently moved to Texas City, Texas, where he spent his entire civilian career as a firefighter. Following his retirement, he moved to Reserve, New Mexico, where he built his own house and enjoyed reading through the copious number of books in his library. Charles Harris passed away on February 25, 1996.

Despite the extreme losses of PQ-17, the Lend-Lease convoys to Murmansk and Archangel did not stop. They couldn't: the USSR desperately needed the materials to gain momentum in order to force the Germans westward. Political pressure between the Allies required the continuation of the convoys and the compromise was made to send another convoy, but only after the twenty-four hour daylight days of summer had passed. PQ-18 was planned for a departure from Iceland on September 2. In the meantime, a risky, high-speed convoy of warships made a transit to Archangel with urgently needed war and humanitarian materiel. On August 13, the *Tuscaloosa*, under the command of Norman Gillette, accompanied by the USS *Rodman* (DD-456), USS *Emmons* (DD-457), and the HMS *Onslaught*, sailed from Glasgow. They were spotted by a German reconnaissance aircraft on August 20. However, a dense fog rolled in, concealing the ships for the remainder of their voyage to Archangel. With less than a twenty-four hour turnaround, they returned for their westward transit, carrying with them 240 survivors from PQ-17. This was the last USSR-bound transit Task Group 39 participated in. Once they delivered their cargo of survivors in Scotland, the ships returned to the United States for much-needed repair work in preparation for participation in the upcoming invasion of North Africa in November.

Medal "For Valor" number 2075707 awarded to Charles Harris. *Courtesy of the Harris family.*

Матрос Iстатьи
(имя)
Чарлз
(отчество)
Клейтон Харрис
(фамилия)

Указом Президиума Верховного Совета СССР награжден медалью „ЗА ОТВАГУ".

№ медали..................

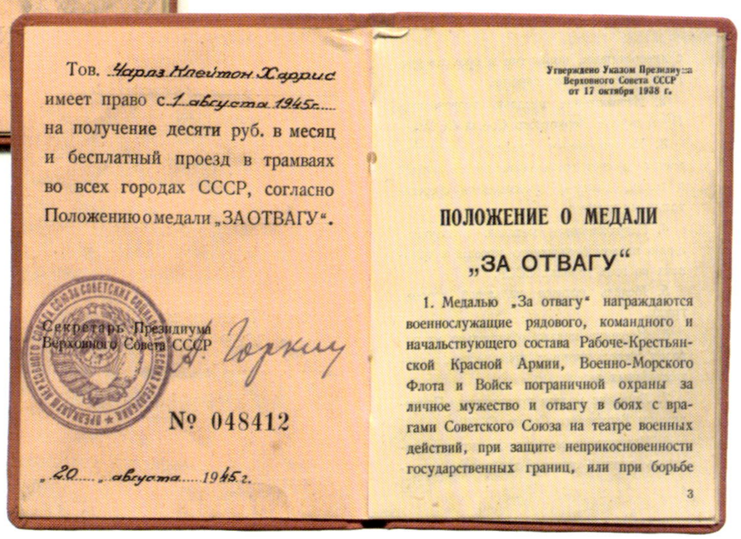

Тов. Чарлз Клейтон Харрис имеет право с 1 августа 1945г. на получение десяти руб. в месяц и бесплатный проезд в трамваях во всех городах СССР, согласно Положению о медали „ЗА ОТВАГУ".

Секретарь Президиума Верховного Совета СССР

№ 048412

20 августа 1945 г.

Утверждено Указом Президиума Верховного Совета СССР от 17 октября 1938 г.

ПОЛОЖЕНИЕ О МЕДАЛИ „ЗА ОТВАГУ"

1. Медалью „За отвагу" награждаются военнослужащие рядового, командного и начальствующего состава Рабоче-Крестьянской Красной Армии, Военно-Морского Флота и Войск пограничной охраны за личное мужество и отвагу в боях с врагами Советского Союза на театре военных действий, при защите неприкосновенности государственных границ, или при борьбе

3

The Soviet medal book to Charles Harris. *Courtesy of the Harris family.*

Chapter 11

Convoy PQ-18 Recipients

Convoy PQ-18, consisting of forty-four ships, set out from Loch Ewe, Scotland, instead of Iceland, due to German reconnaissance over the latter.[1] Much unlike PQ-17, this convoy had a fully dedicated escort force with the addition of the aircraft carrier HMS *Avenger*. The number of warships assigned to the convoy was an astounding seventy-six, an impressive collection of firepower to counter any potential *Luftwaffe* or *Kriegsmarine* attackers. The Germans, however, had not failed to recognize the reaction to PQ-17. The *Luftwaffe* had increased their number of torpedo bombers in northern Norway to ninety-two, along with 133 dive-bombers. This was in addition to the strengthened *Kriegsmarine* position, increasing their number of U-boats dedicated to patrolling the convoy route. The stage was set for a potentially epic battle for the delivery of goods to the USSR.

The convoy was first spotted by German aircraft on September 8, six days out from Loch Ewe. As with the run of the *Tuscaloosa* a month before, a dense fog closed in and for the next four days, they were undetected by the Germans. Despite the protection of the fog, Lieutenant (jg) Wesley Miller, the Armed Guard commander on the SS *St. Olaf*, noted: "Everybody is jittery as we realize that the zero hour is fast approaching."[2]

First blood was drawn when the HMS *Faulknor* sunk *U-88* on the evening of September 12. The next morning at 7:42 AM, approximately 150 miles southwest of Spitzbergen Island, German aircraft were sighted and the convoy went to general quarters. No attacks were made. However, at 8:55, *U-408* (sunk by Soviet medal recipient Robert Millard two months later)[3] fired four torpedoes at the Soviet merchant *Stalingrad* and the brand-new American Liberty ship *Oliver Ellsworth*. The *Stalingrad*, ahead of the *Ellsworth* in the convoy, was hit first. Seeing the explosion, the master of the *Ellsworth* attempted to zig-zag in their convoy position, but was too late: the ship was hit on the starboard side of number four hatch. Though the ship was still making way, she began to settle in the stern. Undoubtedly influenced by the great losses of PQ-17, the crew immediately turned to abandoning ship. One of the Navy gunners jumped at the stern and was caught in the exposed, turning propeller, killing him. The starboard side lifeboats were swamped and unusable. The port side lifeboats were immediately lowered, but the ship was still moving too quickly for them to be released. The first lifeboat on the port side was hit by a raft let go at the same time, causing it to break apart and sink. The other portside lifeboat, with only two Navy gunners on board, was pushed away from the side of the ship by water pressure and they were forced to cut it loose, lest it capsize and drown the occupants. Another lifeboat overturned as soon as it hit the water, trapping two floating men underneath. Seaman Charles Rotz, in the water without a lifejacket, saw this take place and immediately swam under the lifeboat and rescued Deck Cadet John McKelvey, bringing him up to the surface and pushing him on top of the boat.[4] The forty survivors of the *Ellsworth* were rescued by the HMS Harrier and were taken to Scapa Flow for a return voyage to the United States.

Charles Rotz, *Order of Glory, Third Class*

Seaman Charles Rotz was born to Romanian immigrant parents in Warren, Ohio, on January 27, 1916. He enlisted in the Navy on December 29, 1941, from Cleveland and graduated from recruit training at Great Lakes. Arriving at the Armed Guard Center in Brooklyn on June 24, 1942, he was assigned to the SS *Oliver Ellsworth*. Surviving the sinking of the *Ellsworth* and bravely rescuing John McKelvey, he was awarded the Navy and Marine Corps Medal for heroism. Returning to the United States on the SS *Queen Mary*, he was admitted to the US Naval Hospital in Brooklyn for care of ailments related to the sinking of the *Ellsworth*. Released back to Armed Guard duty, he served on Armed Guard detachments through September 1944. Sent to duty in Newport, Rhode Island, he was again struck by health issues related to his time in the Arctic water. Transferred to the Naval Reserve Armory in Chicago in January 1945, he was subsequently ordered to the Naval Training Center, Dearborn, Michigan. At the completion of his training in May 1945, his health again declined. Discharged on July 21, 1945, he returned to Ohio. Going to work for the Ford Motor Company in their automotive foundry until his retirement, Charles Rotz passed away in Cleveland on March 15, 1979.

The Navy and Marine Corps Medal awarded to Charles Rotz.

The *Oliver Ellsworth* was the first American merchant to sink on September 13, but she would not be the last. At 11:45 AM, the gunners on the SS *Nathaniel Greene* reported seeing a periscope about one hundred yards off their starboard beam. It disappeared and the escorts laid a pattern of depth charges over its last known location. Seven minutes later, twenty He 111 torpedo planes attacked the convoy and escorts, concentrating on the HMS *Avenger*. No damage was done. The same went for the high-level bombing raid that took place at 1:30 PM. An hour later, however, things didn't go as well for the convoy. Wesley Miller recorded:

> *At 1500, hell broke loose overhead as a formation of Focke-Wulf Kuriers crossed us from the starboard beam ... They were perfectly camouflaged so that one could scarcely distinguish them from the clouds above. A terrific anti-aircraft barrage was sent up to greet them as they began to let their bombs fall. Every ship in the entire convoy let loose with their guns. The air literally blazed with 20mm tracers ... The ring of destroyers, the flak cruisers, and the merchant ships gave them everything they had from a thousand guns. The noise was deafening ... On and on came the torpedo planes in an unending line. They darted up then down to confuse the aim of our gunners. Some of the typical torpedo planes were painted solid black with the tips of their wings painted orange or green. They were weird and awful to behold. In spite of our murderous barrage, they swarmed through our fire and the water became alive with torpedoes.*[5]

The Soviet order book to Charles Rotz.

Charles Rotz's Order of Glory, Third Class, and Navy and Marine Corps Medal, together as they were stored for seven decades inside the Soviet order's box.

Approximately thirty Ju 88 bombers and fifty-five He 111 torpedo planes came at the starboard side of the convoy. They were flying low and fast, and concentrated their venom on the starboard-most column and last ships of each row. Coming within fifteen hundred yards of the ships, they launched their torpedoes, all the while dodging the massed anti-aircraft fire of the convoy's gunners. With this being the first significant raid of the convoy, a considerable amount of ammunition was fired wildly by inexperienced gunners. On board the SS *Campfire*, three of the Armed Guard gunners, to include Seaman Albert Wohlers, were hit by bullets from another convoy ship and were seriously wounded.

With the water full of torpedoes, the convoy commodore gave the signal to conduct evasive maneuvers. However, the ships of the last row and the ships on the closest column to the attack did not have time to respond. A torpedo plane dropped its weapon directly through the number two hatch of the American merchant SS *Wacosta,* and it exploded inside her. The *Empire Stevenson*, a British merchant, took a torpedo amidships and her cargo of explosives simultaneously detonated. When the smoke and flame cleared, only an oily slick was left to mark her last known location. Of the *Stevenson*, Miller wrote:

> *The British freighter ... was hit and exploded in one towering sheet of bright yellow flame which reached to the sky. After two minutes time the flames subsided to a mere flickering on the waves. Not a trace of that unfortunate ship could be seen. It was sickening. Not one man survived.*[6]

Order of Glory, Third Class, number 387914 awarded to Charles Rotz.

On the SS *Virginia Dare*, gunner George Goddard brought down one plane with the fire from his twenty-millimeter gun as it passed by; they later watched it disappear into the clouds as a single wing from the plane fell into the sea. There was no time to look for more; the massed attack against the convoy continued with utmost savagery. The SS *Oregonian*, with William Kirby as her Armed Guard commander and Arthur Adler and Lloyd Weeks in her gun crew, was hit simultaneously with three torpedoes on her starboard side, "nearly blowing the starboard side of the ship to pieces."[7] One of the torpedoes impacted the hatch where the ammunition was carried and the resulting explosion blew the bow off the ship. With the side of the hull torn to shreds and the bow missing, the engine room and forward compartments flooded instantly, and the ship began to take a heavy list. Her shifting below-decks cargo, consisting of tanks, railroad rails, raw steel, and a topside cargo of aircraft, only pulled the listing ship farther to starboard. The master immediately called to abandon ship, and the crew scrambled for the lifeboats. In the din and confusion, Lloyd Weeks stayed at his gun, firing at the aircraft, but it was no use; the planes were gone. The crew had no time to launch the lifeboats, many jumped directly into the freezing arctic waters as the *Oregonian* capsized and disappeared beneath the surface. Twenty-seven of the fifty-five-man crew, including six of the Armed Guard detachment, went down with the ship. The survivors, many gagging from ingesting mouthfuls of the fuel oil and saltwater mixture that oozed from the stricken ship, were quickly retrieved from the water. Several Armed Guard gunners and Ensign Kirby were rescued by the HMS *St. Kenan.* The survivors were transferred to the HMS *Somali*, a Royal Navy destroyer escorting westbound convoy QP-14. The luck of the *Oregonian's* crew ran out a second time, as the *Somali* was torpedoed by *U-703* on September 20 and later sank. The survivors of the *Oregonian*, now having been torpedoed twice, were transferred to the HMS *Lord Middleton* for transit back to Scotland.

William R. Kirby, *Order of the Red Star*

William Roy Kirby, the Armed Guard commander on the SS *Oregonian*. *National Personnel Records Center.*

William Roy Kirby was born on September 6, 1914, in Concordia, Kansas, moving to Coffeyville, Kansas, as a young child. He graduated from Field Kindley High School, Coffeyville Community College, Kansas University, and Kansas University Law School, all prior to the start of the war. He joined the Navy on September 16, 1941, and was commissioned on January 16, 1942. Completing the Armed Guard School on April 21, he reported that same week to the Armed Guard Center in Brooklyn. Assigned to the *Oregonian*, he survived the sinking by grabbing a rope that was tossed to him by other survivors and wrapping it around his wrist, as he was too cold to tie it around his waist. In shock from the icy waters, he passed out; his next memory came from the sick bay of the *St. Kenan*. For his valor, he was awarded a Letter of Commendation from the Secretary of the Navy. Returning to the United States, he transferred to flight training for airships at Naval Air Station Lakehurst, New Jersey. On December 15, 1943, he was assigned to his first operational squadron, Blimp Squadron (ZP) 23 in Moffett Field, California. By the end of the following year, he was classified a Senior Pilot, Lighter than Air (LTA). On December 29, 1944, he transferred to ZP-32, also stationed at Moffett Field, conducting anti-submarine patrols off the West Coast. Discharged from active duty on November 25, 1945, he returned to Coffeyville, Kansas. He stayed in the Naval Reserves, eventually retiring as a Commander on August 1, 1967.

As a civilian, he practiced law in Coffeyville for over sixty years, serving as the city attorney, assistant county attorney, the attorney for the Coffeyville Regional Medical Center and Coffeyville Community College, as well as his own law practice. Following his retirement, he served as vice chairman of the Board of Directors at Condon National Bank, president of the Coffeyville Chamber of Commerce, and was an active member in the Rotary and Shriners. He was inducted into the Coffeyville Regional Medical Center Hall of Fame in 1996. William Kirby passed away on January 10, 2004.

Edge numbering of Arthur Adler's Medal of Nakhimov. *Courtesy of the Adler family.*

Arthur L. Adler. *Courtesy of the Adler family.*

Arthur L. Adler, *Medal of Nakhimov*

The most senior enlisted Sailor in the Armed Guard detachment on the *Oregonian*, Arthur Adler was born in Boston, Massachusetts, on June 30, 1916. Following high school, he enlisted in the Navy on March 30, 1936, and served his first enlistment on the USS *Illinois* (BB-7), *Badger* (DD-126), *Texas* (BB-35), *Roper* (DD-147), and the *Tuscaloosa* (CA-37). Reenlisting in 1940, he was assigned to the USS *Prairie State* (IX-15) (she was the former battleship USS *Illinois* (BB-7) converted into a midshipman training school) and was quickly promoted to Coxswain. On April 25, 1942, Adler reported to the Armed Guard Center, Brooklyn. For his coolness and bravery in the sinking of the *Oregonian*, he was awarded a Commendation from the Secretary of the Navy and was promoted to Boatswain's Mate, second class. He went on to serve on the SS *Nishmaha* until September 1943, taking her around the world, and then again as a member of the Armed Guard of the SS *George Cleve*, now as a Boatswain's Mate, first class. On February 22, 1944, he was sunk again, this time by a torpedo from *U-969* off the coast of Bone, Algeria, while the *George Cleve* was transiting in a return convoy bound for Norfolk, Virginia. Chief Boatswain's Mate Adler then reported to USS *LST-593*, participating in the Mindanao Island and Luzon landings in April and May 1945. Discharged on October 10, 1945, he worked as a diamond setter for the company of Lepow & Bomze and later as a diamond and jewel setting teacher at the New York Fashion Institute and the Gemological Institute in New York City. Arthur Adler passed away in Teaneck, New Jersey, on December 17, 1996.

Medal of Nakhimov 5593 awarded to Arthur Adler. *Courtesy of the Adler family.*

The Silver Star and Army Good Conduct Medal awarded to Lloyd Weeks. *Courtesy of the Weeks family.*

Lloyd R. Weeks, *Order of the Red Star*

Born in Columbus, Ohio, on September 6, 1923, Lloyd Richard Weeks attended North High School in Columbus and while still in school, lied about his age and spent a year in the Ohio National Guard as a Private in the Signal Corps. Joining the Navy on January 29, 1942, in Cincinnati, he attended recruit training at Great Lakes before being assigned to the Armed Guard Center in Brooklyn in March 1942. His first ship was the *Oregonian*. Surviving the sinking, he was awarded the Silver Star for his heroism by remaining at his gun, even though abandon ship had already been called and the ship was clearly sinking. Returning to the United States, he was assigned to the *Nishmaha* along with Arthur Adler, serving on her from December 15, 1942 to September 21, 1943. Detached from Armed Guard duty as a Gunner's Mate, third class, he went through amphibious warfare training and was assigned to the USS *LST-981* on March 11, 1944. Serving as the Gunner's Mate in charge of the ordnance department, he transferred from her in December and was assigned to the Naval Ammunition Depot at McAlester, Oklahoma. Discharged from active duty in September 1945, he joined the Army, rising to the rank of Sergeant First Class and serving with Battery "D," 73rd Anti-Aircraft Battalion in Germany. Discharged again in September 1954, he returned to civilian life and began an electrical contracting company with his brother in Ohio. Upon his retirement, he moved to Penn Valley, California. Lloyd Weeks passed away on April 29, 2004.

In the rear of the convoy, the SS *Africander*, a Panamanian ship with an Armed Guard detachment on board, was about to take her turn heading to the bottom of the sea. The *Africander* had already had an exciting voyage to the USSR. In December 1941, she struck a submerged object and had to return to Boston for dry-docking and repair. She left for Halifax with a convoy bound for the North Atlantic on January 8, 1942. On January 11, during heavy seas, she was rammed by another merchant vessel, requiring extensive repair work in Newfoundland. Finally underway for the USSR with a new Armed Guard detachment on board, a serious personality conflict developed between the master and Ensign Kenneth Tipping, the Armed Guard commander. Tipping accused the master of incompetence, drunkenness, and violence, including assault against members of the Armed Guard detachment. In turn, the master accused Tipping of being presumptuous by saying that he:

> *... was twenty-one-years-old, first time at sea and did not know anything about ships and still tried to run the ship and take command from me. I had to put him in is his place and tell him what to do and what not to do.*[8]

This conflict, at least in a direct manner, ceased on September 13. As the convoy maneuvered to avoid the incoming German attackers, her Armed Guard detachment swung into action, firing on the attacking planes and watching two of the aircraft burst into flames and crash into the water. However, it was too little, too late: two aerial torpedoes struck the *Africander* on the starboard side, aft of her number three hold. Tipping was knocked off his feet from the force of the explosion and no sooner than he attempted to get back up, he was deluged by a tremendous volume of water that had been sent aloft by the blast. Peering over the side of the pilothouse rail, Tipping watched the deck aft of the hold rise and settle, distorting itself in a shape never before seen.[9] The steering gear was put out of commission and the watertight bulkhead doors were blown open by the explosion. Flooding in the stern of the ship was out of control and the master decided to abandon ship. The *Africander* was last seen lying on her side, slowly sinking below the waves. The survivors were retrieved shortly by the rescue vessels and returned to Scotland, where they embarked for Boston with the other PQ-18 survivors, returning on October 15.

Order of the Red Star number 366455 awarded to Lloyd Weeks. *Courtesy of the Weeks family.*

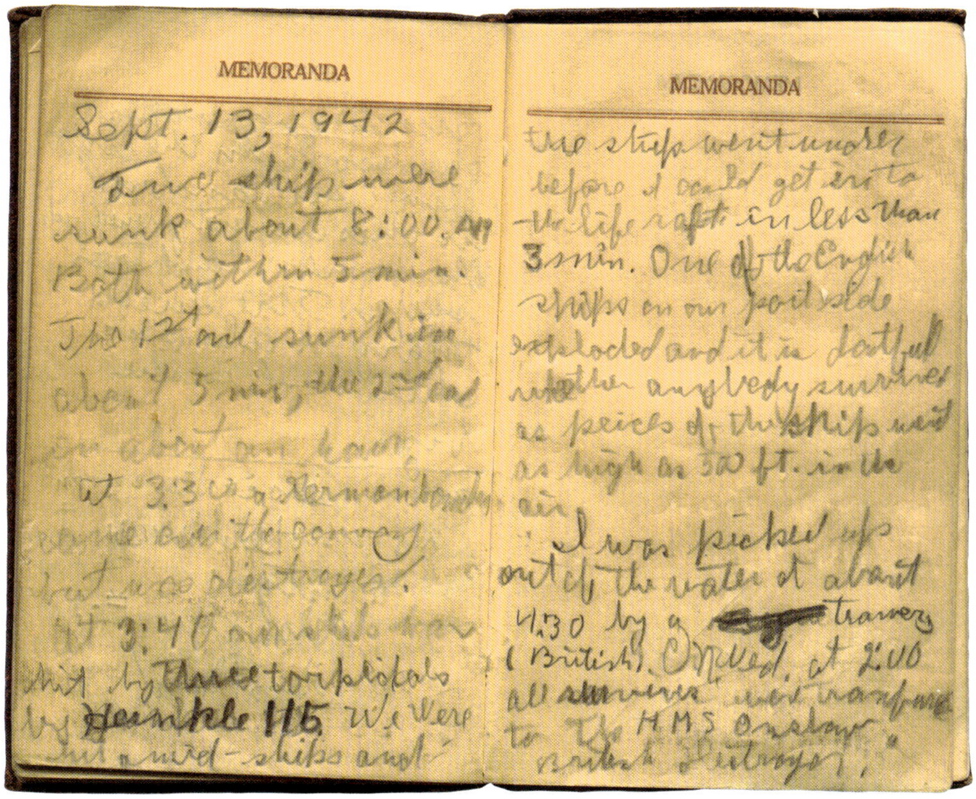
MEMORANDA

Sept. 13, 1942

MEMORANDA

Entry from the journal of Lloyd Weeks, describing the German attacks of September 13, 1942. *Courtesy of the Weeks family.*

Имя, отчество и фамилия

Второй пулеметчик III класса

Ллойд

Р. Уикс

Подпись владельца книжки

1. Награжден Указом Президиума Верховного Совета Союза ССР от 18 февраля 1944 г. орденом Красной Звезды №: 366455

2. Имеет право, начиная с 1 Марта 1944 г. на получение орденских денежных выдач и на другие льготы и преимущества, согласно Общему положению об орденах Союза ССР.

3. Книжка бессрочная.

Секретарь Президиума Верховного Совета СССР

№ 122032

1 Марта 1944 г.

Утверждено постановлением ЦИК и СНК Союза ССР от 7 мая 1936 г.

ОБЩЕЕ ПОЛОЖЕНИЕ
об орденах Союза ССР.

1. Орден Союза ССР является высшей наградой за особые заслуги в области социалистического строительства и обороны Союза ССР.
2. Центральным Исполнительным Комитетом Союза ССР учреждены следующие ордена Союза ССР: „Орден Ленина", „Красное Знамя", „Красная Звезда", „Трудовое Красное Знамя" и „Знак Почета".
3. Орденами Союза ССР могут награждаться как отдельные граждане, так и войсковые соединения и воинские части Рабоче-Крестьянской Красной Армии, предприятия, учреждения и организации.
4. Награжденные орденом Союза ССР могут быть за новые заслуги повторно награждены тем же или другим орденом Союза ССР.

3

The Soviet order book to Lloyd Weeks. *Courtesy of the Weeks family.*

Kenneth W. Tipping (right), the Armed Guard commander on the SS *Africander*. *Courtesy of the Tipping family.*

Kenneth W. Tipping, *Order of the Red Star*

Africander's Armed Guard commander was Kenneth William Tipping. Born on November 6, 1919, in Maywood, New Jersey, he attended Andover Academy before Princeton, where he graduated in 1940 with honors in modern languages. Joining the Navy on May 28, 1941, he was commissioned in January 1942 after attending the Naval Reserve Midshipman School at Northwestern University in Chicago. First assigned to the Armed Guard Center in Brooklyn, he was immediately sent to the *Africander* as the Armed Guard commander. Surviving the sinking of the ship on September 13, he arrived back in the United States and was subsequently sent to the Armed Guard School in Little Creek as an instructor for the four-inch deck gun. In June 1943, he was transferred to the Submarine Chaser Training Center in Miami in preparation for his next assignment. On October 16, 1943, coincident with the commissioning of the ship, he became the executive officer of the USS *Culpeper* (PC-1240), a *PC-461* class submarine chaser. Fleeting up to become the commanding officer of the *Culpeper*, he later took command of USS *PC-1130*, conducting routine convoy and ship escort duties in the South Pacific.

Discharged to civilian life on December 2, 1945, Tipping attended Cornell Law School, serving as a member of the Law Review, and was admitted to the New York Bar in 1949. First working for the law firm of Milbank, Tweed, Hope, and Hadley, he joined the legal department of the Asiatic Petroleum Corporation and Shell Caribbean Petroleum Company in 1951. In 1953, he moved to Caracas to work directly with the Shell Venezuelan oil concessions. One year later, following his return to the United States, he headed the legal department and later became the assistant secretary of Asiatic Petroleum. Kenneth Tipping passed away suddenly on November 23, 1960.Along with the *Africander* and the *Oregonian*, the SS *John Penn* did not survive the day. Positioned almost in the center of the convoy, just astern of *Campfire*, forward of *William Moultrie*, and to the port side of *Nathaniel Greene*, her Armed Guard detachment threw everything they had at the incoming planes, but it was not enough. Two torpedoes impacted the *Penn*; one at the engine room, and one at the number three hold. The explosion blew Ensign Blake Howard, the Armed Guard commander, stationed on the bridge, off his feet and down to the main deck twenty feet below, severely injuring his wrist. One of the gunners was thrown off his mount, and the men in the engine room were killed instantly. The ship immediately slowed as water rushed through the holes in the hull, readily flooding the open compartments. With no ability to stem the flooding, and no engine room to provide propulsion, the order to abandon ship was given. The crew and the Armed Guard gunners left the ship in orderly fashion, and were rescued by the HMS *Eskimo* and HMS *Harrier* for a return trip to Scotland, and from there, the United States, sailing on October 23 on board the SS *Axel Johnson*.

Order of the Red Star number 1553974 awarded to Kenneth Tipping. *Courtesy of the Tipping family*.

Blake C. Howard, Jr., *Order of the Patriotic War, Second Class*

A newspaper photo showing Blake Howard (left) and Latney Farmer (right) receiving their awards for convoys PQ-18 and PQ-17 (respectively). *US Navy photo via the Farmer family.*

Blake Clinton Howard, Jr. was born on January 15, 1919, in St. Louis, Missouri. He attended the Georgetown University School of Foreign Service for two years before joining the Navy on August 10, 1940. Commencing active duty on October 1, 1941, he was commissioned and reported to the Armed Guard Center in New Orleans on April 25, 1942. Subsequently, he was ordered to the *John Penn*, a brand-new Liberty ship, recently outfitted with her weaponry. Surviving the attack on the *Penn*, he was awarded a Letter of Commendation and the Purple Heart, the latter for the permanent nerve damage he sustained in his wrist as a result of the torpedoing. Howard remained on duty at the Armed Guard Center in New Orleans for the duration of the war and was discharged on November 18, 1945. Returning to St. Louis, he remained in the Naval Reserves, finally receiving his discharge on July 19, 1957 as a Lieutenant Commander. Blake Howard passed away in St. Louis on July 20, 1982, and is buried in Calvary Cemetery and Mausoleum.

September 13 was by far the bloodiest day for convoy PQ-18 yet. The attacks did not end with the massed torpedo raid, and only progressed in their severity. The *Luftwaffe* returned again at 4:30 PM and at 9:30 PM. During the latter attack, Seaman Frank Gay on the *Virginia Dare* brought down a Ju 88, blasting it with his twenty-millimeter gun until the starboard engine burst into flames and it crashed about one mile astern of the ship.[10] At 3:30 AM on the morning of September 14, the British escort oiler *Athel Templar* was torpedoed and burst into flames reaching far into the sky, but did not explode. Aircraft attacked at 12:30 PM and again at 1:15 PM. The men of the *Virginia Dare* fought hard to repulse the attackers. Within a matter of minutes, they would become a legend of the Murmansk Run.

This 1:15 PM raid on September 14 consisted of eighteen torpedo bombers using the tactic of cruising just above the wave tops, popping up within visual range to orient themselves to the convoy, and then reducing altitude to disappear under the horizon until almost directly over the hapless ships. Like a cavalry charge in a war long ago, the aircraft, grouped no more than one hundred yards apart and thirty feet off the water, headed directly toward the convoy, below the height of the masts on many of the ships. They split into smaller groups just off the bow of the *Nathaniel Greene*, crossing no more than one hundred feet from her. One of the *Greene's* merchant mariner crew, twenty-two year old Paul George Gill, kept a journal of that day and recorded the following in his diary:

> *Back at our gun stations we spotted the enemy planes to the starboard of the convoy. My God! I said, look at them come! There's no use trying to count them! They're torpedo bombers! Their squadrons looked like swarms of attacking Hornets! All of our guns were trained on them as they flew up ahead of the convoy ... They were splitting into two separate formations – and now we were aware of their intentions – half of them were to attempt to destroy our naval escort, and the other half to destroy the merchantmen! As the enemy approached, this vessel let go the first shot from the convoy with the 3.50 AA* [three-inch deck gun] *and an eight second fuse from our forward gun and made a direct hit on the squadron leader, blowing his fuselage in two! All of convoy vessels opened fire on the attackers.*[11]

Letting loose with everything they could, Roy Billings and his gunners on the *Greene* knocked down the lead bomber right off their bow with their three-inch gun. Two more were shot down off the bow, two off the port side, and one off the starboard. In the words of John Laird, the Armed Guard commander on the SS *Virginia Dare*, six of the aircraft that came down the side of the *Greene* flew "madly down the columns, between ships, towards our end of the convoy."[12] When the first was in range, Chief Boatswain John Harshaw, a veteran of the First World War and passenger on the *Dare*, let loose with his twenty-millimeter gun, setting the plane's port engine on fire. It was then finished off by an escort ship. Subsequently, the second aircraft flew through, and he was shot down by Seaman Cecil Graff, catching fire and crashing into the water. The third was caught in the crosshairs of *Dare's* three-inch deck gun. The gun's pointer, John Harmon, fired exactly when the aircraft was just over five hundred feet away. His aim was perfect: the aircraft instantly blew up, mid-air, scattering burning wreckage into the sea and onto the bow of the *Dare*.

The remaining three aircraft continued through the convoy and two were brought down by *Dare* gunners, one by Seaman George Goddard, the other by Rex Robertson, both firing their twenty-millimeter guns. The final aircraft passed ahead of the SS *Campfire*, where Seaman Donald Biggs filled it full of twenty-millimeter rounds. Banking down the side of the *Virginia Dare* in the direction of the *Nathaniel Greene*, John Harshaw opened up with his gun and the plane streaked with fire. On board the SS *William Moultrie*, Ensign Jeremiah Mahoney took credit for the final blow to the plane as his three-inch deck gun sent a round into its fuselage. He watched in horror as the aircraft began to cartwheel, out of control, directly into the American merchant SS *Mary Luckenbach*, laden with one thousand tons of ammunition. The resulting explosion caused by the strike of the aircraft combined with its never-released ordnance, created one of the most graphic and horrifying images of the war: the *Mary Luckenbach* instantly exploded into a giant ball of flame and smoke.

Wesley Miller watched the plane from his gun station on the *St. Olaf*:

> *Finally, one Junkers 88 rose to a higher altitude and heads across our bow about two hundred yards ahead. My 3"50 gunner burst a shell under him. The motor of this bomber began blazing … On fire and losing altitude, this bomber headed toward the fourth and fifth columns. I watched him carefully to see him crash. It was then that I saw a sight never to be forgotten. The pilot of this plane, undoubtedly knowing that he was doomed, deliberately dove his flaming bomber with its cargo of death onto the mid decks of the US ship,* Mary Lukenbach. *There was a great boiling mass of greyish black smoke and flame, which must have reached a thousand feet in height, as the* Mary Luckenbach *was literally blown to atoms with all her crew.*[13]

The shock wave from the explosion was so great that the crew of the *Greene*, the ship closest to the *Luckenbach*, believed they had been hit and were sinking. Shrapnel rained down with explosive force from all directions, causing mass destruction on the decks of the *Greene, Campfire,* and *Virginia Dare*. Daniel Rooker, the Armed Guard commander on the SS *Campfire*, on the other side of the *Luckenbach*, recalled the force of the explosion:

> *Our ship seemed to lift clear of the water and then plunged downward with solid water surging over our main deck. I was sure our bottom had been ripped out and we would sink. Chunks of steel hurtled at us with the force of bullets, riddling lifeboats and superstructure.*[14]

On board the *Greene*, Paul Gill wrote:

> *I was in the Port Side machine gun nest on the poop deck with Blackie – he manned the gun as I directed the gun laying. As he concentrated on his line of fire I sighted the most threatening target for Blackie to lay his gunfire on. God! We had to move fast! There was no time for indecision! The enemy aircraft were machine-gunning us as well and were just as determined as we were in our gunfire! Our ship was now zigzagging as bombs were dropping around us. The master on the bridge sighted two torpedoes coming right at us on our port bow! "Hard left wheel!" He ordered the quartermaster. The ships heading swung to port to attempt to dodge the torpedoes. As we swung ship, our stern went towards the SS* Mary Luckenbach *which was falling back from abeam of us to our starboard quarter. Frantically searching for the next threatening enemy plane for Blackie to direct his gunfire at I saw the SS* Mary Luckenbach *directly astern of us and then a flash of flame split the heavens above it as the blast of the explosion hit me and I yelled to Blackie to "Duck!" at the top of my lungs and quickly we fell to the deck of the gun nest.*
>
> *The force of the SS* Mary Luckenbach's *explosion was terrifying! Our vessel was lifted from the sea and shook violently as the obliterated ship fell upon us in shrapnel form! In split second action we appraised our situation. We were in a dense cloud of black smoke, thick with the smell of gunpowder from the explosion, not knowing whether we were to remain afloat or disappear beneath the sea. We climbed over the gun nest wall on to the poop deck and then dove over its rail to the main deck below and crawled to cover. Tons and tons of shrapnel continued to fall about us, in every size, in cruel and grotesque shapes and patterns.*
>
> *Visibility about our gun stations was gradually clearing. The bridge and the midships housing were not yet visible. The afterdeck rigging was in ribbons, the crates of deck cargo were blown apart, and the deck cargo of army tanks for Stalingrad appeared to be in ruins. Everything within sight was battered from the concussion and vacuum created by the explosion. Our clothing was ripped and torn from the blast and saturated with fragmented steel from shrapnel. We were not yet aware of the extent of injuries that were incurred by our men. The forward part of the ship must have been blown to bits. God help those poor shipmates!*
>
> *I looked over the ship's side and the ship's propeller was turning slowly. Unsure whether we would remain afloat, or sink, I was uncertain what we should do. Dive overboard and swim clear of the ship's suction beneath the sea, or hang on and wait for rescue from a destroyer? Rescue*

was highly unlikely considering how the enemy quickly destroyed our crippled merchant vessels following yesterday's combat action.

As I pondered our fate, the heavy black smoke started to lift and the shrapnel stopped falling. Looking forward, the bridge started to appear. It had not blown up as I had feared! Then the ship's whistle sounded to report to our boat stations to abandon ship! I made sure that all of the men that were in the after gun stations were accounted for and on their way to the lifeboats. Before leaving for the gun stations for the lifeboats, I remembered one last thing I had to do.

When I was on watch the night before the captain said to me, "Mr. Gill, during today's battles I noticed that none of our American ships flew their ensign. Now, if we had our stars and stripes flying from the gaff!" I replied "Aye, aye, sir!" and promised when we went into battle again I would make sure to send our stars and stripes flying.

Today's enemy action was so time pressing that I completely overlooked my commitment to the captain. Now that the abandon ship alarm had been sounded, and the crew was manning the lifeboats, I remembered my orders and made my way to the mainmast. I removed the ensign from its locker, bent it on its halyard, and aloft she went! When the men saw the stars and stripes flying from the gaff of the mainmast they broke out in cheers. I felt a lump in my throat and overwhelmed with emotion and thought "What heroes! We have so much to fight for!"[15]

The Navy Commendation Medal awarded to Blake Howard.

On the *Greene*, they believed they had been torpedoed by another aircraft that had distracted them from the ones the *Dare* shot down, as they had spotted four torpedoes dropped on their port side, as well as an aerial bomb with a parachute. Billings' gunners were busy firing at their aircraft when the *Luckenbach*, stationed two hundred yards off their starboard quarter, exploded. As recorded by Paul Gill, the blast was so ferocious and so devastating; the decks of the *Greene* were in absolute chaos. Billings was surprised anyone was still alive: his own helmet and earphones had been ripped off by the concussion.[16]

Taking inventory of his men, he saw three of his men covered in blood: Norman Hyams had received a piece of shrapnel in his right elbow, removing almost all of the skin from the back of his arm and causing extensive nerve damage throughout the rest of his lower arm and hand. Clarence Marihugh took a bullet through his left shoulder, and had shrapnel in his right leg. Charles Walters had a piece of shrapnel that traveled through his left boot, taking with it part of two toes. Not a single one of them had left their station, despite their wounds.

The physical devastation to the ship was almost total. According to Roy Billings:

All the cargo boxes on deck were smashed by the concussion. About ten doors and some bulkheads were blown down and smashed ... The cast iron ventilators buckled. Shrapnel and scraps were covering the deck. A piece of angle iron penetrated my starboard four inch ready box and went through a shell, missing the primer by less than an eighth of an inch. Glass ports were smashed. The hospital aft was practically demolished ... The pointer's platform on the four inch gun had completely disappeared and the pointer's site was nearly ruined. A side plate [from the Luckenbach] *about two feet square was found on deck. Bullets were picked up all over the deck (both tank ammunition from the* Luckenbach *and bullets fired at us by the planes) ... Every gun station has been marked by shrapnel and bullets ... How everyone topside was not killed or injured seriously I don't know. It is impossible to put into words the force of the explosion or the amount of debris that hit the ship.*[17]

On the *Moultrie*, Mahoney watched the *Greene* drop out of formation, "... her after deck smoking badly, and her crew preparing to abandon ship ... Her deck cargo splintered from stem to stern."[18] During this attack, the *Moultrie* claimed four aircraft, with hits on a total of seven. The attacks, albeit on a smaller scale, continued throughout the rest of the day, but the Allied ships suffered no further casualties. For their actions on this day, the *Virginia Dare*, *William Moultrie*, and *Nathaniel Greene* became three of the nine civilian ships during the Second World War to receive the Gallant Ship Unit Citation from the United States War Shipping Administration.[19]

Roy M. Billings, Armed Guard commander for the SS *Nathaniel Greene. US Navy photo.*

Roy M. Billings, *Order of the Patriotic War, First Class*

On the *Nathaniel Greene*, Roy Murray "Josh" Billings commanded the Armed Guard detachment. Born in Wisconsin on July 8, 1920, he was a "Ninety Day Wonder," commissioned shortly after his twentieth birthday on November 14, 1940. His first duty station was in the USS *Astoria* (CA-34), operating out of Pearl Harbor, Territory of Hawaii. Being at sea during the December 7, 1941, attack, the *Astoria* made the transit back to Pearl and shortly thereafter, he was transferred to the Armed Guard Center, Brooklyn, New York. In March 1942, he was ordered to the SS *Nathaniel Greene*. After several uneventful transits on the eastern coast of the United States, the *Greene* departed for Archangel in May 1942. Along with other merchant vessels who later took part in convoy PQ-18, she waited through the summer in Loch Ewe, Scotland, and on September 2, finally departed for Archangel. After surviving the transit and following their arrival in the Soviet Union, the *Greene* completed unloading cargo on October 6, and got underway in a westbound convoy on November 17. On December 4, they departed Loch Ewe, Scotland, for the United States, but were turned around and ordered to return to Scotland to conduct cargo transport between Great Britain and North Africa in support of Operation *Torch*.

On February 24, 1943, having been overseas for the better part of ten months, the *Greene* got underway from Mostaganem Harbor, Algeria, with a cargo of one-thousand tons of foodstuffs and vehicles bound for Algiers. At 1:53 PM, the first of two German torpedoes struck the starboard side of the *Greene*, with the second torpedo following less than a minute later. The *Nathaniel Greene*, brave survivor of the Murmansk Run, began to settle by the bow as water quickly began to enter her ruptured hull. Simultaneously, a group of enemy aircraft approached, launching three torpedoes at the stricken vessel. Despite the Armed Guard's best efforts to stop the aircraft (they destroyed one) the torpedoes struck home, eliminating any chance of keeping the *Greene* afloat. The HMS *Brixton* arrived and towed the *Greene* to where she could be beached on the coastline. Billings remained with a handful of Armed Guard gunners on the *Greene* until they determined she was safe from further attack, and at that point, left the ship. The survivors boarded the USS *Anne Arundel* (AP-76), and arrived in the United States on August 3.

Billings served his final year of active service on the USS *Connolly* (DE-306), taking part in the Iwo Jima and Okinawa operations in the Pacific. Released to Reserve status, he was later recalled during the Korean War to serve as the executive officer of the Military Sea Transportation Service Office, Pusan, Korea, from December 1, 1951, to May 12, 1952. He retired as a Captain in the Naval Reserve on July 1, 1965.

As a civilian, he graduated from the University of Southern California following his wartime service and later earned an Executive MBA from Princeton. He worked for the Johns Manville Company, where he eventually became the senior vice president for International Operations before retirement. Roy Billings passed away in Pasadena, California, on May 28, 1981.

Harry M. Gossman, *Medal "For Valor"*

Harry M. Gossman. *Courtesy of the Gossman family.*

The senior enlisted Sailor on the *Greene* was Boatswain's Mate, second class, Harry Madison Gossman. He was born in Cincinnati, Ohio, on November 10, 1909, and joined the Navy on September 14, 1927. He first served on the USS *West Virginia* (BB-48) before being transferred to the USS *Wyoming* (BB-32), where he spent the next three years. Gossman then served on the USS *Leary* (DD-158), USS *Clark* (DD-361), and the USS *Augusta* (CA-31) in the Far East. During the *Augusta's* overhaul at the Mare Island Naval Shipyard, he was transferred to the Headquarters, Eleventh Naval District, where he worked until sent to Armed Guard duty on February 27, 1942. He remained with the Armed Guard, rising to the rank of Boatswain's Mate Chief and receiving a Letter of Commendation from the Secretary of the Navy for his bravery on the *Greene*, until transferred to the USS *PGM-9* on July 30, 1944. Here, he participated in multiple engagements in the Pacific, conducting small-scale shore bombardment. On December 31, he transferred to the fleet rescue tug, USS *ATR-21*, where he spent the remainder of the war. The next year, he transferred to Naval Station Argentia, Newfoundland and subsequently remained there for the following four years. On January 2, 1949, he returned to sea duty on the USS *Canisteo* (AO-99) out of Norfolk. His final tour was as a recruiter in Orange, Texas. Gossman retired on March 18, 1952 as a Boatswain's Mate Chief. As a civilian, Gossman moved to Ocean Springs, Mississippi, and became the building attendant at the Air Ground Operations School at Keesler Air Force Base in 1957. He followed this by becoming a Pinkerton guard, and later, a city patrolman. He passed away unexpectedly on January 1, 1969, and is buried in Crestlawn Cemetery, Ocean Springs.

Подпись владельца удостоверения

Штюпочный старшина
(имя)

Харри
(отчество)

Мэдисон Госсман
(фамилия)

Указом Президиума Верховного Совета СССР награжден медалью „ЗА ОТВАГУ".

№ медали..................

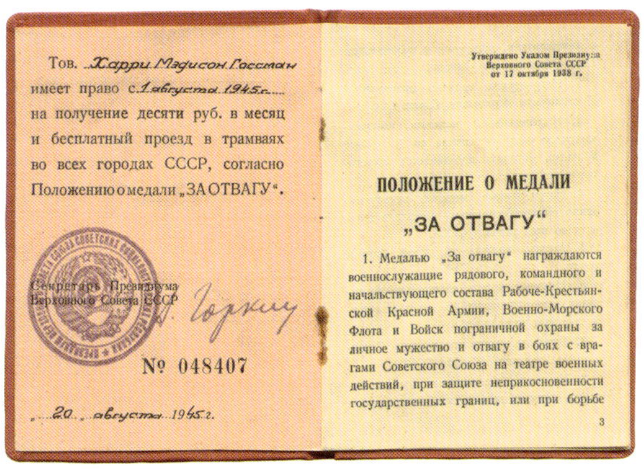

Тов. Харри Мэдисон Госсман имеет право с 1 августа 1945 г. на получение десяти руб. в месяц и бесплатный проезд в трамваях во всех городах СССР, согласно Положению о медали „ЗА ОТВАГУ".

Секретарь Президиума Верховного Совета СССР

№ 048407

„20" августа 1945 г.

Утверждено Указом Президиума Верховного Совета СССР от 17 октября 1938 г.

ПОЛОЖЕНИЕ О МЕДАЛИ „ЗА ОТВАГУ"

1. Медалью „За отвагу" награждаются военнослужащие рядового, командного и начальствующего состава Рабоче-Крестьянской Красной Армии, Военно-Морского Флота и Войск пограничной охраны за личное мужество и отвагу в боях с врагами Советского Союза на театре военных действий, при защите неприкосновенности государственных границ, или при борьбе

3

The Soviet medal book to Harry Gossman. *Courtesy of the Gossman family*.

Medal "For Valor" number 2075703 awarded to Harry Gossman. *Courtesy of the Gossman family*.

Alexander LaGue as a Chief Airship Rigger at the end of the war. *Courtesy of the LaGue family.*

Alexander LaGue, *Medal "For Military Merit"*

Boatswain's Mate, second class, Alexander LaGue hailed from New Bedford, Massachusetts. Born in Woonsocket, Rhode Island, on December 21, 1918, he left school after eighth grade to work in the textile mills as a weaver while also working for his father as an interior house painter. In 1936, he began working for John D'Eon of Gloucester, Massachusetts as a commercial deep sea fisherman in the North Atlantic waters, harvesting scallops. Not content with his education, he put himself through three years of night school for loop repair at the New Bedford Textile School and a year of dead reckoning navigation at the New Bedford Technical School. Active in the community, he also served as a Scoutmaster for two years before joining the Navy on October 6, 1941. Brought in as a Coxswain because of his extensive life experience, he was sent directly to USS *YP-212*, the ex-*Centaur,* a yard patrol craft operating out of Boston. In May 1942, he was given a month of Armed Guard training before being sent to Iceland as a replacement Armed Guard gunner. Attached to the *Nathaniel Greene*, he distinguished himself under fire and received a Letter of Commendation from the Secretary of the Navy. Promoted to Boatswain's Mate, first class, on April 16, 1943, he requested transfer for lighter-than-air aviation duty. Following his lighter-than-air (LTA) qualification, his rate was changed to Airship Rigger, first class and he was assigned to an airship crew out of Lakehurst, New Jersey. Promoted to Chief Airship Rigger on January 1, 1945, he was discharged from active duty on September 6, 1945. As a civilian, he returned to scalloping, and subsequently became a police officer, a job he held until his retirement. Alexander LaGue passed away on August 16, 1976.

The Soviet order book to Norman Hyams. *Courtesy of the Hyams family.*

Norman E. Hyams, *Order of Glory, Third Class*

Norman E. "Duke" Hyams was one of the *Greene's* gunners. Born in New York City on August 26, 1909, he enlisted in the Navy on January 4, 1942, from Los Angeles. Promoted to Coxswain, he reported to the Armed Guard Center in New Orleans on February 27, 1942. Prior to his service on the *Nathaniel Greene*, he was promoted to Gunner's Mate, second class. Surviving the attacks on the *Greene*, he earned a Letter of Commendation from the Secretary of the Navy along with a Purple Heart for his shrapnel wound. Returning to the United States, he spent the next six months recovering from his wound, which affected the use of the fingers on his right hand for the rest of his life. Due to his wound, he was found unfit to continue his service to the Navy, and he was discharged on November 8, 1943. As a civilian, he returned to New York, where he worked as a paper salesman and retired in 1977. He moved to Florida but after the death of his wife returned to New York in 1992. Norman Hyams passed away on November 8, 2007, and is buried in Arlington National Cemetery.

Order of Glory, Third Class, number 387951 awarded to Norman Hyams. *Courtesy of the Hyams family.*

A close-up of the reverse of the Order of Glory, Third Class, to Norman Hyams. Following receipt of the medal, he had it engraved to read: Norman E. Hyams/G.M. 2/c U.S.N./14 Sept.1942. *Courtesy of the Hyams family.*

Clarence H. Marihugh, *Order of Glory, Third Class*

Another gunner was Clarence Henry Marihugh from Defiance, Ohio. Born on April 22, 1924, he finished ninth grade before leaving school in 1939 and working for Kettering Golf Club as a greens keeper. Joining the Navy on January 20, 1942, he entered active service on February 7, followed by recruit training at Great Lakes. Assigned to the Armed Guard Center in Brooklyn, his first ship was the *Nathaniel Greene*. Surviving the transit to the USSR, he returned to the United States and remained with the Armed Guard until May 1944. Unfortunately, the wounds he received during the actions on the *Nathaniel Greene* caught up to him and he was hospitalized for a month. Returning on limited duty, he was placed as the Master at Arms in charge of administration at Naval Air Field (NAF) Columbus, Ohio. Recovered fully, he spent the remainder of the war on the fire and crash crew at NAF Columbus. Discharged as a Boatswain's Mate, second class, on October 13, 1945, he returned to civilian life. Not content out of the military, he enlisted in the Army on January 3, 1946, and remained on active duty until July 1, 1962, when he retired as a Chief Warrant Officer. Returning to Defiance, he passed away on February 1, 1985, and is buried in Riverview Memorial Gardens.

Charles E. Walters, *Order of Glory, Third Class*

Charles E. Walters. *National Personnel Records Center.*

Charles Edgar Walters, also wounded on the *Nathaniel Greene*, was born on January 31, 1921 in Girard, Illinois. Moving to California, he worked for R.G. Watson in Bakersfield as a crane operator before moving to Meridian, California, in October 1941. Enlisting out of San Francisco on December 20, he attended recruit training in San Diego, and then reported to Armed Guard training at the Destroyer Base in the same location. Transferred to the Armed Guard Center in New Orleans, he was assigned to the *Nathaniel Greene* as his first ship. Removed from the ship and taken to Scotland, he spent time in the Naval Hospital in Glasgow, Scotland, before being placed on temporary duty in Londonderry awaiting transfer back to the United States. Returning to New Orleans and serving as part of the Armed Guard on the SS *Pan Rhode Island*, he was transferred to the Naval Advanced Base Personnel Depot, San Bruno, California. This was in preparation for being sent to Navy 3149, a forward supply base on Calicoan Island in the Philippines. He remained here until being sent back to the United States for continued hospitalization due to the wounds he received on the *Greene*. Spending the remainder of the war at Naval Hospital Oak Knoll, in Oakland, California, he was discharged on November 27, 1945. Moving back to Meridian, California, he worked as a mechanic at Marysville Tractor and Equipment Repair. Charles Walters passed away in Meridian on December 3, 1993.

Jeremiah E. Mahoney, *Order of the Patriotic War, First Class*

Jeremiah Ehret Mahoney, Armed Guard commander on the SS *William Moultrie. National Archives.*

On the Gallant Ship *William Moultrie*, Jeremiah Ehret "Jay-Ehret" Mahoney served as the Armed Guard commander. Born on April 15, 1917, to New York Supreme Court Judge Jeremiah T. Mahoney, the one-time president of the Amateur Athletic Union (AAU) and founder of the Pan-American Games, he was a top-ranked water polo player, competing on the 1939 Mid-Ocean Championship Team prior to joining the Navy on April 10, 1942. Immediately assigned to the *William Moultrie* as the Armed Guard commander, he was awarded the Silver Star for his valor exhibited on the Murmansk Run as part of convoy PQ-18. Returning to the United States, he initially taught at the Armed Guard School in Little Creek, Virginia before his assignment to the USS *Monitor* (AP-160), serving on her in the Pacific theater. His final assignment of the war was at the Military Sea Transportation Service Port Office in New York prior to his discharge from active duty on November 8, 1945. Remaining in the Naval Reserves, he retired on March 28, 1969, with the rank of Commander.

As a civilian, he attended Columbia University Law School and passed the New York Bar in 1949, joining his father's law firm. His occupation as a lawyer was greatly overshadowed by his athletic involvement, however. He was a water polo referee at the All Olympic Games from 1948-1976, the team manager of the US Pan-American water polo team in 1951 and

1955, Chairman of the National Water Polo Committee from 1950-1955, Chairman of the Amateur Athletic Union (AAU), Chairman of the US Olympic Committee from 1950-1955, Secretary of the International Water Polo Committee, and inductee in both the USA Water Polo Hall of Fame and the International Swimming Hall of Fame. He was a famed traveler, circumnavigating the globe, and a world-renowned collector of American Indian artifacts. Jeremiah Mahoney passed away on November 12, 1970.

The Silver Star awarded to Jeremiah Mahoney, privately engraved with his name and presentation date on the reverse. This is the same engraving hand as the Silver Star to Ralph Boucher in Chapter 12.

William R. Abbott, *Medal of Ushakov*

William Abbott. *National Personnel Records Center.*

William Robert Abbott was born in Boston, Massachusetts on October 5, 1912. Following high school graduation, he went to work as an investigator for the Standard Service Bureau of Boston, a business-investigating agency. Seeing war on the horizon, he enlisted in the Navy on September 3, 1940 and served his first year on the USS *Siren* (PY-13), a converted yacht on patrol duty off the East Coast. On November 18, 1941, he reported to the Armed Guard Center and served as a member of the Armed Guard on the SS *Exeter* and SS *Edward L. Dohenny*, conducting transits to ports within the United States. Now a Coxswain and the most senior enlisted member of the Armed Guard crew, he reported to the SS *William Moultrie* on June 23, 1942, under the command of Jeremiah Mahoney. For valor exhibited during the around-the-clock attacks while en route to Archangel, Abbott received a Letter of Commendation from the Secretary of the Navy. Offloading their cargo, the *Moultrie* departed the USSR on November 17, and after a tumultuous crossing through heavy winds and seas that killed one of the members of the merchant crew, they arrived in New York Harbor on Christmas Eve. Wearing the rank of Boatswain's Mate, second class, Abbott left the *Moultrie* on December 28, and remained attached to the Armed Guard Center until he was released from active duty on May 5, 1943. He was officially discharged on August 17, 1944. He returned to work for the Standard Service Bureau and was active in local politics, unsuccessfully running for the Massachusetts state legislature in 1949. In September 1950, he was appointed as a deputy sheriff for Norfolk County and served until his retirement. He passed away after a long illness on October 20, 1982.

Richard E. Hocken, *Medal "For Military Merit"*

The master of the *William Moultrie* was Richard Ernest Hocken. Born in England on June 30, 1875, he graduated from high school in Bodmin, England in 1894. Heading to sea, he became master of his first ship in 1904, though he had been qualified as a master since June 1898. Moving to Brooklyn, he became a naturalized citizen on September 3, 1920, but moved to France in 1922 and remained there for three years. Relocating back to New York, he joined the Seas Shipping Company in 1929 and served as master of the SS *Maine* and SS *Pipestone County*. On the *Pipestone County*, he was torpedoed off Cape Henry, Virginia on April 21, 1942. Surviving that sinking, he was given command of *William Moultrie* and left for the Murmansk Run shortly thereafter. Because of his valor shown on their way to the USSR, he was promoted to the rank of Commander in the US Maritime Service in April 1943. Finishing the war as the master of the SS *Sea Dolphin*, he was awarded the Merchant Marine Distinguished Service Medal on September 13, 1946 for his actions on the *William Moultrie*, the same day of his promotion to Captain in the Maritime Service. Richard Hocken passed away in 1948.

John L. Laird, *Order of the Red Star*

John Landers Laird, the Armed Guard commander on the SS *Virginia Dare. US Navy photo.*

The third and final ship to earn the Gallant Ship citation on September 14 was the *Virginia Dare*. John Landers Laird, her Armed Guard commander, was born on August 6, 1920, and joined the Navy from Minneapolis, after attending the University of Minnesota. Commissioned on November 14, 1940, he was serving on the USS *Colorado* (BB-45) when he received orders to Armed Guard training at the Destroyer Base, San Diego. Assigned to the Armed Guard Center in New Orleans, he was subsequently sent to the *Virginia Dare* as the Armed Guard commander. Earning the Silver Star for his valor and leadership during the transit to the USSR, he returned to the United States on the SS *Hollywood* and was assigned to the USS *Ira Jeffery* (DE-63), a newly commissioned destroyer escort conducting convoy operations in the North Atlantic. In June 1944, he was transferred to the brand-new USS *Missouri* (BB-63) and remained on her throughout the rest of the war. Transferred to the USS *Iowa* (BB-61) to return to the United States, he spent a short time on the USS *Coral Sea* (CVA-43) before being discharged from active duty on August 2, 1946.

Remaining in the Naval Reserves, he was recalled for active duty on September 21, 1950, and served on the USS *Belle Grove* (LSD-2) and at Great Lakes, Illinois, before being discharged on December 15, 1953, as a Commander. Returning to civilian life, he became a hotel manager for hotels in Ridgecrest, California, and Nogales, Arizona. Retiring to Tucson in 1993, he passed away on October 2, 2000.

Five of the gunners on the *Virginia Dare* received Letters of Commendation from the Secretary of the Navy, and later, Soviet medals, for their exhibited heroism on September 14, 1942. They were: John Harmon, Frank Gay, George Goddard, Cecil Graff, and Rex Robertson.

John H. Harmon, *Medal of Nakhimov*

John H. Harmon. *Courtesy of the Harmon family.*

John Henry Harmon was born on May 5, 1919, in Denver, Colorado. Enlisting out of Denver on January 7, 1942, he was sent to the Armed Guard Center in New Orleans following recruit training. Like the others, his first ship was the *Virginia Dare*, where he earned his Commendation for his actions as the pointer on the *Dare's* deck gun. Returning to the United States, he spent the remainder of the war attached to CUB 11 and CUB 14, advanced base units created for establishing medium-sized advanced fuel and supply bases at remote locations. His final duty station was in Mare Island, California, on the staff of Headquarters, Twelfth Naval District. Discharged as a Gunner's Mate, second class, he moved to Inglewood, California. He had a fifty-one year career with Three-D Plastics in Burbank, working in sales and marketing. Following his retirement, he maintained a role as a consultant for the company until 1999, when he moved to Santa Ynez, California. John Harmon passed away on September 11, 2000.

Cecil B. Graff, *Medal of Nakhimov*

Also from Colorado, Cecil Billy Graff was born in Weldona on August 8, 1922. He worked as a farm hand for his father from 1936 until he joined the Navy on January 6, 1942. Taking part in recruit training in San Diego, he was attached to the Armed Guard Center in New Orleans and subsequently became part of the Armed Guard detachment on the *Virginia Dare*. Awarded a Commendation from the Secretary of the Navy for September 14, where he served as one of the *Dare's* twenty-millimeter gunners, he returned to the United States and was assigned to the Armed Guard gunnery school in Little Creek, Virginia, as an instructor. Returning to the Armed Guard in March 1943, he was assigned to the Liberty ship SS *Henry George*, where he made a round-the-world cruise, suffering significant storm damage as well as the constant threat of enemy submarines. Released from Armed Guard duty as a Gunner's Mate, second class in January 1944, he attended Advanced Gunner's Mate school and reported to the USS *Astoria* (CL-90) in May 1944, along with fellow Soviet medal recipient Lieutenant Louis Marks, as part of the ship's commissioning crew. Spending the remainder of the war in the Pacific, he was discharged in September 1945 as a Gunner's Mate, first class. He returned to the Midwest and worked in the oil fields of Colorado and Wyoming as a drilling engineer until his retirement in 1982. Cecil Graff passed away on October 14, 2014.

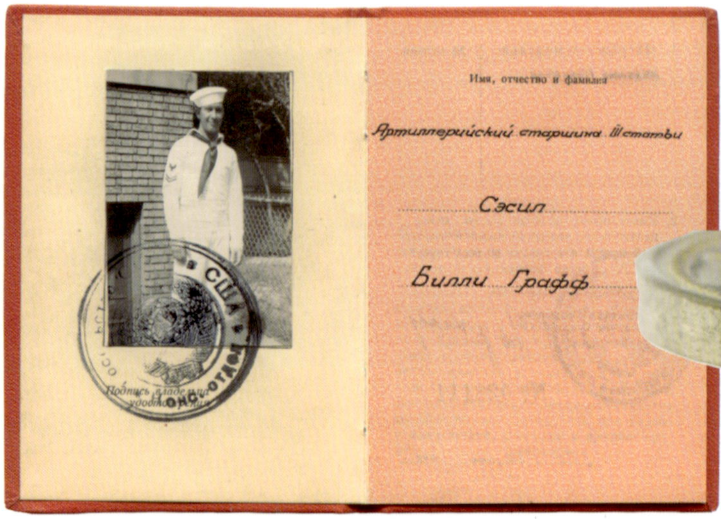

Edge engraving on the Medal of Nakhimov to Cecil Graff. *Courtesy of the Graff family.*

The Soviet medal book to Cecil Graff. *Courtesy of the Graff family.*

Medal of Nakhimov number 5599 awarded to Cecil Graff. *Courtesy of the Graff family.*

Frank C. Gay, *Medal of Nakhimov*

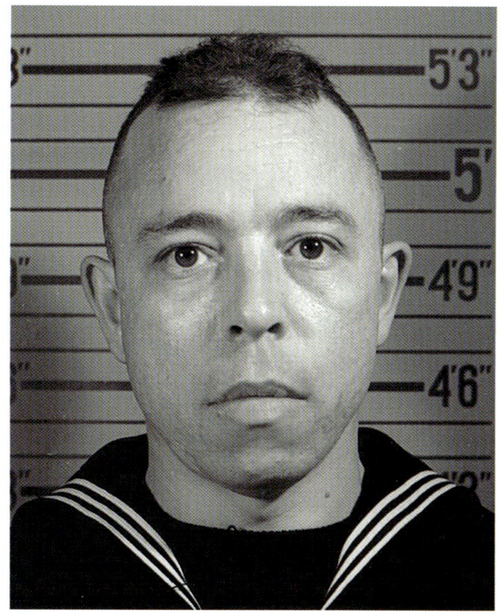

Frank C. Gay. *National Personnel Records Center.*

Another gunner from Colorado was Frank C. Gay. Born on May 4, 1911, he worked at the Gates Rubber Company prior to joining the Navy on January 8, 1942. Attending recruit training in San Diego, he was assigned to the Armed Guard Center in New Orleans, and subsequently, to the *Virginia Dare*. Returning to the United States, he was later reassigned to the SS *Joseph Nicollet*. Leaving Armed Guard duty in March 1944 as a Gunner's Mate, first class, he reported to the USS *Dover* (PG-8) the Spanish-American War veteran gunboat used for Armed Guard training in Louisiana. On October 10, 1944, Gay reported to the USS *Boulder Victory* (AKA-227) in preparation for their maiden voyage into the Pacific. On December 20, while in the Palau Islands en route to Manus, the *Victory* struck a floating mine, tearing an eighteen by thirty-two foot hole in the number three hold. It was only by sheer providence the ship did not explode and sink: the number three hold was filled with five-inch gun projectiles, and only two exploded through the skin of the ship. She ingloriously returned to the United States after temporary repairs were made, and was still in overhaul when the war ended.

Discharged from active duty on October 2, 1945, Gay moved back to Colorado and returned to work at the Gates Rubber Company, alongside PQ-17 survivor and Soviet medal recipient Andrew Mathson, eventually retiring as a belt manufacturing supervisor. Frank Gay passed away on March 19, 1974, and is buried in Fort Logan National Cemetery.

George C. Goddard, *Medal of Nakhimov*

George Goddard. *National Personnel Records Center.*

Gunner's Mate, third class, George Cecil Goddard hailed from El Rito, New Mexico. Born on September 7, 1913, in Cimarron, New Mexico, he worked as a District Forest Ranger for the New Mexico United Pueblos Agents before joining the Navy on January 7, 1942. He reported to the *Virginia Dare* on March 17, 1942, and stayed on board until March 1, 1943, leaving as a Gunner's Mate, third class. He next reported to the SS *Julian Poydras*, remaining there until December. Next, he served on the SS *Cape Rivers*, followed by the SS *Dove*. Finally, in April 1944, he reported to the SS *Sea Perch*, and remained on board until January 6, 1945. Leaving the *Sea Perch* as a Chief Gunner's Mate, he was discharged from the Navy on November 6, 1945. Residing in New Mexico and in Sonora, Mexico, he passed away on September 14, 1995. George Goddard is buried in Santa Fe National Cemetery, Santa Fe, New Mexico.

Rex E. Robertson, *Medal of Nakhimov*

Rex Eldon Robertson, who shared one "kill" of a German aircraft with George Goddard, was born on April 20, 1920, in Dunmore, Kentucky. Finishing the tenth grade at Kiser High School in Dayton, Ohio, he became a coal truck driver for Acme Coal Company. Leaving there in January 1940, he spent one year as a tree trimmer for Dayton Power and Light Company, followed by another year as a brake fluid mixer at the Delco Brake Division of General Motors. On February 10, 1942, he joined the Navy, going through recruit training at Great Lakes. He reported on May 25 to the Armed Guard Center in Brooklyn, and was subsequently assigned to the *Virginia Dare*. Returning to the United States, he was then assigned to the PQ-17 veteran SS *Benjamin Harrison* as the gun captain on the three-inch deck gun. Departing New York on March 4, 1943, as part of convoy UGS-6, she was scheduled to land her cargo of food, machinery, ammunition, trucks and tanks in Oran, Algeria. Twelve days later, she took two torpedoes from *U-172* in the starboard side, just below the number five hold. She sunk very slowly, but several members of the crew caused panic on deck and as a result, three men were killed during the course of abandoning ship.[20] The survivors were picked up by the Panamanian motor merchant *Alan-A-Dale* and landed in Oran on March 24.

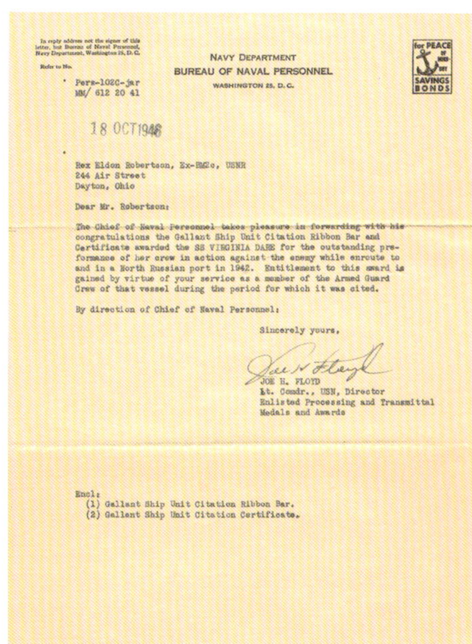

In reply address not the signer of this letter, but Bureau of Naval Personnel, Navy Department, Washington 25, D. C.

Refer to No.

Pers-102C-jar
MM/ 612 20 41

NAVY DEPARTMENT
BUREAU OF NAVAL PERSONNEL
WASHINGTON 25, D. C.

for PEACE ... SAVINGS BONDS

18 OCT1946

Rex Eldon Robertson, Ex-BM2c, USNR
244 Air Street
Dayton, Ohio

Dear Mr. Robertson:

The Chief of Naval Personnel takes pleasure in forwarding with his congratulations the Gallant Ship Unit Citation Ribbon Bar and Certificate awarded the SS VIRGINIA DARE for the outstanding preformance of her crew in action against the enemy while enroute to and in a North Russian port in 1942. Entitlement to this award is gained by virtue of your service as a member of the Armed Guard Crew of that vessel during the period for which it was cited.

By direction of Chief of Naval Personnel:

Sincerely yours,

JOE H. FLOYD
Lt. Comdr., USN, Director
Enlisted Processing and Transmittal
Medals and Awards

Encl:
(1) Gallant Ship Unit Citation Ribbon Bar.
(2) Gallant Ship Unit Citation Certificate.

Letter that accompanied the Gallant Ship Citation ribbon bar and certificate to Rex Robertson for his service on the SS *Virginia Dare*. *Courtesy of his daughter, Evelyn Ann.*

Returning to the Armed Guard Center in Brooklyn, Robertson was next assigned to the SS *J.F. Cooper* on June 21, 1943. He remained on the *Cooper* until January 1944, when he was transferred to Little Creek for amphibious training for his next assignment. Promoted to Boatswain's Mate, second class, he was assigned to the pre-commissioning crew of USS *LSM-208* on May 23, 1944. She was commissioned in June, and by February 1945 they were in Pearl Harbor, Hawaii, en route to duty in the Pacific theater. During the remaining months of the war, they saw a remarkable amount of duty, with Robertson serving as the acting Chief Boatswain's Mate in charge of Deck Division and the ship's Master at Arms. During the invasion of Okinawa, they survived several close calls with kamikaze aircraft, and landed the Army's 713th Flame Thrower Battalion ashore on Purple One beach. She ended the war in Tokyo Bay on August 29, 1945. Moving back to Dayton following his discharge on December 19, 1945, he returned to his old job at Delco, working as a job setter for the next thirty years before retiring. Rex Robertson passed away on December 15, 2003, and is buried in Woodland Cemetery, Dayton.

Rex Robertson (second from right) with some shipmates during the war. *Courtesy of his daughter, Evelyn Ann.*

Edge engraving on the Medal of Nakhimov awarded to Rex Robertson. *Courtesy of his daughter, Evelyn Ann.*

Medal of Nakhimov number 1303 awarded to Rex Robertson. *Courtesy of his daughter, Evelyn Ann.*

John H. Harshaw, *Order of the Patriotic War, Second Class*

Onboard the *Dare* was a passenger by the name of John Harrison "Jack" Harshaw. Leaving the United States, he was a Chief Boatswain, and by the time of his arrival in Archangel, he had been promoted to Ensign at age forty-nine. However, his career was far lengthier than most other Ensigns. Born on October 29, 1893, in Ardmore, Oklahoma, he enlisted in the Navy in 1911. Receiving his recruit training on Goat Island in San Francisco Bay, he was initially assigned to the armored cruiser USS *Colorado* (ACR-7), followed by the USS *South Dakota* (ACR-9), USS *Cleveland* (CL-19) and the USS *Navajo* (AT-52) a fleet tug based in the Territory of Hawaii. By 1917, he was a Chief Yeoman, serving on the USS *Brooklyn* (CA-3) in Vladivostok as part of the Allied Expeditionary Force. While ashore, he met the daughter of a Russian colonel who had commanded a regiment in the Tsar's army, and they got married, contrary to the standing orders of the AEF. He was subsequently transferred to duty at the US Embassy in Tokyo, and from there, orchestrated the escape of his wife's family from the now-USSR. His following tours included the USS *Aroostook* (CM-3), the USS *Isabel* (PY-10), and the USS *Huron* (CA-9), serving under future-admiral Robert Giffen. Harshaw had retired in December 1936 as a Chief Yeoman, following a tour at the Staff Headquarters, Twelfth Naval District. Harshaw went to work in the personnel department of Pan American Airways System in December 1936. Following the start of the war, the Navy desperately sought Russian linguists and, since he was a relatively recent retiree, Harshaw requested to return to active duty on December 8, 1941. Promoted to Chief Boatswain and sent to Russian language school in Washington, DC, he was transported as a passenger on the *Virginia Dare* to Archangel to assume the duties of Assistant Naval Attaché. However, when the convoy was attacked, the tall Texan refused to be quarantined in the safety of the lower decks (if there were such a thing anyway). Manning a twenty-millimeter machine gun along with gunners who were born after he became a Chief Petty Officer, he personally accounted for shooting down two German aircraft on September 14. Surviving the transit, he immediately escorted sixty tons of cargo for the US Embassy by rail to Moscow, perilously close to the front lines and with extreme hardship. Returning to the north, he assumed his duties as Assistant Naval Attaché and War Shipping Administration Representative in Archangel with great vigor, at once being promoted to Lieutenant from Ensign.

John Laird (left) and John Harshaw on the deck of the SS *Virginia Dare*. *Courtesy of the Harshaw family.*

Harshaw remained in the USSR through September 1946, traveling between Murmansk, Archangel, Moscow, the Crimea, as well as the occupied Soviet territories. Awarded a Commendation from the Secretary of the Navy for his actions on the *Dare*, he later was awarded the Order of the British Empire in January 1945 and the Bronze Star Medal in September of the same year by the US Mission to Moscow. Returning to the United States, he returned to inactive duty in March 1947 and was retired in 1949 as a Commander. Moving back to San Francisco, he resumed his previous job, eventually rising to become chief of personnel for Pan American before his retirement in 1959. His final years were spent traveling around the world, and constantly recording observations he made as a civilian and sending them to the Navy Department for analysis by intelligence experts. John Harshaw passed away on September 15, 1964, and is buried in Golden Gate National Cemetery, San Bruno, California.

John Harshaw (middle) stands with Captain Walker, RN, senior British Naval Officer in Archangel, and Soviet Rear Admiral Papanin. *Courtesy of the Harshaw family.*

John Harshaw (left) stands with Rear Admiral C.E. Olsen, Chief of the Naval Division of the U.S. Military Mission to USSR and members of the Naval Attaché's office during their visit to Archangel from Moscow in 1944. *Courtesy of the Harshaw family.*

John Harshaw with his wife at the end of his naval career. Note his ribbon for the Order of the Patriotic War, Second Class (lowest bar, far right). *Courtesy of the Harshaw family.*

Subsequent attacks on convoy PQ-18 occurred throughout the remainder of the day on September 14. However none of them had the intensity or caused the damage of the first major attack. The next day, a high level attack took place at 1:30 PM but with no casualties. Although this attack was a seeming non-event due to the fact that no one died and no ships sank, every attack during the course of the Murmansk Run could potentially spell disaster for the convoy. Part of the journal entry for September 15, written by Wesley Miller eloquently conveyed the feeling in the convoy:

> *The clouds are heavy overhead. Balloons are raised to seventeen hundred feet as we prepare for a bombing attack. We feel that something "special" is being prepared for us today ... You simply feel it in the air. At 12:15, it came with all of its fury. Huge columns of water rose skyward as one thousand pound (or larger) bombs showered around us from four-motored Focke-Wulf Kuriers ... The clouds are too heavy to see the enemy only once in a while ... They continue to drop bombs blindly from a great height. As one wave would drop its load, another would arrive to take its place. This went on for three hours and forty-five minutes without a letup. We could merely stand with gaping mouths watching the clouds for a glimpse, listen to the weird drone overhead, and wonder if our luck would continue to hold out.*[21]

September 16 and 17 were quiet; the latter day saw the addition of four Soviet destroyers to the convoy. The next morning, Cape Kanin was sighted at 6:05 AM, but they were not yet safe: at 10:25 AM, a group of fourteen He 111 torpedo bombers attacked the convoy. Using the same tactics as before, the aircraft let go an oceanful of torpedoes at the same instant. Five torpedoes were aimed directly toward the SS *White Clover*. Her veteran master, Julius Lintlom, skillfully maneuvered the ship using course and speed changes to weave his ungainly merchant through the oncoming torpedoes, with one missing the bow by a scant ten feet.

On board the SS *Kentucky*, Ensign William Farrar, the Armed Guard commander, spotted an inbound torpedo at 10:30. Despite maneuvering the ship, the torpedo struck the number two hatch on the starboard side. The explosion was sufficiently violent to blow the hatch cover into the rigging, buckled the stanchions in the wheelhouse and chart room, and carried away the port side of the bridge. Fire broke out in the officer's quarters and quickly began to spread throughout the ship. The master made the decision to abandon ship, and had the lifeboats lowered. Farrar went through the ship hazarding his own life by bravely passing through burning compartments and receiving burns on his face and hands to ensure no one was left behind. Upon his arrival back on deck, he observed all of the lifeboats already rowing away from the sinking ship. Jumping into the icy water, he swam as hard as he could to a bullet-pocked raft and his fellow survivors pulled him on board. Thirty minutes later, the crew was rescued by the Royal Navy minesweepers *MMS-203* and *MMS-950*. They were put ashore in Archangel at 12:30 PM on September 22.

Close-up of the reverse of John Harshaw's Navy Good Conduct Medal, showing that it was awarded at the American Embassy, Tokyo, Japan, on June 3, 1919. *Courtesy of the Harshaw family.*

Reverse of John Harshaw's US and foreign medals. *Courtesy of the Harshaw family.*

US and foreign medals belonging to John Harshaw. They are: the Bronze Star Medal, Navy Commendation, Navy Good Conduct, World War I Victory, Nicaraguan Campaign number 9975, Mexican Service 1548, Yangtze Service M. No.839, the Order of the Patriotic War, Second Class, No.557261, and the Order of the British Empire. *Courtesy of the Harshaw family*.

William H. Farrar, *Order of the Red Star*

William Farrar onboard his ship, the USS *Sarpedon* (ARB-7) c.1945. *Courtesy of the Farrar family.*

William Hunter Farrar was born on August 28, 1917, in Arkansas City, Kansas. He attended Arkansas City High School and the Kemper Military Academy before attending the University of Texas. Joining the Navy on July 27, 1940, he was commissioned on September 12, 1941, following training at the Reserve Midshipman School at Northwestern University. Reporting to the Armed Guard School on March 24, 1942, he completed his training and reported to the Armed Guard Center in Brooklyn on April 27. Subsequently assigned to the *Kentucky*, he remained on her until she sank on September 18, receiving a Letter of Commendation from the Secretary of the Navy for his heroism. Following a two-month wait, where he received a Commendation from the Assistant Naval Attaché for his bravery in fighting a fire on the roof of a hotel during a bombing raid, he left Archangel on November 17 and returned to Scotland on a Royal Navy cruiser with convoy QP-15. While in Scotland, he had the opportunity to meet the King and Queen of England, an experience that stayed with him for the remainder of his life. Returning to the United States, he was ordered to the USS *Lash* (PYc-31), a converted yacht used for training at the Armed Guard School in Gulfport, Mississippi. Serving on *Lash* as both the gunnery officer and later the commanding officer, he subsequently received orders to take command of the USS *Sarpedon* (ARB-7), undergoing retrofit into a battle damage repair ship. Following three months of school, he reported to the crew of the *Sarpedon*, and commissioned her on March 19, 1945. Farrar took the *Sarpedon* to Okinawa to serve as a repair ship for warships damaged by the continual aerial attacks, remaining there for the duration of the war. He was released from active duty on February 27, 1946, but remained active in the Naval Reserve, eventually retiring as a Lieutenant Commander on September 1, 1962.

As a civilian, he worked for the Continental Oil Company, starting as an accountant and working his way up to being an executive in the comptroller's department before his retirement in 1982. William Farrar passed away in Wichita, Kansas, on April 25, 1989, and is buried in Riverview Cemetery in his hometown of Arkansas City.

Order of the Red Star, number 1553975 awarded to William Farrar. *Courtesy of the Farrar family.*

With the sinking of the *Kentucky*, the at-sea travails of PQ-18 were over. On the evening of September 19, the convoy reached the Dvina River, leading to Archangel. Unlike their previous convoy, twenty-seven out of the original thirty-nine merchant vessels arrived to unload their cargo for the Soviet Union. Of the survivors, fifteen were US-flagged merchants, including the SS *Exford*, *St. Olaf*, *Patrick Henry*, *Sahale*, *Lafayette*, *Campfire*, *White Clover*, and the *Schoharie*.

It took the *Exford* almost two days to make it to their anchorage in Archangel. Initially anchored near the mouth of the Dvina River, her Armed Guard commander, Coxswain John Currant, wrote: "The wind is terrific and the waves are like mountains."[22] In their attempt to remain in one place, they lost two anchors and anchor chains before starting in to Archangel. Not but a few hours after they were moored in port, the German bombers came overhead. Currant wrote in his journal:

> *As soon as it got dark the alarms went off and about fifteen minutes later the fireworks started. Big bombers were all over dropping incendiary bombs and some heavy bombs. They drop many flares around us to light up the area for a target. They circle around our docks and encircle us with flares and things don't look so good. Some bombs drop nearby but no serious damage was done. As we stand on the decks at our gun stations, we get hit by falling shrapnel and it can be heard dropping on the sheds, dock, and on our steel deck. Some pieces are quite big and would injure a person if hit directly.*[23]

On September 30, he recorded: "Archangel seems to be the place that has to take it. Many fires were started and it looks like the whole city is ablaze."[24] When the smoke cleared on October 1, they saw: "About six small blocks have been burned in the residential district and about the same amount in the suburban districts. Some houses were directly hit by big bombs and were leveled out over the landscape. Not a very pretty sight."[25]

John H. Currant, *Order of Glory, Third Class*

John Currant, who served as the Armed Guard commander on the SS *Exford*. *Courtesy of the John Currant family.*

The *Exford* arrived back in New York on January 31, 1943. John Howard Currant, now a Boatswain's Mate, second class, transferred to the SS *Stephen T. Mather*, a new Liberty ship, for the remainder of the war. Born in East Boston, Massachusetts, on January 2, 1918, Currant graduated from Saugus High School and attended Essex Agricultural School for two years before going to work for the New Haven Railroad as an electrician and signal helper. Leaving the railroad, he immediately enlisted in the Navy on June 18, 1941 and following his initial training, served on the USS *Kingbird* (AMC-56), a yacht converted into a coastal minesweeper operating between Boston and Portsmouth, New Hampshire. Transferred to the Armed Guard on June 13, 1942, he was on board *Exford* a day before leaving for Archangel.

Following his service on the *Mather*, Currant was discharged as a Boatswain's Mate, first class, on September 12, 1945. Returning to work for the railways, he spent ten years as a signalman on the Boston and Maine Railroad before moving to California to work for Northrop Aviation as well as several other companies. He retired to Boulder Creek, California, where he passed away on June 15, 1983.

Посольство СССР в США · Конс. отдел

Имя, отчество и фамилия

Шлюпочный старшина

Джон

Х. Кёррант

Подпись владельца книжки

1. Награжден Указом Президиума Верховного Совета СССР от 7 июня 1945 года орденом Славы III степени

2. Имеет право, начиная с 1-VIII-1945 на получение орденских денежных выдач и на другие льготы и преимущества, [illegible] Общему положению об орденах Союза ССР.

3. Книжка бессрочная.

Секретарь Президиума Верховного Совета СССР

№ 222136

15 августа 1945 г.

ОБЩЕЕ ПОЛОЖЕНИЕ
об орденах Союза ССР.

1. Орден Союза ССР является высшей наградой за особые заслуги в области социалистического строительства и обороны Союза ССР.

2. Центральным Исполнительным Комитетом Союза ССР учреждены следующие ордена Союза ССР: „Орден Ленина", „Красное Знамя", „Красная Звезда", „Трудовое Красное Знамя" и „Знак Почета".

3. Орденами Союза ССР могут награждаться как отдельные граждане, так и войсковые соединения и воинские части Рабоче-Крестьянской Красной Армии, предприятия, учреждения и организации.

4. Награжденные орденом Союза ССР могут быть за новые заслуги повторно награждены тем же или другим орденом Союза ССР.

3

The Soviet order book to John Currant. *Courtesy of the John Currant family.*

Order of Glory, Third Class, number 387953, awarded to John Currant. Note how he removed the ribbon from the back of the suspension to make ribbons for his uniform. *Courtesy of the John Currant family.*

Wesley N. Miller, *Order of the Patriotic War, Second Class*

A colorful writer, whose voyage report was later quoted by Samuel Eliot Morrison, Mark Evans, and Nathan Miller (no relation) in their writings about the Arctic convoys, Wesley Norton Miller served as the Armed Guard commander on the SS *St. Olaf.* Born on October 26, 1909, in Hermanville, Mississippi, he attended Millsaps College in Jackson, Mississippi. In 1931, he was hired as the athletic coach for Arcola Public High School. Miller left his teaching role in 1936 and became a salesman for the Delta Implement Company of Greenville and Rolling Fork. He was commissioned in the Naval Reserve in April 1942 and reported to the Armed Guard School in Chicago in May. Following his return from the USSR, Miller was awarded a Letter of Commendation from the Secretary of the Navy for his voyage to Archangel on the *St. Olaf.* Transferring to the SS *Ezra Meeker* immediately following his return, he commanded the Armed Guard detachment through their transit to Sicily in support of the landings there. Subjected to heavy aerial attacks, he earned his second Commendation for action on July 11-12, 1943, and a Silver Star Medal for leading his gunners in shooting down four aircraft during their transit from Oran, Algeria, to Casablanca from July 23 to August 16 of the same year. Leaving Armed Guard duty, he was assigned to the Submarine Chaser Training Center in Miami, Florida, in April 1944, followed by duty at the Amphibious Training Base, Camp Bradford, Virginia, in June. After serving at the office of the Supervisor of Shipbuilding in Evansville, Indiana, for a year, he reported to the Naval Air Technical Training Center in Jacksonville, Florida, where he commanded a school for electric turret technicians on torpedo planes. Discharged from the Navy in 1946, he remained in the Reserves until discharged on October 6, 1953, as a Lieutenant Commander.

As a civilian, Miller returned to Washington County, Mississippi, and worked for the Reliance Life Insurance Company until he retired in 1972. Following his retirement, he became active in Scouting and tennis at the Deer Creek School in Arcola. To honor his many years of service, the 2001 school yearbook was dedicated to him, and he was awarded the 2002 school spirit award. He also served as an alderman for the town of Arcola and on the Board of Trustees for the Delta Regional Medical Center. Wesley Miller passed away on May 13, 2008, and is buried in Leland-Stoneville Cemetery, Stoneville, Mississippi.

Blake Hughes, *Order of the Patriotic War, Second Class*

Order of the Patriotic War, Second Class, number 557279 awarded to Blake Hughes. *Courtesy of the Hughes family.*

The SS *Patrick Henry*, one of PQ-18s survivors, was the first Liberty ship built, commissioned on September 27, 1941, and christened by Mrs. Henry A. Wallace, the wife of the vice president of the United States. The *Henry* went on to steam 175,000 miles during the course of the war, but on this occasion, she was on her maiden voyage to the USSR. Blake Hughes, the *Henry's* Armed Guard commander, was born on June 24, 1914, in New York City. He graduated from Bronxville High School and Dartmouth College. Prior to the start of the Second World War, Hughes attended graduate school at Columbia and at Dartmouth's Tuck School of Business. He additionally earned a *degre de civilization* from the Sorbonne in Paris. With that background, he joined the Naval Reserve on October 14, 1940, and was commissioned shortly thereafter. His first duty station was as a deck officer on the USS *George F. Elliott* (AP-13) a troop transport in the Atlantic. Transferred to Armed Guard duty in January 1942, he served in Brooklyn and out of Newport, Rhode Island, before his voyage to the Soviet Union. Returning to the United States, he was sent to the Armed Guard Gunnery School as an instructor, and before he transferred at the end of his tour, served as the school's executive officer. He reported to the USS *Chase* (DE-158) in November 1943 and made six trans-Atlantic convoys prior to the ship's conversion to a high-speed transport and redesignation as APD-54. Sent to the Pacific, Hughes took part in the Okinawa landings, to include the near-fatal hit *Chase* received from a kamikaze on May 20, 1945. Leaving the *Chase* in July, he reported to the Headquarters, First Naval District, in Boston, and served as war diarist for the district until the end of the war.

Discharged on October 15, 1945, he went into the publishing business. Working for McGraw-Hill, Hughes was the publisher of *Architectural Record* magazine from 1968 to 1981, as well as *House and Home*, *Housing*, and *Architectural Record* books. He additionally founded and was the president of the International Architectural Foundation from 1973 to 1978, dedicated to alleviating the living conditions in third world slums. He also was president of the International Institute for Architecture from 1978 to 1980. Finally, he served as a trustee for Unity College in Maine from 1965 to 1975. Before his death, he penned several books of poetry, short stories, and a novel, and was a noted artist. Blake Hughes passed away on June 11, 2009.

Blake Hughes, Armed Guard commander on the SS *Patrick Henry*. *Courtesy of the Hughes family.*

Maurice Breen, *Order of the Red Star*

The SS *Sahale* left the United States without armament as her original tasking did not include a voyage to the USSR. With a change in convoy routing sending her on the Murmansk Run, she spent forty-five days in a shipyard in Glasgow receiving the modifications to allow her to carry an Armed Guard detachment. Despite the addition of the Armed Guard, the ship was still short-handed, and Thomas Carter, her Armed Guard commander, asked for volunteers from the merchant crew to man the weapons. Maurice Breen, the ship's purser, came forward and was assigned to a fifty-caliber machine gun on the bridge. Receiving two days of instruction on the gun, the ship got underway as part of convoy PQ-18. Even though he could have remained below decks the entire voyage, Breen remained on the bridge; cold, wet, and awake for nearly six days straight. On September 14, he was responsible for personally shooting down one of the German bombers attacking the convoy. Born on July 5, 1907, in New Orleans, Louisiana, Breen graduated from Warren Easton High School and Delgado Trade School. He worked in an auto supply store prior to going to sea. He was thirty-six-years old at the time of his participation in PQ-18, but braved the elements like the Navy gunners nearly twenty years junior to him. Because of his valor during the convoy, Maurice Breen became one of only 148 recipients of the Merchant Marine Distinguished Service Medal during the Second World War. He made multiple trips to the USSR during the war, but with the advent of peacetime, left the Merchant Marine and returned to New Orleans. He also returned to the auto parts industry, working as the district manager for Barrett Equipment Company. Maurice Breen died on April 19, 1956, and is buried in Greenwood Cemetery, New Orleans.

Following their arrival in the USSR, a storm came through on September 19 with such ferocity that the SS *Sahale* lost her anchor and ran aground on the banks of the Dvina River. Held fast, she spent the next week hard aground before she was finally towed off and made her way into port. The *Sahale* wasn't the only ship to spend time aground on the shore of the Dvina. Astern of her were the SS *Lafayette* and the SS *Campfire*.

The Soviet order book to Maurice Breen. *Courtesy of Don and Donna Breen*.

Имя, отчество и фамилия

Казначей

Морис

Бринн

Подпись владельца книжки

Maurice Breen

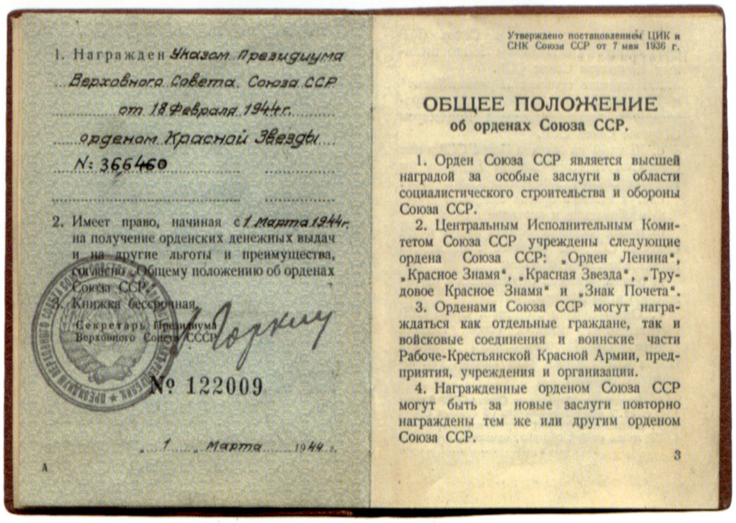

1. Награжден Указом Президиума Верховного Совета Союза ССР от 18 февраля 1944 г. орденом Красной Звезды №: 366460

2. Имеет право, начиная с 1 марта 1944 г. на получение орденских денежных выдач и на другие льготы и преимущества, согласно „Общему положению об орденах Союза ССР".

3. Книжка бессрочная.

Секретарь Президиума Верховного Совета СССР

№ 122009

„1" марта 1944 г.

Утверждено постановлением ЦИК и СНК Союза ССР от 7 мая 1936 г.

ОБЩЕЕ ПОЛОЖЕНИЕ
об орденах Союза ССР.

1. Орден Союза ССР является высшей наградой за особые заслуги в области социалистического строительства и обороны Союза ССР.
2. Центральным Исполнительным Комитетом Союза ССР учреждены следующие ордена Союза ССР: „Орден Ленина", „Красное Знамя", „Красная Звезда", „Трудовое Красное Знамя" и „Знак Почета".
3. Орденами Союза ССР могут награждаться как отдельные граждане, так и войсковые соединения и воинские части Рабоче-Крестьянской Красной Армии, предприятия, учреждения и организации.
4. Награжденные орденом Союза ССР могут быть за новые заслуги повторно награждены тем же или другим орденом Союза ССР.

3

Order of the Red Star number 366460 awarded to Maurice Breen. *Courtesy of Don and Donna Breen*.

Maurice Breen admires his Merchant Marine Distinguished Service Medal and his Order of the Red Star, both awarded for valor on PQ-18. *Courtesy of Don and Donna Breen*.

The Merchant Marine Distinguished Service Medal awarded to Maurice Breen. *Courtesy of Don and Donna Breen.*

George B. Lennig, *Order of the Red Star*

George B. Lennig, Armed Guard commander on the SS *Lafayette. Courtesy of the Lennig family.*

On the *Lafayette*, George Birmingham Lennig cautiously watched the skies for any sign of German aircraft preparing to attack his immobilized ship. Born on July 11, 1913, in Philadelphia, Lennig attended the University of California, Berkeley, and was commissioned via their Reserve Officer Training Corps program on November 19, 1939. His first duty station was the USS *Arizona* (BB-39), arriving on board in December as the fifth division officer, in charge of the battleship's starboard five-inch guns. He was remarkable on board *Arizona* as one of the very first non-Naval Academy graduate officers in the Wardroom and as such did not reflect the "condescending" attitude of many of his fellow junior officers.[26] He had been on board for two years when the *Arizona* was attacked at Pearl Harbor on December 7, 1941. Lennig and another Ensign, Jim Miller, were sent on the hazardous mission to locate Captain Van Valkenburgh and Admiral Kidd during the course of the attack and the ship's subsequent flooding. Finding neither in their search, Lennig took the most direct route off the ship and survived that fateful day.

Without a ship, Lennig was automatically volunteered for Armed Guard duty when the call went forward in late December. Arriving on the *Lafayette* on April 28, Lennig took her to Archangel, distinguishing himself for his leadership throughout the convoy. However, when the *Lafayette* ran aground, his authority was tested. With the ship's civilian master in a drunken stupor, Lennig was ordered to remove his gunners from the ship, along with the rest of the crew. This resulted in significant interest both in Archangel and in the United States. It also caused considerable discontent on the ship itself, with Lennig requesting his Armed Guard detachment be removed from the ship, permanently, upon their return to Liverpool.[27] This did not occur, but Lennig fell ill while the ship was in Liverpool and was hospitalized. This caused him to miss the remainder of the voyage on the *Lafayette*, and it can be assumed that he was not upset by the turn of events. Despite the unusual occurances during the voyage, Lennig was awarded the Silver Star for his heroism during PQ-18. Returning to the United States, he was assigned to the office of Frontier Operations, Western Sea Frontier, responsible for anti-submarine and convoy operations originating from the United States' West Coast. He remained with the Western Sea Frontier until reassigned to the Port Director's Office, 12th Naval District on May 10, 1945. Finishing the war here, he was discharged on September 10, and returned to Berkeley, California.

As a civilian, he remained in California and became a stockbroker in San Diego. In 1965, he moved to British Columbia and lived there for the next year. On September 10, 1966, George Lennig had a sudden heart attack and passed away. He is buried in the Port Coquitlam Cemetery, Port Coquitlam, British Columbia.

The Silver Star presented to George B. Lennig.

SS *Lafayette*, taken approximately 1944 before she was turned over to the Soviets and became the *Novosibirsk*. *National Archives*.

Bernard A. Malloy, *Medal "For Military Merit"*

Bernard Aloysius Malloy served as the radioman on the *Lafayette*. Born on October 6, 1921, he enlisted in the Navy on April 25, 1940. First serving on the USS *Pennsylvania* (BB-38), he survived the attack on Pearl Harbor and transferred to Armed Guard duty on April 12, 1942. Assigned to the *Lafayette* as part of her communications detachment, he received a Letter of Commendation for his actions on the Murmansk Run. He remained with the Armed Guard, serving in both Brooklyn and New Orleans, until November 17, 1944, when he was transferred to the pre-commissioning crew of the USS *Southerland* (DD-748) with the rank of Radioman Chief (acting appointment). Malloy served on *Southerland* in the Pacific theater until October 17, 1945, when he was reassigned to the Receiving Station, Brooklyn, where he received a permanent appointment to Radioman Chief, and then to the Naval Radio Station, Third Naval District, New York. Redesignated a Teleman Chief, he was sent to the US Naval Security Group Activity, Bremerhaven, Germany, where he served until June 1957, and changed rates to Cryptologic Technician Chief. He subsequently served in the Far East until sent to the Naval Security Group Activity, Fort George G. Meade, in Maryland. Promoted to Master Chief here, he was then assigned to Spanish language school in 1965 followed by a tour on the USS *Oxford* (AGTR-1), a communications research and reception ship. Now a commissioned Lieutenant, (Limited Duty Officer) he served his final tour at the Communications Training Center in Pensacola, Florida. Malloy retired on March 21, 1967, and passed away on November 12, 1970.

Junior Wishon receives his documents for his Medal of Ushakov during a ceremony in 1946. *Courtesy of the Wishon family.*

Junior Wishon, *Medal of Ushakov*

Born on April 1, 1920, Junior Wishon enlisted in the Navy on January 20, 1942. Following recruit training, he was assigned to Armed Guard duty and immediately to the crew of the *Lafayette*. During the ship's transit to the USSR, he was specifically commended for his gunnery and received a Letter of Commendation from the Secretary of the Navy. Transferred in October 1943 to the United States Naval Advance Base Personnel Depot, Camp Allen, Virginia, he was promoted to Coxswain and remained there until sent to the personnel detachment at Lido Beach, New York. Following a promotion to Boatswain's Mate, second class, Wishon received orders to CTG 122.10 in Rouen, France, responsible for loading and unloading cargo and prisoners. Detached from there in October 1945, he returned to the United States and was subsequently assigned to the USS *Hancock* (CV-19), then the USS *Antietam* (CV-36). This was followed by a tour at the Naval Auxiliary Air Station, Saufley Field, Pensacola, Florida, before heading back to sea on the USS *Essex* (CVA-9) in July 1953. Transferred from the *Essex* in December 1956, he received orders to Headquarters, Seventeenth Naval District in Kodiak, Alaska. Reporting to the USS *Ticonderoga* (CVA-14) in July 1959 for his final tour, he retired on January 2, 1962 with the rank of Chief Boatswain's Mate. Junior Wishon passed away on August 9, 1991 and is memorialized at Willamette National Cemetery, Portland, Oregon.

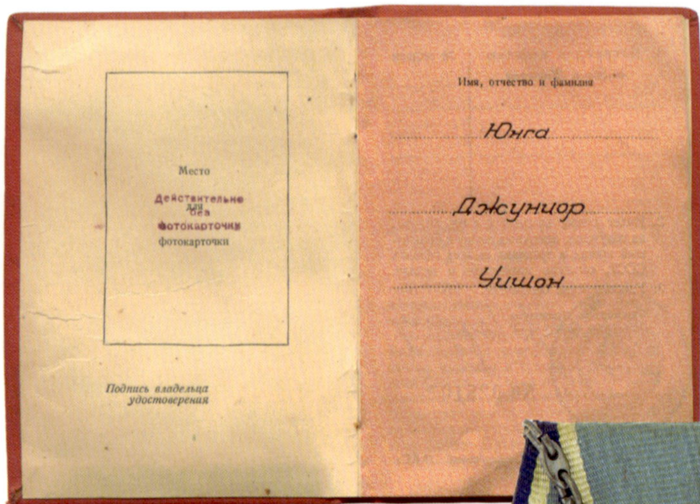

The Soviet medal book to Junior Wishon.
Courtesy of the Wishon family.

Medal of Ushakov number 7520 awarded to Junior Wishon.
Courtesy of the Wishon family.

Kyle V. Johnson, *Medal "For Valor"*

Kyle Vaughn Johnson was born on April 16, 1902 in Clovis, New Mexico. He worked for the Santa Fe and the Southern Pacific railroads in New Mexico and Arizona. While in Arizona, he attended law school and passed the bar in 1930, and began practicing law. With the arrival of the war, he was too old for service in the military branches, so he volunteered for the Merchant Marine. Attached to the *Lafayette*, he volunteered to man the starboard twenty-millimeter Oerlikon gun and was credited with shooting down three German bombers over the course of their transit to the USSR. He was awarded the Merchant Marine Distinguished Service Medal for his valor. He subsequently volunteered for duty on the SS *Maiden Creek II* when he returned to the United States. On March 17, 1944, approximately thirty miles off the coast of Bougie, Algeria, with convoy SNF-17, the *Maiden Creek* was torpedoed at 8:38 AM by *U-371*. The master ordered the ship abandoned, but the damage control efforts were so effective that the ship remained afloat and the crew returned. At 1:00 PM, the ship was hit a second time, and the damage was fatal. Unfortunately the ship's lifeboats were destroyed, broken into splinters by the second hit. The master ordered the ship abandoned and the crew did so by jumping into the open ocean. They were subsequently picked up by a convoy escort vessel. However, during this process, six of the crew were lost, including Kyle V. Johnson. His body was recovered, and he was temporarily buried in Algeria but later moved to Mission Garden of Memories Cemetery, Clovis, New Mexico. The SS *Kyle V. Johnson* was named in his honor.

Daniel J. Rooker, *Order of the Patriotic War, First Class*

Daniel Junior Rooker served as the Armed Guard commander on the SS *Campfire*. Rooker was born on November 13, 1918, in Grand Rapids, Michigan. He graduated from Michigan State University with majors in history, political science, and journalism before joining the Navy on August 15, 1940. Commissioned on September 12, 1941, he was sent to Armed Guard duty and was subsequently assigned to the SS *Campfire*. Awarded the Silver Star for his demonstrated heroism during the Murmansk Run, he was transferred to the Destroyer Base, San Diego, as an Armed Guard gunnery instructor. Following the conclusion of his tour there, Rooker volunteered for submarine service and was sent to the submarine school in New London, Connecticut. Upon graduation, he was first assigned to USS *S-18*, a training submarine in San Diego, but was subsequently assigned to the USS *Ronquil* (SS-396), participating in her final war patrols and earning the Bronze Star Medal and the Purple Heart.

Released from active duty on October 7, 1945, Rooker moved to Miami, where he became the national advertising manager for the *Miami Daily News*. Later moving to Virginia he became the editor of the *Radford News Journal*, working there from 1951 to 1957. From then until 1971, Rooker was the editor and publisher of the *The Southwest Times* in Pulaski, Virginia. That year, he became publisher of the *Charlottesville Daily Progress* and vice president of Worrell Newspapers, Inc. Five years later, he formed his own company, New River Valley Newspapers, and purchased his previous two employers, as well as the *Radford Messenger* and *Blacksburg Sun*. He owned these until 1980, when he finally sold his holdings and retired in 1982. Active in the community, he served as president of the Radford City and Pulaski County Chambers of Commerce, as well as the New River Valley Industrial Association and the Pulaski Golf Club.

Daniel Rooker passed away on June 26, 1993, and is buried in Oakwood Cemetery, Pulaski, Virginia.

The Soviet order book to Daniel Rooker. *Courtesy of the Rooker family.*

Имя, отчество и фамилия

Младший лейтенант

Дэйниел

Дж. Рукер

Подпись владельца книжки

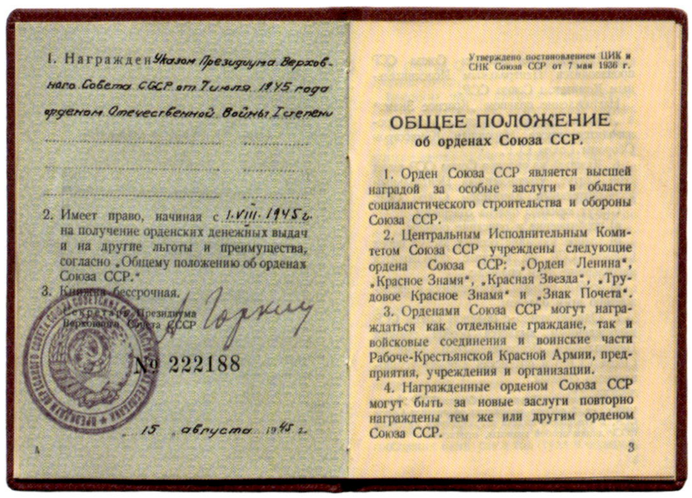

1. Награжден Указом Президиума Верховного Совета СССР от 7 июля 1945 года орденом Отечественной Войны I степени

2. Имеет право, начиная с 1.VIII.1945 г. на получение орденских денежных выдач и на другие льготы и преимущества, согласно „Общему положению об орденах Союза ССР."

3. Книжка бессрочная.

Секретарь Президиума Верховного Совета СССР

№ 222188

15 августа 1945 г.

Утверждено постановлением ЦИК и СНК Союза ССР от 7 мая 1936 г.

ОБЩЕЕ ПОЛОЖЕНИЕ
об орденах Союза ССР.

1. Орден Союза ССР является высшей наградой за особые заслуги в области социалистического строительства и обороны Союза ССР.

2. Центральным Исполнительным Комитетом Союза ССР учреждены следующие ордена Союза ССР: „Орден Ленина", „Красное Знамя", „Красная Звезда", „Трудовое Красное Знамя" и „Знак Почета".

3. Орденами Союза ССР могут награждаться как отдельные граждане, так и войсковые соединения и воинские части Рабоче-Крестьянской Красной Армии, предприятия, учреждения и организации.

4. Награжденные орденом Союза ССР могут быть за новые заслуги повторно награждены тем же или другим орденом Союза ССР.

3

Donald S. Biggs. *Courtesy of the Biggs family.*

Donald S. Biggs, *Medal "For Military Merit"*

Two of the Armed Guard gunners on *Campfire* were recognized by the Soviets: Donald Biggs and Albert Wohlers. Donald Sherman Biggs was born in Detroit, Michigan, on January 12, 1925. Growing up in foster homes, he volunteered for the Navy as soon as he could. Still age sixteen, he enlisted in the Navy on January 20, 1942, and upon completion of basic training in Great Lakes, Illinois, reported to the Armed Guard Center in Brooklyn on April 26. Less than a week later, he was ordered to the SS *Campfire*, where he made her voyage to the USSR. Following his return to the United States, Biggs served as a member of the Armed Guard on the steamships *Colorado* and *Texas Sun* before transferring to the newly-commissioned fleet oiler, USS *Kangaroo* (IX-121), on December 20, 1943. On *Kangaroo*, Biggs steamed over twenty-thousand miles in the Pacific, and was involved in multiple campaigns as a station tanker. With the end of the war, he was released from active duty on November 1, 1945. Biggs worked at the General Motors Buick production facility for thirty years and was a volunteer firefighter for his city of Fenton, Michigan, for forty-seven years before he officially retired. He passed away on January 30, 2001.

Albert F. Wohlers, *Order of the Red Star*

One of the three victims of friendly fire on the *Campfire* during their first taste of combat on September 13 was Albert Franklin Wohlers. Born in Crawford, Nebraska, on April 15, 1917, he enlisted in the Navy on January 29, 1942. He was assigned to the *Campfire* on April 26, just ten days after his twenty-fifth birthday, making him one of the oldest members of the Armed Guard detachment. On September 13, he was shot clear through his torso by a bullet fired from another ship. Seeing him go down, Rooker and the Armed Guard Coxswain, Francis Capobianco, raced to help Wohlers. They assumed the worst: there was no way he could have survived the impact of an anti-aircraft round through his body. However, Wohler's six-foot, two hundred pound frame survived the blast, as it had been a tracer round that entered through his abdomen and departed through his back, searing the ragged edges of the hole as it traveled through and saving his life. Rooker and Capobianco dragged him out of his gun emplacement and to the relative safety of the midship deckhouse. In the process, Capobianco was wounded lightly by friendly fire, but he was able to return to service without extensive treatment. Once bandaged, Wohlers returned to his station and rendered what assistance he could until he was evacuated to the British destroyer HMS *Offa* (G-29) on September 15 for continued medical treatment. For his gallantry and determination, he was awarded the Silver Star Medal and Purple Heart on April 9, 1943. After being released from the US Naval Hospital in Brooklyn, he reported to ACORN 23 in the Pacific on January 27, 1944. With ACORN 23, Wohlers landed on Eyebe Island on March 9, and in conjunction with the 107th Seabee Battalion, began the clearing of the destroyed Japanese defensive emplacements and construction of US Naval Air Base 807 on the tiny strip of land 4,500 feet long and 450 feet wide. While on Eyebe, he received a small package containing his Order of the Red Star, one of only six such awards bestowed in April 1944. He remained on Eyebe Island through June 7, 1945, rising to the rank of Boatswain's Mate, first class. Returning to the United States, he was discharged on September 27, 1945. Living in Gladstone, Missouri, for the remainder of his life, he passed away on November 13, 1997.

SS *Campfire*, taken approximately 1944 prior to her transfer to the Soviets as the *Surkov*. *National Archives.*

Harry F. Ryan, *Medal "For Military Merit"*

Harry Ryan, master of the SS *Campfire* during PQ-18. *Courtesy of the Ryan family.*

The master of the *Campfire* was Harry F. Ryan. Born in Binghamton, New York on January 7, 1899, he graduated from Binghamton Central High School and enlisted in the Navy on May 2, 1917. He served on the USS *North Dakota* (BB-29) until his discharge after the end of the war. On March 1, 1923, he went to sea as an AB (Able Seaman) with the Waterman Steamship Corporation, serving on the SS *Pan American*. He worked his way up through the deck rates, serving on a plethora of ships through the 1920s and 1930s. Earning his master's license in 1937 and taking the SS *Afoundria* to sea on December 15, 1940, as his first ship in the role of master, he served the remainder of his career in that position. During the Second World War he saw intense combat action in every theater of war. In addition to taking the *Campfire* to the USSR, he was master of the second ship into London and took the first ammunition ship, the SS *Lawton B. Evans*, to the newly liberated Anzio beachhead in January 1944. For the week following their arrival, they were continually shelled by German artillery and attacked by *Luftwaffe* aircraft and glide bombs. Surviving the Anzio invasion after shooting down six aircraft and being struck by dud torpedoes twice, he became master of the USAT *Fairland* on April 15, 1944. The *Fairland* was a transport ship taking Marines from the United States into combat in the Pacific, and he participated in the invasions of Saipan and Okinawa. He continued to serve as master of merchant ships throughout the next decade, to include convoy duty during the Korean War. As master of the SS *Choctaw*, he assisted in the evacuation of the US Army forces during the Hungnam redeployment and evacuation in December 1950. In October 1957, he was selected to be the master of the SS *Gateway City*, the first full containership ever built. After forty years at sea, Ryan retired in 1959. Harry Ryan passed away on August 24, 1962, at the Veterans Administration hospital in Biloxi, Mississippi, and is buried in Pine Crest Cemetery, Mobile, Alabama.

The Soviet medal book to Harry Ryan. *Courtesy of the Ryan family.*

The Medal "For Military Merit" number 598607 awarded to Harry Ryan. *Courtesy of the Ryan family.*

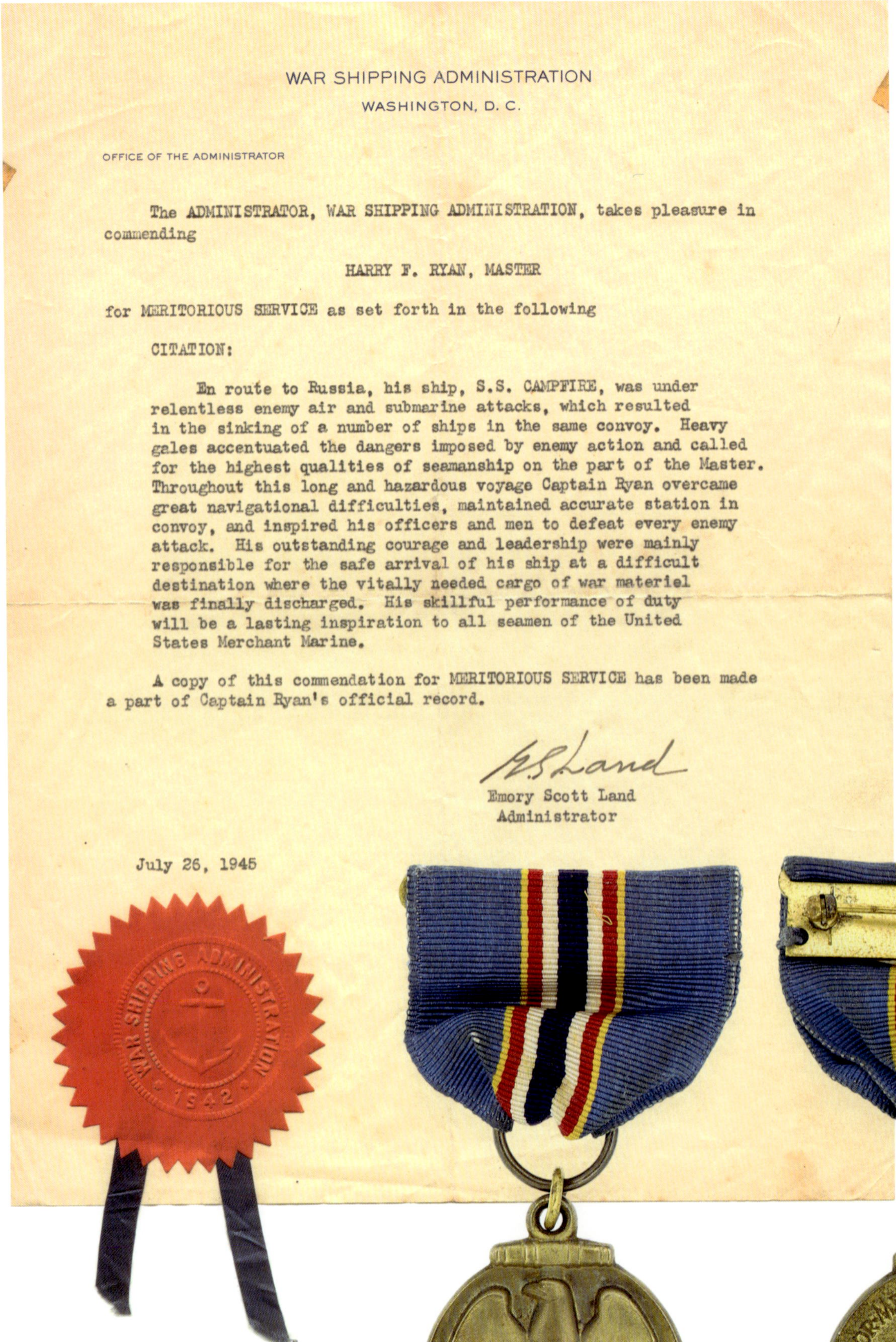

WAR SHIPPING ADMINISTRATION
WASHINGTON, D. C.

OFFICE OF THE ADMINISTRATOR

The ADMINISTRATOR, WAR SHIPPING ADMINISTRATION, takes pleasure in commending

HARRY F. RYAN, MASTER

for MERITORIOUS SERVICE as set forth in the following

CITATION:

En route to Russia, his ship, S.S. CAMPFIRE, was under relentless enemy air and submarine attacks, which resulted in the sinking of a number of ships in the same convoy. Heavy gales accentuated the dangers imposed by enemy action and called for the highest qualities of seamanship on the part of the Master. Throughout this long and hazardous voyage Captain Ryan overcame great navigational difficulties, maintained accurate station in convoy, and inspired his officers and men to defeat every enemy attack. His outstanding courage and leadership were mainly responsible for the safe arrival of his ship at a difficult destination where the vitally needed cargo of war materiel was finally discharged. His skillful performance of duty will be a lasting inspiration to all seamen of the United States Merchant Marine.

A copy of this commendation for MERITORIOUS SERVICE has been made a part of Captain Ryan's official record.

E S Land
Emory Scott Land
Administrator

July 26, 1945

WAR SHIPPING ADMINISTRATION
1942

The citation for Harry Ryan's Merchant Marine Meritorious Service Medal. *Courtesy of the Ryan family.*

The Merchant Marine Meritorious Service Medal, number 101, awarded to Harry Ryan. *Courtesy of the Ryan family.*

Albert Maynard, *Order of the Patriotic War, First Class*

Albert Maynard, Armed Guard commander on the SS *Schoharie. Courtesy of the Maynard family.*

On board the *Schoharie*, Albert "Al" Maynard commanded the Armed Guard detachment. Born in Atlanta, Georgia, on June 22, 1917, he graduated from the University of North Carolina. Working as a banker, he saw the clouds of war on the horizon and joined the Navy on September 21, 1940. Commissioned through the Naval Reserve Midshipman School in Annapolis, Maryland, in July 1941, he attended gunnery school in Tompkinsville, New York, and Little Creek, Virginia, before reporting for Armed Guard duty in November. Sent to the *Schoharie*, he took her to the USSR, and in the process earned the Silver Star for his heroism during the deadly transit. Returning to the United States, he transferred from Armed Guard duty on March 17, 1943. Following three months of training at the Submarine Chaser Training Center in Miami, he reported to the USS *Manlove* (DE-36) as the first lieutenant. Serving on *Manlove* throughout her time in the Pacific, he earned five campaign stars for the sinking of the Japanese submarine *I-32* and convoy escort and patrol operations around Kwajalein, Eniwetok, Ulithi, Manus, and finally, Okinawa. After two weeks on station off the coast of Okinawa, the *Manlove* was hit by a Japanese kamikaze, causing considerable damage and forcing her to head to Guam for repairs. With those complete, she returned to Okinawa until ordered back to the US on July 5, 1945. During their time overseas, Maynard became *Manlove's* executive officer and held that position until his transfer on August 31, 1945.

Discharged from active duty on November 19, 1945, he became a route furniture salesman in Rome, Georgia. Leaving his company a year and a half later, he moved to Belton, South Carolina, and opened Maynard's Furniture Company. The company is still in business and owned by his family today. Al Maynard was active in his business until he passed away from a sudden heart attack the day after Thanksgiving, November 26, 1993. He is buried in Belton Cemetery, Belton, South Carolina.

Julius Lintlom, *Medal "For Valor"*

Julius Lintlom, the master of the SS *White Clover* during PQ-18. *National Archives.*

The skillful and sea-hardened master of the *White Clover*, Julius Waldemar Lintlom, was born in Reval (now Tallinn), Estonia, on June 20, 1892. He first went to sea at the age of fourteen, sailing out of Germany as a ship's quartermaster. In 1909, he went to school in Germany for diesel engineering, and his subsequent voyages were as an engineer. In November 1917, while in the United States, he volunteered for service in the US Army and served as an instructor of maintenance and operations for gas and oil engines at Camp Devens, Massachusetts. Discharged in May 1919, he went to work for the Mississippi Shipping Company, earning his qualifications as chief officer, master, and Mississippi River pilot from Southport, Louisiana, to sea. He then served as a master for the US Tank Ships Company to 1931 and with the Standard Fruit Company from 1931 to 1941. With the increasing wartime need for merchant vessels, he began working for the US Maritime Commission, reconditioning and refitting old freighters. His first, ironically, was the SS *West Jaffrey*, which later sank with future Soviet medal recipients Gifford Starnes and Thomas Delate on board as members of her Armed Guard detachment. He subsequently placed the SS *West Neris* back in service (she was later torpedoed and sunk in 1943) followed by the SS *White Clover*. After eleven months as master of the *Clover* and surviving the Murmansk Run, he then became master of several other ships, to include the SS *Margaret Lykes*, *Michael J. Stone*, *Alexander W. Doniphan*, and *Lake Sapor*. He finished the war as master of the SS *Samuel Nelson* and followed that with service on the SS *Flagstaff Victory* in 1946. As an officer of the US Merchant Marine, he became a Commander on April 10, 1943, and a Captain on October 1, 1946. Retiring not long thereafter from a life at sea, Lintlom moved to Mission Hills, California, where he passed away on January 13, 1983.

In total, convoy PQ-18 lost thirteen ships out of forty; three to submarines and ten to aircraft. In contrast, the Germans expended over 250 torpedoes and lost forty-one aircraft (many with their experienced crews) to include thirty-three torpedo bombers, six dive-bombers, and two long-range reconnaissance aircraft. On November 8, 1942, Operation Torch, the landings in North Africa, began. This brought about the cancellation of convoy PQ-19 as merchant vessels and the Royal Navy escorts were immediately needed to support the landings. For the Germans, this also meant the removal of much of the *Kriegsmarine* and *Luftwaffe* strength in the Arctic to combat the flood of invasion forces in the Atlantic and Mediterranean. This did not mean the voyage to the USSR became any less hazardous: ships were still sent to the bottom of the sea and lives were still tragically lost. However, the *en masse*, continual aerial and subsurface attacks as experienced in PQ-17 and PQ-18 never took place again.

Chapter 12

Operation FB and JW Convoy Recipients

Operation *FB*

Despite the November 1942 Allied opening of a third front in North Africa and the withdraw of some German forces from the Eastern Front to combat the invasion, the Soviet Union still needed Lend-Lease materiel to sustain their defensive momentum. Operation *FB*, the sailing of thirteen ships independently from Iceland at twelve-hour intervals from October 29 to November 2, 1942, took place to fill the immediate lack of supplies resulting from the cancellation of convoy PQ-19.[1] Of the thirteen ships, three returned to Iceland, five were sunk (three by U-boats, two by aircraft) and five, to include the SS *John Walker*, completed their voyage. The *Walker* was number three in the series of ships for Operation FB, and she was underway at 7:00 AM on October 30. The skies were heavily overcast, preventing attacks by German aircraft until November 4, when the cloud cover finally broke. At 9:50 AM, still dark because of the almost perpetual darkness in the Arctic that time of year, the ship was attacked by three Ju 88 dive bombers; each dropping four to six five hundred pound bombs close aboard. Valiantly manning their guns, the *Walker's* Armed Guard detachment threw everything they could at the attackers, preventing any direct hits to the ship, and hitting at least one of the planes. Following that battle, they were again attacked by two more Ju 88s at noon, with a total of thirty bombs being dropped between the two attacks. On November 8, they anchored outside Archangel. That evening, with the harbor pilot on board, they weighed anchor and shortly grounded on an unmarked obstruction. They remained hard aground until November 12, when they had finally discharged a sufficient amount of cargo to lessen their draft to allow tugs to pull them off the obstruction. Reaching port, they offloaded cargo in Molotovsk and later in Murmansk. During this time, the *Walker* fought through multiple air raids over Murmansk on December 26 to 28, with bombs being dropped close enough to spray shrapnel topside and wound two of the crew. Along with PQ-18 veteran *Campfire*, the *John Walker* got underway on December 30 with convoy RA-51 and returned to the United States on February 14, 1943.

Milton A. Stein, *Order of the Patriotic War, Second Class*

Milton A. Stein, the Armed Guard commander on the *Walker*, was born on September 17, 1918, in Los Angeles, California. Following two and a half years at the University of California, Los Angeles, he joined the Army as a Flying Cadet in March 1940. Making a wise decision to part ways with the Army, he left in May and enlisted in the Navy in July. Commissioned an Ensign in October, he was assigned to the USS *Mississippi* (BB-40). Transferred to Armed Guard duty in January 1942, he served as the Armed Guard commander on the SS *Hanley* and the SS *Arizpa* before being assigned to the *John Walker* on August 5. Following his voyage to the USSR, where he earned a Commendation from the Secretary of the Navy, he was assigned to destroyer escort duty. After his training, he reported to the USS *Brough* (DE-148) as the gunnery officer on September 15, 1943. Following the tragic accidental death of the ship's commanding officer during heavy weather at sea, Stein became the ship's executive officer. On September 11, 1944, after less than one year on board, the commanding officer was relieved, and Stein took command. Continuing her convoy escort duties throughout the remainder of the war, Stein relinquished command on October 24, 1945, and was discharged from active duty on January 30, 1946. Returning to California, he founded Stein Construction Company in Studio City, specializing in building commercial and government buildings. He later went to work for Morley Construction Company in Southern California, retiring from them in 1977. After his retirement, he owned and managed a block of rental apartments. Later selling those, he spent time managing his investments and boating off the coast of Southern California.

Order of the Patriotic War, Second Class, number 557271 awarded to Milton Stein.
Courtesy of Milton Stein.

The Soviet order book to Milton Stein.
Courtesy of Milton Stein.

Convoy JW-51A

Very little is written in histories of the Murmansk Run about the eastbound transit experiences of the SS *El Oceano*, *Oremar*, *Richard Bland*, *J.L.M. Curry*, and *El Almirante*, all part of the sixteen-ship Convoy JW-51A, as they were the first convoy since the earliest Lend-Lease convoys to make the transit to the USSR completely unmolested by the Germans.[2] In fact, they had far more action during the trans-Atlantic voyage to Belfast with the torpedoing of several of the ships in their convoy, as the level of U-boat activity in the open reaches of the North Atlantic rose to a crescendo. However, their peaceful Arctic transit abruptly ended when they arrived in Murmansk on Christmas Day 1942. They discovered the season's greeting of "peace to all men" was not part of their cold, continually dark, and very violent reality. Along with the Operation FB veteran *John Walker*, they were subjected to continual German bombardments over the holiday period: four raids on December 26, three on December 27, and five the next day. By the time the *El Oceano* departed the USSR with convoy RA-52 on January 29, 1943, they had been subjected to fifty-five aerial bombardments.

Joseph T. Gillen, Armed Guard commander on the SS *El Oceano. Courtesy of the Joseph T. Gillen family.*

Joseph T. Gillen, *Order of the Patriotic War, Second Class*

The *El Oceano's* Armed Guard commander was Joseph Thomas Gillen, born April 22, 1914, in Wayne, Pennsylvania. His parents ran the local grocery store, and he graduated from St. Katherine's High School and the Philadelphia College of Pharmacy and Science. First working as a pharmacist, he became a chemist-salesman for Merck & Company before the war started. He was commissioned on September 10, 1942 and was sent directly to Armed Guard duty. Arriving in Londonderry, Ireland, without a ship, he was assigned to the *El Oceano*, which had left New York with a Boatswain's Mate in command of the Armed Guard detachment. With three months in the Navy, he took the *El Oceano* to the USSR and heroically directed the gunnery of his men while in port, shooting down a German Me 109 fighter on January 24, 1943. Awarded a Commendation from the Secretary of the Navy for his actions, he returned to the United States and remained with the Armed Guard. First, he served as a gunnery instructor in New York. This was then followed by Armed Guard commander duties on the USAT *Brazil*, the MV *Cape Falcon*, and finally the USAT *Bienville*. Discharged from active duty on January 9, 1946, he returned to Pennsylvania and continued working for Merck, just as before the war. He was working for them when he passed away unexpectedly on August 22, 1968.

Имя, отчество и фамилия

Младший лейтенант

Джозеф

Т. Гиллен

Подпись владельца книжки

Joseph T. Gillen

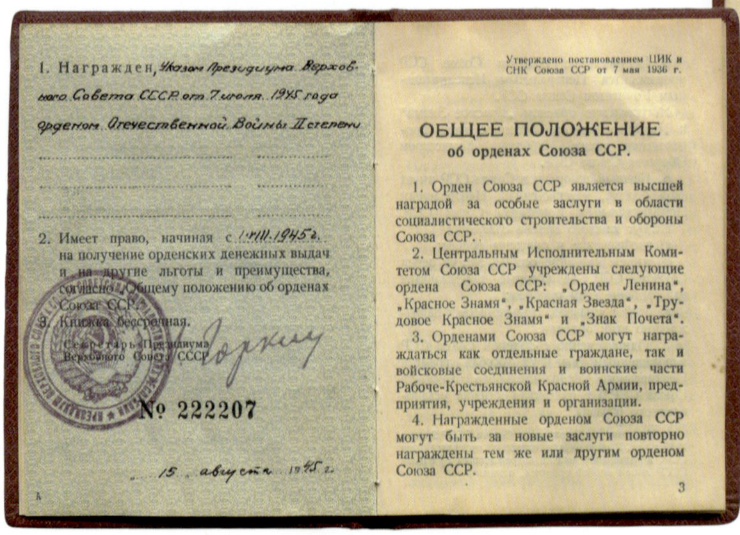

1. Награжден, Указом Президиума Верховного Совета СССР от 7 июля 1945 года орденом Отечественной Войны II степени

2. Имеет право, начиная с 1.VIII.1945 г. на получение орденских денежных выдач и на другие льготы и преимущества, согласно „Общему положению об орденах Союза ССР".

3. Книжка бессрочная.

Секретарь Президиума Верховного Совета СССР

№ 222207

15 августа 1945 г.

Утверждено постановлением ЦИК и СНК Союза ССР от 7 мая 1936 г.

ОБЩЕЕ ПОЛОЖЕНИЕ
об орденах Союза ССР.

1. Орден Союза ССР является высшей наградой за особые заслуги в области социалистического строительства и обороны Союза ССР.

2. Центральным Исполнительным Комитетом Союза ССР учреждены следующие ордена Союза ССР: „Орден Ленина", „Красное Знамя", „Красная Звезда", „Трудовое Красное Знамя" и „Знак Почета".

3. Орденами Союза ССР могут награждаться как отдельные граждане, так и войсковые соединения и воинские части Рабоче-Крестьянской Красной Армии, предприятия, учреждения и организации.

4. Награжденные орденом Союза ССР могут быть за новые заслуги повторно награждены тем же или другим орденом Союза ССР.

3

The Soviet order book to Joseph Gillen. *Courtesy of the Joseph T. Gillen family.*

Order of the Patriotic War, Second Class, number 557277 awarded to Joseph Gillen. *Courtesy of the Joseph T. Gillen family.*

Convoy JW-51B

Consisting of fifteen ships, including the SS *Ballot*, convoy JW-51B sailed from Loch Ewe, Scotland, on December 22, 1942. Their voyage was uneventful until December 26, when they were overtaken by extreme heavy weather. Five ships on the port column of the convoy, including the *Ballot*, got lost due to the weather. The following day, four of the five ships regained position in the convoy, but the disposition of the *Ballot* was unknown. She continued to Kola Inlet traveling independently, missing what became known as the Battle of the Barents Sea, where the German cruisers *Hipper* and *Lützow*, along with six destroyers, attempted to destroy the convoy on December 31. The British convoy escorts, led by Captain Robert St. Vincent Sherbrooke, bravely defended the convoy and drove off the Germans in a series of bold maneuvers that earned Captain Sherbrooke the Victoria Cross.

The voyage of the *Ballot* would have been considered uneventful had they not run aground on Kildin Island on January 2, 1943. In the evening fog, the ship was transiting with the rest of the convoy when a navigation error led them directly onto the rocky coastline. The convoy reacted quickly and that same evening, an attempt was made to pull the *Ballot* off the rocks. This was unsuccessful. Further attempts on January 4 and 5 likewise proved unsuccessful and by the evening of January 5, the ship was nearly full of water, up to the tween-decks and in the engine room. On January 7, they decided to remove all of the crew save for a handful of members of the Armed Guard, the master, and four other civilian crewmen. They remained on board for the following week, living in the galley, without sanitation, heat, or electricity, in the sub-zero Artic winter weather, while the Soviet stevedores removed the ship's cargo. Finally, with the cargo removed, the survivors left the ship on January 14, twelve days after running aground. The *Ballot*, a twenty-one year old Panamanian-registered vessel that was listed as being in "poor condition" even before her transit to the USSR, was left for salvage by the Soviets.[4]

Robert E. Buckbee, *Order of the Red Star*

Robert Edward Buckbee, the Armed Guard commander on the *Ballot*, received a Letter of Commendation from the Secretary of the Navy for his defense of the ship while she was aground on Kildin Island. Born on February 1, 1907, in Urbana, Illinois, he attended the University of Illinois. When the war broke out, he volunteered for service in the Navy, and was commissioned on April 4, 1942. Reporting for Armed Guard duty on June 23, he was assigned to the *Ballot* and took her to the USSR, leaving New York on July 29. Returning to the United States in March 1943, he was detached from Armed Guard duty on June 24. As with many of his peers, Buckbee was sent to the Submarine Chaser Training Center in Miami for training in conjunction with service on a newly commissioned destroyer escort. However, he did not complete the training and was subsequently reassigned to the Support Group, Eleventh Amphibious Base, which later became part of the Eleventh Amphibious Force, responsible for the amphibious landings during Operation Overlord. However, while in Scotland conducting preparations for the invasion, he contracted pneumonia and died on March 25, 1944. His body was returned to the United States in 1949, and he is buried in the Spring Hill Cemetery and Mausoleum, Danville, Illinois.

Robert E. Buckbee, Armed Guard commander on the SS *Ballot*. *National Personnel Records Center*.

Convoy JW-52

On January 17, 1943, fourteen ships left Loch Ewe for Murmansk in convoy JW-52. Included with this convoy were the SS *Cornelius Harnett*, SS *El Oriente*, and the SS *Nicholas Gilman*. Their voyage was relatively uneventful, save for an attack by three German bombers at 12:32 PM on January 24, 1943. The aircraft made their way through the convoy escorts and headed directly for the *Harnett*. The excellent marksmanship of the Armed Guard on the *Harnett,* including the SS *Bellingham* veteran of convoy PQ-17 Raymond Peer, destroyed the first aircraft and damaged the second, with the third breaking off their attack in self-preservation, only to be shot down by the Armed Guard on the *Nicholas Gilman*. The remainder of the voyage took place in heavy winter weather, preventing any further attacks, and they made it to port successfully.

The remaining ships of convoys JW-51A, JW-51B, and JW-52 made the westward return voyage away from the USSR on March 1, 1943 with convoy RA-53, consisting of thirty merchant vessels. Despite the smaller number of attacks experienced on the convoy route since the beginning of the year, the transit was still hazardous.[5] On March 5, they were attacked by a combination of U-boats and aircraft. At 9:30 AM, four torpedo wakes were spotted on the starboard side of the convoy. Despite their evasive maneuvering, the SS *Executive* and the SS *Richard Bland* were both torpedoed by *U-255* (who had earlier sunk the SS *John Witherspoon* and several others during convoy PQ-17). The *Executive* was abandoned almost immediately and was sunk by convoy escort gunfire. However, the *Bland*, with William Carter and other PQ-17 survivors from the *Ironclad*, survived the day's attack, only to be torpedoed again and sunk five days later with a significant loss of life. The first aerial attack came at 2:00 PM, when the convoy was attacked by twelve dive-bombers. The first to drop its bombs was shredded by the accurate gunfire of Gunner's Mate, third class, Mason Houghton on the *Oremar*, and the other attackers were driven off by the determined anti-aircraft fire of the rest of the convoy. That was not the end of the destructive effects of the weather and the enemy on the convoy: on March 9, the SS *Puerto Rican* was sunk by *U-586*, and on that same day, the SS *J.L.M. Curry*, with Romuald Holubowicz on board for his second transit to and from the USSR, floundered and sank in the high seas. All sixty-six members of her crew were rescued.

Gunners load ammunition for the westward transit on the SS *Oremar* at Kola Inlet. *Courtesy of the Houghton family.*

Despite the valor exhibited during the westbound transit of the SS *Oremar*, the stress of the aerial attacks was compounded by the lack of food on board the ship. This was a not an uncommon occurrence during the voyages to the USSR. However, on *Oremar*, it was magnified because of the master's unwillingness to obtain additional food from other ships. James Williams, *Oremar's* Armed Guard commander, wrote:

> *We ran out of potatoes December 28, 1942, and were steadily running out of food since we left Loch Ewe on December 15, 1942. We were completely out of food while alongside the docks in Molotovsk, USSR and when food did arrive it consisted of cheap macaroni, beans, yak, and some milk for our coffee. This food arrived on January 18, 1943, we had been out of food two days then. We departed from Molotovsk on the 25th of January and by the 27th, there was very little food to be had and no milk. On the 28th, we ran out of yeast so we had no bread. The meat was not edible and we lived on rice patties and gravy. Someone stole some powdered pea soup from the cargo which was destined for the Polish Embassy, USSR and when the rice patties ran out, we lived on that for several days. We arrived in Murmansk, February 4, 1943 and by February 7th even the flour used in making biscuits was gone and we were completely out of food again.*[3]

By the time the ship arrived in New York on April 8, they were completely out of food, having run out of the most basic provisions during their westbound crossing of the Atlantic. Several members of the Armed Guard were diagnosed with malnutrition, and all on board had lost considerable amounts of weight from malnourishment.

James D. Williams, *Order of the Patriotic War, Second Class*

James Douglass Williams, the Armed Guard commander on the *Oremar*, was born on June 9, 1918. He enlisted in the Navy in August 1940 and was commissioned at the Naval Reserve Midshipman School at the Naval Academy in May 1941. His first assignment was to the USS *Almaack* (AKA-10) in time to make her first cargo-carrying voyage to Iceland from July to August. Detached upon her return to New York, Williams was sent to Armed Guard duty in November. He was ordered to the SS *El Almirante* on May 1, 1942, having previously commanded three Armed Guard detachments at sea. This time, however, he was bound for the horrors of the Murmansk Run, with several ships that would later take part in convoy PQ-18. However, while in Belfast, a last-minute schedule change turned them back to the United States, where they returned on June 26. He was then reassigned to the *Oremar*, and in convoy with the *El Almirante*, took part in convoy JW-51A. Receiving a Letter of Commendation from the Secretary of the Navy for his heroic work in the return on the voyage to the USSR, he was subsequently transferred to the USS *Prince Georges* (AK-224) to serve as her first lieutenant and cargo officer. In June 1944, he arrived at the Training and Distribution Center at Treasure Island, and spent the next sixteen months there as a department head until his transfer in October 1945. Williams then spent the next year as the flag lieutenant to Commander, Third Fleet. Returning to sea, he served as the air defense officer on the USS *Macon* (CA-132) followed by command of the USS *Rich* (DD-820) in 1948 and the USS *Saufley* (DD-465) in 1951. Subsequently, he served on the staff of Commander, Operational Development Force and on the staff of Commander, Seventh Fleet. Finally, his last four and a half years were spent as the commanding officer of the Naval Reserve Training Center in McAlester, Oklahoma. Williams retired with the rank of Lieutenant Commander on June 30, 1962. Returning to school, he earned a master's degree in Russian history from Oklahoma State University in Stillwater, Oklahoma. He then taught at Merrimack Community College in St. Louis, Missouri, until his death. James Williams passed away on October 24, 1967.

James D. Williams, Armed Guard commander on the SS *Oremar*, photographed in his subsequent role as flag lieutenant in 1945. *Courtesy of J. Douglass Williams.*

Order of the Patriotic War, Second Class, number 557273 awarded to James D. Williams. *Courtesy of J. Douglass Williams.*

Paul L. Hunsinger, *Medal of Ushakov*

The Coxswain with the Armed Guard detachment on *Oremar* was Paul Leonard Hunsinger, who also received a Letter of Commendation from the Secretary of the Navy for his valor during the course of the voyage. Hunsinger was born in Forest City, North Carolina, on January 18, 1925. He enlisted in the Navy on February 3, 1942 and completed recruit training in Norfolk, Virginia. In May, he was sent to Armed Guard duty and reported to the *Oremar* for her voyage to the USSR. Returning to the United States, he remained in the Armed Guard through the duration of the war. He was discharged on November 1, 1945, as a Boatswain's Mate, second class. However, he decided to come back into the Navy and reenlisted on June 18, 1946, but accepted a reduction in rank to Seaman, first class. He served on the USS *Strong* (DD-758) followed by the USS *Tidewater* (AD-31) and the USS *Rowan* (DD-782) where he participated in the invasion of Inchon from September 15 to October 4, 1950. This was followed by a year at Naval Auxiliary Air Station, Sanford, Florida, from 1952 to 1953, and then another year at the Auxiliary Air Station in El Centro, California. Now a Boatswain's Mate, first class, he was transferred to the USS *Bradford* (DD-545), where he served until April 1957. The next two years were spent at the Naval Station, Subic Bay, Philippines, followed by a two-year tour on the USS *Bennington* (CVS-20). His last tour was with the Navy Communications Station, Guam. He retired on December 3, 1962, with the rank of Chief Boatswain's Mate. In his retirement, he returned to Forest City, but moved to Kelseyville, California, in 1976. He became well known for his gardening abilities amongst his friends and passed away on August 3, 1986.

Paul L. Hunsinger. *National Personnel Records Center.*

The Soviet medal book to Mason Houghton. *Courtesy of the Houghton family.*

Mason M. Houghton, *Medal of Ushakov*

Gunner's Mate, third class, Mason Minor Houghton, also of the *Oremar*, received a Letter of Commendation from the Secretary of the Navy for his exceptional gunnery on March 5, 1943. Born on May 6, 1919, in Kingston, Missouri, he graduated from Tarkio High School in 1936 and began helping his father farm three hundred acre tracts of land in Savannah, Missouri. He enlisted on January 8, 1942, in Kansas City. Following recruit training at Great Lakes, he was assigned to Armed Guard duty. His first ship was the SS *El Almirante*, going with her on the return eastbound trans-Atlantic voyage in July 1942. While in Belfast, he was transferred to the *Oremar* and served under James Williams for the voyage to the USSR. Transferred from the *Oremar* in April 1943 following their return to the United States, he reported to the Liberty ship SS *Anthony Wayne* in June, and served on her until January 1944. That April, he reported to the USS *Douglas County* (LST-731) where he participated in the invasions of Guam and Iwo Jima as the leading petty officer in charge of the ship's gunnery division. On August 29, he was rotated back to the United States, and on October 18, 1945, was discharged from the Navy. He returned to Tarkio and farmed for the rest of his life. Mason Houghton passed away on August 13, 2002, and is buried in Home Cemetery, Tarkio, Missouri.

Medal of Ushakov number 7522 awarded to Mason Houghton. *Courtesy of the Houghton family.*

Richard M. Stone, Armed Guard commander on the SS *Cornelius Harnett. Courtesy Lehigh University Special Collections.*

Richard M. Stone, *Order of the Patriotic War, Second Class*

The Armed Guard commander on the *Cornelius Harnett* was Richard Marvin Stone. Born in Niagara Falls, New York, on July 6, 1908, he attended Lehigh University, graduating in 1929, and received his Master's in Business Administration from Harvard Business School in 1931. He taught economics at Niagara University, and in 1932 joined Firestone Tire and Rubber Company. He worked for them in New York City until 1939, when he began working for the Nashua Manufacturing Company in Atlanta and Chicago. In June 1942, he was commissioned in the Navy and was sent to Armed Guard duty. Serving first on the *Cornelius Harnett*, he was awarded the Silver Star for the calmness and professionalism he exhibited that led to his gunners shooting down two aircraft during the attack on JW-52 on January 24, 1943. He was discharged from the Navy in September 1945, and in 1947, established Stone and Company, Inc., an international import/export trading company. During the Eisenhower administration, he served as the representative of the Department of Commerce at trade fairs across Europe. Richard Stone passed away on September 3, 2005, and is buried in Laurel Grove Cemetery, Savannah, Georgia.

Ralph E. Boucher, *Order of the Patriotic War, First Class*

Ralph E. Boucher, Armed Guard commander on the SS *Nicholas Gilman. Courtesy of the Boucher family.*

On board the *Nicholas Gilman* was Ralph Emerson Boucher, born on December 19, 1904, in Friendsville, Maryland. Learning the value of hard work at a young age, he began working with his father, the general manager of a large saw mill in Damascus, Virginia, at the age of twelve. Simultaneously, he began working at a motion picture theater, eventually rising to become the assistant manager before leaving for college in 1922. Earning a bachelor's degree in geology from Roanoke College, he spent the following year as a high school math, history, and civics teacher, before working as a water works manager. In 1929, he moved to New York, where he became the manager in charge and engineer of the water works system for nearly the entire south shore of Long Island. Two years later, he returned to Virginia, where he worked as the general manager of the Roanoke Water Works Company until 1936. During this time, he took night courses in law, graduating with his law degree and passing the Virginia Bar in 1935. Leaving the water business, he became a criminal and corporate attorney until he joined the Navy in 1942.

Unlike many other recipients, who had already been through the hell of the early convoys to the Soviet Union, Boucher boarded the *Gilman* on August 14, 1942, with their first transit being in the Gulf of Mexico and Caribbean. Learning lessons from the six to eight man detachments in the early convoys, Boucher's Armed Guard unit consisted of thirty-one personnel. As they left New York Harbor on December 22, the temperature of -5 degrees (Fahrenheit) was a harbinger of things to come. Experiencing heavy seas crossing the Atlantic, they lost track of the convoy and spent the majority of their transit alone. The *Gilman* got underway to Murmansk as part of convoy JW-52 on January 17, 1943. On January 24, Boucher recorded not only the battle against the German aircraft, but against the elements as well as the gunners of the *Gilman's* Armed Guard strapped themselves to their guns to maintain position against the never-ceasing growth of ice caused by the sub-zero temperatures and splash of heavy seas on the weapons and decks. Arriving in Murmansk, they experienced aerial raids almost hourly, the only respite being on days with heavy snowfall. On February 19, a two-thousand pound bomb landed 150 feet away from the ship. Thirteen Russians were killed instantly, and Boucher's helmet and part of his clothing were blown off in the concussion. Subsequent aircraft dropped multiple 250-pound bombs at thirty-minute intervals. According to his voyage report:

> *Bombing as before – dropping sticks of four* [bombs]. *Sometimes twelve or sixteen hit almost simultaneously; many incendiaries. Murmansk is badly destroyed; nothing left except a few damaged buildings, air raid shelters and the docks – Why the docks? They are rebuilt daily.*[6]

Order of the Patriotic War, First Class, number 25440 awarded to Ralph Boucher. *Courtesy of the Boucher family.*

Surviving the sub-zero temperatures, constant bombing, and twenty-plus hours of darkness every day, the *Gilman* got underway at 10:00 AM on March 1 with convoy RA-53. For his leadership and valor during the voyage to the Soviet Union, Boucher was awarded the Silver Star. Returning to the United States on April 11, he became an instructor at the Armed Guard School in Norfolk, Virginia, until January 1945. Promoted to lieutenant commander, his last duty of the war was on the USS *Gilbert Islands* (CVE-107), where he took part in the invasion of Okinawa. Upon discharge, he remained in the reserves, retiring as a commander in June 1954. As a civilian he returned to Virginia and reestablished his law firm, practicing law until his death on November 10, 1981.

Имя, отчество и фамилия

Лейтенант

Ральф

И. Бучер

Подпись владельца книжки

The Soviet order book to Ralph Boucher. *Courtesy of the Boucher family.*

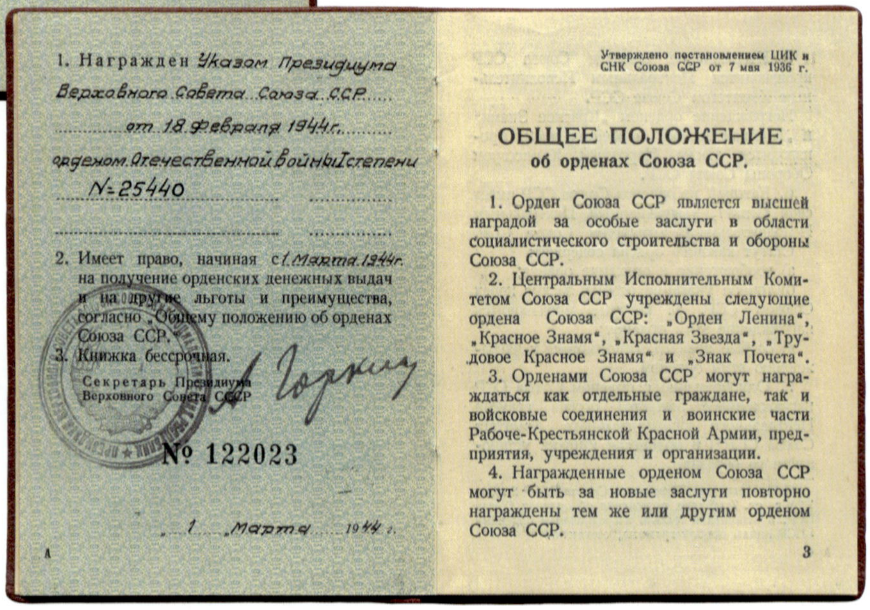
1. Награжден Указом Президиума Верховного Совета Союза ССР от 18 февраля 1944 г. орденом Отечественной Войны I степени № 25440

2. Имеет право, начиная с 1 Марта 1944 г. на получение орденских денежных выдач и на другие льготы и преимущества, согласно „Общему положению об орденах Союза ССР".

3. Книжка бессрочная.

Секретарь Президиума Верховного Совета СССР

№ 122023

1 Марта 1944 г.

Утверждено постановлением ЦИК и СНК Союза ССР от 7 мая 1936 г.

ОБЩЕЕ ПОЛОЖЕНИЕ об орденах Союза ССР.

1. Орден Союза ССР является высшей наградой за особые заслуги в области социалистического строительства и обороны Союза ССР.

2. Центральным Исполнительным Комитетом Союза ССР учреждены следующие ордена Союза ССР: „Орден Ленина", „Красное Знамя", „Красная Звезда", „Трудовое Красное Знамя" и „Знак Почета".

3. Орденами Союза ССР могут награждаться как отдельные граждане, так и войсковые соединения и воинские части Рабоче-Крестьянской Красной Армии, предприятия, учреждения и организации.

4. Награжденные орденом Союза ССР могут быть за новые заслуги повторно награждены тем же или другим орденом Союза ССР.

The Silver Star awarded to Ralph Boucher. The engraving is done in the same hand as the Silver Star awarded to Jeremiah Mahoney and is attributed to the Armed Guard Center. *Courtesy of the Boucher family.*

Walter R. Daley, *Order of the Patriotic War, Second Class*

Walter Daley was the Armed Guard commander on the SS *El Oriente*. Born at Somerville, Massachusetts, on June 8, 1905, he attended Boston College, Columbia University, and graduated from the Massachusetts Institute of Technology in 1935. He worked as a salesman for the Boston Edison Company prior to volunteering for the Navy in August 1942. Promoted to Lieutenant (jg) and sent to indoctrination training on September 10, he was then immediately sent to Armed Guard duty on October 5. Five weeks later, he reported to the Armed Guard Center in Brooklyn and they forwarded him to Liverpool, England, to take charge of the Armed Guard detachment on the *El Oriente*. Arriving on December 4, he found his Armed Guard crew of nine men in complete disarray, with poor morale further exacerbated by the substandard organization, heavy drinking, and low morale of the merchant crew.[7] They had been underway since February 12, 1942, and were just finally unloading their original cargo that had been sitting in their ship for almost ten months. On December 14, their cargo was replaced and reloaded with drums of high-test gasoline below decks and military truck bodies and engines as deck cargo. This was the "official" cargo; as Daley noted in his report, the master personally had fifty cases of whiskey delivered and loaded on the ship for the voyage to and from the USSR.[8]

Four Armed Guard commanders of JW-52 receive awards (left to right): Walter R. Daley, Ralph E. Boucher, Richard F. Mangano (not a Soviet medal recipient), and Richard M. Stone. *Official Navy photo via the Boucher family.*

While in port in Murmansk, moored just forward of the *Cornelius Harnett*, they were attacked by German aircraft seventy-three times. The fifty-ninth attack took place on February 27, 1943, when an Me 109F dropped a 150-pound bomb on the stern of the *El Oriente*, destroying the ship's four-inch gun, killing the starboard side Oerlikon gunner, Seaman Roy A. Robinson, and wounding four other gunners, two of whom were asleep in their quarters at the time of the attack. Returning to the United States, Daley received a Letter of Commendation from the Secretary of the Navy for his bravery shown during the Murmansk run. He received orders to the Armed Guard School at Little Creek, Virginia, as an instructor, and reported on July 4, 1943. He spent the remainder of the war with the Armed Guard in that capacity, receiving his discharge from active duty on July 19, 1945. Returning to West Roxbury, Massachusetts, he resumed his salesman responsibilities with Boston Edison. On December 31, 1948, he had just returned home from a routine employment physical when he died of a sudden heart attack.

Convoy JW-53

The SS *Thomas Hartley*, with a cargo of two PT boats, five Packard PT boat replacement engines, thirty-six cases of PT boat parts, 914 Ford 1½-ton trucks, one hundred Willys Jeeps, sixteen amphibious Jeeps, twenty M5 tractors, 488 cases of Ford truck parts, twenty six hundred spare tires, one locomotive crane and nine flat cars, amongst other cargo, sailed from Loch Ewe on February 15, 1943, along with the SS *Beaconhill* and twenty-four other ships of convoy JW-53. Other than heavy weather that damaged the cruiser HMS *Sheffield* and the aircraft carrier HMS *Dasher* and forced six of the merchant vessels to return to Loch Ewe due to damage or engine defects, their transit was unremarkable. The *Hartley* and *Beaconhill*, whose cargo consisted of 74,028 barrels of alkylate and other components of high-octane aviation fuel, arrived in Murmansk on February 28. From that time forward, both ships endured heavy German aerial attacks. The *Hartley* recorded 169 aerial attacks during her stay in Murmansk, and later, Molotovsk, before she returned to the United States. Due to the coming summer months and increased German air and surface activity, the Soviet convoys were suspended in mid-March 1943. Thus, the ships remaining in the USSR were used to ferry supplies between Murmansk and Molotovsk for the summer months until the weather could again become sufficiently unsuitable as to allow for a safe passage back to Scotland. The ships, including the *Hartley*, *Beaconhill*, *City of Omaha*, *Francis Scott Key*, *Bering*, and *Israel Putnam*, formed what became known as the "Forgotten Convoy of North Russia": conducting local transport duties while awaiting a return convoy. The ships returned with convoy RA-54A, leaving from Kola Inlet on November 1, 1943, after eight months of service in the USSR.

Michael L. Merlo, Armed Guard commander on the SS *Thomas Hartley. Courtesy of the Merlo family.*

Michael L. Merlo, *Order of the Patriotic War, Second Class*

Michael Louis Merlo served as the Armed Guard commander on the *Thomas Hartley*. Born on October 18, 1911, he was commissioned in the Navy on October 12, 1942. Following initial training, he was immediately assigned to the Armed Guard on the *Hartley*. His personal account of his time in the Soviet Union included many more events than were recorded in the official voyage accounts of the ship. During the summer, he was recruited to assist with burning fields far into the interior of the region around Murmansk to create further difficulties for the German attackers. He was additionally offered a visit to Moscow, which he did not accept. Returning to the United States in December 1943, he was subsequently reassigned to the USS *Admiralty Islands* (CVE-99) and took part in the invasions of Iwo Jima and Okinawa. Reassigned to the USS *Franklin D. Roosevelt* (CVB-42), he was discharged from active duty on December 1, 1945. He remained in the Reserves until discharged as a Lieutenant Commander in June 1952. As a civilian, he was employed by the Port Authority of Allegheny County until his retirement. He passed away on September 16, 1988, and is buried in Mt. Lebanon Cemetery, Pittsburgh, Pennsylvania.

Gilbert S. Young, Armed Guard commander on the SS *Beaconhill* shown here as a captain later in his career. *Courtesy of the Young family.*

Gilbert S. Young, *Order of the Red Star*

One of Merlo's fellow long-suffering Armed Guard commanders was Gilbert Stewart Young. Born on March 23, 1920, in Osborn, Ohio, Young was attending Harvard Business School for his MBA when the war started. His patriotic duty overtaking the completion of his degree, he was commissioned in the Navy on August 31, 1942, and was sent directly to Armed Guard duty. Leaving New York on January 3, 1943, he hadn't the faintest idea that he wouldn't return home until the end of the year. Heroically defending the ship through the daily onslaught of aerial attacks in February through June, the *Beaconhill* made almost bi-weekly runs between Molotovsk and Murmansk. With the downturn in enemy attacks during the summer, as the requirements of the war in the Mediterranean moved an ever-increasing number of German assets away from the Arctic, Young made an unprecedented journey to Moscow in July, visiting the staff of the US Embassy as well as capturing a first-hand glimpse of the frontlines of the war on the Eastern Front. Returning to the United States on December 4, 1943, he was subsequently reassigned to motor torpedo boat duty on January 29, 1944. Initially tasked to be the engineering officer for Motor Torpedo Boat Squadron Thirteen, he was rapidly given additional responsibility, eventually becoming the officer in charge of the Motor Torpedo Boat Squadron Floating Equipment Maintenance Unit in October 1944, stationed out of PT Boat Base Seventeen on Samar, Philippines. He held this command until the unit returned to the United States in November 1945. With the conclusion of the war, he was discharged on January 29, 1946, and returned to Harvard to complete his MBA. On February 28, 1947, he returned to active duty, this time as a Supply Corps officer, where he continued his service for the Navy. As a Supply Corps officer, he served on the USS *Monrovia* (APA-31), followed by the Naval Ammunition Depot, Crane, Indiana, Navy Purchasing Office in London, Defense Automotive Supply Center in Detroit, Naval Supply Systems Command in Washington, DC, and finally at the Naval Material Command, Defense Contract Administration Service Region, Atlanta, Georgia. On August 31, 1970, he retired from the Navy with the rank of Captain. Gilbert Young passed away in Whispering Pines, North Carolina, on June 7, 1986.

As the *Beaconhill* and the *Hartley* returned to the United States, the geopolitical situation was drastically different than the same period two years prior when the

Order of the Red Star number 1553970 awarded to Gilbert Young. *Courtesy of the Young family.*

USSR-bound convoys began. Hitler's Germany was now feeling the hemorrhaging of significant losses. Following the defeat of the Battle of the Barents Sea, Grand Admiral Raeder, the Commander in Chief of the *Kriegsmarine*, resigned on January 6, 1943. The German Sixth Army was badly defeated and surrendered at Stalingrad in February 1943, and the German forces in North Africa had fallen in May. Allied forces landed in Italy in September, and the U-boats in the North Atlantic were finally receiving their payback for the previous years of unfettered, unrestricted warfare against the Allies. This was not to say that the Arctic passage was now completely safe for the routine passage of merchant vessels. However, the threat had lessened dramatically, and continued to lower as the war progressed. The last USSR-bound convoy, JW-67, left from Clyde on May 12, 1945, marking the end of one of the most strategically important, yet underappreciated, operations of the Second World War.

Имя, отчество и фамилия

Лейтенант

Гилберт

С. Янс

Подпись владельца книжки

1. Награжден, Указом Президиума Верховного Совета СССР от 7 июля 1945 года орденом Красной Звезды

2. Имеет право, начиная с 1.VIII.1945 г. на получение орденских денежных выдач и на другие льготы и преимущества, согласно „Общему положению об орденах Союза ССР".

3. Книжка бессрочная.

Секретарь Президиума Верховного Совета СССР

№ 222227

15 августа 1945 г.

Утверждено постановлением ЦИК и СНК Союза ССР от 7 мая 1936 г.

ОБЩЕЕ ПОЛОЖЕНИЕ
об орденах Союза ССР.

1. Орден Союза ССР является высшей наградой за особые заслуги в области социалистического строительства и обороны Союза ССР.

2. Центральным Исполнительным Комитетом Союза ССР учреждены следующие ордена Союза ССР: „Орден Ленина", „Красное Знамя", „Красная Звезда", „Трудовое Красное Знамя" и „Знак Почета".

3. Орденами Союза ССР могут награждаться как отдельные граждане, так и войсковые соединения и воинские части Рабоче-Крестьянской Красной Армии, предприятия, учреждения и организации.

4. Награжденные орденом Союза ССР могут быть за новые заслуги повторно награждены тем же или другим орденом Союза ССР.

3

The Soviet order book to Gilbert Young. *Courtesy of the Young family.*

Gilbert Young's US medals, including the Meritorious Service Medal, the American Campaign, European African Middle Eastern Campaign, Asiatic Pacific Campaign, World War II Victory and Occupation medals. *Courtesy of the Young family.*

Chapter 13

Other Convoy Service Recipients

SS *George Clymer*

The convoy system was the lifeblood of transporting supplies from the United States to the in-theater combatants during the Second World War. Because of this, the awarding of Soviet medals was not confined to only those who participated in the Murmansk Run, but was inclusive of others who had distinguished themselves in support of convoy operations in the Atlantic.

On April 11, 1942, while the Murmansk Run was becoming all the more deadly on the other side of the world, Ensign David Pickler and his Armed Guard crew boarded the SS *George Clymer*, with a cargo of mixed war supplies and twenty-four aircraft, in San Francisco. After several quiet port calls in Washington and Oregon, they headed to their final destination of Iran around the Cape of Good Hope to off-load cargo bound for the USSR. On May 10, they completed their transit of the Panama Canal, and on May 13, started their trans-Atlantic voyage. A week later, and approximately halfway across the Atlantic, the ship's main shaft broke due to a faulty weld. As of 10:15 AM on May 30, the ship was drifting at sea, unable to get underway. This was an incredibly undesirable position to be in, made even more untenable by the number of U-boats in the area, not to mention German surface raiders, looking for prey. The ship sent messages to Cape Town requesting assistance, but even the fastest help was days away. If they were sunk, their chances of being found in the middle of the Atlantic were very, very slim.

At 7:48 PM on June 6, two torpedoes struck the *Clymer*, one amidships and one forward on the port side. The Armed Guard immediately went to battle stations to defend the ship. But there was nothing to be found: the sea was absolutely silent. The civilian crew immediately gathered in the lifeboats and abandoned ship, leaving the Armed Guard behind.[1]

Little did the crew know that the German surface raider *Michel* had intercepted their radio transmissions and had raced nine-hundred miles to take part in the action. Waiting just over the horizon, she sent her speedboat, named *Esau*, armed with two torpedoes, to mortally wound the *Clymer*. With the attack complete, the *Michel* retreated some distance away, waiting until the *Clymer's* help arrived in order to add another victim to its already impressive list of kills.[2]

Throughout the night, the Armed Guard remained at their weapons, and the crew huddled in lifeboats, just off the side of the ship. The ship was slowly flooding, but was by no means sinking, so the greatly embarrassed civilian crew re-boarded the ship at 8:00 AM the following morning. At 10:15 AM, a plane passed overhead and signaled that a warship was on its way for assistance. Four hours later, the HMS *Alcantara*, a Royal Navy armed merchant cruiser, arrived. Her commanding officer ordered the *Clymer* abandoned. He intended to assess whether or not they should attempt to salvage the ship the following day. The decision was eventually made to tow the *Clymer* into port. However, at this point, Royal Navy intelligence determined the *Michel* was in the area and the order was quickly changed. On June 9, at 2:15 PM, the first shells from the *Alcantara* tore into the *Clymer*, while her floatplane dropped bombs from above. But the ship refused to sink. For the next three days, the *Alcantara* shelled, depth charged, and bombed the hulk to prevent her from falling into the hands of the enemy. But they did not succeed. The final rounds were fired at 7:00 AM on June 12, and at that point, with the now-capsized *Clymer* having been bombed, holed, and burned beyond recognition, the *Alcantara* left the scene. It is not known why the *Michel* did not attack during the three-day period the *Alcantara* attempted to sink the *Clymer*, but in the end, the survivors were discharged in Cape Town on June 21. The next day, they boarded the British transport HMT *Pasteur* and reported to the Armed Guard Center in Brooklyn, New York, on July 9.

A piece of the American flag taken down from the SS *George Clymer* before she sank. *Courtesy of the Lazetera family.*

David A. Pickler, Armed Guard commander on the SS *George Clymer*. *Courtesy of the Pickler family.*

David A. Pickler, *Order of the Red Star*

David Anderson Pickler, the Armed Guard commander on the *Clymer*, was born on March 14, 1914, in New London, North Carolina. Prior to the war, he graduated from Wake Forest University with a degree in chemistry and then attended the University of North Carolina, earning a master's degree in the same. Commissioned into the Navy on December 12, 1940, he received orders to the USS *Saratoga* (CV-3), reporting on December 25. Answering the call for qualified gunnery officers, he was sent to Armed Guard duty in March 1942. Completing his tour in April 1943, he specialized in an area more along the lines of his education: helium purification. After a month of schooling at Lakehurst, New Jersey, he spent the next two years stationed at Naval Air Station Houma, Louisiana, as the air station's helium officer. In June 1945, he transferred to Naval Air Station Tillamook, Oregon, and spent the next seven months serving in the same billet. Following eleven months at the General Line School in Newport, Rhode Island, he reported to the USS *Boxer* (CV-21) as the damage control assistant. This was followed by a tour on the USS *Lindenwald* (LSD-6) as the executive officer. Subsequent tours at sea included the USS *Charles R. Ware* (DD-865), USS *Luzon* (ARG-2), and command of the USS *Markab* (AD-21). He attended the University of California, Berkeley, graduating with a master's degree in health physics in 1957. His final assignment was as the Naval Liaison Officer for the Lawrence Livermore National Laboratory, where he earned a commendation from the Navy for his work on the Polaris Missile Re-entry Body Coordinating Committee. He retired with the rank of Commander effective December 31, 1960.

After his return to civilian life, he worked at Lockheed, followed by work as a health physicist for the State of California, licensing nuclear reactors for human work environments. In his retirement, he moved to Rossmoor, California, and passed away on January 20, 2006.

The Soviet order book to David Pickler. *Courtesy of the Pickler family.*

Order of the Red Star number 1553973 awarded to David Pickler. *Courtesy of the Pickler family.*

US awarded medals to David Pickler, including the Navy Commendation, American Defense, American Campaign, European African Middle Eastern Campaign, and Asiatic Pacific Campaign medals. *Courtesy of the Pickler family.*

Ernest John Lazetera, *Medal "For Military Merit"*

The two Coxswains on the *Clymer* also received Letters of Commendation from the Secretary of the Navy for their actions. Ernest John Lazetera was born on June 14, 1919, in San Jose, California to parents who had emigrated from Italy. Following his graduation from San Jose High School, he entered the Navy on February 15, 1937. Serving in the deck division of the USS *Cincinnati* (CL-6), he operated in the Atlantic and the Pacific, and was discharged as a Seaman, first class, on June 21, 1940. Returning to San Jose, he worked various jobs, stacking lumber and as a steelworker, until the start of the war. Volunteering for duty, he returned to active service on February 9, 1942, with the rank of Coxswain. Following Armed Guard training, he was sent to the *Clymer*. Promoted to Boatswain's Mate, second class, and subsequently, first class, he served on the SS *Kota Ageong*, followed by the USS *Mission Purisima* (AO-118). Hospitalized due to an appendectomy in May 1943, he spent the next year as a Master at Arms, first at the Armed Guard Center, Treasure Island, California, followed by the cadet quarters at Moffett Field, Naval Air Station. While in the latter location, he requested and was accepted for lighter-than-air duty. Graduating from qualification training on February 29, 1944, Lazetera spent the remainder of the war as a rigger and ground crewman for the Navy's blimp fleet flying from Moffett Field. Discharged on August 11, 1945, he returned to San Jose. First working at San Jose Steel, he then worked for Mayfair Packing Company. He later worked for his uncles' dried fruit business as a supervisor for several of their sites in the Bay Area. Ernest Lazetera passed away on January 15, 2003.

Ernest Lazetera with his bride.
Courtesy of the Lazetera family.

The Soviet medal book to Ernest Lazetera. *Courtesy of the Lazetera family.*

Medal "For Military Merit" number 2551015 awarded to Ernest Lazetera.
Courtesy of the Lazetera family.

Navy Good Conduct Medal to Ernest Lazetera, dated 1940. *Courtesy of the Lazetera family.*

Harvey C. Smalley. *Courtesy of the Smalley family.*

Harvey C. Smalley, Jr., *Medal "For Military Merit"*

The other Coxswain on the *Clymer* was Harvey Carroll Smalley Jr. Born in Omaha, Nebraska, on June 8, 1916, he enlisted in the Navy following his graduation from high school on October 18, 1934. He spent the majority of his four-year enlistment on the USS *Whitney* (AD-4) and was discharged on October 27, 1938. Settling in San Francisco, he worked for the US Weather Bureau and as a handyman for the Postal Telegraph Company. When the war started, he volunteered for service and returned to active duty on February 25, 1942. Immediately sent to Armed Guard duty, he was sent to the *George Clymer* as his first assignment. Surviving the sinking of the *Clymer*, he remained with the Armed Guard for the remainder of the war, serving in the Pacific theater. Discharged on October 14, 1945, he returned to San Francisco and began working for Western Union as a communication equipment specialist. This job took him to Seattle in 1950, where he worked at the Sea-Tac Airport, followed by a promotion and transfer to San Bernardino, California. His last position with Western Union required his move to Oahu, Hawaii. Retiring from Western Union, he was employed by the Department of Defense at McClellan Air Force Base, outside Sacramento. Harvey Smalley passed away on February 10, 1988, and was buried at sea. A memorial for him resides at Golden Gate National Cemetery, San Bruno, California.

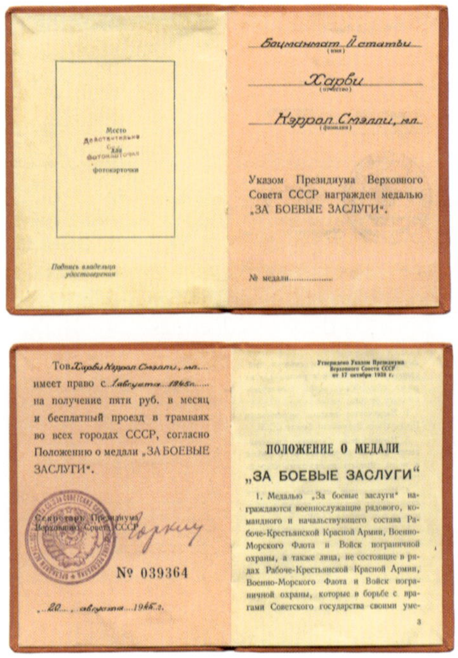

Место для фотокарточки

Подпись владельца удостоверения

Боцманмат II статьи
(имя)
Харви
(отчество)
Кэррол Смэлли, мл.
(фамилия)

Указом Президиума Верховного Совета СССР награжден медалью „ЗА БОЕВЫЕ ЗАСЛУГИ".

№ медали...............

Тов. Харви Кэррол Смэлли, мл. имеет право с 1 августа 1945 г. на получение пяти руб. в месяц и бесплатный проезд в трамваях во всех городах СССР, согласно Положению о медали „ЗА БОЕВЫЕ ЗАСЛУГИ".

Секретарь Президиума Верховного Совета СССР

№ 039364

„20" августа 1945 г.

Утверждено Указом Президиума Верховного Совета СССР от 17 октября 1938 г.

ПОЛОЖЕНИЕ О МЕДАЛИ „ЗА БОЕВЫЕ ЗАСЛУГИ"

1. Медалью „За боевые заслуги" награждаются военнослужащие рядового, командного и начальствующего состава Рабоче-Крестьянской Красной Армии, Военно-Морского Флота и Войск пограничной охраны, а также лица, не состоящие в рядах Рабоче-Крестьянской Красной Армии, Военно-Морского Флота и Войск пограничной охраны, которые в борьбе с врагами Советского государства своими уме-

3

The Soviet medal book to Harvey C. Smalley. *Courtesy of the Smalley family.*

SS *Scottsburg*

Departing New York Harbor on May 25, 1942, with a load of general war cargo and aircraft, the SS *Scottsburg* headed south to her intermediate stop of Trinidad, followed by her final destination in the Middle East. The convoy had broken up and she was proceeding independently about ninety miles west of Grenada when she was struck by two torpedoes at 7:03 PM on June 14. The first slammed amidships on the port side, directly into the engine room, killing both men on watch. Twenty seconds later, the other hit just forward of the bridge, destroying both port lifeboats and blowing damaged cargo all over the decks. Lieutenant (jg) Robert Berry ran up to the bridge, hoping to see the U-boat that fired on them, but there was no trace. For *U-502*, the *Scottsburg* was already being counted as her twelfth kill for this successful patrol and she had already submerged, searching for her next victim. Within ten minutes, the *Scottsburg* was slipping beneath the waves, taking with her the master and three other members of the crew.

After eighteen long hours in lifeboats, the forty-six survivors were rescued by the freighter SS *Kahuku*, which had already picked up seventeen survivors from the SS *Cold Harbor*, also sunk that day by *U-502*. At 8:30 PM on the night of June 15, Berry and the *Kahuku's* Armed Guard commander, Lieutenant (jg) Kammerer, noticed a white light astern of the ship. Unsure what the light was, they altered course and maintained their zig-zag pattern through the water. At 9:02 PM, *U-126* fired a torpedo that hit the ship amidships on the starboard side. The ship slowed to a stop and the master sounded the abandon ship signal. Chaos ensued due to the extra sixty-three survivors on board and the loss of one of the lifeboats during the hit (whether it was lost due to negligence or the torpedo hit was never determined). As the lifeboats moved away from the ship, survivors were plucked from the water wherever they could be found.

Watching from a distance, the captain of *U-126*, Knight's Cross holder *Korvettenkapitän* Ernst Bauer, saw the ship still on the surface and making very little progress sinking. At 10:15 PM, he fired another torpedo at the now-abandoned hulk. Despite the direct hit, the *Kahuku* still refused to sink. At 11:00 PM, he surfaced and proceeded to fire thirty rounds from his deck gun into the ship. Finally, one hit the after magazine, causing a brilliant explosion, and the *Kahuku* slid beneath the waves at 12:20 AM, taking with her the master, five crewman, eight Navy Armed Guards and eight survivors from other ships; seven of whom were from the *Scottsburg*. After picking up survivors through the night, the crews were rescued by the USS *Opal* (PYc-8) and the USS *YP-63* at noon the following day and taken to Trinidad.

Faustin Gallegos, *Order of Glory, Third Class*

Order of Glory, Third Class, number 387915 awarded to Faustin Gallegos. *Courtesy of the Gallegos family.*

Lieutenant Barry, *Scottsburg's* Armed Guard commander, later wrote about the sinking and described Faustin Gallegos:

> *The fair-haired lad of our outfit was Gallegos. It was Gallegos who started the singing; it was Gallegos who organized the jam sessions with his harmonica; it was Gallegos who knew the best stories, who won at poker, who was the first choice of the girls in port. Gallegos was absolutely indifferent to the war, to Navy Regulations, or to any task immediately before him. He could grin his way out of more work than any other man I ever saw. He was lean and long and sandy-haired, and his white teeth flashing in his tanned face gladdened your heart whenever you saw him.*[3]

During the evening of June 15, Gallegos was responsible for saving the lives of many of the crewmembers of the *Kahuku*. Finding an empty raft, he climbed aboard and began retrieving the men out of the water. Adrift from the other survivors, he wasn't discovered until much later the next day, single-handedly rowing the raft with fifteen merchant seaman survivors on board. For his valor, he was awarded a Letter of Commendation from the Secretary of the Navy. Faustin Gallegos was born on January 30, 1923, in Albuquerque, New Mexico, the son of a notable minor league baseball outfielder. Following his father from the East Texas League to the Florida State League, they settled in Miami, Florida. Joining the Navy on February 13, 1942, he attended recruit training in Norfolk, Virginia, and was sent directly to Armed Guard duty. His first ship was the *Scottsburg*, sunk on June 15. At the time of his heroic rescue of fifteen merchant crewmembers, Gallegos had just over four months in the Navy. Requesting transfer from Armed Guard duty, he was assigned to the USS *West Point* (AP-23), where he became an Electrician's Mate, third class, by the time he transferred in January 1945. He was subsequently assigned to the newly commissioned USS *Sarsfield* (DD-837), where he remained, operating out of Boston, until his discharge on October 29, 1945.

Joining the City of Miami Police Department, he spent the next twenty years as an officer in the department, finally retiring as a Sergeant in 1966. He then went to work for Barfield, Inc., manufacturing and maintaining aircraft cabin pressure equipment until his next retirement in 1979. Faustin Gallegos passed away on April 23, 1995.

The Soviet order book to Faustin Gallegos. *Courtesy of the Gallegos family.*

SS *West Hardaway*

Lieutenant (jg) Dan Schwartz boarded the SS *West Hardaway* at Lynnhaven Roads, Norfolk, Virginia, on May 25, 1942, as the ship's Armed Guard commander. Four days later, they departed Norfolk in a southbound convoy bound for Trinidad before making her way to the Suez with a load of general war cargo, coal, and a deck cargo of steam locomotives and railway equipment. By midnight on June 8, they had passed the dispersal point for the convoy and began steaming independently; rarely seeing any other vessels, save for the SS *Kahuku* in the distance on June 14. At 4:00 AM on June 15, the master notified Schwartz that he had received a communication warning of U-boat activity in the area. Extra watches were stationed, and the ship continued on her southern transit. At 2:15 PM, just as they were passing about thirty miles west of Grenada, one of the merchant crew yelled, "torpedo!" Since sinking the *Scottsburg* the day before, *U-502* had been tracking the *West Hardaway* and fired a spread of four torpedoes at her starboard side. One torpedo passed astern, the other passed ahead of the ship. The third torpedo struck right at the number one hold, and the fourth torpedo found its mark at the number two hold. Frantically searching the sea for evidence of the submarine, they found none. Seeing a slick in the water where the submarine may have been, Schwartz had his gunners fire five rounds at the slick, but it was to no avail: *U-502* was already long gone, preparing for her return across the Atlantic and the celebration of an extremely successful war patrol.

Within ten minutes of the first hit, the ship was abandoned and the lifeboats stood three hundred yards off the side of the ship. When it appeared that the *Hardaway* may actually remain afloat for some period of time, Schwartz gathered his gun crew and with the help of the merchant seamen, re-boarded the ship to fire at the U-boat should it surface to give the ship a *coup de grace*. Although one more round was fired at the slick where the U-boat was believed to be, the crew finally left the ship, and she gently slipped below the surface at 3:40 PM, her deck cargo never even shifting as it disappeared below the surface of the sea. On the morning of June 17, the lifeboats made landfall on Margarita Island, off the coast of Venezuela, and were transported to Trinidad on the SS *Maracaibo*, arriving on June 20.

Dan R. Schwartz, *Order of the Red Star*

Dan R. Schwartz, Armed Guard commander on the SS *West Hardaway. Courtesy of the Schwartz family.*

Daniel Richard Schwartz was born on February 27, 1909, in New Britain, Connecticut. Moving to Florida, at a young age, he graduated from Duval High School in Jacksonville in 1925 and attended the University of Florida where he received his bachelor's and Juris Doctorate degrees in 1931. Following admission to the Florida state bar, he formed the law firm of Kitchen and Schwartz. Listening to the radio on December 7, 1941, he heard the announcement that the Japanese bombed Pearl Harbor. He knew what was about to happen, and the following day, went to Naval Air Station Jacksonville to join the Navy. He applied for a commission, and in April 1942, his application was approved, and he was commissioned as a Lieutenant (jg). He was sent to Armed Guard duty and on May 25, arrived on the *West Hardaway*, his first ship. Following his return to the United States following the sinking of the *Hardaway*, he was assigned to the SS *Thomas Hooker*, a Liberty ship with cargo for the upcoming invasion of North Africa. Delivering cargo in Oran Harbor on November 10, 1942, they fought back multiple attacks from enemy aircraft, as the harbor was not yet entirely secured by Allied forces. Making supply runs between Great Britain and North Africa, they were finally allowed to return to the United States in March 1943. On the night of March 5, almost midway across the Atlantic, the weather worsened into hurricane-force winds. The *Hooker* began to crack at the number three hold and developed an ever-enlarging crack from the port to starboard side. With the force of the winds and seas, the crack kept forcibly opening and closing upward of two feet at a time, like the mouth of a large beast. The master made the call to abandon ship. With the crew safely in lifeboats, the ship broke in two and sank to the bottom of the sea. Schwartz and the other survivors were retrieved by the HMS *Pimpernel* (K-71) the following morning. Returning to the United States, he was assigned to the SS *Dartmouth*, a large fuel tanker with 124,776 barrels of eighty-octane motor fuel, and took her from Beaumont, Texas via New York to Oran, Algeria, arriving on May 11, 1943. On May 19, 20, and 25, the *Dartmouth* was attacked by German aircraft on multiple occasions, though no damage was done to the ship.[4]

Following his tour on the *Dartmouth*, he received orders to the USS *Hubbard* (DE-211) and placed her in commission on March 6, 1944. The Hubbard had an exceptional hunter-killer wartime career in the Atlantic, sinking *U-248* on January 16, 1945, and *U-546* on April 24. Detached from the *Hubbard* on VE-Day, Schwartz reported to the USS *Herrmann* (DE-139) as the executive officer. Taking her into the Pacific, their progress toward Japan was stopped by the dropping of the atomic bombs, and they returned to the Atlantic via the Panama Canal. On October 17, 1945, he was released from active duty and returned to Jacksonville, where he continued to practice law, representing motor carrier companies from Alabama to Florida. He was admitted to practice before all Federal courts in Florida, as well as the Federal appellate courts and the US Supreme Court. He was also active in the community, with the Scottish Rite Bodies, the Morocco Shrine Temple in Jacksonville, and as past president of the Jacksonville Downtown Lions Club. Before being elected as a district governor for the Lion's Club, Dan Schwartz passed away on November 16, 1994.

The Soviet order book to Dan Schwartz. *Courtesy of the Schwartz family.*

Order of the Red Star number 1553967 awarded to Dan Schwartz. *Courtesy of the Schwartz family.*

SS *Columbian*

Sailing from New York at almost the same time as the *West Hardaway* and the *Scottsburg*, the SS *Columbian* left Trinidad on June 12, 1942 en route to her following destination of Cape Town, South Africa. At 4:45 PM on June 16, a lookout sighted what they believed to be a submarine. Confirmed in his analysis by the chief officer, the master changed course and remained on their zig-zag pattern into the evening. The weather was beautiful, the sea was calm; ideal conditions for a submarine attack. Thus, extra lookouts were maintained throughout the night. The chief officer, who had stationed himself on top of the pilothouse to have an unrestricted view around the ship, spotted the submarine just off the bow of the ship at 12:03 AM on June 17. The master swung the *Columbian* away from the submarine, almost striking her with the ship's stern as he came around. The submarine, later identified as the Italian Navy *Archimede*, responsible for the sinking of the Panamanian freighter SS *Cardina* on June 15, opened fire on the *Columbian* with her deck gun. Ensign Merrill Stone's rear twenty-millimeter gunner opened up on the sub at almost point blank range and as the *Columbian* increased her distance, the Armed Guard gunners let loose their four-inch stern gun at a range of no greater than two hundred yards. The first round was a direct hit on the conning tower of the *Archimede*, most obviously hitting an ammunition locker as the deck of the submarine instantly exploded, rocking both ships, and the top deck of the submarine was ablaze in a huge column of fire.[5] The *Columbian* fired a second round, again hitting the submarine. At that point, the *Archimede* ceased firing and appeared to be riding lower in the water. Believing they sank the submarine, the crew of the *Columbian* made the best possible speed to clear the area and continue with their transit. Later wartime records indicate the *Archimede* was only damaged during this engagement as she was later sunk by aircraft from VP-83 on April 15, 1943.

Merrill R. Stone, Jr., *Order of the Patriotic War, First Class*

Merrill Rust Stone Jr., the Armed Guard commander on the *Columbian*, was born on November 17, 1917. Graduating from Vanderbilt University in 1940, he joined the Navy on October 8, 1941. Assigned to Armed Guard duty, he served on the *Columbian* and earned the Silver Star for his action with the *Archimede*. Remaining with the Armed Guard service until January 1943, he left sea-going duty to serve as an instructor at the Armed Guard School for the next six months. Receiving orders to the Submarine Chaser Training Center, he graduated from there in August 1943 as part of his schooling to his final duty station as gunnery officer on the USS *Thomason* (DE-203). Stone served on the *Thomason* in the Pacific until November 1944 when he was transferred to the staff of Naval Operating Base Terminal Island before reporting to the USS *Tolovana* (AO-64) as gunnery officer on February 27, 1945. Taking her through the ship's shakedown cruise, he spent the remainder of the war on her in the Pacific, shuttling gasoline between Ulithi and the combat area around Okinawa, which was considered too dangerous for civilian merchant tankers. Once Okinawa was secured, she delivered aviation and automobile fuel from the newly established fuel farm on Okinawa to Ulithi and Ryukyus. The *Tolovana* experienced frequent air attacks but suffered no combat damage. Discharged in late 1945, Stone returned to Nashville and worked for General Shoe Corporation. In 1955, he founded the Merrill Stone Company, a supplier to shoe and boot manufacturers. He passed away on November 19, 2000.

SS *Alexander Macomb*

Departing Buzzard's Bay, Massachusetts, along with thirty-one other ships in convoy BX-27, the SS *Alexander Macomb* got underway for her maiden voyage on July 2, 1942, laden with eleven hundred tons of Lend-Lease explosives, five aircraft, thirty-five tanks, and other military cargo bound for Iceland in order to later continue on to Archangel. During the night of 3-4 July, heavy fog closed in and the master fell behind the convoy ito avoid a collision in restricted visibility, despite being instructed do to otherwise. Lieutenant (jg) Clarence Kelso, the Armed Guard commander, had the ship's guns manned by 5:45 AM to assist as lookouts in the fog. Fifteen minutes later, the fog partially lifted, but no other ships from the convoy could be seen. Coming up to maximum speed to catch the convoy, they began to see the smoke of other ships on the horizon. They were in this condition, approximately 175 miles off the coast of Massachusetts, when struck by a torpedo from *U-215* at approximately 6:38 AM. The torpedo hit the starboard quarter, close enough to ignite some of the ship's explosive cargo. The ship shook violently. The stern gun crew was blown overboard as were several men from the bow gun. Flames enveloped the ship from the bridge all the way to the stern. The master, who had shortly before gone to his cabin, was never seen again as the entire living quarters were engulfed in flames.[6] Lowering what lifeboats they could, the crew and the remaining Armed Guard personnel left the ship in the most expeditious way possible: over the side. During this time, four of the gunners, including Donald Vandiver, climbed into a lifeboat and approached the burning ship, searching for wounded survivors who could not swim away. Putting themselves at extreme risk from flying debris caused by the continuing explosions inside the ship, they rescued eight Navy and merchant sailors before being forced away from the sinking ship.

Photo taken during the rescue of survivors of the SS *Alexander Macomb*. Donald Vandiver is on one of the oars in the lifeboat. *National Archives*.

Within fifteen minutes, two convoy escorts were on scene: the HMS *Le Tiger* (FY-243), which rescued twenty-three crewmembers and eight of the Armed Guard, and the HMCS *Regina* (K-234), which retrieved fourteen crewmembers and eleven of the Armed Guard. Six from the Navy Armed Guard and four crewmembers died in the attack. *U-215*, twenty-five days into her first war patrol, was sunk with all hands by depth charges from *Le Tiger* later that day.

Donald L. Vandiver, *Order of Glory, Third Class*

Donald Lee "Speck" Vandiver was born on March 27, 1920, in St. Joseph, Missouri. Completing the eighth grade, he joined the Civilian Conservation Corps, serving at camp 1734 in Higginsville, Missouri. Leaving the CCC in May 1940 to work as a powderman, determining the placement and charge size for explosives at Hayes Quarry in Bethany, Missouri, he enlisted in the Navy on February 17, 1942. Following recruit training at Great Lakes, he was assigned to Armed Guard duty. Earning the Navy and Marine Corps Medal and Merchant Marine Mariner's Medal for heroism during the sinking of the *Alexander Macomb*, he remained with the Armed Guard throughout the war, taking his discharge from active duty on September 29, 1945, as a Gunner's Mate, second class.

Returning to Bethany, Missouri, he took employment at the Westlake Quarry, in Troy, Kansas, working there as a powderman for twenty-three years. He subsequently worked as a superintendent for the List and Clark Construction Company in Iatan, Missouri, for ten years before retiring in 1987. Residing in Clarksdale, Missouri, Donald Vandiver passed away on May 2, 1991.

Donald Vandiver. *Courtesy of the Vandiver family.*

Order of Glory, Third Class, number 387959 awarded to Donald Vandiver. *Courtesy of the Vandiver family.*

Reverse of the Order of Glory, Third Class awarded to Donald Vandiver. *Courtesy of the Vandiver family.*

Navy and Marine Corps Medal awarded to Donald Vandiver. *Courtesy of the Vandiver family.*

US Merchant Marine Mariner's Medal awarded to Donald Vandiver. *Courtesy of the Vandiver family.*

SS *Kaimoku*

Departing Sydney, Nova Scotia on July 31, 1942, with a load of general cargo, trucks, and fifteen-hundred tons of bombs for the Army Air Force, the SS *Kaimoku* was en route her final destination of Birmingham, England, as part of convoy SC-94. Unbeknownst to the thirty merchant ships and six escorts in the convoy, they headed directly into the German U-boat wolfpack *Steinbrinck*, consisting of eight U-boats.[7]

The first victim of what became a five-day running battle was the Dutch merchant SS *Spar*, sunk by *U-593* on August 5. However, the convoy escorts were effective, and *U-593*, along with another attacker, was driven off. The following day was costly for the German wolfpack: *U-210* was sunk and two additional U-boats were damaged beyond repair and had to head back to port. On August 7, the nine additional U-boats joined the wolfpack, and the convoy became a deadly game of hunter and hunted. The next day, August 8, *U-176* and *U-379* attacked almost simultaneously and within the space of an hour, five merchant ships were sunk. One of *U-379's* victims was the *Kaimoku*.

Ensign Robert Clayton, the Armed Guard commander, recorded:

I heard the merchant ship lookout in the crow's nest shouting and looked in the direction he was pointing. I saw a ship enveloped in grey smoke. The next moment our ship jumped and shuddered and I realized we had been hit. Almost instantly there was another shock that sent pillars of flame and fuel oil skyward amidships completely obscuring my view aft.[8]

As the smoke cleared and it was clear the ship was rapidly sinking, he saw chaos amongst the Armed Guard manning the four-inch gun. Seven men, including Seamen DeGennaro and DeBaun, had just loaded a round into the gun when the torpedoes hit. Seaman McKeon, another member of the gun crew, was slammed by the door of the ammunition ready box from the force of the explosion. Falling from the gun platform and lifeless, McKeon was grabbed by DeGennaro and thrown overboard. Having removed his own lifevest to ensure the unconscious McKeon had one, DeGennaro grabbed a life ring and jumped overboard to assist his unconscious shipmate. Gathering more lifevests in the water, DeGennaro fastened them to McKeon to ensure he would remain afloat until they were picked up by a lifeboat.

Coxswain Clark of the Armed Guard ran aft to the gun platform to help, but either during the explosion of the second torpedo, or from the shifting of the ship during a strong wave, an Army truck on deck broke loose and pinned his leg to the walkway. At some point he was able to get his leg free, but was badly injured in the process. Seaman DeBaun saw him struggling and dragged him over to the starboard rail. Finding a donut raft and wrestling it over the side, DeBaun then threw Clark into the raft and jumped in after him, just as the *Kaimoku* slipped beneath the waves.

The crew was rescued by the Canadian corvette HMCS *Battleford*, with the loss of two members of the Navy Armed Guard. They were safely put ashore in Gourock, Scotland, on August 13. As for the convoy, seven more ships were sunk before they reached port. *U-379*, responsible for sinking the *Kaimoku* and the British merchant *Anneberg*, was sunk on August 8 by the escort vessel HMS *Dianthus*. Both DeGennaro and DeBaun were awarded the Navy and Marine Corps Medal for lifesaving on the high seas.

Louis DeGennaro, *Order of Glory, Third Class*

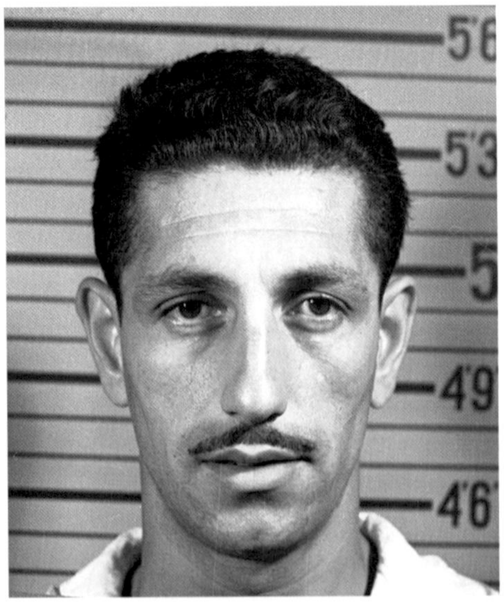

Louis DeGennaro. *National Personnel Records Center.*

Louis DeGennaro was born in New York City on March 23, 1914, but was raised in Italy until 1919. At the age of fifteen, he became a barber at Nota's Barber Shop in Brooklyn. However, he had to leave the line of work because of his poor arches, so he became a house painter. He was in the painting business when the war started. Feeling his patriotic duty, he enlisted in the Navy on March 17, 1942. After initial recruit training in Great Lakes, he was sent for Armed Guard duty. Assigned to the *Kaimoku*, he survived her sinking and was taken to Northern Ireland. While in Londonderry, he was given orders to the SS *Richard Bland* (formerly of PQ-17 and later sunk in convoy RA-53) on August 19, 1942. However, this was not long lived as injuries he sustained during the sinking of the *Kaimoku* prevented his further service in the convoy. He returned to Brooklyn on December 2, 1942, and remained in the Naval Hospital for the next four months. He changed rates and became a Painter, third class, due to his previous civilian experience and for the remainder of 1943 supervised prisoners conducting building maintenance projects. In March 1944, he was sent to California and became part of Air Transport Squadron (VR) 2, based out of Alameda, along with fellow Soviet medal recipient Theodore Thueson. He finished the war as a member of the squadron's ground crew and was discharged on December 16, 1945. Returning to Brooklyn, he passed away on August 15, 1988, and is buried in Calverton National Cemetery, Calverton, New York.

Garnett DeBaun receives his Order of Glory in 1946. *Courtesy of the DeBaun family.*

Garnett C. DeBaun, *Order of Glory, Third Class*

Garnett Curry DeBaun was born in 1921. He joined the Navy from Indiana on December 26, 1941, and attended initial training at Great Lakes. From there, he was sent to Armed Guard duty, and his first ship was the *Kaimoku*. Surviving the sinking, he was taken to Londonderry and, along with DeGennaro, assigned to the *Richard Bland*. However, DeGennaro didn't make the Murmansk convoy, so DeBaun ventured as the sole *Kaimoku* survivor to the USSR in convoy JW-51A. Returning with convoy RA-53 with the PQ-17 *Ironclad* survivors on board, they were torpedoed, but again DeBaun survived. Picked up by the HMS *Eclipse*, he returned to the United States on the *Queen Elizabeth* in March 1943. Reassigned to the USS *Colahan* (DD-685) as a Gunner's Mate, third class, he took the ship from the Atlantic to the Pacific, in charge of her forty-millimeter gun battery. On *Colahan*, he participated in strikes against Palau, Mindanao, Leyte, Samar, and Southern Luzon; landings on Palau, strikes in the Manila area, against Calamian Group, Nansei Shoto Island, Formosa, Hong Kong, Hainan Island, French Indo-China, Okinawa, and Iwo Jima. With this remarkable record, now a Gunner's Mate, first class, DeBaun was transferred back to the United States and served as part of shore patrol for Headquarters, Ninth Naval District, in Chicago. Discharged on June 3, 1952, he settled in Sullivan, Indiana, and later, Southern California, where he spent the remainder of his life.

SS *Stone Street*

By the time Coxswain Joseph Chatterton arrived on the SS *Stone Street*, formerly the SS *Clara*, a captured Italian merchant ship, she was already a long-serving veteran of the Murmansk Run, having survived convoy PQ-12. She got underway from New York on July 6, 1942, bound for Great Britain as part of convoy BX-28. Traveling in the same convoy was a ship named the SS *William Moultrie*, bound for the USSR, which would later gain notoriety as a member of convoy PQ-18. The *Stone Street*, however, was delayed in Nova Scotia for repair work and eventually made it to Belfast, Ireland on August 20 as part of convoy HX-202. She next moved to Garston, and finally, to Liverpool. Leaving as part of ON-127 on September 4 to return to New York, she was one of thirty-three ships in the convoy. Unfortunately for ON-127, four days into their transit they crossed into the thirteen-boat wolfpack *Vörwarts*.[9] For the next four days, a running battle ensued. The first attack came at 12:30 PM on September 10 when the merchants SS *Elisabeth van Belgie*, *Fjordaas*, and *F.J. Wolfe* were torpedoed. The *Stone Street*, which had fallen behind the convoy due to mechanical difficulties, watched as these ships fell behind the convoy, either sinking or attempting repairs. At 5:15 PM, the tanker SS *Empire Oil* was torpedoed but remained afloat. Six hours later, so was the SS *Empire Thackery*. Believing they spotted a surfaced U-boat, the Armed Guard on the *Stone Street*, commanded by Lieutenant (jg) Granville Geisert, opened fire with their four-inch deck gun, but they were unsuccessful at hitting the target.

The next morning, September 11, opened with the torpedoing of the SS *Marit II*, and later, the sinking of the *Empire Oil* (which had been damaged the day before) and the torpedoing of the SS *Hindanger*. (The latter two ships were sunk by Joachim Deecke with the *U-584*, which was later sunk by Wilma Fowler and Letson Balliett on October 31, 1943.) By this time, the convoy had been under attack for over twenty-four hours. No one had slept; everyone was on edge. Ships were being sunk or damaged every few hours and the handful of convoy escorts seemed to have little success against the U-boats (in fact, only one U-boat, *U-659*, was damaged by the escorts, limping back to France for repair). The *Stone Street*, due to producing excess smoke from a furnace leak, and their continued straggling, was finally ordered to leave the convoy in order to give the other ships the best chance of survival. This was a certain death sentence for the old ship, but the entire convoy could not be risked; this was simply a sacrifice of war.[10]

At 10:45 AM on September 12, the *Stone Street*, now steaming independently, was struck amidships on the port side by a torpedo. The seas were rough and within minutes, the ship was listing to forty-five degrees. They continued underway, but there was no way they could remain afloat. The master gave the order to abandon ship to avoid being on board should the unseen U-boat decide to give the sinking hulk a *coup de grace* and expedite her trip to the bottom of the sea. Attempting to launch the lifeboats in heavy seas on a ship about to capsize led to chaos amongst the civilian crew. One boatswain was crushed when his lifeboat lowered incorrectly. One Navy gunner drowned by jumping overboard without a lifejacket and another was mangled in the still-turning screw as he was carried over the side by a heavy wave. Coxswain Joseph Chatterton ended up in the water, but was hauled into a lifeboat with the ship's master.

Minutes later, *U-594* surfaced, almost directly under the master's lifeboat, capsizing it and tossing the occupants into the water. Rescued from the sea and brought on board the U-boat, *Oberleutnant zur See* Friedrich Mumm, the submarine's commanding officer, began interrogating the survivors, looking for the master. After a brief time of attempting to hide, Captain Anderson, the *Stone Street's* master, came forward, and Mumm took him as a prisoner. Releasing the others with food, alcohol, and cigarettes, they debarked the U-boat in two rafts and began the long wait for rescue. After four days, the survivors of the *Stone Street* were pulled from the sea by the SS *Irish Larch*, which landed them at St. John, New Brunswick, on September 23. Of the crew of the *Stone Street*, forty were rescued, one taken prisoner, and thirteen were never seen again.

Joseph J. Chatterton, Jr., *Order of Glory, Third Class*

Joseph Chatterton. *Courtesy of the Chatterton family.*

Born on February 17, 1919, in Salem, Massachusetts, Joseph John Chatterton, Jr. was raised in Salem. He had served in the Civilian Conservation Corps with Company 1152, followed by six years in the Naval Reserve, being discharged on June 18, 1941. He worked at the General Electric River Works Plant in Lynn, Massachusetts, as a machinist helper. With the start of the war, he signed up for the Navy on December 9, 1941. Brought in directly as a Coxswain, he was assigned to USS *YP-211*, patrolling Boston and Portsmouth. In May 1942, he volunteered for Armed Guard duty and on June 20, 1942, arrived at the Armed Guard Center in Brooklyn. He was subsequently assigned to the *Stone Street*, where he was awarded a Letter of Commendation from the Secretary of the Navy for his heroic actions on September 10 through 13, 1942. He remained with the Armed Guard through the end of the war and was discharged as a Gunner's Mate, first class, on August 9, 1945. Returning to Lynn, he became a firefighter and served the City of Lynn for thirty-five years until his retirement. Joseph Chatterton passed away on March 1, 2001, and is buried in Saint Joseph Cemetery, Lynn, Massachusetts.

1. Награжден Указом Президиума Верховного Совета СССР от 7 июля 1945 года орденом Славы III степени

2. Имеет право, начиная с 1-VIII-1945 г. на получение орденских денежных выдач и на другие льготы и преимущества, согласно „Общему положению об орденах Союза ССР."

3. Книжка бессрочная.

Секретарь Президиума Верховного Совета СССР

№ 222135

15 августа 1945 г.

Утверждено постановлением ЦИК и СНК Союза ССР от 7 мая 1936 г.

ОБЩЕЕ ПОЛОЖЕНИЕ
об орденах Союза ССР.

1. Орден Союза ССР является высшей наградой за особые заслуги в области социалистического строительства и обороны Союза ССР.

2. Центральным Исполнительным Комитетом Союза ССР учреждены следующие ордена Союза ССР: „Орден Ленина", „Красное Знамя", „Красная Звезда", „Трудовое Красное Знамя" и „Знак Почета".

3. Орденами Союза ССР могут награждаться как отдельные граждане, так и войсковые соединения и воинские части Рабоче-Крестьянской Красной Армии, предприятия, учреждения и организации.

4. Награжденные орденом Союза ССР могут быть за новые заслуги повторно награждены тем же или другим орденом Союза ССР.

3

The Soviet order book to Joseph Chatterton. *Courtesy of the Chatterton family.*

Order of Glory, Third Class, number 387952 awarded to Joseph Chatterton. *Courtesy of the Chatterton family.*

SS *Pan York*

The SS *Pan York* left Boston on July 13, 1942, and joined a convoy bound for Iceland, where she arrived on August 5. Following several delays in Iceland, the *Pan York* commenced her westward voyage back to the United States. First stopping in Argentia, Newfoundland, on September 3, she received orders to form a convoy and head for Montreal. At 1:36 AM on September 7, they weighed anchor in Argentia and were underway. Not finding their convoy, they proceeded independently to Sydney, Nova Scotia, arriving on September 8. Five days later, now part of a twenty-three-ship convoy, they weighed anchor and were once again headed to Montreal. The following day, September 15, was a beautiful day with the convoy transiting off the coast of New Brunswick. Nothing was out of the ordinary, and they were enjoying the sunny weather and perfectly calm sea approximately three miles east of Cape des Rosier, New Brunswick, when *U-517* fired a spread of four torpedoes at 12:35 PM. Two torpedoes missed; one impacted the rocky coastline and the concussion was recorded as having broken 123 windows in the small fishing village up to a mile away.[11] The other torpedoes ran true: one struck the Dutch merchant SS *Saturnus*, and the other, the Norwegian SS *Inger Elizabeth*. Both ships sank quickly, with their survivors scrambling into lifeboats. General alarms were sounding across the convoy, and the Armed Guard crew on the *Pan York* spotted the U-boat's periscope in the middle of the convoy. As soon as the other ships were clear, they opened fire with their five-inch gun, blasting eight rounds at the partially surfaced submarine. When the smoke from the last round cleared, the submarine was not seen again. Eyewitnesses from the SS *Royalite* stated that at least two rounds from the *Pan York* struck the submarine, and the HMS *Salisbury* and HMS *Arrowhead* moved in with depth charges for the final kill. Unfortunately, *U-517* survived the engagement, though she would be sunk two months later. The adventures of the convoy weren't yet over, as the following morning, both ships in front of the *Pan York* were torpedoed by *U-165*. Her captain, *Fregattenkapitän* Eberhard Hoffman, also claimed damaging the *Pan York*, but no damage was recorded by the ship. As with *U-517*, the lifespan of *U-165* shortly came to an abrupt end; she was sunk with all hands by a depth charge attack two weeks later.

Herbert M. Sonneborn, Jr., *Order of the Red Star*

Herbert M. Sonneborn, Jr., Armed Guard commander of the SS *Pan York*. *Courtesy of the Sonneborn family.*

Herbert Mone Sonneborn Jr. was born on June 18, 1911 in Baltimore, Maryland. Attending the University of Virginia from 1928 to 1935, he graduated with his LLB and was accepted to the Virginia Bar the same year, followed by New York Bar in 1937 and West Virginia Bar in 1938. He worked in the firm of Liebowitz and Schuman from 1935, Wise, Greenewald, and Moskowitz until 1937, both in New York City. He then moved to Wheeling, West Virginia, where his family lived, to work for the firm of McGinley, Paull, and Petropalus until October 1941. He finally became part of the family business, working as the secretary of the board of directors at The Hub Department Store, until joining the Navy in April 1942. Commissioned as a Lieutenant (jg), he was sent to Armed Guard duty and directly to the *Pan York*. In December 1942, he was transferred to the SS *Samuel Johnson*, and in April 1943, shifted to the SS *Cape Douglas*. Leaving the Armed Guard service with a promotion to Lieutenant at the end of 1943, he received orders to the USS *Arlington* (AP-174) as the first lieutenant and damage control officer. The *Arlington* served as the West Coast APA pre-commissioning crew training ship, conducting training cruises out of Seattle and Treasure Island. During the course of the war, they trained ninety-three crews, totaling just over twenty-five thousand personnel. In March 1944, he became the *Arlington's* executive officer and remained in this capacity through November 1945, when he was discharged from active duty. Returning to Wheeling, he returned to working at The Hub, working as both the secretary to the board of directors and the merchandise manager, with oversight of the store's 150 employees. He eventually rose to president of The Hub, but sold the store and began working as a securities advisor for Hazlett, Burt, and Watson, Inc., in 1967. He retired from Hazlett as a vice-president in 1996. Active in the community, he served on the board of directors for the Wheeling Hospital for many years. Herbert Sonneborn passed away on August 3, 2003, and is buried in Greenwood Cemetery, Wheeling.

SS *Wade Hampton*

On February 18, 1943, the SS *Wade Hampton*, loaded with eight-thousand tons of general war cargo, including explosives as well as two motor torpedo boats and crates of auto parts on the aft deck, departed New York as one of the seventy-one ships in convoy HX-227. She was bound for Loch Ewe, then Murmansk. Despite reports that U-boats were trailing the convoy, nine days out of port the *Hampton* dropped behind the convoy in order to secure cargo that had been shifting due to heavy seas, causing a thirty-six degree list to starboard. With the shifting of cargo to create an even keel, the *Hampton* ended up seventeen miles behind the convoy. However, by the evening of February 28, she had almost regained all lost distance and was approximately two miles behind the convoy. At 8:39 PM, she was struck by two torpedoes fired by *U-405*. Both torpedoes struck the port side within four seconds of each other and literally blew off the stern of the ship. The propeller, most of the shaft, and all of the steering gear disappeared in the explosion, and water immediately filled the engine room. Despite the loss of the latter one-fifth of the ship, the *Hampton* remained afloat, though dead in the water and tossed about powerlessly in the seas. Ensign Kendall Cram, the Armed Guard commander, hurriedly manned the guns strike back, but no submarine could be seen.

The master gave the order to abandon ship as it was evident that she could not remain afloat, and all hands took to their lifeboats. Ensign Cram, assigned to lifeboat number one, refused to leave the ship as two of his Navy gunners assigned to the boat were not present. Leaving the safety of the lifeboat and allowing those present to lower it into the water, he ran back into the ship to find the gunners. Minutes later, he was spotted by the lifeboat occupants dragging the two injured gunners to the main deck along with a third gunner. He found a raft and placed the two injured men into it. However, the second gunner got tangled in the securing line and to prevent him from drowning, Cram let go the line holding the raft to the ship. This forcefully took the raft away from the ship, far out of reach. Ensign Cram then took the last remaining life ring and gave it to the third gunner so he could make it to the raft. With that self-sacrificing action, the crew watched as Cram jumped into the water to swim to the raft, but he was forced under by the waves and was never seen again.

Sixty-five survivors were rescued by the HMS *Vervain* (K-190) three hours later. At dawn, the *Vervain* rescued the master and the chief engineer. Both had stayed with the ship to free the torpedo boats and use them to aid in the rescue, but they were unable to do so. The master, an aging man in poor health who had been recalled out of retirement to participate in convoy duty, refused rescue to go down with the ship but was pulled from the ship by the chief engineer when the *Vervain's* small boat appeared. Four civilian crew and five Navy gunners, including Ensign Cram, were lost. Eight months later, *U-405* was sunk after being rammed by the USS *Borie* (DD-215) on the night of October 31, 1943, as recounted in Chapter 3.

Kendall H. Cram, *Order of the Patriotic War, First Class*

Kendall H. Cram, Armed Guard commander on the SS *Wade Hampton. Courtesy of the Cram family.*

Kendall Hutchinson Cram was born in Songio, Korea, on March 26, 1913, the son of a Methodist missionary serving overseas. Moving to Nashville and attending Hume-Fogg High School, Cram made a name for himself as a champion tennis player and outstanding basketball player both there and at Tulane University, where he served as captain of the tennis team until his graduation in 1935. Following graduation from George Peabody College in Nashville with his master's degree in 1937, Cram returned to Tulane to become the graduate manager of student activities and director of alumni relations. With the outbreak of the war, he volunteered for the Navy and was commissioned on July 28, 1942. Subsequently, he was sent to Armed Guard duty out of New Orleans, arriving at the command just before Thanksgiving. He was assigned to the *Wade Hampton*, making a transit in US coastal waters with the ship before participating in the trans-Atlantic convoy HX-227. Following the sinking of the *Hampton*, Kendall Cram was posthumously awarded the Silver Star and the Purple Heart for the heroism that cost his life. That year's Tulane yearbook was dedicated in his honor, a brave man who served his nation with the ultimate sacrifice.

The posthumous Silver Star and Purple Heart awarded to Kendall Cram. *Courtesy of the Cram family.*

Order of the Patriotic War, First Class, number 247515 awarded to Kendall Cram. *Courtesy of the Cram family.*

SS *Henry Wynkoop*

Departing New York ten days after the *Wade Hampton* on February 28, 1943, the SS *Henry Wynkoop* was headed for Belfast with a mixed cargo of war supplies as part of convoy HX-228. What was not known at the time was that the Germans had changed their message coding system, and as such, the Royal Navy suffered a momentary loss of information on the location of the U-boat wolfpacks. Thus, HX-228 was routed directly across the patrol line of wolfpack *Neuland*. The convoy remained together in a group of approximately sixty ships until March 8, when heavy seas caused the cargo on the *Wynkoop* to shift, causing a three-degree port list. Dropping out of the convoy to resecure the moving cargo, they were escorted by the Free French corvette *K-58*, who remained with them until they reapproached the convoy. Unaware of what was happening below the surface, the convoy had entered the territory of the waiting wolfpack. Just as they were about to slide back into their position in the convoy, the sub alert signal sounded across the convoy. Almost immediately, the British merchant *Tucurinca* was torpedoed by *U-221* at 5:26 PM. Five minutes later, the *Andrea F. Luckenbach*, carrying a partial cargo of explosives, was also hit. Flames reached three-hundred-feet in the air and a mushroom cloud could be seen for miles. Darkness descended on the convoy, but adrenaline was running high. John McNaughton, the Armed Guard commander on the *Wynkoop*, noted that the men who went to bed slept in rubber suits and life preservers – if they could sleep at all.

At 10:15 PM, *U-590* torpedoed the SS *Jamaica Producer*, sending flames into the air. The convoy commodore gave the order to scatter, sending merchant vessels and escorts into a mass of weaving and maneuvering ships, causing several close calls and the sounding of collision alarms in the darkness. Less than thirty minutes later, the American merchant SS *William C. Gorgas* was hit by the *U-757*, tearing a gigantic hole in the side of the ship and killing the men on watch in the engine room. The *Gorgas*, a short distance forward of the *Wynkoop*, refused to sink, though she was being overtaken by the other vessels in the convoy. *Korvettenkapitän* Friedrich Deetz, the captain of the *U-757*, waited patiently for the *Gorgas* to sink. Finally frustrated, and with other ships to include the *Wynkoop* and military escorts from the convoy moving within sight of his position, he fired the *coup de grace* and watched the *Gorgas* slip below the waves. This was not without risk, however, and the explosives carried by the *Gorgas* detonated underwater, lifting up and shaking *U-757*, causing severe damage and injuries and preventing the sub from diving.

McNaughton had just fallen asleep when he was awakened by the violent shaking of the ship and the ringing of the general alarm on the *Wynkoop*. Reporting to the bridge and attempting to sort through the confusion, he discovered that the *Gorgas* had been torpedoed and sunk ahead of them and that the merchant crew of the *Wynkoop* believed they had either been hit by a torpedo as well, or had possibly rammed the submarine. The engines were shut down and the steam release valves were opened. Together with the shouting of the crew, the darkness of night, and the sounding of the alarm, an unbelievable cacophony of noise and confusion ensued. Considering that three ships of the convoy had been torpedoed and sunk earlier in the day and with chaos quickly developing on the ship, the civilian crew and some of the Navy gunners scrambled into lifeboats, lowering them over the side and moving as quickly away from the ship as possible.

However, McNaughton wasn't entirely convinced the ship was sinking. Making a hasty inspection, he saw nothing apparently wrong with the ship, and in fact, the perpetual list to port had been corrected. He ordered his gunners (save for several who had already left in lifeboats) to man the five-inch gun platform to protect the ship. Twenty-six members of the merchant crew and seven Armed Guard gunners in the lifeboats, already far from the *Wynkoop*, were picked up by *K-58* and the SS *Stuart Prince* the following day. With all but eighteen of the crew gone, McNaughton and his Armed Guard gunners stood in for the civilian mariners, taking their watches in the engine room, the galley, as lookouts, and in the radio room. The undamaged but lightly-manned *Wynkoop* arrived in Belfast safely at 7:00 PM on March 14, marking the end of one of the more unusual episodes of the Armed Guard during the war.

John T. McNaughton, *Order of the Patriotic War, Second Class*

John Theodore McNaughton, the Armed Guard commander on the *Wynkoop*, was born in Bicknell, Indiana, on November 21, 1921, but was raised in Pekin, Illinois, moving there in 1927 when his father bought the *Pekin Daily Times* newspaper. Graduating from DePauw University in Greencastle, Indiana on May 31, 1942, he joined the Navy on July 8, 1942 and following his commissioning on August 10 was assigned to Armed Guard duty in New Orleans. Completing his tour with the Armed Guard, he received orders to a newly commissioned destroyer escort. After attending the Submarine Chaser Training Center in Miami, he reported to the USS *Paul G. Baker* (DE-642). On the *Baker*, he served eighty days off the coast of Okinawa, continually plagued by the threat of kamikazes. With victory in the Pacific, the *Baker* returned to the United States and McNaughton was discharged on March 12, 1946. Returning to civilian life, he attended the Harvard University School of Law, graduating in October 1948. He earned a Rhodes scholarship the same year, receiving his LLB from Oriel College at Oxford University.

McNaughton then returned to Pekin, where he joined the family business, becoming the editor of the *Pekin Times* from 1951 to 1953. In 1952, he ran for the US House against incumbent Republican Harold Velde but lost. The next year, he left the *Times* and joined the faculty of the Harvard Law School to work on nuclear arms control issues. It was while working on the Harvard faculty that he was brought into the Kennedy presidential administration, becoming the assistant secretary of defense for international security affairs in 1961 and later, general counsel for the Department of Defense. In this position, he became the close confidant to Secretary of Defense Robert McNamara, drafting many of the memoranda McNamara delivered to President Johnson encouraging the use of substantial US forces to the Republic of Vietnam. He likewise was the architect of the strategy of limited air war, resulting in the Rolling Thunder bombings of North Vietnam. As the war in Vietnam progressed, John McNaughton was nominated to become the fifty-ninth Secretary of the Navy. Making it through the confirmation process and in the Senate, he was two weeks away from being sworn in when he was tragically killed above Hendersonville, North Carolina, on July 19, 1967. On that day, Piedmont Airlines Flight #22 collided with a Cessna 310. All eighty-two people onboard, including McNaughton, his wife, and younger son, perished. He was buried with a formal military ceremony at Arlington National Cemetery.

John T. McNaughton, Armed Guard commander on the SS *Henry Wynkoop. Courtesy of the McNaughton family.*

John McNaughton (far right) during one of President Kennedy's cabinet meetings. He is seated next to General Lyman Lemnitzer, chairman of the Joint Chiefs of Staff. *Courtesy of the McNaughton family.*

1. Награжден Указом Президиума Верховного Совета СССР от 7 июля 1945 года орденом Отечественной Войны II степени

2. Имеет право, начиная с 1-VIII-1945 г. на получение орденских денежных выдач и пользоваться льготы и преимущества, согласно Общему положению об орденах Союза ССР.

№ 222210

15 августа 1945 г.

Утверждено постановлением ЦИК и СНК Союза ССР от 7 мая 1936 г.

ОБЩЕЕ ПОЛОЖЕНИЕ
об орденах Союза ССР.

1. Орден Союза ССР является высшей наградой за особые заслуги в области социалистического строительства и обороны Союза ССР.

2. Центральным Исполнительным Комитетом Союза ССР учреждены следующие ордена Союза ССР: „Орден Ленина", „Красное Знамя", „Красная Звезда", „Трудовое Красное Знамя" и „Знак Почета".

3. Орденами Союза ССР могут награждаться как отдельные граждане, так и войсковые соединения и воинские части Рабоче-Крестьянской Красной Армии, предприятия, учреждения и организации.

4. Награжденные орденом Союза ССР могут быть за новые заслуги повторно награждены тем же или другим орденом Союза ССР.

The Soviet order book to John McNaughton. *Courtesy of the McNaughton family.*

Order of the Patriotic War, Second Class, number 557280 awarded to John McNaughton. *Courtesy of the McNaughton family.*

SS *Alcoa Prospector*

Leaving New York on April 2, 1943, the SS *Alcoa Prospector* participated in convoys NG-353 to Guantanamo, GZ-28 to Cristobal, and then steamed independently to Fremantle, Australia, arriving on May 18. She then transited the Indian Ocean and into the Arabian Gulf, arriving at Basra, Iraq, on June 7. Following a short stay in Abadan, Iran, and then back to Basra, the *Prospector* left on July 2, arriving in Khasab Bay, Oman, on July 4. Underway the following day for Aden, Yemen, she was transiting in convoy PA-44 with ten other merchants and two escorts. At 10:10 AM, they were about seventy miles northwest of Muscat, Oman, when she was torpedoed by the Japanese submarine *I-27*. The *I-27*, under the command of Lieutenant Commander Toshiaki Fukumura, was on her seventh war patrol. She had been operating in the Gulf of Oman since May 7 and had already sunk four ships.[12] However, *I-27* was not entirely successful this time: the *Alcoa Prospector* was damaged but escaped. The torpedo had entered the number four hold, and the resulting blast had bent the propeller shaft at the bulkhead entering the engine room. Five minutes after the blast, the master made the call to abandon ship, even before determining the extent of the damage. However, Lieutenant (jg) Robert Nisbet, the Armed Guard commander, refused to leave the ship, believing it would potentially remain afloat for an indefinite period. The convoy continued on their transit, but the Indian corvette, HMIS *Bengal* remained in their vicinity, retrieving the survivors from the *Prospector*. As darkness fell, the captain of the Bengal convinced Nisbet and his ten gunners to leave the *Prospector* as he felt very certain the submarine would return during the night to serve the *coup de grâce*.

Robert Nisbet and his gunners, pictured here soaked in oil, lacking basic facilities, and baking under the hot sun, maintained guard on the SS *Alcoa Prospector* until it safely reached port. *Courtesy of the Robert A. Nisbet family.*

At daybreak on July 6, Nisbet, his gunners, and five of the merchant crew returned to the *Prospector* and conducted damage control to stem the flooding and keep the ship afloat. Two days later, the *Bengal* received orders to return to Karachi with the survivors of the *Prospector*. *Bengal's* captain requested Nisbet to abandon his ship and return with the other survivors. To this request, Nisbet replied: "Do not consider ourselves survivors as the vessel is still afloat. Will remain aboard ship."[13] On July 9, the Anglo-Iranian Oil Company fleet tugs *Zurmand* and *Tavana* towed the *Prospector* to Bandar Abbas, Iran, where they waited until July 16 for authorities from the War Shipping Administration to arrive and inspect the ship. As they waited on the powerless ship, Nisbet and his crew remained on board as the ship's defense, cooking topside with scrap lumber, drinking fresh water they located in the forward head (bathroom) and sleeping on the decks as the temperatures reached 130 degrees during the day. The ship was finally towed Bombay, India, where she underwent an extensive period of repair to regain her seaworthiness. Robert Nisbet and his gunners were returned to the United States and received Letters of Commendation from the Secretary of the Navy for their valor in the protection and salvage of the ship.

Robert A. Nisbet, *Order of the Patriotic War, Second Class*

Robert Alexander Nisbet was born on November 15, 1911, in Pittsburgh, Pennsylvania. He graduated from Lehigh University in Bethlehem, Pennsylvania, with a bachelor's degree in Industrial Engineering in 1933. First working for the Dravo Contracting Company, he worked on the construction of locks and dams on the Ohio and Kanawa Rivers. In 1937, he went to work for Pittsburgh Plate Glass, working for them in Oklahoma, West Virginia, and Pennsylvania. Four years later, he changed careers and went to work in the personnel department of the Talon Company. With the war starting, he took a leave of absence from Talon and joined the Navy. Reporting for active duty on June 15, 1942, as a Lieutenant (jg), he was assigned to Armed Guard duty. His first ship was an Esso tanker, the SS *Wallace E. Pratt*, making oil runs into the Amazon to obtain cargo before traveling to New York and Halifax. His next ship was the Liberty ship SS *Henry L. Benning*, taking cargo bound for the Soviets through Iran via the Pacific Ocean. His third ship was the *Alcoa Prospector*. Surviving the torpedoing by *I-27* and the subsequent misery of guarding a floating hulk, he left Armed Guard duty following his return to the United States. Following training at the Submarine Chaser Training Center in Miami, he became a Navy officer instructor at Princeton University, followed by an NROTC instructor at the University of Southern California. Before the end of the war, he was moved north and became the V-12 Program officer at the University of the Pacific in Stockton. Following his discharge on December 13, 1945, he returned to civilian life, working again for the Talon Company. With the outbreak of the Korean War, he was recalled to active duty on March 26, 1951, and served in the Office of Naval Material in Washington, DC Released from active duty on July 16, 1953, he remained active in the Naval Reserves, and retired as a Captain on November 15, 1971. In the meantime, as a civilian, he worked for Scovill Manufacturing in New Jersey, Georgia, and Connecticut as a salesman. Nisbet retired in 1968 and went to work for the Picatinny Arsenal in Dover, New Jersey, as a civilian supervisor in the ammunition section. He finally retired permanently in 1977 and enjoyed traveling until he passed away on August 21, 1991. He was placed in the Columbarium at Arlington National Cemetery.

Order of the Patriotic War, Second Class, number 557265, awarded to Robert Nisbet. *Courtesy of the Robert A. Nisbet family.*

The Soviet order book to Robert Nisbet. *Courtesy of the Robert A. Nisbet family.*

SS *Sharpsburg*

The SS *Sharpsburg* left New York in convoy CU-13 on January 31, 1944, with a cargo of 123,000 gallons of 130-octane aviation fuel bound for the US Army Air Forces in Great Britain. Heading to Liverpool, she picked up the harbor pilot near midnight on February 12. However, the fog was so thick that the ship had to anchor before entering port. Weighing anchor at 12:01 PM on February 13, they transited for less than thirty minutes before anchoring again due to the lack of visibility. Finally, at 12:42 PM on February 14, they weighed anchor and headed into the River Mersey, leading to Liverpool. At 1:07 PM, she collided with the Norwegian tanker MT *Bralanta* while maneuvering through the fog. The *Bralanta* had just departed Liverpool with convoy ON-224 bound for the United States and also had a cargo of fuel. The *Bralanta* tore a seventeen-foot hole in the side of the *Sharpsburg*, right at the location of the latter's number three storage tank and both ships caught on fire. With fuel hemorrhaging from the side of the *Sharpsburg*, the surface of the water was engulfed in flames. The crew of the *Bralanta* was able to gain control over the fire on board, but despite the best efforts of the merchant crew and the Navy Armed Guard gunners on the *Sharpsburg*, she became a raging inferno. Twenty minutes after the collision, it was evident the fire could not be controlled on *Sharpsburg* and the master sounded the signal to abandon ship. The crew and the gunners left the ship in the most expeditious means possible; some in lifeboats and some directly over the side, attempting to find patches of water free from the burning fuel. With their fire extinguished on board, the *Bralanta* put a lifeboat down into the burning water with a volunteer crew and they proceeded to pull fuel-soaked survivors from the *Sharpsburg* out of the sea. A short time later, a Royal Navy destroyer and minesweeper came to assist with damage control and the rescue of survivors. Between the crews of all four ships, they were able to gain control over the conflagration. By 3:00 PM, the fire was out on enough of the *Sharpsburg* so her master and Wilson Rutherford, the Armed Guard commander, along with a volunteer crew, could return to the ship. Working through the night and into the next day, they directed continuing damage control efforts that finally led to extinguishing the flames and saving the ship. Wilson Rutherford was awarded the Bronze Star Medal and the other members of the Armed Guard received Letters of Commendation from the Secretary of the Navy. Five volunteer rescuers from the *Bralanta* became the last recipients of the The Camp and Villaverde Medal, issued a total of thirty-seven times by the Liverpool Shipwreck and Humane Society since its inception in 1872.[14]

SS *Sharpsburg*, taken approximately at the same time as the collision. *National Archives.*

Wilson D. Rutherford, *Order of the Patriotic War, Second Class*

Wilson Douglas Rutherford was born on August 24, 1910, and graduated from Johns Hopkins University in 1931. Although his father owned Rutherford Field, an airport near Baltimore, Rutherford and his brother concentrated on four-wheeled vehicles and purchased an automobile repair shop, Dolphin Radiator Repair Works, prior to the war. Joining the Navy on May 1, 1943, he was assigned to Armed Guard commander duty following his training at the Naval Training School, Cornell University. Surviving the collision of the *Sharpsburg* on February 14, 1944, and earning the Bronze Star Medal for heroism, he returned to the United States. Subsequently, he was assigned to a new program, the Armed Guard Inspection Service working out of the offices of the Port Director in Baltimore. He was responsible for a litany of activities, from introducing the new Armed Guard crew to their respective ships to inspecting onboard weaponry, making maintenance reports, and spot-checking the Armed Guard crews on the ships in the port. Holding this responsibly for the remainder of the war, he finished his service and was discharged on May 21, 1946, with the rank of Lieutenant. He returned to the auto repair business and lived in Towson, Maryland. Wilson Rutherford passed away on November 25, 1961, and is buried in Baltimore National Cemetery, Baltimore, Maryland.

PART III

Chapter 14

Additional Recipients

Henry K. Hewitt, *Order of Kutuzov, First Class*

Admiral Henry Hewitt receives the *Legion d'Honneur* and the *Croix de Guerre* from the government of France during a ceremony in 1945. *National Archives.*

Admiral H. Kent Hewitt was born on February 11, 1887, in Hackensack, New Jersey. He entered the Naval Academy in 1903 and graduated with his fellow future admirals Giffen and Spruance with the class of 1907. Serving on the USS *Missouri* (BB-11), part of the "Great White Fleet" on their round-the-world tour as a passed midshipman, he was commissioned on September 13, 1908. In April 1910, he reported to the USS *Connecticut* (BB-18), followed by the USS *Flusser* (DD-20) and the newly commissioned USS *Florida* (BB-30). After six years of duty at sea, he reported to the Naval Academy as a mathematics instructor on September 16, 1916, and was promoted to Lieutenant in December. On June 30, 1916, he took command of the USS *Eagle*, a gunboat conducting patrol and survey duties off the coast of Haiti. After a year on the Eagle, he then took command of the USS *Dorothea*, another civilian vessel turned gunboat. With the war in Europe in force, he was sent to Brest, France, to take command of the USS *Cummings* (DD-44), where he earned the Navy Cross for his valor in commanding the *Cummings* through submarine and mine-infested waters as a convoy escort. Following a short tour in command of the USS *Ludlow* (DD-112), he returned to the Naval Academy in June 1919, this time serving as an instructor of electrical engineering and physics. After two years at the Academy, and now a Commander, Hewitt received orders to the USS *Pennsylvania* (BB-38) as the gunnery officer. Until he attended the War College in July 1928, he held successively senior billets as a gunnery officer, to include head of the gunnery section in the Division of Fleet Training in the Office of the Chief of Naval Operations, the gunnery officer and aide to the Commander, Battleship Divisions, Battle Force, and later, as the Battle Force gunnery officer. Following his graduation from the War College, he served on staff there for two years. In June 1931, he assumed command of Destroyer Division Twelve. One year later, Hewitt was promoted to Captain and served as the operations officer to the Commander of the Battle Fleet. After a year in that job, he again reported to the Naval Academy, this time as the Head of the Department of Mathematics, where he remained for the next three years. Hewitt assumed command of the USS *Indianapolis* (CA-35), becoming well known for transporting President Roosevelt to the Pan American Conference in Buenos Aires. Relieved in July 1937, he served as chief of staff to Commander, Cruisers Scouting Force until ordered to become the commanding officer of the US Naval Ammunition Depot in Puget Sound, Washington.

Promoted to Rear Admiral in December 1939, he took command of the US Special Service Squadron in Panama, followed by Commander, Cruiser Division Eight. In June 1941, he became Commander, Cruisers Atlantic Fleet. At this point, the war was in full force in Europe, and Hewitt was in charge of the oversight of the United States neutrality patrols. Following the United States' entry into the war, he was charged with the oversight of convoy escort duty for the initial Lend-Lease and troop convoys heading to Europe. In April 1942, he took charge of the newly formed Amphibious Force, Atlantic Fleet, tasked with establishing an amphibious capability in the Atlantic theater. Following the invasion of Morocco in November 1942, he was promoted to Vice Admiral and shortly thereafter, established the US Eighth Fleet, headquartered in Algiers, under the Supreme Allied Command of General Eisenhower. Operating from the Mediterranean, Hewitt commanded the naval landing of Sicily in July 1943, followed by the landings at Salerno in September and at Anzio in February 1944. Finally, he commanded the Allied Forces for the invasion of Southern France in August 1944. Remaining in command of the Allied naval forces in the Mediterranean, Hewitt was promoted to Admiral in April 1945. Relieved on April 12, he returned to the United States. During his time in theater, he earned his second Navy Cross for the invasion of Italy, both the Navy and Army Distinguished Service Medals for the invasion of Morocco, a second Army Distinguished Service Medal for the invasion of Southern France, and a second Navy Distinguished Service Medal for his service as Commander, Eighth Fleet.

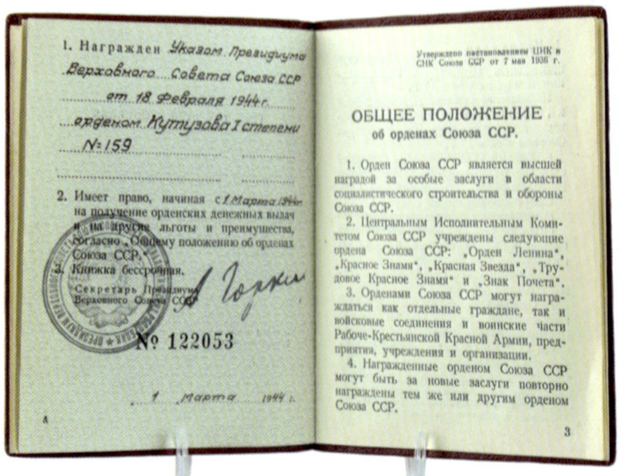

The Soviet order book to Admiral Henry Hewitt. *Courtesy of the US Naval War College Museum, Newport, RI; gift of Mrs. Floride Hunt Hewitt.*

Following his return to the United States, he served on the board investigating the attack on Pearl Harbor. On August 1, 1945, he returned to Europe and assumed command of the Twelfth Fleet, in charge of all US Naval Forces, Europe. A year later, he reported to the Naval War College in an advisory capacity and remained there until becoming the representative of the Chief of Naval Operations on the Military Staff Committee of the Security Council of the United Nations. Following forty-six years of active duty service, Admiral Hewitt retired on March 1, 1949. Retiring to Middlebury, Vermont, he died on September 15, 1972. The *Spruance*-class destroyer USS *Hewitt* (DD-966), commissioned on September 25, 1976, was named in his honor.

The Order of Kutuzov, First Class, number 159 awarded to Admiral Henry Hewitt. *Courtesy of the US Naval War College Museum, Newport, RI; gift of Mrs. Floride Hunt Hewitt.*

Admiral Hewitt's full-sized medal bar consisting of the Navy Cross, Dominican Campaign, Navy Expeditionary Medal, and the World War I Victory Medal with Destroyer bar. *Courtesy of the US Naval War College Museum, Newport, RI; gift of Mrs. Floride Hunt Hewitt.*

The post-World War II miniature medal bar of Admiral Hewitt, including US medals as well as medals from Allied nations. Interesting to note is the ribbon used to indicate the award of the Order of Kutuzov (third from the right on the second row). *Courtesy of the US Naval War College Museum, Newport, RI; gift of Mrs. Floride Hunt Hewitt.*

John McGinnis, after his retirement from the Navy. *Courtesy of the McGinnis family.*

John A. McGinnis, *Order of the Red Star*

John Alber McGinnis was born in Shasta, California, on July 30, 1905. Enlisting in the Navy on November 23, 1920, he was initially ordered to the USS *New York* (BB-34) in March 1921. This was followed by service on the USS *Texas* (BB-35) and the USS *California* (BB-44). On September 30, 1923, he reported to the USS *Borie* (DD-215) in the Far East, remaining on her until October 1927. After returning to the United States, he served on the USS *Worden* (DD-288) and at Naval Air Station Pensacola before receiving orders to Asia again. As a Yeoman, he served on multiple ships for short periods of time, to include the USS *Smith Thompson* (DD-212), the gunboat USS *Luzon* (PG-47), USS *Bulmer* (DD-222), the USS *Rochester* (CA-2), and the USS *McCall* (DD-400). While stationed on the *Luzon*, he was cited for bravery for actions on September 16 through October 27, 1930, against Chinese bandits and communists. As a Lewis machine gunner, he remained at his battle station throughout numerous attacks from shore batteries and small arms fire on the Yangtze River. In August 1941, now Chief Yeoman McGinnis, who had married a Russian woman while stationed in China, received an unusual set of orders: to serve in the office of the US Naval Attaché in Kuibyshev, USSR, where the Soviet government had moved expecting the fall of Moscow. Following a three-month transit through a nation reeling under the Nazi onslaught, he reported to the Attaché's office in the southern USSR on January 28, 1942. With the start of the Lend-Lease convoys, the offices of an Assistant Naval Attaché were established in Murmansk and Archangel, and McGinnis made the lengthy transit by railroad to the far north. Arriving in the early summer during the height of the bombardment of Murmansk, he was again cited for bravery in rescuing Soviet civilians and military personnel during the bombing of the city from March 20 to July 3, 1942. With this citation came a recommendation for promotion to Chief Ship's Clerk. As the single enlisted Sailor at the office of the Assistant Naval Attaché, he worked tirelessly to establish good relations with the Soviets, maintain liaison with the British, placate civilian ship's masters, monitor the treatment of survivors, and serve as an overall go-between for the Assistant Attaché's office and the waterfront. On January 12, 1943, he was awarded the Legion of Merit, an exceptionally unusual award to a Navy enlisted person, for: "exceptionally meritorious conduct in the performance of his services to the Government of the United States as the only assistant to the Assistant Naval Attaché stationed in North Russia."[1] William Carter wrote about McGinnis in his book *Why Me, Lord?*:

> *He was quite a social person, and loved to entertain in small groups ... He entertained lavishly and frequently, and seemed to be the unofficial host for the US presence in Archangelsk. Although he appeared to be an expert in his field, he was also very good at glad-handing the Russian dignitaries and spreading good will for our side. He was a handsome man and a charming host and seemed to have a natural talent for entertaining, which he obviously enjoyed doing.*[2]

Transferred to the US Embassy, Moscow, in September 1944, he finally received orders back to the United States, reporting to the office of the Chief of Naval Operations that November. The next month, he reported to the Eleventh Naval District in San Diego, and remained there until the end of the war. In September 1945, he moved across country to serve at the New York Naval Shipyard and retired from active duty on May 9, 1946. He then attended Oklahoma A & M, graduating with a degree in horticulture. Returning to California, he became a ranger for the California Department of Parks and Recreation, serving in both Southern and Northern California until his second retirement. John McGinnis passed away on July 17, 1984, and is buried in Tucson, Arizona.

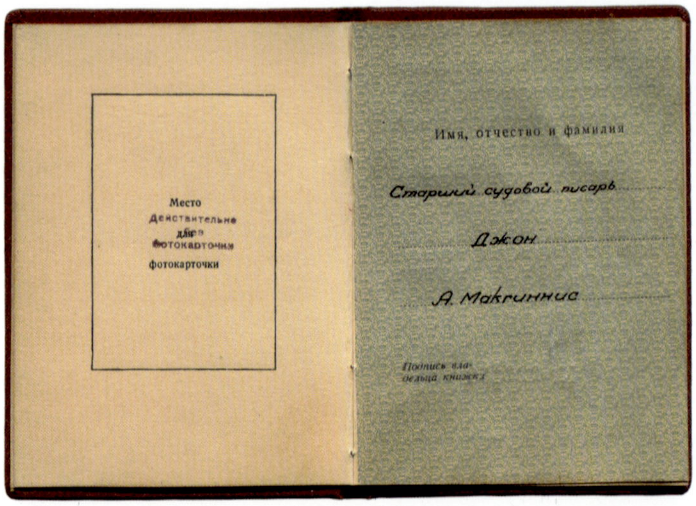

Место
для
фотокарточки

Имя, отчество и фамилия

Старший судовой писарь

Джон

А. Макгиннис

Подпись владельца книжки

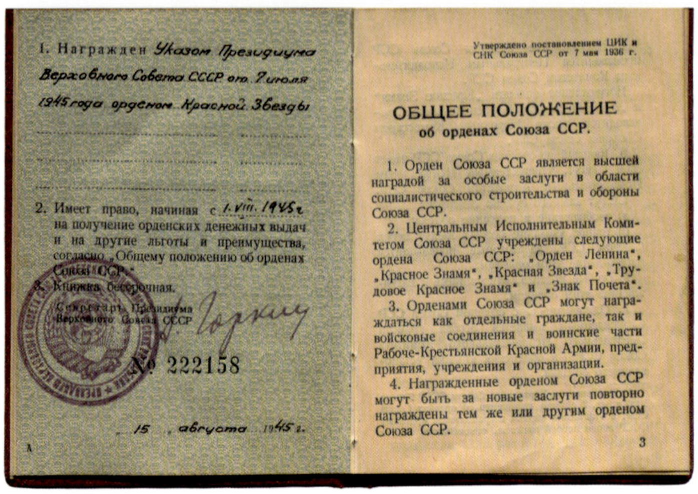

1. Награжден Указом Президиума Верховного Совета СССР от 7 июля 1945 года орденом Красной Звезды

2. Имеет право, начиная с 1.VIII.1945 г. на получение орденских денежных выдач и на другие льготы и преимущества, согласно „Общему положению об орденах Союза ССР."

3. Книжка бессрочная.

Секретарь Президиума Верховного Совета СССР

№ 222158

15 августа 1945 г.

Утверждено постановлением ЦИК и СНК Союза ССР от 7 мая 1936 г.

ОБЩЕЕ ПОЛОЖЕНИЕ
об орденах Союза ССР.

1. Орден Союза ССР является высшей наградой за особые заслуги в области социалистического строительства и обороны Союза ССР.

2. Центральным Исполнительным Комитетом Союза ССР учреждены следующие ордена Союза ССР: „Орден Ленина", „Красное Знамя", „Красная Звезда", „Трудовое Красное Знамя" и „Знак Почета".

3. Орденами Союза ССР могут награждаться как отдельные граждане, так и войсковые соединения и воинские части Рабоче-Крестьянской Красной Армии, предприятия, учреждения и организации.

4. Награжденные орденом Союза ССР могут быть за новые заслуги повторно награждены тем же или другим орденом Союза ССР.

3

The Soviet order book to John McGinnis. *Courtesy of the Pagnotta family.*

Close-up of the reverse of John McGinnis' Navy Good Conduct Medal, dated 1931. *Courtesy of the McGinnis family*.

The reverse of the award bars on John McGinnis' Navy Good Conduct Medal, showing his naming on both. *Courtesy of the McGinnis family*.

Order of the Red Star number 1553953 awarded to John McGinnis. *Courtesy of the McGinnis family*.

The US medals awarded to John McGinnis, to include the Legion of Merit number 6344, Navy Good Conduct, and Yangtze Service Medal M. No.2392. *Courtesy of the McGinnis family*.

Reverse of the US medals awarded to John McGinnis. *Courtesy of the McGinnis family*.

George D. Roullard as a Captain, taken sometime in the late-1950s. He is wearing the ribbon for his Order of the Red Star in the middle of his bottom row. Also notable is his wearing of the pre-May 1941 style hat device. *Courtesy of the Roullard family.*

George D. Roullard, *Order of the Red Star*

One of the Assistant Naval Attachés in North Russia, and later Vladivostok, was George Dee Roullard. Born in Windsor, Colorado, on June 11, 1910, he attended Idaho Falls High School and Hall's Preparatory School before joining the class of 1933 at the Naval Academy. Following his commissioning, he reported to the USS *Lexington* (CV-2) and spent the next year serving as a gunnery and engineering division officer. In 1934, he transferred to the gunboat USS *Tulsa* (PG-22), where he again served as a gunnery officer and this time as a communications officer until his transfer in 1936. He then reported to the USS *Bulmer* (DD-222) and later, the USS *Whipple* (DD-217) as the torpedo officer and first lieutenant. For the next two years, he was on the USS *Pensacola* (CA-24) and USS *Nitro* (AE-2) as the gunnery division officer and in January 1940 reported to the USS *Memphis* (CL-19) as the assistant engineering officer. Roullard was in this billet when he was selected in July 1941 to serve as the Assistant Naval Attaché at the US Embassy in the USSR. Initially assigned as the officer in charge of the Attaché's office in Archangel until the end of 1942, Roullard was transferred to Vladivostok to serve as the single Navy representative in the port for the duration of the war. Remaining in the Soviet Union until August 1946, he then transferred to Washington, DC, to serve on the Navy Department staff. In 1949, he was selected for a one-year tour in command of the US Naval Operating Base, Grodnal, Greenland. Subsequently, he assumed command of the USS *Shelton* (DD-790) in 1950, and took her into action on both coasts of Korea during the Korean War.

Following a successful command tour in *Shelton*, he reported again to the Navy Department, working with the Strategic Plans section. Returning to sea in 1953, he took command of the USS *Taluga* (AD-52). In December 1954, Roullard became the inspector general for the Fifteenth Naval District. This was followed by his next command, that of Destroyer Squadron One. At the end of 1957, he reported to the Seventeenth Naval District, also serving as the inspector general, and four months later, became the chief of staff of the Alaskan Sea Frontier and Seventeenth Naval District.

Retiring in 1960, he returned to school and earned his teaching credential at San Diego State University. From 1962 to 1975, he taught algebra at Coronado High School in Coronado, California, and finally retired. George Roullard passed away on May 31, 1986

Order of the Red Star number 1693874 awarded to George Roullard. *Courtesy of the Roullard family.*

George Roullard's US-awarded medals, including the Navy Commendation, China Service, European African Middle Eastern Campaign, Asiatic Pacific Campaign, World War II Victory, and UN Korea. *Courtesy of the Roullard family.*

PART IV

CHAPTER 15

PROCESS OF AWARDING SOVIET MEDALS TO THE NAVAL SERVICES

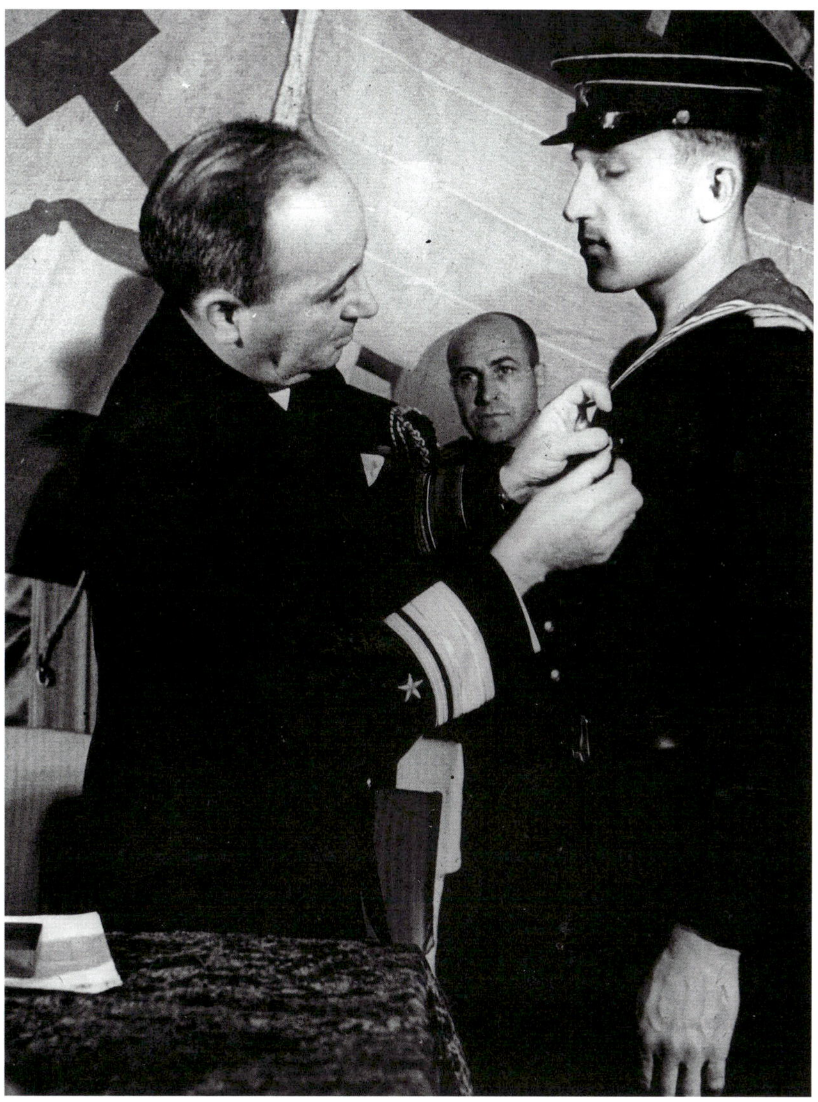

Admiral C.E. Duncan presents the US Navy Distinguished Service Medal to Petty Officer First Class V.N. Lenkov, Soviet Navy, in a ceremony in June 1943. *Courtesy of the Navy Memorial Foundation.*

The awarding of medals to foreign recipients is not a new phenomenon: it is an important means to ensure solidarity and goodwill between allies and has taken place since decorations for valor originated. The first significant motion the Soviet Union made to award medals to US citizens for their contribution in the Second World War came from a note dated May 20, 1943, where the Soviets requested permission from the US Secretary of State to award medals to four Army Air Force pilots working in Fairbanks Alaska for "their exemplary work in testing airplanes and assisting Soviet aviators who are taking over American airplanes."[1]

On September 6, 1943, the Charge d'Affaires of the USSR in the US requested permission to award one Order of Suvorov First Class and one Order of Kutuzov First Class to "outstanding representatives of our Armed Forces in the Mediterranean theater of war" along with twenty-five orders and medals to members of the Army and Army Air Force "who have distinguished themselves," and fifteen to members of the Navy and ten to members of the Merchant Marine who have "shown courage in transporting military equipment to the Northern ports of the Soviet Union."[2]

Secretary of the Navy Frank Knox approved the awarding of the medals on September 15 to members of the Navy,[3] and Emory S. Land, of the War Shipping Administration, approved the awarding on September 23 to members of the Merchant Marine.[4] On a letter dated November 1, Edward R. Stettinius Jr., acting Secretary of State, requested each of the services to submit names for the award recipients. He stated:

> *As you may recall the American Ambassador in Moscow on June 22 awarded American decorations to certain outstanding individuals of the Soviet armed forces. The Soviet recipients of the awards were chosen by the Soviet Government and it would appear that in the present instance the Soviet Government expects this Government to designate those members of its armed forces to whom it is desired that the Soviet decorations should be awarded.*[5]

The War Shipping Administration submitted their list of ten names on December 10, and the Navy submitted their list on December 13. The presentation ceremony for these first twenty-five awards took place in the Chinese Room of the Mayflower Hotel on April 11, 1944.[6] This awarding was not without internal conflict, however. President Roosevelt was deeply concerned about offending Winston Churchill, who maintained a mercurial relationship with Stalin, by the receipt of the Soviet awards, and on March 17, 1944, directed Henry Stimson, Secretary of War, to confer with Field Marshal John Dill, Senior British Representative on the Combined Chiefs of Staff, to determine the British feeling on the awards. In a letter dated March 18, Stimson wrote to Roosevelt that according to Field Marshall Dill: "...in view of the importance of not offending Stalin, we ought not hesitate a moment and he [Dill] would undertake to make it clear to his people what the situation was."[7]

At this point, it is not clear if Field Marshall Dill was aware of the previous awardings of Soviet medals to members of the British armed forces that had taken place on February 19 and 26, 1944, or the in-process awarding of decorations awarded by Presidium decree dated March 21 to members of the British merchant marine service.[8]

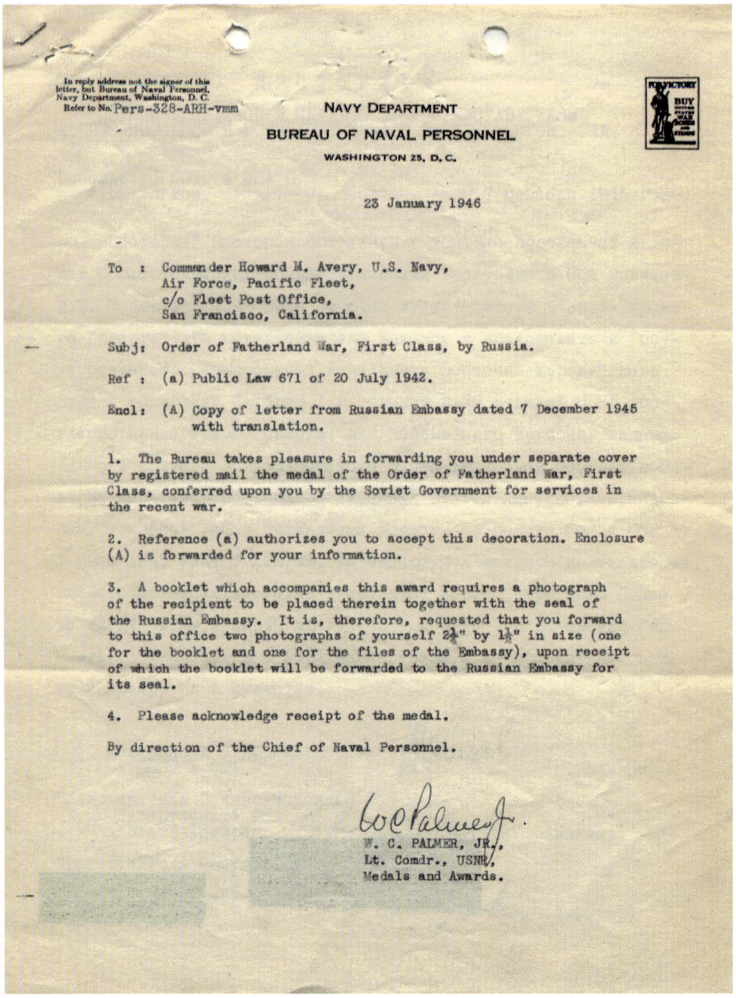

In reply address not the signer of this letter, but Bureau of Naval Personnel, Navy Department, Washington, D. C.
Refer to No. Pers-328-ARH-vmm

NAVY DEPARTMENT
BUREAU OF NAVAL PERSONNEL
WASHINGTON 25, D. C.

23 January 1946

To : Commander Howard M. Avery, U.S. Navy,
Air Force, Pacific Fleet,
c/o Fleet Post Office,
San Francisco, California.

Subj: Order of Fatherland War, First Class, by Russia.

Ref : (a) Public Law 671 of 20 July 1942.

Encl: (A) Copy of letter from Russian Embassy dated 7 December 1945 with translation.

1. The Bureau takes pleasure in forwarding you under separate cover by registered mail the medal of the Order of Fatherland War, First Class, conferred upon you by the Soviet Government for services in the recent war.

2. Reference (a) authorizes you to accept this decoration. Enclosure (A) is forwarded for your information.

3. A booklet which accompanies this award requires a photograph of the recipient to be placed therein together with the seal of the Russian Embassy. It is, therefore, requested that you forward to this office two photographs of yourself 2¼" by 1½" in size (one for the booklet and one for the files of the Embassy), upon receipt of which the booklet will be forwarded to the Russian Embassy for its seal.

4. Please acknowledge receipt of the medal.

By direction of the Chief of Naval Personnel.

W. C. PALMER, JR.,
Lt. Comdr., USNR,
Medals and Awards.

The initial letter that was received by the recipients informing them of their soon-to-be arriving award. It states the requirement for each recipient to submit a photograph for inclusion in the document they would later receive. *Courtesy of the Avery family.*

On April 8, 1944, Roosevelt approved a policy removing the State Department from the process of receiving and holding foreign military medals for the various military departments until congressional approval could be granted for their awarding.[9] This unfortunately eliminated a portion of historical documentation regarding future awards, in particular the 190 awards bestowed in 1945. However, with the documentation that remains, we know that George M. Abbott, a representative of the State Department, was given a short tutorial about the medals by Mr. Zubilin, second secretary of the Soviet Embassy. In his comments, he noted:

> *In a conversation with Mr. Zubilin, he explained to me that the grant of a decoration by the Soviet Government carries with it a number of privileges. The bearer is entitled to free admission to any public bath in Russian [sic] and to free transportation on streetcars, busses, and subways in any city in the Soviet Union. In addition he receives every year a free pass on the Soviet railroads entitling him to make one trip to any point in the Soviet Union and return. Finally, the decoration carries with it a small monthly pension for life. The amount varies according to the Order and the class with a maximum of twenty rubles per month. The Order of Suvorov does not carry with it all of the above privileges, in particular the life pension and the annual railroad pass.*
>
> *I was shown the decorations which are to be given out on April 11. The boxes contain in addition to the medal: (1) a small booklet with a place on the first page for the holder's photograph and details regarding his status and rank in the Order; (2) the railroad pass referred to above; (3) a small booklet about one-half inch thick, each page of which consists of an application for the monthly pension which is to be filled out, signed and presented for payment.*
>
> *Mr. Zubilin explained in the United States the pension would be paid at the Soviet Embassy. He pointed out that each decoration bears a serial number and cannot be replaced if lost.*[10]

On April 10, in discussion with Major Leon Bell, Assistant Chief of Staff, G-1, of the War Department and George Abbott, it was decided that only the medals with their appropriate order or medal document would be given to the recipients in the presentation ceremony the following day, and the documents for the pension and railroad pass would be retained by the War Department to determine the legality of accepting the monetary reward. Of note, the War Shipping Administration did authorize the medal recipient's acceptance of the pension, as they were not subjected to the same regulations as the members of the armed forces who received the medals.[11]

Following the ceremony on April 11, with the War Shipping Administration receiving the medals on April 17 (as their medals were received by the Navy Department during the ceremony), the matter of obtaining photographs for the order and medal books arose. The medals in the possession of the respective military and civilian departments were held in abeyance until photographs could be received from the recipients, and at that time, the documents were sent to the Soviet Embassy for final sealing. Only then were the documents with their medals sent to the commands of each recipient.[12]

On October 26, 1944, Ambassador Anatoly Gromyko sent a letter to Cordell Hull, the Secretary of State, requesting the approval of a second awarding of medals to the Navy. In his letter, he states:

> *The Soviet Government, placing high value on the services of American seaman engaged in convoy work from the United States of America to the Soviet Union wishes to reward by the bestowal of medals and orders of the USSR on persons of the lower ranks of the American Navy who have distinguished themselves in the organization and execution of convoys.*[13]

This awarding was approved on December 20, 1944, by James Forrestal, Secretary of the Navy, via Edward Stettinius.[14] A month later, on January 20, 1945, Nikolai Novikov, the Charge d'Affaires of the USSR, forwarded a list of award types, classes, and numbers to be awarded to "men of the American Navy who have distinguished themselves." In the State Department translation of this document, the Order of the Patriotic War was incorrectly translated as "Order of the Fatherland War," giving rise to the erroneous naming of the award that persisted throughout the awarding process and subsequent decades.[15] The list of awardees generated by the Navy Department was subsequently sent to the Soviet Ambassador on March 21, 1945, including the names of 190 recommended Navy and Coast Guard recipients of Soviet medals. Where this list originated, or who determined the eligible recipients for these awards, based on what criteria, is unfortunately lost to history. This list was approved on July 14, 1945, by decree of the Presidium of the Supreme Soviet of the USSR dated July 7, 1945.

Five months later, on December 7, 1945, in a presentation ceremony at the Soviet Embassy, Nikolai Novikov delivered the 190 medals to Rear Admiral Thomas B. Inglis, the Director of Naval Intelligence. This ceremony automatically produced a flurry of press releases within the span of the next week, notifying several of the recipients of their award far before they were notified by the Navy Department. In at least one case, this prompted the inquiry of a recipient's father to Rear Admiral Inglis as to the location and status of the medal, as the awarding was announced so far in advance of the medals being officially delivered to the recipients.[16]

In most cases, following the administrative processes of the Navy Department at the time, the medals were forwarded to the respective naval districts for further distribution to the enlisted medal recipients. Depending on the naval district, the presentation ceremony itself ranged from a simple mailbox delivery to an elaborate, public ceremony as in the case of Oman Nelson. For those enlisted recipients still on active duty, the medals were mailed to their commands for presentation. In one particular case, the box for the medal was received at the command with the medal missing.[17] The presentation to officers varied greatly, with most being delivered via registered mail to the recipients at their home of record or current command.

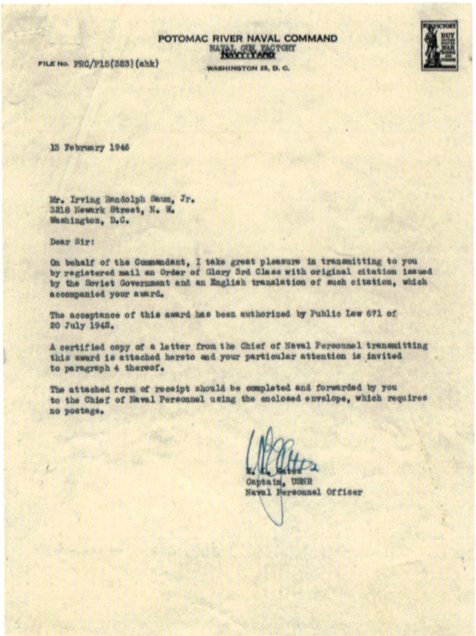

POTOMAC RIVER NAVAL COMMAND
NAVAL GUN FACTORY
~~NAVY YARD~~
WASHINGTON 25, D. C.

FILE No. PRC/P15(323)(ahk)

15 February 1946

Mr. Irving Randolph Saum, Jr.
3218 Newark Street, N. W.
Washington, D.C.

Dear Sir:

On behalf of the Commandant, I take great pleasure in transmitting to you by registered mail an Order of Glory 3rd Class with original citation issued by the Soviet Government and an English translation of such citation, which accompanied your award.

The acceptance of this award has been authorized by Public Law 671 of 20 July 1942.

A certified copy of a letter from the Chief of Naval Personnel transmitting this award is attached hereto and your particular attention is invited to paragraph 4 thereof.

The attached form of receipt should be completed and forwarded by you to the Chief of Naval Personnel using the enclosed envelope, which requires no postage.

Captain, USNR
Naval Personnel Officer

A

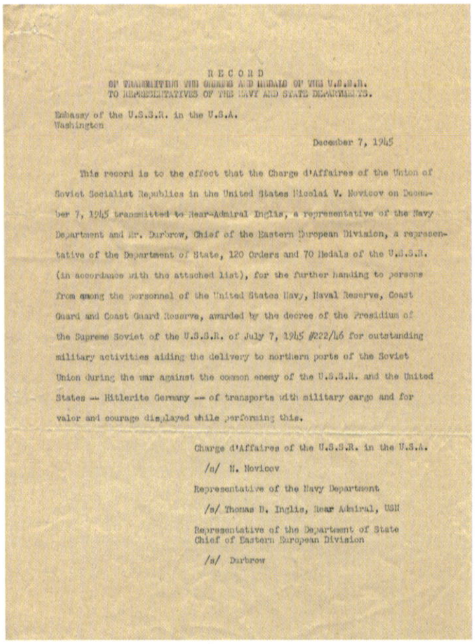

RECORD
OF TRANSMITTING THE ORDERS AND MEDALS OF THE U.S.S.R.
TO REPRESENTATIVES OF THE NAVY AND STATE DEPARTMENTS.

Embassy of the U.S.S.R. in the U.S.A.
Washington

December 7, 1945

This record is to the effect that the Charge d'Affaires of the Union of Soviet Socialist Republics in the United States Nicolai V. Novicov on December 7, 1945 transmitted to Rear-Admiral Inglis, a representative of the Navy Department and Mr. Durbrow, Chief of the Eastern European Division, a representative of the Department of State, 120 Orders and 70 Medals of the U.S.S.R. (in accordance with the attached list), for the further handing to persons from among the personnel of the United States Navy, Naval Reserve, Coast Guard and Coast Guard Reserve, awarded by the decree of the Presidium of the Supreme Soviet of the U.S.S.R. of July 7, 1945 #222/46 for outstanding military activities aiding the delivery to northern ports of the Soviet Union during the war against the common enemy of the U.S.S.R. and the United States -- Hitlerite Germany -- of transports with military cargo and for valor and courage displayed while performing this.

Charge d'Affaires of the U.S.S.R. in the U.S.A.
/s/ N. Novicov
Representative of the Navy Department
/s/ Thomas B. Inglis, Rear Admiral, USN
Representative of the Department of State
Chief of Eastern European Division
/s/ Durbrow

B

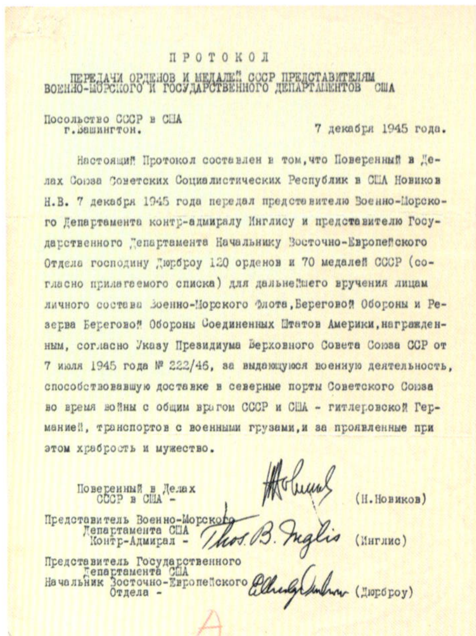

ПРОТОКОЛ
ПЕРЕДАЧИ ОРДЕНОВ И МЕДАЛЕЙ СССР ПРЕДСТАВИТЕЛЯМ
ВОЕННО-МОРСКОГО И ГОСУДАРСТВЕННОГО ДЕПАРТАМЕНТОВ США

Посольство СССР в США
г.Вашингтон.

7 декабря 1945 года.

Настоящий Протокол составлен в том, что Поверенный в Делах Союза Советских Социалистических Республик в США Новиков Н.В. 7 декабря 1945 года передал представителю Военно-Морского Департамента контр-адмиралу Инглису и представителю Государственного Департамента Начальнику Восточно-Европейского Отдела господину Дюрброу 120 орденов и 70 медалей СССР (согласно прилагаемого списка) для дальнейшего вручения лицам личного состава Военно-Морского Флота, Береговой Обороны и Резерва Береговой Обороны Соединенных Штатов Америки, награжденным, согласно Указу Президиума Верховного Совета Союза ССР от 7 июля 1945 года № 222/46, за выдающуюся военную деятельность, способствовавшую доставке в северные порты Советского Союза во время войны с общим врагом СССР и США - гитлеровской Германией, транспортов с военными грузами, и за проявленные при этом храбрость и мужество.

Поверенный в Делах СССР в США - (Н.Новиков)
Представитель Военно-Морского Департамента США Контр-Адмирал - Thos. B. Inglis (Инглис)
Представитель Государственного Департамента США Начальник Восточно-Европейского Отдела - (Дюрброу)

C

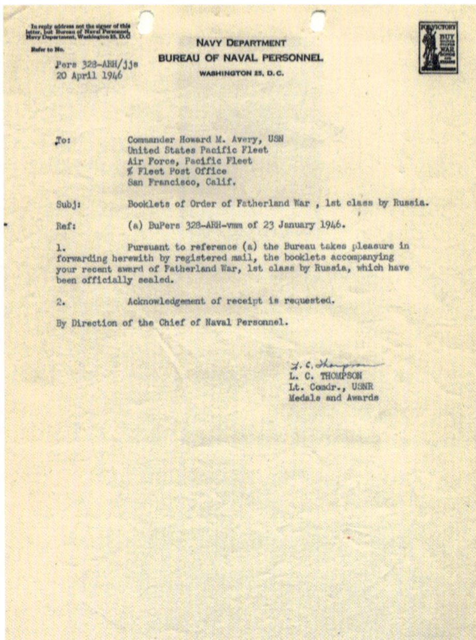

In reply address not the signer of this letter, but Bureau of Naval Personnel, Navy Department, Washington 25, D.C.
Refer to No.
Pers 328-ARH/jjs
20 April 1946

NAVY DEPARTMENT
BUREAU OF NAVAL PERSONNEL
WASHINGTON 25, D. C.

To: Commander Howard M. Avery, USN
United States Pacific Fleet
Air Force, Pacific Fleet
% Fleet Post Office
San Francisco, Calif.

Subj: Booklets of Order of Fatherland War, 1st class by Russia.

Ref: (a) BuPers 328-ARH-vmm of 23 January 1946.

1. Pursuant to reference (a) the Bureau takes pleasure in forwarding herewith by registered mail, the booklets accompanying your recent award of Fatherland War, 1st class by Russia, which have been officially sealed.

2. Acknowledgement of receipt is requested.

By Direction of the Chief of Naval Personnel.

L. C. Thompson
L. C. THOMPSON
Lt. Comdr., USNR
Medals and Awards

D

A) In the cases of enlisted recipients, the award was given to their nearest Navy command for transmittal. This letter, to Irving Saum, is from the Naval Gun Factory of the Potomac River Naval Command in Washington, DC. *Courtesy of the Saum family.*

B and C) Each recipient received the declaration providing the basis for the award, both in Russian and in English. *Courtesy of the Avery family.*

D) When the documents were complete, they were forwarded out under separate cover and another letter was sent informing the recipient they were about to receive the documents. *Courtesy of the Avery family.*

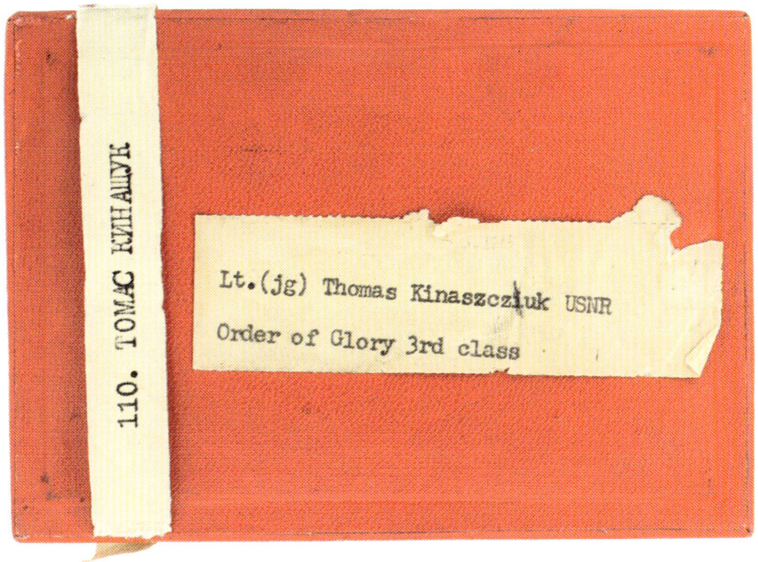

The documents and awards were sent in slightly different boxes. However, this was not always consistent and with some recipients, the boxes were identical. This box contained the documents for Thomas Kinaszczuk. *Courtesy of the Kinaszczuk family.*

The medal box did not have the velvet lining of the order box, it was lined with simple, off-white cardstock. This Medal of Nakhimov was awarded to Robert Henderson. *Courtesy of the Henderson family.*

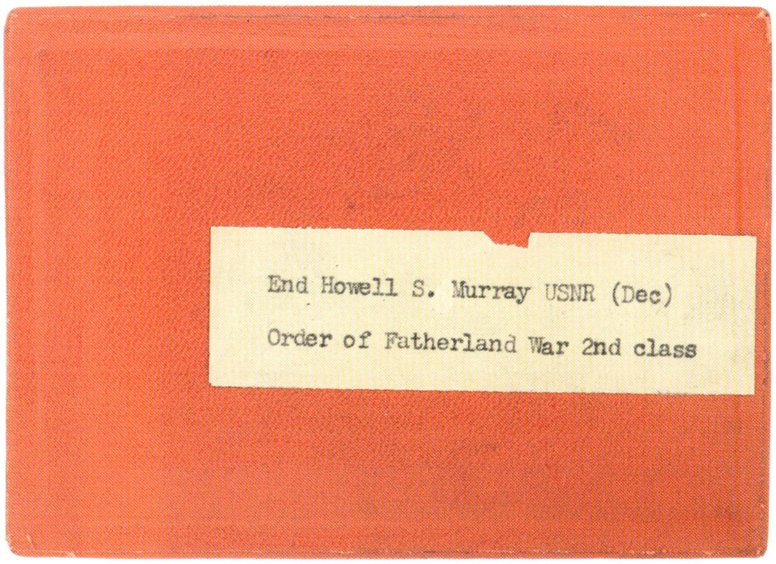

The recipients who were no longer living had the inclusion of the word "Deceased" (abbreviated as "Dec") on their boxes. This box was sent to the family of Howell Murray. *Courtesy of the Murray and Herman families.*

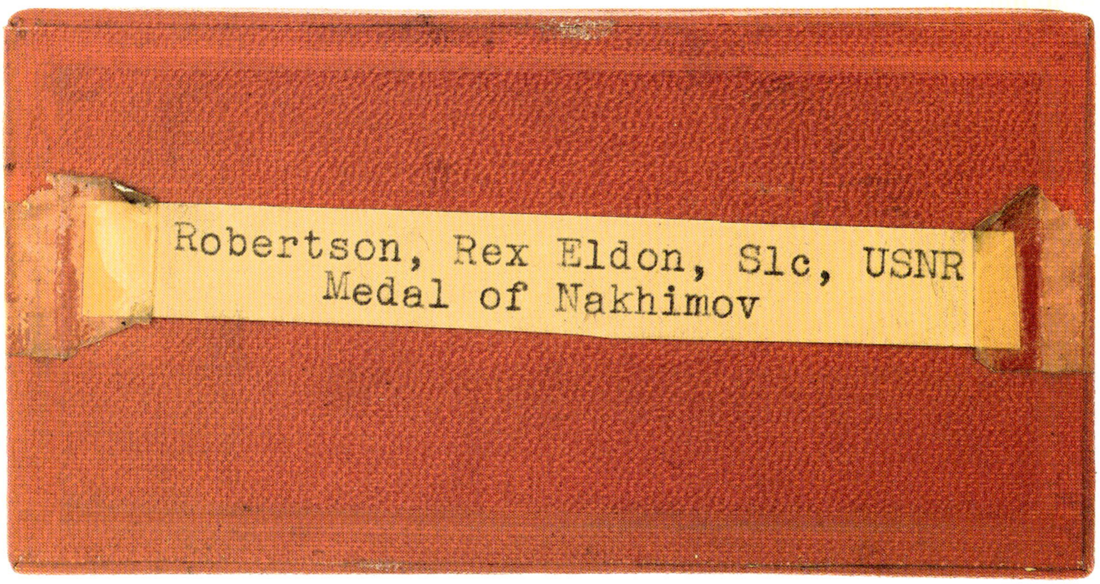

The medal recipients received their decorations in a slightly smaller red box. This box contained the Medal of Nakhimov to Rex Robertson. *Courtesy of his daughter, Evelyn Ann.*

This is the Medal "For Valor" awarded to Charles Harris. *Courtesy of the Harris Family.*

The box was very closely fitted to the documents. These are the medal book and pension document to Robert Henderson. *Courtesy of the Henderson family.*

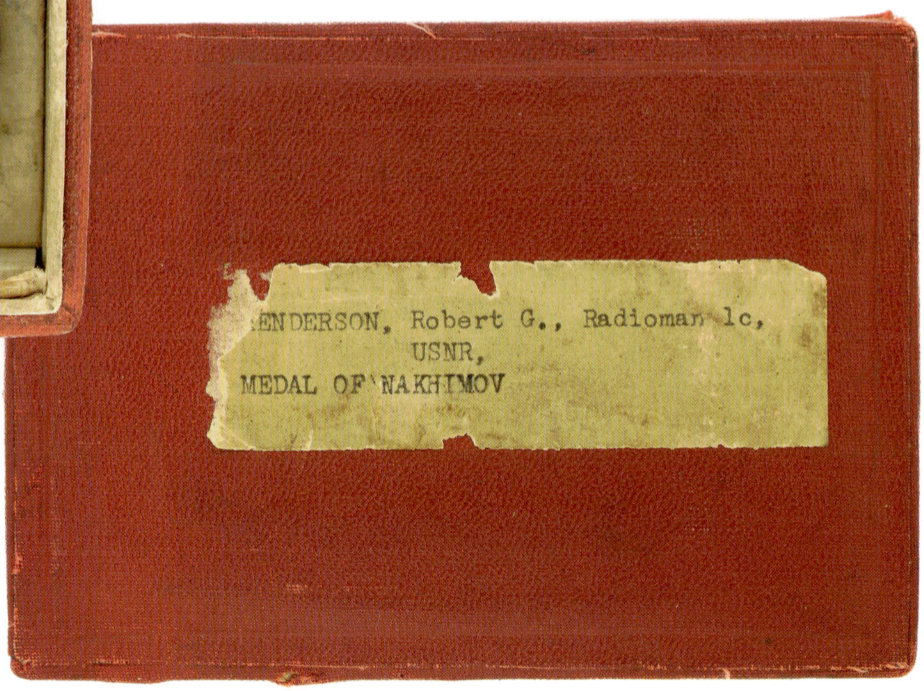

All recipients received their documents in the same type of box. This box contained the documents for the Medal of Nakhimov to Robert Henderson. *Courtesy of the Henderson family.*

The highest awards different from the others by not having the name labels taped to the boxes. Instead, they were placed on top of the box, and later, depending on the recipient, were retained in the box. *Courtesy of the US Naval War College Museum, Newport, RI; gift of Mrs. Floride Hunt Hewitt.*

The highest awards, including that of the Orders of Kutuzov and Suvorov, were presented in a brown leatherette covered box with a blue velvet base and a cream silk pocket for the order book. *Courtesy of the US Naval War College Museum, Newport, RI; gift of Mrs. Floride Hunt Hewitt.*

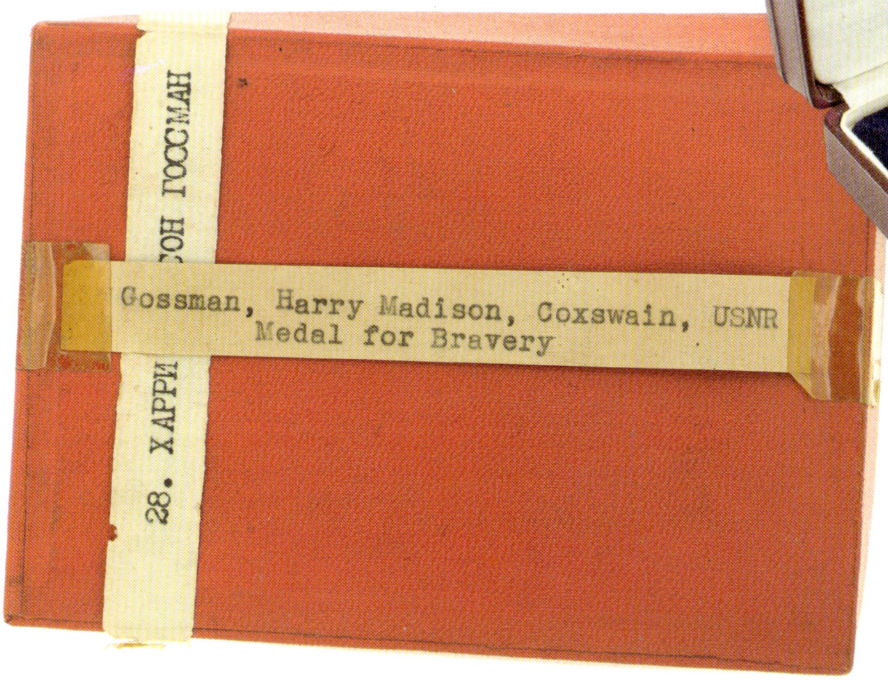

The reason for the varied labels is not known. This box contained the documents for Harry Gossman. *Courtesy of the Gossman family.*

Often, the small boxes were a repository for random souvenirs from the recipient's time in the USSR. Merlin Houdeshell used his boxes to house several documents he brought back from his time in Archangel. *Courtesy of the Houdeshell family.*

You Are Cordially Invited to Attend a Special

PROGRAM

and Medal Presentation

at the Walhalla School Gym

Wed., March 27th 8 p.m.

Oman Nelson to Be Decorated

A veteran of nearly four years with the Navy, Oman Nelson, GM second class, a former resident of Maddock, now a member of the Walhalla Hardware Co., Inc., will be presented with a Navy Award by Lieutenant Commander D. J. Schultz of the United States Navy Public Information office at Bismarck.

3 Exciting War Films 3

Official War Actions Taken At the Spectacular Battles of the

2nd Philippines Sea, Okinawa & Iwo Jima

An Especial Invitation Extended to Veterans of These Historic Battles

Program Sponsored by American Legion

While many recipients received their awards by registered mail, several took part in large, organized ceremonies. This large poster was used to announce the awarding ceremony for Oman Nelson on March 27, 1946. *Courtesy of the Nelson family.*

Comdr. Howard S. Roberts, right, and Lt. Robert W. Hayman, left, are included on the list of 190 Navy and Coast Guard men who recently were awarded medals by the Soviet government. Comdr. Roberts received the Order of the Red Star and Lt. Hayman the Order of Glory, 3rd class. These medals were given to them for outstanding military activities aiding the delivery of transports with military cargo to northern parts of the Soviet Union and for valor and courage displayed in the performance of their duties.

Rear Admiral Thomas B. Inglin, USN, Chief of Naval Intelligence, accepted the awards in behalf of the recipients at a ceremony held at the Soviet Embassy in Washington.

Other medals awarded included: Order of the Fatherland, War, First Class; Order of the Fatherland War, Seccnd Class; Medal for Bravery; Meial for Merit in Action; Medal of Ushakov; and Medal of Nakhimov.

Used as a background in the above picture is the Russian citation accompanying aviation training officer Robert's award. Lt. Hayman, ATD instruction pilot, received a similar citation, also written in Russian.

Some awards were announced by local or military newspapers. This collage was published by the base newspaper for Naval Air Station Fort Lauderdale, where both Robert Hayman and Howard Roberts were stationed. *US Navy via the Hayman family.*

Presentation ceremonies ranged from simple to elaborate. Ward Gemmer receives his China Service medal, his Order of the Patriotic War, and a Commendation in the same ceremony. He is holding the red box for the Soviet medal, as well as both documents. *Courtesy of the Gemmer family.*

Jack Stewart receives his Order of Glory during a presentation ceremony in 1946. The red box for the medal is seen in the left hand of the officer shaking Stewart's hand. *Courtesy of the Stewart family.*

Romuald Holubowicz receives his Medal "For Military Merit" in a presentation ceremony at the Merchant Marine Academy in 1944. *Courtesy of the Holubowicz family.*

This photo was taken immediately following the award ceremony where William Schilbe, since discharged from the Navy, received his Order of the Red Star. Close inspection shows that it was affixed to the lip of his jumper pocket. *Courtesy of the Schilbe family.*

Chapter 16

Pension for Award Recipients

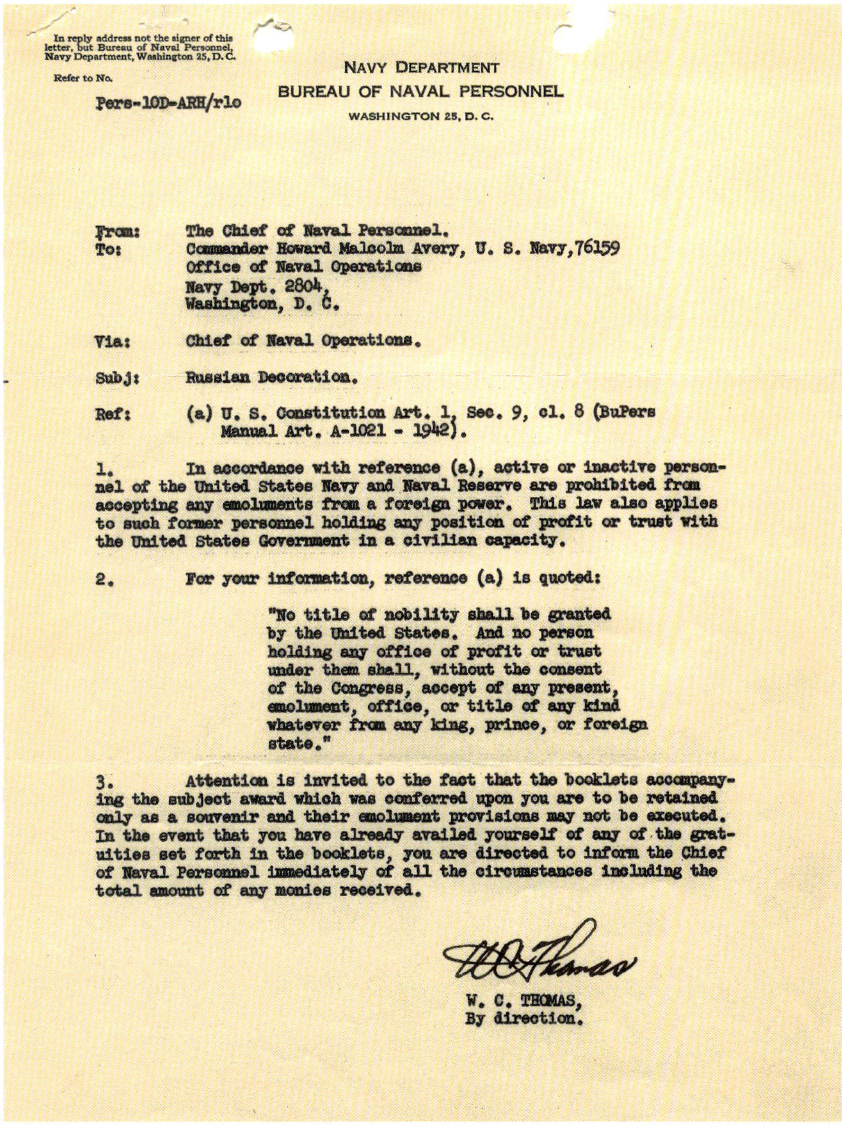

In reply address not the signer of this letter, but Bureau of Naval Personnel, Navy Department, Washington 25, D.C.

Refer to No.

Pers-10D-ARH/rlo

NAVY DEPARTMENT
BUREAU OF NAVAL PERSONNEL
WASHINGTON 25, D. C.

From: The Chief of Naval Personnel.
To: Commander Howard Malcolm Avery, U. S. Navy,76159
Office of Naval Operations
Navy Dept. 2804,
Washington, D. C.

Via: Chief of Naval Operations.

Subj: Russian Decoration.

Ref: (a) U. S. Constitution Art. 1, Sec. 9, cl. 8 (BuPers Manual Art. A-1021 - 1942).

1. In accordance with reference (a), active or inactive personnel of the United States Navy and Naval Reserve are prohibited from accepting any emoluments from a foreign power. This law also applies to such former personnel holding any position of profit or trust with the United States Government in a civilian capacity.

2. For your information, reference (a) is quoted:

> "No title of nobility shall be granted by the United States. And no person holding any office of profit or trust under them shall, without the consent of the Congress, accept of any present, emolument, office, or title of any kind whatever from any king, prince, or foreign state."

3. Attention is invited to the fact that the booklets accompanying the subject award which was conferred upon you are to be retained only as a souvenir and their emolument provisions may not be executed. In the event that you have already availed yourself of any of the gratuities set forth in the booklets, you are directed to inform the Chief of Naval Personnel immediately of all the circumstances including the total amount of any monies received.

W. C. THOMAS,
By direction.

The pension booklet was forwarded to the recipients "only as a souvenir" according to the letter that accompanied the document. Sent separately from the actual booklet, this letter may not have reached all of the recipients. *Courtesy of the Avery family.*

Along with the box containing the order or medal booklet and the pension booklet came a letter stating plainly that the monetary reward, as represented by the booklet of pension coupons, could not be accepted:

> *Your attention is invited to Article I, Section 9, Clause 8 of the United States Constitution which prohibits the acceptance of a monetary gratuity from a foreign government for service performed in the line of duty. Therefore, the booklets are forwarded merely as mementoes of the award.*

Despite the firmly worded letter, several recipients accepted the monetary reward from the USSR, as the Soviet government was willing to send the pensions to the recipients as per Soviet policy of the time. In the case of Sheldon Kinney, his family related that he had received the pension checks coincident with the documents. Knowing this was not correct, he returned the checks to the Embassy without accepting the money.[1] David Kellogg and Norman Hyams both accepted the pension, and were later written about by the Associated Press, appearing in newspapers across the country.[2] In contrast, Joseph Gillen and Harrison Smith accepted the pension but never gained notoriety from it. As fewer than half of the pension booklets bestowed on US Navy award recipients were viewed during the writing of this book, it is not fully known how many recipients accepted the pension in 1946 and 1947, but it can be assumed that it was not entirely uncommon.

Like Kellogg and Hyams, Morton Wolfson also made the papers for accepting the Soviet pension.[3] However, unlike his peers, he retained the correspondence regarding the pension, thus providing a rare look into the receipt of the monetary reward.

Wolfson had corresponded with the Soviet consulate several times following the receipt of his medal. The first time was to obtain lengths of ribbon for the medal so he could then wear the ribbon on his ribbon bars. (It can be assumed that, due to the number of photographs existing of the recipients wearing the corresponding ribbon on their ribbon bars, this was a common practice, as the ribbon material was not obtainable through military tailors in the United States.) The Soviets were happy to assist and provided him with several lengths of ribbon for his Order of the Patriotic War, First Class.[4]

Pension documents that were used were processed through the Consulate General of the USSR in New York. This booklet shows the recipient accepted payment for twenty-nine months. *Courtesy of the Joseph T. Gillen family.*

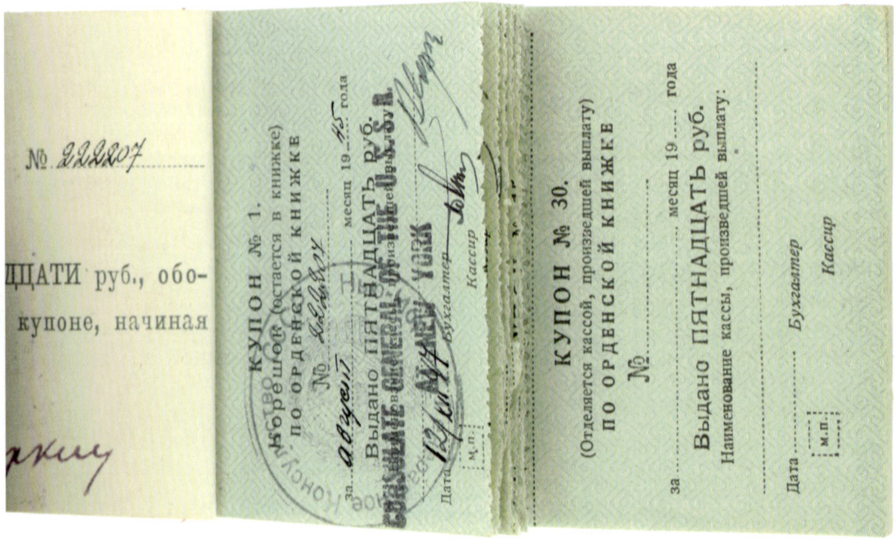

The pension could be redeemed at any Soviet consulate. David Kellogg, quite possibly the most well known recipient, received his pension from the Consulate General of the USSR in San Francisco. *Courtesy of Tom and Kathie Kellogg, Seattle, Washington.*

The second time was his request of the payment for his pension. Once again, the consulate was happy to oblige his request and in two separate transactions, sent him $476.17 (an average exchange rate of eighty-two-cents to the ruble) to satisfy his pension between August 1945 and December 1947.[5]

On December 12, 1947, he received a letter requesting confirmation by the Navy Department if he had indeed accepted this money. He replied in the affirmative that he had on December 18. A reply dated January 20, 1948, informed him that:

> *For your information, you are not the sole offender. I can also assure you that the Chief of Naval Personnel will do all in his power to render a favorable decision for you. In any case, he does not consider it to be a matter of discipline.*
>
> *The Judge Advocate General has given a decision that it is illegal for you to accept the money. However, there is now a question of ethics which will be determined. The determination of this question will be in the hands of the Department of State, and they will decide whether or not it will be ethical and/or practicable to refund to the Russian Government the monies collected by several Reserve officers. You will be notified as soon as a decision has been reached.*[6]

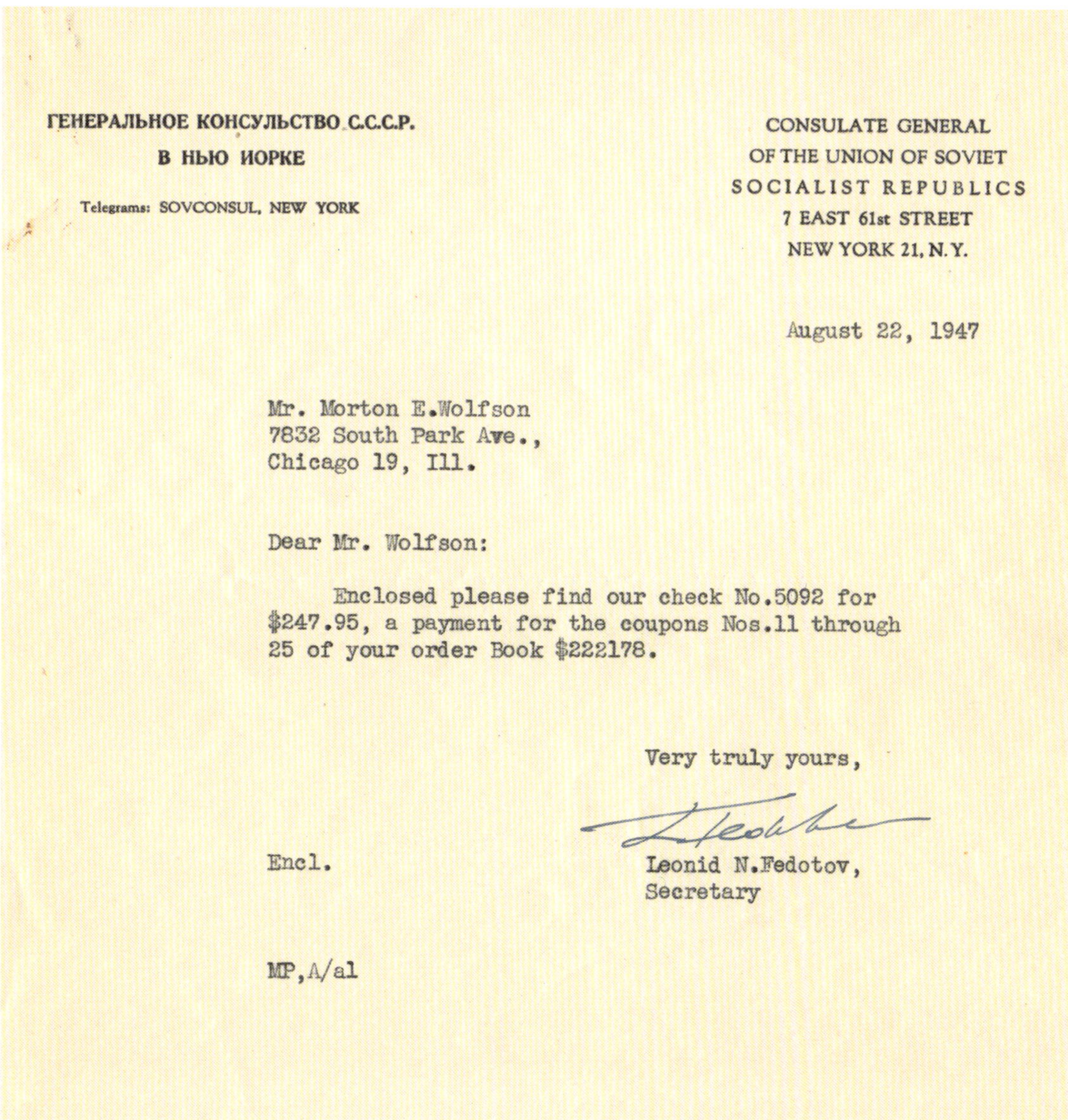

ГЕНЕРАЛЬНОЕ КОНСУЛЬСТВО С.С.С.Р.
В НЬЮ ИОРКЕ

Telegrams: SOVCONSUL, NEW YORK

CONSULATE GENERAL
OF THE UNION OF SOVIET
SOCIALIST REPUBLICS
7 EAST 61st STREET
NEW YORK 21, N.Y.

August 22, 1947

Mr. Morton E.Wolfson
7832 South Park Ave.,
Chicago 19, Ill.

Dear Mr. Wolfson:

Enclosed please find our check No.5092 for $247.95, a payment for the coupons Nos.11 through 25 of your order Book $222178.

Very truly yours,

Leonid N.Fedotov,
Secretary

Encl.

MP,A/al

The recipient was not required to be present to receive his pension. This letter accompanied the check for pension to Morton Wolfson from the Consulate in New York City. *Courtesy of the Morton E. Wolfson family.*

According to reporting at the time, it was later determined that officers of the Naval Reserve could retain their payments, whereas it was illegal for anyone remaining on active duty to keep any money received from the Soviet government.[7]

On September 10, 1947, a decree by the Presidium of the Supreme Soviet of the USSR eliminated the pensions and transportation privileges of medal recipients, effective January 1, 1948. The declaration stated that the Presidium had:

> *taken into consideration the many proposals of order and medal holders of the USSR regarding the abolition of monetary payments for orders and medals and several other exemptions granted the holders and regarding the directing of the funds released to the reconstruction and development of the national economy of the USSR.*[8]

Thus, as of January 1, 1948, any question regarding the continuing acceptance of the pension was no longer relevant; the pension no longer existed.

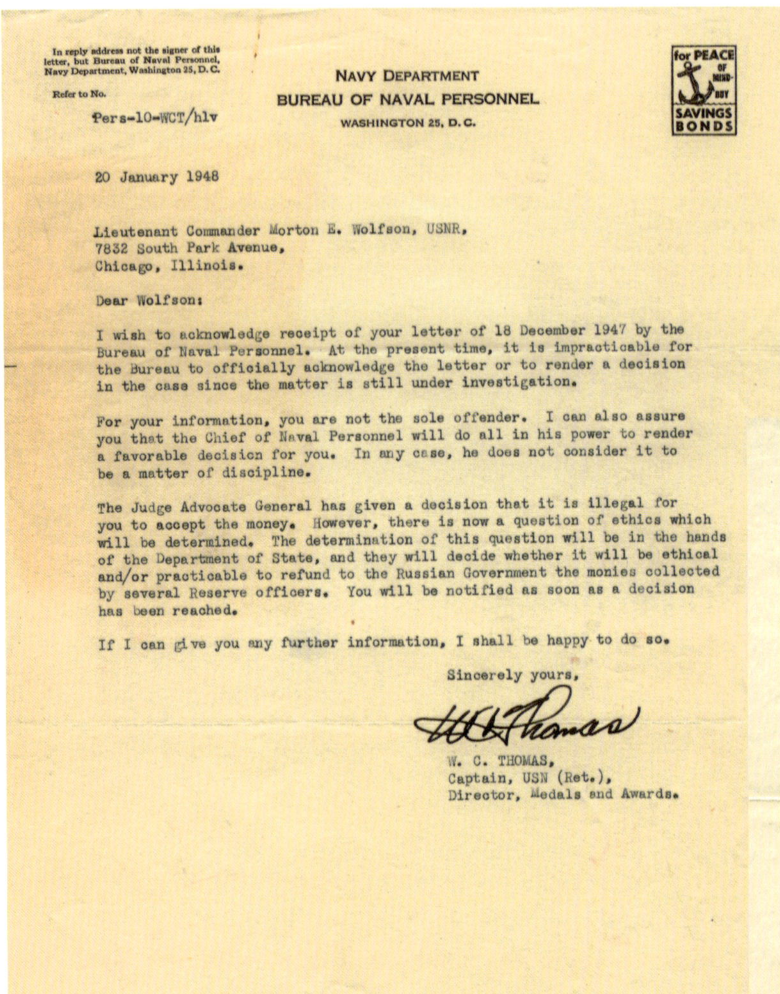

In reply address not the signer of this letter, but Bureau of Naval Personnel, Navy Department, Washington 25, D. C.

Refer to No.
Pers-10-WCT/hlv

NAVY DEPARTMENT
BUREAU OF NAVAL PERSONNEL
WASHINGTON 25, D. C.

for PEACE OF MIND BUY SAVINGS BONDS

20 January 1948

Lieutenant Commander Morton E. Wolfson, USNR,
7832 South Park Avenue,
Chicago, Illinois.

Dear Wolfson:

I wish to acknowledge receipt of your letter of 18 December 1947 by the Bureau of Naval Personnel. At the present time, it is impracticable for the Bureau to officially acknowledge the letter or to render a decision in the case since the matter is still under investigation.

For your information, you are not the sole offender. I can also assure you that the Chief of Naval Personnel will do all in his power to render a favorable decision for you. In any case, he does not consider it to be a matter of discipline.

The Judge Advocate General has given a decision that it is illegal for you to accept the money. However, there is now a question of ethics which will be determined. The determination of this question will be in the hands of the Department of State, and they will decide whether it will be ethical and/or practicable to refund to the Russian Government the monies collected by several Reserve officers. You will be notified as soon as a decision has been reached.

If I can give you any further information, I shall be happy to do so.

Sincerely yours,

W. C. THOMAS,
Captain, USN (Ret.),
Director, Medals and Awards.

Following the news coverage of the medal recipients receiving pensions from the Soviets, the Navy Department requested the amount of pension received from the Soviets by each recipient. This letter was the response to Morton Wolfson's acknowledgement of receiving the pension. *Courtesy of the Morton E. Wolfson family.*

As the Merchant Marine recipients were allowed to receive the pension, they continued to do so until the pension was discontinued for all medal recipients by the Presidium of the Supreme Soviet on January 1, 1948. *Courtesy of Don and Donna Breen.*

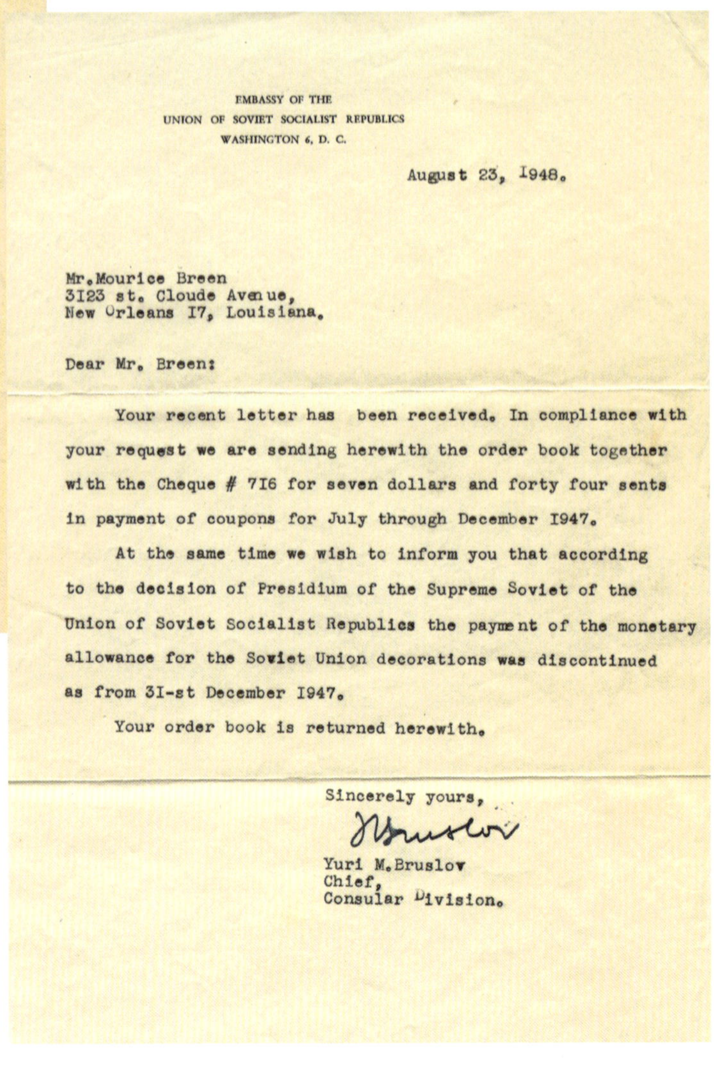

EMBASSY OF THE
UNION OF SOVIET SOCIALIST REPUBLICS
WASHINGTON 6, D. C.

August 23, 1948.

Mr. Mourice Breen
3123 st. Cloude Avenue,
New Orleans 17, Louisiana.

Dear Mr. Breen:

Your recent letter has been received. In compliance with your request we are sending herewith the order book together with the Cheque # 716 for seven dollars and forty four sents in payment of coupons for July through December 1947.

At the same time we wish to inform you that according to the decision of Presidium of the Supreme Soviet of the Union of Soviet Socialist Republics the payment of the monetary allowance for the Soviet Union decorations was discontinued as from 31-st December 1947.

Your order book is returned herewith.

Sincerely yours,

Yuri M. Bruslov
Chief,
Consular Division.

CHAPTER 17

THE COLD WAR EXPERIENCE AND OTHER AWARDS TO AMERICAN VETERANS

Edward Hoban wears his Medal "For Military Merit" at his change of command ceremony on October 5, 1962. Eight days later, the Cuban Missile Crisis began. *Courtesy of the Hoban family.*

The experience of Soviet medal recipients and the Cold War

George Roullard wears his Order of the Red Star ribbon (lowest right) on his uniform. This photo dates from the late-1940s, prior to his service in the Korean War. *Courtesy of the Roullard family.*

An oft-heard myth is that many of these awards were hidden away or destroyed during the McCarthy-era "Red Scare." Through this research, only three families reported that their relative actually discarded the medal due to potential political ramifications. Others refused to talk about it. The daughter of David Pickler recalled her father telling her in a very stern voice: "You will not say anything about the Red Star." He never gave any reasons, he simply ingrained in them that it would be a "horrible embarrassment" to the family if anyone found out. It was only when she was about fifteen that he took her to the bank deposit box and showed her the medal, treating it as if it was "poisonous."[1]

In the main, however, there is no evidence to suggest recipients of Soviet medals during the Second World War were in any way overtly prejudiced against during the decades after the war.

In the case of John McNaughton, who rose to high political prominence on the national scale during the years of the Kennedy and Johnson presidential administrations, several thorough FBI interviews were conducted to grant his security clearance. A Freedom of Information Act (FOIA) request for his FBI interviews brought forward several comments about his Soviet medal. In a memo dated November 25, 1964, from Special Agent Marcus E. Sharpe, mentioned that somebody (name redacted) recalled McNaughton:

> *... then served in the United States Navy and recalls that he read write-ups in the local press regarding his experiences as the Commander of a destroyer escort in the United States Navy during World War II. He recalled that one of the stories printed about his experience during World War II had to do, if he recalled correctly, with his being a gun captain on a destroyer escort on the Murmansk Run. He recalled this story had to do with his bringing in his ship after it had been torpedoed. He stated if he recalled correctly that John T. McNaughton was the recipient of a citation or decoration not only by the United States Government but also by the Government of Russia in regards to his experiences.*[2]

John McNaughton made no effort to hide his award. Special Agent Sharpe recorded in the transcripts of his interview:

> *He* [McNaughton] *indicated he had been in the United States Navy serving from July 29, 1942 to April 12, 1946, that he was separated from the United States Navy as a Lieutenant serving under Serial No.178433. He indicated that he was on the Murmansk Convoy Run and that due to his service in the United States Navy on a destroyer escort that he had received a letter of commendation from the Secretary of the Navy Frank Knox and had also been awarded the Order of the Fatherland by the Russian Government.*[3]

Despite McNaughton's open remarks about his Order of the Patriotic War, he was still granted his clearance and went on to have a remarkably successful career in Washington, DC before his untimely death. From these excerpts, as well as from the images of the ribbons for the awards being worn in photographs of recipients throughout the book, it can be safely surmised that most "ordinary" recipients were rarely troubled or harassed about their awards by the US government during the Cold War.

While in Alaska toward the end of his career, George Roullard can be seen wearing his Order of the Red Star on the right lapel of his uniform at a formal function. *Courtesy of the Roullard family.*

Leonard Harmon's ribbon bar. He continued to wear the ribbon for his Order of Glory, Third Class, throughout his career.

Other medals bestowed by the Russian and Soviet governments

A note should be made here about the awarding of other Soviet medals during the Second World War. Coincident to the approval of these awards early in the summer of 1945, numerous other Soviet decorations were bestowed in the field where US Army and Soviet forces met in Europe. These awards, sadly, were not documented by either the War or State Department to a large measure and the records are thus extremely incomplete. The final awards bestowed by the Soviets on Americans were officially approved on January 21, 1947, when eighty-seven US Army personnel received orders and medals, bestowed in a ceremony that took place on March 12, 1947:

> *In connection with the successful completion of operations against the common enemy – Hitlerite Germany – and the valor and gallantry displayed, as well as the organization and successful execution of work of transporting military supplies from the United States to the Soviet Union.*[4]

Due to the commencement of the Cold War, no further military orders or medals for meritorious service or heroism were known to have been bestowed for the next forty-five years. However, starting in 1985, all veterans of the Murmansk Run, as well as the other recipients of Soviet medals, were allowed to receive the Soviet commemorative medal "40 Years of Victory in the Patriotic War." The same process took place for subsequent commemorative medals, including the medals "50 Years of Victory" and "60 Years of Victory" in 1995 and 2005, respectively.

Order of the Patriotic War, Second Class, number 369802, awarded May 14, 1945, by General Lieutenant Zakhvataev, Commander, 4th Guards Army, to Colonel Oscar W. Koch, US Army. Colonel Koch was General Patton's intelligence officer (G-2) in Africa and Europe.

Norman Hyams' "Forty Years" medal in the case of issue. *Courtesy of the Hyams family.*

The medal "Forty Years of Victory in the Patriotic War" awarded to Norman Hyams. Interestingly, it is not the version of the award intended for issue to foreign recipients. *Courtesy of the Hyams family.*

„СОРОК ЛЕТ ПОБЕДЫ
В ВЕЛИКОЙ ОТЕЧЕСТВЕННОЙ ВОЙНЕ
1941—1945 гг."

УДОСТОВЕРЕНИЕ

Норман И.
Хиамс

ВРУЧЕНА ЮБИЛЕЙНАЯ МЕДАЛЬ

„СОРОК ЛЕТ ПОБЕДЫ
В ВЕЛИКОЙ ОТЕЧЕСТВЕННОЙ
ВОЙНЕ 1941—1945 гг."

М.П.

Президент
Российской Федерации

„15" ноября 1993 года

The document for the medal "Forty Years of Victory in the Patriotic War 1941-1945" (1985) awarded to Norman Hyams. Note that that he received this medal eight years after it was authorized. *Courtesy of the Hyams family.*

Following the end of the Cold War and the fall of the Soviet Union, relations between the former Allied nations normalized and for the first time since 1947, personal military decorations were awarded to veterans of the Second World War for their part in aiding the Russians toward victory over Nazi Germany. On April 27, 2012, 190 Medals of Ushakov were awarded by the government of the Russian Federation to the Allied veterans of the Arctic convoys in a gesture of appreciation and goodwill, acknowledging the sacrifice and heroism exhibited so many decades before. Due to the combined list of Allied recipients, consisting of veterans from Australia, New Zealand, and the United States, the exact number awarded to Americans is not known.

One of the recipients was John Haynes, a gunner on the SS *Eldena* during convoy PQ-13, under the command of Frederick Fink. As with most of his peers, his first trip to the USSR was his last; he volunteered for flight duty shortly after his return. Later selected for flight training, he was a qualified Naval Aviator by the time the war ended. Remaining a Naval Reservist, he retired as a lieutenant commander in July 1965. As a civilian, he traveled around the world as a pilot and manager for the Federal Aviation Administration, building an amazing biography that would only be fitting for someone who survived the horrors of the journey to the USSR above the Arctic Circle.

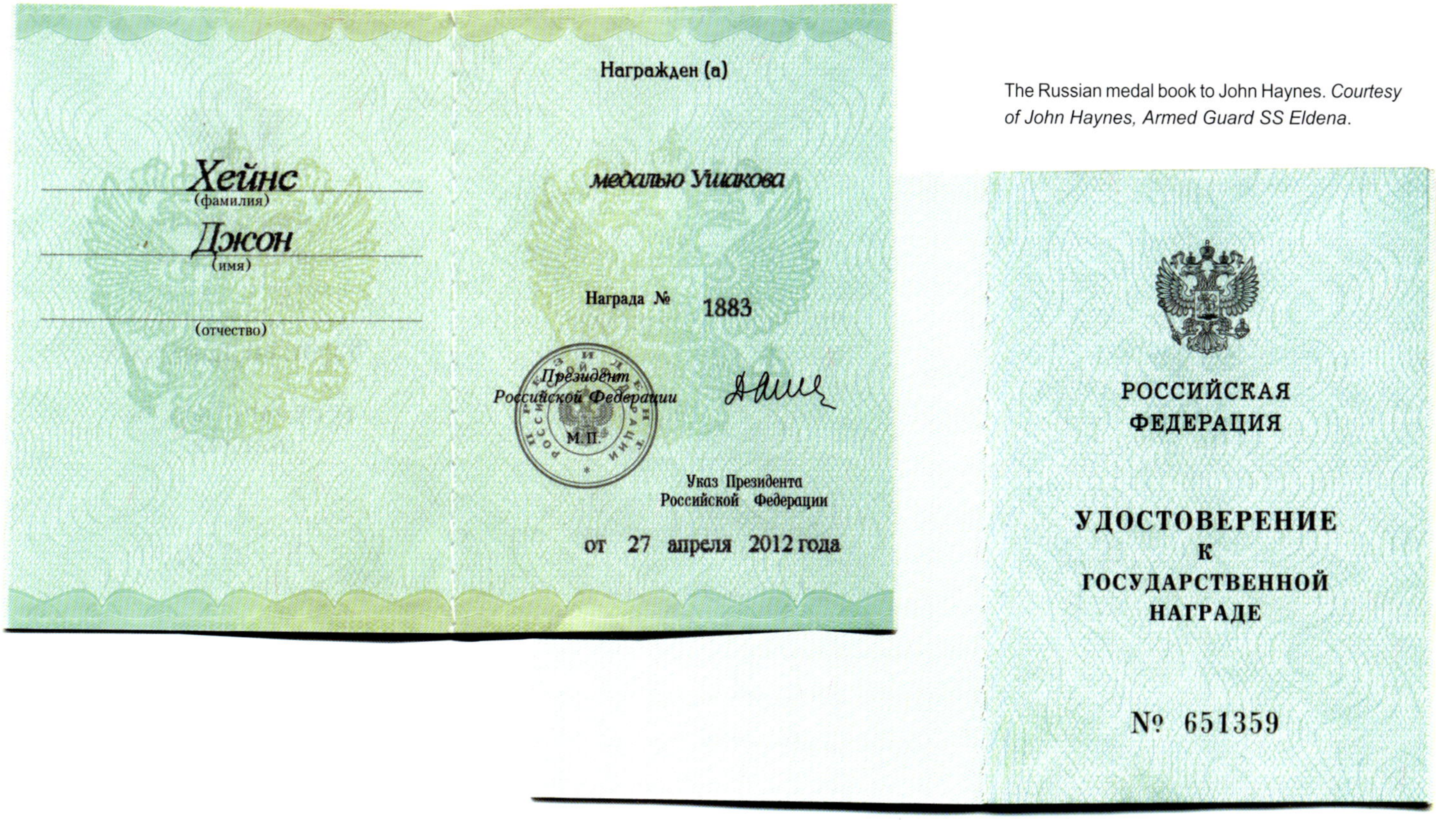
Награжден (а)

Хейнс
(фамилия)
Джон
(имя)
(отчество)

медалью Ушакова

Награда № 1883

Президент
Российской Федерации
М.П.

Указ Президента
Российской Федерации
от 27 апреля 2012 года

РОССИЙСКАЯ
ФЕДЕРАЦИЯ

УДОСТОВЕРЕНИЕ
К
ГОСУДАРСТВЕННОЙ
НАГРАДЕ

№ 651359

The Russian medal book to John Haynes. *Courtesy of John Haynes, Armed Guard SS Eldena.*

Medal of Ushakov number 1883 awarded to John Haynes. *Courtesy of John Haynes, Armed Guard SS Eldena.*

APPENDICES

APPENDIX 1

ALPHABETICAL CITATIONS FOR SOVIET MEDAL RECIPIENTS[1]

Abbott, William Robert, *Medal of Ushakov*
As a member of the US Navy Armed Guard crew aboard a US merchant vessel operating in the North Atlantic during a period of seven days of almost constant bombing, submarine and aerial torpedo attacks from an extraordinary number of enemy units, Boatswain's Mate Abbott contributed greatly by his remarkable endurance, capability and bravery to the completion of the voyage with its valuable cargo.

Adams, Norman Owens Whitehurst Jr., *Order of the Patriotic War, Second Class*
As commanding officer of a US Navy Armed Guard aboard a US merchant vessel operating in the North Atlantic, Ensign Adams successfully repulsed very severe enemy aerial attacks lasting for many days and enabled his ship to arrive safely in port without materiel damage.

Anderson, Edward Thomas, *Medal "For Military Merit"*
As member of the US Navy Armed Guard crew aboard a US merchant vessel operating in the North Atlantic which underwent numerous and violent attacks by enemy aircraft subjecting the vessel to continuous bomb fire, he contributed materially in the defense of his ship. In spite of physical exhaustion and intense eyestrain after twenty-eight hours at their gun stations, the crew kept up an anti-aircraft barrage that inflicted damage upon the enemy. However, in spite of their heroic defense, the vessel, seriously damaged by falling bombs, was sunk.

Anderson, Emmett Dotson, *Medal of Nakhimov*
As a member of the US Navy Armed Guard crew of a US merchant vessel operating in the North Atlantic when that vessel was attacked by enemy aircraft and became separated from the remainder of the convoy, he continued to man his gun until the vessel sank. Suffering from hunger and exposure, he was rescued from a lifeboat after ten days in the North Atlantic.

Anderson, Philip Randolph, *Order of Glory, Third Class*
As pilot of a US Navy patrol bomber in the face of heavy and accurate enemy gunfire that severely damaged his place, Ensign Anderson pressed home his attack and inflicted damage upon the enemy by strafing.

Adler, Arthur Leslie, *Medal of Nakhimov*
As petty officer of the US Navy Armed Guard crew of a US merchant vessel operating in the North Atlantic when the vessel to which he was attached was subjected to sustained attacks by enemy submarines, high level bombers and torpedo bombers, Boatswain's Mate Adler contributed materially to the defense of his vessel and to the destruction of several enemy planes. When the vessel was struck by aerial torpedoes and its ammunition exploded, he accomplished the successful abandonment of the rapidly sinking ship under most difficult conditions with a maximum of coolness and efficiency.

Andrews, Clyde Neil, *Order of the Red Star*
His ship, carrying vital war material to Russia, was without defense armament except for two .30 caliber machineguns mounted, without protective shielding, on the bridge. During six days of continuous attack, he manned one of these guns, and aided in successfully standing off numerous dive-bombing attacks. Subsequently, while homeward-bound his vessel was lost due to enemy action and while transferring the injured to the lifeboats he exhibited exceptional courage with complete disregard for his own safety.

Avery, Howard Malcolm, *Order of the Patriotic War, First Class*
As commanding officer of Composite Squadron Nine during the period September 24, 1943 to November 10, 1943, Lieutenant Commander Avery participated in a large number of attacks on enemy submarines, displaying unfailing high standards of aggressiveness, airmanship and personal bravery which resulted in the destruction of a number of submarines. Twice in the face of heavy anti-aircraft fire he was personally responsible for the destruction of an enemy submarine in the North Atlantic.

Balliett, Letson Samuel, *Order of the Red Star*
As pilot of a US Navy torpedo bombing plane operating in the North Atlantic, Lieutenant (jg) Balliett, in the face of enemy anti-aircraft gunfire, delivered successful bombing and strafing attacks against an enemy submarine, contributing greatly to the destruction of the enemy vessel.

Baughan, Robert Louis, *Order of the Patriotic War, Second Class*
As executive officer of a US destroyer operating in the North Atlantic, when the commanding officer was seriously wounded, assumed command and continued effective gunfire against an enemy submarine until the enemy vessel was abandoned by its crew and sank.

Billings, Roy Murray, *Order of the Patriotic War, First Class*
As commander of a United States Navy Armed Guard crew on board a US merchant ship operating in the North Atlantic from September 13 to 21, 1942, Ensign Billings, with dauntless courage and marked ability and with the ship rocked by explosion, bulkheads blown down and smashed and otherwise seriously damaged, remained at his station with his crew and successfully defended the vessel against heavy enemy submarine and air attack.

Biggs, Donald Sherman, *Medal "For Military Merit"*
As a member of the US Navy Armed Guard crew of a US merchant vessel operating in the North Atlantic when the vessel sustained numerous submarine and aircraft attacks, Seaman Biggs, despite direct exposure to enemy strafing, remained at his station and shot down the enemy plane, thus contributing individually to the successful completion of the voyage of this vessel.

Blake, Renald Henry Jr., *Medal "For Valor"*
As a member of the US Navy Armed Guard crew of a US merchant vessel operating in the North Atlantic when heavily attacked upon numerous occasions by enemy aircraft, Gunner's Mate Blake successfully defended his ship, contributing to the successful completion of her voyage.

Bloch, Jules Hirsch, *Order of the Patriotic War, First Class*
As commanding officer of a US Navy Armed Guard aboard a US merchant vessel operating in the North Atlantic, Ensign Bloch successfully repulsed enemy air attack for many days, thereby enabling his ship to arrive safely in port without damage.

Boucher, Ralph Emerson, *Order of the Patriotic War, First Class*
Exhibited courage and heroism in command of the US Navy Armed Guard unit serving on board a US merchant ship engaged in transporting military equipment to the ports of Northern Russia.

Bourg, Eli Philip, *Medal "For Military Merit"*
As member of the US Navy Armed Guard crew aboard a US merchant vessel operating in the North Atlantic which underwent numerous and violent attacks by enemy aircraft subjecting the vessel to continuous bomb fire, he contributed materially in the defense of his ship. In spite of physical exhaustion and intense eyestrain after twenty-eight hours at their gun stations, the crew kept up an anti-aircraft barrage that inflicted damage upon the enemy. However, in spite of their heroic defense, the vessel, seriously damaged by falling bombs, was sunk.

Brinn, Rufus Timothy, *Order of the Red Star*
Exhibited courage and heroism in command of the US Navy Armed Guard unit serving on board a US merchant ship engaged in transporting military equipment to the ports of Northern Russia.

Breen, Maurice Jr., Merchant Marine, *Order of the Red Star*
Early in the war, his unarmed ship was in a British port when ordered to join a convoy to Russia. Two fifty caliber machine guns were mounted on the bridge and Breen, with only two days of training, volunteered to man one of these guns, although his duty as Pursuer did not require him to be above deck during enemy attacks. He serviced his gun throughout a six days running battle with enemy submarines, bombing planes, and torpedo planes. During the course of this prolonged action, he aided materially in standing off repeated attacks and alone succeeded in bringing down an enemy two-motored bomber.

Brokas, Alex Xavier, *Order of Glory, Third Class*
As pilot of a US Navy torpedo bomber in the North Atlantic during a period of intensive aerial anti-submarine operations under generally unfavorable weather conditions, Lieutenant (jg) Brokas successfully pioneered night escort carrier aircraft operations in the Atlantic. Upon one occasion, in spite of heavy anti-aircraft fire, he launched a combined projectile and depth bomb attack that severely damaged an enemy submarine.

Brown, Philip Bausche, *Order of the Patriotic War, Second Class*
As executive officer of a US destroyer operating in the North Atlantic, Lieutenant Brown assisted his commanding officer in a long, drawn out action with an enemy submarine. He personally manned a machine gun and, in the face of heavy enemy counter-fire at short range, assisted in clearing exposed personnel from the deck of the submarine.

Brown, Thomas Edward, *Medal "For Military Merit"*
As member of the US Navy Armed Guard crew aboard a US merchant vessel operating in the North Atlantic which underwent numerous and violent attacks by enemy aircraft subjecting the vessel to continuous bomb fire, he contributed materially in the defense of his ship. In spite of physical exhaustion and intense eyestrain after twenty-eight hours at their gun stations, the crew kept up an anti-aircraft barrage that inflicted damage upon the enemy. However, in spite of their heroic defense, the vessel, seriously damaged by falling bombs, was sunk.

Brown, Willard Wilkins, *Order of the Patriotic War, First Class*
As commanding officer of a United States Navy Armed Guard aboard a US merchant vessel operating in the North Atlantic, Lieutenant Brown by his courage and tenacious devotion to duty, successfully defended the merchant vessel against numerous and vicious enemy air and submarine attacks which enabled the vessel to survive the hazardous voyage with negligible damage.

Buckbee, Robert Edward, *Order of the Red Star*
As commanding officer of a US Navy Armed Guard aboard a US merchant vessel operating in the North Atlantic, when the ship was badly damaged by the enemy, Lieutenant Buckbee remained aboard with certain members of his crew and successfully protected the vessel during salvage operations against enemy air attack in spite of prevailing bad weather, thus enabling the ship to be saved.

Carraway, Howard Ernest, *Order of the Red Star*
As commanding officer of a US Navy Armed Guard aboard a US merchant vessel operating in the North Atlantic, Ensign Carraway successfully defended the ship to which he was attached through a prolonged period of constant submarine and air attack by enemy forced, enabling her to safely complete her voyage.

Carter, William Allen, *Order of the Patriotic War, First Class*
As commanding officer of a United States Navy Armed Guard aboard a US merchant vessel, Lieutenant (jg) Carter succeeded in repeatedly driving off enemy air attacks and, in spite of faulty operation of guns due to continuous dense fog and damp weather, successfully defended his vessel, enabling her to complete her voyage in the North Atlantic.

Casey, Milton Clayton, *Medal "For Military Merit"*
As member of the US Navy Armed Guard crew aboard a US merchant vessel operating in the North Atlantic which underwent numerous and violent attacks by enemy aircraft subjecting the vessel to continuous bomb fire, he contributed materially in the defense of his ship. In spite of physical exhaustion and intense eyestrain after twenty-eight hours at their gun stations, the crew kept up an anti-aircraft barrage that inflicted damage upon the enemy. However, in spite of their heroic defense, the vessel, seriously damaged by falling bombs, was sunk.

Cassidy, Oswald Irvin, *Medal "For Valor"*
As a member of the US Navy Armed Guard crew of a US merchant vessel operating in the North Atlantic that was subjected for a continuous period of six days to enemy aerial and torpedo attacks, he contributed materially to the defense of his ship. Upon one occasion the ship was separated from the convoy and was struck below the waterline by a torpedo that failed to explode. Through the efforts of the gun crew, all attacks were successfully repulsed, serious damage inflicted upon the attackers, and the ship was enabled to successfully complete her voyage.

Chatterton, Joseph John Jr., *Order of Glory, Third Class*
As a member of a US Navy Armed Guard crew of a US merchant vessel operating in the North Atlantic, Boatswain's Mate, second class Joseph John Chatterton, Jr. and the fellow members of his crew participated in a running battle for over four days against persistent raids by a number of enemy submarines. Upon the eventual sinking of the vessel to which he was attached, he abandoned ship only after operation of his guns became impossible and he exhibited heroic courage during four exhausting days in the cold, heavy seas of the North Atlantic until finally rescued from a life raft.

Church, John Howard, Jr., *Order of the Patriotic War, Second Class*
As commanding officer of a US destroyer escort operating in the North Atlantic as part of a task force, Lieutenant Commander Church entered into a heavy concentration of enemy U-boats, resulting in the probable destruction of an enemy submarine.

Cole, William, *Order of Glory, Third Class*
As pilot of a severely damaged plane operating in the North Atlantic, Lieutenant Cole exhibited extraordinary airmanship and unusual skill in flying his plane through 240 miles of hazardous conditions in order to bring his wounded crew within safe reach of medical attention rather than bail out over the sea.

Cooper, George Clifford, *Medal of Nakhimov*
As a member of the US Navy Armed Guard crew of a US merchant vessel operating in the North Atlantic when that vessel was attacked by enemy aircraft and became separated from the remainder of the convoy, he continued to man his gun until the vessel sank. Suffering from hunger and exposure, he was rescued from a lifeboat after ten days in the North Atlantic.

Corbus, John, *Order of the Patriotic War, First Class*
As commanding officer of a United States submarine, Commander Corbus overcame tactical disadvantage and, notwithstanding the danger inherent in the situation, attacked and probably sank an enemy submarine in the North Atlantic.

Collins, Wilbur Plummer, *Order of the Patriotic War, First Class*
As commanding officer of a US Navy Armed Guard aboard a US merchant vessel operating in the North Atlantic, Ensign Collins successfully defended his ship from a series of low-level dive-bombing and strafing attacks while lying in anchor in a foreign port in the North Atlantic.

Cram, Kendall Hutchinson, *Order of the Patriotic War, First Class*
As commanding officer of a US Navy Armed Guard aboard a US merchant vessel operating in the North Atlantic, upon the occasion of the sinking of that vessel by a surprise enemy submarine attack, Ensign Cram remained at his station and manned his guns despite the order "Abandon Ship," leaving only after all opportunity to counterfire had passed and after saving the lives of two members of his crew.

Currant, John Howard, *Order of Glory, Third Class*
As petty officer in charge of the Armed Guard crew aboard a US merchantman operating in the North Atlantic, Coxswain Currant successfully defended the vessel to which he was attached through an extraordinary number of attacks by enemy submarine and repeated waves of bombers and torpedo planes, thus enabling his ship to safely reach port and discharge her cargo.

Daley, Walter Roche, *Order of the Patriotic War, Second Class*
As commanding officer of a US Navy Armed Guard aboard a US merchant vessel operating in the North Atlantic under repeated and heavy aerial bombing by enemy forced and extremely adverse weather conditions, Lieutenant Daley successfully defended the vessel to which he was attached.

Davis, Lowell Levon, *Order of Glory, Third Class*
As pilot of a Navy patrol plane operating in the North Atlantic when sighting an enemy submarine on the surface, Lieutenant Davis successfully attacked through enemy anti-aircraft fire with the result that the enemy submarine was badly damaged and probably sunk.

DeBaun, Garnett Curry, *Order of Glory, Third Class*
As a member of the US Navy Armed Guard crew of a US merchantman operating in the North Atlantic upon the occasion of the torpedoing and sinking of that vessel, Seaman DeBaun, with utter disregard for his own safety, remained aboard the rapidly sinking ship to assist a wounded shipmate, both of them being eventually picked up by a rescue vessel.

DeCottes, Eaton Pleasants, *Medal "For Military Merit"*
As member of the US Navy Armed Guard crew aboard a US merchant vessel operating in the North Atlantic, he contributed greatly to the defense of his ship during numerous attacks by enemy aircraft and submarines. The courageous and efficient defense of the vessel contributed greatly to the successful completion of an extremely important mission.

DeGennaro, Louis, *Order of Glory, Third Class*
As a member of the US Navy Armed Guard crew of a US merchant vessel operating in the North Atlantic upon the occasion of the torpedoing and sinking of that vessel, although himself wounded, Seaman DeGennaro remained behind to assist a wounded comrade, both of whom were eventually picked up by a life raft.

Delate, Thomas Edward, *Order of the Red Star*
As commanding officer of a US Navy Armed Guard aboard a US merchant vessel after the ship had been severely damaged while discharging cargo in a northern foreign port, Lieutenant Delate successfully defended his ship against repeated heavy enemy air attack and assisted materially in the defense of the port, thus enabling his ship to be repaired and complete her voyage.

Delhom, James Joseph, *Order of Glory, Third Class*
As co-pilot of a US Navy bombing plane, Lieutenant (jg) Delhom attacked a surfaced submarine in the face of heavy enemy anti-aircraft fire. Although explosion of shells disrupted the bomb release system, repeated attacks were made with the damaged plane in the face of withering enemy fire and without regard for personal safety.

Desgalier, Marcel Jr., *Order of the Patriotic War, Second Class*
As commanding officer of a US Navy Armed Guard aboard a US merchant vessel operating in the North Atlantic, when subjected to numerous severe enemy air attacks, Ensign Desgalier successfully defended his vessel, enabling her to return to port without material damage.

Dixon, Thomas Jackson, *Medal "For Military Merit"*
As member of the US Navy Armed Guard crew aboard a US merchant vessel operating in the North Atlantic, he contributed greatly to the defense of his ship during numerous attacks by enemy aircraft and submarines. The courageous and efficient defense of the vessel contributed greatly to the successful completion of an extremely important mission.

Dole, Charles Everett, *Medal "For Valor"*
As a member of the US Navy Armed Guard crew of a US merchant vessel operating in the North Atlantic upon two occasions, while subjected to heavy enemy and torpedo attack, Boatswain's Mate Dole aided in the successful defense of his ship, thus contributing to the successful completion of her voyage.

Duncan, Francis Lee, *Medal "For Military Merit"*
As member of the US Navy Armed Guard crew aboard a US merchant vessel operating in the North Atlantic which underwent numerous and violent attacks by enemy aircraft subjecting the vessel to continuous bomb fire, he contributed materially in the defense of his ship. In spite of physical exhaustion and intense eyestrain after twenty-eight hours at their gun stations, the crew kept up an anti-aircraft barrage that inflicted damage upon the enemy. However, in spite of their heroic defense, the vessel, seriously damaged by falling bombs, was sunk.

Dyer, Bradford Mayo, *Order of Glory, Third Class*
As second pilot of a US Navy plane operating in the North Atlantic, although wounded, Ensign Dyer remained in the second pilot's seat and assisted the pilot during long and exhausting flight to near land. After a landing at sea, he displayed heroism in assisting to rescue the remainder of the crew.

Enloe, George Albert, *Order of Glory, Third Class*
As pilot of a US Navy patrol bomber plane when a fully surfaced enemy submarine was sighted, Lieutenant Enloe attacked through heavy enemy gunfire with the result that the submarine was probably sunk during these repeated attacks.

Farmer, Arthur Latney, *Order of Glory, Third Class*
As a member of the US Navy Armed Guard aboard a US merchant vessel operating in the North Atlantic, Coxswain Farmer courageously manned his gun during persistent raids and assisted materially in the maintenance of timely and effective fire against overwhelming odds.

Farrar, William Hunter, *Order of the Red Star*
As commanding officer of a US Navy Armed Guard aboard a US merchant vessel operating in the North Atlantic, after having led his crew valiantly when subjected to violent submarine and air attack, Ensign Farrar displayed heroism in the rescue operations when his ship was torpedoed and sunk.

Fetherston, Edward Michael, *Order of the Red Star*
His ship, carrying vital war material to Russia, was without defense armament except for two thirty-caliber machine guns mounted, without protective shielding, on the bridge. During six days of continuous attack, he manned one of these guns, and aided in successfully standing off numerous dive-bombing attacks. Subsequently, while homeward-bound his vessel was lost due to enemy action. In abandoning ship he exhibited exceptional courage with complete disregard for his own safety and personally rescued an injured and helpless fireman.

Fink, Frederick Strong, *Order of the Patriotic War, First Class*
As commanding officer of a US Navy Armed Guard aboard a US merchant vessel, Ensign Fink fought off numerous attacks from airplanes, surface ships and submarines while underway in the North Atlantic and, in addition, successfully defended his ship against severe bombing attacks while in port.

Forney, Junior Clyde, *Order of Glory, Third Class*
As pilot of a US Navy bombing plane when an enemy submarine was sighted upon the surface, Lieutenant Forney pressed home his attack in the face of heavy enemy anti-aircraft fire and contributed greatly to the destruction of the enemy submarine.

Fowler, Wilma Sim, *Order of the Red Star*
As pilot of a US Navy torpedo bomber plane, Lieutenant Fowler sighted two enemy submarines on the surface and, in spite of heavy anti-aircraft fire, made an extremely accurate bombing attack that contributed materially to the probable sinking of the enemy vessel in the North Atlantic.

Friday, Albert DeLloyd, *Medal of Nakhimov*
As a member of the US Navy Armed Guard crew of a US merchant vessel operating in the North Atlantic when that vessel was attacked by enemy aircraft and became separated from the remainder of the convoy, he continued to man his gun until the vessel sank. Suffering from hunger and exposure, he was rescued from a lifeboat after ten days in the North Atlantic.

Gallegos, Faustin, *Order of Glory, Third Class*
As member of a US Armed Guard crew on board a US merchant vessel operating in the North Atlantic upon the occasion of the torpedoing and sinking of that vessel, Seaman Gallegos rendered valuable assistance in picking up survivors and assisting them to board another vessel. Upon the torpedoing of the second vessel nineteen hours later, he again rendered heroic service in the assisting of rescue of survivors.

Gannon, John Walter, *Medal "For Military Merit"*
As member of the US Navy Armed Guard crew aboard a US merchant vessel operating in the North Atlantic which underwent numerous and violent attacks by enemy aircraft subjecting the vessel to continuous bomb fire, he contributed materially in the defense of his ship. In spite of physical exhaustion and intense eyestrain after twenty-eight hours at their gun stations, the crew kept up an anti-aircraft barrage that inflicted damage upon the enemy. However, in spite of their heroic defense, the vessel, seriously damaged by falling bombs, was sunk.

Gay, Frank C., *Medal of Nakhimov*
As a member of the US Navy Armed Guard crew of a US merchant vessel operating in the North Atlantic when that vessel was attacked by enemy aircraft and became separated from the remainder of the convoy, he continued to man his gun until the vessel sank. Suffering from hunger and exposure, he was rescued from a lifeboat after ten days in the North Atlantic.

Gemmer, Ward Leverne, *Order of the Patriotic War, Second Class*
Exhibited courage and heroism as a member of a US Navy Armed Guard unit serving on board a US merchant ship engaged in transporting military equipment to the ports of Northern Russia.

Giffen, Robert Carlisle, *Order of Suvorov, Second Class*
Senior US Naval officer operating with the British Home Fleet and who was charged with preparations for and operated in connection with North Russian convoys.

Gillen, Joseph Thomas, *Order of the Patriotic War, Second Class*
As commanding officer of a US Navy Armed Guard aboard a US merchant vessel operating in the North Atlantic, although subjected to heavy enemy submarine and air attacks, Ensign Gillen successfully defended his vessel enabling her to return to port without damage.

Gillette, Norman Campbell, *Order of Suvorov, Third Class*
Commanded a US cruiser that made an urgent trip to Murmansk through enemy infested waters to deliver especially important and greatly needed supplies.

Goddard, George Cecil, *Medal of Nakhimov*
As a member of the US Navy Armed Guard crew of a US merchant vessel operating in the North Atlantic when that vessel was attacked by enemy aircraft and became separated from the remainder of the convoy, he continued to man his gun until the vessel sank. Suffering from hunger and exposure, he was rescued from a lifeboat after ten days in the North Atlantic.

Gossman, Harry Madison, *Medal "For Valor"*
As a member of the US Navy Armed Guard crew of a US merchant vessel operating in the North Atlantic when subjected to a week of almost continuous assaults by enemy submarines, torpedo planes, and bombers, Coxswain Gossman participated in the successful defense of his ship. On one occasion, when the ship was temporarily disabled and separated from the convoy, it underwent several attacks which were successfully repulsed, thus enabling the vessel to reach her destination and discharge vital war cargo.

Graff, Cecil Billy, *Medal of Nakhimov*
As a member of the US Navy Armed Guard crew of a US merchant vessel operating in the North Atlantic when that vessel was attacked by enemy aircraft and became separated from the remainder of the convoy, he continued to man his gun until the vessel sank. Suffering from hunger and exposure, he was rescued from a lifeboat after ten days in the North Atlantic.

Grandey, Ernest Edwin Jr., *Medal "For Valor"*
As a member of the US Navy Armed Guard crew of a US merchant vessel operating in the North Atlantic that was subjected for a continuous period of six days to enemy aerial and torpedo attacks, he contributed materially to the defense of his ship. Upon one occasion the ship was separated from the convoy and was struck below the waterline by a torpedo that failed to explode. Through the efforts of the gun crew, all attacks were successfully repulsed, serious damage inflicted upon the attackers, and the ship was enabled to successfully complete her voyage.

Green, William Joseph, *Order of Glory, Third Class*
As a member of the forward engine room crew of a US destroyer in action against an enemy submarine in the North Atlantic when the forward engine room was hold and took water so rapidly as to endanger both the engine room and the ship, Chief Machinist Mate Green remained faithfully at his post, leaving his station only at the order of his superior officer and when it became apparent that the ship would sink.

Grotenrath, John Gellert Jr., *Order of the Red Star*
As commanding officer of a US Navy Armed Guard aboard a US merchant vessel operating in the North Atlantic, Lieutenant Grotenrath defended his vessel under almost continuous air attack for a period of four days, abandoning ship only after his vessel bad been so severely damaged that all hope of saving it had been lost.

Gudat, Walter John, *Order of the Patriotic War, Second Class*
As commanding officer of a US Navy Armed Guard aboard a US merchant vessel operating in the North Atlantic under heavy and almost continuous submarine and air attacks for many days, Ensign Gudat successfully defended his vessel and inflicted serious damage upon the enemy.

Guyton, James Nathan, Jr., *Medal of Nakhimov*
As a member of the US Navy Armed Guard crew of a US merchant vessel operating in the North Atlantic when that vessel was attacked by enemy aircraft and became separated from the remainder of the convoy, he continued to man his gun until the vessel sank. Suffering from hunger and exposure, he was rescued from a lifeboat after ten days in the North Atlantic.

Hall, Leland, *Medal "For Valor"*
As a member of the US Navy Armed Guard crew of a US merchant vessel operating in the North Atlantic that was subjected for a continuous period of six days to enemy aerial and torpedo attacks, he contributed materially to the defense of his ship. Upon one occasion the ship was separated from the convoy and was struck below the waterline by a torpedo that failed to explode. Through the efforts of the gun crew, all attacks were successfully repulsed, serious damage inflicted upon the attackers, and the ship was enabled to successfully complete her voyage.

Handshuh, Harold Leo, *Order of Glory, Third Class*
As pilot of a US Navy fighter plane in offensive action against an enemy submarine in the North Atlantic, Ensign Handshuh made successful strafing attacks against two enemy surfaced vessels, in spite of heavy anti-aircraft fire, scoring many hits and contributing largely to the probable sinking of the submarine.

Harkins, William Thomas, *Medal of Nakhimov*
As a member of the US Navy Armed Guard crew of a US merchant vessel operating in the North Atlantic when that vessel was attacked by enemy aircraft and became separated from the remainder of the convoy, he continued to man his gun until the vessel sank. Suffering from hunger and exposure, he was rescued from a lifeboat after ten days in the North Atlantic.

Harmon, John Henry, *Medal of Nakhimov*
As a member of the US Navy Armed Guard crew of a US merchant vessel operating in the North Atlantic when that vessel was attacked by enemy aircraft and became separated from the remainder of the convoy, he continued to man his gun until the vessel sank. Suffering from hunger and exposure, he was rescued from a lifeboat after ten days in the North Atlantic.

Harmon, Leonard Edward, *Order of Glory, Third Class*
As pilot of a US Navy bombing plane operating in the North Atlantic, Lieutenant Harmon successfully attacked a surfaced enemy submarine in the face of heavy enemy fire, making repeated attacks with his damaged plane without regard for personal stafety.

Harris, Charles Clayton, *Medal "For Valor"*
As a member of the US Navy Armed Guard crew of a US merchant vessel operating in the North Atlantic that was subjected for a continuous period of six days to enemy aerial and torpedo attacks, he contributed materially to the defense of his ship. Upon one occasion the ship was separated from the convoy and was struck below the waterline by a torpedo that failed to explode. Through the efforts of the gun crew, all attacks were successfully repulsed, serious damage inflicted upon the attackers, and the ship was enabled to successfully complete her voyage.

Harshaw, John Harrison, *Order of the Patriotic War, Second Class*
As a member of the US Navy Armed Guard crew on board a US merchant vessel operating in the North Atlantic while his ship was subjected to numerous severe enemy air and submarine attacks necessitating manning stations through eight days of continuous alerts, Chief Boatswain Harshaw successfully conducted his gunfire in a manner which enabled the ship to which he was attached to reach its destination without damage.

Hay, Sidney Miller, *Order of the Patriotic War, Second Class*
As commanding officer of a US destroyer escort operating in the North Atlantic. When a tanker in convoy was torpedoed, Lieutenant Commander Hay proceeded to the scene of the attack and, with depth charges, forced the enemy vessel to the surface, took it under highly effective and accurate gunfire, participating in a series of attacks that resulted in the destruction of an enemy submarine.

Haycraft, Cecil Ray, *Order of Glory, Third Class*
As plane captain of a US Navy plane during operations in the North Atlantic when his plane was badly damaged by gunfire, Aviation Chief Machinist's Mate Haycraft exhibited heroic courage in assisting in rescuing a wounded comrade. After the wounded and injured had been taken off, although the plane was rapidly filling with water, he assisted in taxiing the plane toward the beach.

Hayman, Robert William, *Order of Glory, Third Class*
As pilot of a US Navy torpedo bomber upon sighting a fully surfaced enemy submarine during operations in the North Atlantic, Lieutenant (jg) Hayman immediately repeatedly attacked with every weapon at his disposal and probably destroyed the enemy submarine.

Heim, Elbert Stewart, *Order of the Red Star*
As pilot of a US Navy fighter plane in action in the North Atlantic, Lieutenant (jg) Heim maintained contact on a group of enemy submarines. He immediately made a determined strafing attack on the largest and most heavily armed of the group in spite of a heavy barrage of anti-aircraft fire by all submarines in the group and repeated these attacks at close range, thus enabling two submarines to be subjected to unopposed bombing attacks by other planes resulting in destruction to one submarine

Henderson, Robert Glenn, *Medal of Nakhimov*
As a member of the US Navy Armed Guard crew of a US merchant vessel operating in the North Atlantic when that vessel was attacked by enemy aircraft and became separated from the remainder of the convoy, he continued to man his gun until the vessel sank. Suffering from hunger and exposure, he was rescued from a lifeboat after ten days in the North Atlantic.

Henry, Alexander Smith, *Order of the Red Star*
After completing delivery of vital war material, his ship was anchored in a Russian port awaiting formation of a homeward-bound convoy when an aerial bomb attack blew in several of the stern plates and frames of his ship. Captain Henry, by the exercise of exceptional ingenuity, caused his ship to be beached by her own tackle on a nearby mud flag. For two months, a period in which the crew were often called to defend themselves, or to assist in the defense of the port, against extensive enemy air activities, he led his crew in effecting repairs that again put the ship in a seaworthy condition.

Hewitt, Henry Kent, *Order of Kutuzov, First Class*
Commanding US Naval Forces in North African waters, an outstanding representative of our armed forces in the Mediterranean theater of war.

Hill, Harry Wilbur, *Order of Kutuzov, Second Class*
The senior US Naval officer operating with the covering force, accompanying an escorting convoys to North Russia.

Hoban, Edward Connor, *Medal "For Military Merit"*
As member of the US Navy Armed Guard crew aboard a US merchant vessel operating in the North Atlantic, he contributed greatly to the defense of his ship during numerous attacks by enemy aircraft and submarines. The courageous and efficient defense of the vessel contributed greatly to the successful completion of an extremely important mission.

Hocken, Richard Ernest, *Medal "For Military Merit"*
Setting out into a force eight gale, in which all ships of the convoy suffered heavy weather damage, the convoy was under almost uninterrupted attack from Nazi planes and submarines. In the course of the long running battle, his ship was directly attacked thirteen times, and was credited with downing eight planes and scoring direct hits on twelve others. On one occasion, a combined attack by Axis high-level bombers and submarines, four torpedoes were launched at the stern of the ship. One of the torpedoes sank before reaching the vessel; another was fired at by the guncrew and it exploded, and by alert maneuvering the Master eluded the other two. On another occasion, a torpedo sighted approaching off the beam was successfully dodged. By his maintenance of an alert watch, and by his skillful seamanship, he largely contributed to the delivery of an essential cargo of military supplies to our Russian allies.

Hodson, Norman Douglas, *Order of the Red Star*
As pilot of a US Navy fighter plane operating in the North Atlantic, on two occasions Lieutenant Hodson successfully strafed an enemy submarine sighted on the surface, in one case in the face of heavy anti-aircraft fire, thus enabling the submarine to be subjected to unopposed attacks by his companion bombers.

Hoffman, Norman Cullen, *Order of the Patriotic War, First Class*
As commanding officer of a United States Destroyer Escort he delivered an extremely accurate attack which severely damaged and forced an enemy submarine to the surface where it was later destroyed by gunfire and ramming during operations in the North Atlantic.

Hogan, Gerald Griffin, *Order of the Red Star*
As pilot of a US Navy torpedo bomber, having sighted a fully surfaced enemy submarine, Lieutenant Hogan delivered an extremely accurate and damaging bombing attack in the face of heavy anti-aircraft fire, contributing largely to the complete destruction of the submarine.

Holt, Stewart Baldwin, *Order of Glory, Third Class*
As pilot of a US Navy torpedo bomber plane operating in the North Atlantic, upon sighting an enemy submarine on the surface, Lieutenant Holt immediately attacked with all weapons at his command and probably destroyed the enemy submarine as it was attempting to escape by crash diving.

Holubowicz, Romuald, *Medal "For Military Merit"*
While serving as a Cadet-Midshipman on vessels delivering vital war material to Russia, he was subjected to repeated air and torpedo attacks. On three occasions ships on which he was serving were lost due to enemy action. At all times his conduct was in keeping with the best traditions of the sea.

Hopgood, Robert Brown, *Order of the Red Star*
As pilot of a Navy patrol plane operating in the North Atlantic, Lieutenant (jg) Hopgood engaged an enemy submarine and so severely damaged the enemy vessel that it was abandoned and sunk.

Horn, Joseph Donald, *Order of the Red Star*
As pilot of a US fighter plane operating in the North Atlantic, upon sighting an enemy submarine, Ensign Horn immediately commenced strafing and maintained a deadly and effective fire, thus denying the use of its defensive anti-aircraft battery by the enemy vessel, and enabling his companion bombers to probably destroy the submarine.

Horton, Leonard Durwood, *Medal "For Valor"*
As a member of the US Navy Armed Guard crew of a US merchant vessel operating in the North Atlantic that was subjected for a continuous period of six days to enemy aerial and torpedo attacks, he contributed materially to the defense of his ship. Upon one occasion the ship was separated from the convoy and was struck below the waterline by a torpedo that failed to explode. Through the efforts of the gun crew, all attacks were successfully repulsed, serious damage inflicted upon the attackers, and the ship was enabled to successfully complete her voyage.

Houdeshell, Merlin Gaylord, *Medal "For Military Merit"*
As member of the US Navy Armed Guard crew aboard a US merchant vessel operating in the North Atlantic which underwent numerous and violent attacks by enemy aircraft subjecting the vessel to continuous bomb fire, he contributed materially in the defense of his ship. In spite of physical exhaustion and intense eyestrain after twenty-eight hours at their gun stations, the crew kept up an anti-aircraft barrage that inflicted damage upon the enemy. However, in spite of their heroic defense, the vessel, seriously damaged by falling bombs, was sunk.

Houghton, Mason Minor, *Medal of Ushakov*
As a member of the US Navy Armed Guard crew aboard a US merchant vessel operating through the North Atlantic war zone, subjected to viciously persistent submarine attacks and relentless bombing day after day by large numbers of enemy planes through heavy seas, floating mines and intense cold, Gunner's Mate Houghton contributed largely by his courage and vigilance to the successful completion of the voyage and the delivery of vital war cargo.

Howard, Blake Clinton Jr., *Order of the Patriotic War, Second Class*
As commanding officer of a US Navy Armed Guard aboard a US merchant vessel operating in the North Atlantic while subjected to serious and continued air attacks, Ensign Howard successfully defended his vessel although wounded by the explosion of an enemy torpedo hit.

Hughes, Blake, *Order of the Patriotic War, Second Class*
As commanding officer of a US Navy Armed Guard aboard a US merchant vessel operating in the North Atlantic while subjected to severe aerial and submarine attack for many days, Lieutenant (jg) Hughes successfully defended the vessel to which he was attacked, enabling it to reach its destination without material damage.

Hunsinger, Paul Leonard, *Medal of Ushakov*
As a member of the US Navy Armed Guard crew aboard a US merchant vessel operating through the North Atlantic war zone, subjected to viciously persistent submarine attacks and relentless bombing day after day by large numbers of enemy planes through heavy seas, floating mines and intense cold, Coxswain Hunsinger contributed largely by his courage and vigilance to the successful completion of the voyage and the delivery of vital war cargo.

Hutchins, Charles Harris, *Order of the Patriotic War, First Class*
As commanding officer of a US destroyer operating in the North Atlantic, Lieutenant Hutchins engaged and destroyed two enemy submarines, one by ramming and in the face of heavy opposition from gunfire and depth charges.

Hyams, Norman Erwin, *Order of Glory, Third Class*
As a member of the US Navy Armed Guard crew of a US merchant vessel operating in the North Atlantic when subjected to numerous attacks by enemy submarines, torpedo planes and bombers throughout a week of almost continuous attack, Gunner's Mate Hyams, although wounded, contributed largely to the destruction of certain enemy planes and enabled the vessel to which he was attached to reach her destination and discharge vital war cargo.

Johnson, Kyle Vaughn, *Medal "For Valor"*
While serving as number one gunner on a twenty millimeter Oerlikon he aided materially over a period of eight days in repelling a series of enemy aerial attacks, and is credited with shooting down three enemy planes and assisting in the destruction of two others. His coolness under attack, and the resulting accuracy of the fire of his gun contributed immeasurably to the safety of the ship, and served as an inspiration to other members of the crew.

Johnson, Roy Walter, *Order of Glory, Third Class*
As second pilot of a US Navy patrol bomber, Ensign Johnson skillfully aided the plane commander in evading enemy air attack and successfully attacked an enemy submarine, contributing largely to the sinking of the enemy vessel.

Jones, Dallas Harding, *Order of Glory, Third Class*
As a member of a crew of a US Navy patrol bomber during a successful attack against an enemy submarine, in spite of enemy gunfire, Aviation Chief Ordnanceman Jones manned his station with courageous devotion to duty, contributing to the success of this attack and the probable destruction of the enemy vessel.

Jones, Harry Jr., *Medal "For Valor"*
As a member of the US Navy Armed Guard crew of a US merchant vessel operating in the North Atlantic when heavily attacked by enemy aircraft, he successfully defended the vessel to which he was attached inflicting damage upon the attacking planes. Later, when the vessel was torpedoed and sunk, he was rescued after three days in a lifeboat in the North Atlantic.

Kellogg, David McDougall, *Order of the Patriotic War, First Class*
As commander of a US destroyer escort operating in the North Atlantic at considerable risk from enemy gunfire and torpedoes, Lieutenant Commander Kellogg closed the range at maximum speed and rammed an enemy submarine ensuring its immediate sinking.

Kinaszczuk, Thomas, *Order of Glory, Third Class*
As pilot of a US Navy bombing plane operating in the North Atlantic on convoy coverage, upon sighting a surfaced enemy submarine approaching the convoy at high speed, Lieutenant (jg) Kinaszczuk immediately attacked and, with disregard for enemy fire and damage to his plane, successfully sank the enemy vessel.

Kinney, Paul Bruce, *Order of the Red Star*
As second pilot of a US Navy patrol bomber operating in the North Atlantic, Lieutenant (jg) Kinney so maneuvered the plane and assisted the plane commander in an attack upon an enemy submarine in spite of enemy gunfire that there was no resulting damage to the plane and the submarine was probably sunk.

Kinney, Sheldon Hoard, *Order of the Patriotic War, First Class*
As commanding officer of a US destroyer escort operating in the North Atlantic, having sighted an enemy submarine on the surface, Lieutenant Commander Kinney immediately attacked and sank the enemy vessel.

Kirby, Elden Samuel, *Medal "For Military Merit"*
As member of the US Navy Armed Guard crew aboard a US merchant vessel operating in the North Atlantic which underwent numerous and violent attacks by enemy aircraft subjecting the vessel to continuous bomb fire, he contributed materially in the defense of his ship. In spite of physical exhaustion and intense eyestrain after twenty-eight hours at their gun stations, the crew kept up an anti-aircraft barrage that inflicted damage upon the enemy. However, in spite of their heroic defense, the vessel, seriously damaged by falling bombs, was sunk.

Kirby, William Roy, *Order of the Red Star*
As commanding officer of the US Navy Armed Guard crew aboard a US merchant vessel operating in the North Atlantic when his ship was subjected to violent submarine and air attack, Ensign Kirby valiantly led his men to combat the enemy and when the ship was torpedoed and sunk he displayed heroism in the rescue of his crew.

Kroeger, Lewis William, *Medal "For Valor"*
As a member of the US Navy Armed Guard crew of a US merchant vessel operating in the North Atlantic that was subjected for a continuous period of six days to enemy aerial and torpedo attacks, he contributed materially to the defense of his ship. Upon one occasion the ship was separated from the convoy and was struck below the waterline by a torpedo that failed to explode. Through the efforts of the gun crew, all attacks were successfully repulsed, serious damage inflicted upon the attackers, and the ship was enabled to successfully complete her voyage.

Kroetz, Rudolph Henry, *Order of the Patriotic War, First Class*
As commanding officer of a US Navy Armed Guard aboard a US merchant vessel operating in the North Atlantic, Ensign Kroetz successfully defended the merchant vessel during a series of persistent raids by enemy aircraft and submarine attacks and eventually reached port.

LaGue, Alexander, *Medal "For Military Merit"*
As a member of the US Navy Armed Guard crew of a US merchant vessel operating in the North Atlantic while subjected to numerous assaults by enemy submarines, torpedo planes and bombers, Boatswain's Mate LaGue's gun crew contributed to the destruction of at least eight enemy planes, thereby enabling his ship to successfully complete her voyage and discharge vital war cargo.

Laird, John Landers, *Order of the Red Star*
Exhibited courage and heroism in command of the US Navy Armed Guard unit serving on board a US merchant ship engaged in transporting military equipment to the ports of Northern Russia.

Larson, Maurice Elvin, *Medal "For Military Merit"*
As member of the US Navy Armed Guard crew aboard a US merchant vessel operating in the North Atlantic which underwent numerous and violent attacks by enemy aircraft subjecting the vessel to continuous bomb fire, he contributed materially in the defense of his ship. In spite of physical exhaustion and intense eyestrain after twenty-eight hours at their gun stations, the crew kept up an anti-aircraft barrage that inflicted damage upon the enemy. However, in spite of their heroic defense, the vessel, seriously damaged by falling bombs, was sunk.

Lazetera, Ernest John, *Medal "For Military Merit"*
As petty officer of the US Navy Armed Guard crew aboard a US merchant vessel operating in the North Atlantic when the vessel was torpedoed by the enemy, her main shaft broken, and the ship was unable to proceed, he contributed materially to the defense of his ship. While drifting, she underwent enemy attack. The Armed Guard crew remained at their battle stations from the moment of attack until it was finally necessary to abandon ship.

Leahy, Joseph Donald, *Medal of Nakhimov*
As a member of the US Navy Armed Guard aboard a US merchant vessel operating in the North Atlantic, Radioman Leahy manned his battle station with courage and efficiency in the face of large-scale enemy raids upon his convoy. When his ship was separated from the convoy and finally sunk, he carried on until ordered to abandon ship and thereafter heroically assisted in the rescue of his shipmates.

Lennig, George Birmingham, *Order of the Red Star*
Exhibited courage and heroism in command of the US Navy Armed Guard unit serving on board a US merchant ship engaged in transporting military equipment to the ports of Northern Russia.

Lessard, Paul Oscar, *Medal of Nakhimov*
As a member of the US Navy Armed Guard crew of a US merchant vessel operating in the North Atlantic when that vessel was attacked by enemy aircraft and became separated from the remainder of the convoy, he continued to man his gun until the vessel sank. Suffering from hunger and exposure, he was rescued from a lifeboat after ten days in the North Atlantic.

Lintlom, Julius Waldemar, *Medal "For Valor"*
The convoy of which his vessel was a part was under concentrated air and torpedo attack for five days, but his coolness and courage served as an example to all hands, and his leadership was of such a high caliber that the behavior and efficiency of the ship's entire company was beyond reproach and resulted in the safe delivery of a cargo of war material to Russia. By expert seamanship, he skillfully maneuvered his vessel so as to evade five aerial torpedoes that were simultaneously approaching his ship. In addition he found time to closely observe the action of these aerial torpedoes so he could submit a comprehensive report to the senior naval officer present.

Mahoney, Jeremiah Ehret, *Order of the Patriotic War, First Class*
Exhibited courage and heroism in command of the US Navy Armed Guard unit serving on board a US merchant ship engaged in transporting military equipment to the ports of Northern Russia.

Malloy, Bernard Aloysius, *Medal "For Military Merit"*
As a member of the US Navy Armed Guard crew of a US merchant vessel operating in the North Atlantic while subjected to prolonged and sustained attacks by enemy bombers, torpedo planes and submarines, Radioman Malloy contributed materially to the defense of his ship and the destruction of seven enemy planes, enabling the vessel to which he was attached to successfully complete her voyage.

Marihugh, Clarence Henry, *Order of Glory, Third Class*
As a member of the US Navy Armed Guard crew of a US merchant vessel operating in the North Atlantic when subjected to numerous assaults by enemy submarines, torpedo planes and bombers after a week of almost continuous attack and in spite of his wounds, Seaman first class Marihugh courageously performed his duties, thereby contributing greatly to the successful completion of the voyage and discharge of vital war cargo.

Marks, Louis Davidson, *Order of the Red Star*
As commanding officer of the US Navy Armed Guard crew aboard a US merchant vessel operating in the North Atlantic, Lieutenant (jg) Marks assisted in the frustration of large-scale raids upon the convoy for a period of eight days. In a recurrent engagement, he continued the action against overwhelming odds until the vessel was finally sunk and abandoned without personnel injury or loss of life.

Mason, Donald Francis, *Order of Glory, Third Class*
Operating from established bases in the North Atlantic, Lieutenant Mason conducted extensive submarine search and convoy coverage flights in the face of constant hazards due to icing, low visibility, blizzards, and high winds in a land type plane. Earlier, as pilot of a US Navy patrol plane, he attacked an enemy submarine that was severely damaged and undoubtedly destroyed.

Mathson, Andrew Oliver, *Medal "For Valor"*
As a member of the US Navy Armed Guard crew of a US merchant vessel operating in the North Atlantic that was subjected for a continuous period of six days to enemy aerial and torpedo attacks, he contributed materially to the defense of his ship. Upon one occasion the ship was separated from the convoy and was struck below the waterline by a torpedo that failed to explode. Through the efforts of the gun crew, all attacks were successfully repulsed, serious damage inflicted upon the attackers, and the ship was enabled to successfully complete her voyage.

Maynard, Albert, *Order of the Patriotic War, First Class*
As commanding officer of a US Navy Armed Guard aboard a US merchant vessel operating in the North Atlantic, Lieutenant (jg) Maynard and his crew repulsed numerous enemy aerial attacks and enabled the merchant vessel to eventually reach port.

Maddalena, Arthur Daniel Jr., *Order of the Patriotic War, First Class*
As commanding officer of a US Navy Armed Guard aboard a US merchant vessel operating in the North Atlantic, Ensign Maddalena successfully defended his ship through numerous hazardous engagements with enemy dive bombers, torpedo planes and submarine, driving off numerous and almost continuous attacks and thereby enabling his vessel to successfully reach port.

McDole, John Wallace, *Medal "For Valor"*
As a member of the US Navy Armed Guard crew of a US merchant vessel operating in the North Atlantic when heavily attacked by enemy aircraft, he successfully defended the vessel to which he was attached inflicting damage upon the attacking planes. Later, when the vessel was torpedoed and sunk, he was rescued after three days in a lifeboat in the North Atlantic.

McDonald, Arthur Jr., *Medal of Nakhimov*
As a member of the US Navy Armed Guard crew of a US merchant vessel operating in the North Atlantic when that vessel was attacked by enemy aircraft and became separated from the remainder of the convoy, he continued to man his gun until the vessel sank. Suffering from hunger and exposure, he was rescued from a lifeboat after ten days in the North Atlantic.

McGinnis, John Alber, *Order of the Red Star*
As the only assistant to the Assistant Naval Attaché in a foreign port in the far North Atlantic under conditions which entailed great personal danger, Chief Ship's Clerk McGinnis assisted materially in establishing the Naval Attaché's Office and, through his efforts, the welfare of US vessels and their crews and survivors from vessels lost en route was kept at a standard well in advance of what might have been reasonably expected under the existing circumstances.

McLane, William McNair, *Order of Glory, Third Class*
As pilot of a US Navy torpedo bomber, sighting two fully surfaced enemy submarines, Ensign McLane immediately attacked and, coordinating his efforts with those of his fighter plane, sank the enemy submarine during operations in the North Atlantic.

McNaughton, John Theodore, *Order of the Patriotic War, Second Class*
As commanding officer of a US Navy Armed Guard aboard a US merchant vessel operating in the North Atlantic, although subjected to heavy enemy submarine attack, Ensign McNaughton successfully defended his ship and enabled her to reach her destination with no serious damage.

Merlo, Michael Louis, *Order of the Patriotic War, Second Class*
As commanding officer of a US Navy Armed Guard aboard a US merchant vessel operating in the North Atlantic, repeatedly subjected to enemy aerial bombing both at sea and in a friendly foreign port, Lieutenant (jg) Merlo successfully defended the ship to which he was attached.

Millard, Robert Carpenter, *Order of Glory, Third Class*
As pilot of a US Navy patrol plane operating in the North Atlantic, upon sighting an enemy submarine on the surface, Lieutenant Millard immediately dived to the attack and before the enemy could fire a shot in its defense, severely damaged and probably sank the enemy vessel.

Miller, Wesley Norton, *Order of the Patriotic War, Second Class*
As commanding officer of a US Navy Armed Guard aboard a US merchant vessel operating in the North Atlantic, although subjected to severe bombing by enemy planes, Lieutenant Miller successfully defended the ship, enabling her to complete the voyage without casualty.

Moon, Don Pardee, *Order of Alexander Nevsky*
Senior US naval officer in destroyers of the covering force escort groups for North Russian convoys.

Murray, Howell Sherer, *Order of the Patriotic War, Second Class*
As commanding officer of a US Navy Armed Guard aboard a US merchant vessel operating in the North Atlantic under almost constant air and submarine activity for six days, Ensign Murray successfully defended his ship, enabling her to arrive safely at her destination.

Nelson, Oman Ambrose, *Medal "For Military Merit"*
As member of the US Navy Armed Guard crew aboard a US merchant vessel operating in the North Atlantic which underwent numerous and violent attacks by enemy aircraft subjecting the vessel to continuous bomb fire, he contributed materially in the defense of his ship. In spite of physical exhaustion and intense eyestrain after twenty-eight hours at their gun stations, the crew kept up an anti-aircraft barrage that inflicted damage upon the enemy. However, in spite of their heroic defense, the vessel, seriously damaged by falling bombs, was sunk.

Newman, Edwin Booth, *Medal "For Military Merit"*
As member of the US Navy Armed Guard crew aboard a US merchant vessel operating in the North Atlantic, he contributed greatly to the defense of his ship during numerous attacks by enemy aircraft and submarines. The courageous and efficient defense of the vessel contributed greatly to the successful completion of an extremely important mission.

Nightingale, Thomas, *Medal "For Valor"*
As a member of the US Navy Armed Guard crew of a US merchant vessel operating in the North Atlantic when heavily attacked by enemy aircraft, he successfully defended the vessel to which he was attached inflicting damage upon the attacking planes. Later, when the vessel was torpedoed and sunk, he was rescued after three days in a lifeboat in the North Atlantic.

Nisbet, Robert Alexander, *Order of the Patriotic War, Second Class*
As commanding officer of a US Navy Armed Guard aboard a US merchant vessel after the ship had been torpedoed and was being abandoned by its crew, Lieutenant Nisbet realized that the ship was not sinking and he and ten of his men remained aboard for eleven trying days despite danger of further attack and succeeding in expediting the crippled ship's salvage.

Norton, George John, *Order of the Red Star*
Exhibited courage and heroism as a member of a US Navy Armed Guard unit serving on board a US merchant ship engaged in transporting military equipment to the ports of Northern Russia.

Orem, Howard Emery, *Order of Kutuzov, Third Class*
As acting chief of staff to the senior US naval officer in the area, acted as liaison officer with British escorting forces and with convoy commanders in connection with North Russian convoys.

O'Savage, Joseph, *Medal "For Valor"*
As a member of the US Navy Armed Guard crew of a US merchant vessel operating in the North Atlantic, Boatswain's Mate O'Savage heroically aided in the defense of his ship against enemy submarines and aircraft. On one occasion, when a submarine was sighted close aboard, serious damage was inflicted upon it. He contributed greatly to the successful completion of the voyage of the vessel to which he was attached.

Ours, John Jacob, *Medal "For Valor"*
As a member of the US Navy Armed Guard crew of a US merchant vessel operating in the North Atlantic when heavily attacked by enemy aircraft, he successfully defended the vessel to which he was attached inflicting damage upon the attacking planes. Later, when the vessel was torpedoed and sunk, he was rescued after three days in a lifeboat in the North Atlantic.

Pagnotta, Mario James, *Order of Glory, Third Class*
When the destroyer to which he was attached was holed in action against an enemy submarine, Machinist's Mate Pagnotta remained at his station in the forward engine room and endeavored to reduce the flow of water into the ship and to complete repairs in his damaged engine room to keep it in operation, leaving his station only after the water had risen neck deep and being specifically ordered to do so by the engineer officer, in the North Atlantic.

Parker, Milton, *Medal "For Valor"*
As a member of the US Navy Armed Guard crew of a US merchant vessel operating in the North Atlantic when heavily attacked by enemy aircraft, he successfully defended the vessel to which he was attached inflicting damage upon the attacking planes. Later, when the vessel was torpedoed and sunk, he was rescued after three days in a lifeboat in the North Atlantic.

Peer, Raymond Peter, *Medal "For Valor"*
As a member of the US Navy Armed Guard crew of a US merchant vessel operating in the North Atlantic that was subjected for a continuous period of six days to enemy aerial and torpedo attacks, he contributed materially to the defense of his ship. Upon one occasion the ship was separated from the convoy and was struck below the waterline by a torpedo that failed to explode. Through the efforts of the gun crew, all attacks were successfully repulsed, serious damage inflicted upon the attackers, and the ship was enabled to successfully complete her voyage.

Perdue, Luther William, *Medal "For Valor"*
As a member of the US Navy Armed Guard crew of a US merchant vessel operating in the North Atlantic when heavily attacked by enemy aircraft, he successfully defended the vessel to which he was attached inflicting damage upon the attacking planes. Later, when the vessel was torpedoed and sunk, he was rescued after three days in a lifeboat in the North Atlantic.

Pernell, James William, *Medal "For Valor"*
As a member of the US Navy Armed Guard crew of a US merchant vessel operating in the North Atlantic when heavily attacked by enemy aircraft, he successfully defended the vessel to which he was attached inflicting damage upon the attacking planes. Later, when the vessel was torpedoed and sunk, he was rescued after three days in a lifeboat in the North Atlantic.

Perret, Francis Peter, *Medal "For Valor"*
As a member of the US Navy Armed Guard crew of a US merchant vessel operating in the North Atlantic that was subjected for a continuous period of six days to enemy aerial and torpedo attacks, he contributed materially to the defense of his ship. Upon one occasion the ship was separated from the convoy and was struck below the waterline by a torpedo that failed to explode. Through the efforts of the gun crew, all attacks were successfully repulsed, serious damage inflicted upon the attackers, and the ship was enabled to successfully complete her voyage.

Phillips, Willie H., *Medal "For Valor"*
As a member of the US Navy Armed Guard crew of a US merchant vessel operating in the North Atlantic when heavily attacked by enemy aircraft, he successfully defended the vessel to which he was attached inflicting damage upon the attacking planes. Later, when the vessel was torpedoed and sunk, he was rescued after three days in a lifeboat in the North Atlantic.

Pickler, David Anderson, *Order of the Red Star*
As commanding officer of the US Navy Armed Guard crew aboard a US merchant vessel operating in the North Atlantic when that ship was torpedoed, Ensign Pickler remained aboard with his crew after the ship had been otherwise abandoned for a period of twenty-four hours despite the possibility of imminent sinking and further enemy attack.

Pollard, Francis Costello, USCG, *Order of the Patriotic War, First Class*
As commanding officer of a US Coast Guard cutter, although handicapped by inadequate equipment and a limited number of depth charges, Lieutenant Commander Pollard successfully attacked and probably sank an enemy submarine in the North Atlantic.

Porter, Wallace Stevens, *Order of Glory, Third Class*
As pilot of a US Navy torpedo bomber when an enemy submarine was detected in the North Atlantic, Lieutenant (jg) Porter successfully coordinated bombing attacks that forced the enemy vessel to the surface where it was completely destroyed by bombing and strafing attacks.

Richards, Floyd Eugene, *Medal of Ushakov*
As a member of the US Navy Armed Guard crew aboard a US merchant vessel operating in the North Atlantic, Signalman first class Richards manned his battle station with courage and efficiency in the face of large scale raids upon the convoy and succeeded in influencing damage upon the enemy, abandoning the vessel only at the last moment when his guns could no longer be of use.

Ricks, Robert Byron, *Order of the Patriotic War, First Class*
As commanding officer of a US Navy Armed Guard aboard a US merchant vessel operating in the North Atlantic, Lieutenant (jg) Ricks successfully attacked an enemy submarine at close range.

Roberts, Howard Stowe, *Order of the Red Star*
As pilot of a carrier based torpedo plane, having sighted an enemy submarine on the surface, Lieutenant Commander Roberts immediately delivered a dive attack which resulted in the complete disabling of the submarine and, by accurate machine gun fire, the enemy crew was prevented from manning their guns and the submarine eventually sank.

Robertson, Rex Eldon, *Medal of Nakhimov*
As a member of the US Navy Armed Guard crew of a US merchant vessel operating in the North Atlantic when that vessel was attacked by enemy aircraft and became separated from the remainder of the convoy, he continued to man his gun until the vessel sank. Suffering from hunger and exposure, he was rescued from a lifeboat after ten days in the North Atlantic.

Rooker, Daniel Junior, *Order of the Patriotic War, First Class*
As commanding officer of a US Navy Armed Guard aboard a US merchant vessel during persistent attacks by enemy bombers in the North Atlantic and in most adverse weather conditions, Ensign Rooker successfully defended his ship, enabling her to finally return to port and discharge valuable cargo.

Rotz, Charles, *Order of Glory, Third Class*
As a member of the US Navy Armed Guard crew aboard a US merchant vessel operating in the North Atlantic, when forced to abandon ship by the torpedoing of his vessel, Seaman first class Rotz dived off the sinking ship without a life jacket and, when trapped beneath the capsized lifeboat and nearly exhausted, he successfully rescued a shipmate at the risk of his own life.

Roullard, George Dee, *Order of the Red Star*
For accurate fulfillment of assignments of the command in securing sea communications during the war.

Rutherford, Wilson Douglas, *Order of the Patriotic War, Second Class*
As commanding officer of a US Navy Armed Guard aboard a US merchant vessel operating in the North Atlantic when, after collision with another vessel in the convoy, the ship was abandoned, Lieutenant (jg) Rutherford returned with a volunteer crew and supervised the hazardous and exhausting work of extinguishing fire and assuring the ship's safety.

Ryan, Harry F., *Medal "For Military Merit"*
Despite tremendous gales and continuous attacks from large numbers of German aircraft and submarines, he successfully conducted his ship, with its valuable cargo of war materiel, to a Russian port. By exact and expert station keeping in the face of almost insurmountable difficulties, and by competent leadership, he was largely instrumental to the defense of his own vessel and in the infliction of serious damage upon the enemy. His outstanding courage, endurance and skillful seamanship on the above occasion were in keeping with the highest traditions of the men who serve on the sea.

Saum, Irving Randolph, *Order of Glory, Third Class*
When the destroyer to which he was attached was holed and in danger of sinking during operations in the North Atlantic, Machinist's Mate Saum descended into debris filled water in the flooded engine room in order to secure the drain valves and permit pumps to be used in controlling the water.

Schilbe, William Alfred, *Order of the Red Star*
As a member of the US Navy Armed Guard crew of a US merchant vessel operating in the North Atlantic during a mass enemy attack by twenty-six enemy planes, Gunner's Mate Schilbe, upon two occasions, so ably assisted in the defense of the ship to which he was attached through twenty-eight hours of exhausting effort, that his ship was enabled to successfully complete her voyage.

Schill, Gustav William Jr., *Medal "For Military Merit"*
As member of the US Navy Armed Guard crew aboard a US merchant vessel operating in the North Atlantic, he contributed greatly to the defense of his ship during numerous attacks by enemy aircraft and submarines. The courageous and efficient defense of the vessel contributed greatly to the successful completion of an extremely important mission.

Schwartz, Dan Richard, *Order of the Red Star*
As commanding officer of the US Navy Armed Guard crew aboard a US merchant vessel operating in the North Atlantic, when the ship to which he was attached was torpedoed and believed sinking, Lieutenant (jg) Schwartz fired several rounds at the slick of the enemy submarine. When the ship had been abandoned it became evident that it would not sink immediately, whereupon Lieutenant (jg) Schwartz returned with volunteers and continued the action until the ship was struck by a second torpedo and sank shortly thereafter.

Schwartz, Norbert Lewis, *Order of Glory, Third Class*
As petty officer in command of the US Navy Armed Guard crew aboard a US merchant vessel operating in the North Atlantic after the ship to which he was attached had been torpedoed and abandoned and after seven days in lifeboats, Coxswain Schwartz was highly instrumental in the rescue of his crew under extremely difficult and trying conditions.

Sessions, William Alton, *Order of the Patriotic War, First Class*
As commanding office of a US vessel operating in the North Atlantic, Lieutenant Commander Sessions, in the face of enemy fire, rammed and sank an enemy submarine that had previously torpedoed a US ship in convoy.

Sharp, William Stewart, *Medal "For Military Merit"*
As a member of the US Navy Armed Guard crew of a US merchant vessel operating in the North Atlantic, Coxswain Sharp contributed to the successful defense of his ship against attacking enemy planes. In the midst of one heavy bombing attack when one of his guns became disabled, disregarding the danger and difficulties involved, he repaired the gun in time to enable his ship to continue in action.

Sherbring, Milton John, *Order of Glory, Third Class*
As pilot of a US Navy torpedo bomber having sighted an enemy submarine at periscope depth, Lieutenant Sherbring immediately attacked and by depth bombs forced the enemy vessel to the surface and further assured its complete destruction by repeated attacks, during operations in the North Atlantic.

Shipley, Francis Marion Jr., *Medal "For Valor"*
As a member of the US Navy Armed Guard crew of a US merchant vessel operating in the North Atlantic during numerous encounters with enemy submarines, airplanes, and surface vessels, Boatswain's Mate Shipley contributed materially to the defense of his ship, infliction of damage upon the enemy and the successful completion of the voyage.

Sissler, Bernard Charles, *Order of Glory, Third Class*
As pilot of a US Navy torpedo bomber having sighted an enemy submarine at periscope depth, Lieutenant (jg) Sissler immediately attacked and by depth bombs forced the enemy vessel to the surface and further assured its complete destruction by repeated attacks.

Smalley, Harvey Carroll, *Medal "For Military Merit"*
As petty officer of the US Navy Armed Guard crew aboard a US merchant vessel operating in the North Atlantic when the vessel was torpedoed by the enemy, her main shaft broken, and the ship was unable to proceed, he contributed materially to the defense of his ship. While drifting, she underwent enemy attack. The Armed Guard crew remained at their battle stations from the moment of attack until it was finally necessary to abandon ship.

Smith, George Thornewell, *Order of the Patriotic War, Second Class*
As commanding officer of a US Navy Armed Guard aboard a US merchant vessel operating in the North Atlantic. Both while at sea and at port the ship was subjected to heavy attack by air and submarine, and Ensign Smith successfully defended the vessel, enabling her to complete her voyage.

Smith, Harrison, *Order of the Patriotic War, Second Class*
As commanding officer of a US Navy Armed Guard aboard a US merchant vessel operating in the North Atlantic, Lieutenant (jg) Smith successfully defended his ship against numerous attacks by enemy planes, enabling the ship to which he was attached to successfully complete her voyage.

Smith, William Benton Conway, *Order of Glory, Third Class*
As first mechanic of a severely damaged plane operating in the North Atlantic, Aviation Machinist's Mate Smith assisted the first and second pilot in conducting a long over-water flight until the plane landed close ashore. In the rescue operations that followed, although wounded, he assisted materially in rescuing the other occupants of the plane.

Sonneborn, Herbert Mone Jr., *Order of the Red Star*
As commanding officer of the US Navy Armed Guard crew aboard a US merchant vessel operating in the North Atlantic, Lieutenant (jg) Sonneborn, upon several occasions, successfully defended his ship against enemy submarine attack, during one which the submarine was sighted in the middle of the convoy and severe damage inflicted upon it by the guns of the Armed Guard crew.

Spann, Percy Leon, *Medal "For Valor"*
As a member of the US Navy Armed Guard crew of a US merchant vessel operating in the North Atlantic when heavily attacked by enemy aircraft, he successfully defended the vessel to which he was attached inflicting damage upon the attacking planes. Later, when the vessel was torpedoed and sunk, he was rescued after three days in a lifeboat in the North Atlantic.

Starnes, Gifford Harmon, *Medal "For Military Merit"*
As petty officer of the US Navy Armed Guard crew aboard a US merchant vessel operating in the North Atlantic while undergoing numerous attacks by enemy aircraft, Gunner's Mate Starnes successfully defended the ship and inflicted damage upon the enemy, thus enabling the vessel to which he was attached to successful complete her voyage.

Stein, Milton A., *Order of the Patriotic War, Second Class*
As commanding officer of a US Navy Armed Guard aboard a US merchant vessel, although subjected to heavy air attack, Lieutenant Stein successfully defended the ship to which he was attached, enabling her to complete her voyage with no considerable damage in the North Atlantic.

Stewart, Jack Howard, *Order of Glory, Third Class*
As pilot of a US Navy fighter plane, Lieutenant (jg) Stewart upon two occasions at sighting a surfaced enemy submarine, immediately delivered strafing attacks in the face of enemy anti-aircraft fire and assisted materially in the destruction of the enemy vessels.

Stone, Merrill Rust, Jr., *Order of the Patriotic War, First Class*
As commanding officer of a US Navy Armed Guard aboard a US merchant vessel operating in the North Atlantic, Ensign Stone conducted a running fight with gunfire with an enemy submarine causing a violent explosion aboard the enemy vessel which was last seen apparently sinking, thus extricating his vessel from a perilous encounter without damage to the ship or crew.

Stone, Richard Marvin, *Order of the Patriotic War, Second Class*
As commanding officer of a US Navy Armed Guard aboard a US merchant vessel operating in the North Atlantic and while unloading in a friendly foreign port the ship was subjected to extremely heavy aerial bombing attacks, Lieutenant Stone successfully defended his ship, enabling her to discharge her cargo and complete her voyage.

Sulton, John Rueben, *Order of Glory, Third Class*
As pilot of a US Navy torpedo bomber in the North Atlantic, having sighted an enemy submarine at periscope depth, Lieutenant (jg) Sulton immediately attacked and by depth bombs forced the enemy vessel to the surface and further assured its complete destruction by repeated attacks.

Tepuni, William, *Order of Glory, Third Class*
As pilot of a US Navy patrol plane during operations in the North Atlantic, upon sighting an enemy submarine, Lieutenant Tepuni immediately attacked, seriously damaged, and probably destroyed the enemy vessel.

Thompson, Allan Anthony, *Medal "For Military Merit"*
As member of the US Navy Armed Guard crew aboard a US merchant vessel operating in the North Atlantic which underwent numerous and violent attacks by enemy aircraft subjecting the vessel to continuous bomb fire, he contributed materially in the defense of his ship. In spite of physical exhaustion and intense eyestrain after twenty-eight hours at their gun stations, the crew kept up an anti-aircraft barrage that inflicted damage upon the enemy. However, in spite of their heroic defense, the vessel, seriously damaged by falling bombs, was sunk.

Thompson, Paul Waite, *Order of the Patriotic War, Second Class*
As commanding officer of a US Navy Armed Guard aboard a US merchant vessel operating in the North Atlantic, Lieutenant (jg) Thompson successfully defended the ship to which he was attached through seven attacks by enemy torpedo planes, thus enabling her to complete her voyage.

Tipping, Kenneth William, *Order of the Red Star*
As commanding officer of the US Navy Armed Guard crew aboard a US merchant vessel operating in the North Atlantic, Ensign Tipping defended his ship from enemy bombing and torpedo planes over an extended period, inflicting serious damage upon the enemy.

When the ship was finally sunk by enemy torpedoes, he displayed heroism in enabling the entire crew to escape without injury.

Townsend, Frank Floyd, *Medal "For Valor"*
After completing delivery of vital war material, his ship was anchored in a Russian port awaiting formation of a homeward-bound convoy when an aerial bomb attack blew in several of the stern plates and frames of his ship. By the exercise of exceptional ingenuity, he aided in beaching the ship by her own tackle on a nearby mud flag. For two months, a period in which the crew were often called to defend themselves, or to assist in the defense of the port, against extensive enemy air activities, he led his crew in effecting repairs that again put the ship in a seaworthy condition.

Thueson, Theodore Stanley, *Order of Glory, Third Class*
As pilot of a US Navy patrol bomber, in the face of intense enemy gunfire, Lieutenant Thueson conducted continuous strafing attacks against an enemy submarine until it submerged.

Trahan, Senua, *Medal "For Military Merit"*
As member of the US Navy Armed Guard crew aboard a US merchant vessel operating in the North Atlantic which underwent numerous and violent attacks by enemy aircraft subjecting the vessel to continuous bomb fire, he contributed materially in the defense of his ship. In spite of physical exhaustion and intense eyestrain after twenty-eight hours at their gun stations, the crew kept up an anti-aircraft barrage that inflicted damage upon the enemy. However, in spite of their heroic defense, the vessel, seriously damaged by falling bombs, was sunk.

Ulrich, Charles Monroe, *Order of the Patriotic War, First Class*
As commanding officer of a US Navy Armed Guard aboard a US merchant vessel operating in the North Atlantic, Ensign Ulrich defended his vessel against heavy enemy bombing attacks and strafing fire from enemy airplanes.

Vandiver, Donald Lee, *Order of Glory, Third Class*
As member of the US Navy Armed Guard crew of a US merchantman operating in the North Atlantic, when the vessel to which he was attached was torpedoed and quickly enveloped in flames, under extremely difficult conditions and with great personal risk, Seaman first class Vandiver greatly contributed to the rescue of twelve men of the crew.

Walters, Charles Edgar, *Order of Glory, Third Class*
As a member of the US Navy Armed Guard crew of a US merchant vessel operating in the North Atlantic, when subjected to numerous attacks by enemy submarines, torpedo planes and bombers for a period of over a week, Coxswain Walters valiantly manned his station and contributed to the destruction of at least eight enemy planes. Although wounded in one of these attacks, he continued to perform his duties until the attacking planes had left. His heroic conduct contributed to the safe arrival of his ship at her destination with a vital war cargo.

Wanless, Robert Hume, *Order of the Patriotic War, First Class*
As commanding office of a US destroyer escort operating in the North Atlantic, Lieutenant Commander Wanless, in a series of successfully executed and well-coordinated attacks, damaged and forced an enemy U-boat to the surface where the enemy vessel was sunk by heavy and well-directed gunfire.

Watson, John Belton, *Order of Glory, Third Class*
As pilot of a US Navy torpedo bomber in the North Atlantic, having sighted an enemy submarine at periscope depth, Lieutenant Watson immediately attacked and by depth bombs forced the enemy vessel to the surface and further assured its complete destruction by repeated attacks.

Webb, Paul Neil, *Order of the Red Star*
As a member of the US Navy Armed Guard crew aboard a US merchant vessel operating in the North Atlantic while that vessel was undergoing severe and continuous aircraft attack, Seaman first class Webb remained at his gun after it had been abandoned by the other members of the crew and continued his fire at the enemy until wounded. In further attacks upon his rescue ship, he continued himself heroically throughout a six-hour dive-bombing attack.

Weeks, Lloyd Richard, *Order of the Red Star*
Exhibited courage and heroism as a member of a US Navy Armed Guard unit serving on board a US merchant ship engaged in transporting military equipment to the ports of Northern Russia.

Welch, Brian Grant, *Order of the Patriotic War, First Class*
As commanding officer of a US Navy Armed Guard aboard a US merchant vessel, Lieutenant Welch succeeded in driving off continued and persistent attacks by enemy aircraft until a violent explosion ripped open the starboard side and enveloped the ship in flames. Lieutenant (jg) Welch, although blocked by raging fire and hampered by flooding decks, supervised the abandonment of the rapidly sinking vessel until all members of his crew had gone over the side, during operations in the North Atlantic.

Wilcox, Robert, USCG, *Order of the Patriotic War, First Class*
As commanding officer of a US destroyer escort in offensive action against an enemy submarine in the North Atlantic, Lieutenant Commander Wilcox successfully forced the enemy vessel to the surface by depth charges where it was sunk by gunfire and final ramming by an attacking destroyer escort.

Williams, Hubert, *Medal "For Military Merit"*
As member of the US Navy Armed Guard crew aboard a US merchant vessel operating in the North Atlantic which underwent numerous and violent attacks by enemy aircraft subjecting the vessel to continuous bomb fire, he contributed materially in the defense of his ship. In spite of physical exhaustion and intense eyestrain after twenty-eight hours at their gun stations, the crew kept up an anti-aircraft barrage that inflicted damage upon the enemy. However, in spite of their heroic defense, the vessel, seriously damaged by falling bombs, was sunk.

Williams, James Douglass, *Order of the Patriotic War, Second Class*
As commanding officer of a US Navy Armed Guard aboard a US merchant vessel operating in the North Atlantic, although subjected to prolonged enemy aerial attacks, Lieutenant Williams successfully defended the ship to which he was attached, thus enabling the vessel to complete her voyage without damage.

Wilson, Harry Parks, *Medal "For Valor"*
As a member of the US Navy Armed Guard crew of a US merchant vessel operating in the North Atlantic and for eight consecutive days while unloading in an Allied port his ship was subjected to numerous attacks by enemy bombers, submarines and destroyers. Coxswain Wilson contributed materially to the successful defense of his ship, enabling her to complete her voyage and successfully discharge her vital cargo.

Wishon, Junior, *Medal of Ushakov*
As a member of the US Navy Armed Guard crew aboard a US merchant vessel operating in the North Atlantic, Apprentice Seaman Wishon valiantly fought off the recurrent waves of enemy planes, remaining at his gun under repeated attacks and assisted materially in the destruction of seven hostile aircraft. By his courageous efforts, he contributed materially to the safe completion of the voyage of the ship to which he was attached and the delivery of vital war cargo.

Wohlers, Albert Franklin, *Order of the Red Star*
Exhibited courage and heroism as a member of a US Navy Armed Guard unit serving on board a US merchant ship engaged in transporting military equipment to the ports of Northern Russia.

Wolfson, Morton Eugene, *Order of the Patriotic War, First Class*
As commanding officer of a US Navy Armed Guard aboard a US merchant vessel operating in the North Atlantic, Lieutenant (jg) Wolfson defended his vessel against a mass enemy air attack by enemy aircraft and enemy submarines until, after twenty-eight hours of fighting, the merchant vessel, disastrously crippled by falling bombs, sank.

Wright, Hugh Patrick, *Order of the Patriotic War, Second Class*
Exhibited courage and heroism as a member of a US Navy Armed Guard unit serving on board a US merchant ship engaged in transporting military equipment to the ports of Northern Russia.

Wright, Kenneth Leon, *Order of Glory, Third Class*
As pilot of a US Navy patrol bomber, in the face of heavy enemy fire, Lieutenant (jg) Wright pressed home his attack and, in coordination with other planes, contributed greatly to the sinking of an enemy submarine.

Yingling, Albert Oney, *Medal "For Valor"*
As a member of the US Navy Armed Guard crew of a US merchant vessel operating in the North Atlantic that was subjected for a continuous period of six days to enemy aerial and torpedo attacks, he contributed materially to the defense of his ship. Upon one occasion the ship was separated from the convoy and was struck below the waterline by a torpedo that failed to explode. Through the efforts of the gun crew, all attacks were successfully repulsed, serious damage inflicted upon the attackers, and the ship was enabled to successfully complete her voyage.

Young, Gilbert Stewart, *Order of the Red Star*
As commanding officer of the US Navy Armed Guard crew aboard a US merchant vessel operating in the North Atlantic, when subjected to repeated aerial attack by the enemy while in convoy, Lieutenant Young successfully defended the vessel to which he was attached and inflicted serious damage upon the enemy.

Appendix 2

Serial numbers of Soviet medals awarded to the US Sea Services

The following list of serial numbers, observed, extrapolated, and from archival sources were compiled during the course of writing this narrative. Serial numbers extrapolated and directly obtained from documents located in the State Archives of the Russian Federation have been interspersed with serial numbers directly observed in the writing of the book.

An extrapolation of the serial numbers for the 1944 awarding can be considered very accurate based on the sequential serial numbers of those observed and noted in the Archives. For the awarding event that took place in 1945, an extrapolation of serial numbers is difficult but not entirely impossible. It appears that the award numbers follow the original version of the Ukaz (declaration) of the Supreme Soviet, dated July 7, 1945. However, there are several gaps in the award numbers as well as at least one case of numbers awarded out of sequence making the extrapolation close, but not guaranteed to be completely accurate.

There is an interesting detail worthy of note regarding the sequential serial numbering of the awards. Assuming these medals were delivered to the Soviet Embassy as a sequentially serial numbered block of unissued medals, the observed serial numbers for the 1945-awarded Orders of the Patriotic War, First Class Red Star, Glory, Third Class and the Medal "For Valor" range beyond the actual numbers bestowed upon the naval personnel contained in this book. Thus, there are sequentially numbered medals within the observed range that were not awarded to naval recipients, but were quite possibly awarded to others via the Soviet Embassy in Washington, DC

The unusual out of sequence serial numbers of the Order of the Red Star to George Roullard and the Medals of Nakhimov awarded to Emmett Anderson, Rex Robertson, and William Harkins must also be noted. George Roullard's Order of the Red Star was awarded locally by decree of the Soviet Pacific fleet commander for his service as the Assistant US Naval Attaché in Vladivostok, whereas all of the other awards were issued by decree of the Presidium of the Supreme Soviet. Thus, his Order of the Red Star was sourced from a different block of award numbers than the others.

The three low-numbered Medals of Nakhimov, however, were awarded by decree of the Supreme Soviet but are outside the range of other observed serial numbers for the Medal of Nakhimov. The reason for this is not known, and there were no documents available to reveal any rationale for the unusual numbers. Interesting to note is that the issue of the Russian newspaper *Krasnii Flot* (translated as *Red Fleet*) published on July 7, 1945, Robertson, Anderson, and Harkins are listed as the last three of the fifteen recipients of the Medal of Nakhimov, and coincidentally, their serial numbers are from a different block of awards. Further, the book *Cavaliers of the Medal of Nakhimov*, by Russian author Nikolai Efimov, a comprehensive and complete listing of all recipients of the medal lists only three Medals of Nakhimov between serial numbers 1301 (Anderson) and 1312 (unknown). The other

Medals of Nakhimov within this range appear to have been unissued, or perhaps the records of who they were issued to were lost over the course of time. It is possible that the medals were included at random with the other sequentially serial numbered awards at its origin in Moscow or Leningrad, or perhaps they were included from an older stock available at the Soviet Embassy, but the actual reason will unfortunately never be known.

Order of Kutuzov, First Class
159 Hewitt, Henry

Order of Kutuzov, Third Class
6654 Orem, Howard

Order of the Patriotic War, First Class
1944
25440 Boucher, Ralph
25441 Mahoney, Jeremiah*

1945
247502 Kellogg, David
247503 Sessions, William **
247504 Wanless, Robert
247505 Hoffman, Norman **
247506 Hutchins, Charles **
247507 Brown, Willard **
247508 Wolfson, Morton
247509 Carter, William
247510 Maynard, Albert **
247511 Ricks, Robert **
247512 Welch, Brian **
247513 Billings, Roy **
247514 Collins, Wilbur **
247515 Cram, Kendall
247517 Kroetz, Rudolph
247518 Maddalena, Arthur **
247519 Rooker, Daniel **
247520 Stone, Merrill **
247521 Ulrich, Charles **
247522 Fink, Frederick **
247523 Pollard, Francis **
247524 Wilcox, Robert **
247525 Corbus, John **
247526 Kinney, Sheldon
247527 Avery, Howard

Order of the Patriotic War, Second Class
1944
34841 Wright, Hugh*
34842 Gemmer, Ward

1945
557260 Baughan, Robert
557261 Harshaw, John
557262 Church, Howard **
557263 Brown, Philip
557264 Miller, Wesley **
557265 Nisbet, Robert
557266 Stone, Richard **
557267 Daley, Walter **
557268 Merlo, Michael **
557269 Rutherford, Wilson **
557270 Smith, Harrison **
557271 Stein, Milton
557272 Thompson, Paul **
557273 Williams, James
557275 Desgalier, Marcel
557276 Bloch, Jules **
557277 Gillen, Joseph
557278 Gudat, Walter
557279 Hughes, Blake
557280 McNaughton, John
557282 Murray, Howell
557283 Smith, George
557284 Howard, Blake **
557285 Hay, Sidney **

Order of the Red Star
1944
366451 Brinn, Rufus
366452 Laird, John*
366453 Lennig, George*
366554 Norton, George*
366455 Weeks, Lloyd
366456 Wohlers, Albert*
366457 Henry, Alexander*
366458 Andrews, Clyde*
366459 Fetherston, Edward*
366460 Breen, Maurice

1945
1553951 Hodson, Norman
1553952 Hopgood, Robert
1553953 McGinnis, John
1553954 Webb, Paul ***
1553955 Roberts, Howard ***
1553956 Buckbee, Robert ***
1553957 Delate, Thomas ***
1553958 Hogan, Gerald
1553959 Balliett, Letson
1553960 Grotenrath, John
1553961 Kinney, Paul ***
1553962 Marks, Louis ***
1553963 Puckett, David
1553964 Sonneborn, Herbert ***
1553965 Fowler, Wilma
1553967 Schwartz, Dan
1553970 Young, Gilbert
1553971 Carraway, Howard
1553972 Kirby, William ***
1553973 Pickler, David
1553974 Tipping, Kenneth
1553975 Farrar, William
1553976 Horn, Joseph

1553978 Schilbe, William
1693874 Roullard, George

Order of Glory, Third Class
387901 Cole, William
387902 Mason, Donald
387903 Millard, Robert
387904 Harmon, Leonard ***
387905 Sulton, John ***
387910 Jones, Dallas
387911 Haycraft, Cecil
387912 Smith, William ***
387913 Saum, Irving
387914 Rotz, Charles
387915 Gallegos, Faustin
387916 DeBaun, Garnet ***
387919 Davis, Lowell ***
387920 Tepuni, William ***
387921 Watson, John ***
387922 Forney, Junior
387923 Holt, Stewart
387924 Enloe, George ***
387926 Brokas, Alex
387927 Delhom, James ***
387929 Kinaszczuk, Thomas
387931 Porter, Wallace
387933 Wright, Kenneth
387934 Sissler, Bernard
387935 Stewart, Jack
387936 Thueson, Theodore ***
387938 Hayman, Robert
387939 Sherbring, Milton
387940 Anderson, Phillip ***
387941 Dyer, Bradford
387942 Johnson, Roy
387943 McLean, William ***
387944 Hudson, Bert
387945 Handshuh, Harold ***
387946 Green, William ***
387950 Pagnotta, Mario
387951 Hyams, Norman
387952 Chatterton, Joseph
387953 Currant, John
387954 Farmer, Arthur ***
387956 Schwartz, Norbert
387957 Walters, Charles ***
387959 Vandiver, Donald
387960 Marihugh, Clarence ***
387961 DeGennaro, Louis ***

Medal "For Valor"
1944
525482 Johnson, Kyle*
525483 Townsend, Frank
525484 Lintlom, Julius*

1945
2075701 Dole, Charles
2075702 Shipley, Francis ***
2075703 Gossman, Harry
2075704 Perret, Francis ***
2075705 Yingling, Albert ***
2075706 Peer, Raymond ***
2075707 Harris, Charles
2075708 Blake, Renald
2075709 Perdue, Luther ***
2075710 McDole, John
2075711 O'Savage, Joseph ***
2075712 Hall, Leland
2075715 Ours, John Jacob ***
2075716 Nightingale, Thomas ***
2075717 Pernell, James
2075718 Wilson, Harry
2075719 Spann, Percy
2075720 Jones, Harry ***
2075721 Parker, Milton ***
2075722 Phillips, Willie
2075723 Horton, Leonard ***
2075724 Grandey, Ernest
2075725 Cassidy, Oswald ***
2075726 Kroeger, Lewis ***
2075731 Mathson, Andrew

Medal "For Military Merit"
1944
598607 Ryan, Harry
589608 Hocken, Richard*
598609 Holubowicz, Romuald

1945
2551001 Malloy, Bernard ***
2551002 Brown, Thomas ***
2551003 Anderson, Edward ***
2551004 Duncan, Francis
2551005 Thompson, Allan ***
2551006 Williams, Hubert ***
2551008 DeCottes, Eaton ***
2551009 Dixon, Thomas
2551010 Newman, Edwin
2551011 Starnes, Gifford
2551012 Bourg, Eli ***
2551013 Hoban, Robert
2551014 Schill, Gustav
2551015 Lazetera, Ernest
2551016 LaGue, Alexander ***
2551017 Smalley, Harvey ***
2551020 Sharp, William
2551021 Biggs, Donald ***
2551022 Kirby, Elden
2551023 Gannon, John ***
2551024 Casey, Milton ***
2551025 Larson, Maurice ***
2551026 Nelson, Oman ***
2551027 Trahan, Senua ***
2551028 Houdeshell, Merlin ***

Medal of Ushakov
7518 Richards, Floyd†
7520 Wishon, Junior
7521 Abbott, William†

7522 Houghton, Mason
7523 Hunsinger, Paul†

Medal of Nakhimov
1301 Anderson, Emmett†
1303 Robertson, Rex
1311 Harkins, William†
5589 Harmon, John††
5590 McDonald, Arthur
5591 Henderson, Robert
5592 Cooper, George††
5593 Adler, Arthur
5594 Leahy, Joseph
5595 Gay, Frank††
5596 Guyton, James††
5597 Goddard, George ††
5598 Lessard, Paul††
5599 Graff, Cecil
5600 Friday, Albert

* These serial numbers were not observed, but were extrapolated based on trends seen on medals included in the writing of this book. The author is confident that these serial numbers would be correct if the original medals were ever located.
** These serial numbers were not observed, but were obtained by Nikolai Efimov from the State Archive of the Russian Federation. It must be noted that these cannot be fully guaranteed correct, as the Archives do list several awards that do not concur with what was observed by the author. This includes the Order of the Patriotic War, Second Class, noted by the Archives as having been awarded to Norman Adams, but was observed having been awarded to Marcel Desgalier. Similarly, the number noted by the Archives as having been awarded to Desgalier was actually awarded to Blake Hughes. For the majority of numbers recorded by the Archives and those observed by the author, however, there is a perfect match.
*** These numbers were not observed but were extrapolated based on observed serial numbers and corresponding patterns in the original Ukaz (declaration) of the Supreme Soviet dated July 7, 1945. Notable in the number lists for the Order of Glory and the Medal "For Valor" are several gaps of award numbers. It is impossible to know if the actual award numbers were awarded on one side of the gap or the other, but the most educated extrapolation by the author has been included here. With that caveat noted, these numbers should be deemed relatively accurate and should an award without document be discovered, there is a very good likelihood that it belonged to the person ascribed to it in this list.
† These serial numbers were not observed but were listed in the books *Cavaliers of the Medal of Nakhimov* and *Cavaliers of the Medal of Ushakov* by Nikolai Efimov. Number 7519 appears to have been unissued.
†† These serial numbers were also not observed and were listed in the *Cavaliers of the Medal of Nakhimov* book. However, the list in the book is not an exact match for those observed by the author. The book lists Albert Friday with 5589, but the medal in the possession of his family is number 5600. Similarly, Arthur McDonald is listed as being awarded 5600, but his family still retains number 5590. John Harmon's medal could not be located by the family, but he is listed in the book with serial number 5590. As this medal belonged to Arthur McDonald, it can be assumed that he was most likely awarded number 5589, which is listed in the book as having been awarded to Albert Friday as the other book-listed and author-observed serial numbers match.

George Cooper's Medal of Nakhimov was lost en route to his command in 1946 (the box arrived, sans medal). With his family unwilling to participate in the research for the book, it is unknown if he ever received a duplicate or replacement medal, thus the number cannot be confirmed. Finally, it is notable that Efimov's book lists no recipient for 5597, and likewise does not list George Goddard as a recipient. Since Goddard had no surviving family and the location of his medal is unknown, it is an educated estimate on the part of the author to list him as a potential recipient of Medal of Nakhimov number 5597.

Appendix 3

Soviet Medal Statutes[1]

Order of Suvorov

1. The Order of Suvorov is awarded to Red Army commanders for distinguished accomplishments in managing troops, organizing combat operations, and displaying decisiveness and persistence in the execution which, as a result, achieved victory for the homeland in the Patriotic War.

2. The awarding of the Order of Suvorov is by decree of the Presidium of the Supreme Soviet of the USSR.

3. The Order of Suvorov has three classes:

Order of Suvorov, First Class

Order of Suvorov, Second Class

Order of Suvorov, Third Class

4. The Order of Suvorov, First Class is awarded to front and army commanders, their deputies, chiefs of staff, chief operational managers, and branch chiefs (artillery, air force, armored, and mortar):

For excellently organized and conducted front or army level operations devastating a numerically superior force.

For a skillfully conducted encirclement of a numerically superior enemy, resulting in the full destruction of enemy personnel and capture of his arms and equipment.

For displaying initiative and decisiveness in choosing and executing the main thrust against an enemy which not only devastated the enemy, but allowed the follow-on pursuit by friendly forces.

For a skillfully conducted deception operation that crushed the enemy and destroyed his ability to regroup or employ reserves.

5. The Order of Suvorov, Second Class is awarded to corps, division, and brigade commanders, their deputies, and chiefs of staff:

For fully organizing a combined arms operation with a sudden, decisive attack using the least number of forces necessary to destroy an enemy corps or division.

For the breakthrough of an enemy defensive belt; development of the breakthrough and subsequent, relentless pursuit, encirclement, and destruction of the enemy.

For conducting defensive operations against a numerically superior encircling enemy and break out from the encirclement while preserving the unit's combat capability, arms and equipment.

For conducting a brigade or larger size armored raid deep into the enemy rear area which significantly affects the enemy and allows for the successful accomplishment of an army level operation.

6. The Order of Suvorov, Third Class is awarded to regimental, battalion, and company commanders, and regimental chiefs of staff:

For choosing the decisive point of a bold, direct attack against a superior enemy and destroying him.

For stubborn resistance against a superior enemy's attack, involving both the able holding of his unit's position and an effective transition to the attack.

The Order of Suvorov was awarded the following number of times:

Order of Suvorov, First Class: 393 (0 to the US Navy)

Order of Suvorov, Second Class: 2,862 (1 to the US Navy)

Order of Suvorov, Third Class: 4,012 (1 to the US Navy)

Order of Kutuzov

1. The Order of Kutuzov is awarded to Red Army commanders for a well-developed and well-conducted operational plan at the front, army, or independent large unit level that caused heavy enemy destruction and preserved our forces' combat capability.

2. The awarding of the Order of Kutuzov is by decree of the Presidium of the Supreme Soviet of the USSR.

3. The Order of Kutuzov has three classes:

Order of Kutuzov, First Class

Order of Kutuzov, Second Class

Order of Kutuzov, Third Class

4. The Order of Kutuzov, First Class is awarded to front and army commanders, their deputies, and chiefs of staff:

For a well-developed and executed front or army level operation that resulted in the destruction of the enemy.

For a well-developed and well-executed plan with organized mass counterattacks that forced the retreat of major enemy units, with heavy casualties, and allowed friendly forces to occupy new forward lines with minor losses to materiel, manpower, or combat readiness.

For a capably organized operation of major units against superior enemy forces that exhausted the enemy, destroyed his personnel and materiel, and preserved friendly strength in a constant state of readiness for a decisive assault.

5. The Order of Kutuzov, Second Class is awarded to corps, division, and brigade commanders and their chiefs of staff:

For exceptional persistence in holding off an attack of a superior enemy and retaining occupied positions employing a well-organized fire support system, use of terrain, troop counterattacks, armor or aviation and turning the battle into a decisive and successful assault.

For a well-conducted, decisive action, in a difficult situation and while facing a superior enemy, which caused heavy destruction to the enemy.

For a capable defense of an occupied position, while surrounded by a superior enemy, and a successful breaking out that preserved friendly combat readiness.

For the organization of a friendly force's struggle against superior enemy armored or air forces causing heavy enemy losses and forcing his withdrawal.

6. The Order of Kutuzov, Third Class is awarded to the regimental, battalion, and company commanders and their executive officers:

For initiative displayed in conducting an assigned battle, causing the enemy heavy losses as a result of a sudden, bold attack.

For the capture of a massive enemy strongpoint with minimal friendly losses, successful consolidation, and defeat of enemy counter-attacks.

For the organization of a successful pursuit operation against a retreating enemy that destroyed his forces and material and quickly neutralized enemy delaying positions.

For destroying enemy communications and disabling his rear area garrisons and bases.

For a capably developed battle plan, employing combined arms with a successful outcome.

The Order of Kutuzov was awarded the following number of times:

Order of Kutuzov, First Class: 675 (1 to the US Navy)

Order of Kutuzov, Second Class: 3,326 (1 to the US Navy)

Order of Kutuzov, Third Class: 3,328 (1 to the US Navy)

The Order of Alexander Nevsky

1. The Order of Alexander Nevsky is awarded to Red Army commanders displaying personal courage, boldness, bravery, and capable command in combat for the homeland in the Patriotic War that secured our unit's success.

2. The awarding of the Order of Alexander Nevsky is by decree of the Presidium of the Supreme Soviet of the USSR.

3. The Order of Alexander Nevsky is awarded to divisional, brigade, regimental, battalion, company and platoon commanders:

For displaying initiative in choosing the decisive moment for a bold, surprise attack on the enemy and inflicting heavy enemy casualties, with minor friendly losses.

For completing a well-executed, combined arms attack, resulting in either complete destruction of the enemy, or the destruction of a large part of a superior enemy.

For an artillery unit commander's persistent suppression of a superior enemy artillery unit, destruction of an enemy artillery position suppressing our unit's advances, destruction of a bunker complex, or disruption of an enemy armor attack, and causing heavy enemy losses.

For a tank unit commander's successful mission accomplishment, with heavy enemy personnel and equipment losses, while preserving his unit's combat capability.

For an aviation unit commander's successful completion of a series of sorties, which cause heavy enemy losses, while returning with his unit, without losses, to base.

For initiative in disrupting or destroying an enemy's engineer obstacles, and supporting a successful passage of friendly troops.

For managing uninterrupted, multi-faceted communications, and the timely restoration of damaged communications, thereby guaranteeing a friendly unit's success.

For a bold and decisive landing (airborne, sea, or dismounted troops), with minimum casualties, resulting in the enemy's destruction and overall mission accomplishment.

The Order of Alexander Nevsky was awarded 43,638 times (1 to the US Navy)

The Order of the Patriotic War

1. The Order of the Patriotic War is awarded to enlisted and officer ranks of the Red Army, Navy, NKVD troops, and partisan detachments who displayed bravery, fortitude, and courage in combat for the Soviet homeland and also to servicemen, who by their actions, enabled our troops' successful combat operations.

2. The awarding of the Order of the Patriotic War is by decree of the Presidium of the Supreme Soviet of the USSR.

3. The Order of the Patriotic War has two classes:

Order of the Patriotic War First Class

Order of the Patriotic War Second Class

The higher class is the First Class.

The class of the order bestowed upon the individual is directed by decree of the Presidium of the Supreme Soviet of the USSR.

4. The Order of the Patriotic War First class is awarded to those:

Who have struck and destroyed an especially important objective in the enemy rear area.

Who have courageously carried out their responsibilities as an aircraft crewmember on a mission in which the navigator or pilot received the Order of Lenin.

Who as a crewmember of a:

Heavy bomber, destroyed four aircraft

Long-range bomber, destroyed five aircraft

Short-range bomber, destroyed seven aircraft

Ground attack aircraft, destroyed three aircraft

Fighter, destroyed three aircraft

Who as a crewmember of a:

Heavy bomber, completed twenty successful sorties

Long-range bomber, completed twenty-five successful sorties

Short-range bomber, completed thirty successful sorties

Ground attack aircraft, completed twenty-five successful sorties

Fighter, completed sixty successful sorties

Long-range reconnaissance aircraft, completed twenty-five successful sorties

Short-range reconnaissance aircraft, completed thirty successful sorties

Artillery spotter aircraft, completed fifteen successful sorties

Aviation communication aircraft, completed sixty successful sorties from friendly territories and thirty successful sorties involving landing in territory occupied by the enemy.

Transport aircraft, completed sixty successful sorties from friendly territories and fifteen successful sorties involving landing in territory occupied by the enemy.

Who organized accurate and uninterrupted administration of aviation units.

Who organized accurate and well-planned staff work.

Who managed to repair a damaged aircraft that made a forced landing in enemy territory and got it airborne.

Who repaired no fewer than ten aircraft at a forward airbase under enemy fire.

Who, under enemy fire, managed to evacuate supplies from an airbase and sabotaged the base, thereby prohibiting the enemy from using it.

Who personally destroyed two heavy or medium tanks or three light tanks (armored cars); or three heavy or medium tanks or five light tanks (armored cars) as a member of a gun crew.

Who suppressed no fewer than five enemy batteries with artillery fire.

Who destroyed no fewer than three enemy aircraft with air defense fire.

Who, as a tank crewmember, successfully accomplished three combat missions which destroyed enemy fire support or personnel or destroyed no fewer than four enemy tanks or four anti-tank guns in battle.

Who, while under enemy fire, recovered no fewer than three damaged tanks from the battlefield.

Who, disregarding danger, was the first into the enemy's defensive positions, decisively destroyed them, and gave our troops the ability to quickly capture the enemy line.

Who, while under enemy fire, repaired a bridge or pontoon which was damaged by the enemy.

Who, under enemy fire, either fixed a bridge or crossing which was destroyed by the enemy, or who, under orders, personally blew up a bridge or crossing under enemy fire to delay enemy movement.

Who, under enemy fire, technically or personally established communications or fixed communications equipment damaged by the enemy that supported friendly, uninterrupted combat activities.

Who, in battle, and by their own initiative, moved an anti-tank gun or artillery pieces to an open position and fired point-blank at an attacking enemy.

Who commanded a battalion, company or platoon and destroyed a superior enemy.

Who participated in a cavalry raid, charged into the enemy, and destroyed them.

Who captured an enemy artillery battery in combat.

Who, as a result of personal reconnaissance, determined the enemy's defensive weak points and led our troops into the enemy's rear area.

Who sunk an enemy ship or two enemy transports as a crewmember of a ship, plane, or coastal artillery gun.

Who organized and successfully conducted a naval landing on enemy territory.

Who, under enemy fire, steered their damaged ship to safety.

Who captured and brought back an enemy combat ship to a friendly port.

Who successfully cleared a mined approach to the enemy's bases.

Who, by successfully clearing mines, secured the safety of our navy's activity.

Who successfully repaired the damaged portions of a ship, thus restoring its defensive capability or allowed it to return to base.

Who successfully organized our troop's materiel-technical support, thus contributing to the destruction of the enemy.

5. The Order of the Patriotic War Second Class is awarded to those:

Who courageously carried out their responsibilities as an aircraft crewmember on a mission in which the navigator or pilot received the Order of the Red Banner.

Who have as a crewmember of a:

Heavy bomber, destroyed three aircraft

Long-range bomber, destroyed four aircraft

Short-range bomber, destroyed six aircraft

Ground attack aircraft, destroyed two aircraft

Fighter, destroyed two aircraft

Who as a crewmember of a:

Heavy bomber, completed fifteen successful sorties

Long-range bomber, completed twenty successful sorties

Short-range bomber, completed twenty-five successful sorties

Ground attack aircraft, completed twenty successful sorties

Fighter, completed fifty successful sorties

Long-range reconnaissance aircraft, completed twenty successful sorties

Short-range reconnaissance aircraft, completed twenty-five successful sorties

Artillery spotter aircraft, completed ten successful sorties

Aviation communication aircraft, completed fifty successful sorties from friendly territories and twenty successful sorties involving landing in territory occupied by the enemy.

Transport aircraft, completed fifty successful sorties from friendly territories and ten successful sorties involving landing in territory occupied by the enemy.

Who managed to repair, master, and employ in combat, a captured enemy aircraft.

Who repaired no fewer than five aircraft at a forward airbase under enemy fire.

Who personally destroyed a heavy or a medium tank or two light tanks (armored cars); or two heavy or medium tanks or three light tanks (armored cars) as a member of a gun crew.

Who destroyed enemy fire support with artillery fire or mortars, thus allowing the successful actions of our troops.

Who suppressed no fewer than three enemy batteries with artillery or mortar fire.

Who destroyed no fewer than two enemy aircraft with air defense artillery.

Who destroyed no fewer than three enemy firing positions with his tank, thus allowing the successful penetration of the enemy line by our troops.

Who, as a crewmember of a tank, destroyed no fewer than three enemy tanks or artillery pieces in battle.

Who, under enemy fire, recovered from the battlefield no fewer than two tanks disabled by enemy fire.

Who destroyed an enemy tank on the battlefield or the enemy rear area with grenades, "Molotov" cocktails or explosives.

Who led their battalion, company, or platoon out of an enemy encirclement, without loss of weapons or materiel, and shattered the enemy.

Who infiltrated into the enemy's positions and destroyed no less than one heavy gun, three mortars or three machine guns.

Who, at night, have taken out an enemy forward post or captured it.

Who downed an enemy aircraft with their personal firearm.

Who struggled with a numerically superior enemy, not given up any ground, and caused heavy enemy losses.

Who organized and supported uninterrupted communications, under difficult combat conditions, between the command and subordinates throughout a battle, which enabled the successful operations of our troops.

Who, as a member of a ship, aircraft, or coastal gun crew, sunk or damaged an enemy combat ship or transport.

Who captured and returned an enemy transport to a friendly port.

Whose timely discovery of the enemy thwarted an attack on a ship or base.

Who successfully maneuvered their ship which resulted in sinking or damaging an enemy ship.

Who, with capable work, ensured the successful combat activities of a military unit or ship.

Who organized smooth, materiel-technical support to combat units, thereby contributing to the unit's success.

6. Those awarded the Order of the Patriotic War may receive subsequent awards of the same Order for new feats and distinctions.

7. The Order of the Patriotic War is worn on the awardee's right breast.

8. Cities, units, and institutions may be awarded the Order of the Patriotic War.

9. Civilians may be awarded the Order of the Patriotic War.

10. The Order of the Patriotic War and order booklet are to be awarded posthumously to the deceased awardee's family and kept by them in memory of the deceased.

11. Revocation or rescindment of the Order of the Patriotic War is by the Presidium of the Supreme Soviet of the USSR.

12. Foreigners may be awarded the Order of the Patriotic War for their contribution to the successful combat operations for the Soviet homeland.

The Order of the Patriotic War was awarded the following number of times:

Order of the Patriotic War, First Class: 324,903 (25 to the US Navy; 2 to the US Coast Guard)

Order of the Patriotic War, Second Class: 951,652 (26 to the US Navy; 1 to the US Coast Guard)

The Order of the Red Star

1. The Order of the Red Star is established for awarding great achievements in defending the USSR in war, as well as the state security in peace.

2. The Order of the Red Star is awarded to:

Servicemen of the Soviet army, Navy, Border Guards, Internal Troops, associates of the Committee of State Security USSR, and also enlisted and command elements of the Organs of Internal Affairs.

Military units, ships, enterprises, establishments, and organizations.

3. The Order of the Red Star is awarded:

For personal courage and bravery in battle, excellent organization and capable combat leadership that facilitates the success of our troops.

For a unit's successful combat activity that causes significant enemy losses.

For achievement in securing state security and the inviolability of the state border of the USSR.

For courage and bravery displayed in combat or on duty involving the risk of life.

For exemplary accomplishments of the command's special assignment and other achievements during peace time.

For great achievements in supporting the high state of military readiness, excellent results in combat and political training, fielding new military equipment and other achievements strengthening the defensive might of the USSR.

For achievements in developing military science and equipment and training the cadre of the Armed Forces of the USSR.

For achievements in strengthening the defensive capabilities of the governments of the socialist brotherhood.

4. The award of the Order of the Red Star is in accordance with the Ministry of Defense of the USSR, Ministry of Internal Affairs of the USSR, and the Committee of State Security of the USSR, respectively.

5. The Order of the Red Star is worn on the right breast, and in the presence of other orders of the USSR, is situated after the Order of the Patriotic War Second Class.

The Order of the Red Star was awarded approximately 4 million times (27 to the US Navy; 4 to the Merchant Marine):

The Order of Glory

1. The Order of Glory is awarded to enlisted ranks and aviation junior lieutenants who distinguish themselves by displaying glorious feats, bravery, courage, and fearlessness in combat for the Soviet homeland.

2. The Order of Glory has three classes:

Order of Glory First Class

Order of Glory Second Class

Order of Glory Third Class

The highest class is the First Class; the awarding is sequential: Third Class Second Class and First Class.

3. The Order of Glory is awarded to those who:

Were the first to valiantly storm an enemy position, thereby guaranteeing the unit's success through personal bravery.

Continued to accomplish the mission from a burning tank.

Saved a unit banner from the enemy's imminent capture.

Personally killed ten to fifty enemy personnel with small arms fire.

Disabled no less than two enemy tanks with an anti-tank rifle.

Destroyed, with hand grenades, one to three tanks on the front lines or in the enemy's rear area.

Destroyed no less than three enemy aircraft with machine-gun or artillery fire.

Disregarding danger, were the first into an enemy bunker and decisively destroyed it.

Found enemy defensive weak points in a personal reconnaissance which allowed friendly soldiers into the enemy's rear area.

Personally captured an enemy officer.

Took out an enemy watch post or captured it.

Personally penetrated into the enemy's position and resourcefully and bravely destroyed a machine-gun or mortar.

Destroyed an enemy supply depot while on a night sortie.

Saved their commander's life while under a great threat of danger.

Returned to the unit after being bandaged.

Destroyed an enemy aircraft with their personal small arm.

Ensured their unit's success by destroying the enemy's indirect fire capability with artillery or mortar fire.

Under enemy fire, cleared the way for their attacking unit through enemy barbed-wire obstacles.

While risking their life, rendered aid in the course of a battle to the wounded under enemy fire.

Continued to fire from a disabled tank, thereby fulfilling their mission.

Drove their tank directly into an enemy convoy, destroyed it and continued to push on to complete the mission.

Destroyed, with their own tank, one or several heavy guns or destroyed no less than two enemy machine-gun nests.

Gathered valuable information about the enemy while on reconnaissance.

As a fighter pilot, destroyed in aerial combat, two to four enemy fighters or three to six bombers.

As an aerial navigator, destroyed two to five enemy tanks, three to six locomotives, a train at a train station or en route, or no less than two aircraft at an enemy airbase as a result of an aerial raid.

As an aerial navigator, destroyed one or two enemy aircraft in aerial combat as a result of their initiative.

As a crew-member of a daylight bombing raid, destroyed a train column, bridge, ammunition depot, fuel depot, battalion or higher enemy headquarters, train station or track section, electro-station, dam, military vessel, transport, cutter, or no fewer than two enemy aircraft at an airbase.

As a crew-member of a light bomber on a night run, destroyed an ammunition depot, fuel depot, enemy headquarters, train column, or bridge.

As a crew-member of a long-range night bomber, destroyed a train station, ammunition depot, fuel depot, port armament, naval transport, train column, or bombed an important factory or industrial center.

As a crew-member of a bomber, during a daylight raid, downed one to two enemy aircraft in aerial combat.

As a member of a reconnaissance party, successfully carried out their mission and gathered valuable information about the enemy.

4. The award of the Order of Glory is by decree of the Presidium of the Supreme Soviet of the USSR.

The Order of Glory, Third Class was awarded 997,815 times (45 to the US Navy).

The Medal "For Valor"

1. The medal "For Valor" is established as an award for personal courage and bravery displayed in the defense of the Socialist Homeland and in the performance of military duty.

2. The medal "For Valor" is awarded to servicemen of the Soviet Army, Navy, Border Guards, Internal Troops and other citizens of the USSR.

The medal "For Valor" can also be awarded to foreign individuals.

3. The awarding of the medal "For Valor" is for personal courage and bravery displayed:

In combat with enemies of the Socialist Homeland.

In the defense of the state boundary of the USSR.

In the performance of military duty in conditions involving risk of life.

4. The medal "For Valor" is worn on the left breast, and in the presence of other orders and medals of the USSR, is positioned after the orders.

The Medal "For Valor" was awarded approximately 4.5 million times (25 to the US Navy).

The Ushakov Medal

1. The Medal of Ushakov is established as an award for courage and bravery displayed while defending the Socialist Homeland at sea, in war as well as peace.

2. The Medal of Ushakov is awarded to soldiers and sailors, petty officers and non-commissioned officers, chief petty officers and warrant officers of the Navy and Naval Border Guards.

3. The Medal of Ushakov is bestowed for personal courage and bravery displayed:

In naval combat with enemies of the Socialist Homeland.

In the defense of the state naval boundary of the USSR.

In the execution of a Navy or Naval Border Guard's ship or unit's combat mission.

In the performance of military duty in conditions involving risk of life.

4. The Medal of Ushakov is worn on the left breast and in the presence of other medals of the USSR, is positioned after the medal "For Valor."

The Medal of Ushakov was awarded approximately 15,000 times (5 to the US Navy).

The Medal "For Military Merit"

1. The medal "For Military Merit" is established as an award for active assistance in successful combat operations and increasing troop combat readiness.

2. The medal "For Military Merit" is awarded to servicemen of the Soviet Army, Navy, Border Guards, Internal Troops, and other citizens of the USSR.

The medal "For Military Merit" can also be awarded to foreign individuals.

3. The awarding of the medal "For Military Merit" is:

For skillful, bold combat actions displaying initiative, causing the successful accomplishment of a unit's combat mission.

For courage displayed in the defense of the state border of the USSR.

For excellent accomplishments in military and political training; developing new military equipment; supporting the high level of a unit's training; and other achievements occurring on active military service.

4. The medal "For Military Merit" is worn on the left breast and in the presence of other medals of the USSR, is positioned after the Medal of Ushakov.

The Medal "For Military Merit" was awarded approximately 5 million times (25 to the US Navy).

The Nakhimov Medal

1. The Nakhimov Medal is established as an award for excellence in defending the Socialist Homeland and active assistance in the successful completion of a Navy or Naval Border Guard's ship or unit's combat mission.

2. The Nakhimov Medal is awarded to soldiers and sailors, petty officers and non-commissioned officers, chief petty officer and warrant officers of the Navy and Naval Border Guards.

3. The Nakhimov Medal is bestowed for:

Skillful, bold action displaying initiative while enabling successful completion of a ship or unit's combat mission while at sea.

For courage displayed in the defense of the state naval boundary of the USSR.

For self-sacrifice displayed in the performance of military duty or other acts involving a risk of life while on active duty.

4. The Nakhimov Medal is worn on the left breast and in the presence of other medals of the USSR, is positioned after the medal "For Military Merit."

The Nakhimov Medal was awarded approximately 13,700 times (15 to the US Navy).

Appendix 4

Translations of the Soviet Order and Medal Books to US Navy Recipients

Unlike medals presented by the United States, the orders and medals bestowed by the Soviet Union required specific, formal documentation in order to prevent cases of "stolen valor" and potential fraud. These documents, known as the Order Booklet (Ordenskaya Knizhka) and the Medal Booklet (Udosteverenie K Medali) identified the exact awards earned by a recipient. Without these documents, a person wearing a Soviet order or medal could potentially be charged with the crime of wearing unearned awards. Further, these documents provided the rules, responsibilities, and entitlements of the holder. In addition to bearing the serial number of the recipient's award (which was not done during the 1945 awarding, in an unusual breech of standard Soviet protocol) the number of each booklet was inscribed in the bearer's corresponding pension document. This allowed authorities to cross-reference the bearer's pension booklet with that of his or her Order or Medal Booklet in an attempt to prevent fraud from taking place. Further confirmation of the identity of the bearer included their photograph, sealed with an official stamp of the Soviet Union, in these cases, from the Soviet Consul, inside the front cover of the booklet. In a labor-saving measure, the requirement for the photograph was waived in the years immediately following the end of the war, and the photograph-less documents were overstamped with the wording "valid without photograph." This appendix provides a translation of the booklets awarded to the United States sea service recipients in 1944 and 1945.

Page One

Given Name, Patronymic Middle Name, Last Name
Signature of the bearer of the book.

Page Two

1. [The bearer] Is awarded [the listed award]

2. [The bearer] Is entitled to the monetary grants accompanying the Order as well as other privileges and preferences, beginning on [date], in accordance with the general rules relating to the orders of the USSR.

3. This book has no expiration date.

The secretary of the Presidium of the Supreme Soviet of the USSR. [Signed] A. Gorkin [with serial number of the order book]

Page Three

General rules relating to orders granted by the USSR.

1. An order granted by the USSR is the highest award for special merits in the field of socialist construction and in the defense of the USSR.

2. The Central Executive Committee of the USSR has established the following orders of the USSR: the Order of Lenin, the Order of the Red Banner, the Order of the Red Star, the Order of the Red Banner of Labor, and the Order of the Badge of Honor.

3. An order of the USSR may be bestowed on individual citizens as well as upon military units of the Red Army, factories, institutions, and organizations.

4. The recipients of an award of the USSR are entitled to additional orders of the same or any other category for new achievements.

Page Four

5. The Central Executive Committee of the USSR is the one to grant an order of the USSR. In wartime the Order of the Red Banner and the Order of the Red Star are also being awarded by the People's Commissar of the Defense of the USSR.

6. Each order of the USSR has its own rules approved by the Central Executive Committee of the USSR. The rules relating to each order are as follows:

a) the appearance and description of the order.

b) the detailed designation of the special service rendered to the USSR for which the order in question is being awarded.

c) special rules pertaining to the award of the respective order.

Page Five

7. Simultaneously with the granting of an order of the USSR the recipients are given a special certificate by the Central Executive Committee of the USSR and a book of the order bearer of a designated example.

* Note: by order of the Presidium of the Supreme Soviet of the USSR dated 2 June 1939, article 7 of the general regulations regarding the granting of orders of the USSR, the grant of a special certificate to the recipient of an order of the USSR has been abolished.

8. An order of the USSR is worn on the left side of the chest. Army units, factories, institutions, and organizations affix the order of the USSR to their banners.

9. The recipients of an order of the USSR are granted the following monetary awards at the expense of the state: for the Order of Lenin – 25 rubles a month; for the Order of the Red Banner – 20 rubles a month; for the Orders of the Red Banner of Labor and Red Star – 15 rubles a month; and for the Order of the Badge of Honor – 10 rubles a month. These monetary awards are in addition to the wages or payments by the Red Army or pensions the recipients may already be receiving and are not based on the amount of such payments.

10. The bearer of an order of the USSR is entitled to free transportation on the railway and steamship lines once a year (round trip).

Page Six

11. The bearer of an order of the USSR is entitled to free transportation on the street cars in every city of the USSR.

12. The duration of service required to be entitled a pension, to disability pensions, and to pension on other basis is reduced by one third in the case of a bearer of an order of the USSR.

13. The bearer of an order of the USSR is exempt from the payment of income taxes and from any deductions from wages or Red Army pay for their dwelling and up to a maximum of 6000 rubles annually. If the taxes are more than 6000 rubles per year, the bearer must only pay the 6000 deductible.

14. The bearer of an order of the USSR is entitled to a reduction of 10% to 50% in his rental in the houses where the rate is established by the local Soviet.

Page Seven

The size of the reduction is determined by the local Soviet. Any space above the regular allotment and every additional space is paid for by the bearer of the order according to the regular rate.

15. The privilege of reduced rentals is extended to the family of the bearer of the order in case the bearer dies. This privilege applies to: his wife, minor children, and elderly parents.

16. The amount of the pension to be paid to the family of the bearer of the order in case of his death is to be determined on the basis of the amount of allowance received by the deceased, his pension, and the additional payments received by him in connection with the holding of the order.

17. The bearers of orders of the USSR are to be exemplars in the performance of their duties as required by law of all citizens of the USSR.

18. Only the Central Executive Committee of the USSR has the right to revoke an order of the USSR. The grounds for the revocation of the order may be either a court sentence or the commission of degrading acts by the bearer of the order.

Page Eight

19. Unauthorized wearing of an order of the USSR will be punishable as a criminal offense.

By order of the Presidium of the Supreme Soviet of the USSR dated May 20, 1942, the Order of the Patriotic War, First and Second Class has been established.

The higher of the two orders is the First Class. The order is worn on the right side of the chest.

The monetary awards are: for the order of the First Class – 20 rubles; for the order of the Second Class – 15 rubles per month.

The bearers of the Order of the Patriotic War are entitled to the same privileges and preferences as established by the general regulations governing the orders of the USSR.

An Order of the Patriotic War that is awarded posthumously is to be given to his family together with the order book so that they may keep it as a memento.

Page Nine

Rules of the procedure wherein bearers of the orders of the USSR are to receive the privileges and preferences that they are entitled to by the general regulations governing the orders of the USSR.

1.The personal book of the bearer of the order of is the essential document for the receipt of the privileges and preferences granted by the general regulations governing the orders of the USSR.

2. The book of the bearer of an order is valid indefinitely.

3. The established monetary awards in connection with the orders are to be paid by the State Savings Banks on the basis of a special order by the general administration of the State Savings Banks and the general office of the People's Commissariat of Finance of the USSR.

Page Ten

4. In case of the death of the bearer of an order the amounts to be paid for the previous month as well as the current month are paid to members of the family of the deceased who were his dependents, and the month the death occurred is paid in full.

In order to receive these monetary payments the family of the deceased makes an application to the respective Savings Bank, supplying the following: a death certificate, an affidavit stating the composition of the family of the bearer of the order, naming the ones who were being supported by him, and the documents relating to the order of the deceased.

5. The privilege of free transportation on the railway, waterways, and streetcars is granted only to the bearer of the order. This privilege is not extended to the members of the family of the bearer of an order.

6. The documents for the free transportation of the bearer of an order are the special travel tickets issued to the book of the bearer of the order.

Page Eleven

7. The tickets mentioned in paragraph 6 entitle the bearer of the order to the following:

a) free use of a seat in first class and in first class cabins.

b) travel in all passenger trains – not excluding post and express trains as well as on the steamers of all the river and ocean lines.

8. The bearer of an order of the USSR is supplied with a single-use ticket for each year. The single-use ticket gives the bearer of the order the right to one trip.

The term "one trip" stands for a return journey from the station (dock, port) where the trip starts to the station (dock, port) of the destination and return.

For each separate journey, one single-use ticket is used. The single-use ticket may be filled out only for such destination for which passenger tickets are being sold and also for alternate (railway-waterway) destinations.

The itinerary is filled out by the ticket official of the railway station, the dock, or port of embarkation in accordance with the request of the ticket holder.

Page Twelve

The single-use ticket is to be presented to the ticket office for punching or stamping of the respective coupon reading "going" at the start of the journey and "returning" on the return trip.

The single-use ticket is good for a trip any time within the calendar year designated on that ticket, regardless of the time when the trip starts and will become void at midnight on December 31st of that year.

The ticket cannot be used the following year.

9. The single-use ticket is not valid for any journey if not accompanied by the respective order book of the order bearer (that is – the book of the same serial number). The order book is to be presented together with the ticket at the ticket office of the railway station, dock, or port at the starting point of the journey, as well as to inspectors on the trains and steamers.

10. Travel in a sleeper of a through train is permitted only upon prepayment of the extra fare required for travel in such trains.

Page Thirteen

11. In cases not foreseen in these regulations, the instructions of the People's Commissariat of Transport governing free tickets will be applied.

12. For the free use of streetcars in all cities, the bearer must only present his order book.

This is a page-by-page translation of the medal book (it could also be translated as a medal certificate) that was awarded with the Medals of Nakhimov and Ushakov. The medals "For Valor" and "For Military Merit" to US Navy and Merchant Marine recipients had medal booklets that had been specifically printed for those medals, and are considered to be the type normally seen with pre- and early-wartime awards to Soviet citizens. In the USSR, these books discontinued during the war as the cost and administrative burden to have specific documents for each type of medal was a bureaucratic nightmare. Thus, all Soviet holders of medals received the same documents issued to the US Navy recipients of the Medals of Nakhimov and Ushakov as it was a document created to represent all of the regulations for all medals of the USSR. The translation of the updated (for the time) universal medal document is included here.

Page One

Photo of bearer

Page Two

Given Name, Patronymic Middle Name, Last Name

Page Three

1. Medal awarded: [name of medal] Number of Medal [number]
2. [The bearer] is entitled to monetary grants as well as free transportation on street cars in all cities of the USSR, beginning on [date], in accordance with this medal's general rules.
3. This certificate has no expiration date.

The secretary of the Presidium of the Supreme Soviet of the USSR. [Signed] A. Gorkin [with serial number of the order book] and Date

Page Four

EXCERPT

From the General Rules relating to medals awarded by the USSR – "For Valor," "For Military Merit," "For Labor Heroism," and "For Labor Excellence."

The Medal "For Valor" may be awarded to enlisted military personnel, commissioned and non-commissioned officers of the Red Army of workers and peasants, Russian Navy Fleet, and Border Guard Units for display of outstanding personal courage and valor in combat against enemies of the Soviet Union, while defending national borders of the USSR, or in fight against saboteurs, spies and other enemies of the Soviet state.

Page Five

The Medal "For Military Merit" may be awarded to enlisted military personnel, commissioned and non-commissioned officers of the Red Army of workers and peasants, Russian Navy Fleet, and Border Guard Units and also civilians who, putting their lives at great risk, showed initiative, skill and performed acts of heroism, contributing to success during combat.

The Medal "For Labor Heroism" is awarded to workers, peasants, laborers, engineers and technicians, household workers, employees of transportation, construction, cooperative and trade organizations, scientific and cultural facilities, who, selflessly laboring, are being the forerunners of advancement of socialism; who set an example of using technology in manner of Stahanov;

Page Six

who set stellar standards of productivity, push forward in the development of science, technology and culture.

The Medal "For Labor Excellence" is awarded to workers, peasants, laborers, engineers and technicians, household workers, employees of transportation, construction, cooperative and trade organizations, and scientific and cultural facilities to recognize the outstanding labor efforts, high productivity standards, and achievements in development of science, technology and culture.

The awarding of medals is carried out by the Presidium of The Supreme Soviet of the USSR.

The medal is pinned and worn on the left side of the chest.

The USSR medal recipients are granted the following monetary awards at the expense of the state: "For Valor" – 10 rubles per month, "For Military Merit" – 5 rubles per month, "For Labor Heroism" – 10 rubles per month, "For Labor Excellence" – 5 rubles per month.

Monetary awards can be collected at any State Savings Bank throughout the USSR.

Page Seven

Medal recipients are entitled to free use of public street cars throughout all the cities of the USSR.

Medals can only be revoked by the Presidium of the Supreme Soviet of the USSR.

"For Valor" medal recipients must continually show the example of personal courage, valor and fortitude in our struggle with the enemies of the Soviet state and must be a model to all other citizens in fulfilling their civil obligations.

"For Labor Heroism" medal recipients must wear it with honor, serve as an example of conscientiousness in fulfilling their public duties, and serve as a model of good conscience and diligence in fulfilling their civil obligations.

"For Military Merit" and "For Labor Excellence" medal recipients must wear their medal with honor and serve as an example of conscientiousness and diligence in fulfilling their civil obligations.

Page Eight

Rules pertaining to the bestowal of the "For Valor" and "For Military Merit" medals were established by the Decree of the Presidium of the Supreme Soviet of the USSR on October 17, 1938.

Rules pertaining to the bestowal of the "For Labor Heroism" and "For Labor Excellence" medals were established by the Decree of the Presidium of the Supreme Soviet of the USSR on December 27, 1938.

NOTES

Chapter 1

1. Message 282317 from COMTASKFOR 4 to CINCLANT dated January 29, 1942.

2. ibid.

3. Letter dated July 19, 1945, from the Navy Department Board of Decorations and Medals to the Secretary of the Navy.

4. Ragnar Ragnarsson comment on http://www.vpnavy.org/vp73_1940.html

5. Roy Grossnick, Vol. 2, *Dictionary of American Naval Aviation Squadrons,* 704.

6. The narrative is sourced from Commander Patrol Squadron Seventy Three letter to the Secretary of the Navy serial number VP-73/P15-A9-8, dated June 24, 1942.

7. The Distinguished Flying Cross was approved through the Commander, Task Group 24.6, but the final award presented was an Air Medal. The determination to downgrade was not included with the documents available to me.

8. *Santa Fe New Mexican*, "LASL accident victim released from hospital," June 12, 1978.

9. Nisetle, Axel. *German U-Boat Losses During World War II Details of Destruction.*

10. A similar light was used during the attack on *U-1229*, discussed in Chapter 2.

11. Discussed in Chapter 2.

12. Based on the combat awards or service of a particular officer, the Navy Department had the authorization to promote the officer to the next higher rank upon retirement. The promotion would be in title only; no other benefits were given to the recipient, nor was the rank ever worn on active duty. Thus, it was said that the promotion was simply for the recipient's "tombstone."

13. *German Submarine Sunk off the Province of La Coruna.* Office of Strategic Services report dated November 11, 1943.

14. *US Navy Fleet Air Wing Seven Newsletter*. Volume 3, Issue 1, Publisher Unknown, 2000.

15. *Administrative Report Concerning PB4Y-1 Airplane Bureau Number 32022, 103-B-7 (G)* dated October 5, 1943.

16. Dallas Jones, in an interview with the author, July 2013.

17. *Chicago Tribune*, "Crash of Jet Traced in Part to Turbulence," February 15, 1963.

Chapter 2

1. Interrogation of survivors from *U-860.*
2. Interrogation of survivors from *U-1229.*
3. ibid.
4. Interrogation of Survivors from *U-569.*
5. Letter from Admiral J.H. Sides, Commander in Chief, US Pacific Fleet, to H.S. Roberts dated June 7, 1961.
6. Letter from Commander, Fighting Squadron Eighty-Two to Mrs. Heim, dated April 2, 1945.
7. Report of internment, WD QMC Form 1042, dated November 25, 1947.
8. A detailed account of the last days of the IJN *Kumano* can be found at the website: http://www.combinedfleet.com/atully04.htm.
9. Quoted from Avery's Legion of Merit award citation.

Chapter 3

1. Handshuh discovered *U-256* and *U-220* at the same time. *U-256* escaped, and he sank *U-220.* This is discussed in Chapter 2.
2. The story of the sinking of the SS *Wade Hampton* is recorded in Chapter 13.
3. Interrogation of Survivors from *U-856.*
4. ibid.
5. USS *Gandy* (DE-764) Contact and Action Report.
6. Report on the Interrogation of Survivors from *U-233.*

Chapter 4

1. Factual History of the USCGC *Northland* July 1941 to September 1945.
2. Citation for Pollard's Legion of Merit
3. USS *Herring* – Report of Third War Patrol dated April 13, 1943.
4. Letter from Commander, US Naval Forces in Europe to Commander in Chief US Fleet, Subject *USS* Herring – *Third War Patrol* dated May 22, 1943.
5. ibid.

Chapter 5

1. Albert Weeks, *Russia's Life-Saver*, 108-109.
2. ibid. 109.
3. Paul Kemp, *Convoy! Drama in Arctic Waters*, 18.
4. Albert Weeks, *Russia's Life-Saver,* 6.
5. ibid. 42-43.
6. ibid. 8-9.
7. ibid. 67, 141-152.
8. Paul Kemp, *Convoy! Drama in Arctic Waters*, 16.
9. Thomas Delate, in an interview with the author, December 2013.
10. *United States Naval Administration in World War II Office of Naval Operations: History of the Naval Armed Guard Afloat.*
11. Although no written policy has been found, the fact that only one of all of the Armed Guard participants covered by this book returned for a second voyage to Russia would be indicative of the rarity of making subsequent voyages, in contrast to the routine return trips made by the civilian merchant mariners.

Chapter 6

1. Letter from the Commandant, First Naval District, to the Chief of Naval Operations dated January 30, 1942.
2. Paul Kemp, *Convoy! Drama in Arctic Waters*, 42.
3. Naval Armed Guard Voyage Report for SS *Mormacmar.*
4. Memo dated June 8, 1942, regarding receipt of a call from Admiral Fairfield regarding the Russian government rewarding the entire crew with one month's pay.

5. Note in the SS *Dunboyne* Armed Guard file from "Clay" (unknown) to a LCDR Cleave, stating: "This Armed Guard officer rates a Navy Cross for shooting down 2 planes and general excellence of performance of duty." When or why the award was downgraded to a Silver Star is not known.

6. *San Diego Union* "Eaton P. DeCottes Funeral Scheduled," December 10, 1963. Note: I have found no other evidence to corroborate this claim. Based on the dates of his arrival and departure from the *Day*, as well as the lack of any evidence from the War Diary of USS *LST-464* from this time period, I believe this claim may fall more into the category of "legend" than reality.

Chapter 7

1. Letter from the Port Director, Third Naval District to the Chief of Naval Operations dated July 14, 1944, subject *Voyage reports of 22 vessels scuttled and beached to form breakwaters at "Omaha" and "Utah" Beachheads, Normandy, France.*

2. This disaster is discussed more thoroughly in Chapter 8.

Chapter 8

1. Michael Walling, *Forgotten Sacrifice*, 96.
2. *Annapolis Capital*, "Services set for Adm. Hill," July 20, 1971.
3. Naval Armed Guard Voyage Report for SS *Expositor.*
4. Naval Armed Guard Voyage Report for SS *Zebulon B. Vance.*
5. Bernard Rubinstein, *Who's Who in the Maritime Industry*, 86-88
6. ibid.
7. Marc Desgalier, interview with the author, September 2003.

Chapter 9

1. Naval Armed Guard Voyage Report for SS *American Robin.*
2. Michael Walling, *Forgotten Sacrifice*, 132.
3. Naval Armed Guard Voyage Report for SS *City of Joliet.*
4. Naval Armed Guard Voyage Report for SS *American Robin.*
5. Paul Kemp, *Convoy! Drama in Arctic Waters*, 57.
6. Naval Armed Guard Voyage Report for SS *City of Joliet.*
7. Naval Armed Guard Voyage Report for SS *Richard Henry Lee.*
8. Paul Kemp, *Convoy! Drama in Arctic Waters*, 95. Michael Walling, *Forgotten Sacrifice*, 172-175.
9. Naval Armed Guard Voyage Report for SS *American Robin.*
10. Justin Gleichauf, *Unsung Sailors*, 90.
11. *New York Times*, "Ray Holubowicz, Father of Shipping Containerization, Dies at 88," January 10, 2013.
12. War Diary, USS *Swasey* (DE-248) December 1, 1943 to January 3, 1944.
13. Commander, Eastern Sea Frontier, War Diary January 1, 1944, through February 29, 1944.

Chapter 10

1. *Translation of the final report on Operation "Rosselsprung" (Attack on PQ.17) submitted by Admiral Carls (Gruppe Nord) on 12.7.1942.* National Archives.

2. A thorough discussion of all aspects of PQ-17 is unfortunately beyond the scope of this book. Should they find it interesting, the reader is encouraged to conduct further research on the topic via some of the books listed in the Bibliography.

3. Hughes, Daniel J. (ed.) *Moltke on the Art of War: Selected writings.* New York: Presidio Press, 1993, p. 45-47.

4. David Irving wrote a dedicated work about PQ-17 titled *The Destruction of Convoy PQ-17.* This is the landmark work on the subject, and well worth the time to read in full. The convoy is also discussed in nearly every book about the Arctic convoys as it was truly the most costly (in terms of cargo and human losses) of any convoy of the entire Murmansk Run.

5. The *Richard Bland* is covered in Chapter 12, as well as in detail in William Carter's book *Why Me, Lord?*

6. Commendation of H.P. Wright by Commanding Officer, Armed Guard Unit, Ex-SS *Christopher Newport*, dated September 11, 1942.

7. Naval Armed Guard Voyage Report for SS *Christopher Newport*.

8. ibid.

9. Unpublished journal of Robert Henderson, dated 1942. Courtesy of the Henderson Family.

10. ibid.

11. Naval Armed Guard Voyage Report for SS *William Hooper*.

12. David Irving, *The Destruction of Convoy PQ-17*, 142.

13. ibid. 128-133.

14. ibid. 132.

15. Naval Armed Guard Voyage Report for SS *Washington*.

16. ibid.

17. ibid.

18. Henderson journal.

19. A comment must be made here about conflicting information and the difficulty of trying to find the actual "facts" in order to write about them properly. The author has seen the numbers of survivors of the SS *Olopana* ranging from zero to thirty-four. Some sources say six survived. Others say six died, and the remaining survived a terrible ordeal on the lifeboats at sea. The story of a Russian eyewitness claims there were actually twelve survivors (*Sea Power*, December 2000, published by the Navy League of the United States).

20. Henderson journal.

21. Naval Armed Guard Voyage Report for SS *Washington*.

22. Henderson journal.

23. Naval Armed Guard Voyage Report for SS *Peter Kerr*.

24. Confidential memorandum dated October 30, 1942, subject: *Summary of Statements by Survivors of the US, SS* Peter Kerr, *6647 GT, armed freighter, owned and operated by the Pacific-Atlantic Steamship Company*.

25. Naval Armed Guard Voyage Report for SS *Daniel Morgan*.

26. ibid.

27. Arthur Moore, *A Careless Word, a Needless Sinking*, 300.

28. As a matter of historical interest, *U-255* survived the war and was eventually sunk as a towed target by the British in December 1945. Her commanding officer, Reinhart Reche, earned the Knight's Cross during the war, eventually retired as a Captain from the *Bundesmarine* in 1974, and passed away peacefully on March 3, 1993.

29. Arthur Moore, *A Careless Word, a Needless Sinking*, 190-191.

30. Quoted from his Application for Enlistment, dated January 16, 1942.

31. As recounted in Chapter 3.

32. Naval Armed Guard Voyage Report for SS *El Capitan*.

33. Naval Armed Guard Voyage Report for SS *Benjamin Harrison*.

34. Naval Armed Guard Voyage Report for SS *Troubadour*.

35. *Ocala Star-Banner*, "Florida Newspaper Headliner Winner," April 17, 1963.

36. *Ft Pierce News Tribune*, "Troubadour." December 26, 1976.

37. Peer thus became the only Soviet medal recipient to make two trips on the Murmansk Run. The biography for his second Armed Guard commander is in Chapter 11.

38. *The Evening Post* (Wellington, NZ). "When Wellington Faced a Wartime Disaster," April 23, 1954.

39. Undated and unattributed newspaper clipping. Courtesy of the Harris Family.

Chapter 11

1. Michael Walling, *Forgotten Sacrifice*, 213.

2. Naval Armed Guard Voyage Report for SS *St. Olaf*. It is interesting to note that Wesley Miller's report, though not in the standard terse "military" format at the time (for which he was gently reprimanded and made to re-write it, as per an attachment with the report dated December 14, 1942) turned out to be an exceptional resource for historians. It has been used in several histories of the war and the Arctic convoys, to include use by the foremost historian of the Navy during the war, Samuel Eliot Morison.

3. And described in Chapter 1.

4. The Armed Guard report states that Rotz saw two men under the lifeboat, but only states that he rescued John McKelvey. What happened to the other man trapped under the lifeboat is not known. John McKelvey was sadly killed less than three months later, when his subsequent ship was torpedoed and sunk four hundred miles south of Iceland. There were no survivors.

5. Naval Armed Guard Voyage Report for SS *St. Olaf.*

6. ibid.

7. Naval Armed Guard Voyage Report for SS *Oregonian.*

8. *Investigation called by War Shipping Administration to ascertain facts concerning certain incidences that took place on board the Panamanian SS Africander on her last voyage*, conducted by Captain F.E. Cross, Assistant Marine Superintendent, Washington, DC, and Captain R.E. Pendleton, District Marine Superintendent, War Shipping Administration, dated November 6, 1942.

9. Naval Armed Guard Voyage Report for SS *Africander.*

10. Naval Armed Guard Voyage Report for SS *Virginia Dare.*

11. Unpublished journal of Paul George Gill, dated 1942. Courtesy of Evan Smith.

12. Naval Armed Guard Voyage Report for SS *Virginia Dare.*

13. Naval Armed Guard Voyage Report for SS *St. Olaf.*

14. Naval Armed Guard Voyage Report for SS *Campfire.*

15. Journal of Paul Gill.

16. Naval Armed Guard Voyage Report for SS *Nathaniel Greene.*

17. ibid.

18. Naval Armed Guard Voyage Report for SS *William Moultrie.*

19. The complete list can be accessed at: http://www.usmm.org/gallantships.html.

20. Arthur Moore, *A Careless Word, a Needless Sinking*, 31.

21. Naval Armed Guard Voyage Report for SS *St. Olaf.*

22. Unpublished journal of John Currant. Courtesy of the Currant Family.

23. ibid.

24. ibid.

25. ibid.

26. *Report of Voyage SS Lafayette From New York to Archangel, USSR – Addenda to.* Dated December 14, 1942.

27. Paul Stillwell, *Battleship Arizona*, 210.

Chapter 12

1. Michael Walling, *Forgotten Sacrifice*, 224.

2. ibid. 230.

3. Naval Armed Guard Voyage Report for SS *Oremar.*

4. Naval Armed Guard Voyage Report for SS *Ballot.*

5. The stories of these ships are recounted earlier in Chapter 12.

6. Naval Armed Guard Voyage Report for SS *Nicholas Gilman.*

7. Naval Armed Guard Voyage Report for SS *El Oriente.*

8. ibid.

Chapter 13

1. Naval Armed Guard Voyage Report for SS *George Clymer*. David Pickler's family relayed that he was extremely bitter about this event for many years. An interesting note to the whole scenario is that every contemporary record of the events I had access to seemed to indicate that the *Clymer* was abandoned as soon as the *Alcantara* arrived. This was followed by an immediate departure from the area upon being alerted to the presence of the *Michel*. However, the Naval Armed Guard report written by David Pickler records the day-by-day attempted sinking of the *Clymer* by the *Alcantara*, clearly ending on June 12. Why the *Alcantara* remained in the area for five days after being alerted to the presence of the *Michel*, and why the *Michel* did not attack is something I was unable to determine through my research.

2. James Duffy, *Hitler's Secret Pirate Fleet*, 171-173.

3. Bob Berry, *Gunners Get Glory*, 77.

4. Naval Armed Guard Voyage Report for SS *Dartmouth*.
5. Naval Armed Guard Voyage Report for SS *Columbian*.
6. Naval Armed Guard Voyage Report for SS *Alexander Macomb*.
7. Gordon Williamson, *Wolfpack: The Story of the U-Boat in World War II*
8. Naval Armed Guard Voyage Report for SS *Kaimoku*.
9. Gordon Williamson, *Wolfpack: The Story of the U-Boat in World War II*
10. Dedicated coverage of the SS *Stone Street's* sinking can be found in Leonard Amborski's book: *The Last Voyage: Maritime Heroes of World War II*. His brother was killed when the ship sank, and he dedicated many years to completing the story of the last days of the ship; far more than I can account for in this book.
11. Naval Armed Guard Voyage Report for SS *Pan York*.
12. A nearly day-by-day log of the employment of the *I-27* can be found at: http://www.combinedfleet.com/I-27.html.
13. Naval Armed Guard Voyage Report for SS *Alcoa Prospector*.
14. From http://www.liverpoolshipwreckandhumanesoc.org.

Chapter 14

1. Citation for McGinnis' Legion of Merit.
2. William Carter, Why Me Lord?, p.19.

Chapter 15

1. Telegram from the US Ambassador to the USSR to the Secretary of State dated May 20, 1943. File number 093.612/20.
2. Letter from Cordell Hull to Henry Stimson dated September 9, 1943. File number 093.612/21A.
3. Letter from Frank Knox to Cordell Hull dated September 15, 1943. File number 093.612/22.
4. Letter from Emory Land to Cordell Hull dated September 24, 1943. File number 093.612/24.
5. Letter from Edward Stettinius to Emory Land dated November 1, 1943. File number 093.612/26.
6. Letter from Cordell Hull to Emory Land dated April 10, 1944. File number 093.612/30.
7. Memo to the President from Henry Stimson dated March 18, 1944. File number 093.612/48.
8. From copies of *Pravda*, dated February 19, 1944, February 26, 1944, and March 21, 1944. Retrieved by Captain Igor Kozyr from the Russian State Library.
9. Telegram from Cordell Hull to the American Embassy, Moscow, dated April 8, 1944. File number 093.612/54A.
10. Department of State Memorandum of Conversation between Mr. Bohlen (State Department) and Mr. Zubilin (Soviet Embassy) dated March 13, 1944. File number 093.612/50.
11. Department of State Memorandum of Conversation between Vice Admiral A.P. Fairfield, Maritime Commission, and Mr. Abbott dated April 8, 1944. File number 093.612/66. Also, Department of State Memorandum from Mr. Abbott dated April 8, 1944. File number 093.612/69.
12. Memorandum dated April 13, 1944, from Mr. Abbott to Mr. Muir. File number 093.612/70. Also Letter from Henry Stimson to Cordell Hull dated May 3, 1944. File number 093.612/73.
13. Letter from Ambassador Gromyko, Soviet Embassy, to Cordell Hull dated October 26, 1944. File number 093.612/10-2644.
14. Letter from Cordell Hull to Ambassador Gromyko, dated December 20, 1944. File number 093.612/10-2644.
15. Translation from the Department of State Central Translating Division of the Soviet Embassy letter dated January 20, 1945. File number 093.612/1-2045. This is in spite of the fact that the order, during the 1944 awardings, was called the "Order of Patriotic War" in the State Department press releases.
16. Letter from Rear Admiral Thomas Inglis to Herbert Sonneborn Jr., dated January 9, 1946.

17. In the case of George Cooper. His package arrived at the command opened, with the medal missing. It is not known if it was ever replaced.

18. In 1944, the wrong photograph was attached to the wrong book, but was corrected. In 1945, at least one observed incorrect book was sent to the wrong recipient. Unfortunately, because the other recipient (to whom the book correctly belonged) no longer had their document, it is impossible to know how much of a cascade effect this had on getting the correct documents to the correct recipients.

Chapter 16

1. As per Sheldon Kinney's family in an interview with the author, December 2013.

2. David Kellogg's photo made the AP newswire and was published profusely around the country on December 5 and 6, 1947. Norman Hyams was on the AP newswire on March 18, 1948.

3. *Chicago Daily Tribune,* "Russia Cancels Pension It Paid Yank War Hero," March 1, 1948.

4. He was provided two hard-mounted ribbons in the regulation Soviet uniform size and a two-inch length of ribbon for mounting himself.

5. See image of letter dated August 22, 1947.

6. From letter dated January 20, 1948, from W.C. Thomas to Morton Wolfson. See image.

7. *Chicago Daily Tribune,* "Russia Cancels Pension It Paid Yank War Hero," March 1, 1948.

8. Letter from Soviet Embassy to Maurice Breen dated August 23, 1948.

Chapter 17

1. Recollections from the family of David Pickler. Interview with the author, February 2014.

2. Interview conducted by Special Agent Marcus E. Sharpe with unknown individual (name redacted from FOIA) on November 16, 1964. Page 2.

3. Interview conducted by Special Agent Marcus E. Sharpe with unknown individual (name redacted, but believed to have been McNaughton based on factual statements) on or about 16 to 24 November 1964. Page 7.

4. Letter from Nikolai Novikov (Soviet Embassy) to George Marshall dated January 21, 1947. File number 093.612/1-2147.

Appendix 1

1. From the original State Department Files 093.612 and held at the National Archives.

Appendix 2

1. McDaniel and Schmitt, The Comprehensive Guide to Soviet Orders and Medals, 85-86, 99-100,123-124, 129-133, 163, 190-192, 210, 216, 219, 227. Used with permission. Note: the names of medals in the book vary slightly due to the differences in translation between authors.

Bibliography

Books

Enlisted Naval Aviation Pilots, Nashville, TN: Turner Publishing, 2002.

Ships of the Esso Fleet in World War II, New York: Standard Oil Co. of New Jersey, 1946.

Amborski, Leonard E. *The Last Voyage: Maritime Heroes of World War II*, Williamsville, NY: Ambor Press, 2001.

Andrews, Lewis M. *Tempest, Fire & Foe: Destroyer Escorts in World War II and the Men Who Manned Them*, Victoria, BC: Trafford Publishing, 2004.

Berry, Robert B. *Gunners Get Glory*, New York: Bobbs-Merrill Co., 1943.

Blair, Clay. *Hitler's U-Boat War*, New York: Random House, 2000.

Bunker, John: *Heroes in Dungarees: The Story of the American Merchant Marine in World War II,* Annapolis: Naval Institute Press, 1995.

Busch, Rainer and Röll, Hans-Joachim. *German U-boat Commanders of World War II: A Biographical Dictionary,* Annapolis: Naval Institute Press, 1999.

Carey, Alan C. *Osprey Combat Aircraft 34: PV Ventura/Harpoon Units of World War 2,* Oxford, UK: Osprey Publishing, Ltd., 2002.

Clark, J. W. *SSS*, Kings Point, NY: American Merchant Marine Museum, 2000.

Carse, Robert. *Cold Corner of Hell*, New York: Doubleday-Garden City, 1969.

Carter, William A. *Why Me Lord? The Experiences of a US Navy Armed Guard Officer in World War II's Convoy PQ 17 on the Murmansk Run,* Millsboro, DE: William Carter, 2007.

Duffy, James P. *Hitler's Secret Pirate Fleet: the Deadliest Ships of World War II,* Westport, CT: Praeger Publishers, 2001.

Dupra, Lyle E. *We Delivered! The US Navy Armed Guard in World War II,* Manhattan, KS: Sunflower University Press, 1997.

Efimov, Nikolai V. *Cavaliers of the Medal of Nakhimov*, St Petersburg, Russia: Central Military Naval Archive, 2012.

Efimov, Nikolai V. *Cavaliers of the Medal of Ushakov*, St Petersburg, Russia: Central Military Naval Archive, 2011.

Gleichauf, Justin F. *Unsung Sailors: The Naval Armed Guard in World War II*, Annapolis: Naval Institute Press, 1990.

Grossnick, Roy A. Vol 2., *Dictionary of American Naval Aviation Squadrons,* Washington, DC: Naval Historical Center, Department of the Navy, 1995.

Hague, Arnold and Ruegg, Bob. *Convoys to Russia, 1941-1945.* Kendal, UK: World Ship Society, 1993.

de Hartog, Jan. *The Captain*, New York: Atheneum, 1966.

Haynes, John L. *Frozen Fury: The Murmansk Run of Convoy PQ-13*, Baltimore: PublishAmerica, 2010.

Hughes, Blake. *Loves and Consequences,* Pittsburgh: Dorrance Publishing Co., 2005.

Irving, David. *Destruction of PQ-17*, New York: Simon & Schuster, 1968.

Kelshall, Gaylord T. *The U-boat War in the Caribbean*, Annapolis: Naval Institute Press, 1994.

Kemp, Paul. *Convoy! Drama in Arctic Waters,* Edison, NJ: Castle Books, 2004.

Maher, Robert A. and Wise, James E. Jr. *Sailors' Journey into War*, Kent, OH: Kent State University Press, 1998.

Moore, Arthur R. *A Careless Word...A Needless Sinking*, Hallowell, ME: The Knowlton & McLeary Co., 1998.

Morison, Samuel E. *History of US Naval Operations in World War II. Vol. 1: The Battle of the Atlantic*, Champaign, IL: University of Illinois Press, 2001.

Niestle, Axel. *German U-Boat Losses During World War II: Details of Destruction,* Annapolis: Naval Institute Press, 1998.

Ragnarsson, Ragnar. *Osprey Combat Aircraft 65: US Navy PBY Catalina Units of the Atlantic War,* Oxford, UK: Osprey Publishing, Ltd., 2006.

Roscoe, Theodore. *United States Destroyer Operations in World War II,* Annapolis: Naval Institute Press, 1953.

Rubenstein, Bernard J., ed. *Who's Who in the Maritime Industry*, New York: 74 Degrees West Co., 1946.

Schofield, B. B. *The Russian Convoys,* New York: Ballantine Books, 1967.

Stillwell, Paul. *Battleship Arizona: an illustrated history*, Annapolis: Naval Institute Press, 1991.

Syrett, David. *The Defeat of the German U-Boats: The Battle of the Atlantic*, Columbia, SC: University of South Carolina Press, 1994.

Taylor, Theodore. *Battle in the Arctic Seas. The Story of Convoy PQ 17*, New York: Thomas Y. Crowell Company, 1976.

Walling, Michael G. *Forgotten Sacrifice: The Arctic Convoys of World War II,* Oxford, UK: Osprey Publishing, 2012.

Weeks, Albert L. *Russia's Life-Saver: Lend-Lease Aid to the USSR in World War II*, Lanham, MD: Lexington Books, 2010.

Wiegand, Brandon T., ed. *Index of Decorations and Orders Announced in* All Hands *and Its Predecessors, Prior to 1950*, Brackenridge, PA: D-Day Militaria.

Wihelmsen, George N., ed. *US Navy – Marine Corps – Coast Guard Silver Star Awards for World War II,* San Francisco: George Wilhelmsen, 2004.

Wilde Jr., E. Andrew, ed. *The USS* Borie *(DD-215) in World War II: Documents and Photographs*, Needham, MA: E. Andrew Wilde Jr., 2001.

Williamson, Gordon. *Wolfpack: The Story of the U-Boat in World War II*, Oxford, UK: Osprey Publishing, Ltd., 2005.

Wynn, Kenneth. *U-Boat Operations of the Second World War.* 2 vols, Annapolis: Naval Institute, 1998.

Y'Blood, William T. *Hunter-Killer*, Annapolis: Naval Institute Press, 1983.

Directories and Associations

1948 V-Five Directory, Annapolis: V-Five Association of America.

2003 Register of Alumni, Annapolis: The United States Naval Academy Alumni Association, Inc..

Government Publications

Director of Naval History. *United States Naval Administration in World War II Office of Naval Operations: History of the Naval Armed Guard Afloat.*

http://www.ibiblio.org/hyperwar/USN/Admin-Hist/173-ArmedGuards/index.html

Navy Department. *Register of Commissioned and Warrant Officers of the United Sates Navy and Marine Corps July 1, 1944*, Washington, DC: US Government Printing Office, 1944.

—. *Register of Commissioned and Warrant Officers of the United States Naval Reserve July 1, 1944,* Washington, DC: US Government Printing Office, 1944.

—. *Register of Retired Commissioned and Warrant Officers, Regular and Reserve, of the United States Navy and Marine Corps July 1, 1966,* Washington, DC: US Government Printing Office, 1976.

—. *Register of Retired Commissioned and Warrant Officers, Regular and Reserve, of the United States Navy September 30, 1972*, Washington, DC: US Government Printing Office, 1972).

War Diaries

USS *Joyce* (DE-317) April 1944
USS *Gandy* (DE-764) April 1944
USS *Peterson* (DE-152) April 1944
VB-103, August 1943, November-December 1943, January-February 1944
VB-105, November-December 1943, October 1944
VP-73, June 1942
VP-82, January-March 1942
VP-84, December 1942, April 1943
VP-125, April 1943

Anti-Submarine Engagement After Action Reports (ASW-6)

Patrol Wing Eight, Patrol Squadron Eighty-Two serial A16-3(02) dated January 28, 1942

Report of U-Boat Sighting and Attack by Aircraft, serial number Rey04/20/8/42, dated August 20, 1942

Report of Anti-Submarine Action by Aircraft, VB-103 Report No. 3 dated August 13, 1943.

Report of Anti-Submarine Action by Aircraft VB-103 Report No. 5, dated November 11, 1943.

Report of Anti-Submarine Action by Aircraft VB-110 Report No. 1, dated November 10, 1943

USS *Joyce* (DE-317) Contact and Action Report dated 16 April 1944

USS *Gandy* (DE-764) Contact and Action Report dated 16 April 1944

USS *Champlin* (DD-601) Action with enemy submarine- report of. DD601/A16-3 serial 030 dated 10 April 1944

Reports of Interrogation, U-boat Prisoners of War

Interrogation of Survivors from *U-1229*, Sunk August 20, 1944. Dated September 27, 1944

Interrogation of Survivors from *U-569*, Sunk May 22,, 1943. Dated June 19, 1943

Interrogation of Survivors from *U-856*, Sunk April 2, 1944. Dated May 27, 1944

Preliminary report on the interrogation of survivors from *U-860* sunk on June 15, 1944. Dated July 6, 1944

Naval Armed Guard Voyage Reports

The voyage report records are located within the National Archives, Record Group 38, Chief of Naval Operations, Office of the Deputy Chief of Naval Operations (Logistics), Naval Transportation Service, Armed Guard Files compiled 1934-1946. For the sake of uniformity and alleviate confusion, they have all been listed as "Naval Armed Guard Voyage Reports" though their actual subject lines varied depending on the author and regulations at the time. The reports for the following ships were used for compiling the narrative for this book:

SS *Africander*
SS *Alcoa Prospector*
SS *Alexander Macomb*
SS *American Robin*
SS *Ballot*
SS *Beaconhill*
SS *Bellingham*
SS *Benjamin Harrison*
SS *Campfire*
SS *Christopher Newport*
SS *City of Joliet*
SS *Columbian*

SS *Cornelius Harnett*
SS *Daniel Morgan*
SS *Dartmouth*
SS *Deer Lodge*
SS *Dunboyne*
SS *Effingham*
SS *El Almirante*
SS *El Capitan*
SS *El Oceano*
SS *El Oriente*
SS *Eldena*
SS *Exford*
SS *Expositor*
SS *Exterminator*
SS *Francis Scott Key*
SS *George Clymer*
SS *Heffron*
SS *Henry Wynkoop*
SS *Ironclad*
SS *John Penn*
SS *John Walker*
SS *John Witherspoon*
SS *Kaimoku*
SS *Kentucky*
SS *Lafayette*
SS *Larranaga*
SS *Massamar*
SS *Michigan*
SS *Mormacmar*
SS *Mormacrio*
SS *Nathaniel Greene*
SS *Nicholas Gilman*
SS *Oliver Ellsworth*
SS *Oregonian*
SS *Oremar*
SS *Pan Kraft*
SS *Pan New York*
SS *Pan York*
SS *Patrick Henry*
SS *Peter Kerr*
SS *Richard Bland*
SS *Richard Henry Lee*
SS *Sahale*
SS *Schoharie*
SS *Scottsburg*
SS *Seattle Spirit*
SS *Sharpsburg*
SS *St. Olaf*
SS *Stone Street*
SS *Syros*
SS *Thomas Hartley*
SS *Troubador*
SS *Virginia Dare*
SS *Wade Hampton*
SS *Washington*
SS *West Cheswald*
SS *White Clover*
SS *William Hooper*
SS *William Moultrie*
SS *Yaka*
SS *Yorkmar*

Index to Recipients